The Selected Letters of Mary Moody Emerson

The Selected Letters of

MARY MOODY EMERSON

Edited by

Nancy Craig Simmons

THE UNIVERSITY OF GEORGIA PRESS

Athens and London

This publication has been supported by a grant from the National Endowment for the Humanities, an independent federal agency.

Designed by B. Williams & Associates
Set in Linotron 202 Sabon by Tseng Information Systems, Inc.
Printed and bound by Maple-Vail

The paper in this book meets the guidelines for permanence and durability of the Committee on Production Guidelines for Book Longevity of the Council on Library Resources.

Printed in the United States of America

97 96 95 94 93   C 5 4 3 2 1

LIBRARY OF CONGRESS CATALOGING IN PUBLICATION DATA
Emerson, Mary Moody, 1774–1863.
    [Correspondence. Selections]
    The selected letters of Mary Moody Emerson/ edited by Nancy Craig Simmons.
        p.   cm.
    Includes bibliographical references and index.
    ISBN 0-8203-1462-5 (alk. paper)
    1. United States—Intellectual life—1783–1865.   2. Emerson, Ralph Waldo, 1803–1882—Biography—Family.   3. Emerson, Mary Moody, 1774–1863—Correspondence.   4. Women—United States—Correspondence.   I. Simmons, Nancy Craig.   II. Title.
E164E46   1993
973.5'092—dc20
[B]   92-5076
                                                                           CIP

British Library Cataloging in Publication Data available

Frontispiece: Mary Moody Emerson (1774–1863).
Silhouette by Williams (before 1810).

M.M.E.'s style is that of letters,—an immense advantage—
admits of all the force of colloquial domestic words, &
breaks, & parenthesis, & petulance—has the luck &
inspiration of that,—has humor, affection, & a range from
the rapture of prayer down to details of farm & barn & *help*.

All her language in writing was happy but inimitable as if
caught from some dream.

—Ralph Waldo Emerson, *MME Notebook 3*

Contents

Mary Moody Emerson Genealogy

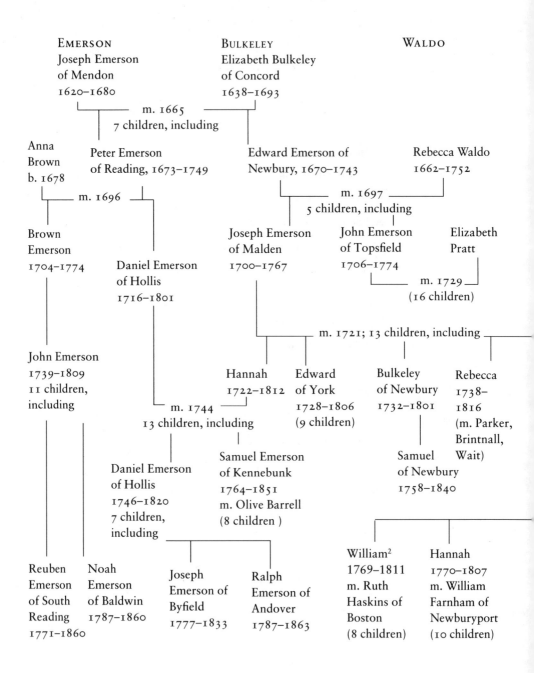

EMERSON
Joseph Emerson
of Mendon
1620–1680

BULKELEY
Elizabeth Bulkeley
of Concord
1638–1693

WALDO

m. 1665
7 children, including

Anna
Brown
b. 1678

Peter Emerson
of Reading, 1673–1749

Edward Emerson of
Newbury, 1670–1743

Rebecca Waldo
1662–1752

m. 1696

m. 1697
5 children, including

Brown
Emerson
1704–1774

Daniel Emerson
of Hollis
1716–1801

Joseph Emerson
of Malden
1700–1767

John Emerson
of Topsfield
1706–1774

Elizabeth
Pratt

m. 1729
(16 children)

John Emerson
1739–1809
11 children,
including

m. 1721; 13 children, including

Hannah
1722–1812

Edward
of York
1728–1806
(9 children)

Bulkeley
of Newbury
1732–1801

Rebecca
1738–
1816
(m. Parker,
Brintnall,
Wait)

m. 1744
13 children, including

Daniel Emerson
of Hollis
1746–1820
7 children,
including

Samuel Emerson
of Kennebunk
1764–1851
m. Olive Barrell
(8 children)

Samuel
of Newbury
1758–1840

William[2]
1769–1811
m. Ruth
Haskins of
Boston
(8 children)

Hannah
1770–1807
m. William
Farnham of
Newburyport
(10 children)

Reuben
Emerson
of South
Reading
1771–1860

Noah
Emerson
of Baldwin
1787–1860

Joseph
Emerson of
Byfield
1777–1833

Ralph
Emerson of
Andover
1787–1863

List of children in the next generation follows; this list includes the
nieces and nephews with whom Mary Moody Emerson corresponded
or whom she mentions in her letters.

MOODY   SEWELL   BLISS   WALKER

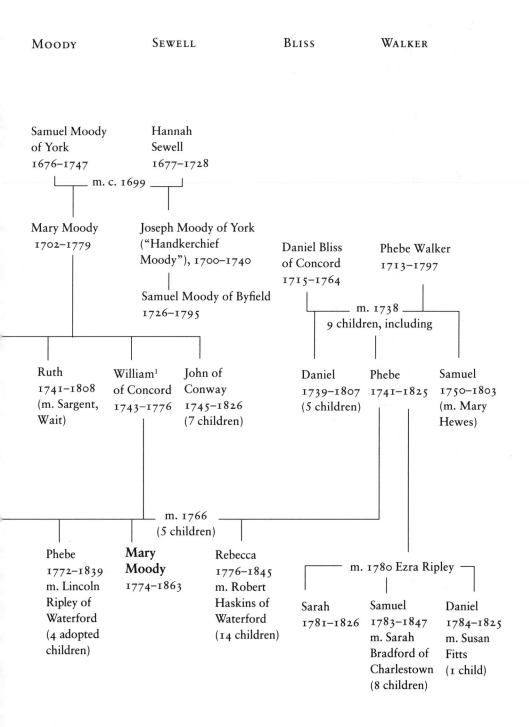

Samuel Moody
of York
1676–1747

Hannah
Sewell
1677–1728

m. c. 1699

Mary Moody
1702–1779

Joseph Moody of York
("Handkerchief
Moody"), 1700–1740

Daniel Bliss
of Concord
1715–1764

Phebe Walker
1713–1797

Samuel Moody of Byfield
1726–1795

m. 1738
9 children, including

Ruth
1741–1808
(m. Sargent,
Wait)

William[1]
of Concord
1743–1776

John of
Conway
1745–1826
(7 children)

Daniel
1739–1807
(5 children)

Phebe
1741–1825

Samuel
1750–1803
(m. Mary
Hewes)

m. 1766
(5 children)

Phebe
1772–1839
m. Lincoln
Ripley of
Waterford
(4 adopted
children)

**Mary
Moody**
1774–1863

Rebecca
1776–1845
m. Robert
Haskins of
Waterford
(14 children)

m. 1780 Ezra Ripley

Sarah
1781–1826

Samuel
1783–1847
m. Sarah
Bradford of
Charlestown
(8 children)

Daniel
1784–1825
m. Susan
Fitts
(1 child)

Genealogy of Mary Moody Emerson *(continued)*

Children of Hannah and William Farnham
John Hay Farnham 1791–1833
Mary Farnham 1792–1816
Louisa Farnham (Dewey) 1794–1864
Charlotte Farnham 1796–1862
Daniel Farnham 1797–1824
William Farnham 1799–1819
Phebe Farnham (Cobb) 1801–1875
Sybil Farnham (Lambard) 1801–1887

Children of William and Ruth Haskins Emerson
Phebe Bliss Emerson 1798–1800
John Clarke Emerson 1799–1807
William Emerson[3] 1801–1868
Ralph Waldo Emerson 1803–1882
Edward Bliss Emerson 1805–1834
Robert Bulkeley Emerson 1807–1859
Charles Chauncy Emerson 1808–1836
Mary Caroline Emerson 1811–1814

Children of Rebecca and Robert Haskins
Rebecca Haskins (Hamlin) b. 1799
Thomas Waldo Haskins b. 1801
Phebe Haskins (Chamberlain) b. 1803
Robert Haskins b. 1804
William Emerson Haskins b. 1806
Ralph T. Haskins b. 1808
Lincoln Ripley Haskins 1812–1860
Samuel Moody Haskins b. 1813
Hannah Haskins (Parsons) b. 1814
Sarah Haskins (Ansley) b. 1816
Charlotte Haskins (Cleveland) b. 1822

Adopted children of Phebe and Lincoln Ripley
Martha Robinson
Martha Bliss ("Patty")
Noah Ripley
Ann Brewer (Sargent Gage) 1794–1876

Genealogy of Mary Moody Emerson *(continued)*

Children of Samuel and Olive Barrell Emerson
George Barrell Emerson 1797–1881
Ralph Emerson b. 1806

Son of Joseph Emerson
Alfred Emerson 1812–1897

Son of Reuben Emerson
Charles Milton Emerson 1802–1881

Children of Samuel and Sarah Bradford Ripley
Elizabeth Bradford Ripley b. 1819
Mary Emerson Ripley (Simmons) b. 1820
Christopher Gore Ripley b. 1822
Phebe Bliss Ripley b. 1824
Ezra Ripley b. 1826
Ann Dunkin Ripley (Loring) b. 1829
Sophia Bradford Ripley (Thayer) b. 1833

Children of Ann and Leander Gage
Phebe Hovey Gage 1821–1880
Frances Gage (Cousens) 1823-1904
Irene Bliss Gage (Warren) 1824–1873
Thomas Hovey Gage 1826–1909
Ann Louisa Gage (Foster) 1828–1878
George Gage b. 1834

Illustrations

Abbreviations

REH	Rebecca Emerson Haskins
RHE	Ruth Haskins Emerson
RTH	Ralph T. Haskins
RWE	Ralph Waldo Emerson
SAB	Sarah Alden Bradford
SBR	Sarah Bradford Ripley
SR	Samuel Ripley
THG	Thomas Hovey Gage
TTS	Thomas Treadwell Stone
WE^1	William Emerson (1743–76)
WE^2	William Emerson (1768–1811)
WE^3	William Emerson (1801–68)
WE^4	William Emerson (1835–86)
WEC	William Ellery Channing

DEPOSITORIES AND COLLECTIONS

MCR-S	The Arthur and Elizabeth Schlesinger Library, Radcliffe College, Harvard University, Cambridge, Mass.
MH	Houghton Library, Harvard University, Cambridge, Mass.: MH: 000 = RWEMA, bMS Am 1280.226; MH: 220(00) or 225(00) = bMS Am 1280.220 or bMS Am 1280.225
MH-AH	Andover-Harvard Theological Library, Harvard University, Cambridge, Mass.
MT/EW	Joel Myerson Transcription, Collection of Dr. Ethel Emerson Wortis (Privately Owned)
MT/MH	Joel Myerson Transcription, RWEMA
MWA	American Antiquarian Society, Worcester, Mass.
RWEMA	Ralph Waldo Emerson Memorial Association Collection, Houghton Library, Harvard University, Cambridge, Mass.
T	Tolman Transcripts, Houghton Library, Harvard University, Cambridge, Mass.
ViU	University of Virginia Library, Charlottesville, Va.
VtMiM	Egbert Starr Library, Middlebury College, Middlebury, Vt.

PRIMARY AND SECONDARY SOURCES

| Ahlstrom | Sidney Ahlstrom. *A Religious History of the American People.* New Haven: Yale University Press, 1972. |

AWW	*American Women Writers.*
Charvat	William Charvat. *Emerson's American Lecture Engagements: A Chronological List.* New York: New York Public Library, 1961.
CS	Ralph Waldo Emerson. *The Complete Sermons of Ralph Waldo Emerson.* 3 vols. to date. Ed. Albert J. von Frank, Teresa Toulouse, Andrew Delbanco, and Ronald J. Bosco. Columbia: University of Mo. Press, 1989–.
CW	Ralph Waldo Emerson. *The Complete Works of Ralph Waldo Emerson.* Ed. Joseph Slater et al. 5 vols. to date. Cambridge: Harvard University Press, 1971–.
DAB	*Dictionary of American Biography.*
Days	Walter Harding. *The Days of Henry Thoreau.* New York: Dover, 1982.
DNB	*Dictionary of National Biography.*
"EH L"	Elizabeth Sherman Hoar. "Elizabeth of Concord: Selected Letters of Elizabeth Sherman Hoar (1814–1878) to the Emersons, Family, and the Emerson Circle." Ed. Elizabeth Maxfield-Miller. Part 1, *SAR 1984*: 229–98; Part 2, *SAR 1985*: 95–156; Part 3, *SAR 1986*: 113–98.
EL	Ralph Waldo Emerson. *The Early Lectures of Ralph Waldo Emerson.* Ed. Stephen E. Whicher, Robert E. Spiller, and Wallace E. Williams. 3 vols. Cambridge: Harvard University Press, 1959–72.
ETE L	Ellen Tucker Emerson. *The Letters of Ellen Tucker Emerson.* Ed. Edith Emerson Webster Gregg. 2 vols. Kent, Ohio: Kent State University Press, 1982.
Gougeon	Len Gougeon. *Virtue's Hero: Emerson, Antislavery, and Reform.* Athens: University of Ga. Press, 1990.
Howe	Daniel Walker Howe. *The Unitarian Conscience: Harvard Moral Philosophy, 1805–1861.* Cambridge: Harvard University Press, 1970.
IpsE	Benjamin Kendall Emerson. *The Ipswich Emersons.* Boston: David Clapp, 1900.
J	Ralph Waldo Emerson. *The Journals of Ralph Waldo Emerson.* Ed. Edward Waldo Emerson and Waldo Emerson Forbes. 10 vols. Boston: Houghton Mifflin, 1909–14.
JMN	Ralph Waldo Emerson. *The Journals and Miscellaneous Notebooks of Ralph Waldo Emerson.* Ed. William H. Gilman et al. 16 vols. Cambridge: Harvard University Press, 1960–82.

L	Ralph Waldo Emerson. *The Letters of Ralph Waldo Emerson*. Ed. Ralph L. Rusk. Vols. 1–6. New York: Columbia University Press, 1939. Ed. Eleanor Tilton. Vols. 7–8. New York: Columbia University Press, 1990–91.
LCD	*Lempriere's Classical Dictionary.*
Life of RWE	Ralph L. Rusk. *The Life of Ralph Waldo Emerson*. New York: Columbia University Press, 1949.
LJE L	Lidian Jackson Emerson. *The Letters of Lidian Jackson Emerson*. Ed. Delores Bird Carpenter. Columbia: University of Mo. Press, 1989.
Lyceum	Kenneth Walter Cameron. *The Massachusetts Lyceum during the American Renaissance*. Hartford, Conn.: Transcendental Books, 1970.
MF L	Margaret Fuller. *The Letters of Margaret Fuller*. Ed. Robert N. Hudspeth. 5 vols. Ithaca: Cornell University Press, 1983–88.
Milton	John Milton. *John Milton: Complete Poems and Major Prose*. Ed. Merritt Y. Hughes. Indianapolis: Bobbs-Merrill, 1957.
"MrsSR"	Elizabeth Hoar. "Mrs. Samuel Ripley." In *Worthy Women of the Nineteenth Century*, ed. Mrs. O. J. Wister and Miss Agnes Irwin, 113–227. Philadelphia: Lippincott, 1877.
MWW-M	Elizabeth Amelia Dwight. *Memorials of Mary Wilder White*. Ed. Mary Wilder Tileston. Boston: Everett Press, 1903.
OED	*Oxford English Dictionary.*
OFL	Ellen Louisa Tucker. *One First Love: The Letters of Ellen Louisa Tucker to Ralph Waldo Emerson*. Ed. Edith W. Gregg. Cambridge: Harvard University Press, 1962.
PJ	Henry David Thoreau. *The Writings of Henry D. Thoreau: Journal*. Ed. Elizabeth Hall Witherell, William L. Howarth, John C. Broderick, Robert Sattelmeyer, Thomas Blanding, Mark R. Patterson, William Rossi, Leonard N. Neufeldt, and Nancy Craig Simmons. 4 vols. to date. Princeton: Princeton University Press, 1981–.
QR	*Quarterly Review.*
RevSR	James B. Thayer. *Reverend Samuel Ripley of Waltham*. Cambridge: John Wilson, 1897.
Sanborn	Franklin Benjamin Sanborn. *Recollections of Seventy Years*. 2 vols. Boston: R. G. Badger, 1909.

SAR | *Studies in the American Renaissance.* Ed. Joel Myerson. Boston: Twayne, 1977–82; Charlottesville: University Press of Va., 1983–.

Shakespeare | William Shakespeare. *The Riverside Shakespeare.* Ed. G. Blakemore Evans. Boston: Houghton Mifflin, 1974.

TR | Perry Miller, ed. *The Transcendentalists: An Anthology.* Cambridge: Harvard University Press, 1950.

W | Ralph Waldo Emerson. *The Complete Works of Ralph Waldo Emerson.* Ed. Edward Waldo Emerson and James Elliot Cabot. 12 vols. Boston: Houghton Mifflin, 1903–4.

Waterford | *The History of Waterford, Oxford County, Maine, 1775– 1875.* Portland, Maine: Hoyt, Fogg, and Donham, 1879.

Wright | Conrad Wright. *The Beginnings of Unitarianism in America.* Boston: Starr King, 1955.

Acknowledgments

An edition such as this is a collaborative adventure. The collaboration involves many people, across time and space. The adventure is mostly the editor's, because, as with any quest, she cannot know at the outset of her journey what she will discover along the way, and each discovery opens a new path that could not have been anticipated. As I have worked on the letters of Mary Moody Emerson over the past decade, I have often thought of how greatly I was blessed by my experiences in this work.

The first collaboration, of course, is between the editor and the writer of the texts. When the writer has said, as Mary Emerson did on one occasion, that "not a scrap [of my manuscripts] is to see print as many deceased persons have had their papers," the editor must hope that she would be forgiven for publishing private correspondence. On another level, editing, like biography, requires intense participation in the mental and physical life of the subject. Through reading and transcribing every located letter written by Mary Moody Emerson and creating a context for understanding the correspondence, I have come to know her and her world intimately. I still do not understand her fully, but I have come to appreciate Mary Emerson for who she was and what she had to teach.

The collaboration extends backward also to those who so valued Mary Emerson's writing that, two centuries after the first letters were written, the manuscripts remain to be read and edited. In this group belong especially the Emerson family, James Elliot Cabot (Emerson's literary executor and the subject of my doctoral dissertation), Ann Gage and her heirs, and the depositories that house the manuscripts. Other co-workers from the past are the people—Waldo Emerson, George Tolman, Edward Waldo Emerson, Waldo Emerson Forbes, Ralph L. Rusk, William Gilman, and the many other editors of Emerson's *Journals and Miscellaneous Notebooks*—whose transcriptions and publication of some of the letters alerted people like me to the fact of their existence, made us aware that here, indeed, was a treasure trove waiting to be discovered.

For permission to publish the letters from manuscripts in their collections, I am indebted to the Houghton Library of Harvard University and to the Ralph Waldo Emerson Memorial Association; the American Antiquarian Society, Worcester, Mass. (the Gage Family Papers); the Andover-Harvard Theological Library, Harvard Divinity School (the Frederic Henry Hedge papers and the Henry Wilder Foote papers); Middlebury College (Special Collections,

Starr Library); and the University of Virginia Library (Ralph Waldo Emerson Collection [#6248-A], Manuscripts Division, Special Collections).

Other particular sources of information have enriched this edition in special ways. I am indebted to Michael Wortis for permission to quote from manuscripts in the private collection of Dr. Ethel Emerson Wortis and to Joel Myerson for permission to quote from his transcriptions of these papers. The Ralph Waldo Emerson quotation used as the epigraph is reproduced by permission of the Houghton Library of Harvard University and the Ralph Waldo Emerson Memorial Association [MH:bMS Am 1280.148].

To the people in the libraries that house the manuscript letters, who made possible my use of very fragile materials, I owe a tremendous debt. I appreciate especially the support of Rodney Dennis, Curator of Manuscripts for the Houghton Library, Harvard University, and Trustee of the Ralph Waldo Emerson Memorial Association, and James L. Lewis, head of the Houghton Reading Room. During my many months of work on the manuscripts and annotations, Mr. Lewis's excellent staff provided everything I needed; Thomas Noonan, Susan Halpert, Melanie Wisner, Jennie Rathbun, Denison Beach, and Emily Walhout remained cheerful, patient, diligent, and professional even during those hectic times when it seemed that most of the world's scholars were demanding Houghton materials. At the Antiquarian Society, Sidney Berger, Thomas Knoles, Marie Lamoureux, Dianne Rugh, and Joyce Tracy provided valuable assistance and answers to all sorts of questions. At Middlebury, Robert Buckeye was a wonderful host, and Michael Plunkett and his staff made my visit to the University of Virginia's Alderman Library enjoyable. My most exciting library experience was courtesy of Alan Seaburg, Curator of Manuscripts at the Andover-Harvard Theological Library. Mr. Seaburg heard the name Wilder when I described my search for additional manuscript letters and connected it with the large, uncataloged Henry Wilder Foote collection of materials, still in boxes in the library's basement—and invited me to search them. Mary Emerson came alive in new ways as I sifted through four generations of treasures from a family who knew her.

I have enjoyed a special kind of collaboration with Phyllis Cole, who from the beginning of my work on this project shared materials and ideas and encouraged, supported, questioned, and corrected me all along the way. Her rich knowledge, her wonderful sense of humor, and her hospitality during our annual meetings of the Mary Moody Emerson Society have made this a very human adventure. No one has contributed more to my growing appreciation of Mary Moody Emerson and to the final shape of this edition than Phyllis, whose work on Mary Emerson's "Almanacks" and generational study of the Emersons provides the feminist standpoint we need to reenvision a woman traditionally seen only in relationship to her famous nephew. Phyllis introduced me to Joan Goodwin (the third member of the Mary Moody Emerson Society), whose work centers on Sarah Bradford Ripley, Mary Emerson's "long loved Friend & Sister." Joan too became a real friend, sharing her transcriptions of Ripley family papers, her knowledge of the Ripleys, and her enthusiasm for our shared subjects. I appreciate also the contribution of Evelyn Barish, who had once considered editing these letters herself. Evelyn graciously relinquished her claim to this project and offered advice and information.

Two other people deserve special thanks for their enormous support and contributions to this edition. Early in my scholarly career, Eleanor Tilton welcomed me to her wonderful Morningside Heights apartment and invited me to use the files of Emerson-related materials she had taken over from Ralph L. Rusk. Throughout my work on this project, Eleanor graciously answered questions and provided additional materials, serving as an inspiration while challenging me to develop my own skills as a researcher. The other important person has been Joel Myerson, who first answered my questions about the feasibility of this edition back in 1982 and has supported every step of the process since those first discussions. Joel shared with me early versions of Elizabeth Maxfield-Miller's transcriptions of the letters of Elizabeth Hoar (subsequently published in *Studies in the American Renaissance*) and his invaluable transcriptions of the Emerson brothers' correspondence, and he has continued to contribute to the final product in innumerable ways.

Over the years, I learned much from the people I worked with through the Textual Center for the Writings of Henry D. Thoreau; there I built a bridge from my preacademic career in textbook and newspaper publishing to scholarly editing. From William L. Howarth, Thomas Blanding, Elizabeth Witherell, Carolyn Kappes, Leonard Neufeldt, Kristin Fossum, and Robert Sattelmeyer I gained valuable editorial skills that were necessary to make the multitudinous decisions required for editing texts such as these.

Creating a context for the letters was essential, as I realized very early. Letters that seemed slight or obscure began to glow when I discovered what Mary Emerson was talking about. In my attempt to pin down every obscurity in the letters, I began with the collections of Virginia Tech's Newman Library and profited especially from its microfilm collection of older periodicals and its excellent interlibrary loan services. I owe special thanks to Paul Metz, Scottie Cochran, Lucy Cox, Glenn McMullen, Anita Malebranche, Sue Fritz, and Gordon Hogg. I also found much information in the collections of other libraries I visited for various reasons: at Smith College, the University of Indiana, Emory University, the Library of Congress, and the Schlesinger Library of Radcliffe College. To the wonderful librarians at the Concord Free Public Library, Marcia Moss and Joyce Woodman, I owe my greatest debt in this department. Descending into the air-conditioned vaults of the Concord Special Collections on a muggy summer day is a trip back in time, to a Concord past that still lives under Marcia's and Joyce's loving care. They have been extremely generous in many ways, helping me to locate materials, providing photographs for illustrations, and answering my endless questions about Concord people, places, and events.

After Concord, the major place in Mary Moody Emerson's life was Waterford, Maine. During our sabbatical in the fall of 1989, my husband and I traveled to Waterford to see and learn what we could. There (thanks to Phyllis Cole) we met some wonderful people, especially Margaret Merry Sawyer, the acknowledged authority on Waterford history, and Sylvia Sawyer Sebelist. Margaret showed us around Waterford on two raw and blustery days, helping us to discover the probable location of Mary's Elm Vale farmhouse, the graves of her family and friends, and other places she would have known. Through Margaret I made my closest contact with Mary Emerson: she introduced me to an old woman whose husband's grandmother had boarded Mary Emerson in her home. Here was someone who had known someone who had known Mary Moody Emerson. This lady did not want to gossip about Mary Emerson, to tell the things that Waterfordians considered scandalous. She preferred to remember Mary as a great theologian. Sylvia Sebelist proved to be an indefatigable researcher of obscure Waterford facts, genealogy, and Maine and New England history.

As I review my files of annotation materials, I am newly aware of how many people have been involved in creating the context for these letters. In addition to those mentioned above, others who have helped by answering specific questions include Tom Blanding of Concord; Rebecca J. Bates and Patrice Donoghue of the Harvard University Archives; Joyce Butler of the Brick Store Museum, Kennebunk, Maine; Hilbert Campbell of the Virginia Tech English Department; Inese Gruber of the Windham (Maine) Public Library; Dianne M. Gutscher of the Bowdoin College Library; Judith Ann Schiff of the Yale University Library; Marianne Ventura of the Newburyport Public Library; Douglas Emory Wilson, textual editor for the Emerson edition; and Guy Woodall of Tennessee Tech.

Institutional and financial help has come in various ways. The National Endowment for the Humanities provided initial funding for this project in the form of a summer stipend that supported my purchase of microfilm copies of many of the letters and my transcription of about one hundred letters in the summer of 1983. A Travel-to-Collections Grant from the National Endowment for the Humanities made it possible to perfect the letters in the Houghton Library, and a grant from the American Philosophical Association helped support research in Cambridge, Concord, Worcester, and Waterford. Two half-year sabbaticals from Virginia Tech in 1988 and 1989 made these trips possible. Further support came from the Virginia Tech Foundation; the College of Arts and Sciences, Virginia Tech; and the Department of English and the Center for Programs in the Humanities at Virginia Tech. The many months I spent working in Cambridge would not have been possible without the wonderful hospitality offered by Bette and Chris Noble.

I have also been helped by several of Virginia Tech's graduate students, who for brief periods in the summers aided various stages of this project. Most important was Sabrina Kirby, who in the summer of 1986 helped me complete the keyboarding of the bulk of the letter transcriptions. Sabrina also helped organize the transcripts so that I could begin to work on them. The next year, Rich Dooner further helped with organization, especially with setting up the calendar of letters that I have used. In 1989, Peter Donahue worked nobly on annotation questions for the 1830s, a particularly difficult period.

I also owe a great deal to those involved in shaping my manuscript into its final form—especially Len Hatfield of the Virginia Tech English Department, who cheerfully answered my computer-related questions; Nancy Grayson Holmes, my editor at the University of Georgia Press, whose extraordinary energy has kept this project moving rapidly; the several readers Nancy enlisted, who let me know what readers did and did not want in an edition such as this; and Brenda Kolb, who did a superb job of copyediting the typescript and asking the right questions.

And finally, my colleague and husband, Len Scigaj, provided the best support of all: his belief that I could complete this task, even at those times when I doubted my abilities and its worth. His encouragement, optimism, and joyful willingness to accompany me on my quest made everything possible.

Mary Moody Emerson: Woman Writing

"Where does a woman write, what does she look like writing, what is my image, your image, of a woman writing?"[1] Ursula Le Guin's questions haunt me as I think about how to introduce this selection of the letters of Mary Moody Emerson. They are an extraordinary record of woman writing. We know, of course, that she wrote: thousands of pages of manuscript letters and spiritual diaries survive, along with numerous comments about her in print, even passages from her writing published in connection with the life and work of her well-known nephew Ralph Waldo Emerson. But the image of her as woman writing is obscured by the more familiar emphasis on her stern Calvinism, her role as a father figure for her Emerson nephews, her eccentricities, her great "velocity." The letters here, most of them published for the first time, reveal, instead, a woman of great intelligence, a woman challenged and excited by intellectual questions, passionately engaged with her subjects and her audience, using language to express the great truths that were the object of her life's pilgrimage. They also show us a woman negotiating the difficulties created by "single blessedness" in a culture that viewed wife- and motherhood as woman's vocation.

The question of where she wrote is complicated, because the setting was always changing: like the old pilgrims, Mary liked to point out, she rarely stayed "but a month at a place" (MWA). The datelines of her letters often identify towns in which she was staying—Boston, Concord, Waterford, Waltham, Hartford, Newburyport, Ashfield, Belfast—but the houses must often be inferred. Her life as a single woman and a boarder gave her one advantage often denied the woman writer, a room of her own, and at times she mentions writing after midnight, perhaps in moonlight, in the quiet after the family has gone to sleep. Nevertheless, lack of a warm fire or a good lamp, or the desire for company, often led her to the common parlor, where the noise of conversations and family activities interrupted her. Still, she wrote and wrote: letters, her "Almanack," minireviews, metaphysical speculations.

Often she began letters on Sunday afternoons (abbreviated "Sab. PM") and wrote on into the evening, until, as she would note, "bad light" precluded writing clearly. "You must pardon this scrool," she would explain. At other times she wrote from hotels or stagecoach stops. Her letters inform about other adverse conditions: poor pens; a shortage of writing paper; her inability to locate the letter she is responding to or the book she wants to quote from;

the sound of the stagecoach or the arrival of the bearer for the letter, both of which necessitated a hasty close.

Trying to form an image of her writing is also complicated by a paucity of visual representations of her: no painting exists, no daguerreotype survives to help us see this woman (whom contemporaries often described as a small whirlwind). It is hard to see her seated, engaged in her work. Did she write at a table? Did she use a lap desk (she refers at times to her secretary)? Did she sit on a settee, with papers and books strewn about her? The one surviving pictorial representation made during her lifetime is a paper silhouette, cut before 1810 and reproduced as the frontispiece of this edition, which suggests a rather elegant and delicate young woman, frozen in profile. Only N. C. Wyeth, in his painting *Thoreau and Miss Mary Emerson*, has attempted to construct a visual image for us, and he imagines a sweet-faced, elderly woman wearing an old-fashioned bonnet, seated in a large wing chair, and knitting, while a handsome, young Henry Thoreau leans forward from his rocking chair to look intently into her eyes.[2] But Mary Emerson did not knit; she was neither adept at nor interested in the usual domestic occupations performed by women. Reading, writing, and conversing were her vocations.

Once, when she had experienced "favored omens" of her imminent departure from earthly life, Mary Emerson wrote to her friend Ann Gage about the disposition of her manuscripts, which she hoped might provide "sympathy" to others in "age & solitude"—but, she added, "Not a scrap is to see print as many deceased persons have had their papers." Yet she also indulged in the thought of being remembered through her writings, at the same time that "the love or the esteem or censure of others" seemed irrelevant in the face of immortality (MWA).[3] A great deal of this literary estate survives: almost 900 letters written between 1793 and 1862 to more than fifty people, as well as over one thousand pages of her "Almanack," the spiritual diary she kept for fifty years.[4] This edition prints 334 of the letters, selected to reveal the range of her voice and correspondence over this seventy-year span. Although Waldo Emerson thought of using some of them to tell the "interior & spiritual history of New England" (*JMN* 7:446), his single product was the essay "Mary Moody Emerson," published posthumously from the fragmentary lecture read to the New England Women's Club in 1869.[5] Embedded in his essay are numerous extracts from her letters and "Almanack."

Until now, the only other printed primary materials available to scholars interested in her writing have been extracts included in George Tolman's monograph, *Mary Moody Emerson* (1929); twenty-three excerpts or whole letters printed as part of Emerson's journal (1909–14, 1961–82); and passages quoted in James Elliot Cabot's memoir of Emerson, by Ralph L. Rusk in Emerson's *Letters* (1939) and *Life* (1949), and by a few other editors of works that are less well known. Eleanor Tilton's recently published volumes of additional Emerson letters have finally made Waldo's side of this correspondence available in accurate and accessible texts, and, in her notes, Tilton erty, mortgages, and rents and her own desire for mental stimulation often prompted her to spend long periods, from a month to several years, visiting and boarding elsewhere. (Less than half of the period from 1810 to 1850 was actually lived at Waterford.) Part of almost every year she spent with her family in Boston, Concord, and Waltham, with the remainder lived in towns all over New England. At times she writes pitifully of saying good-bye, of passing Vale for the last time—only to return later. When she could not return to the Vale, she might board in Waterford with friends or relatives: another sister, Phebe, was married to Waterford's first Congregational minister, Lincoln Ripley (brother of their stepfather Ezra), the first link to Waterford.

The attractions of Vale, her early experiences as nurse or nanny, her hard-won independence from marriage and the ties that bind—all must have contributed to Mary Emerson's attempt to refuse the part for which she seemed to be destined: as maiden aunt or surrogate father for the children of her brother, William, who died in 1811, leaving a Boston-bred widow and six children under the age of ten. Despite sister-in-law Ruth's urging that she make her home with them (and help not only with the children but also with the boarders Ruth hoped would support them), for six years after her brother's death Mary Emerson divided her time among the families at Boston and Concord, even returning to Waterford (with five-year-old Charles) for much of 1813. The War of 1812 brought her back to Boston in 1814, and soon after celebrating peace in February 1815, she moved with the Emersons for the fourth time in sixteen months. By the fall of 1817—when Ralph Waldo left home for Cambridge—Mary believed Ruth could do without her. Now forty-three years old, she returned to Vale, the place she chose to call home.

But Vale was never to be a permanent home. The letters after 1817 give us some sense of her wanderings, preserving the rhythms of visits and encounters, journeys forth from and returns to the farm. These moves chronicle her outer life for four decades; the inner life is the subject of her writing. (Writing to Waldo in 1830, she exclaimed, "I send you and Almanack! 'Catch me'—Soberly—I will not till you return the others. They are my *home*—the only images of having existed.") For this reason, I have not attempted to print a chronology of her life, for, beyond a few serious illnesses and her moves, such a list would have chronicled events—the marriages, births, deaths, accomplishments, and publications—in the lives of others, not in her own. Instead, the Calendar of Residences at the beginning of each section after part 1 tracks her movement from one address to the next; in the six introductions, I suggest how her life intersects with the lives of her correspondents.

In 1850, Elm Vale was sold. Now in her late seventies and eighties, Mary Emerson became a full-time "pilgrim," unsuccessfully seeking the "home for life" of which she dreamed. She boarded frequently in Concord and other New England towns until her final move in 1859 to Williamsburgh (Brooklyn), New York, where she lived her last, increasingly enfeebled, years under the care of niece Hannah Haskins Parsons. She died on 1 May 1863, a few months before her eighty-ninth birthday.

also prints some extensive extracts from Miss Emerson's letters. Before the computer simplified word processing, the sheer volume and complexity of these letters daunted several would-be editors, and only recently have a few intrepid scholars begun to use the manuscript sources in new ways.[6]

As Waldo Emerson recognized, these letters provide a unique source of information about a remarkable woman in a remarkable age. During the crucial period spanned by Mary Emerson's life—from the American Revolution to the Civil War—a young United States struggled to define itself, federalism yielded to more democratic values, religious orthodoxy came into conflict with Unitarianism and then Transcendentalism, and the great shadow of slavery loomed over the democratic experiment. In this volume, students of R. W. Emerson will find much concerning his relationship with his aunt and her formative influences on him. Moreover, Mary Emerson's writing testifies to what Jean Baker Miller has called "the variety of ways of being in the world that different women have constructed" and the vast "storehouse of creativity" that new scholarship on women has revealed. The work of Phyllis Cole, in particular, has begun to place this writing in the context of feminist scholarship, which seeks to "rethink the larger network of cultural traditions and social structures."[7] Here we find a woman negotiating her freedom beyond marriage, practicing a vocation that is closest to theology, and transforming the minor genre of letter writing into a major vehicle for free discussion.

Our portrait of Mary Moody Emerson—eccentric, demanding, rigid, Calvinistic, always in old age—comes largely from a younger generation, who did not know her until she was in her forties. In one frequently cited account, Frank Sanborn claimed her full height was only four feet, three inches; but she was eighty-one years old when he met her for the first time, in 1856, and, according to an earlier piece by Sanborn, she was about five feet tall. She was a woman of incredible energy: according to Waldo, she spun faster than the other tops. He also called her the "representative" figure of an older New England. Many are the reports that she always dressed in white (though references to dress fabrics in her letters dispel that notion), wore out several "shrouds," slept in a bed shaped like a coffin, and dwelt on death and the worm. Her disregard for social conventions is legendary: anecdotes stress her vagabond life, outspoken directness and obtuse questions, preference for the conversation of men, ability to say the most disagreeable things in the least time, strange eating habits, demanding nature, inability to manage finances, and quarrels with her landladies.

Like all round characters, Mary Emerson combined seemingly contradictory qualities: despite her emphasis on humility, she admitted she possessed the "cardinal virtue of *pride*" (MH: 834); contemning honor and ambition, she was supremely aware of the distinction attached to the Emerson name, which she traded on frequently. Her reputed distress at her most famous nephew's apostasy was countered by her excitement in engaging in the theological debate he stimulated. And she was a very youthful Sibyl: Elizabeth Hoar described her as having steely blue eyes, as always fair, with rosy skin that never wrinkled, and bobbed yellow hair that never grayed—and never quite stayed confined in its old-fashioned mobcap. Elizabeth Palmer Peabody told Mary in 1845, "You do not exhibit any of this death-in-life which I complain of—but coquette with life like a girl of fifteen—who knows herself sovereign and can afford to play with *All*" (MWA). In 1855 Henry Thoreau described her as, at age eighty-one, the "youngest person in Concord." When she reached her forties she began to use glasses for reading, and in her eighties, she was still riding horseback for exercise.[8]

Among Mary Emerson's "eccentricities" was her decision not to marry or become dependent on anyone. Instead, she turned a small inheritance into a living arrangement designed to serve her well—as it would have, had she not lived so much longer than she had anticipated. Unmarried, refusing to live as a poor relation, and unequipped for any other occupation, the Aunt Mary the younger generation knew moved about New England as she pleased, turning up to visit for weeks or months at a time, boarding at distant places, always searching for the excitement offered by solitude, society, and intellectual exercise.

The plain facts of her life are quickly told. Born in Concord on 25 August 1774, the fourth child and third daughter of Phebe Bliss and William Emerson (another daughter was born before Mary was two years old), Mary was, as she later punned, "in arms"—her mother's—during the battle of Concord, fought at the bridge close by the family home, the "Manse" built by her father in 1769. Her mother, the daughter and wife of Concord ministers, was (in Sanborn's terms) a "stately and cultivated lady" whose life was drastically changed by the American Revolution. Mary was less than two years old when her father—minister at Concord, son of the minister at Malden, and grandson of ministers who served at Concord, York, and Newbury—marched off as a chaplain with the Continental army. William's death at Rutland, Vermont, a few months later, in October 1776, deprived the child of father, mother, siblings, and home.

Instead of the Manse at Concord, Mary grew up in Malden, where she alone was sent to stay with widowed grandmother Mary Moody Emerson; after her grandmother's death in 1779, she remained in Malden with her childless aunt and uncle, Ruth Emerson and Nathan Sargeant (or Sargent). In 1780 her mother married Ezra Ripley, the new Concord minister, and they produced a second family, while Mary was unofficially adopted by the Sargeants—with the provision, it seems, that Aunt Ruth's portion of the grandmother's estate should come to Mary. (As one of five daughters, Mary's monetary prospects were extremely slim.) Also living in Malden was another aunt, Rebecca Emerson Brintnall, who was considered "insane" by the early 1780s. Thus, Mary spent her early "orphanship" (as she called this period of her life)[9] with genteel women in straitened circumstances. Mary was excluded

from all that her brother inherited, and in this her life epitomized woman's situation in a patriarchal culture. But she was not the tragic victim that writers such as Phillips Russell have created, with his description of her wandering "desolately from one house to another," cursed with a "mind which found no companionship, lacking any normal outlet or channel for her energies." Mary's solution to the problem of being a woman in this culture was both unique and personally satisfying.

In 1791, when she was seventeen, Mary went to live in fashionable Newburyport with her sister Hannah, who had recently married William Farnham, a bookseller from a liberal and cultured family; after less than two years in Newburyport she returned to Concord to help out in the home of her mother, an invalid who was "confined to her chamber most of her life,"[10] and stepfather. Thus Mary spent her early adulthood caring for the Farnham family (Hannah left ten living children when she died in 1807) and three generations of Blisses, Emersons, and Ripleys in Concord. Probably it was during these years that she eagerly listened to her brother and his friends from Harvard discuss Milton and discovered that the untitled poem she had found in her aunt's house and loved was *Paradise Lost*.[11] Her grandmother Bliss died in 1797, and when her aunt Ruth (widowed in 1798) remarried in 1802, Mary returned to Malden to live with new uncle Samuel Waite and Aunt Ruth. This six years was a delightfully happy period in her life; though she felt profoundly ignorant on the theological topics that her aunt and uncle frequently debated, finally, as she approached her thirtieth birthday, she had her first opportunity to develop her own knowledge.

Despite her apparently meager formal education[12] and heavy responsibilities for the young and the sick (she was an excellent nurse), Mary Emerson also managed to read, visit, converse—to enjoy, in other words, an intellectual and social life. She began friendships and correspondences with the elegant Mary Wilder Van Schalkwyck of Concord (whose marriage to Daniel White of Newburyport in 1807 resulted from Mary's matchmaking), Ann Brownfield of Newburyport, Sarah Hurd of Concord, and other young women (very few of these letters survive), and in 1804 and 1805 she wrote, as "Constance" to Mary Van Schalkwyck's "Cornelia" in a fictional epistolary conversation published in the *Monthly Anthology and Boston Review*.[13] In 1807 she turned down a proposal of marriage.

Perhaps the most important event in this outer life occurred between 1812 and 1813, when, through a complicated legal and financial maneuver, Mary Emerson invested her legacy from Aunt Ruth (who died in 1808) in a farm at Waterford, Maine, that she called Elm Vale. She shared the property with Rebecca and Robert Haskins, her sister and brother-in-law, in a secret arrangement that was the source of much rancor between Mary and her relations. For almost forty years, her home was this secluded farmhouse nestled among Waterford's gentle mountains and thirteen ponds or lakes, and close to Mutiny Brook and the cemetery—even though disputes over the prop-

Those of Mary Emerson's letters that have survived (probably less than half of those she must have written) record her continuing conversation with the people in this world she crisscrossed for so many years.[14] In 1832 her nephew Charles tried to explain how their conversation affected him:

> How often I think of your sister Hannah's critique on you—"There's Mary—Death, Judgment, & Eternity, nothing else will do for her". I think of it, because when I sit down to write to you, I involuntarily go through a mental process that answers to what Cousin talks about—"finding one's East"—I poise myself on my principles—& undertake simply to tell what is going on in the inner soul, after all the gates of disguise & deceit are passed. What is it to you, how I flutter or creep, through this day's show, or that day's drudgery? And how cold would you feel the style which should affect the Epicurean, & skim over the top of things, as if there were no depths to sound, & no wounds of the spirit to probe. (MT/MH)

Waldo—who reread her letters frequently—felt this power throughout his life, especially when experiencing doubts about his own creative powers and his profession. "*How rich the world is!* I said on reading a letter of M. M. E.," he exclaimed in 1839 (*JMN* 7:220). Rereading Mary's letters in 1843, he wrote, "Never any gave higher counsels . . . nor played with all the household incidents with more wit & humor" (*JMN* 8:391). Two years earlier, he had appreciated her letters as the work of "Genius always new, frolicsome, musical, unpredictable." He went on to describe their style and effect: "What liberal, joyful architecture, liberal & manifold as the vegetation from the earth's bosom, or the creations of frost work on the window! Nothing can excel the freedom & felicity of her letters,—such nobility is in this self rule, this absence of all reference to style or standard: it is the march of the mountain winds, the waving of flowers, or the flight of birds" (*JMN* 7:442).

While this baroque style was both admired and imitated by Waldo, its exuberance often precludes clarity. Mary's method is far different from that prescribed by the classical curriculum at Harvard, where her grandfathers, father, brothers, cousins, and nephews received their educations. Nephew William thought that Carlyle's description of the fantastic style of Richter could also be applied to that of his aunt, and the boys traded jokes about the latest "ludicrous profoundness" of a "she-Isaiah . . . alive to the comedy of her pretensions & costume [who] quotes as wildly as she talks" (*L* 1:242), as Waldo described a recent communication from his aunt in 1828. Letters begin in medias res and stop abruptly; spelling, punctuation, and grammar are careless; they are maddeningly allusive; their language ranges from the wonderfully poetic and highly rhetorical to the grandiose and trite. Nevertheless, in the best letters, the form is rich and fluid: it circles and weaves together topics appropriated from reading, conversation, and the lives and letters of correspondents, making the writing of Mary Emerson more difficult than if she were logical and linear.[15]

Reading these letters can prove a daunting experience. Mary recognized that she wrote obsessively on "one subject . . . the joy of reason & sensibility," or religion; and she conceded that her "homilies" might be as tedious as a "thrice-told tale" (MH: 670). Filled with questions and exclamations, her letters are also elusive: they require "much commentary," as Waldo recognized (*JMN* 16:15). Still, especially with that commentary (provided in this edition through both extensive annotation and introductory material), it is possible to appreciate her uniquely provocative voice; to discover the "she-Isaiah," the "weird-woman of her religion"; to see the "lightnings of [her] ladyship's satire" and hear her "hortatory eloquence," as her nephews described her and her writing in 1832 and 1828 (MT/MH).

The letter was Mary Emerson's art form, which she used to counsel, provoke, engage, inspire, and always challenge her audience. In her earliest letter, she calls herself an "epistler of *common size*," and numerous statements about the method, value, and purpose of letters indicate this was not a form she practiced casually. She strove to make each letter, as she did with each meeting with an interesting person, a "conversation" rather than a mere "narration" of facts (MH: 220[76]). Most often, her letters are feminized sermons on texts appropriated from her culture, especially as that culture was mediated by her correspondents.

A good example of how she uses texts from her correspondents' lives is a letter, written in February 1826 at Elm Vale, to nephew Charles Emerson, then a sophomore at Harvard. Mary's topics derive from Charles's letters to her over the past half year: society's advancement toward perfectibility; the Grecian oracles, the topic for the upcoming dissertation competition at Harvard; Charles's New Year's greeting; and his reference to Mary as a "weird woman." In each case, though the text is borrowed, Mary uses it to express her own ideas. Without apparent argument, she questions the idea of societal perfection by substituting the "higher order" toward which God is moving, the millennium; and she offers the present state of the law ("cumbered" by the "rubbish of barbarous ages") as a counterexample to his claim. A fantastically mixed metaphor perfectly embodies her own sense of the incomprehensible complexities of the legal system: law is "so loaded with [rubbish] and with artificial (and I fear fraudulent) apparatus that it takes years of the flower of life to pass thro' their dadalian volumns and . . . often the rights of an individual are lost in their involutions." From this she moves to her larger view: fifty years hence, perhaps, the law may be "regenerated" (with the help of her nephews, she hints) by a return to "those few grand principles" sufficient to all legal practice.

Other topics from Charles's letter receive similar treatment: though she wants to read his essay on the Grecian oracles, she immediately uses the subject for her own miniessay, an imagined re-creation of the human journey after the flood. Charles's New Year's greeting opens the door for her view of time, which she expresses in a cryptically poetic passage built on an image of the self as the pointer (or "gnomon") on a sundial, which marks time by its own shadow; but the time toward which she points is incomprehensible to her. Charles's epithet "weird woman" prompts her to define herself: "I who live so as to try never to offend by one singular word—whose whole time is devoted to one & the same object, pray you spare my age & vocation."

In each case, Mary relocates herself at the center of Charles's text, makes his tenor serve as vehicle for her object: to regenerate the world through perception of a few grand principles. To some extent, this is a variation on the Puritan moralizing habit. But her use of this technique in many letters goes beyond such an inheritance; her transformation of the events and ideas of her correspondents' lives is a way of insinuating herself into their texts. Whereas Beatrice Didier has called the letter the "place of conflict"[16] between woman's desire to write and society's silencing of her, the "society" of letter writing opens Mary's mind by giving her a place to speak. Her method is organic; her thoughts grow naturally out of the texts she takes from her correspondents. She creates a feminized version of orthodox realities: a universe designed and controlled by an all-powerful God; the authority of Scripture and the testimony of revelation; human depravity and the need for redemption by Christ, but one in which the God-given gift of inquiry is the guiding spark, and feelings (or "affections") are the enabling power.

It is impossible to appreciate these letters without some idea of the religious view of reality Mary Emerson took for granted. For Waldo her writing was "the best example I have known of the power of the religion of the Puritans in full energy. . . . The central theme of these endless diaries, is, her relation to the Divine Being" (*JMN* 16:15–16). She practiced what she preached to seventeen-year-old Ann Brewer in 1811: "Make religion the great business of your life. Accept with humble zeal every possible method of improving yourself. [Contemplate] *Death, Judgment* and *Eternity*" (MWA).

"Religion" was central to her life, and she held steadfastly to some of the outward forms of an earlier Puritanism (such as her solemn observance of fast days and her refusal to travel on Sunday). However, she was less "Puritan" than the word connotes to many people, less Calvinistic than the legends about her suggest.[17] Jonathan Edwards's statement in his preface to *Freedom of the Will* adequately describes her basic position: "Of all kinds of knowledge that we can ever obtain, the knowledge of God, and the knowledge of ourselves, are the most important. As religion is the great business, for which we are created, and on which our happiness depends; and as religion consists in an intercourse between ourselves and our Maker; and so has its foundation in God's nature and ours, and in the relation that God and we stand in to each other; therefore a true knowledge of both must be needful in order to true religion."[18] Like Edwards, she stressed "connection" and "relation," not separation and sin. She saw life as a "web" of "eternity," the "long woven scheme of man's creation and redemption." The practice of religion was the discovery of the "golden links w'h bind [the individual] to the great end of existence" (MH: 704). She urged Waldo to study the "relations that bind the universe and God" (MH: 863), desired to know the "intimate relations . . . of the other world with our souls," and constantly saw correspondences, analogies, and emblems in nature, a harmony between works and word. Reason connected her with Being; nature connected with spirit, cause with effect.

Mary Emerson's theological position was actually quite complex. Writing to Elizabeth Hoar in 1846, she said, "I who never know nor talk of sects can be fed with crumbs every where. tho' I rarely enter a Chh." Her "religion" combined orthodoxy with the more rational and evangelical tendencies alive in her day. Just as Waldo, in his 1837 Phi Beta Kappa address, insisted on the excitement of being born in an age of revolution, when old meets new, Mary Emerson rejoiced that she lived in an era of intense theological dispute: "In the wanderings of your imajanation, dear Charles," she asked in 1829 (in a letter Waldo probably reread only a few months before composing "The American Scholar" in 1837), "can you find a world where it is likely there are such differences in theology?" Rather than despairing, she found her time a "period of wonderfull revolutions," as new and old views clamored to be heard: Calvinistic, Trinitarian, liberal, old and new Unitarian, orthodox, Universalist, materialist, Deist, humanitarian, Arian, Socinian, pantheist, transcendentalist. She claimed to follow the "religion of Paul," calling herself a "bible theist," an "old Unitarian," and "orthodox." In fact, she advocated a middle position between "coarse damnatory Calvinism," many of whose doctrines she found "horrible" and "exclusive," and the timid, easy faith of the liberals or "new Unitarians," as she called them. Her theology was broad enough to encompass both God's sovereignty and human freedom, both God's benevolence and man's sin and redemption—and the nexus was the human mind.

In many respects, her theology closely resembled the post-Awakening, liberal, Arminian position that began to develop in about 1734. As Conrad Wright shows, in this period New England liberals rewrote Christian theology to conform to the basic principles of the Age of Reason, shifting the emphasis from the inscrutable sovereignty of God and innate human depravity to the benevolence of God and humans' free agency in working out their own salvation. The new doctrinal position that emerged combined Arminianism, supernatural rationalism, and anti-Trinitarianism.[19] Her grandfather, father, and brother played important roles in the early stages of the shift from orthodox to liberal religion, after the Awakening's revivalism and the theology of Edwards and his heirs had done their work and the Revolution had radically changed the social and political landscape. Her maturity coincided with intellectual movements of great influence: the "Unitarian controversy" that began with the appointment of Henry Ware, Sr., to the Hollis professorship at Harvard in 1805, when Harvard Unitarians clashed with the Andover orthodox and when William Ellery Channing emerged as the leader of Unitarianism; Americans' discovery of German metaphysics in the 1820s and 1830s; and the transcendentalist challenge that grew out of this ferment.

For the "bible theist," Scripture provides the only secure proof of the truths arrived at by human reason and experience. Mary Emerson's theology rested on a very traditional bedrock. She stated it simply in an 1825 letter to Waldo: "Man has deeply fallen. An Enymy *hath sown tares*. A friend is plucking them up—is renovating the fallen & guilty." She proceeded to reiterate this scheme, paraphrasing the words of Saint Paul, for which another baroque artist (George Frideric Handel) created a memorable setting: "*As by means of Adam* sin *entered and death so* by *means of a divine* man *death & sin are destroyed!*" (1 Cor. 15:21).

This account, written for twenty-one-year-old Waldo when he was considering studying for the ministry, restates her earliest epistolary expression of her religious ideas, written thirty years earlier to her future sister-in-law Ruth Haskins, when Mary herself was twenty-one. Much like Anne Bradstreet in "Contemplations," the writer finds her subject in the appearance of nature on one exquisite October day, which led her with "wonder and inquiry" to meditate on the fall in Eden, on the sad loss of happiness of this first pair, but without imputing to them a legacy of original sin. "How aggravating and painfull to see them falling by that very capacity, freedom of will," that could raise them, she exclaimed. At the same time, she stressed the whole scheme of redemption and man's reinstatement to divine favor. She goes on to emphasize the essentially Arminian belief in human potential: she speaks emotionally of the "power of man" to rise above his fallen state, through "persevering dilligence and activity to regain what is lost . . . and secure the offer of life and glory."

Most of the homilies or sermons in these letters, however, explore non-biblical texts drawn from Mary Emerson's wide reading in theology, philosophy, and literature, and they reveal her Enlightenment interests in "evidences," natural and supernatural, external and internal, and her joy in the harmony between Scripture and the voice within, history, nature, and philosophy. "Without evidence [faith] has no charms," she insisted, and she believed the inquiring human spirit was designed to lead the mind to God. In the "earthly Eden of xianity . . . the intellect gathers most effectually the fruit from the tree of knowledge," she asserted; ten years later, she called reason the "godlike spark . . . ordained to thread it's way to the first Cause—to find it's origin—to build it's faith by it's own sternest laws." Her thought was never static: each encounter with a new idea led to a new synthesis. By 1832 she had arrived, through her explorations of German thought, at a more "transcendental" expression of the paradox of the will: she speaks of the only true philosophy—the religion of Paul—as the "divine personal agency as of your own consciousness—God within the heart but not the heart."

However, these appeals to the intellect never obscured Mary Emerson's emphasis on the primacy of the "affections," often experienced in rapturous encounters with nature. The theme of her earliest letters is the "feelings of the human heart"; later she called these nonrational experiences "miracles," and

miracles, she asserted, are "the foundation of our faith." In 1830 she worried
about Charles's "lack of enthusiasm" and "sacred fire," and she reminded him
that "one great ice berg is a shallow theology" (MH: 681). Reason meant not
"cool thoughts," but emotional experiences, found in the mystical, idealistic, and Platonic side of Puritanism as well as the intuitionist moral sense
described by the English philosopher and theologian Richard Price and the
Scots philosopher Thomas Reid. The unassailable sense of Being, the "it is," as
Samuel Clarke expressed it,[20] was the spark that set the mind in motion; consciousness, feelings, the connection between God and the self, created "moral
epochs" or the "*feeling infinite,*" which was evidence of immortality. She repeatedly stresses the joy of religion, the excitement of the "ardent enlarged
mind" as it pursues "the glorious prize of immortal glory," and the importance
of nature as a source of "symbols of character human & divine."

Despite her enthusiasm and her open-minded quest for religious knowledge, Mary Emerson never repudiated her ancestors' sense of the mysterious,
the inexplicable, the inscrutable nature of God, of the "divine agency," and
of what she frequently calls "the enigma of human nature." As was the case
with Melville and Hawthorne, these dark questions fascinated her and drove
her inquiries. She trusted in an infinite design, but one image for that design
was a "measureless dial" with dread and veiled "numbers." She faced head-
on the complex issues of sin and atonement ignored by the liberals, while she
avoided the extreme doctrines of innate depravity and election. In her Chris-
tology, which was essentially Arian, Jesus is the eternally created Son of God
and necessary mediator in the redemption of humankind. His death and sacrifice are an "astonishing apparatus" miraculously constructed to reveal God's
will and attributes, as do Scripture and the book of nature. Like Edwards,
she arrived at a paradoxical synthesis of the problem of free will and divine
providence: "necessity . . . in its' perfect accordance with . . . liberty."

Her letters are full of wonderful expressions of this remarkable "scheme"
devised by God, of the "divine econymy" that unites chance and Providence,
the "liberty of the creature & the agency of Creator": she describes "liberty . . . girdled . . . within the infinite Orb of Being" (MH: 679) and claims
that "Destiny allows of much freedom." The "true metaphysicks," she insists,
is the "glorious secret" that God is in all; this is the "ground fact" that makes
us free agents.

The continuing presence of this harsh, stern, demanding thread in her religious framework has led to Mary Emerson's being classified as a latter-day
Puritan. She believed the liberal school had failed to deal with questions of
necessity, "the nature of man & of the origin & nature of evil," the origin
and meaning of Christianity. In their emphasis on God's benevolence and
man's potential, the liberals had lost sight of eternity. Even the Scriptures, she
admitted, "are misterioss there," for they cast both "light & darkness" on
these matters—but, she adds in a significant image, "Perhaps it is this feeling
[of "misteriossness"] which leads us on with unwearied curiosty to search

it's meaning, as we should follow some supernal vision that was always the same yet never the same." This was the gleam she followed in her letters and conversation.

Comparing God to a human father in his 1828 sermon "Likeness to God," William Ellery Channing asked, "And what is it to be a father? It is to communicate one's own nature, to give life to kindred beings; and the highest function of a father is to educate the mind of the child, and to impart to it what is noblest and happiest in his own mind." It is hard to imagine Mary Emerson reading this sermon without thinking of the father she had never really known, the education she had missed, and the pilgrim life she had led. In connection with the subject of war, she wrote, in 1832, "Of the widows & orphans—Oh I could give facts of the long drawn years of imprisoned minds & hearts w'h uneducated orphans endure. But it is among the means of discipline and no worse than other warfare with poverty and ill & ignorance." Perhaps it was her marginal position in society, as a woman and "orphan," cut off from her inheritance, that made her cling at times to a stern view of God's sovereignty and human weakness, of God's inscrutability and incomprehensible plan—to a gap between God and human that prevented her, finally, from accepting the transcendentalists' belief in the God within. Within this spiritual reality, her own suffering made sense.

At the end of his lecture-essay "Mary Moody Emerson," Waldo commented sardonically that, despite the appeal of his aunt's "arcana," "it is easy to believe that Cassandra domesticated in a lady's house would have proved a troublesome boarder" (*CW* 10:432). She has indeed proven difficult to domesticate. But, like Mary herself, these letters are perhaps most welcome in small doses—which is, after all, how her regular correspondents experienced them. Usually arriving fortnightly or monthly, a letter was written on a 9 ¾-by-15-inch sheet of old-fashioned, heavy ivory or thin, pale-blue paper bought by the quire and folded to give four full sides, the last typically reserved for the address. The folded letter was sealed with a wax wafer—often red, or black flecked with green, if she could get it—stamped with the thimble that had pressed against more letters than needles (*JMN* 3:98).

In black ink now faded to brown, she filled at least three sides of each folded sheet with an elegant, slightly spindly, not entirely ladylike hand: right-sloping, angular, her handwriting was characterized by bold downstrokes and many loops (which make distinguishing both capital letters and lowercase vowels particularly difficult). She frequently used the space on the address side for afterthoughts or continuations (in the style of Richardson, as she explained). Typically she caught up on family matters first (marriages, illnesses, deaths, moves, distinctions), asked questions and made requests, and continued a dialogue, at the same time that she was writing her sermon on a text from her correspondent's life and letters. Each letter contains a world of ideas, as passed through her personal lens of family, religion, and the revolutionary period in which she lived.

It should not be surprising that this "auction of the mind" (I borrow Emily Dickinson's metaphor for publication) of Mary Moody Emerson has been so long in coming. From her handwriting to the volume of her output, from the complexity to the tediousness of many of her missives, these letters present a challenge to general reader and editor alike. However, this edition, through its judicious selection of letters to significant correspondents on representative topics, makes it possible to see her and her world anew. I hope it will enable a new generation of readers and scholars to see beyond the anecdotes and around the eccentricities, to see into the mind and heart of a remarkable woman writer who obviously had something to say to her contemporaries and who can continue to speak to ours.

NOTES

1. Ursula K. Le Guin, "The Fisherwoman's Daughter," *Dancing at the Edge of the World: Thoughts on Words, Women, Places* (New York: Harper and Row, 1989), 213.

2. Francis H. Allen, ed., *Men of Concord and Some Others as Portrayed in the Journal of Henry David Thoreau*, with illustrations by N. C. Wyeth (Boston: Houghton Mifflin, 1936), pl. 4. The painting is in the Concord Free Public Library.

3. Abbreviations of depositories are used to identify locations of manuscripts cited in the Introductions and notes. Citations of letters by MME not printed in this edition that are in the RWEMA Collection (MH) will be further identified by one of two notations: "MH: 000" designates a letter in bMS Am 1280.226(000); "MH: 220(00) or 225(00)" refer to bMS Am 1280.220(00) or 1280.225(00). Non-MME manuscripts will be cited by depository designation only. My use of Joel Myerson's transcriptions of letters by the Emerson brothers is indicated by "MT/MH" (where the manuscript is in the RWEMA Collection) or "MT/EW" (where the manuscript is in the Ethel Wortis Collection).

4. To date, the most significant work on MME is by Phyllis Cole. In "The Advantage of Loneliness: Mary Moody Emerson's Almanacks, 1802–1855," in *Emerson: Prospect and Retrospect*, ed. Joel Porter (Cambridge: Harvard University Press, 1982), 1–32, Cole describes the spiritual diary (she discovered MME's manuscript in the uncataloged RWEMA Collection) and begins to explore it as a major woman's text. In "From the Edwardses to the Emersons," *CEA Critic* 49 (Winter 1986–Summer 1987): 70–78, Cole reflects further on MME's place within the larger generational history of the Emersons, especially the family-centered "opposing culture" of women (71), the basis for her forthcoming book on MME. A useful genealogical chart of the Emersons is on p. 78.

5. RWE, "Mary Moody Emerson" (W 10:399–433), a portrait that James Elliot Cabot believed was "somewhat softened by [Emerson's] veneration" (*A Memoir of Ralph Waldo Emerson* [Boston: Houghton Mifflin, 1887], 1:30).

6. The lesser-known sources include several by Franklin B. Sanborn, who prints portions of six letters in "A Concord Note-Book," *The Critic* 48 (Feb., Apr. 1906): 154–60, 338–50; Sanborn reprints this material in *Recollections of Seventy Years*, 2 vols. (Boston: R. G. Badger, 1909); *Sixty Years of Concord, 1855–1905*, ed. Kenneth W. Cameron (Hartford, Conn.: Transcendental Books, 1975); and *The Personality of Emerson* (Boston: Charles Goodspeed, 1903). *RevSR* includes excerpts from three letters by MME (as well as many letters from SR to MME); manuscripts for these letters

seem to be among the now-lost Ames family papers, privately owned, transcribed by Joan Goodwin in 1954. *MWW-M* prints portions of four letters by MME (all but one located in MH-AH).

Along with a few additional anecdotes in Edward W. Emerson's *Emerson in Concord* (Boston: Houghton Mifflin, 1889), RWE's and Sanborn's accounts have served as the major texts for most subsequent writing about MME, which skews the material in several ways (as the following titles suggest): R. F. Dibble, "She Lived to Give Pain," *Century Magazine* 112 (July 1926): 326–32; Van Wyck Brooks, "The Cassandra of New England," *Scribner's Magazine* 81 (Feb. 1927): 125–29; and Rosalie Feltenstein, "Mary Moody Emerson: The Gadfly of Concord," *American Quarterly* 5 (Fall 1953): 231–46. An earlier Sanborn piece is "Thoreau's *Autumn* and Mary Moody Emerson," dated 13 Sept. [1892], in *Transcendental Writers and Heroes*, ed. Kenneth Walter Cameron (Hartford, Conn.: Transcendental Books, 1978), 97–98. Remarkably few scholars have made use of George Tolman's more liberal and varied selection of texts (from both her letters and her "Almanack") in his *Mary Moody Emerson* (privately printed, by Edward Waldo Forbes, in 1929), read at the Concord Antiquarian Society in 1902. MME has always figured in some way in RWE's biography, with perhaps the most interesting earlier comments appearing in O. W. Firkins, *Ralph Waldo Emerson* (Boston: Houghton Mifflin, 1915), esp. 4–8, and Phillips Russell, *Emerson: The Wisest American* (New York: Brentano's, 1929), 19–30. Ralph L. Rusk's edition of the letters and his *Life of Ralph Waldo Emerson* print extracts from previously unpublished manuscripts; and Tilton's two volumes of additional letters continue the tradition. Publication of *JMN* provided additional materials for exploring connections between RWE and MME, including many (but not all) of the letters between them that RWE copied there. Scholars who have used this material include John McAleer, *Ralph Waldo Emerson: Days of Encounter* (Boston: Little, Brown, 1984); David R. Williams, "The Wilderness Rapture of Mary Moody Emerson: One Calvinist Link to Transcendentalism," *SAR 1986*: 1–16; Lawrence Rosenwald, *Emerson and the Art of the Diary* (New York: Oxford University Press, 1988); and Alan D. Hodder, *Emerson's Rhetoric of Revelation* (University Park: Pa. State University Press, 1989). While Williams has used the "MME Notebooks" (MH) into which RWE and his son Edward copied many extracts from MME's manuscripts, none of these studies draws on the manuscripts themselves.

The "intrepid" scholars are Phyllis Cole (see above, n. 4), and Evelyn Barish, whose *Emerson: The Roots of Prophecy* (Princeton: Princeton University Press, 1989) is the first major study since Rusk's *Life* to make extensive use of these materials. See also Barbara Packer, "Origin and Authority: Emerson and the Higher Criticism," in *Reconstructing American Literary History*, ed. Sacvan Bercovitch (Cambridge: Harvard University Press, 1986), 67–92.

7. Jean Baker Miller, *Toward a New Psychology of Women*, 2d ed. (Boston: Beacon Press, 1986), xii, xvi; Cole, "Edwardses to Emersons," 71.

8. Most of these stories are preserved in sources cited in nn. 5, 6, above, and *JMN*; see also the articles on MME in *DAB* and *Notable American Women, 1607–1950: A Biographical Dictionary*, ed. Edward T. James, Janet Wilson James, and Paul S. Boyer, 3 vols. (Cambridge: Harvard University Press, 1971), 1: 580–81; HDT, *Journals* (Boston: Houghton Mifflin, 1906; Princeton: Princeton University Press, 1981–); Susan Loring, "Reminiscences of Concord," *The Concord Saunterer* 17, no. 3 (Dec. 1984): 12–17; [F. B. Sanborn], untitled obituary notice, *Boston Commonwealth*, 8 May 1863; and

EPP's tribute to MME, in Thomas Hovey Gage, Jr., *Notes on the History of Waterford, Maine* (Worcester, Mass., 1913), 54–57. For EH's comments, see *MWW-M*, 109–17, probably the source for Sanborn's use of the same material. HDT's comment is in a letter to H. G. O. Blake, 9 Dec. 1855 (*The Correspondence of Henry D. Thoreau*, ed. Walter Harding and Carl Bode [New York: New York University Press, 1958], 401–2). In this biographical overview I have drawn freely on printed and manuscript sources concerning MME; much family information comes from *IpsE*.

9. MME called her early years in Malden a "slavery of poverty and ignorance and long orphanship" ("Almanack," Phyllis Cole transcription).

10. "Reverend Samuel Ripley," *Christian Examiner* 44 (Mar. 1848): 178.

11. Somewhat different versions of this story are told by EH in *MWW-M*, 114, and RWE, "Mary Moody Emerson."

12. Whereas Tolman says MME "attended the district school" in Malden (4), Barish, *Emerson*, assumes she had "little or no schooling" (39). MME is silent on the subject.

13. See Introduction to part 1, n. 6. Phyllis Cole first recognized MME's authorship of the "Constance" letters ("Nature Within and Without," New World Colloquium, Concord, Mass., 6 Jan. 1988, 5–8). Three other publications (all printed anonymously) are an obituary notice of LG, *Christian Witness* (Boston), 13 May 1842; a fictional piece, "Meeting of Two Friends after Long Separation by Death" ("from a fragment of 1830"), *Portland Register*, 27 June 1846, rpt. in *Christian Register* (Boston), 22 Aug. 1846; and an article, "The Sabbath," *Middlesex Freeman* (Concord), 14 Nov. 1851. " 'The Woman': A Reminiscence," *Christian Register*, 24 Jan. 1852, signed "An Octogenarian," may have been written by MME, but heavily revised by someone else.

14. Most of MME's surviving correspondence is addressed to her family and to ASG and EH, both of whom she came to consider her nieces. However, references in her letters make it clear that she corresponded extensively with Sarah Hurd; MWW; Ann Bromfield Tracy; niece Louisa Farnham Dewey and her husband Orville; TTS; her sisters Hannah Farnham, PER, and REH; and their children, numerous Emerson cousins, and others. Very few of these letters survive. Other references point to additional letters addressed to her major correspondents.

15. Compare, for example, Edmund Wilson's puzzled response to Harriet Beecher Stowe's style (*Patriotic Gore* [New York: Oxford University Press, 1962], 34–35) to RWE's description of MME's writing: both point to a need to consider these features in the context of a "feminist poetics": to look at what Elaine Showalter calls the "social dimensions and determinants of language use, the shaping of linguistic behavior by cultural ideals" ("Feminist Criticism in the Wilderness," in *The New Feminist Criticism*, ed. Showalter [New York: Pantheon, 1985], 259–60).

16. In *Le Journal intime* (Paris: Presses Universitaires de France, 1976), 11, Beatrice Didier calls the letter "le lieu d'un conflit."

17. See, for example, the entry for Sarah Alden Bradford Ripley in *Notable American Women*: "When Mary tried to force her own grim Calvinism on [Sarah], she refused to accept a creed that might close her mind 'against the light of truth' " (164). Three recent examples of the persistence of this label of Calvinist are McAleer, *Ralph Waldo Emerson*, 34; Lawrence Buell, *New England Literary Culture* (Cambridge: Cambridge University Press, 1986), 168; and David M. Robinson, "Historical Introduction," *CS* 1:3. On the other hand, David R. Williams recognizes the difficulty

of codifying her position, and he distinguishes between the "literal and legal side of Calvinism" and MME's more "imaginative and lively" version ("Wilderness Rapture," 4). Eleanor Tilton concludes that MME was "just what she claimed to be: an old-fashioned Unitarian. She cannot be called a Calvinist" (*L* 7:3). Although I would argue that MME was moving beyond old-fashioned Unitarianism, Tilton's term is usefully free of connotations of rigidity, narrowness, and dogmatism. MME communicates an open and joyful vision of a meaningful universe of connections presided over by a designing God, who is first discovered in *"those keen vibrations of soul which . . . immortalizes moments and which give to life all the zest of enjoyment."*

18. Jonathan Edwards, *Freedom of the Will*, ed. Paul Ramsey, vol. 1 of *The Works of Jonathan Edwards*, ed. Perry Miller, Sydney E. Ahlstrom, John E. Smith, et al., 7 vols. to date (New Haven: Yale University Press, 1957–), 133.

19. Conrad Wright, *The Beginnings of Unitarianism in America* (Boston: Beacon Press, 1955), 3–5, 252; see also Ahlstrom, 391–402.

20. Samuel Clarke, *A Demonstration of the Being and Attributes of God: Works, 1738* (New York: Garland Publishing, 1978), 2:527.

Editor's Note

THE MANUSCRIPTS

The vast majority (about 730 items) of Mary Moody Emerson's manuscript letters are in the Ralph Waldo Emerson Memorial Association Collection in the Houghton Library, Harvard University. The second largest collection (122 items) is in the Gage Family Additional Papers of the American Antiquarian Society. The Egbert Starr Library of Middlebury College is the depository for 18 manuscripts, 16 of which seem to be letters; 11 letter manuscripts are in the library of the Andover-Harvard Divinity School, and 3 in the Ralph Waldo Emerson Collection, the University of Virginia Library. The large private collection of manuscripts owned by Ethel Emerson Wortis and transcribed by Joel Myerson includes only 1 letter by Mary Emerson. Letters or portions of letters that do not seem to survive in manuscript are printed in Sanborn (3), *RevSR* (2), *JMN* (3), and *MWW-M* (1).[1]

Because of the condition of some of the manuscripts and the ways in which they have been cataloged, it is impossible to arrive at an exact number of surviving letters. Although many leaves of the "Almanack" are badly scorched around the edges, remarkably few of the letters were damaged in the fire at Waldo Emerson's house in 1872. However, separated letters, numerous fragments and scraps, miscellaneous writings (from the "Almanack" to obituaries and brief reviews), and single manuscripts containing separate letters or notes to different people all complicate the picture. In RWEMA, almost every item has been separately cataloged, except for letters to several persons in a single manuscript. In MWA, most of her letters have been separated from other Gage family correspondence and placed in three thick folders, somewhat chronologically arranged; in my work at MWA I discovered 4 more items scattered among other materials, as well as separated materials that belonged together. Nothing by Mary Emerson was known to exist in MH-AH until Phyllis Cole discovered 1 letter, and I later discovered 10 more; these were subsequently cataloged.

The copy-text for each letter printed here is the holograph (with one exception, a copy in an unknown hand); the depository for each manuscript (and, for RWEMA manuscripts, the complete finding number) is indicated in the unnumbered textual note following each letter. The note also describes pertinent details not part of the letter proper—usually address, postmark, and endorsement. Whereas researchers have often used George Tolman's more legible transcriptions of the bulk of the letters in RWEMA, I transcribed all of the letters from photocopies of the holographs and then perfected my transcriptions of the letters selected for publication by reading them against the manuscripts. I have also read Tolman's transcriptions and used them to help with difficult readings.

Letters are arranged in chronological order. In the case of undated letters, I have assigned a probable date, wherever possible; where no such assignation is possible, undated letters are printed at the end of the year to which they most probably belong.

EDITORIAL TREATMENT

Any printing of a handwritten document stereotypes the original in ways that make it easier to read, thus changing the reading process. While it is important to render the handwritten words as accessible as possible, certain limits on editorial privilege are set by natural variations in the author's style. My goal in this edition has been to print a large and representative sample of Mary Emerson's correspondence in a form that will make the letters available to a wide spectrum of readers without eliminating those stylistic features that make her unique. I have tried not to tamper with the shapes of the mental handwriting—unorthodox punctuation and spellings ("curiosty," "independance," "goverment," "weake," "popolare," "nessicity," and so forth); ungrammatical, confusing, or awkward expressions; frequent use of abbreviations—that reveal the mind in process, in the act of writing, just as the ink on the page traces that act. Much that a very liberal modern editor might change (to correct or improve the texts, as Tolman was wont to do) has been left as Miss Emerson wrote it. These features do make reading these letters a little more difficult, but they also make up the substance of her peculiar style, which was a result of her having not been educated alongside her brother, William, and was perhaps a sign of her rebellion against what he represented. Because I believe that the whole letter was her artistic form, most letters are printed in their entirety; omissions are indicated by a conspicuous, three-asterisk sign to mark the ellipsis.

On the other hand, given the fact that Mary Emerson is not a recognized author with a published body of work, I have not attempted to follow the exacting editorial standards outlined in the _Statement of Editorial Principles and Procedures_, published in a revised edition in 1972 by the Center for Editions of American Authors of the Modern Language Association. This edition of Mary Emerson's letters does not include, for example, tables of emendations, alterations, end-of-line hyphenations, or textual variants. I will, however, deposit in the Houghton Library of Harvard University a list of individual instances of silent emendations.

Mary Emerson's idiosyncratic style presents certain challenges. A special problem is created by her use of old-fashioned symbols for money: for example, throughout her life she wrote in terms of pounds and shillings rather than dollars and cents. Tolman chose to render her pound sign (#) as a dollar sign ($); but Mary Emerson's failure to make the switch is characteristic. In the few cases where she also speaks of shillings, I have tried to represent her symbol as closely as possible: ⁵⁄ₘ. Another case in which I have decided not to emend this writer's particular habits is in her occasional use of the apostrophe to make the plural of a noun that ends with *s,* such as "genius' " and "exegesis'," or the singular form of a verb, such as "[he] hypothesis'."

In cases when obvious errors are either significant or unresolvable, a note may be used to explain the problem, but the printed text retains the manuscript reading. For example, in 1850 she writes "sole" where "soul" seems to be required, but to emend here would erase the trace of a possible pun.

Editorial Symbols

The letters are printed in straight text, with the following exceptions: a superscript ⁿ indicates a textual note; a superscript numeral indicates an informational footnote; braces (sometimes called "curly brackets") indicate an unrecovered letter or word due to a blot, tear, or burn; and brackets indicate an editorial interpolation, almost always a mark of punctuation but occasionally a word, where the omission would cause a serious misreading.

Textual Notes

Textual notes point to dubious or alternative readings of words (alternative readings from the Tolman transcripts are designated T, and a few variants in Waldo Emerson's transcriptions are designated *JMN*). Textual notes also selectively report substantive authorial alterations to the text, using the symbols adopted by the editors of *JMN*: angle brackets to indicate canceled material, and up- and down-arrows (↑ ↓) to indicate added material. Nonsubstantive alterations include corrections of obvious errors (such as interlineation of an omitted but necessary word or insertion of a missing letter), simple additions, and cancellations of meaningless material, such as incomplete false starts. Substantive alterations represent a significant change of thought (as when the writer changes "imbitters" to "impresses" or cancels a complete phrase). A textual note is also used where it helps to explain a confusion in the printed text that results from interlineation of a second word without cancellation of the first, as in "greatness of a nation literature," where the manuscript reads "nation ↑ literature ↓ ." Textual notes also point to other problems or solutions, such as a word that may be canceled or a possible meaning for an obscure abbreviation.

Informational Notes

Informational notes clarify a number of things: they identify correspondence mentioned or implied, persons, references to reading and other allusions, quotations, and events, and they provide, when needed, cross-references to other letters and notes. Full information on persons and publishing information for books and articles read by Mary Emerson will be included at their first mention; subsequent mentions of these persons and works will be identified only if obscure in the letter (the reader should consult the index to locate the first reference). In the case of references to and quotations from other manuscript sources, I follow the policy outlined in note 3 to the Introduction. Unidentified items are usually ignored in the notes.

Datelines

All datelines are printed as they appear in the holographs (dates added by others are mentioned in the notes), even when it is clear that information in a given dateline is incorrect. However, information is added in brackets as needed to make each dateline as complete as possible. Dates added in other hands are reported in the notes, which also discuss problems with dating particular letters.

Silent Emendations

Many features that result from handwriting or the fragility of the manuscripts would be merely confusing were they reproduced in the printed text. Where the manuscript is blotted, torn, or burned but the missing letters or words are obvious from the context, they are silently added. Where the letter *l* or *b* is inadvertently crossed, or where a *t* is uncrossed (a notable example is "immorlats" for "immortals"), no mention is made of the error, unless there is doubt as to her intention. Where words are not finished at line or page breaks but the intended word is obvious, the word is silently completed; conversely, where words or syllables are repeated at line or page breaks, the extra word or syllable is silently omitted.

In the following cases, I have also emended the printed text without report:

Missing or extra pen strokes. Where missing or extra strokes or loops create apparent misspellings that impede reading, or where two letters seem to be collapsed (one written over or inside the other), I have silently supplied the missing letters in cases where strict fidelity to the written word would prove confusing or distracting. These slips of the pen result in such apparent misspellings as "inpired," "exmption," "advesity," "incitng," "pleasue," "obsure," "recipocal," "souce," "pevent," "possiblity." A special case is the word "principle," which most often lacks either *n* or *c*; in all cases I have silently emended the word to read "principle," rather than "priciple" or "priniple." Other words contain an extra loop, creating spellings such as "conveniience" and "everey." In all cases, the word is written correctly elsewhere.

Metatheses. In Mary Emerson's handwriting, letters are frequently transposed, resulting in common errors, such as "freind," "liesure," "thier," and "persume," all of which are printed as written, because they do not seriously impede reading. The problem of *ei* versus *ie* is compounded both by the similar formation of these letters and by the frequent extreme-right placement of the i-dot. However, in the case of a metathesis that results in a more difficult spelling, such as "spets" (steps), "counrty" (country), "scloded" (scolded), "Agens" (Agnes), "Montagin" (Montaign), "deit" (diet), "prhase" (phrase), "Stwo" (Stow), the word is normalized and printed correctly in the text, without a note.

Letters s/z. In the years before her handwriting matured, before 1810, Miss Emerson's *s* and *z* can be distinguished easily. Later, these two letters become almost identical. In cases where it seems possible to distinguish these letters, I have printed what I see. In other cases I have printed what seems to be her usual practice. Close inspection of the manuscripts indicates that she was inconsistent in her spelling of words such as "idolise," "apologize," "recognize," "sympathize," "realised," and "analyse." An exception is her spelling of Elizabeth Hoar's name, which is almost always written "Elis." or "Elisabeth."

Words that are incomplete or contain extra syllables. "We" is emended to "wear," "b" to "by," "revelalation" to "revelation," "grieveded" to "grieved."

Unhyphenated words. Unhyphenated words that are broken at ends of lines are silently joined. In the case of words that may be hyphenated compounds broken at ends of lines, I have followed Mary Emerson's usual practice for these words. Because she rarely hyphenated compound words, only one hyphenated compound occurs at a line break in this edition: "Daphne-like" at 169:23. All other end-of-line hyphenations result from the typesetting process.

Incomplete alterations. Incomplete alterations are completed or reported as textual notes: "you ↑ seem to ↓ felt" is silently emended to "you seem to feel."

Underlining. Words underlined in the manuscript are printed in italics; double underlining is reported in a textual note; words partially underlined in the manuscript are printed as though they were completely underlined, unless the partial underlining seems meaningful: for example, "*un*principled," "*dis*claiming."

Punctuation. On the whole, I have not regularized unorthodox punctuation. For example, I have left the apostrophe in the possessive pronoun "it's" or "its'" (a typical feature of eighteenth-century orthography) wherever it occurs; I have not added apostrophes to possessive forms of nouns that lack them, and I have not repositioned misplaced apostrophes. Where periods or commas fall outside of quotation marks, I have left them as they appear. I have not supplied missing periods at the ends of sentences, and I have reported (in brackets) the few instances where I have added a comma or a dash. In cases where a sentence ends with a period and is then followed by an afterthought, I have retained the superfluous period. However, I have silently supplied any missing halves of paired punctuation marks (quotation marks, parentheses, and dashes) when their correct placement can be determined. Often, for example, she ends a passage with a quotation mark, but if it is impossible to determine where the quotation was supposed to begin, no quotation mark has been added. I have also made these marks consistent where she has begun with one (such as a single quotation mark or an opening parenthesis) and ended with another (such as a double quotation mark or a dash).

A special problem occurs with Mary Emerson's use of two different sizes of parentheses: she may enclose parenthetical material using normal, large parentheses, two commas, or an intermediate form that looks like smaller, lower parentheses. Where the smaller parentheses seem intentional (for example, at times the opening "low" parenthesis occurs at the beginning of a line), I have printed a normal parenthesis.

Paragraphing. Though new paragraph indentations occur far less often than one would wish, I have resisted the temptation to break up the many very long paragraphs into smaller units. I have, however, added a paragraph indentation in the following cases: where the previous line ends considerably short, and the next line is flush left; where the previous line ends slightly short but the next line is flush left and begins a new topic; where a new topic begins flush left at the top of a new page; where significant extra space has been left in the middle of a line and the topic changes; and where a line space is followed by a new paragraph without a paragraph indent.

Vertical space and positioning of text. Vertical space (often one line above and below salutations and closings, and between paragraphs) is eliminated in the printed text. I have retained one line of vertical space when it separates portions of a single letter written at different times or to different individuals. Additional vertical space in the manuscript is reduced to a single line of space in the printed text. Horizontal placement of datelines, salutations, and closings is regularized to approximate the writer's practice.

Page breaks in the manuscript are not indicated in the printed text. Unusual placement of text is not noted unless there is doubt as to where it belongs or it seems to require comment (such as a message written on the outside, and therefore intended to be read before the rest of the letter, rather than merely added as an afterthought). These situations are reported in informational notes.

Authorial footnotes. Mary Emerson's own notes to her letters are indicated by single asterisks (her own usual notation is an "^{x}" or an asterisk); these notes are printed at the end of her letter, regardless of the page on which they appear in the letter.

Authorial abbreviations. I have not expanded Mary Emerson's abbreviations ("w^d" for "would," "xianity" for "Christianity," "opp^y" for "opportunity," "aff^y" for "affectionately," "W—d" for "Waterford," "C—d" for "Concord," and so forth. Abbreviations frequently terminate in superscripts;

these are regularized and printed as roman superscripts throughout, even when they may have been underlined or marked with one or more dots below in the manuscript. In cases where her abbreviations are confusing or obscure, I have printed the abbreviated word as it appears in the manuscript and used a textual note to explain what it probably stands for, such as "trans^s.] *probably abbreviation for* transcendentalism" and "im^t] *probably abbreviation for* immortality." In the case of her frequent use of initials for names, see the list of abbreviations or the informational notes used to identify those that are not clear from the context.

A special case is the word "received," which is rarely spelled in full: it may occur as "receved," "receed," "rceved," "rceed," "rievd," and other forms. Whether this is the result of abbreviation or missing strokes, in all cases I have chosen to print the complete word.

Inside addresses. The names of recipients (such as "Mrs. Emerson") sometimes written at the left margins at the ends of letters, are silently omitted.

NOTE

1. For a complete list of all located letters and locations, see my "Calendar of the Letters of Mary Moody Emerson," to be published in *SAR 1993*; letters printed in this edition are marked there with asterisks. Sources mentioned here are discussed in n. 6 to the Introduction.

PART I

1793–1809

In July 1793, when she wrote her earliest surviving letter, Mary Emerson was nineteen years old. The last letter in this chapter was written in 1809, when she was thirty-five. For the entire seventeen-year period, only thirty-nine letters survive, very few when compared to the hundreds of letters we have from each decade between 1820 and 1860 and too few to permit the construction of a detailed calendar of residences for these years. From the thirty-nine letters I have selected twenty-four, to eight correspondents. While they reveal that Mary Emerson was by no means always "in old age," they also indicate that her young womanhood contained the seeds of her later character, the religiously centered yet independent "herb and berry woman" of Waldo's mythologizing.[1]

President George Washington began his second term in 1793, and John Adams and Thomas Jefferson served as the second and third presidents of the new United States in these years. Yet no mention of political events occurs in the letters. Instead, the letters document Mary's transition from her childhood home to her adult home. From 1793 to 1797, home was the parsonage (or Manse) at Concord, which she called "the best place in the world for me; who seldom wander from home without loosing ground in my spiritual Journey." Her Concord family included her mother, Phebe Emerson Ripley; her stepfather, Ezra Ripley; her grandmother Phebe Walker Bliss; her Emerson sisters Phebe (two years older than Mary) and Rebecca (two years younger); and her Ripley half siblings, Sarah, Samuel, and Daniel, who in 1793 were twelve, ten, and nine years old. Older sister Hannah had married William Farnham of Newburyport in 1790, and brother William had been ordained and settled as minister at Harvard, Massachusetts, in 1792. Before this, Mary had lived mostly in Malden with her grandmother and aunts, until she went to Newburyport in 1791 for a couple of years to help care for the first of many nieces and nephews, the first two Farnham children, who were born in 1791 and 1792.

Much later, when she was fifty-eight years old, Mary recalled her determination to provide for herself at this time: "The first use I made at 19 of the knowledge of imperishable matter was, in gaity, to tell my sisters after all, *I* must have place to exist in however it seemed so difficult" (MH: 719). Finding her own place was indeed difficult. In 1796 William married Ruth Haskins; their first child, Phebe, was born in 1798. In 1797 grandmother Bliss died and sister Rebecca married Robert Haskins, and Mary left Concord. For the next five years she divided most of her time between Malden (where her uncle Nathan Sargeant died in 1798) and Newburyport, but she still visited regularly at Concord and Boston (where her brother William moved his expanding family in 1799, when he became minister to the First Church). By 1803, all of her siblings were married and her half siblings grown up: Samuel and Daniel were at Harvard College, and Sarah remained at home and cared for their mother; sister Hannah Farnham had recently given birth to her ninth child, and sister-in-law Ruth Emerson had had her fourth—Ralph Waldo Emerson; in Waterford, sister Rebecca Haskins now had three children. Aunt Ruth had recently remarried, to Samuel Waite, and Mary returned to Malden for several years, calling this newly constituted family the "happiest" she could imagine. In 1805 she attended the birth of the last Farnham child; in 1805, 1807, and 1808, Emerson nephews Edward, Robert Bulkeley, and Charles were born; and she continued to travel between Malden, Concord, Boston, and Newburyport.

Although no letters are dated from Waterford, Maine (which she would consider home after 1813), Mary was there earlier. In 1800 her sister Phebe had married the Reverend Lincoln Ripley, who was the brother of their stepfather, Ezra, and who had recently become the Congregational minister at Waterford. Later that year, sister Rebecca Haskins and her husband moved to Maine as well. Mary probably visited for the first time in 1801.[2] In 1805 William and Ruth's second child, John Clarke (b. 1799), was sent to stay with his Waterford aunts in the hope that the mountain air would improve his health, and a letter from Mary to Ruth Emerson (1805 or 1806), which reported on John Clarke's welfare, may have been written at Waterford. By September 1806, however, Mary was back at Newburyport, where her brother wrote to her and related Waite's description of "the condition of his family as hopeless unless you returned" (MH).

Mary did return to Malden, but she sold her property there (which she co-owned with Samuel Waite) in January 1807. According to George Tolman, who studied Malden records and family documents, over the years Aunt Ruth's first husband, Nathan Sargeant, had purchased from Ruth's siblings more than half of the estate of Mary's grandmother Mary Moody Emerson. In 1791 he signed over this property to the Reverend Peter Thacher (Tolman assumes this was to prevent its seizure by creditors and, by an earlier agreement, to ensure its being inherited by Mary Emerson.) In 1796, soon after Mary became twenty-one, Thacher conveyed the property to " 'Mary Moody Emerson of Concord, singlewoman,' " and she signed a lease that allowed the Sargeants to stay there for the remainder of Ruth's life. After her husband died in 1798, Ruth continued to hold the lease until her marriage to Waite in 1801, when Mary sold part of the property to Waite and leased the remainder until 1807. In that year, she and Waite sold it for three thousand dollars, three-fifths of which was her portion. Tolman believed that, despite Mary Emerson's frequent complaints that she had somehow been defrauded in this transaction, "she got more of the purchase money than she was entitled to" (4–5).

About this time (she was now thirty-three years old) she refused an offer of marriage from "Mr. Austin of Charlestown," a lawyer, according to a note on Waldo Emerson's manuscript of his lecture "Mary Moody Emerson" (MH). She was in Newburyport at the time of sister Hannah's death (probably from tuberculosis) in March 1807. For two more years she moved between Concord, Boston, Malden, and Newburyport. In 1808 aunt Ruth Waite died, and within a year Waite married the "insane" aunt Rebecca Parker Brintnall. A month later (May 1809—the last letter of this part) Mary Emerson tells her friend Mary Wilder White of her plan to go to Waterford, though she claims indifference to place and describes herself as the most at "*loose ends* of all the world." [3]

The range of correspondence and subjects in these letters indicates that Mary Emerson was not as deprived as her later memories and complaints suggest; her youth was not, as one writer has described it, always "bare and severe, completely unadorned by any variety, gaity, or possibilities of choice." [4] She was involved in the social life of her small, family-centered circle, with its never-ending cycle of marriage, birth, and death. Indeed, her geographical movements of this time were usually determined by these events. In 1793 she responded to her brother's question as to whether or not " 'any of us girls are courted' " with a resounding "No!" With the local gentlemen the question was always, "Is there money? Are there lands?" (MH: 1047). She read current literature, wrote and published some literary pieces, read, traveled, visited in fashionable homes, conversed and counseled, attended the theater, and played matchmaker. At Malden, she later recalled, she developed her first "taste for books and the idea of a friend" from a Mrs. Dexter, "a woman whose strong sense and taste rendered her interesting" (MWA); there, too, she met Ruth Haskins of Boston, who often visited her Malden grandmother and aunts. Mary actively encouraged her brother to consider "the aimable Ruth" in 1795, and eighteen months later they were married. In September 1806 she arranged a meeting between Mary Van Schalkwyck and Daniel White, a Newburyport lawyer and friend; eight months later they were married. [5]

Though the letters in this part contain disappointingly little evidence of reading and other intellectual experiences in these years, other sources help to fill out this meager picture: two manuscript lists of books (made by her brother, William, and her friend Mary Van Schalkwyck) indicate the wide range of reading available to her, from theology and sermons (which she could also borrow from Ezra Ripley) and devotional literature to poetry, English periodical essays, plays, classical authors in translation, history, and travels (MH, MH-AH, and *MWW-M*, 393–95). Four of the nine surviving letters from William to Mary, written between 1803 and 1811, mention books she has requested or he is sending. In 1807 William indicates that he sends a book to her at Malden each week by way of a Mr. Barrett (MH).

Mary's friendship with Mrs. Van Schalkwyck and, beginning in May 1804, William's position as editor of the *Monthly Anthology*, opened a wide door to nontheological literature. As editor, William not only had access to the wide variety of books reviewed in the *Anthology* each month but also was someone to whom she dared send writing for publication. In the epistolary conversation she and Mary Van Schalkwyck published in five installments between July 1804 and July 1805, Mary Emerson played the part of "Constance" to her friend's "Cornelia" in elevated discourses on death, the imagination, the study of nature, and biography.[6] Their common theme might be the bliss, described by Alexander Pope in *An Essay on Man*, of one who "looks thro' Nature up to Nature's God" (4:323).

It is true, however, that much of young Mary Emerson's time was spent playing a different sort of Constance—as nursemaid or *garde-malade*. The description comes from Mary Van Schalkwyck, who went on to explain that Mary Emerson's concern for "all the little wants and comforts of an invalid, together with her sublime views of immortality, render her peculiarly fitted for her charge."[7] The dominant tone of her writing from the beginning indicates her piety and testifies to how fully she lived her life in accordance with religious beliefs and principles that were well formed before she turned twenty.

Mary Wilder Van Schalkwyck provides the best glimpses of Mary Emerson's social self in these years. She had grown up in Concord, married the French émigré son of a West Indian sugar planter when she was nineteen, followed him to Guadeloupe, where they encountered first a slave insurrection in 1801–2 and then tropical diseases that killed Mrs. Van Schalkwyck's beloved brother, Henry, and her husband. Barely escaping death herself, Mary Van Schalkwyck returned to Concord, a twenty-two-year-old widow, in 1802. As children growing up in Concord, Mary and her brother, Henry, had been friends of Sarah and Daniel Ripley for many years, but the two Marys probably did not begin their friendship until 1803, the year of the first surviving letter from Mary Van Schalkwyck to Mary Emerson, who was six years her senior. The beautiful and cultured young widow found in the older woman a special quality she repeatedly praised to her friends. "Had I . . . eloquence," she wrote in 1805, "I would describe the influence of religion on the mind, the temper, and the life of this uncommon woman; as it is, I despair doing justice to her" (209).

Still, she comes close, as in this description written in 1807 to her fiancé, Daniel Appleton White: "You know not how much I owe her. Courageous in correcting, and generous in commending, she stimulates her friends to the pursuit of excellence, by every motive and by every method that piety, good sense, and affection can suggest" (262). To her friend Susan Lowell, she writes, "Her society ever fortifies and elevates above the events of life. Regarding nothing as evil which tends to moral improvement, she places sickness, sorrow, and death in a sublime and consolatory point of view" (249). Another description, this one in a letter to Sarah Ripley, comes from 1806, when Mary Van Schalkwyck's mother was dying: "Mary beam'd on us the day before yesterday—& like a minist'ring Angel, consol'd—fortified—& elevated. The happiness that results from a connection—with her—is it not nearly without alloy? We can suffer no anxiety on her account— She is beyond the reach of *real* misfortune—& this is the inestimable privilege of loving those who rest on the arm of Omnipotence" (MH-AH).

Mary Emerson as seen by her friends is quite different from the complex psychological being who emerges from Phyllis Cole's study of the "Almanack," which Mary began in these years. Recognizing that these diaries represent an "exploration of solitude," Cole finds here the voice of "piety-in-exile": of an isolated woman poised between extreme Calvinism and extreme Arminianism, between self-denial and self-affirmation, between a loathing and an exhilaration for life.[8] The letters occupy a middle ground between the external view of her friends and the intense inner searching of the private and confessional spiritual diary. While they do suggest her movement through and then out of her various families in Malden, Concord, Boston, and Newburyport and ultimately to her own future at Elm Vale in Maine, at every point they also show her rooted in a Christian tradition that not only sustained, encouraged, and excited her but also was demonstrated through her life. Repeatedly she reminds friends and correspondents of their connection with the infinite. Present humility and trials are linked to future happiness, while the virtues of the interested heart are contrasted with the hopeless pursuits and vacant minds of the ambitious. The momentary, the present, the transitory are always raised to the viewpoint of eternity.

With the exception of a few letters to her brother, most of the letters in this part seem rather juvenile, forced, and artifically literary. Coy pleas for attention, repartee about who is being courted by whom, elaborate epistolary contracts, Latinate diction, a profusion of relative clauses and prepositional phrases heaped one atop the other, and apologies for her inadequacies—all suggest a rather sheltered young woman who is eager to please. Nevertheless, as early as 1806, her brother was critical of her "obscure style of writing, consisting of bloated figures, far-fetched allusions, and turgid words," her "illegible chirography, [and] bad orthography," which often rendered her "sublime epistles" perplexing; and he complained that while she could "hurl . . . shafts of satire," she was unwilling to receive them. He advocated "plain facts, just thoughts, simple expressions, and right spelling." For "plain Christians," he counseled, "religion consists in being intelligible as teachers, and useful in society" (MH).

William had spelled out this utilitarian model of Christian epistolary excellence three years earlier in the first of a series of letters addressed to "misses, of from twelve to fifteen years old," which was printed in the *Boston Weekly Magazine*. He outlined three rules to follow when "conversing" on paper: the writer should choose her subject matter according to her relationship to her correspondent (though these thoughts should seem "natural" rather than learned); she should dress her thoughts carefully and neatly, not ostentatiously; and she should work to achieve a clear and beautiful handwriting.[9]

Such counsel, as well as her reading in eighteenth-century polite and theological literature, profoundly affected Mary Emerson's style. In 1806, however, we begin to hear a different voice. In that year she still writes to Rebecca Thoreau in the self-conscious fashion she would always adopt for those she considered her superiors: "I am pleased to be able to afford you a moment's gratification, in humble addition to those resources of constant enjoyment which you are so largely furnished with in those prospects which you are constantly drawing nearer to realize in that animated & spiritual existence which so fully possess your ambition." [10] In the same year, a letter to brother Samuel Ripley begins, "Your letter which bore indubitable marks of coming from the heart gave me positive pleasure. Your situation, your pursuits, your resolutions & your success in the cause of virtue meet my sympathy & respect." Yet from this same year, another letter, probably written at Waterford and addressed to her sister-in-law Ruth, flows simply and naturally: "My dear Sister," she begins, "is anxious to hear by this time the history of her little Son."

This voice is newly mature and assured, the public version of the voice of solitude that Mary Emerson had been exploring in Concord and Malden during this period. The years before 1809 correspond to the model of the "female" moratorium described by Carolyn Heilbrun (an idea borrowed from Erik Erikson): the period when the individual appears "to be getting nowhere . . . [and] unclear as to what [her] aims might be," while she is actually preparing for some future, though unrecognized, "task" and moving toward an "unconscious decision to place [her] life outside the bounds of society's restraints and ready-made narratives." [11] It is no accident that this voice speaks first in what may be her earliest surviving letter from Waterford; for Mary Emerson's decision, three years later, to locate herself at Elm Vale constituted her definitive break with the social plot from which she was removing herself.

NOTES

1. Feltenstein, "Mary Moody Emerson," 231, calls her "one of those women whom we can never imagine except in old age"; RWE's comment is in *L* 1:343.

2. WE[2] (Boston) to REH (Waterford), 2 Nov. 1801, asks whether MME is with Rebecca or Phebe (MH).

3. Two letters addressed to MME at Waterford survive: MWW to MME, 27 Aug. 1809 (MH-AH); and WE[2] to MME, 23 Oct. 1809, in which he urges her to return to "come home . . . and help to alleviate the burdens of a minister of religion" (MH).

4. Feltenstein, "Mary Moody Emerson," 232.

5. David Greene Haskins suggests that MME and Ruth Haskins were related through the Waites of Malden (*Ralph Waldo Emerson: His Maternal Ancestors* [Boston, 1887; Port Washington, N.Y.: Kennikat Press, 1971], 40); however, the connection may have been Aunt Rebecca's first husband, Jacob Parker, whose mother was Mary Upham (*IpsE*, 125). Ruth Haskins's mother was Hannah Upham.

6. Cornelia to Constance, *Monthly Anthology* 1 (July 1804): 393–95; Constance to Cornelia, ibid., 1 (Aug. 1804): 453–54; Constance to Cornelia, ibid., 1 (Dec. 1804): 646–47; Cornelia to Constance, ibid., 2 (Feb. 1805): 72–73; Constance to Cornelia,

ibid., 2 (July 1805): 342–44. Constance also contributed an extract from Richard Price on morals to the Aug. 1804 number (456–57) and a letter to the editor, "designed as a compliment to the preface of our first volume," dated 25 Jan. 1805 and printed in 1805 in volume 2 (140–41). In it Constance urges the editor not to forget the importance of "theological sentiments" among the more worldly fare of the *Anthology.*

7. *MWW-M,* 208–9.

8. Cole, "Advantage of Loneliness," 4, 8, 13.

9. "Letter 1: Aug. 24, 1790," *Boston Weekly Magazine; or, Ladies' and Gentlemen's Magazine* 2 (19 Nov. 1803): 13.

10. WE[2]'s first rule: "If she is your superiour, you certainly should suffer no trifling ideas to escape your pen, whilst writing to her; but should be careful to introduce such subjects, as would lead you rather to ask her opinion, than hazard your own. If your correspondent is an equal, it is optional with you to select and discuss your favorite topicks. Good sense, however, as well as politeness, seems to require, that you consult the disposition and taste of your friend; for if you do not please, you will not probably improve her" (*Boston Weekly Magazine,* 19 Nov. 1803).

11. Carolyn Heilbrun, *Writing a Woman's Life* (New York: Ballantine, 1988), 49–51.

1793

To William Emerson[2]

Concord   July 29   —93

Well, my good Brother, have you selected the rank I might take in order to fill some of those mighty voids between you & some epistlory correspondents? What exalted seat may I humbly take to form one link of the descending chain that connects you with an epistler of *common size*? When mounted you the *demi* throne? From whence you distribute the shallow streams of applause, bleakly murmuring with hard pebbled sattire. And my ambiguous letter the dark cause of your bright effussions. What brilliant effects! However, right well guesed (*if not judged*) the judicious Rebecca[1] at the fault you would perceive in the letter of an ill fated composuist. But *disrobed* of *reverence,* for a moment hearken! All the perplexed ideas that can be huddled in the discovered cell of an ambiguous head is not so discordant as the gargon of {inf}lating & flattering sounds. These, good Sir, will not—cannot harmonize in my *nicely tuned* ears. But er'e the uncouth vibration has ceased to irritate my perceptions, I pray my understanding may receive a shock, sufficient to disperse the clouds that have hitherto obscured the clear *hemmisphere of perspecuity.* Thus—& *too* much for the answer of your first head. Now for a part of the alphabet, that you anounce with as much ease, as when a school boy. "*Fine girls all*" Yes. But may be L[2] is *finer* than you imagan. As follows—that the more compressed atmosphere of reason & sense might be too powerful for her fine wrought nerves; and alass! she *may evaporate* in the fumes of sensibility, & thus become *extinct in the world* of *reason*! In short, she is too much of the woman to be angel. P. might breath a more *dense climate* without *suffucation*—but she appears to need a luxuriant, yet purified softness to assimulate to a feminine seraph. Of B. I alass! am ignorant—and how timid & apprehensive is ignorance! Yet, I will hope that she not already so fixed in her orbit that she will not easily yeild or soar in compliance with a united soul. For can you be too ambitious in a choice, which you would joy to have approved, by more worlds than one? Happy the kindred souls that shall hereafter bask in the same beams of equal glory! But I retract, & must ask pardon for amusing myself at the expense of your time & patience. Your letter & the sedateness of the night have diffirent aspects & may excuse a smale *jumble* of ideas if any thing of the kind should be observed. I will close with the petetion that you will ever consider me in the light of a *friend & Sister*. An idea that shall forever soften each care & pain that may be felt

by the, then, happy & affectionate
Mary Emerson

The family are well, & w^d send love were it not for their tyrant Morpheus. I hope he will leave Becca early to receive mine.

Aha! the morning brings Mr H.[3] no corrections, no inspections of my letter. Take *your dear sister Mary* as she is; tho'tless & persuming & you are welcome to all her productions. I congratulate you, & all who love you that you are preserved from the trouble of a *visitation*[n] to Concord.

I wish thee well!
Mary.

MH: bMS Am 1280.226(1046). *Addressed:* The Reverend William of / Harvard. *Endorsed:* Miss M. M. Emerson. / July 31. R. / Jan. 22. 1794. A.

    visitation] ⟨second⟩ visitation; second *possibly not canceled*

    1. Sister Rebecca Emerson, then sixteen years old.

    2. Probably Lucy Grosvenor, daughter of the former minister at Harvard, the Reverend Ebenezer Grosvenor (d. 1788). MME to WE[2], 25 Feb. 1795, responds to her death on 8 Feb. (MH: 1048). P. and B., below, are unidentified.

    3. Mr H.: possibly Hurd, probably the bearer of the letter.

1795

To WILLIAM EMERSON[2]

Concord, M[ar]. 17 —95.

My dear Brother,

    What would I give to possess, for ten minutes, the art of persuasion! But on what subject can I interest your imaganation or touch your heart? How excite a resolution that will bring you to partake of the pleasures of Concord?

Shall I recall the image of these pleasures which are past with the irrecoverable flight of days and years, and paint the joys that were wont to swell your bosom when in the once loved habitation of your[n] father? No! a retrospection like this, would but serve to soften and lull the soul to repose. It is the prospect, the dear hope of future bliss which awaken its desires and tempts to enterprize. Shall I name the means by which you may, at least, partake of the bliss of others? You would already realize it; by contemplating the joyfull countenances and gladdened hearts of twelve or thirteen persons, if your approach was announced   Imagine the almost breathless messengers each one striving first to articulate the news in the ears of a Sick parent and grandparent. Imagine the effect such an information will create in the health and spirits of those you love and revere, and tell me if I needed eloquence[n] to inform you that the former (health) has failed in our Mother for these five weeks and in Gran'r [1] for this some time. But a harder task remains; and for your sake only I again wish for eloquence. I want to remind you of charms that shall have a different aspect, that can lay no claim to filial or fraternal obligations. I want to remind you of Haskins and Larkin,[2] that you may make arrangments for proceeding farther than C. Do you remember that such names exist, or has the cold & solitary winter left you so philosophized that you are insensible to the sounds? You appear solemn and sublime, and I am tempted to erace the name of a lady. Should I omit personalities, and aim at description; talk of love, and faintly trace some of the ever interesting delights which result from the culture of this *animated friendship,* methinks it would not relish on your taste, which, not vivified by sensibility, as corrected by understanding, would be disgusted rather than entertained. How is it my dearest B. are you altered or is my imajanation lost the idea[n] of your relaxation from duty and labour. Be it as it may, of the amiable Ruth I *must* write. And yet I have nothing new to write, but cannot withstand the *something* that almost forces my pen along. I have already told you that she is virtues self. And I repeat it, that in her look and manners is combined every thing which gives an idea of the whole assemblage of mild and amiable virtues. Added to this a natural good understanding and a uniform[n] sense of propriety which characterizes her every action and enables her to make a proper estimate of every occurance. Yet true it is, my dear Ruth, thou dost not possess *those energies,—those keen vibrations of soul* which seizes pleasure—which immortalizes moments and which give to life all the zest of enjoyment! But why should I regret this incapasity? If thou wert thus formed, thou wouldst be a very different being from what thou now art. The tear of commiseration which is now wont to fill thine eye would too often, e're it reached the lucid orb, be drenched in culturing some luxuriant flower which the fervid fancy creates at the sight of woe. The sigh of meekness and gratitude[n] would frequently be suppressed by the anxious throb of vanity and the triumps of self exultation. A thousand unborn sensations would impede the gentle accents of benevolence, which now dwell on those lips that seem open but in the cause of virtue!

Figure 1. Mary Emerson's
Concord Grandparents,
the Reverend Daniel Bliss
(1715–64) and Phebe
Walker Bliss (1713–97).
Courtesy the Ralph Waldo
Emerson Memorial
Association.

Are you out of all patience W. or will you listen a moment to ye name of *her* whose eye is lustre and whose voice is melody? Elisa[3] is truly amiable, and bids fair under an ingenuous culture, to be great and noble. At present, enervated by too much praise, her heart beats thick at the distant sound of applause! Pleasure dances before her glowing fancy with a thousand unsubstantial charms. But soon will her *ever yeilding* mind banish delusion and imbrace the unadulterated essence of virtue. Alass! that this eager desire of fame[n] should be placed so near the female heart! How fatal does it prove to the real improvement of this ill fated sex!!!

Were I to feel it nessesary to apoligize for the freedom[n] and frequency of my epistles, I should at once cease to enjoy the ease & pleasure with which I relax from every care and employment to converse with you.

From a friend and sister
Mary Emerson

MH: bMS Am 1280.226(1051).
your] ⟨thy⟩ ↑ your ↓
eloquence] ⟨to wish for⟩ eloquence
idea] ⟨remembrance⟩ ↑ idea ↓
uniform] ⟨native⟩ ↑ uniform ↓
gratitude] ⟨greatness⟩ gratitude
fame] ⟨notice⟩ ↑ fame ↓
freedom] ⟨lenght⟩ ↑ freedom ↓

    1. Mother Phebe Bliss Emerson Ripley (1741–1825); grandmother Phebe Walker Bliss (1713–97).

    2. Haskins: "the amiable Ruth" mentioned below, whom WE[2] married in Oct. 1796; Miss Larkin is unidentified.

    3. Probably Eliza Grosvenor, a sister of Lucy (see MME to WE[2], 29 July 1793, n. 2), mentioned by WE[2] in his diary for Mar. and Apr., following Lucy's death (MH).

To WILLIAM EMERSON[2]

Concord, Aug. 12, 1795.

My dear Brother,

    I remember you once complimented me by saying I appeared contented. I wish my present feelings did not render it difficult for me to recollect what constitutes tranquility. But I do not ask for the joys of life. No, I deserve not happiness if my mind does not afford it. Contentment, when not the effect of stupidity, is the genuine offspring of heroism, a heroism which triumphs over the struggles of ambition, and strenghtens the soul to bear the painfull and disgusting ills of life in noble expectation of future enlargement. But I am too often forced to compare the sensations of my mind[n] to those which we experience, by striving to distinguish a great variety of objects, which are presented to our eyes, by the feeble light of an expiring taper. Tho' perhaps I do not give you an idea of my feelings; but I can do no better. I sometimes endeavour to recall the images which my warmer fancy, in earlier days of liberty and leisure, was wont to present. But for want of some culturing hand, those few flowers have fallen and withered; even before they could be distinguished from the comcomitant weeds of error and folly which are not, as yet, extirpated. Alass! how often do I feel inadequate to the task; and how apt is the feeble mind to look around for *some culturing,* some encourageing hand. From this fruitless search I return to my own heart; and wrap myself in this one solitary, yet precious design, that of keeping free from guilt. I am aware that most of your sex would say[n] my dejection was merely the effect of that passion which in youth, always seeks an object for its exercise. I promise you, my Brother, it is no such thing. My passions are not restless; besides I should scorn to shelter the weakness that renders me insufficient to my own happiness, in the indulgence of a passion which for the most part, tends to enervate the female mind, and renders it avaricous of the smalest applause. It is the exercise of the more pure and more disinterested feelings of the soul, which are called friendship, which can call into action whatever is great and lovely in the human heart. What will not the reverence, the gratitude which friendship inspires bring to maturity! But on this subject, about which I have always formed the most delightfull conjectures, let me now be silent. Tho' it is not ten days ago since I thou't that thy shades, Oh Harvard,[1] fostered that celestial plant. In thy peacefull retreats, said I, will its luxuriant fruit yeild a flavor at which even angels will be delighted, while they wonder to behold the children of men already partaking their joys! But alass, will this flower never be suffered to decorate this rude and inclement soil   A flower whose virtues would rob the clime of all its inclemency. Will it always be vulnerable to the rash invader! will it always shrink from the look of suspision! Surely this can not be always the case. No, I had rather imagine that solitude and *perhaps* disappointment had chilled that bosom which I have hithertoo honoured as a sanctuary where friendship and devotion (those kindred flames) were most dear, and most reverenced. But I am so far from supposing that this bosom has lost its native hospitality, that I have ventured, for this once, to seek a charitable asylum to the murmurs of a discontented mind.

Fare well! Mary Emerson.

MH: bMS Am 1280.226(1049). *Addressed:* The reverend W. Emerson. / Harvard. *Endorsed:* Miss M. M. Emerson. / Sep. 14, 1795. R. / Sep. 15. 1795. A.

mind] ⟨intellectual powers⟩ ↑ mind ↓
say] ⟨attribute⟩ ↑ say ↓
1. WE[2] was settled as minister at Harvard, Mass., in Aug. 1792.

To Ruth Haskins

Concord   Oct.   1795

How do you do my dear Ruthe? This is the first convenient moment I have had to make this enquiry since I saw you, and when I parted with you, it was in prospect of returning to Boston. At my coming home I realized the loss we had sustained by your departure; and the loss of that animation which the "countenance" of a friend inspires. Yes, my friend, I look towards the river but not with "*those elegant perceptions*" which the delightfull sensations of admiration, esteem & mutual friendship excited in my own heart, as well as that of my dearest W.—— No, the verdure of the grass is gone. The leaves of the tree, under which we sat, are withered and fallen. The hill on which we rambled, is become barren. The sun has, since, cut short his journey, and the skies begin to frown. But, the face of nature is constantly changing and now threaten's a dismal appearance; the subjects on which we dwelt are ever the same, always interesting and sublime. Tho' so many ages have passed, yet we look back on the origin of our existance with wonder and inquiry. And what can more excite them? than to contemplate the sad & wonderfull reversion of the innocence and happiness of the first of our race? To behold them in habits of friendship & daily intercourse with heaven and possessed of the power to perpetuate it. How aggravating and painfull to see them falling by that very capasity, freedom of will, which could give to virtue all its merit and to obedience its reward. But if this retrospect humbles depresses & enervates the mind the prospect of the redemption of mankind by our Saviour raises and animates *it* to the enobleing exercises of gratitude & praise. We ought perpetually to rejoice that man is reinstated in the divine favor; placed anew in the station of probation, and possesed of the power to continue in it. Yet still he has the power of self destruction, and alass! most of our race fall from the remaining innocence of our native state, and debase the noble traces which were not destroyed by the first fall. But we do not forfeit life. We rise when we believe; we repent and become the expectants of immortality and glory; not by own merits, but in consequence of our love & obedience to the great Redeemer.

Does not the reflection of these things excite to more persevering dilligence and activity to regain what is lost; to cherish what remains and secure the offer of life and glory; to extirpate the bad habits we have willfully gained, and those propensities which we have the misfortune (*not the guilt*) to find inherent in us from the natural tendency of our first parents transgression! All this is placed in the power of man by the blessing and aid of Heaven. Yet that dillijence and self denial which alone call down these blessings are difficult to be gained.

We are loath to consider *this,* chiefly, as a scene of *danger & duty* and the ardent desire of ease and present pleasure, are, at first almost inextinguishable. But why do I say *we?* when I talk to you Ruth   Surely you have conquered or have never felt those passions which render the practice of virtue difficult. *Then Pray for your friend!* If I were not *such,* I should apoligize for the lenght & freedom of this epistle   But I studied in the choice of my subject that which I tho't would be most interesting to you and I concluded that the serious would be most acceptable.

My parents & sister desire particular remembrance to you & yours. I regret that Phebe cannot gratify herself by writing but you & Elisa will excuse her.

My love to Sister Ladd[1] & every one of the rest. Your gratefull and truly affectionate

Mary Emerson.

MH: bMS Am 1280.226(964). *Addressed:* Miss R. Haskins / Boston / Designed for the care / of / Sam[l] Bliss Esq[r].

1. MME's sister Phebe (1772–1839); RHE's sisters Elizabeth Haskins (1771–1853) and Mary Haskins Ladd (1766–1839).

To WILLIAM EMERSON[2]

Concord, dec. 27, 1795.

My dear Brother,

I received your letter with a delight to which my heart had long been a stranger. I rejoiced to know that *you lived,* were in health, and the subject of the *pleasures* of this life; for I involuntarily began to think of you as one who was once dear, but had long since departed to some happier reigions. I am not gloomy, nor by any means jesting. I am glad you remember us and our little concerns. We are all well. Sam[l] is on the recovery from the scarlet fever, which he has had favorbly.[n] We are made happy by the return of my sister B.[1] whose virtues have suffered no diminution by the change of circumstances & power[n] of fashion.

I am at Concord. It is the best place in the world for me; who seldom wander from home without loosing ground in my spiritual Journey. Mr & Mrs W.[2] sent, very politely, for me to pass "a week or two" with them which I did, about the last of oct. As I thought it prudent to decline their invitation for the winter, I carried my refusal with me. I found by experience in the course of a short week, what I had before reluctantly beleived, that without *money* or uncommon merit I had no right to expect much from uncommon professions of friendship. However, we parted with those civilities which are customary in the commerce of the world. I heartily rejoice that such disappointment do not make me quarrel with myself or the prevailing constitution of the world. Humble at the knowledge of both I ought to be. I moreover gain this religious knowledge by every days experience, that to be happy here & forever, I must be *meek and lowly in heart.* Will you laugh at me, if I tell you, that I never feel the influences of humility less than when I see you, hear you speak and feel animated by your smiles. Thus true it is that moments of prosperity, especially when thus unusual, are not favorable to the growth of this lowly virtue. Pray for me, my dear Brother, that I may serve God with that awe & reverence which his perfections demand, and feel that joy & delight which such a service ought always to create. I hope I am not deceived in the sincerity of my obedience, or my views of Jesus Christ when I think of dying for I can think of death with some sattisfaction & much hope. I then feel the need of a saviour in all the amiable characters which he bears. To feel more my guilt and my dependance is what I wish.

Figure 2. Mary Emerson's birthplace, the Manse, Concord.
Courtesy Concord Free Public Library.

My parents present love. and Sister P. & R & S.[3] My mother urges you to visit us. I dare not censure you even by a tho't, but I am certain you are unconscious of the power you possess to make happy your parents & Sisters as you certainly would do by a timely attention in visiting them & writing to them. Methinks, you have forgotten how to estimate the smiles of those[n] you love, but are so little conversant with. I should not say so much but I think you can easily augment the happiness of many deserving & affectionate friends.

It is not without some restraint on my pen that I get along as I have done in my last letters without mentioning *any friend*. Without selecting some feature in that picture[n] of virtue to dwell on. But I resolve to be cautious, and even silent in my wishes. I entertain a delightfull presage that you will one day be blest with the richest gift of Heaven, a *wise & lovely* woman!

I am your affectionate & obliged Sister
M. Emerson.

I wish you would send "elegant extracts"[4] as Miss C wishes for it. Mr L. has returned and the deserving H. I hope will at lenght be happy.

MH: bMS Am 1280.226(1050). *Addressed:* The rev. W Emerson. *Endorsed:* Miss M. M. Emerson. / Dec. 30. 1795. R. / Jan 13, 1796. A.

favorbly.] ⟨rather⟩ favorbly.

power] ⟨fileness⟩ ↑ power ↓

those] ⟨sattisfaction⟩ those

that picture] ⟨the character⟩ that picture

1. Half brother SR, then twelve years old; sister Rebecca Emerson.

2. WE[2] to Phebe Emerson, 13 Oct. 1795, says MME "has a proposal" from Mr. and Mrs. Woodbridge (probably of Newburyport) which "would be advantageous to her in a literary way" (MH).

3. Sisters Phebe and Rebecca, and probably half sister Sarah Ripley.

4. *Elegant Extracts in Prose* and *Elegant Extracts in Poetry*, titles of popular anthologies edited by Vicesimus Knox, first published in London, 1784 and 1790.

1796

To Ruth Haskins

Concord, Mar. 26. 1796.

My dear friend,

I have, at lenght, the very great sattisfaction of sending you the sermons of Mr. Foster. I must beg leave to give you some account of their journey from Harvard, which commenced about the first of feb. when my brother came to Concord, but in calling at Stow, he left the books at the house of a friend, who sent them to a house in C. where they remained some time before they reached us. We have been studious to gain conveyance for them to you; but in vain till now. So you must not tax us with neglect, tho' we have had the appearance of it hithertoo. I feel impatient for you to enjoy the reading of these excellent sermons; or I should take more pleasure in detaining them for our own reading. And now, my dear Ruthe, permit me to beg the favor of your sentiments on these sermons   Particularly the fourth & tenth of vol. 1, and the 2 & 5 & 6 & 9 & 14 & 15 of the second vol. the only ones I have had time to read or hear since they came.[1] I hope you will be so obliging as to give me your opinion of whatever is peculiar to Mr. F. as a preacher. I do not mean to read any thing as infallible but the scriptures; and believe I am not so prejudiced in favor of any sermons, but that I should be willing to reject any thing that was too liberal as well as any thing too rigid, on my conviction. Sure I am, I had rather err on the extreme of the latter than the former. But the danger and folly of building devotion on superstitious errors (I think) is very well proved in the 5th sermon I mentioned.

I have just been to visit my honored Granmother[2]   As I knew it would please my friend to hear directly from her, I told her to whom I was writing. She presents her kindest love to you and your family; and says you must go on as you have begun, to forget the things of the present moment and press on toward the great mark of christian perfection. I tell my granmar' it is an interesting sight to contemplate the various ages, and their respective employments, in our numerous family. When I go into her chamber (where she has been confined for these six weeks) she appears to be making those preparations which bespeak a speedy departure from all earthly cares. This appearance[n] is interesting, tho' not by no means gloomy. No, methinks we should rather congratulate a friend who was just closing a long and laborious journey, tho' thier external appearance bore the tokens of hardship and discipline; a discipline which was purifyed[n] their souls, and hardships that were fortifying the spirit to bear, with resignation, the last painfull conflicts of yeilding nature. To hear an aged & zealous christian talk of the vanity of this world, and the prospects of another, makes the charms of the former to fade & diminish. But is it not in vain to wish to begin life with the same views with which the aged terminate it. It is in vain, if we follow the native impulses of natural inclination. But let us rejoice & be thankfull that there *is a wisdom,* which the children of men may possess, so *pure and heavenly* that even the young possesor of *it* shall find a growing indifference to the pleasures of this life, and a refined taste for those which flow more imediately from the great Source of blessedness. How animated do I feel, my dear Ruthe, at the bare mention of such an *indifference*—of possessing such an elevated *taste*—and yet I fear I make little or no progress to the attainment—or surely I should not so often take so deep an interest in the trifles of the passing moment—an *interest,* which, alass, often betrays me into follies, which occasions the deepest regret to myself, tho' the *more happy & calmn observer* is a stranger *only* to the error. Whoever knows me knows my errors; therefore you, my friend, must forgive me many, and fail not often to ask, for me, a pardon, where only the riches of pardoning grace may be found.

It seems a very long time since I heard or saw any thing from you. Let it not be long I beseech you before you write. My respects to your parents and love to your Sisters. We depend on seeing some of the family soon. Tell Elisa[3] I long to see her for many more reasons than I can well mention in writing. I expected a letter from her before this.

I am in haste and when I begun these letters I did not think to have spent half an hour in writing.

From your sincere & gratefull friend & well wisher

Mary Emerson.

MH: bMS Am 1280.226(965).
appearance] ⟨reflection⟩ ↑ appearance ↓
was purifyed] ⟨had⟩ ↑ was ↓ purifyed
1. James Foster, *Sermons*, 4 vols. (London, 1755).
2. Phebe Walker Bliss.
3. Elizabeth Haskins.

1797

To Ruth Haskins Emerson

Concord   May 19, 1797.

My dear Sister,

The dispersion of our family this afternoon[1] affords me an hour of solitude, which is gratefull, *only* as I am at leisure to devote it to you. I am mortified that I have suffered my little pursuits to prevent answering your letter of last dec.; especially as I think early attentions peculiarly proper to new connections.[2] How have you done, my dear sister, since your visit at Concord? I wish to see you here again so much, that I know not but I may wish for some unfavorable incident. I feel habitually interested in your concerns & happiness, yet (for I had no leisure with your hon'd Mother) am a stranger to your tho'ts & actions. What do you say about this delightfull season? Does not Harvard give you an idea of some shady retreat which might have been placed in the garden of Eden! A heart like yours, methinks, cannot be untouched— uninterested at this delightfull season! And if *interested* then happy. The first concern I feel for my friends, and the first dread for my self is on account of those parts of life in which pursuit is tasteless and hope is famisht. I have tho't whether the weaker sort of people suffer from *this satiety,* as they appear to be kept awake by the incidents of the hour. But whenever I form an idea of a person with great strenght of mind, I immediately conceive them courageous enough to meet these tasteless moments & vigour sufficient to put to flight indifferent ones. But I cannot readily conjecture, how people of sensibility who are not influenced, at times, by the animating prospects of eternity nor deluded by the splendor of life can maintain that engagedness & alacrity w'h are so apparent. For my own part, I acknowledge (for the first time) I cannot long contemplate the splendid, the busy, nor the tranquil scenes of this life without sensations of apathy. I have conceived but perhaps with more fancy than reason, of a state of misfortune in which the mind would be so exerted as to rise above the weakness I have been endeavouring to describe. A vacant mind, not a pained one, methinks, is alone conscious of weakness.

How abundantly may we rejoice, my friend, that piety can supply to the feeble, what the stronge possess by nature. An acquaintance with a Being infinitely blessed, can alone chastise the fileness of the human mind, can only sufficiently supply us with hopes to brighten the dark and stimulate the inactive scenes of life. Suffer me to add to an epistle, already I fear, too lenghty that I wrote not to sympathise with you on the score of these infirmities, as I believe you to be remarkably exempt from them, from the native constancy of your temper & from habits of virtue. May firmness & tranquility be the rich rewards of your labour.

Our Family are well except Gran'mar'. Sister P. appears at times to be *well*. They are ignorant of my writing & ye rest are absent. You may ever believe them affectionate in remmembering you. My best love to my brother and to your Sister. The former has *not written to his sisters since he was married*! My love to cousin Samuel whom we depend on seeing at Election. Nancy too, I antisipate seeing, soon, with pleasure.[3]

> I am my dear Sister yours with affection
> M Emerson

MH: bMS Am 1280.226(966). *Addressed:* Mrs Emerson / Harvard. *Endorsed:* Miss Mary Emerson. / Received May 27, 1797.

1. MME's sister Rebecca married Robert Haskins, brother of WE[2]'s wife, RHE, on 18 May 1797, the occasion for the family gathering in Concord.

2. Ruth Haskins and WE[2] were married 25 Oct. 1796.

3. Grandmother Bliss; sister Phebe; brother WE[2], RHE's sisters Elizabeth and Nancy Haskins; "cousin Samuel" may be the "Sam. Bliss" mentioned in MME to WE[2], 18 Oct. 1798. The *Bliss Family Genealogy* includes no cousin Samuel. MME's uncle Samuel Bliss (1750–1803) was a loyalist who emigrated to Canada at the time of the American Revolution and married Mary Harwood in 1779; their only child, Mary Harwood Bliss (1783–1868), married Deacon Samuel Hewes of Boston.

1798

To WILLIAM EMERSON[2]

Mal.   18 Oct. 1798

How does my dear brother, his wife and daughter?[1] I long to ask you a thousand questions respecting your health wealth & happiness. But I am the more patient, as I hear so good accounts from Harvard, from the ladies who have lately visited it. My every inquiry after Phebe, is gratified by a description of her infant graces. I trust we shall early discover in her those *languid* "looks that deeply pierce the soul, where with the light of tho'tfull reason mixed, shines lively fancy and the feeling heart."[2] Our Sister, they say, blessed with health, vigorously pursues the pleasures & the duties of her calling. Well; how blessed a thing is it to be phisically as well as morally happy! Please to give her my tenderest love. I should like, very much, to write to her at this time but I like better to write to my reverend brother, who has had a long respite from my epistolary company. Your last cause of complaint was your inability to observe a punctuality with me. I do not exact it; pray write as I do to you, only for pleasure. I thank you for the two last letters you have honored me with. I am instructed by their instructions, flattered by their flattery.

What news at Harvard my brother? We have, here, a perpetual dearth. I paid a visit to Concord a few days since and there I expected to have collected a stock of livliness for the season. But my sister met with an accident which rather discoulered my visit. She is now very well, and at home, and her arm in a fine way of recovery. Save that, every thing was auspicious at the Mansion.[3] They (the ladies) are very fortunate in their matrimonial prospects, most of them, rather; for instance, our friend Miss Minot and Miss Brown. Speaking of the latter reminds me of her lover.[4] How rapidly he succeeds in his wishes respecting a settlement! I admire that man! and greatly hope his early sucess is not a bad omen of his future fortune. Sarah, our sister, too figures in the circle of the gay with no smale pretentions to merit. In truth, one cannot, without a little philosophy, behold the charms of youth & read her ardent promises, and not wish to forget half a dozen years of the dull number. Here, your sex have the advantage of ours. Your vanity is seldom in danger of injury by the number of your years. You either welcome their approach as the means of your advancement, or find them the only security for respect. But poor woman had rather forfeit her tittle to superiorty than her claims to youth, and is even tempted to adopt folly, than own wisdom, if she be called the child of experience.

I have had agreable accounts from Newburyport in a letter from my sister[5] this week. Tell Mrs. Emerson, if you please, her parents, Dr Kast & lady, Mr & Mrs Ladd and Misses F. Haskins & S. Kast have gone to L. Compton: I believe they return this week.[6]

My kindest love to Mary & Sam. Bliss.[7] I have by me a letter, which I bro't from Concord written by the former, that I read^n with pleasure and astonishment.

Farewell my dear brother! May you forget every misery as waters that have passed away. May thine age be clearer than the noonday, & thou shine forth like the morning![8] M Emerson.

MH: bMS Am 1280.226(1053). *Endorsed:* Miss M. M. Emerson. Oct. 19, 1798. R. / Oct. 21, 1798. A.
    read] *possibly* rceed (*abbreviation for* received)

1. First child of WE² and RHE, Phebe Ripley Emerson, born 9 Feb. 1798, died 28 Sept. 1800.

2. James Thomson, *The Seasons*, "Spring," 433–35.

3. Half sister Sarah Ripley (1781–1826), then seventeen years old, at the Manse in Concord.

4. Sally Minot (b. 1780) and Tilly Merrick (1755–1836), both of Concord, were married 25 Dec. 1798. MME seems to misuse "latter" to mean "former": that is, to refer to Miss Minot and Merrick's settlement of his mother's large estate following her recent death. Merrick graduated from Harvard in 1773, served in the embassy of John Adams to France and Holland during the American Revolution, was captured twice by the British, and became a successful merchant in Amsterdam. After the war he entered business in Charleston, S.C., where he owned several large plantations. In 1797 he was almost ruined by poor ventures, and, after his mother's death the following year, he returned to Concord. Miss Brown is unidentified: Elizabeth Brown and Samuel Potter Prescott, both of Concord, were married 7 June 1798.

5. Sister Hannah Farnham (1770–1807).

6. RHE's sister Hannah and her husband, Dr. Thomas Kast; probably their daughter, Sally Kast; sister Mary and William Ladd; sister Fanny Haskins, then twenty years old. Little Compton, R.I., was the home of William and Sarah Gardner Ladd, two of whose children married siblings of RHE.

7. See MME to RHE, 19 May 1797, n. 3. Mary is probably Samuel's daughter.

8. Cf. Job 11:16–17.

1799

To Ruth Haskins Emerson

Mal.   Jan 20   —99.

Dear Sister,

I have so long defered the pleasure of writing to you, that I feel somthing too much like a Stranger to you in the epistolary way. I confess that I have been faulty in neglecting you as a correspondent; I am the readier to own this, as I feel conscious of a fault only in the exterior of attention to a sister whose happiness is a daily subject of my wishes. However, tho' we understand each other too well to be punctilious, I motion that in future we recognize each other a little oftner as correspondents, friends & sisters by the means of pen & ink. If you agree to this & will honor me with one letter to three of mine I shall think myself well off.

Have you read Woolsencraft's works,¹ about which we were so warmly disputing the last time I saw you? I hope you have; for I am persuaded that if you have read it *candidly* (& otherwise my sister could not read) your prejudices (which seem to have arisen from a partial knowledge of our Auther's sentiments) will be almost wholly removed, and if possible new motives given to your virtuous exertions. Miss W—'s theology, I think, bad; and some of her theories intricate; but still her pages may be characterized by one of her quotations. "Pleasure was for the inferior kind; but glory, virtue Heaven for man designed."[2] Were her modes of education adopted I believe we should find less of *that softness* in girls which lays a foundation for many future ills in thier lives; and less of that voluptuousness in men, which so often ener-vates their understandings, and gives unreasonable women such a dominion over thier passions. If you should ever honour "the rights of woman" with a reading I beg you would give me your opinion of it. Do you own the book my sister? If you do, & can at any time spare it I shall be obliged by the loan of it.

I must again disappoint myself of visiting you so soon as I expected. I can-not make it agreable to pass any time with you at present, my sister; but I keep an eye on the promise I made you; and beg you to call on me whenever you are without a Sister or Cousin; I shall count that time (in which I can cheer your solitude, or releive one embarrassment) among the most precious parts of my life. However, I intend to pay you a little visit, with some sister or other, before the sultry season. If you should come to Boston as my brother intimated, I shall rejoice to see you at Malden. Pray do not disappoint us.

I saw Mrs Ladd a moment the day but one, she is yet about. Becca has been unwell, but is better. My Aunts are well & send love.[3] My best love to my dear Brother.

Kiss your daughter for me; & remind my cousins[4] of me.

I am, dear Mrs Emerson,
Your affectionate Sister
M Emerson.

MH: bMS Am 1280.226(967). *Addressed:* Mrs. Ruth Emerson. / Harvard. / To the care / of / Mr Haskins. *Endorsed:* Miss Mary Emerson. / 1799.

1. Mary Wollstonecraft (1759–97), author of, among other books, *Thoughts on the Education of Daughters* (1787) and *A Vindication of the Rights of Women* (1792).

2. Anna Laetitia Barbauld, quoted by Wollstonecraft in a note to chap. 4 of *A Vindication of the Rights of Women.*

3. Sister REH; MME's aunts Ruth Sargeant and Rebecca Brintnall.

4. Probably Samuel and Mary Bliss.

1801

To Rebecca Thoreau

Portland   Mar. 31 1801

Alass, my dear Mrs Thorough, what shall I say to you? I approach you not insensible to your situation; but feeling unable to offer you consolation.[1] You have shed the bitterest tears—you still utter the language of affliction. Could the fondest friend wish you to possess less sensibility to so heavy a loss?

Grief restrained by piety, & mourning love sanctified by devotion, are among the most acceptable sacrifices offered at the shrine of religion! A christian methinks can never be comfortless. The rememberance of the piety of your departed husband must, at times, illume the dark cloud which hangs over you. It will make you feel your alliance with a future & happy state, with sentiments animating, as those inspired by faith. *Thy will be done*, methinks, is inscribed on your every hour! Soon may it's balsamic power heal the anguish which is so severe. Soon may you feel the fruits of affliction tending to sublimate your affections, & increase your zeal for a world where you will meet in higher forms of life, those whose joy & pride you constituted here.

Please to present my love to your daughters.[2] I heartily sympathise with them in their loss of a tender & amiable parent. May the God of the *fatherless* take them & the little ones into his favor & keeping.

My sister[3] wishes to be affectionately remembered to you, with her sorrow for your affliction and best wishes for your consolation & comfort. She is rather feeble at present, joins me in wishing you to give our duty to our parents & love to our brother & Sister. I believe I cannot write them, as the bearer of this is in haste.

I heard of Mr. T—s death but a few hours since, without any of its circumstances or time.

Farewell, my dear friend, I forbear to add more; tho' so much might be said, when I consider the greatness of the duties which have devolved on you, and the gloom which at present surrounds you. But feeble indeed would be every thing I could suggest, compared to the strenght of your own resources, and the height to which you will endeavour to carry the sacred virtues of the parent & instructress. Accept my repeated wishes for the restoration of your tranquility; wishes dictated by gratitude as by friendship. Yes, my dear Mrs. Thorough, I shall always remember the tokens of your kindness received by my friends, & myself with pleasure.

Yours &c
M Emerson.

MH: bMS Am 1280.226(1293). *Addressed:* Mrs. Rebecca Thorough / Concord. / To the care of Mr. T. Haskins Boston. *Postmarked:* Boston. MS / Apr / 17.

1. Rebecca Kettell Thoreau was the second wife of John (Jean) Thoreau (grandfather of HDT), who died on 7 Mar. 1801, aged forty-seven, "after contracting a cold while patrolling the streets of Boston in a severe rainstorm when it was thought an anti-Catholic riot was imminent" (*Days*, 5).

2. Rebecca was the stepmother of eight children from John Thoreau's first marriage: Elizabeth, Jane, Mary, Nancy, Sarah, Maria, John (HDT's father), and David.

3. Sister: Either Hannah Farnham (Newburyport), or PER or REH (both of Waterford). The reference to illness suggests Hannah, who died in 1807.

1802

To Ruth Haskins Emerson

Newburyport　Feb. 26　—1802

My dear Mrs. Emerson,

I expected to have been obliged to have passed thro' Boston on my way hither, when I intended to have paid my respects to your parents & sisters; to have thanked Elisabeth[1] for her attention to me in the purchase of those things, & to have obeyed the dictates of duty & inclination in passing a social hour with you. An intercourse which cercumstances at one time & real indisposition at another forbad, when I saw you; but they did not prevent my heart from honoring you for that sensibility & those virtues which I observed time had not diminished. But that in future your sensibility might not be wounded by meeting with me, my dear Ruthe, let me beg of you not to think of any thing that has passed, to asure you that I esteem myself happier than when with you, for which I can easily assign one of the real causes, however, lessening it may be to my merit. Solitude & reflection place objects in a light inexpressibly different from that which they assume amid society & labour. At every retrospection, I have made of the time passed with you, I turn with disgust from the zeal with which I entered into the tributes of fashion & parade; & tho' I neglected every personal one, yet I feel certain that under the specious pretext of family honor, I should have continued to depart from the perpetual claims of simplicity, reason & piety. I should have forgotten that visiated appetites & passions were the unhappy causes of injured charity & murdered time. While I wish you to congratulate me on my escape from temptation; I heartily felicitate you on the possession of those virtues which render you calm & tranquil amid the cares, the pleasures & honors of life. I could not but reflect on these qualities when I last saw you & observed their happy effects by the order & elegance which prevailed at your table.

After again finishing all that relates to our earthly intercourse—about bidding you farewell, my dear Ruthe, suffer me to console myself with the antisapation of cementing our imperfect freindship at some other stage of our existance; when I doubt not of beholding you—& of tracing the perfection of those very virtues which I once tho't (when ignorant of myself & the unavoidable lot of humanity) you possessed in their fullest extent. I shall see you at that period when the splendor of tables & talents will be alike forgotten in the rubbish of the world—when you will remember with rapture—that you sought suffering merit—that you cheered the desponding, honored the virtuous, tho' in obscurity & entered with holy zeal into every feeling of suffering humanity.

Thus may you *abundantly* & joyfully[n] pass the ordeal of perfect charity & love is the affectionate wish of

M Emerson.

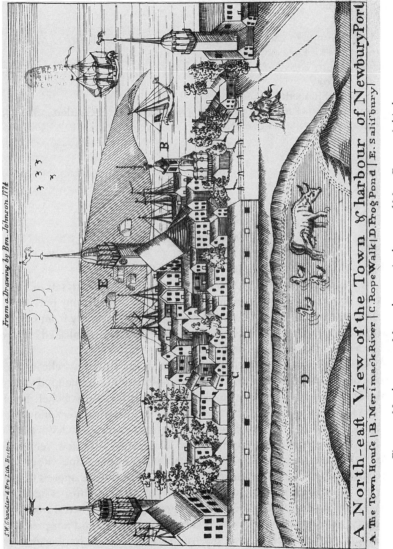

S.W. Chandler & Bro. Lith. Boston.

From a Drawing by Ben. Johnson. 1774

A North-east View of the Town & harbour of NewburyPort.

A. The Town House | B. Merimack River | C. Rope Walk | D. Frog Pond | E. Salisbury

Figure 3. Newburyport, Massachusetts, in the year of Mary Emerson's birth.

"*All is well*" *with us* who jointly present salutations to Mr Emerson & yourself, to which my sister adds a request that you would take the charge of Charlotte for a few days after Pa'pa[2] brings her to Boston, till she can make provision for her return home.

MH: bMS Am 1280.226(972). *Addressed:* Mrs Emerson. / Boston. / Mr Sawyer. *Endorsed:* Miss M. Emerson.

joyfully] *mostly covered by large ink smear (possibly cancellation);* fully *written above and canceled*

    1. Probably Elizabeth Haskins.

    2. Sister Hannah Farnham of Newburyport; her daughter Charlotte, then eight years old. Pa'pa is stepfather Ezra Ripley.

1803

To Ezra Ripley

Mal.   Feb. 24 1803.

Honored Sir,

    As you were good enough to ask me to write, I avail myself of the liberty with pleasure. And with anxiety to hear of the health of my parents, and what has become of Phebe.[1] I have not heard one word directly from Concord since I left it; except by Mr Haskins. Is your health, Sir, established? Has my Mother left her chamber? Is Sarah well?

    My Uncle & Aunt[2] & myself are very well, and I sincerely believe constitute one of the happiest families in the world. Whoever is acquainted with the simplicity of our lives, will not think me ostentatious in this belief. But the evident sattisfaction which these good people enjoy, arises very much from the absence of those turbulent & vexatious circumstances which have hithertoo almost constantly followed them. And as the mind of man never can rest in absolute quietude, my Aunt often finds cause of complaint, either in the depredations of a Cat, or the loss of a hen; and when she is disposed for more elaborate difficulties, the religious scepticism of Mr Wait affords her opportunity for the display of her controversial powers—and I often think I might be a party were the arguments about subjects on which I did not profess the profoundest ignorance. However, my Aunt, flatters herself that his universalism will be shaken by an attack the next sabbath, from Tutor Emerson,[3] who Mr Green tells us, called there this week to propose an exchange.

    As the situation respects myself, Sir, I acknowledge with gratitude it's pleasures and advantages. I feel them so sensibly at times, that I feel what I never did before a dread of loosing them. I think too of the greatness of my accountability for days & nights of health & spirits in which I have no object of attention but my own mind. I ask, my dear Sir, an interest in your prayers, for my progress in knowledge & peity. You will excuse the egotism of my epistle as my observation is bounded by so few objects. Please to commend me dutifully to my dear Mother & tenderly to my sister, & freinds.

From hon. Sir, your dutifull daughter.
M. Emerson.

Uncle & Aunt send much love to my parents & Sister and say nothing would give them more pleasure than a visit from them.

MH: bMS Am 1280.226(1235). *Addressed:* Reverend Ezra Ripley. / Concord. *Endorsed:* M. M. Emerson—Malden.

1. Probably PER of Waterford.

2. In Jan. 1802, Ruth Emerson Sargeant married Samuel Waite of Malden.

3. Probably second cousin Joseph Emerson (1777–1833), who was a tutor at Harvard from 1801 to 1803 and who was ordained in Sept. 1803.

1805

To William Emerson[2]

Conc. Feb. 7 [1805]

Dear brother,

The book you so unexpectedly sent me is unfortunately left at Malden, where it is safe. If you should need it I will send to my Uncle[1] to carry it to Boston. I went thro' it, rapidly and should like to again if convenient. I went thro' it with a sattisfaction I cannot express—it has raised me from darkness to light. I feel thanks to be poor—indeed, in sending me that book, my brother, you have confered a greater favor than I ever received from any created being, and I will never forget it. *I am here* and I wish you could see you here— I am at a loss what to think of Sarah. God is good!

You would have suitable remembrances if any knew of my writing. Only think at Malden beneathe the shelter of that eastern mountain—with a lowring sky & the works of the Celtic bard[2] in my hand I had dared to try to imitate him but adieu to every thing & to you. Pray for your

Sister M

MH: bMS Am 1280.226(1056). *Addressed:* Rev. Mr. Emerson / Boston / Politeness of Mr Cabot. *Endorsed:* Miss M. M. Emerson / 1805 feb 5 D. —— 7. R.

1. Samuel Waite.

2. Perhaps the book WE[2] has sent, possibly Thomas Gray, *The Bard* (1775), or one of James Macpherson's "Ossianic" works, *Fragments of Ancient Poetry* (1760) or *Fingal: An Ancient Epic Poem* (1761).

To WILLIAM EMERSON[2]

Tuesday Morn. [May 1805]   Beverly

My dear Brother,

I hope my sister yourself and sons are well. Sarah will tell you of our journey and how much inquiry was made after you both. and how we have an additional relation called Hannah Bliss.[1]

I write to solicit you to insert the letter in the Anthology which I shewed you when in Boston.[2] I left it at Rebecca's. It is a favorite production of your sister's, and she thinks it no smale compliment to your understanding to ask the indulgence of her taste[n] when it is so different from yours. I intended to have written it better at N—t but I did not feel well enough; tho' when there I conversed with Hannah Sawyer by accident on the subject of Unwin[3] and am desirous to publish the letter.

Give my love to all not omitting Edward Bliss[4]

Yours &c
M Emerson.

MH: bMS Am 1280.226(1055).

taste] ⟨weakness⟩ taste

1. Niece Hannah Bliss Farnham, born in Newburyport on 4 May 1805.

2. A letter from Constance (MME) to Cornelia (Mary Van Schalkwyck) comparing Samuel Johnson and William Hayley (whose life of the poet William Cowper appeared in 1803–4) as biographers was published in the *Monthly Anthology* 2 (July 1805): 342–44.

3. Hannah Farnham Sawyer (1780–1865), of Newburyport, possibly a cousin of MME's brother-in-law William Farnham; Mary Unwin, with whom Cowper boarded for much of his life. In her Constance letter (see above, n. 2), while discussing Johnson's "ungentle" treatment of his subjects, MME speculates on how he would have treated Cowper: "And what too would have become of the pious and venerable Unwin," whose friendship was a "testimony to the strength and inviolability of an attachment, in which all the passions of the heart were not interested" (343)?

4. WE[2] and RHE's fifth child, Edward Bliss Emerson, was born in Boston on 17 Apr. 1805.

To RUTH HASKINS EMERSON

thursday   [1805]

My dear Sister,

I thank you for your tender care of me. I hope you got home well. My love to my brother   He says ask him *any question in theology* and he will answer it. I wish him to explain the 73[d] proposition of Dr Jebb's in the 2[d] vol. respecting the philosophy of prayer.[1] I believe it was the 73. There is no part of my visit I remember with so much gratitude as my brother's conversation[n] on religion, however removed from *my* belief, they discovered his goodness &c.

The sufferings of my head while at your house ended in tow or three days confinement with medicine; and the good things you gave me enabled me to go thro' them.

Figure 4. The Reverend William Emerson (1769–1811),
brother of Mary Emerson.

I hope you will send the rest of Johnson's life[2] next thursday. My love to cousin Mary and my wish that she would not with her present time for reading attempt this work. It requires much reading to read it. And often religious ablution.[n] Such especially as the 511 page. Speaking of this all important subject of religion my dear Ruthe, with which you may remember we parted, there is no religious tract of more importance to me than Dod's rise & progress. the 26 chap especially should be read often and the 27 especially for you.[3]

In haste. farewell
M Emerson

My kind love to Mary R. & the children

MH: bMS Am 1280.226(979). *Addressed:* Mrs Emerson.
conversation] conversation(s); s *possibly not canceled*
ablution] sic *in MS; possibly* absolution *intended*

1. John Jebb, *Works Theological, Medical, Political, and Miscellaneous . . .*, 3 vols. (London, 1787): "Prayer, philosophically considered, may, by altering the affections of my mind, put me into that state, according to which, the course of divine providence renders me capable of blessings: popularly considered, i.e. in the effect, and as a secondary affection, it is to be supposed as working an alteration in the mind of God, our creator, governor, and judge. This seems to be the case. July 1773, but it cannot be worthily performed, unless the latter idea prevails at the time" (proposition 73, 2:164–65).

2. Probably James Boswell's biography of Samuel Johnson; but see also preceding letter, n. 2.

3. Philip Doddridge, D.D., *The Rise and Progress of Religion in the Soul*, a very popular series of addresses with meditations and prayers, first published in 1744; MME to SAB, [1813?], wrote, "Dr D. (tho not ranked among calvinistic divines) is far from the prevailing and fatal errors of the present day, in which religion is represented as merely a convenient, pleasant, political advantage, whose obligations are comfortable with the love of pleasure and the pursuit of ambition. This work represents the pursuits of the christian as occupying the whole soul with the pure and real love of glory, and with the use of means highly arduous and elevating" (MH: 1261).

1806

To Rebecca Thoreau

Mal. Jan 15 1806.

You say my dear Mrs Thoreau, that three lines of my writing will give you pleasure. I am pleased to be able to afford you a moment's gratification, in humble addition to those rich resources of constant enjoyment which you are so largely furnished with, in those prospects which you are constantly drawing nearer to realize in that animated & spiritual existence which so fully possess your ambition; and in the peculiar blessings of family and situation.

A christian with a native happy disposition, with society to their taste, with those they love, and over whose happiness they can exert an influence; perhaps, gives an observer as perfect an idea of the life the blessed lead above, as can be in the present state. This week, my friend, you share particularly my sympathy; as Daniel tells me it is designed for the marriage of our dear & amiable Miss White.[1] Suffer me to add my congratulations; on her restoration and prospects. You will feel in no common degree the loss of her society, nor interest in her future happiness. In the painfull conflict of your various emotions you will feel that serenity which faith alone can inspire. My love to your dear Girls, whose privation in the seperation with their friend will undoubtedly cost them some pangs. Tell Jane[2] I am pleased by her kind notice; but marvel how she could help calling on me; I do not think I could have passed a house which contained the smalest of your family. *Yours* too I esteem for their comfort, but especially as a mark of your tenderness.

What have you been reading, my friend, if your more active more important duties have permitted you to read? But I strongly suspect that the revolution in your circle has ingrossed some of your reading hours. Reading, however indispensable to inlarge the mind of early youth, when compared with the ardent exercise of the faculties may bear no more proportion to virtue than a fine picture does to it's original. We find those whose minds are the most stored with all that genius and science can bestow, yet suffer alike with others, periods of stupor and apathy, in which pursuit is tasteless, and hope inactive. To give interest to such portions of time, to redeem, as it were one's existence from such an untimely grave, what can supply the mind with energy but a sense of its' awfull responsibility, and the prospect that the future proportion of its' reward will be according to it's dilligence. But indeed my dear & estimable freind why should I have taken my time to paint to you what is so familiar? Indeed, I meant it not, but a scarcity of subjects, and a reluctance to part with you, made me linger thus on a subject on which, I might only give you an idea of my wants and your own fullness. Therefore I hasten to bid you adieu.

M Emerson.

Give my love to our lovely friend MVS[3] & whatever duty & affection can dictate to my parents & Sister.

MH: bMS Am 1280.226(1294). *Addressed:* Mrs. Rebecca Thoreau / Concord. / Left at Deacon Whites.

1. "Daniel" is probably MME's half brother Daniel Ripley. Betsy White, Rebecca Thoreau's niece, married the Reverend Joseph Pickering of Woburn, Mass., on 13 Mar. 1806. The Whites and Thoreaus lived next door to each other on the town square in Concord.

2. Jane Thoreau, Rebecca's stepdaughter.

3. Mary Wilder Van Schalkwyck (1780–1811). In May 1807 MVS married Daniel Appleton White (1776–1861), who had boarded with the Farnhams in Newburyport.

Figure 5. Home of Dr. Isaac Hurd, Concord, stepfather of Mary and Henry Wilder; drawing by Henry Wilder. Courtesy Concord Free Public Library.

To Samuel Ripley

Newburyport No[v]. 7. [1806]

My dear Brother,

Your letter which bore indubitable marks of coming from the heart gave me positive pleasure. Your situation, your pursuits, your resolutions & your success in the cause of virtue meet my sympathy & respect.[1] Go on, I again say as I have often said to my progressing brother, go on & prosper in resisting temptation in acquiring fame—not that which is puffed from the fleeting breath of frail interested prejudiced mortals—but that which inevitably awaits at some sure tho' uncertain period the faithfull discharge of duty. Ah, my dear Samuel, how grand & weighty the consideration that a few revolutions of this little world and we shall enter a scene where not the splendor of talent nor the most extensive influence will be nessecary to a passport to everlasting life   But where those whose feeble pen restricted their comprehension to the humblest & most solitary duties, yet who wholly & faithfully embraced them, will be adjudged truly honorable & illustrious at the ordeal of perfect rectitude.

But I need not reciprocate these sentiments with you, my brother, however pleasant is the sympathy, for your distance from home renders intelligence more interesting than any speculations, which already reside in your own mind. Our honored parents are well. Sister F. is convalescent—essentially so, we believe. She is at Concord for a little while. Her family are well. Our dear Sarah[2] is in good health & spirits. You mentioned her visit at this place. It proved not less fortunate for herself than for the family she cherished; if the acquisition of friends who know how to appreciate her and were capable of loving her is desirable. A Miss Jackson of Boston, Miss Bromfield[3] (now of this Town) saw admired & loved our Sister with an interest by no means uninteresting. That she made no more conquests in the male world was owing to their scarsity or insensibility. Yet at present the reign of love & matrimony is triumphant. The Miss Sawyers you know—but to estimate their talents accomplishments &c &c you must see more of them. H—h will be married to Capt Lee in Jan. At the same time, MaryAnn will be to a Mr Scyleur Son to Gen. Scyleur.[4] The beau monde will have no longer a center to which their revolutions are attached & from which they derived most of thier lustre. I very much regret that MaryAnn leaves this part of the Country.

Our lovely freind M. S—k[5] is well & prosperous. I am writing from my freind's Mrs F—[6] who desires her remembrance.

Adieu my dear brother
MM Emerson.

MH: bMS Am 1280.226(1244). *Addressed:* Mr. Samuel Ripley / at Mr Taloe's / Washington City. *Endorsed:* M. M. Emerson / Nov. 7. 1806.

1. Before his graduation from Harvard in 1804, SR had gone to Va. to work as a tutor for the family of Colonel John Tayloe of Mount Airy (considered at the time the most splendid mansion in Va.) and the city of Washington.

2. Sister Hannah Farnham's tenth and last child, Hannah Bliss, died on 11 Oct. 1806. MME filled her sister's place at Newburyport during the fall of 1806, while Mrs. Farnham traveled for her health (*MWW-M*, 244). "Our dear Sarah" is half sister Sarah Ripley.

3. Ann Bromfield (1777–1856?), later Ann Tracy, was not—despite Philip Young's claim—Herman Melville's illegitimate half sister, identified by Young as Ann Middleton Allen Tracy (1798–1869) ("Small World: Emerson, Longfellow, and Melville's Secret Sister," *New England Quarterly* 60 [Sept. 1987]: 382–402). Daughter of John and Ann Roberts Bromfield of Newburyport, Miss Bromfield met Mary Wilder and Antoine Van Schalkwyck at Newburyport following their marriage in June 1801 (*MWW-M*, 98–99). In 1824 Ann Bromfield married a retired Congregational minister, the Reverend Thomas Tracy of Biddeford, Maine—not Nathaniel Tracy, scion of the prominent Newburyport family (Young, "Small World," 389–90). On this family, see *MWW-M* and Josiah Quincy, "Memoir of John Bromfield," *The History of the Boston Athenaeum, with Biographical Notices* (Cambridge, 1851), 73–104.

4. The daughters of Dr. Micajah Sawyer of Newburyport were both married on 20 Jan. 1807: Hannah Farnham Sawyer married George Gardner Lee of Boston, and Mary Anna Sawyer, Philip Jeremiah Schuyler of Rhinebeck, N.Y. Schuyler was a son of General Philip Schuyler, for a time commander of the American Northern Army during the revolutionary war.

5. MVS.

6. Several letters mention a Mrs. Frothingham at Newburyport, whom MME sometimes refers to as "Cousin." MME's cousin Samuel Emerson (1758–1840) of Newburyport married two Frothingham women, Sarah in 1783 and Lois in 1814 (the two women were not sisters), who may be related to this Mrs. Frothingham.

To Ruth Haskins Emerson

[1806]

My dear Sister

Is anxious to hear by this time the history of her little Son.[1] He is very well; and what is delightfull to me (in addition to his uncommon mental affairs) he is gay & affect. He does his Mother honor by his manners; but his bodily habits, to an observer, are defective. They should be formed to more hardihood, in my opinion, such habits are lastingly important. He cuts a poor figure in walking & worse at running; and as to any thing so brave as swinging, he will not be courted, nor induced by my ridicule or example   But such habits belong to a Father. Any nursery Maid can teach a child to read but never will form to independance. Now how fine a plan, after the beams of the morning have extinguished the epictetan lamp of your husband, for him to expose himself & the boys to the cold air before thier bodies are relaxed by artificial heat?

Speaking of this gentleman, my dear Ruthe, what a change in his countenance since his tour to the east.[2] Pray never let him breathe your close atmosphere so long again without a journey. A world of life and sentiment has taken the place of that frigid apathy which had taken dominion of all his features and sat uncontrouled whenever he became a hearer in publick. I was prepared for this illumination by his Journal, it contained evident symptoms of a resucitation *at the heart.*

I wish you to pay attention to procure me some of the *largest* kind of writing paper. The money is in your stocking, not letter paper but the thinest & largest of the other. The books I borrowed are ready to go home, I wish for Sir Wm Jones[,] female biography & power of genius;[3] if my brother has nothing newer & better.

You cannot have Rebecca.[4] As it was uncertain whether you w^d take her her mother was afraid to skip so good an offer as presented. I merely mentioned a great coat for her if you had any thing in the house, you only are a judge what she is indebted to.

Adieu.

M Emerson

William desire Duty
I shall pay you when my rents are due! hem!

MH: bMS Am 1280.226(975). *Addressed:* Madam Ruth Emerson. *Endorsed:* Miss Mary M. Emerson / 1806.

1. In 1805 and 1806, WE[2] and REH's second child, John Clarke (1799–1807) stayed at Waterford with his aunts.

2. On 19 Sept. 1806 WE[2] wrote from Otisfield to report on his travels to various places, including Andover, Reading, Salem, Windham, Londonderry, and Litchfield, with a visit to his son John Clarke at Waterford (MH).

3. Possibly *Memoirs of the Life, Writings, and Correspondence of Sir William Jones*, by Lord Teignmouth, reviewed in the *Monthly Anthology* of July 1805, or a volume of William Jones's *Works*, published in several editions beginning in 1799. The "female biography" may be *The Female Revolutionary Plutarch, Containing Biographical, Historical, and Revolutionary Sketches, Characters, and Anecdotes*, by the author of the *Revolutionary Plutarch* and *Memoirs of Tallyrand* (London, 1805, 1806). The Oct. 1805 number of the *Monthly Anthology* included a review of *The Powers of Genius: A poem, in Three Parts*, by John Blair Linn (Philadelphia, 1802).

4. Probably niece Rebecca Emerson Haskins of Waterford, b. 1799.

1807

To Ruth Haskins Emerson

[4 Mar. 1807]

My dear Sister,

I most heartily sympathise with you about this sad affair of bad eyes in your husband. In truth nothing can of this life's concerns be so important to a man's body. I know you are surrounded with skill and means of every kind to recover him. But, my dear Ruth, allmost every thing depends on you—

keep him from taking any cold—watch him or some ill favored moment will convey cold or light in a bad direction; tho' he will be very attentive, few men are uniformly so. I know your intentions, but you have never drank of this cup of privation as myself. Too much bracing or relaxation is of the utmost importance; and good spirits are fine tonics for the optical nerves.

Your sympathy & prayers I have for this scene of sickness & misfortune to this family. Hannah's mind is calm & firm, and appears strikingly natural. She says little, but truly affecting. Who would have tho't that she would have failed so fast—indeed I never expected this—but you can have no idea of the greatness of her release.[1] Still, my dear Ruth, this mortal accountability is important, at a dying hour. I hope my brothers health will permit his coming soon. You cannot easily realize how much I want to see him. I am very sorry I said any thing the evening he went away that displeased him for a moment. I will never do so again. Indeed to see him here I should be willing not to speake once."Sarah[2] is here tho' I wished her to return least her health s^d not be attended. But H—h wishes to have her friends about her and Sarah could not bear to leave her so I have the benefit of her society & assistance *and feel sattisfied that if she is prudent her health is secure.* Farewell.

M Emerson

If convenient send a few osters.
    March 4

No need of osters[3]

    MH: bMS Am 1280.226(976). *Addressed:* Rev. Mr Emerson / Boston / Rev. Mr Ripley.
    once.] once. ⟨What ever of feeling & sympathy a visitor expresses⟩
    1. Sister Hannah Farnham died at Newburyport on 27 Mar. 1807.
    2. Half sister Sarah Ripley.
    3. Written on outside.

To Rebecca Thoreau

NY. Port.   Ap. 7 —7.

My dear and always valued friend,
    I have heard of your sickness and restoration with sympathy for your family, and delight at your recovery. It is a long time since we exchanged the pleasures and pains which await our daily path by any kind of intercourse. But I have very often tho't of you, and felt that this afflicted family was often the subject of your faith and sympathy. It is not natural to associate the idea of death with those we loved, whom we viewed as nessecary to the comfort of many and with whom we expected a longer journey and happier scenes. Yet what is more futile than human calculations and human hopes! Among the few who are connected with me, I regreted to lose one who had for many years taken an interest in whatever concerned me. I now rejoice in her dis-

mission from labour, anxiety and all the temptations, which inevitably attend more or less a mortal state. In retracing the scenes of Hannah's life, which first interested me, I remember her at your house and the high enjoyment she discovered. She loved you very early, and has in late years always mentioned you as a Mother with interest and peculiar approbation. What greater pleasure can a christian of sensibility taste in this weary world, than to recall the memory of those who have died with the conviction of having added to their pleasures and shared their esteem? My sister was able to speake but very little, and seldom ventured on tender subjects. When at Boston she expressed much gratitude for Sarah's attention to her in the summer. No sister, in truth, was ever more tender and assiduous than our dear Sarah; and whoever shares her heart will be sure of finding an affectionate and sympathising freind.

How are your children? Remember me to them with kindness.

May God bless us my dear freind and prepare us to die with the most eminent advantages to religion & ourselves

M Emerson.

MH: bMS Am 1280.226(1295). *Addressed:* Mrs Thoreau. / Concord / D. A. White Esqr.

To Ruth Hurd

Concord   Oct —   [180]7

Good morning my lovely friend.[1] Your call was too pleasant to be easily forgotten; would I could return it for an hour personally.

How is your health and all whom *accident* has placed in the same room? No wonder you laughed at my formal attention to one of your companions. True, there was "time enough hereafter"—but what of attention to those we esteem when *you* are absent compared to *that* when you are present. Think I know nothing of *complaisance?*[n] I dont how to spell the complacant word. And do you know the extent of my delicacy in not asking you to tell the cause of coldness between you and Mrs —? I hope you will appreciate my self denial, and not tax me with stupidity. But, apart from the restraint, which prudence imposed, least you might possibly regret too frank a moment, I preferred another time for a subject which must be interesting as it involves character, in a degree.

Character my charming Miss Hurd—how delicate and unspeakably important in a christian! Shall I ask you in confidence, if that of a woman entering the publick & responsible *one* of wife and Mistress would not appear to more (more than we now name) advantage, if a more simple or rather a style wholly removed from splendor was adopted? But who has strenght! *Where is the model to be found!* Who will first despise imitation and fashion?

I shall go to N.P. probably next spring. Do tell me, you will be there also, tho' you may go ever so many times before. If convenient, will you let me know when the excellent Miss Bromfield is in C—n?[n] I cannot direct a letter to her at hazard, or call without the certainty of seeing her. I feel glad you were so sensible to the charms of intellect &c in Mrs Lee. I am enjoying the sweets of tranquility and friendship with my valued freind & her family. If my letter needs excuses make them yourself; and remember my ostensible one in the last request. Yours affectionately

M M Emerson.

MH: bMS Am 1280.226(1222). *Addressed:* Miss Ruth Hurd / Charlestown / Mr. I. Hurd. *Endorsed:* Oct. 7th 1807 / Miss Mary Emerson; 1807 *added below dateline by RH.*

complaisance] MME first wrote *complascence*

C—n] *probably abbreviation for* Charlestown

1. Ruth Hurd (b. 1784), of Charlestown, Mass., was a "cousin" by marriage of MVS (see below, MME to MWW, 29 Apr. 1809, n. 7). In 1824 Ruth became DAW's third wife.

1808

To Mary Wilder White

Mal.   March 14. —8

Yes, my dearest freind, the interest of my *little expected* has taken many of my tho'ts. And I once went so far as to provide it with a wet Nurse, in case you could not discharge that task yourself.[1] But I have no fear on your account in any way—a degree of solicitude to hear good news is never so pleasant as to have heard it. But the cercumstance of the Nurse is this. A woman whose *constitution temper* & integrity fitted her uncommonly for this office applied to me for advice in disposing of herself. I told her of the possibility of your needing her and persuaded her to wait. Since that time I have heard that she was guilty of harshness to a nurse child which she took to board. Tho' nothing really injurious to it, yet alters my recommendation of her. But as I had promised to write you, I told her I would, & must also acquaint you with her misconduct. It is among the possibilities, that you may employ her. I should not be afraid of her in my own house. A desperate state of poverty and inexperience with children make some little apolygy for her neglect. But I had gone so far with her concerns, that at any rate I could not withdraw all my efforts in her behalf. Oh, my lovely Mary, what would I give to hear from you. How does my freind do? Give him the affectionate remembrance of a Sister interested in all his concerns.

Yes, we do not need, perhaps, like new freinds the constant aid of letters. I cannot but think our connection will be favored by Heaven. Never surely was one formed less like those in the world—leages[n] of pleasure or interest. When it became particular, I do not remember that the eclat my freind had in the world ever came into my mind to influence me in soliciting her love. Adieu.

M Emerson.

I intended to have written to our excellent Miss B— am disappointed. Remember me.[2]

MH-AH. *Addressed:* Mrs White.
leages] *illegible; possibly* hopes
 1. MWW and DAW's first child, Mary Elizabeth, was born on 27 Mar. 1808 and died the following Oct.
 2. Written on outside; Miss Bromfield.

1809

To Mary Wilder White

Ap. 29 —9

My dear friend,
 I recieved your letter, and advice, and note from your husband with feelings of gratitude. You both were very good. And I *dont know*, but stupidity prevents my attention to the Bethlehem plan—but some how I dont think any thing about it.[1] I will, however, attend to what you have said. No one surely could interest me more, than you whose judgment and taste I have so great respect for. I mentioned the other day, what you tho't to Mrs Codman,[2] but the indirect tendency of what she said was discouraging. *She had been there.* As yet I have said nothing of the matter to my brother. He says much about my living with him, and the scheme is often very pleasant; still I have been so long at liberty "have loved it so well,"[3] that I intend to indulge it for the summer and may visit a number of freinds in the Country. Your health, my dear frend, is very good I hear. You are surely very much favoured; and greater ones are in succesion I trust. Your *lot is fallen in a pleasant place and* you have a *goodly heritage.*[4] Surrounded with the best of society and those interested in your welfare, you are richly distinguished. Remember me to the Miss Searls and Mrs. Greenleaf.[5]

Those sermons you sent to Sarah are excellent. So are the "letters from the Mountains"[6] tho' not in the same view exactly. These present us with a very interesting picture of a good wife, Mother and freind—and with some of the pretty flowers of literature.

I have no news. You know how unwell your sister is.[7] I think her very unwell indeed. Sarah was there last night— Your Mother was well.

I was in Boston the other day and went to the theatre. I had often inveighed against it, and when I came to see for myself, concluded it more injurious to taste, sentiment and all that is respectable in it's effect, in forming a christian than I had even suspected. It was Romeo & Juliet. The spirit of S— was most cruelly injured—and as it is a play the most destitute of sentiment and the most seductive to the passions I saw, perhaps, a cariture of stage effect.

Adieu my friends "may the broad hand of the Almighty cover you." [8]

Yours kindly
M Emerson.

MH-AH. *Addressed:* Mrs Mary A White / Newburyport.

1. After her return to Concord in 1802 as a twenty-two-year-old widow, MVS considered joining the Moravian community at Bethlehem, Pa. (*MWW-M*, 97, 152, 209, and MVS to MME, 12 Nov. 1805 [MH-AH]). Perhaps she had suggested this to MME.

2. Probably Catherine Amory Codman (1769–1831), widow of John Codman (1755–1803), whose Boston home was on Hanover Street.

3. Compare Shakespeare, Sonnet 73: "To love that well, which thou must leave ere long."

4. Cf. Ps. 16:6.

5. "Aunt" Mary Russell Searle was a close friend of DAW in Newburyport; widowed in 1796, she was the mother of two sons and at least five daughters: Fanny (b. 1783), Margaret (b. 1785), Mary (b. 1790), Sarah (b. 1792), and Lucy (b. 1794). "Aunt" Greenleaf was another close family friend.

6. [Mrs. Anne (MacVicar) Grant], *Letters from the Mountains: Being the Real Correspondence of a Lady, between the Years 1773 and 1803,* 2 vols. (Boston, 1809).

7. Sally Hurd, stepsister of MWW as a result of the remarriage (in 1790) of her mother, Mary Flagg Wilder, to Dr. Isaac Hurd of Concord. MWW to MME, 27 Aug. 1809, says Sally does not have long to live (MH-AH); she died 29 Nov. 1809.

8. Cf. Exod. 33:22.

To Mary Wilder White and Daniel Appleton White

Boston   May 24   —9

My heart has bowed with yours, my best friends, in gratitude for the preservation of your health, my dear M—, and the welcome addition to your family.[1] *What shall you render* in new efforts of love & consecration[n] to your Heavenly Father who so often repeats the healing and almighty power of saving your life when in iminent danger, will be the gratefull motto of every hour of your existence. Oh may your united offerings ascend with those sacrifices which the Angel of the covenant offers *"with much incense."*

I never had your letter till monday night. I have been absent from C—d three weeks. And in truth it was welcome! I thank you for mentioning my visit to you—but if so soon you visit Concord I might there expect the pleasure; and it would have been a peculiar gratification. But it will probably be a long time before I even go there. I intend going to Waterford & indeed expected to have been there almost by this time, but my brother persuades me from one time to another to put it off and thinks Boston the best[n] place on most accounts. And (I dont exactly know how to account for it) I am so indecided, so indifferent as to the place of my abode, that I form no plans and seem to be

Figure 6. Silhouettes of Daniel Appleton White (1776–1861) and Mary Wilder White (1780–1811).

the most at *loose ends* of all the world. If I should go as I expect I wish to go by Water to Portland—but wherever I am, you shall hear, and if convenient I am sure you will afford me the pleasure of knowing how you go on. And when you can mention the apparent state &c &c of the F—s[2] I shall be glad.

I have a great many things to say but it is late and I am very tired with walking. I go out but seldom but today I have been very busy, and in tow instances so much disap^t that I feel the more weary. I hoped to see a good deal of Ann B.[3] and find she is going as soon as found and Miss Searle too. I did not hear of her till last eve. Ann looks in very good health which gave me more pleasure as it was unexpected.

Farewell, my dear friends, with feelings of, I believe, not everyday sympathy I bid you farewell.

M M Emerson.

MH-AH. *Addressed:* Daniel A. White Esqr / Newburyport. / Miss M. Searle. *Endorsed:* Miss Emerson / 1809.

consecration] conseration *in MS; possibly* consideration *intended*
best] ⟨only⟩ best
1. MWW and DAW's second child, Elizabeth Amelia, born 4 May 1809.
2. Probably the Farnhams.
3. Bromfield.

PART 2

1810—1819

1810   Waterford (all year?).

1811   Waterford (Jan.); Boston, Concord, Newburyport (late Jan.–Dec.).

1812   Boston (Jan.–June); Concord (July–Sept.?); Boston (Oct.–Dec.).

1813   Boston (Jan.); Waterford (Feb.–Dec.).

1814   Waterford (Jan.–Mar.?); Concord (Apr.); Newburyport, Boston, Summer and Bennet Sts. (Apr.–Oct.); Concord (Nov.–Dec.).

1815   Concord, Malden (Jan.–Sept.?); Boston, Beacon St. (Oct.–Dec.).

1816   Boston, Beacon St. (Jan.); Concord (Feb.); Boston (Mar.–Oct.); Boston, Hancock St., with visit to Andover and Newburyport? (Nov.–Dec.).

1817   Concord (Jan.); Boston, Hancock St. (Feb.); Concord (Mar.); Boston, Hancock and Essex Sts. (Apr.–Aug.?); Exeter, Dover, Portland (Aug.–Sept.); Waterford (Oct.–Dec.).

1818   Waterford, with possible trips to Northampton and Portland (Jan.–Nov.?); Concord (Dec.).

1819   Concord (Jan.); Newburyport, Boston, Essex St. (Feb.–Mar.?); Waltham (Apr.); Concord, with possible visit to Conway (May?–Nov.); Boston, Essex St. (Dec.).

The period from 1810 to 1819 was a politically charged decade including the presidency of James Madison (1808–17); the rapid western expansion of the United States; "Mr. Madison's War," as New Englanders derisively called the war declared against England on 19 June 1812; and the postwar economic inflation that marred President James Monroe's "era of good feeling." The British embargo did not reach New England ports north of New London, Connecticut, until April 1814. Indeed, people in eastern New England were affected little by the events that were destroying Indian villages and white settlements, forts and ships, along the frontier, around the Great Lakes, and in the mid-Atlantic region and that were creating economic havoc in areas cut off by the British blockade, including, by the end of 1813, Long Island and New York. In August 1814 the British burned Washington, and in September British forces landed in Maine. The troops finally reached Boston only a few months before the Treaty of Ghent formally ended the war on 24 December 1814. Mary Moody Emerson's view of these events is probably typical of those not directly affected: her letters never mention them until the British approach Charlestown in September 1814, when Boston prepared for a siege. After news of the treaty finally reached the United States on 11 February 1815, Mary Emerson hailed "the auspicious gift of peace"—which she immediately raised to a higher level by reminding her nephew William that "to those whose aims are high and lofty in the holy world of morals, all terrestrial events 'pass away as the waters,' only as they subserve his future salvation" (MH: 1064). Rather than national or political events, the network of her family relationships was central to Mary Moody Emerson in these years. The image of a spider web is appropriate here, because her major effort was to escape entrapment.

In 1810, when the decade begins, the web was complicated indeed. In Boston, brother William Emerson was very ill, having suffered a severe hemorrhage of the lung in 1808; five of his seven children were still living, and Ruth was pregnant again. In 1811, a few months after the birth of Mary Caroline, William died of a stomach tumor, leaving Ruth with six children under the age of ten. By the end of the decade, nephews William and Waldo were at Harvard (William graduated in 1819); Mary Caroline had died; Bulkeley's psychological problems had required much special care; and Edward, who suffered his first serious illness while a student at Andover in 1817, had delayed his entrance at Harvard for a year. In Concord, mother Phebe Ripley was almost seventy years old in 1810; during her frequent illnesses throughout the decade, half sister Sarah was her primary caretaker in Mary's absence. In 1818 Sarah was very ill. Half brother Daniel began to practice law, suffered a severe illness in 1813, and may have gotten into some kind of trouble (Sanborn claims he was involved in a duel)[1] that led him to move to New Orleans by 1816. The elder Ripley brother seemed most favored: ordained in Waltham in 1809, Samuel persuaded Sarah Bradford (whom Mary called her "new-found favorite" in 1814) to marry him in 1818.

In Malden, Uncle Samuel Waite died in 1815, and his third wife, Rebecca Emerson Parker Brintnall Waite, died the next year. This left Mary with no Malden connections except for a Mrs. Tufts, Samuel Waite's daughter from his first marriage, whom she tried to befriend. In Newburyport, eighteen-year-old Mary and sixteen-year-old Louisa Farnham headed a motherless family of five younger siblings; though their father, William Farnham, lived for almost twenty more years, he seems to have been rather helpless, and as the girls grew up, they supported the family by teaching school. The eldest brother, John Hay, graduated from Harvard in 1811 and probably stayed in Boston to work: in 1813 Ruth Emerson reported that he called often and that Mary was in charge of a school in the house while Charlotte taught school in town and Louisa managed the family (MH). In 1814 Mary Emerson went to Newburyport to help care for Mary Farnham when she had rheumatic fever; this niece died two years later. In 1819 twenty-year-old William Farnham died at sea.

In Waterford, Maine, in 1810, Rebecca and Robert Haskins had six children under the age of eleven; by the end of the decade four more had been born (one died at the age of two in 1813). Robert Haskins was having a difficult time making a living as a farmer. The Lincoln Ripleys, with no children of their own, always had a house full of "adopted" and foster children. During this period disagreements between Lincoln Ripley and his congregation led to his dismissal in 1820. Probably in 1810 Mary began her lifelong friendship with sixteen-year-old Ann Brewer, who was adopted by the Ripleys in 1802.

Beyond this wide circle of family lay the friends and "cousins" she visited, wrote to, and mentioned: Mary Wilder and Daniel White in Newburyport, whose third daughter was born six months before her mother's death in 1811; the Haskins sisters in Boston and their parents (mother Hannah Upham Haskins suffered a paralytic stroke in 1813, and father John Haskins died in 1814); Ruth Emerson's brothers, successful Boston businessmen, and her married sisters and their families; cousins Samuel, Elizabeth, and Martha (Patty) Emerson of Newburyport; Uncle John Emerson, after 1816 her father's only living sibling; friends Ann Bromfield, Ruth Hurd Rogers (whose husband of three years died in 1814); her oldest female friend, Mrs. Dexter, who died in 1816; and many others.

From every side, claims competed with Mary's decision, in 1809, to light out for Maine. She had been in Waterford a scant six months when her brother asked her to return and help his boys (both their bodies and their minds) with her "healing attentions" (MH); in February 1811, when Ruth was about to deliver her last child, he urged her to come from Concord by the earliest stagecoach (MH). She probably responded to his plea; she seems to have spent most of 1811–12 in the Boston area. Her own health was excellent, as reported in a letter written in October 1812 to Ann Brewer: "Nothing to prevent constant exercise   And last week I walked to Malden & back [to Boston] the next day. Nothing can be more enchanting than the Country at this solemn season" (MWA). She returned to Waterford in February 1813 but came back to Massachusetts in April 1814, when the war finally approached Boston; she probably did not return again to Waterford until October 1817, when she began to date her letters from "Elm Vale" rather than "Waterford" or "Main." When Mary wrote in 1813 of her plan to stay in Waterford, Ruth was astonished and explained how much she had counted on her, pointing out the impropriety of being alone, without a "female friend or companion in the house," with her new (presumably male) boarder (MH). In 1818 half sister Sarah Ripley wrote plaintively from Concord, where she had "suffered very much with the ague or rheumatism in my head" and was "sick & solitary." She closed by comparing her situation with her elder sister's: "Ah often dear Mary do I think of your leisure & retirement & hope you remember one who surrounded with cares needs all the aid of devotion & grace" (MCR-S). Ruth had said much the same thing a month earlier, when she compared her small circle of cares with those of Mary, who was "elevated & ennobled by the priviledges of retirement & a more intimate communion with God" (MH). By November 1818, some disagreement with Robert Haskins had forced Mary from Vale once again.

Although she bragged about her "uninterrupted solitude," it must have been difficult for Mary Emerson to resist these appeals to serve in the traditional female roles of nurturer and caretaker. But she had long ago learned how to cope with her sense of other people's needs when they began to engulf her. Her apparent insensitivity to her brother's condition in 1810 derives from this need to *be* "myself." Her last surviving letter to her brother, William, is a declaration of independence. Comparing her "emigrations" to the imaginative flights of English novelist Ann Radcliffe, Mary claims an important difference: her movements not only "preserve life" but also "gratify the feelings of my relations." Bravely she announces that she so enjoyed the trip by stagecoach to Waterford that "I shall never feel reluctant to removeals [or] be laughed out of them."

Over 130 letters document these years in which Mary Emerson worked to define her vocation in the context of the "solitude" she had decided upon by settling at Waterford; of these, 56, addressed to sixteen different correspondents (primarily Ann Brewer, Sarah Bradford, and Ruth Emerson) are printed here.

The calendar of Mary Emerson's residences reveals the ongoing struggle between her need for independence and the claims of her various families. She spent all or most of 1810, 1813, 1817, and 1818 at Waterford; for most of 1811

and 1812 she was in Boston, with visits to Concord, Malden, and Newburyport. After William's death in May 1811, his widow desperately sought Mary's
help with children and boarders, and when Mary returned to Waterford in
1813, she took Charles and Bulkeley with her.

Probably in April 1814, when the war was approaching New England,
Mary returned to Boston to help Ruth. Over the next three years she moved
at least six times with the Emersons: from Summer Street to Bennet Street in
Boston and then to the Manse at Concord; back to Boston, possibly to the
Haskinses' home on Rainsford Lane, before going to Beacon Street, Hancock
Street, and finally Essex Street. By this time, Mary had decided that Ruth
could do without her (or that she could do without Ruth), and in August 1817
she headed for Waterford. She remained at Elm Vale probably through the
fall of 1818, but she spent all of 1819 moving between Concord and Waltham,
ignoring Ruth's pleas for help.

Even more than her refusal of marriage, Mary Emerson's decision to purchase Elm Vale seems to have been the event that transformed her life from
a "conventional to an eccentric story."[2] The deaths of her brother and her
friend Mary White, both of which occurred in 1811, accentuated her sense
of the vanity of human wishes and her desire for the solitary, nunlike life she
imagined for herself at Vale. Her decision to settle in Elm Vale, as the place
she had chosen (and which had chosen her) to practice her vocation, should
be viewed in the context of her grandfathers', father's, brothers', and uncles'
ministerial settlements at York, Malden, Concord, Harvard, Boston, Waterford, Waltham, and Conway. Unfortunately, her letters say nothing about
this decision; other evidence indicates she had arranged to purchase the farm
by the summer of 1813, though the transaction was not completed until the
following spring.[3]

Most of what Mary said about this purchase survives in letters from the
1840s and 1850s, after she had decided to sell the farm. From these accounts
we learn that in 1805 Robert Haskins (Ruth Emerson's brother, who had married Mary's sister Rebecca) used his inheritance to buy at South Waterford
land known as the Pollard place. By 1809, when the Haskinses already had six
children, Robert had fallen into debt and had to be rescued by his brothers,
Thomas and Ralph, who purchased the mortgage but allowed the family to
remain as tenants. Robert probably continued to be unable to pay his rent or
taxes regularly, and in 1811 Ralph Haskins was tempted to rid himself of the
responsibility for his shiftless brother when a stranger named Wyman offered
him fifteen hundred dollars for the farm.

Instead, after some dickering, Ralph sold the mortgage to Mary so that the
Haskinses could continue at Vale as her tenants.[4] Mary invested eleven hun-
dred dollars of her inheritance from Aunt Ruth (the result of the sale of the
Malden property, which netted Mary about eighteen hundred dollars), while
Robert, who swore he would "never work on a farm without ownership"
(MH: 1082), contributed four hundred dollars (probably a loan from Ralph)

to gain owner's rights. For his share, he received a ten-year lease, negotiated some sort of "bond" with Mary that made him appear to be the owner, and was obligated to pay interest (between sixty and eighty dollars a year) on Mary's share. For her part, Mary gained a home where she could live as a paying boarder as well as an income in the form of interest on her "investment" (which she insisted was not a loan) and the hope of future profit should property values increase. She expected to take full ownership once the lease with Robert expired.

Ideally, this was a mutually beneficial contractual arrangement for both parties: as she later recalled, Mary could "house a destitute family" while providing for her own social security. Sworn to secrecy regarding their arrangement, Mary maintained that "the world of waterford never discovered . . . till after '45 the all important fact" of the real ownership of the farm. By that time, Robert Haskins fully believed he was the owner and tried to prevent a sale by denying Mary any rights. But even in the period of the first lease, she found it difficult to realize the ideal. No sooner had she settled at Waterford than Ruth needed her in Boston; and even after she managed to return in 1817, new frictions developed in her relationship with Robert and eventually led to her five-year "exile" from Waterford, which began at the end of 1818. The separation was painful: she longed to return, she wrote Ann Brewer, "to recover the associations of some of the dearest holiest part of my life. Oh bitter were the tears I shed at passing Elm Vale for the last time" (MWA).

This was a period of intense female friendships, as suggested by the predominance of letters to Ruth, Sarah, and Ann. The correspondence with Sarah Bradford provides the best view of the role Mary Emerson hoped to play in her relationships with other women. It also shows Sarah helping to shape that role. Of about forty surviving letters to Sarah Bradford (later Ripley), perhaps twenty-six come from this decade. Almost thirty letters to Mary from Sarah also survive, most of them also from this period.[5] The fourteen printed in part 2 represent best the tenor of their conversation. Here Mary begins to develop a new voice, one familiar from Waldo's transcriptions of later letters to him. This is the voice in which Sarah urges her to speak, arguing that their friendship is different from that owed to family, that they are privileged to share a speculative, open, and free discourse. Even though Sarah was almost twenty years younger than Mary, they established the relationship of equals that William Emerson's rules for epistolary conversation describe. Encouraged by Sarah, Mary writes some of her most bewildering letters as she reaches for a public style to speak these thoughts heretofore saved for her "Almanack." (In the 1820s and 1830s, the disjunction between the private "Almanack" and the public letter is sometimes bridged through her inclusion of "Almanack" pages with—or as—letters.) Despite William's complaint in 1806, these letters are the first to seem really incomprehensible in places; this new voice defies logic, order, and control, and seems to speak instead from some genius raised by enthusiasm. The letters to Sarah are allusive and argumentative in new ways. In them, Mary Emerson explores what it means to write as a woman for another woman.

For the biographer interested in the diachronic dimension of Mary and Sarah's friendship, these letters can be frustrating. Neither woman was much rooted in ordinary time structures, and their letters from the years before Sarah's marriage to Samuel Ripley in 1818 are extremely difficult to date. While 1809 has been cited as the first year of their friendship, the letters contain insufficient evidence to support that date and indeed suggest that the two women became friends in 1812, when Sarah was nineteen.[6] Problems with dating result partly from Sarah's notorious failure to date her letters or to endorse those she received—that is, to write on the outside, in the businesslike way the Emerson men did, the date of receipt and answer or at least the date of the letter.

Moreover, Mary fell under Sarah's spell, and the way she adjusted her voice to that of her new correspondent not only prefigured her relationships with her Emerson nephews and Elizabeth Hoar but also made these later conversations possible. Sarah, younger and much better educated, opened up for Mary vistas on the classics, literature, philosophy, and science. Sarah read ancient languages, knew science and mathematics, speculated widely about theological issues, drew a wonderful picture of the evolution of the classical mind, and dared to speak her mind. She was accomplished, sociable, and had her pick of the eligible and educated young men of the day. Mary quickly rose to the style and level of discourse that Sarah sought. When writing to Sarah Bradford, Mary eschews the high plain of polite abstraction that characterizes her letters to Mary and Daniel White, Ruth Hurd, and Rebecca Thoreau. Instead, encouraged by her new friend, Mary Emerson allows herself to engage in the intellectual dialogue that Sarah demands—at the same time that Sarah begins to plead her own sense of propriety as an excuse for not joining more fully in her friend's "enthusiasm." Their correspondence testifies to the ability of these two women to engage each other in genuine dialogue.

While the content of these letters varies considerably, Mary Emerson's religious vision remains constant. As we read, we can watch her shaping her thoughts in an increasingly baroque prose, as necessary to her vision as Milton's was to his. With her brother William, she had dared to use this voice in 1810, despite his emphasis on clarity. With her Emerson nephews, she looked forward to the time when she could commence a "collegiate correspondence" (MH: 990)—when they would become intellectual "equals." With Sarah Bradford, Mary learned to shape this style for a woman she considered her equal; and, almost immediately, she began to use it in her letters to Waldo.

NOTES

1. Sanborn, *Recollections* 2:358.
2. Heilbrun, *Writing a Woman's Life*, 39.
3. The details of this purchase remain unclear. RHE to MME, 20 July 1813, gives

an imprecise report on a recent transaction between her brother, Thomas Haskins, and MME, which suggests he considered her involvement in the Waterford farm at this time merely a loan (MH). Another document refers to a deed dated 8 July 1814 and indicates that Ralph Haskins (another of Ruth's brothers) was part owner until 1821, when he conveyed the deed to "100 ½ acres of land together with the dwelling house and other buildings thereon situated in the town of Waterford" to MME (MH). A deed from Robert Haskins dated 23 Dec. 1820 turns over to MME three additional lots, or about ninety acres, less a small piece of land that had been sold for the Methodist meetinghouse. In another document of the same date, MME leased the whole property to Robert Haskins: an "Estate . . . which formerly belong^d to Ralph Haskins & contains about one hundred & ninety acres" (MH).

4. An undated letter from Ralph Haskins to MME rejects her offer of thirteen hundred dollars for the Vale farm. He goes on to explain: "I wish to serve Robert & that was my motive in offering the farms on the low conditions I have named. I should not sell them so low to strangers. Robert is willing to take them on the terms offered, & to have the Vale farm deeded to you on your giving an obligation to reconvey it to him on his paying you the debt of 1200 or what it amounts to & interest" (MH). The terms of the first lease can be inferred from a second "Indenture," dated 23 Dec. 1820, which leased to Robert Haskins "a farm in the town of Waterford . . . with the Dwelling house & other buildings thereon, . . . to hold for the term of six years from this date, yielding & paying there for the rent of Sixty six dollars per annum from this date. Which said rent is to be in lieu of interest provided the said Robert purchases the s^d estate agreeable to an obligation he holds of s^d Mary, to sell him s^d estate, otherwise it is to be paid to said Mary as stipulated in this above written contract. & at the end of said term he promises (if he does not purchase as agreed on above) to quit & deliver up s^d premises to the Lessor or her attorney. & s^d Robert agrees to pay all taxes thereon during the s^d term of six years also that he will not call on or charge the s^d Mary for any repairs or improvements which he may make there on" (MH).

5. Many of the letters written by SAB (later SBR) are in the Sarah Alden Ripley Collection (MC 180, MCR-S); a large number are printed in "MrsSR," 113–227.

6. SBR to George Simmons, [?] 1844, recalls that MME heard of her "when I was sixteen years old as a person devoted to books and a sick mother, sought me out in my garret without any introduction, and, though received at first with sufficient coldness, . . . did not give up till she had enchained me entirely in her magic circle" ("MrsSR," 175–76). Consequently, EH dates SAB's "earliest letter" to MME "about 1809" ("MrsSR," 120), a date accepted in all subsequent discussions of their relationship.

1810

To William Emerson[2]

W— Jan. 30 1810.

Dear Brother,

I thank you for the notice you take of me now and then by writing. I should have written to you, perhaps, more if I had not been kept back by diffidence. I hope your dear wife and children are well— Our honored parents, brothers and sisters. I know your omitting to mention those freinds, and to inquire after these, is not owing to insensibility to the best affections, but from a pressure of extensive engagements, that I can form no idea about. Sister H.[1] has good health, but never for an hour, appears to enjoy herself, which is more than I can always account for from cercumstances even the most adverse.

You appear in fine health and spirits; and as usual are pleased to profess a devotion to the present world, and an ignorance of the future. The curiosty which men of genius have excited, and a desire to pry into their plans and pursuits, has been universal, and never taxed with impertinence. The coldness and scepticsism of many great men about another state of existence, has often seemed almost nessecarily connected with their education and condition; and their misguided passion for immortality appears the immediate cause of many of those revolutions in the world, which will forever perpetuate their names. Were you, my brother, placed in the Athens of the world—surrounded with those visions of glory which hover over Patriots and Philosophers—forming splendid freindships—or with the Genius of Avignon,[2] immortalising the misterious passions of the heart, your predilection for this life would be less unaccountable.

But when one considers your birth, your education which was nessecarily unfortunate, your profession, your lot in a Country struggling rather for means of subsistence, than glory, in a crisis of the world too, when the Elijahs of the Chh, are watching, in holy jealously, for their alters, and looking for some amelioration of human misery; your fondness for the present is wonderfull! You are likewise, by a happy intuition, well acquainted with the frame of the human mind—a frame so adapted to the revelation of another life, that the internal evidences[n] of many, may be said, to be matter of "knowledge" rather than faith. Though it must be owned this revelation involves many things hostile to human passions and habits. You represent a prevailing attention to the improvement of the mind, as inducing gloom. This has been the opinion of a large proportion of people; but of those, generally, who are wholly fitted to the few aspects of pleasure and convenence which pass before their senses in their own houses, and at places of publick festivity. But to those, who profoundly yeild themselves to the prospects of improvement, the darkest hallucinations of a religious imajanation, are less pitiable than any species of atheism.

Farewell, my brother. With much love to your family, brother D. B. R. I am your affec[n] Sister

M M Emerson.

If you do not know where Miss A—s lodgings are, please to send the letter to Miss P.[3]

I wish Mrs Emerson would send Doddridge's rise & progress. my shoes.[n] And I wish you would loan me Barlow.[4]

MH: bMS Am 1280.226(1057). *Addressed:* Rev. Mr Emerson. / Boston. *Endorsed:* Miss M. M. E./ 1810 Jan. 30d / Feb. 9. — r./ 20 — a.

internal evidences] ⟨faith⟩ ↑ internal evidences ↓

Doddridge's . . . shoes.] ↑ Doddridge's rise & progress. ↓ my shoes.

1. REH.

2. Possibly Italian poet Petrarch (1304–74), who celebrated Avignon and nearby Fontaine-de-Vaucluse during his residence at the splendid court of Pope Clement VI.

3. Probably historian Hannah Adams (1775–1831) and Lydia Prentiss (1790–1855), daughter of the Reverend Caleb Prentiss of Reading, Mass.

4. Possibly a volume by Joel Barlow (1754–1812), American poet and diplomat; author of the verse epic *The Vision of Columbus* (1787) and a satiric poem *The Conspiracy of Kings, with a note on Mr. Burke*, published in Newburyport in 1794, among other works.

To William Emerson[2]

W— June 24 [1810]

Dear Brother

You *will* talk of coolness and calmness in religion— Let Angels and burning Seraphs be calm—let *man* struggle and agonize for truth, while any thing remains to be done or known relating to his salvation   The least prospect of the christian's futurity, should awaken unremitting efforts. Should ages intervene thier ponderous weight before the soul reassumes activity, yet *it will* become acquainted with a Being nessecary and eternal—it *will* at some grand and awfull period become acquainted with its relations to the will and agency of that Being. To common readers of the bible, it appears strange that learned Ones endeavour to divest it of every thing to excite fear. No analogies in nature in the history of man, and Providence or Grace itself bespeake an econyomy which does not operate on the mind of man in exciting wonder fear hope and terror tho' more of joy and faith. If a late famous Philosopher said that it required the utmost exertion of fortitude to contemplate the physical attributes of the Deity, what must be the emotions of those who contemplate the God of the bible—the Auther of a perfect law which remains and will forever remain in full force, who have not confidence that their feeble destinies are united to this Being by a miraculous interposition of mercy.

Ah, my dear brother could live with yourself—   —far away from those vain and ambitious objects w'h constantly press on the senses, and enter into every literary pursuit. Could you commune with nature sublime and tranquil, contemplate dead men's bones—and take leave of the earth, hastening to revolutions—that light of genius, which your sultry air and diet have not yet extinguished, would rekindle, and aspire to the skies—that benevolence which in the days of youth glowed in your eyes would be animated with celestial enthusiasm. Visions of happiness would visit your imajanation, and whilst you diffused light over socity, you would be elevated above the world!

I hoped you would have been particular in speaking of our unfortunate

THE FIRST CHURCH, (CHAUNCY PLACE),
1808—1868.
THE REV. WM. EMERSON, MINISTER,
1808—1811.

Figure 7. The First Church, Chauncy Place, Boston.

brother.[1] Alass! the day that saw him defy the athority of God, and injure the best principles of socity. Give him my love if worth the acceptance. But I believe I have displeased my sister Sarah in a letter I wrote about it, for she omits answering it.

Sister H— thanks you for her letter. Mr H— is gone today and cannot write about your farm. Farewell.

M—y M—y E—n

MH: bMS Am 1280.226(1058). *Addressed:* Rev. Mr Emerson / Boston / Rev. Mr Gardiner. *Endorsed:* Miss M. M. Emerson. 1810 /. Oct. 15 d / — 20 r / — nov 7 a.

1. References in family correspondence indicate that half brother Daniel Ripley's hot temper got him into trouble, and Sanborn says he was involved in a duel (*Recollections* 2:358); Mary may be referring to the duel here.

To WILLIAM EMERSON[3]

Waterford, June, 24, 1810

My dear Nephew,

I am so much pleased with your letter that I take the first oppurtunity to thank you for it. The subjects were very proper which you mentioned. I am glad to hear that John Hay[1] is capable of speaking an oration well; but it would be more pleasant to hear that he was very fond of reading his bible, or had some opportunity of obliging some poor person. I do not mean that he is not fond of doing both; but I only mean that learning, or being spoken well of by gentlemen, is of no consequence compared to being pious and benevolent.

You, my dear William, are nine years old. In those years how many weary steps and anxious thoughts have you cost your dear parents. And many pleasant ones also. But it is now time for you to reflect on your condition, as a being who has been sent into this world for a short time to prepare for a world which will always exist. If you fear God, and serve Him, He will accept of your services and make you unspeakably happy. You may be sure He will, because you read in the holy scriptures, how Jesus Christ, Gods only Son, came into this world and died for Sinners. It is for his sake, that God bestows so many and so invaluable blessings upon us.

I often think of you and your brothers, and remember whatever I saw modest and affectionate in you with delight. A man possessed of amiable dispositions is always sure of happiness, and without those, tho' he were a President or Govenor would be despicable.

Give my love to R Waldo. I shall write to him very soon

Your affectionate Aunt
M—y M—y Emerson

MH: bMS Am 1280.220(75). *Addressed:* Master William Emerson / Boston. *Endorsed:* M. M. Emerson / June 1810.

1. Possibly WE[3]'s cousin, John Hay Farnham (b. 1791) of Newburyport, who graduated from Harvard in 1811.

To WILLIAM EMERSON[2] AND RUTH HASKINS EMERSON

Waterford   Oct. 16. [1810]

My dear Brother,

I received your last by mail and was entertained by its high flown compliments. I think you must lately have refreshed your imajanation with some pages of Don Quixot—and have wandered with Mrs R— in some of her emigrations.[1] *Mine* it is true are some what like hers, tho' more honorable, for they not only preserve life, but alternately gratify[n] the feelings of my relations. I injoyed my last stage journey so well, that I shall never feel reluctant to removeals, and never intend to be laughed out of them. The next I make, may be in a state incident to old age, that of being deaf. I have for four or five weeks been troubled with a partial deafness in one ear. The drum has been so irittable that noise was injurious and any business. My physician if such he may be called "that shape hath none"[2] has electricised it very often. The cause is intirely owing to an improper state of the bile and is of the nervous kind. This he at lenght perceives and there is no doubt but will be removed when my health is better. If you apprehend any danger you may mention it to some of the Faculty—but on the whole I hardly think it worth while—as it is not certainly a local complaint; and it might appear extravagant to think the loss of an ear very important to one at 36.

But how shall I keep that village school with "spectacles bestride"?[3]

Your affe[t] Sister

M Emerson

My dear Sister

I hope you and every body are well. All are well here and send love. You would be pleased to see your brother—tho' you would feel for their many embarressments. Becca[4] has but tow beds. Are you willing to send mine? If so, you can put it in a box covered with that old ticking, and inclose the counterpayne, my muff, and walking shoes   I shall send to C— for the muff to be sent to you. Direct the box to D[r] Coe. Portland.

The labourer asks for the pay done on Mr Emersons farm.

Your affec[t] Sister.

I wish you would send me a box of dentifice from Randall. Brother Ralph has a dollar of mine I believe and Dodd[s][5] Rise & Progress. Some Wafers. Please to seal the inclosed letters. Mr. Farrar tarries tow or three days in Boston. Dont forget to give my love to brother D B R—

MH: bMS Am 1280.226(1059). *Addressed:* Rev. Mr Emerson / Boston. *Endorsed:* M. M. E. / to her brother.

gratify] ⟨realize⟩ ↑ gratify ↓

1. Cervantes's *Don Quixote* and Ann Radcliffe, English author of Gothic novels.

2. Milton, *Paradise Lost* 2:666–67: "The other shape, / If shape it might be call'd that shape had none."

3. Possible allusion to Cowper's description of ministers who "strain celestial themes / Through the prest nostril, spectacle-bestrid" (*The Task* 2:438–39).

4. Sister REH, at Waterford.

5. Philip Doddridge.

1811

To Mary Wilder White and Daniel Appleton White

W— Jan. 15, 1811.

Your letter my dear friends made me glad at the bottom of my heart. Your health, your children, your gratitude to the Giver of all good gave me the images of yourselves still dear & interesting. It is true, I had begun to look back on our connection, as on some rainbow vision which had dawned on my obscurity—shed its' influence—and was no more—but it might be the *promise* of some future scene of more permanent love. This pleasant thought soothed the conviction, that if indeed, you had concluded to drop me, it was a dictate of cooler refined judgment, which the deepest reflections on my manners[n] approved. How singular and happy for mortals is the misterious office of religion—that at the same time it gives us to feel unworthy of the blessings of the *present*, it gives us every thing to expect in a *future* life. I view your course, estimable Pair, as including the very best of earthly passions,— and as terminating in every thing for which man appears by the will of his Creator destined.

I never heard of your indesposition last summer, dear Mary—but *somehow* I do not connect the idea of illness in *you* with unhappiness. It rather seems like renewing an opp[y] for your fortitude and your husbands unaffected[n] tenderness. Your Elisabeth is at the most interesting age in infancy. Your Isabell has a fine name. You will in time[n] remind the world that the Stanley family has a real existence I trust.[1]

Are your friends & acquaintance well? I hoped to hear of the charming Ruth, probably now Mrs. Rogers[2] Remember me affectionately to the Miss Searls. Their good Gramother is no more. She always appeared a chearfull hospitable lady. Our dear Sarah had indeed been called to much bodily sufferings—and of course my family to much affliction.

Do let me hear from you whenever it is intirely pleasant and convenient. A thousand things render writing a task to Heads of families, of which I know nothing; but promise to accept every line with gratitude however distant the time may be, if you will not trouble yourself, dear Sir, to make any more apoligies. To your sprightly request to know if I was going to marry, I asure you, I have met with no opp[y] that interested my heart for one moment, nor even flattered my vanity. My occupations are much the same as at Malden—but rendered more pleasant, as I am not even of so much consequence as when there. So that when I dine by myself or with the family no notice is taken of the change. Were I less ignorant, *it seems*, I could not so well enjoy the few books I have.

Adieu dear friends

Yours affectionately

M—y M—y Emerson

MH-AH. *Addressed:* Daniel A. White Esq[r] / Newburyport. / Miss M. W. Bliss.
manners] ⟨self⟩ manners
unaffected] unaffected ⟨and interesting⟩
in time] ⟨soon⟩ ↑ in time ↓
 1. The Whites' third daughter, born 12 Dec. 1810, was first named Isabella Hazen for a favorite relative. After her mother's death on 29 June 1811, she was baptized Mary Wilder White. Allusion to Stanley is unclear. MME seems to hope one of their children will bear this name, but no Stanley appears in family records.
 2. In 1806, Ruth Hurd became engaged to Abner Rogers (d. 1814) of Newburyport, a lawyer and close friend of DAW's; they were not married until 18 June 1811.

To MARY WILDER WHITE AND DANIEL APPLETON WHITE

Boston   Ap. 13, 1811.

My dear friends,

You are afflicted still. But *you* are recovering Mary. My Brother recovers no more. God is taking him away and blessed be his name.[1] How much better oh infinitely better than to outlive his mind, his exertions, his friends! Should it not be the prayer of every christian that they may not survive any of these, but especially his *moral improvement*! And unhappy must the One be, who is so wedded to life as to loose a desire[n] to depart when their improvements stagnate.

But I *feel* not much of these great things—an unaccountable heaviness weighs down my spirit—pray for me—that a situation so painfull and admonishing may be improved. I long to see you—do if possible write.

The Physicians think it advisable their Patient should try the sea a little— it may revive—but not at all probable any benefit worth the trouble.

Farewell.

M—y M—y Emerson

MH-AH.
desire] *possibly* decree
 1. WE[2] died 12 May 1811. MME continued to believe MWW would recover and wrote an encouraging letter to DAW and MWW on 24 June 1811 (MH: 1298); MWW died 29 June 1811.

To Ezra Ripley

Boston   July, 3, 1811

Hon^d Father

Ruthy sends her duty to you and thinks it may have a very good effect on W^m if you should be surprised with the unwelcome intelligence that he is not so good a Schollar as he might be. Mr Bigelow[1] called here last sat. and after a particular conversation in which he was pressed to know W^m's standing he observed that if his school of 60 were divided into 4 parts W^m would be in the second, as to behaviour and scholarship—that he might by dilligence and activity as well in the *first*. He was particular that the child might not know this from him—as he endeavoured to exert all his influence as Master. Sister E. thinks this information will come with more energy from you, Sir, and that so important a deficiency should be as it were immediately communicated—and that she has not seen Mr B. since W^m's absence is a fact.

We also regret that W^m has a notion of being a merchant—and we aim to direct his taste in a manner that he shall not^n feel his self will stimulated.

I long to hear from Sarah *how* and where she is.

Your dutifull daughter
MME.

4. Brother Robert has bo't a chaise and sets out on monday for home. I tho't I w^d mention it to Sarah—if she has a mind to go—I w^d tarry at C—   I wish to visit the westward and as I dont hear particularly from sister Becca— think not to return at this time especially as this season is not favorable to making the application I s^d like there.

MH: bMS Am 1280.226(1236). *Addressed:* Rev. Mr Ripley / Concord / Miss Bliss.
shall not] shall ↑ not ↓ (not *possibly canceled*)
1. William Biglow, headmaster of Boston Public Latin School until 1814.

1812

To Ann Brewer

Boston   Jan 26. 1812.

What can be the reason of Martha's rejection? Is it because of another?[1] Is it because she cannot esteem? *She does well.* because she *cannot love? She does well.* or from independance of matrimony to make her better—and a desire to consecrate herself more eminently to God? These questions you will perhaps answer. Life is so fleeting that it's events appear very trivial whenever we realize eternal interests. It is well to marry, and it is well not to marry.

But what are you doing Girls? You, Ann, write without elegance & taste— because without simplicity. You seem to have no distinct idea of what you mean to convey when you begin a sentence—   You *feel* much but express yourself confusedly. I disliked the note—you trifled with serious words &

Figure 8. Ezra Ripley (1751–1841), stepfather of
Mary Emerson.

ideas. You reflected on sects. which is always illiberal. I will return it that you may be more carefull to improve your self in every thing. An ardent inlarged mind pursuing the glorious prize of immortal glory should never *putter and quidle* for one moment. I s^d not be so severe (for I am very severe) but you are apt to *appear* slow & *particular*. Now you Martha & all compare yourselves with none—and have no opp^y for humility. And I shall write solely to strive to put you all a little in the blessed ground of humility. I always said it, when at W^d, and I think of you all, as I've seen you at meeting, and about your houses, Mrs Farrar & Susan and all—thinking *how good I am*—how correct—how much better than the poor gay creatures who dance go to parties of pleasure. Well I hope to be humbler after this—it puts in my head a great many things you will justly tax me with and above all my pride which is often so insupportable to myself that I am sure it must be to others, especially those who care about me. But let us not be too willing to acknowledge our faults— let a sense of our awfull responsibility to a heart searching God and our holy vocation so often defiled, fill us with shame and contrition. It is for want of vigilance, zeal industry we so live.

That I have so written is my dear Ann because I love you.

Farewell   May God bless you with the richest gifts of his love
MME.

I send the letter as you desire my advice in writing. and if you are not sincere you are paid by my sincerity. Read my speech about pride to Martha & Susan.

MWA. *Addressed:* Ann Brewer.

1. MME implies that AB's adoptive sister, Martha Robinson, has rejected an offer of marriage. Martha remained unmarried and cared for their adoptive father, the Reverend Lincoln Ripley, until his death in 1858. Martha Bliss, another adopted child in this family, was called Patty.

To Ann Brewer
Boston   Ap 20 1812.

My dear Ann,

Where abouts in the journey of life, moral, intellectual & sublime art thou? Does the rapidity of the planets which carry about your body mark the rapid growth of your mind. Are your ideas clear on those subjects which you attempt to understand? Are your faculties concentered in the great & infinite subject of moral perfection? Does every new day awaken new and holier ambition?

Love to Martha & Susan. Mrs Hewes[1] is nicely.

Your aff^t friend
MME

MWA. *Addressed:* Ann Brewer.

1. Probably Mary Bliss Hewes.

To Ann Brewer

Boston   June 13 1812.

Dear Ann,

Thank you for writing—spend not time so much in thinking of frailty, as in fervent penitence & reformation. Yesterday I was a spectator to the most solemn & interesting scene I ever wittnessed Mr B—s funeral.[1] Would you, Girls, could have seen it. The lying vanities of the world there lost thier hold. The world appeared in its' true colures. Genius, fame, all that endeared existence suddenly arrested. How little did *one's self* appear when the splendid character of the Deceased thrilled thro' the soul. We ought to contemplate distinguished gifts of God to be humble. It is His will that some of his favored children should climb the heights of virtue & honor by a rapid career—be called amidst their growing[n] honors, to leave a world in tears. But you shall have the sermon. But amidst the humiliation of comparison and the bitter regret that an intellectual luminary is removed from this dark world, we are led most deeply to contemplate the state of the dead. *There* in the world of retribution, talents but give weight to awfull responsibility—*there* no wreaths of fame intwine immortal brows, but as the heart has been *humble, sincere, disinterested resigned* and *contrite*! The labours of piety & learning which employed the Deceased can never excite our emulation—   His numerous friends—his electrifying influence on soceity—his capacious powers, his profound researches after truth can never even be appreciated by us—   *But we can* be less frivolous less talkative—less engaged in trifles—less languid more alive to the great things which are going forward to bring to pass the purposes of God.

Give my love to all who ask; Mrs Farrar[2] thank her for her kind letter. Yours in good will

MM Emerson

The solemnity of the scene was increased by the gloom of the day. The Chh is large & dark—the organ (w'h played at the entrance & departure of the procession) is deeply toned—the bell is the heaviest—   The assembly[n] large—   The aged minister who prayed had wittnessed the death of many of the pastors of that Chh. He seemed the picture of age & sorrow bending over death & ruin. It was with difficulty the Preacher could perform his office for tears. As the afflicted Sisters[3] entered, supported by friends, a thrill of sympathy pervaded the assembly. And there was no moment of consolation to sympathy, so powerfull, as when the Orator[4] observed that at any interval[n] of reason *the departed was observed to be engaged in prayer to God.*

If you have sensibility I shall not regret the trouble of writing.

MWA. *Addressed:* Ann Brewer.
growing] ⟨thickening⟩ ↑ growing ↓
assembly] ⟨croud⟩ assembly
interval] ⟨moments⟩ interval

1. Joseph Stevens Buckminster, brilliant pastor of Boston's Brattle Street Church, died on 9 June 1812 at the age of twenty-eight.

2. A Waterford neighbor, either Mrs. Calvin Farrar or Mrs. Josiah Farrar.

3. Lucy Buckminster Farrar, wife of John Farrar (Hollis professor of mathematics at Harvard beginning in 1807); Eliza Buckminster (later Lee) (1794–1864) became a writer of fiction; Mary Buckminster married Samuel Lothrop in 1829.

4. The Reverend John Thornton Kirkland (1770–1840), president of Harvard College from 1810 to 1828, preached the funeral sermon on a text from Job 16:19, "Thou destroyest the hope of man."

To Ralph Waldo Emerson

Concord, July, 26, 1812.

I have but a moment to write, as company is expected to tea—but I could not fail of acknowledging yours which gave me pleasure. You it seems, my dear Ralph, wrote in haste; so you can sympathise with me. It is well we have not the affairs of the nation to guide, as our little avocations render us already so busy. 8 o'k eve. My dear dear Ralph, I this moment received letter from W^m, for which I thank him a thousand times. I rejoice you have received any { } not because of the honor, but because it denotes worth in yourself. Go on, my dear Waldo, and exert every nerve to gain the favor of God and the good will of the worthy part of society will follow. I sometimes antisapate the time when you shall be at man's estate, the Protector of your beloved Mother and Sister, with emotions of hope and pleasure. How delightfull the thought that your virtues shall honor the memory of your Father! How much more valueable than the applause of a multitude! Charles is very well grows ambitious of being the man. He was with me, coming from Lincoln on friday, we were out in a violent shower, he was alarmed at first & cried, but soon conquered his feelings and laughed begged I would not tell the family he cried.

Your affectionate Aunt.
MM Emerson.

MH: bMS Am 1280.226(812). *Addressed:* Master R W. Emerson / Boston.

To Sarah Alden Bradford

[1812?] [1]

My latest freind & sweetest freind, I send the shawls least you s^d need them, & to request you to come *tomorrow*. Fail me not & tarry here either to dine or to *sleep*. You will feel anxious to know the termination of our route. We arived without any ill to my darling—for my old carcase it does not fare better but worse for scenes of pleasure & festivity & libations to Ceres which sometimes prove so healthy to debility generally injure me. And then how natural to reflect that the abstinence & every day labours of the house are the best means for promoting the pure & fervid race of peity. How perpetually have I said tho' a long journey never will I deviate after pleasure— So you will not think it the least *deviation* of affection if I do not fullfill somthing of an engage^t to come again.

Give my regards to your parents   apoligise to your Mother for my not sitting with her as I told her I w^d for you came in to read to me at the moment I was going into the parlour. Love to Martha she must place her black eyes on good books. & come & see me in my lonely abode.

Remember that I feel a great respect to the Sheriffs family[2] for their goodness to mine.

Let me see you tomorrow

MME.

MH: bMS Am 1280.226(1257). *Addressed:* Miss S. A. Bradford / Charlestown.

1. Dating uncertain; letter possibly written from Concord, where MME took nephew CCE for a visit in the summer of 1812.

2. "Sheriff" Samuel Bradford, one of WE[2]'s parishioners, was, according to RHE, the Emersons' " 'greatest earthly benefactor' " after WE[2]'s death (*Life of RWE*, 84).

To Charles Chauncy Emerson

[1812?]

My own dear boy,

I send you a little cake, as a remembrance of our sweet friendship. And I would have it answer a nobler purpose. Let the milk, flour and eggs of which it's constituent parts are composed represent the solid virtues of your character, The sugar it's sweetness—the flavor of its fruit and the fragrance of it's spices be emblamatical of the ornaments and graces of your soul. But especially let the white incrustation be a type that the lovely veil of modesty will be a cover even to your virtues. It is this which inhances the value of goodness itself, and renders it useful and dignified.

If Mother will permit you to go to school the first letter you write with your own hand shall be rewarded by

MME.

Fig to Bulkley.

MH: bMS Am 1280.226(631). *Addressed:* Master C C Emerson. *Endorsed:* M M Emerson / (V)O T.

1813

To Phebe Bliss Emerson Ripley

Boston   Jany 19, 1813.

The first time I use this date is to express my love & respect for my honored parent.[1] Oh may this year bear in it's course some peculiar blessing for my Father, Mother and Sister. The sorrows of the past are gone—   Every day obliterates their memory. Every day does more—it hastens to bury it's own load of care and ignorance and suffering beneathe the endless future. Every thing is transient and mutable but the corruptions of the heart. These defy the power of days and years—and the efforts of religion itself. Nothing less than parting soul and body will rid us of these diseases and render the spirit the constant abode of truth, meekness and charity. How great such a *parting*. How astonishing the effect of that instant which frees the soul from lugging a putrifying "unearthed" carcase, which bears down every aspiring thought, darkens every vivid imajanation, confounds every intellectual process, and what is altogether more deplorable, narrows and chills every disinterested affection! Is it strange that the Apostle who once had a glimps of an unbodied state should so eagerly long to be rid of *a body of sin and death*? This happy man was distinguished by such a rapture as added^n energy to all his after life; but when he really did put off mortality it is not likely, he experienced more joy than other Saints, tho' of the most ignorant order, who had *tasted of the same measure* of grace. How delightfull, my dear Mother, that not only Paul, but every soul who has drank into the same spirit will be delivered from sin & stupidity forever! In the usual course of things you, Madam, appear nearer this change than your children. How many years of feeble, irksome life may some of them dragg, after you have entered on your eternal state. What an advantage does this probability give you in prospect over them. You may already be touching the period of all that is grand in existence! You may be near the unveiled knowledge of the will of God—and the practice of that *will* in spotless perfection! The pious friends you have mourned over, may be in daily expectation of welcoming you to some mansion of your Saviours. Oh, my dear Mother, how interesting and solemn will this eventfull departure be—leaving a world in which you have sojourned so long. How unspeakable the joy to leave it with out any lingering desire for it's comforts—without a claim from any of its poor and afflicted inhabitants unfullfilled. Oh my dear Mother may your sun set clear—and may every year of your mortal life be fruitfull of these dispositions which will be most promotive of your own and our sanctification. How much good you may yet procure your dear family can only be known when all hearts are disclosed. Could I ever hope to be a means of adding to your comfort dear Madam, how earnestly should I look forward to the period of your latest age. Ruthe desires her duty and most affectionate wishes to our honored Parents, says she daily thinks of you and trusts she is remembered in your daily petitions.

As to Sarah we have so long been disappointed in not seeing her that we resolve to say no more; Sarah will be here today, or this week will certainly bring her. We are sure that wherever she is, she is aiming at the highest of all objects and living under the favor of the highest Being. My affectionate remembrance to Mrs. Thoreau. I will write to her if I can give her any plea- sure. Present *if proper* my congratulatory remembrance to Mr Hoar,[2] who I think inquired after me Sarah said. William has been confined at home with a sore throat for nearly a fortnight; but with a good appetite he promised every day to be better, till thursday his Mother had a physian and since he has kept chamber. Today Dr W.[3] called again says he is getting well but must not come down too soon. W^ms health has been so much endangered in years past that every complaint gives anxiety. The rest are finely. Your dutifull daughter

MM Emerson

MH: bMS Am 1280.220(77). *Addressed:* Mrs Phebe Ripley / Concord / Mass. / Hon^d by Mr Hoar.

added] ⟨gave⟩ ↑ added ↓

1. Another letter, to Rebecca Thoreau, is dated 14 Jan. (MH: 1296; see last para- graph); the date of the letter printed here may be 9 Jan., and the apparent "1" (which does not look like MME's usual "1") a stray mark, thus making valid MME's claim that this is her first letter for the new year, 1813.

2. Samuel Hoar (1778–1856) graduated from Harvard in 1802 and began practic- ing law in Concord in 1805.

3. Probably Boston physician and surgeon John Collins Warren (1778–1856), like WE[2], a founding member of the Anthology Society.

To Sarah Alden Bradford

[Jan.? 1813?]

It is past midnight—   Oh does every response of that bell carry us for- ward to the grand office!—   Oh each echo of it warns us, as with an Angel's voice, to prepare for that period when the Herald of Omnipotence shall say *time shall be no more!* Transporting moment—when sin and time & death shall divide this wretched globe no longer. Will it ever arive? Is it possible— faith weary and weak cannot grasp the too rich idea—too grand for her feeble exercises! Yet somthing illumines the cloud which hangs over eternal Provi- dence at times like these. Oh how grand are these events when viewed as contrould—nay, ordained by Him who rideth on the tempest of war and ter- ror and saith peace to a contending world. It was always delightfull to find Homer & Virgil marshalling their armies by the direction of Jupiter & his ladies, and the interest their deities pleased to take in human affairs was very pleasant. Ideas of power & wisdom are adapted to delight—   Then how grand joined to benevolence & mercy. Think oh think, my beloved Sister, in immortality of our connection with the first great Cause. What a weight— what a glory this to our existence! Creation of an immortal does this—but *redeemed re*created in the image of Gods Son & forever united to the right hand of God, beyond the claims of *Principalities and Power*. What a wonder to all the universe & will forever continue so in the plan of redemption! Almighty God, in mercy to the wretched human race, hasten to unviel the scheme w'h involves the happiness of myriads!—   Oh hasten to unfold it's yet unknown glories—to burst on a ruined world, an oppressed groaning creation, the full splendor of it's consumation! Angels and Seraphs will rise a louder note of praise than ever echoed thro the riegions of Hosannahs. Where then will be the depravity of human nature? Where thus that deep mysterious secret, of whose origin and end & nature bafle the profoundest to fathom? Oh shall we be forever & eternally rid of its defiling invincible power! Oh let us pray, my darling fellow Traveller to eternal scenes, for the coming of our great Master to arrange his family. May our account be adjusted—   *What have I said*   Oh may mercys richest balm be applied to *my* case—for verily *I have fallen short in every thing* & in many guilty. May your *redoubled talents* be crowned with immortal—with distinguished splendor—by splendor I think not of fame—but of partaking more of the approbation of Him *who is the resurrection*! What pursuits—what growing knowledge will be yours! Yet love, ineffable love will transcend all. Good night. W^m is sick[1] & this has been a most anxious ev^g.

MH: bMS Am 1280.226(1268).

1. WE³'s illness mentioned in other letters from Jan. 1813 suggests this undated letter may have been written at that time.

To Sarah Alden Bradford

[1813?]

Near tow o'k Morning. When shall I see you thou soother of my dark life? The Miss S—[1] will come some day & take tea, but if W^m does not get well soon I know not when. He was out this morning & seems tolerable

Shall you be in wednesday? Do go and hear for me, for I shall have no ticket

I was at a very splendid smale party at Miss Searls last friday. You were spoken off by Mrs Richard Sullivan. Well, she is the most lovely & excellent woman I ever saw or imajaned! *It was good to be there* in view of the finest objects of divine favor. Oh what excursions does the soul make? Your letters have a similar effect. I read one today which interested me when nothing else could. Multiply them—continue to brighten my path w'h is at times so stale so wearisome from the cercumstances which surround me that it seems almost insupportable. Were the soul raised by faith how insensible w^d it be of repressing objects. Burn this I pray you. Write me long long letters. Yours most aff^t

MME

Tuesday Morn.
Many thanks for the last letter & flower. Martha was very kind. I wish I could have seen her.

MH: bMS Am 1280.226(1266). *Addressed:* Miss S. A. Bradford / Charlestown.
    1. Probably the Searles.

To WILLIAM EMERSON[3]

Waterford, Feb. 22, 1813.

My dear Nephew,
    You may well imajane with what emotion I take my pen to write to "a man of your parts and profound erudition." But as the gentlest candour and warmest good nature are often^n concomitant with astonishing talent, I make bold to address you. And without offense let me say that however lofty the pinicle of fame on which you are mounted, however vast the multitude of your admirers, and magnificent your power, if you have not an open ingenuous temper, & humble, pious heart, your memory, after a few uncertain days, will perish, or your name be mentioned with contempt. Riches are but the dust of the earth; honor, which cometh from the breath of man, empty as air, & learning but the collection of other men's property. Would you be great, throw aside your pomp, descend into the tomb—behold there that *the worm is thy sister, and corruption* thy appointment. Seek not for *honor and glory* on this earth, hastening itself to destruction. Pass the few days in which it carries thee on it's surface in purifying thyself for the society of all the truly great and good in the universe. Fill with faithfullness, the rapid moments, that thy Mother may rejoice in *a wise son*—that the poor and ignorant may be the happier that thou wast born.^n With the same portion of respect with which I began this bold epistle, and with renewed affection I subscribe myself your affectionate Aunt

M M Emerson

MH: bMS Am 1280.226(1060). *Addressed:* William Emerson A.B.C.D. / Boston.
Endorsed: Miss M. M. Emerson / February 22^d 1813 / Answered ——.
    often] ⟨always⟩ ↑ often ↓
    born.] born ⟨in their day⟩.

To Ruth Haskins Emerson

Waterford, Feb. 28, 1813.

My dear Sister,

It is with many recollections of the past, that I feel myself at so great a distance from you. When I reflect how closely we have been united by the dead and by the living—how much we have conversed on the greatest of all subjects, the harmony and kindness so unbroken—I feel some gratitude—and some hope that we have not lived together in vain. You will feel, of course, a void in my absence. But I fervently hope, it will be filled with better thoughts than I could afford. Oh my sister, may your future life be as different from the past as the clear light of day from the dawning twilight. May you go on with renewed zeal to *the stature of a perfect man in Christ*. May each of your dear children forever be the holier and consequently the happier for your exertions in piety, your firmness of truth, your disinterestedness, your whole devotion of soul to whatever is lovely.

But of Charles I have said nothing. He is finely in health and gayer in spirits from his increased society than at home. I tarried at home today. He says he has been very happy and *pretty* good, and I promised to write it. He often speaks of you and home, and I shall wish to promote this remembrance. At present I feel very glad you judged best to send him—find no "reasons" even that Mrs Ripley acknowledges now. And reading better than William stimulates him. This I dont like and trust it will wear off. Should Rebecca[1] go, which seems probable, you will have the pleasure of bestowing attention less interested, than on your own children, and thus taste the highest pleasure this side the other world. Your manner will benefit her. Never do I think was a journey and different scenes more nessecary. God will prosper the plan I trust. Let her be cheerfull and her mind expand to new objects. But of all virtues make her frank, open and ingenously confident. Torpor and timidity, those foes to all that is great and pious, she is naturally inclined to, *there,* may all your instructions aim   But of all things dont let her indulge my dear Babe.[2] I think she is injuring these little ones very much. She has much of a dizzy head ache—cannot rise early I fear. * * * I think it much best that you should have a child in exchange, if your freinds notice your situation. It w^d be giving wrong impressions for them to think tow children were taken care off without your expense.[3] I think *to myself,* that probably Rebecca may return with Mr. Farrar but nothing of the kind is said. I wish you w^d send me a book of geography like the one I asked you to put up, & charge it to me & a geography still *less* w^d be usefull. Some coffee at 20 cents I s^d like soon—   It might be best to procure it, if no opp^y to send it. This is good enough but takes more than double the quantity   As to my clothes if Rebecca *needs* use the slip. I wish you w^d find some pieces of my ginum slip. Mrs Ripley's tea is missing & one of the caps for me. I forgot at the time of talking our monied affairs the muslin & locke—but I will do right in the end. Please to send me a little books w'h are about.

Figure 9. Ruth Haskins Emerson (1768–1853), sister-in-law of
Mary Emerson, as a young woman.

You will ask if I feel as I used to describe. I do and tho' I dont make any calculation on books, yet am constantly employed to the extent of my power. And how happy for you and I my dear for whom the world has little charms and we still less for society that the livliest enjoyment is wholly independant on time place and situation—that the human mind is made for *effort* and *there* it is destined to find it's honor and peace. Sister Betsey was mistaken about our suspicions being ill founded—tho' we are comfortable for the present, & I doubt not shall be provided for. Sister Becca has not a word of complaint and is more reserved towards me it seems than ever. Phebe is so unwell as to keep her room sends much love to you.[4] So does Bulkly who is as gay as ever, but looks thin. I fear he is not well—his appetite appears unnatural. As to Rebecca's school, do as you think best. I tho't if she could go to Mr How's school mornings I w^d easily defray a quarter— She needs writing, composition arithmetic & any thing. You will do wisely I trust.

Tuesday. 2 March. We are disappointed about Rebecca's going today—but hope to send her some time this week. Farewell dear Sister. Daily as I live you are the object of my prayers & wishes. Fail not to do the same

MM Emerson

MH: bMS Am 1280.226(984).

1. MME paid the expenses for Rebecca Haskins, her fourteen-year-old niece, to attend school and board with the Emersons in Boston during the first half of 1813 (MH).

2. WE[2] and RHE's last child, Mary Caroline Emerson, then two years old.

3. MME indicates she has taken nephews RBE (age six) and CCE (age five) to Waterford.

4. RHE's sister Betsey Haskins and MME's sisters REH and PER.

To RUTH HASKINS EMERSON

Main *May 12* 1813.

My dear Sister,

This day brings you fully to my mind and occupies my thoughts with your concerns.[1] With you it is consecrated to the memory of the best of husbands—how sweet is the duty to recall his virtues— Oh how plainly can I remember his youthfull ardor, his zeal in pursuit—his frankness, his candour his happy love of beholding and doing justice to the merit of others—how well he loved to contribute to the light and happiness of others. I remember his unhappiness—his defects—these are painfull—but a duty—especially as I conceive them to have arisen in great measure from corrupted views of the gospel. Oh how differently would that ardent mind have left the world had it viewed sin and human depravity as the gospel, I think, represent them—had he viewed Jesus Christ, in his astonishing characters, as some have believed— with what fervid solemn delight would he have taken leave of a world of sin and sorrow! At least these are in general the natural effects of a stronge

faith. The recollection of his last years and last days will always be gloomy—
tho' I believe his piety and his endeavours to serve the interests of virtue, as
far as they were disinterested found acceptance—and that he is now sharing
that salvation of which we all know so darkly in this world. *But why these
remarks,* any one who did not know my design in making them would ask?
I *make them because I love you*—and think the nearer the exampel is bro't
the better. Your very great responsibility often fills my mind. Oh Ruthy may
you have grace to leave nothing undone in forming those children to *faith
in a Redeemer—to humility—to honesty* and disinterestedness. I do believe
one of the most powerfull engines of the Enymy of Souls is the belief in *materialism.* An idea of *no soul* is most dangerous to the incessant labours the
soul requires   The surety that the scriptures give of an immediate entrance
on judgment and eternity when realised, gives the soul an ardor in duty which
perhaps no other sentiment, besides the omnipresence of God can do. Oh
what importance that this be felt ourselves and inculcated on the children.
That the best motives have fail'd in education appears to be the case for a
time—but the seed will spring up in time if watered with constant fervent
prayer. With peculiar pleasure your husband heard the idea suggested that
your virtues would appear to more advantage—   With what delight may he
not wittness the fruits of your zealous persevering labours in bringing up the
children in the fear of God. What self renouncement of ease—what a unceasing care of your own conduct to set before them an elevated exampel of a
life removed from a world of sensual low selfish enjoyments? And how peculiarly suited to these habits is the life of a widow? *The crown is taken from
her head*—delicacy and decorum demand that her life should be a *weaned
one*—the strict propriety of your manners oblige you to no sacrifices—nor,
perhaps, from your natural timidity entitle you to much praise—that it is
only what you sacrifice to the glory of God which will give you to rejoice in
another day. I have sometimes amused myself with the hope that Providence
would put you in a state of independance, and give you an earthly Protector.
But I have repented of this levity—I have no hopes—but those which respect
your future character in a world where God alone is the Judge and Reward-
ing merit—and where we are rewarded[n] not *for* our works but in *proportion*
to them. Oh my dear Sister how fully I rejoice in your virtues—how fully I
should rejoice in a situation which I have hoped for—but it is because I am
shortsighted—a humble claim on the world from our accomplishments and
situation is the best preparative for a better state. Oh lay aside every anxiety
for yourself and children to appear genteel. And while you exert every nerve
to save the children from abject dependance on the world, you will at the
same time enable them to bestow enough to keep the habit or to implant the
holy lesson of charity. Caroline—oh Ruthy, if her temper *is not subdued*—if
she acquires base and selfish habits—   Oh Ruthy how great is your responsibility! I shall have no part in it any more—a weight is taken of my mind,
by this disposition of Providence as I felt how far short I came in the most

important of all duties. You may think I spend much labour in exhortation. Suffer me to say it is not because I do not fear *Physician heal thy* self[2]—but I do think it an indispensable duty to overcome such *fear*. The more we say to others, the more solemn our obligations to live up to all demands of christian perfection. You say nothing of your daily spending time—of Mrs Waters— of your intercourse with your family. You will now more naturally fall into former habits of attachment to them as you are more alone. Give them my respects and love. Betsey I suppose is as much engaged in *publick* schemes of benefiting the world as ever.

How is Rebecca? If she should be in need of some trifling change in her pocket you will not let her be perplexed as I have money with you. My love to Miss Paines Sally and all—Bradfords Mary W. and any who inquire   I wish for the crape I left.[n] Please to procure me a quire of the cheapest letter paper like the sheet I send to you. and one of the common. If tea is risen one pound will answer. I hope you have procured me some chocolate like the other as it is essential to my strenght. An exclusive use of it instead of coffee and tea, has been highly beneficial.

MH: bMS Am 1280.226(986).
rewarded] ⟨accepted⟩ ↑ rewarded ↓
left.] I left. ⟨and the kid shoes.⟩
1. MME writes on the second anniversary of her brother's death.
2. Luke 4:23.

To SARAH ALDEN BRADFORD

W— May 12. 1813.

Dear Sarah,

Many thanks for your letter—its' frankness—it's freindship—but dearer still its' piety. But, pardon me, if I say you know not yourself. You *are not* so cold—so indifferent in religion. Were you, I should venture to say, you did not think of that august period, when every failure will have consequences which in this dreaming state we can never apprehend. I should venture to urge you to *new* efforts—perhaps exertions out of the usual course of religious habits are even nessecary to keep the soul in a progressive state. I should venture farther—(as you know me enough not to suspect me of a levelling principle in this instance) would inquire if the pursuit of literature *was not dangerous to an exclusive ardor in christian perfection?* Who ever kindled the torch of divine love at the lamp of human knowledge? Who ascribes his zeal in edifying others, his purity & heavenly mindedness to his scientific pursuits? Speaking of others—my dear Sarah, never take up with narrow views on this subject—it seems the least questionable of all pursuits—after one's own salvation—more—it is intimately connected with it—is *it not indispensable to it?* How many good people (those at least whom we are bound in charity to call good) who deceive themselves with the idea of being too humble to dictate—but perhaps at bottom is a fear that their exhortations should impose on themselves certain virtues which *at present* they wish to exclude? But to the matter of knowledge I hope you will take good notice of Foster's essays, his last letters especially I trust you will *study*. Miller's "retrospect" which you intend reading; where he reviews the effect of advancement in every department of knowledge, except divine, are to this purpose.[1] I know you, my lovely young freind, I believe, and I know your studies are pursued with the best intentions, they are not to make you splendid, but usefull. Go on and prosper—let me share some of these pleasures by recounting them— had you not been thus occupied, above the croud, who pursue pleasure in amusements, I had never known the sattisfaction of hoping to share in your affections. You are a dear lover of nature—   Some other time, I will describe the deep solitude and the rural beauty which surrounds me. Today is a memorable day to me—and religious subjects of the highest import are the most congenial—it is the anniversary of my brother's death. You love nature—precious sentiment—and how greatly wise "to look thro' nature up to natures God."[2] And how wise, to search His goverment in the records of history. But have not the profoundest Students been left cheerless and bewildered amid the difficulties which nature and the gloomy facts of history afforded, unless led and instructed by the truth of revelation? Oh how much readier is the only infallible way to wisdom—the study of the God of the bible! There are explained the miseries of man—and there are they remedied in the glorious plan of redemption! Were there any other display of God's character in the universe equal to this, would the very Angels be represented as desiring to contemplate this preeminent scheme of divine benevolence? The astonishing characters which meet in Jesus Christ can, it seems, be only subjects of faith, of wonder and the warmest gratitude till hope is turned into fruition. Till that sublime moment—let us pray for each other—and there may the affection which is sanctioned by our pursuit of religion be perfected.

Write by the Bearer of this if you are not better employed. Write what your Father says about "the times"—write about the prospects of a Society, in re-settling a Minister,[3] in which I shall always take an interest. My respects to your family.

Adieu M.M. Emerson.

MH: bMS Am 1280.226(1258). *Addressed:* Miss Sarah Alden Bradford / Boston.

1. John Foster, *Essays in a Series of Letters on the Following Subjects . . .* , 2 vols. (Boston, 1811). The last letters ("Essay 4") are on the "unchristian tendency" of classical literature, "modern polite literature," and modern philosophers and essayists. In *Brief Retrospect of the Eighteenth Century*, 2 vols. (New York, 1803), Samuel Miller, a Princeton Calvinist, lamented that metaphysics was attacked with contempt as "useless," "unintelligible," and "absurd" as Scottish commonsense philosophy gained ascendency (Howe, 31, 323).

2. Pope, *An Essay on Man* 4:332.

3. Reference to the First Church's efforts to find a minister to succeed WE[2]; RHE to MME, 11 June 1813, reports that John L. Abbot has been selected and the church wants her to board him, which is a "trial," though she could not refuse (MH).

To Samuel Ripley

Main   Oct. 3 [1813]   sab Eve

My dear Brother,

I have so little intercourse with many of my family, that I am in the habit of passing over the few intervening points of time, and contemplate our future connection in a world where love and freindship will be perfected. That *future* of our life becomes very familiar to one who is in uninterrupted solitude. Would to the great Auther of all good, that the pure and exalted dispositions preparatory to that state were concomitant with its' expectation. Your situation, my dear S., so awfully responsible, and so favorable to the highest exercises of christianity often employs my thoughts and most fervent wishes.[1] It always seems, to me, that a minister who deeply embraces the gospel, whose spirit is imbued with the grand and astonishing truths of his ministry, is of all mortals, most like the spirits above, who are employed in acts of benevolence. To him how idle is all knowledge which does not make him a more faithfull messenger of love to the miserable— How vain and contemptible the breath of man which wafts any applause but that of gratitude for the *bread of life*.

Oh my Brother, may God honor you by making you an instrument of the richest blessing to your own socity, and to others. If you can spare time from your more important claims, do write. What is your opinion of the Successor of our Brother?[2] What is the appearance of that society? Your freind Hurd is settled. *Is it where Mr Thacher was?* How is your class Mate Thacher,[3] in health & popolarity? Sad case for a *christian minister* to be popolar in the usual conception of the word with the world. Have you any books one or tow, that I could keep till an opp^y occurs next winter to return them, such as are very interesting. Can you loan me some numbers of the Edinburgh review? I have excleastical history and other history enough.

I have parted with my idol Charles. Do observe him and let me know some time hence your opinion. Farewell dear Brother   Yours

affectionately
MM Emerson

If you do not write I shall think it because you could not read this. Excuse it, the pen is bad!

MH: bMS Am 1280.226(1245). *Addressed:* Rev. Samuel Ripley / Waltham / Mrs L. Ripley. *Endorsed:* M. M. Emerson.
1. SR studied theology at Harvard from 1807 to 1809, before being ordained at Waltham.
2. John L. Abbot.
3. The Reverend Isaac Hurd (1785–1856) graduated from Harvard College in 1806.

The Reverend Peter Thacher, minister at Malden from 1770 to 1784, was pastor of Brattle Street Church, Boston, from 1785 until his death in 1802; he was succeeded by J. S. Buckminster, who died in 1812, and Edward Everett, who took the post in 1814. Hurd may have served in the interim. Samuel Cooper Thacher (1785–1818), son of Peter Thacher, graduated from Harvard in 1804 with SR and became pastor of New South Church, Boston, in 1811.

1814

To Sarah Alden Bradford

Fast day   P. M. [Apr.? 1814?]

Dear dear Sarah,

I take the light of a day which, perhaps, ought not to afford any such indulgences—but the opp^y is here, and my mind far from that state of solemn concentration which forbids the joyfull duties of friendship. Would to that Being, *from whom every good thought* descends, it were! Oh how cold & stupid are publick Assemblies! Do you think the very Heathen did not seek to propitiate their gods with more devotion, in time of danger, than Christian Soceities do?[1] What solemn fasts were kept by Jews at the express command of God? How sublime was the intercourse of Daniel with Heaven not only for himself, but for a nation! Can there be this side the invisible world one subject so full of contemplation of the highest kind, as that of a human Intercessor with God for his fellow Sinners! What a life does it require! How holy, how spotless, how strongly connected with the great Purchaser of all human blessings! Do write on this and every thing without the form of letter if less trouble and in that of M.S.

But, my beloved Girl, "your friendship for me gives you much uneasiness." Then why maintain it. Must I be the only One who enjoys much? *But what is the matter?* My hardness of remark, my ungentle warmth alone must be the cause—operating on your too susceptible delicate secluded mind which has conversed so elevatedly with the *silent* dead that animal heat and motion of the gross corporal kind quite deranges your ethereal intellectual enjoyments! And other sacrifices you hint at— Now I am not willing you should make any—for my affection is not worth^n them. As to our walk to M— it is a little curious that we may write within sight of each other, & visit ever so often, yet not fall under the wofull imputation of *romantic,* unless we inhale the pure air of the wide atmosphere. Appropos on me alone falls that dreaded denunciation— Here it is true, I have felt a momentary fear—but knowing my affection and motives I forgot it. Yes the affection I feel endears life; it gives me to hope that other objects I shall meet which will make the journey less weary. But what is infinitely more, the attachment we feel for the pious & lowly, unite us more fervidly to the Source of all Good.

Do not be discouraged at the hours of langour which may sometimes take place in retirement. Would you win the prize without fighting the warfare. But if you would understand the whole dispensation of the christian Scheme— feel all its power, and know all its demands as described by a human pen and by one who has practiced all it's duties *Read Willberforce.*[2] Say nothing of my writing for I shall send this by a Stranger—but if he cannot find the way I may enclose it but I am now in haste & eyes ake.

Yours affectionately
MME.

My young friend White passes this week in Concord.

MH: bMS Am 1280.226(1270).

is not worth] ⟨cannot repay⟩ ↑ is not worth ↓

1. In Mass., public fast days were proclaimed for 7 Apr. 1814 as well as 6 Apr. 1815; this letter could have been written in either year.

2. William Wilberforce (1759–1833), British statesman and humanitarian, who secured passage of the bill abolishing England's slave trade in 1807; MME probably refers to his very popular *A Practical View of the Prevailing Religious System of Professed Christians in the Higher and Middle Classes in This Country, Contrasted with Real Christianity* (London and Dublin, 1797).

To Phebe Emerson Ripley

Boston   Sep. 20, 1814[1]

My dear Sister,

You will like to hear by pen from this place, on which for some time so dark a cloud has rested. The publick mind, after tow days from the date of mine to Ann,[2] became in the most anxious and alarmed state, you know. Many of the inhabitants hastened to hide themselves & property in the Country. For the two last sabbaths the petitions of the Clergy denote "fearfull uncertainty" and the most "alarming apperhension." But you know the unhappy division in opinion renders it difficult for an individual to judge of the preponderance of immediate danger. People of good judgment, at the head of socity, think an invasion of this Town probable. At any rate, we know that a most afflictive and humiliating war is depopolating and wasting the property & lives of the Inhabitants! But so dark and misterious is the condition of man, ever since the apostacy, that one war raging, and one Country distroyed, is but an epitome of the whole earth. How should the freinds of Zion give themselves to prayer for the coming of His kingdom, whose reign will be peace & righteousness. As to our unprotected selves we are very calm as to immediate difficulty— But had we any thing to lose we s^d feel very different probably. We did not think of moving till last week many freinds tho't it best   And when we consider the price of wood & provisions which will be the consequence of the troops quarted already here it seems the best thing to go into the Country. But where? Father R has invited us there in case of being obliged to fly. And

Figure 10. Beacon Street and the Common, Boston, about 1812.

Ruthy has concluded, and has indeed sent to propose taking some part of their house & living by ourselves as it is impossible for her to board out with the children. She has been seeking a place for Ann but in vain. Either of her Brothers w^d take one of the boys were it in their power, and were they situated so that she could on the whole think it best. And as business is wholly checked there is not a single place to which either Ed. or Ralph can go. We are contemplating Andover as a good place for Boarders and Mrs T. Haskins has written to her friends today. You would think from this we are *cast down* but we are not. A low and humble state is generally without much change. We have some hope that this house may be given up, in that case Ruthy will not be in danger of immediate difficulty—from debts. This letter will increase your comfort in having Bullkley. *Blessed be God who put it into your heart.* I have been desirous to try some new plan of life; but Ruthy will not consent to our seperation at this time. Should she; can you take me to board and Charles, so as not to suffer any loss? Can I be of service to Becca   Let me know, and whether Susan C. w^d like to take me. If sister B. has any yarn she w^d like me to { } for her, she can send it by Representative. And I w^d like to purchase some of her ½ pound if convenient. You will remember Sister E—s. If I s^d go to W— perhaps Mr Farrar has a seat for me in that carriage he took B. down in. I cannot go in the stage, if there is any less expensive way. And you must remember that my wishing to go depends on cercumstances which do not exist as yet. Only let me know the difficulties &c. Charles is accostomed to a very different diet than when he went to Main before   And perhaps I shall not take him. How is your health and Mr Ripley's. His former anxiety on account of the Country was not ill founded it seems. My love to him & all, and Becca. Your aff^t Sister

MME.

Night   I s^d like to describe the garrison like appearance of this Town, the incessant echo of martial musick, no day nor night excepted, but I have not time on this paper, nor inclination. The revolution of states and worlds is bringing forward to every individual one certain event *the peace of the grave.* All other advantages[n] in the rise & fall of empires is uncertain! * * *

MH: bMS Am 1280.226(1241). *Addressed:* Mrs. Phebe Ripley / Waterford. / Maine. *Postmarked:* BOSTON / MSS / SEP / 2. *Endorsed:* Sept. 14, 1814.
    advantages] ⟨dis⟩advantages
    1. Letter is definitely dated "Sep. 20"; however, both postmark and endorsement suggest that the correct date may be earlier. Stamped postmark contains a "2" followed by a smudge.
    2. MME to AB, 3 Sept. 1814, commented on conditions and her state of mind as Boston prepared for siege: "Surprising what an apathy possesses the publick mind. It is tho't Charlestown, Mass., will be attacked every day on account of the little Navy which is stationed there. Vigorous measures are making to fortify the coast. Christians

ought only to seek the reformation of their Country and rejoice if that be accomplished whatever afflictions attend. The commence^t was brilliant and interesting. I had an invitation from S.A. Bradford whose brother graduated. And I can hardly feel pleased with the moderation I then tho't so wise in refusing. These publick occasions invite the best feelings and make one forget the little cares of home. William has entered. Such was the voice of all Advisers—and in truth there was nothing else to be done. Many boys have entered because there is no business. I went to NP. a month since & tarried a fortnight with Mary F. who was very sick with a rheumatic fever. Charlotte absent & Louisa without any help but a neighbour & Elizabeth. * * * Of Concord I know nothing but that they are well. I came from thence in April and have had no means to visit them since. We can get no Boarders and sister wishes to exchange this house for a smale one. * * * Do you ever suspect I shall be needed at Elm Vale? Do keep an eye out for me. Tho' in the commotions of war I prefer a situation like this. I wish to know what is doing, tho' my means of information are so limited that I know nothing.

"Last eve. we learnt that west india goods were rising. If we should suffer in the article of food it will be painfull for the present but a temporary ill. It will not be inquired a century hence whether you and I departed this life by famine pestilence or sword. They appear equally indifferent to me provided they were equally expeditious in performing the great work for w'h we came into the world for. From young Everet (the Sucessor of Buckminster, the more illustrious star) I have heard sermons of late so powerfull that all the vissisitudes of life lost their power—religion alone triumphed, and the glory of the resurrection morning appeared to open in visions of blessedness on the eye of faith. * * * It was with much regret that I left N.P. for the visit of Main. Oh how dear thy mountains, thy waters, thy trees, & roads?" (MWA).

To Ann Brewer

Boston   Oct. 12. [1814]

Your consequential uncertainty about being *moved*, my dear young friend, lessens not my willingness to write, as while I am your chief Correspondent, this part of the Country, letters will be agreeable. And I am always pleased with yours.

You interest my answer too, in the most effectual way by inquiring after my last found favorite.[1] She has indeed grown up in my affections since my return. Her increasing attentions in our sickness, and our present solitude. She very often comes in from Charelestown (where they have lately removed to a most elegant Seat) sleeps with me, spends part of the eve͠g with Mrs E. & children, animates the boys to study, and becomes herself so animated that I hear her voice up chamber, and can hardly believe it she, who among the fashionable is silent and awkward. However, she is gaining in eclat. Society begin to find that we shall have an Elizabeth Smith.[2] Did I ever tell you, I tho't there was a striking resemblance in character and acquisition? I have forgotten what I have told you about Sarah A. Bradford. She ascribes much to her Instructor— but the greek she acquired alone. She solves a problemn in Euclid, in astronomy, in mathematics, with as much ease as she uses her needle, & as much simplicity as she makes poltices for the sick. But the higher departments of intellect, render her to me more respectable, as I have some vague ideas of the pleasure w'h must result from pursuing reason, when ingaged on moral truth beyond any which can result from mathematical truth. Such as reading "Locke on the human understanding," and the far better theories on the mind, by Reid and Stewart. But her knowledge, critical and practical of the scriptures is her richest possesion, except a heart influenced by their truths. Her habits are as singular as her acquisitions, a steady almost constant refusal to mingle among the gay, tho' her Brothers, high Bucks at Colledge, solicit her, and a new set of acquaintance. Her capasity for business is great. She does much—sews while her little school is going on, w'h consists of a brother whom she is fitting for Colledge, and a sister or tow. She rises early, & when here after waking up our family, goes home to breakfast. Her conversation & letters are full of *heart,* and of course have few professions of love and generally none. She enjoys with enthusiam antient poetry, the study of botany and the intercourse of friendship. But her highest pleasures are those of devotion; and her *very plain* dress and habits of discipline are conformable to the self denying spirit of the gospel. True, as yet a stranger to care, to mortification and sorrow she is as yet a stranger to herself, and in those moments when death appears to her so desirable it may be conjectured she knows not herself. When Caroline died,[3] she was the only Watcher we had & the only *friend* who remained for the following *nights.*[n] No consideration would have tempted one of the Miss Haskins to hazard the danger, I believe tho' they were not asked as they could not leave home. You will remember I do not say what kind of problemns she solves, as I could not make any distinction. All I wish is to represent her justly. She is termed handsome by some, modesty prevails in her face. It is usefull to dwell on the different conditions and talents which prevail in the great family. And the sentiment which gives us *to say, even so Father, for so it hath seemed good to Thee,* conveys a richer pleasure to the soul than all the treasures of knowledge, and the fame of talent. Oh should the pursuits of literature, the researches of science and the dearer pleasures of possessing influence over the hearts & happiness of others, lessen one habit of humble adoration, one effort of disinterested charity, of holy sincerity, here *forever* to be deplored—perhaps in the very kingdom of Heaven, holy regret will mingle for having fallen short! *To do all*—on the brink of time, that single sentiment will fill the soul. In vain to look back on efforts for usefullness, while one *certain* duty, however, humble has been slighted. The thrones of Angels will not fill the soul, we have reason to believe, with a pleasure so great as to have concentrated its' force on the simpel and sober and meek duties which every hour demands in this weary world. When I converse with Sarah, I speake with the contempt of latin & greek which I feel, considered as mere learned acquisitions. What is scholarship, how little does it often do for the head, and nothing for the heart. She can, it is true, live in the ages which have gone bye. With genius and imajanation, she can visit the consecrated abodes of science, which are now succeeded by the desolate dwellings of ignorance and stupidity. But what of retracing the little past[n] of this earth, when a career for future ages is open! Louisa Farnham[4] is a lovely woman, & devoted christian. Yet she is ignorant of even the passing literature of the day. The finest poems lie untouched. It is said she has no taste. It is a mistake—common taste and ambition w[d] lead her to books, but higher duties prevent, and she is happier far than her more literary Sister. I wished to sound her, & to give her new motives of humility; and I spoke of the knowledge w'h many ladies possess. The answer was what I hoped, but dared not expect. "It was true she was ignorant, but of this world so full of guilt and tumult, she was contented to know nothing." I question, if by concentrating her mind to a few simpel principles of our sublime religion, and by uniform attention to the labours of every day, she does not outstrip many of her companions in the race of real glory. The faith is of the old school, and she supports the redicule of her family with unmoved dignity. She has no time to bestow but sabbath evenings in charity   And then she instructs poor children in the great truths of the gospel. I wish you to read this notice of Louisa to her Aunts. And all the better if it will amuse them but *not of Louisa to Rebecca.* While others are struggling to collect some scattered rags of knowledge, and to shine in talk about some scraps of poetry history or languages, she will be contented not to shine, *And superior to shining—can we ask more! Your friend*

MME.

Ask Mr Cushman to buy "Germany"   it will delight him if he has taste & you may borrow it[5]

MWA. *Addressed:* Ann. *Added in pencil:* 1814.

nights.] ⟨days⟩ ↑ *nights* ↓.

past] *possibly* part

1. The "character" that follows is of SAB.

2. *Fragments of Prose and Verse,* by Miss Elizabeth Smith, Lately Deceased (1808). Most of the prose comes from Smith's letters and journals, which her editor, H. M. Bowdler, quotes liberally in his brief "account of her life and character." Something of a prodigy, Smith (1776–1806) was a poet and a translator of German writers and knew several languages, science, and mathematics.

3. Mary Caroline Emerson, born 26 Feb. 1811, died 30 Apr. 1814.

4. MME's niece, Louisa Farnham, born in Jan. 1794, was just five months younger than SAB.

5. Written on outside. Germaine de Staël's *Germany,* published in English in Oct. 1813, was reviewed by Sir James Mackintosh in the *Edinburgh Review* 22 (Oct. 1813): 198–238.

To William Emerson[3]

Friday Morning   [28 Oct. 1814]

Dear W^m

The enrapturing dawn scarsly reflects its beauty sufficient to guide the pen. May the grandeur of the scene in which I first address you from home agur well for our future intercourse.[1] May every morning, which *either mourneth or rejoicest thro'* Him, *who maketh the sun to know his place,* rouse you to His worship, and awe your spirit with His presence! May each, tho' destined to bear no peculiar event, remind you of that morning which will, at some sure and august tho' unprophecied *moment,* dawn on the night of the grave! Ah to what unknown horrors and to what inconceivable transports will that morning of the resurrection awaken the nations of the grave! *Where then will you be?* Oh my dear W^m may you be clothed with celestial beauty in the presence of approving Angels!

Your Grandfather breathed his last mortal sigh at ½ past 6 o'k last eve§. *Blessed are the dead who die in the Lord!*[2] His funeral is appointed to be on monday. Your dear Mother sends much love, and wishes you to come as early as may be in the morning or Sab eve—thinks it will not be worth while for you to walk over tomorrow. Your Granmother & family are comfortable, rather occupied with religious faith & hope than sorrow.

Your friend & Aunt
MME.

Some lady observed you felt your dependent situation too much. Be humble & modest, but never like *dependance.* If you have no unnessecary wants you cannot feel anxious for others. God's bounty is infinite   Be generous and great and you will confer benefits on society, not recieve them thro' life.

MH: bMS Am 1280.226(1062). *Addressed:* William Emerson / Student at H. C. / Cambridge. *Endorsed:* M.M.E.

1. WE[3] began his first year at Harvard College in the fall of 1814.

2. Rev. 14:13. John Haskins died in Boston on 27 Oct. 1814; burial was 31 Oct. from Trinity Church.

To William Emerson[3]

Concord   No[v.] 26 Sat [1814]

Dear W^m

Dr Moody[1] prescribes particular attention to avoid taking cold, as you have so often shook beneathe the oppression of disease.

Have your flannels on and a coat extra whenever you go from home   Avoid the relaxation arising from artificial heat—   Brace your body with air & exercise before going to fire if possible by a few moments in the open air. We wish you to be in health—a diseased dreg on the face of the earth is esteemed a misfortune—but perhaps, the highest advantage to the Soul. when it fixes^n the attention on glory. But health when devoted to God and the cause of holy enthusiasm that is of promoting truth—& disinterested exertions

Send your bundle by Mr Daggot

Love from your dear Mother & Aunts. Ed. is confined with a cold the week past, I am perhaps the more thoughtfull about my absent Patients.

God preserve you dear W^m in his fear and love or, oh, how unhappy your condition.

Your aff^t Aunt
MME.

MH: bMS Am 1280.226(1063). *Addressed:* William Emerson / Student at H. U. / Holliss 3 / Cambridge.

fixes] *possibly* fires

1. The family's name for MME when she played the role of physician. RHE to EBE, 9 Feb. 1817, states, "Dr Mooddy desires his love & begs if you are not well you would come home directly—& he will prescribe—your mother joins in this request also" (MH). Despite the masculine pronoun, "Dr Mooddy" is probably MME.

To Sarah Alden Bradford

[1814?] [1]

My beloved Sarah,

Write me more. Ever you read Dante? Why is that that his infernal reigions are so much more interesting than his celestial? Is not man formed for terror, grandeur? Why then divest christianity of it? You talk of Antients. *If* their poetry does exceed Milton, was it not because they had fewer ideas —their minds more concentrated & fixed on nature, & the cultivation of imajanation? Is it not a certain maxim that minds do not rise much above the age they live in? [2] It seems incomprehensible to me & unjust. But to you acquainted with departed ages can solve this problem. Do you love Tasso? Oh that you could write the history of all you know in miniature? a picture of Antient Greece from your hand, how w^d I idolise painting! But oh do write a portrait of *Edwards on will* and especially give me *Stewart* in short hand. Can you be so disinterested? willing to live so much time for another? It should be communicated to the ignorant—   It may possibly benefit you in the habit of communicating? Tho' your letters appear to me perfect. None of your old musty Acquaintance reconcile you to the doctrine of nesscisty. Do answer my letter about *Jove*. They talked of fate but they knew nothing of the "philosophy of the mind." What do you know about Epictitus. Plato, & that Gentry. Oh how delightfull are thier names! They were ordained to preserve alive some sparks of religion in a dreadfull night of error. But my dear S. your one sentence at closing the short letter is worth all these ages & all the inhabitants of these ages, to you. It is was one of the happiest moments of my life which gave me that letter.

How does the dear little One do?[3] Your eyes I hope are safe. Write more
more to your affectionate freind

MME.

Wednesday late night.

MH: bMS Am 1280.226(1265). *Addressed:* S. A. Bradford.
  1. Dating is uncertain. An undated letter from SAB to MME that begins with an
apostrophe to the Augustan Age (MCR-S) seems to be part of the conversation of
this letter and the next. Both this letter and the next refer to the same idea from de
Staël, and the next letter mentions the "Augustan age." All three letters seem to reflect
MME's renewed friendship with SAB following MME's return to Boston in Apr. 1814.
  2. Attributed to de Staël in next letter.
  3. Possibly CCE.

To Sarah Alden Bradford

[1814?]

No, my darling Girl, it was not the moderation of subdued feeling, nor
the delightfull abstraction of devotion—else I should not have sought enjoyment & improve[t] from home— But a low frigid state incident to years. Had
you flashed with the same illuminating beams of monday I *might* have been
excited—or had the society of your Father been indulged me, I might have
roused. I say all this to prepare the way for your future charity, when I am
torpid. But had any defect been yours, I s[d] not have pursued you. And oh
my dear S. I feel that I can never love you less— I cannot descend even to
mediocrity I must part with those I have so fervidly sought, or go on with
increasing love. Well, well Sarah you seem to know but little of the phylosophy of the *heart* if you think *books* will cure the anxieties of *love*—but not
of *friend*ship. Besides I tho't we concluded that books were insipid when the
pulse of the heart beat high. That subject is interesting in speculation—as a
spectator I love to discuss it— I seldom knew it fail to rouse a listless state
when my young Companion was frank & affected. You made much progress
in this way last eve. I verily believe if I had not been sleepy we should have
discussed this misterious subject with some insight into your views. What
do you think Madame De Stale means by saying no Genius has risen much
above his times? She thinks 16 centuries were lost respecting the progress of
imajanation & the fine arts, but not as it respected the phylosophy of mind
in morals politicks & science.[1] How glad w[d] the christian be to have had
no darkness, barbarism & human degradation remain after christianity had
illumined the earth. But were not the dark ages of paganism darker? What
causes *moral* & *physical* produced the Augustan age? Those relating to christianity are obvious. The Infidel says, you know, that christianity is the cause
of the degradation of letters & mind. Did you ever ask yourself what w[d] be
your practice & feelings if christianity were a fable but the perfections of God

the same we believe them? And you immortal? Well I shall tire you. But I prize your letters, they seem clear gain—but when we converse I have to exert myself, and I fear committing a similar fault to *optimism*.

Your aff[t] friend
MME

Wed. Do pass some time with us after Lecture tomorrow   Miss Adams will be here.

MH: bMS Am 1280.226(1267). *Addressed:* Miss Bradford.
   1. Germaine de Staël, *The Influence of Literature upon Society* (London, 1812), 1:227–28.

1815

To Ann Brewer

Jan. [1815]

Dear Ann,

   Not a line from you. Well no matter, I thought so much of writing to you when I was in a visiting mood at Malden, that I will embody my thoughts, as I can do nothing better this broken up morning. I was there alone in my chamber where I had past so many years. My Uncle was in his coffin in *the room* to *me* once so pleasant. I often visited him in the fore part of the night previous to the funeral.[1] I there retraced his life. That narrow limit of ignorance and earth was occupied with a few material objects. How smale the field for contemplation. But no; that spark[n] of immortality kindled by God, had entered a sphere of existence beyond the comprehension of the greatest mortal! That feeble ray of mind which could never grasp the slightest problemn of science, or connect the feeblest chain of reason, is now united to the Head of *principalities and powers*, and happy, I believe, beyond the greatest Genius living![n] Such, and so grand is the priviledge of death *to a babe in Christ*! Could he have foreseen this period, which disunites him from his beloved estate, would he have devoted with such ardor his faculties to the retaining it. How much of resentment and pride would have been stifled in their birth. Could he have realised the time, when he should not have been connected with one individual spot of earth, more than the whole universe, how many hearts would have been gladdened by the kindness of his aspect, and the openness of his hand. If a man, whose education habits, and native temper *bound him to the soil*, could afford this retrospection, what would a more genial situation afford of blame? Oh, I could never blame him, even when I felt the gripe of his parsimony. At the last years of his life, religion seemed to take all the sway, and shone amidst the darkness of an erroneous faith. I looked at his remains, and I thought of you, my dear Ann, who I suspect, of prizing too highly the advantages of literature and the distinctions of life. Vain advantages, useless distinctions! Lost and contemptible in the infinite grandure of invisible scenes! There humility and love alone will be indispensable.

In these may you advance. I mentioned a book called "Germany,"[2] but it is two # and not nessecary to your real improvement. I found it a different thing from what at first expected. Betsy H— will send your Mother some tracts which I was to procure. I send Charles' bible, as I believe it is an improper appropriation for him to retain it. His Aunt Betsy gave it to him   You may dispose of it. Much love to Martha   wish she would write to me— Sympathise with her in the departure of Hannah. The faith will be called into exercise. Love to Patty and Noah. Affectionate remembrance to Mrs Farrar. Can you tell me of Mary E. Monroe[3]

Your affectionate freind
MME.

Bible cannot go

MWA. *Addressed:* Miss Ann Brewer. *Added in pencil:* [1815?].
spark] ⟨speck⟩ spark
living!] ⟨alive⟩ ↑ living ↓ !
1. Samuel Waite, second husband of MME's aunt Ruth Emerson Sargent Waite, was buried 12 Jan. 1815.
2. See MME to AB, 12 Oct. [1814]. MME's initial response changed, and *Germany* remained one of her favorites.
3. Betsey Haskins; Martha Robinson, Martha (Patty) Bliss, and Noah Ripley, the other adopted children of the Lincoln Ripleys; probably Mary Emerson Monroe, b. 13 Mar. 1813, daughter of Major William Monroe and Achsah Sawyer Monroe of Waterford.

To Phebe Emerson Ripley

Concord   Jan. 22, 1815

Dear Phebe,

I read your letter to Mother with great approbation. Nothing could have been better devised to awaken piety. She appears more sensible of the approach of death—is kind very condescending to me, I dress & read occasionally in her chamber.[1] Indeed, she my Father & Sarah I consider as the dear children of God, whom He is carrying on by very different methods of discipline and suffering to a state of rest and positive happiness. Sarah's trials have been peculiar, & her resignation, I trust, to the divine will genuine & pious. Her exertions for the cause of truth in education, and in confering benefits are noticeable, and flow from principle and feeling. With her ambition, and inability to improve herself in science and literature, calls for constant resignation. With her warmth of affections and no particular object demands nameless efforts of fortitude & charity.

I have been to Malden to the funeral of Uncle Wait. Poor desolate relation-less Aunt[2] lies bedrid, except a few moments when her bed is made. Appears rational for the most part. She is to remain there for three months. This I esteem a great favor. She has enough to support herself for two or three years if no more trouble than at present. Her food is the least & simplest one can conceive— And the time spent about her not an hour in 24. Yet so disagreeable is her conduct and existence to the Wait Family that they will not board her under three dollars nor will any one in Malden. But her food I told them would not amount to 3⅝. I am for taking her to that old chamber myself but she will not consent nor perhaps could I go. The best way in the world is to carry her to your house if it could be practicable. Uncle John, the Town of M. and Cousins[n] at one place or other must contribute to her support. Her annual income is more than { } dollars. I s[d] rejoice to have you take her at 3# and to have her among relations is most desirable. I feel she had a double claim on me as niece. The cause of her inability to stand is the putting out of her hip. I think it possible to have her removed in a waggon. While surrounded with attractive infancy, and blooming youth I fear you will not draw on your selves *all* the blessings which attend on suporting the helpless. Still suffer me to exhort you, while the fleeting day of our life remains, to remember that the labours of an Apostle, and the agonies of a Martyr, avail nothing without growth in meekness, patience and humility. Deficiency in *these*, are our *constitional* sins, let us therefore warn each other and be more abundant in prayer. In Heaven where knowledge and labour cease, charity and love continue. How sublime and enrapturing is the employment of the beatified   It is adoration—admiring infinite perfection.

May we meet there and recognise each other in the mansions of redeeming love.

MM E—n

Mother and Sisters think my proposal approaches insanity. It is the tho't of the moment, but could we practice it, excellent. I am going now to write to Uncle John, whose care she is, to whom she has willed all her property, but on whose exertions I have little dependance; as he is aged & feeble. * * *

MH: bMS Am 1280.226(1242). *Addressed:* Mrs Phebe Ripley.
Cousins] Cousins ⟨Sam⟩
1. MME's mother PBER did not die until ten years later.
2. See preceding letter. Less than a year after the death of Ruth Emerson Sargent Waite (his third wife) in 1808, Samuel Waite had married her sister, Rebecca Emerson Parker Brintnall, who was reputed to be "insane" (*IpsE*).

To John Emerson

Concord   Feb. 1 1815.

My dear Uncle,

I rejoice in the prospect of your Son S. Moody being settled in so pleasant a place.[1] Hope and trust he will be an honor to his name, but more especially to the name of Christ. My Sister Sarah, whose judgment is as good, as her principles and feelings, speakes highly of him. And she had an opportunity to converse with him. I regret that I had no accomodations to offer him, when I saw him at Boston some years since. I still more regret that I saw you so little for the same reason last Spring. Your kind and condescending letters, which I received this week, I thank you very much. Most people, I believe, will think you, Sir, have done perfectly right in resuming your title to the estate of my late Uncle.[2] I know you have done what appeared to you strictly just. And it is true, my Cousins have had the advantage of the estate much longer than the principle is worth.

I wrote to you by the post an account of the death of Uncle Wait. I went to Malden to see my poor Aunt, found her tranquil, but deranged occasionally. I do wish to have her among relations so anxiously, that I have written to my sister Ripley, saying it might be possible to convey her to Waterford, and board her with Phebe. My Mother thinks it a distracted plan. I only mentioned it as a thing for her contemplation against the time I should consult with you. I believe I mentioned in my letter, that the demands for food were so smale and so simpel, that my Aunt's board was trifling, it is the care of her, which is so disagreable to many. The only relief we can find on this afflictive subject is the promises of a faithfull covenant God. In this connection I delight to recall the eminent *piety* and *charity* and faith of our Ancestors. I was gratified by your fervent exhortation which refered to the sufferings of our blessed Lord. To contemplate the great plan of our redemption with increasing light and edification is the only object which renders this low, dark state of existence desirable. But, oh my dear Uncle, with what ease and delight shall we behold in unclouded vision this glorious subject when we drop these heavy troublesome bodies in the grave! I *have* been anxious to discern somthing of the distinctions of faith which kept the Church in such agitations for these 18 Centuries; but I *now* relinquish the pursuit, and am willing to be ignorant of those things which are not essential to a humble and candid practice. I cannot think that it is nessecary to be devoted to the love and service of God, to believe in the proper and underived deity of *His only begotten Son* our Saviour. I should rejoice to be established in trinitarism, if this were the revealed will of God. To an obscure person who has taken no party, is no teacher, has no interest but that of truth, there cannot be expected to be strong prejudices as in publick Teachers who are connected with Sects? On the trinitarian plan, how could Jesus suffer? Is not his expiation a greater mystery than can be presented to the reason of a being like man? How could he suffer? Is it not placing the man Jesus even when united to the Eternal impossable[n] Jehovah, below the martyrs who rejoiced amidst the more tremendous sufferings prepared for them. That there is a mystery in those sufferings (which I rejoice to believe effacious to the expiating human guilt) I have no doubt, but to me, it is one, to which human reason must *submit*, but does not *contradict* all its exercises. For what makes man a subject of the moral gov[t] of God, and an "object" of salvation, but *reason*? True, it is obscured and injured by the apostacy, but not lost and become useless? I have ventured to suggest these observations hoping they would draw from your pen somthing to edify and enlighten.

My parents & Sisters present respects and affectionate salutations to you and my Aunt. Mrs Emerson thanks you for the kind interest you take in her widowed condition. Sarah says she should like to write, but it is not in her power having many and pressing avocations. Do write soon if a convenient opportunity offers to your

very affectionate and dutious Neice
Mary Moody Emerson

My love to all my Cousins.

MH: bMS Am 1280.226(765). *Addressed:* Rev. John Emerson / To the kind care of Jonas Lee Esq[r] / to be given to Mr Childs of Conway / Conway / Mass. *Endorsed:* M. M. Emerson / 1815.

impossable] *possibly* impassable

1. Uncle John Emerson (1745–1826), for fifty-seven years the minister at Conway, Mass., was the younger brother of MME's father, WE[1], and aunts Rebecca and Ruth. His son, Samuel Moody Emerson (1785–1841), was both married and ordained on 1 Feb. 1815 at Chester, Mass., where he remained as minister for three years (*IpsE*).

2. After the death of JE's sister Ruth in 1808, the only other remaining heir to the estate of MME's grandmother Mary Moody Emerson was sister Rebecca, third wife of Samuel Waite; MME suggests that Waite's death (see MME to PER, 22 Jan. 1815) led JE to assert his claim. Following Rebecca's death in July 1816, JE seems to have pressed his claim again: MME to JE, 26 Feb. 1816, says, "I am sorry that I know nothing of the qustion you ask, but I have no doubt of your being *legally* acknowledged the sole heir of my late Aunt" (MH: 767). Waite's handling of the Malden property for MME probably prevented the aunts' shares from going to JE.

To ANN BREWER

After 10 Wed. night. [1815?]

Dear Ann

If I do no more than say a few words it is not because I love sleep or cannot find time. I never saw the period when I had not liesure to write a friend. But because none of you have sent me the least notice. Your Mother, not a word. Still if I had any thing to communicate edifying or intellectual I would do it. We have made the fourth remove within 16 months. The situation of the house is one of the finest.[1] At one side of it lie the dead who have gathered there probably from the first settlements, and still is the resort of the present day. There lie the ambitious, the vain the avaricious, the gay, the beloved & those who had niether fortune friends nor fame. And, we trust, here repose, from their earthly *labours*, those *whose works follow them*, who having *fought a good fight* are *inheriting the promises* and filling their minds with those views of the divine goverment which here they so earnestly sought, but often found perplexed with *clouds & darkness*. Ah precious dust of these pure Souls, who passed the changing ocean of life in secret, unobtrusive, yet fervent faith & charity, whose influence on society was gentle[n] yet refreshing as the dew of Heaven, whose patience and humility were acceptable like the sweet savor which arose from the alter of the Antideluvian! We are surrounded by a Neighbourhood of the highest Class—Otis, Dexter, Sulivan, Emery, Gore[,] Phillips and Eliot;[2] but if we should live here always we s[d] have no intercourse, never see them; therefore you will not wonder that I dwell more on our Neighbours with whom we certainly are connected and with whom we shall one day mingle.

But I like very much to live in sight of these rich people. I like it very much indeed. If I had ever associated with the Gay & great it might not now be so pleasant to be unknown. But not one regret, that ladies do not like to visit where are Boarders

Thursday late Night. Adieu, dear Anna, may the richest gifts of divine mercy rest on your Parents, Martha, Patty, yourself & each member of the family. Adieu for Sister H. intends going tomorrow   How glad how surprised how thankfully did we see her. She appears full of patient endurance and calm resignation. Instead of seeing her every moment *I* alone have seen her the least.

MME—

MWA. *Addressed:* Miss Ann Brewer. *Added in pencil:* 1815 or 1816.
gentle] ⟨secret⟩ gentle

1. Probably the Beacon Street house where the Emersons moved in late Oct. 1815. Four moves in sixteen months dates this letter to Dec. 1815–Jan. 1816: in Sept. 1814, the Emersons left the Summer Street parsonage in Boston and moved briefly to Bennet Street (*Life of RWE*, 40), perhaps staying for a while with the Haskinses on Rainsford Lane; in Nov. 1814, when war approached, they moved to Concord, where RHE remained until Mar. 1815 (MME remained in Concord with some of the boys for a while); MME may have joined the Emersons at Rainsford Lane before moving into the Beacon Street house in Oct. RWE to EBE, 15 Oct. 1816, refers to "Aunt" and describes the view from the Beacon Street house (*L* 1:18–19).

2. Harrison Gray Otis, Samuel Dexter, probably William Sullivan (1774–1839), John Gore, John Phillips (father of five boys, including Wendell Phillips), probably Thomas Amory; Eliot is not identified.

1816

To Ruth Haskins Emerson

Thursday Eve 9. Jan. [1816]

Have no woman who can cook—alas—   Where is Mrs Barrett? I have been expecting a new one from the Country—but this morning sent to Ann of Harvard—[1] Have little expectation of her—   But you will get on—be carried comfortably thro this and the remaining seasons of life, my dear Ruthy.

Never failing are our resources in the meanest departments of the present life. Mother & Sister send much love   they are comfortable. Sarah breakfasted below today. And I am now telling them I will stay for my intended visit— unless you should feel particularly embarressed about help—   In that case, One line will bring me home. Waldo has rested from my teasing him about tilting the chair, & overhawling somthing at every sentence. William is so nervous at times I hope he has kept my place good. Charles I hope does not "slip along without application," and think he imposes on you for studious. *One* such day—may induce a habit of decieving ever to be lamented. But I know if you have time, you will gaurd against every moral evil with ever wakfull vigilance. For if the character of your children are injured *"what have you more"* for this world! And if you impose nothing on him, how irksome will be my school? He had better go to school, anywhere, than secretly dislike the society of One who loves him as I do, and to whom he professes so much. I say this for the future, when I may be at W— as for the present. Is brother Robert expected. Farewell   I feel in health here or I should prefer returning—   As it is I am desirous of coming if in the least nessecary. Yours affectionately

MME.

I remember what you said about change of air—that tho' it were worse it might benefit. I have no great esteem for Concord air tho' somthing has bettered me.

My dear Charles must write.

MH: bMS Am 1280.226(1002).

1. MME to RHE, 1 Mar. [1815], from Concord, where she was helping sister Sarah care for their ailing mother, says she is still attempting to find domestic help for RHE to replace niece Phebe Haskins, age thirteen, who had been helping out in the Emerson household but who was wanted at Concord: "I have prospect of a Girl who now lives at a tavern here with such recommendations that I have partly engaged her to come the 1ᵗ of May if you should want her. . . . I told her if she did all the cooking to your sattisfaction without any *care* she wᵈ have 8/ if she added chamber work or washing she would be paid. But perhaps I sᵈ said no more than 7/6 for cooking if another girl is nessecary. I intend to go the third time and inquire more particularly her capasity. She is tired of a Tavern, where I believe she has been the only Woman. She is daughter to Calvin Warner of Harvard. The present Mistriss recommends her. and her sober modest appearance does the same.

What delightfull weather! Every thing looks pleasant—and the view of the occupations of education, preaching and the care of the sick give the mind to serious and hopefull meditations" (MH: 1005).

To John Emerson

Boston, Sep, 13, 1816.

Honored and dear Sir,

I have been looking for you with considerable anxiety; and especially since I heard that you did not intend coming I have felt much regret. The reason

I am going to give. My Aunt Brintnall has left, I find to my surprise, somthing worth attention. There is a very poor woman (who has a very unprincipled husband) who was daughter to Mr Parker.[1] She has lived considerably on charity, but is able to do better than for many years. Still she labours hard, and has many children. She rode with me to the grave of her mother in law,[2] and observed with modesty, that she had expected to be remembered in the will. Especially she expected to have the few articles of houshold furniture which did belong to her Father tho' most of them were disposed off. I told her I thought it was right and that I would represent to you the cercumstances. My aunt has left a bed or two and some bedding and clothing which would be very acceptable to this poor woman who beginns to be going down the hill of life. I told a number of persons who spoke on the subject, that I should inform you of the articles which I remember to have seen in Mr Parker's house, and that you would do the thing that was right. And so they all told Mrs Tufts, that you would consider her. It appears to me, Sir, but I know very little of what is proper in settling estates, that if I had known my Aunt had any thing to bequeathe, I should have considered it my duty to urge her to bequeathe it to Mrs Tufts—*because* and for no other reason, that my Aunt has been benefited by the Parker estate for these forty years, without having been of any advantage to it. I may judge wrongly, but I submit my opinion to you, Sir, with the fullest respect, and confidence in what you shall do yourself. My only personal interest in the affair is, that as the name of my respected Ancestors is now removed from the Town of Malden, it may be remembered in connexion with every thing just, noble, and charitable. I have always felt a respect for those people and friendship. They are peculiarly given to *censure*—but they have their virtues.

I hope, my dear Sir, your valueable life will long be spared, and that we shall have the sattisfaction of seeing you here this Autumn. My Mother is in a very poor way.[3] Please to give my duty to your wife, and love to each of my Cousins.

My Sister is well and the children. It is with reluctance I have written, but a certainty that it was my duty to you, to the woman and to the cause of justice, I have written, as the only way to inform you of the expectations of the people, as I feared you did not intend coming. Your duteous Niece

Mary M. Emerson.

MH: bMS Am 1280.226(766). *Addressed:* Rev. John Emerson / Conway / Mass. *Postmarked:* Boston [*date illegible*]. *Endorsed:* M. M. Emerson / Letter / 1816—.

1. Rebecca Emerson Parker Brintnall Waite died at Malden, 21 July 1816. Her first husband, Jacob Parker, was forty years old when she married him in 1777; the daughter mentioned here, identified later as Mrs. Tufts, is from his first marriage.

2. MME means stepmother.

3. MME to RHE, Concord, 1 Mar. [1816], writes that her mother has "failed much" since her arrival: "Oh how painful are the ills of old age pain and helplessness. Yet what a short moment is the most lingering age to eternity!" (MH: 1005).

Boston   Oct. 27, 1816.

My dear Ann,

I am glad to hear from you—was not sensible we had lost our intercourse only as distance prevented frequency. How do you get on in christian
perfection? Avoid superstition, and what is called *cant phrases*, if I should
never see you again. I never reflect on your appearance on sabbath with pleasure. *It was not hypocircy*—but to persons of different habits & education
it had the appearance if not of hypocircy of gloomy and mistaken views of
the worship due to the Infinite and happy God. Penitence, & self denial beget
humility, that holy, indispensable virtue, so lovely to all holy beings—   Yet
we do not find the long faced people exceed in that desirable virtue—I have
often found them peculiarly deficent in it. Praise and religious joy beget the
finest sympathies—expand the heart to rejoice in the superior advantages of
others—   This seems the temper peculiar to Heaven! They are talking and
laughing so that I cannot go on. Such is our condition (we need variety) and
the ebulitions of mirth are as innocent as food and sleep, and as rational.
It frequently happens that the longer the mind is bent on invisible subjects
with the more force it returns[n] to earth. Thus have the excentricities of many
Professors injured the cause of religion. A uniform lofty Philosopher in the
heathen world, should make the christian blush. Aim at living as different
from the past as manhood from infancy.

I regret that your mind is so troubled about the cercumstance of your name
&c.[1] What right has any one to know it? But every one has a right to expect fair
dealing—no deceit. I should answer. "The[n] name I bear is not my Fathers—I
am not ashamed of his—but I have no right to publish the errors of his youthfull days of which he has repented. That illegitimate children should suffer
some inconveniences in this life is the law of society, and a duty society owes
to good morals. Were there none, what confusion and guilt would multiply!
I can solemnly exculpate all you suspect. My Father is a man of wealth and
consequence—but a perfect stranger to my adopted parents." Such I should
think would be the language of reason & good sense & *piety*. As your mind
expands—and you learn to appreciate society—thier praise and blame—thier
sympathy and curiosity will be alike indifferent—and you will estimate thier
good will only a means to benefit them, not as a mede to your own vanity.

Solitude and limited views of the world if they do not sublimate, often be-
little the soul—and imajanation is spent in forming pictures of a great and
splendid world which does not exist. To some whose talents and virtues shed
light and influence over nations, the world is of some importance as a medium
of their piety. But blessed obscurity is independant on fame! The richer glories
of a charity devoted to God, of a self renouncement which none but lofty
minds can practice—these—these oh eternity are thy due!

What do you sacrifice to others? In what consists your highest pleasure?
Tell me of these and you will forget your mortal condition

Your friend MM.E.

MWA. *Addressed:* Miss Ann Brewer / Waterford.

returns] ⟨adheres⟩ returns

"The] ⟨my⟩ ↑ "The ↓

1. MME refers to Ann's "illegitimate" birth in 1794: her parents, Daniel Sargent (1764–1842) and Hepzibah Atkins Brown (d. 1800), both of Boston, never married. He was the eldest of six brothers in a respected Boston family. After her mother's death, the child, who was called Nancy, was placed in a foster family in Dorchester, where her father visited her. Upon his marriage to Mary Frazier in 1802, Sargent, with the help of "four gentlemen of Boston" (including the Reverend William Emerson), sent nine-year-old Nancy to Waterford, where she was adopted by WE[2]'s sister and brother-in-law, Phebe and Lincoln Ripley, who changed her name to Ann (or Anne) Brewer. About the time of her marriage in 1820, Ann decided to use her father's name as her middle name. Much of this story is preserved in a correspondence that ASG initiated in 1854 with her father's brother, Lucius Manlius Sargent (MWA).

To Edward Bliss Emerson

Boston   No[v]. 9, 1816.

My dear Ned Bliss,

I thank you for my letter. It was well judged to write me—and its contents were well chosen. I rejoice if you love to join your fellow students in the offices of religion. What is man without piety? The most abject and destitute being in the universe   Exposed to all the winds and waves of life's tempestous ocean, without the pole star of hope to irradiate one of the heavy clouds which threaten to overwhelm his future prospects. Yet it is worthy of the most serious consideration, *in what piety consists*! Prayer is an indispensable requisite—but whether it should be social, and how frequent, is not determined—but should depend on situation and relative dutiees. A penitent, humble, charitable heart which prefers the favor of God to the whole universe is indispensable to salvation, and the only true state of dignified enjoyment. But how much time is to be spent in social prayer, to this purpose, seems very uncertain. Private devotion is called by the most eminent Saints, the richest means of improvement and happiness! And we often have the most deplorable instances of fanaticism and hypocircy in those who make *long prayers* in company—for it sometimes proceeds from ignorance, sometimes from delusion, and not wholly from hypocircy. But these are only hints to guard you against veiwing the holy and sublime duty of prayer with superstition or persumption. It might be an unspeakable benefit for you to attend frequently, were it consistent with your health. But *the night air* is *improper*—especially after the use of a warm and crouded room. Therefore your Mother thinks proper to prohibit your frequent attendance. When the weather and the room and so forth are favorable you may attend sometimes. But you should go to bed uniformly by 9 'k or before. Doctor Moody[1] is ever interested in the health and welfare of the Bliss Patient. But your freinds are more desirous that your mind should expand with inlarged veiws, and your heart be alive to every thing great and generous.

We wish to see but Mother says you had better not come this vacation, from many causes, which your reliance on her wisdom, need not be mentioned. She will send you money soon for wood &c

Your affectionate Aunt
MM Emerson.

MH: bMS Am 1280.226(748). *Addressed:* Master Edward Bliss Emerson / Andover. *Endorsed:* Miss M. M. Emerson.

   1. MME. See MME to WE[3], 26 Nov. [1814].

To Ann Brewer

[1816?]

My dear Ann

Do you progress? What sacrifices are you hourly making—? What obstacles are you incessantly renouncing? Do you feel your own littleness—and often loose your own sinister wants in sympathy for a world of sorrow & darkness? Do you get the better of that particular set way of doing every thing—such as puting on your clothes with the consumption of unnessecary time which has the *appearance* of selfishness? Do you rise superior—or rather grow in that grace of graces, *humility* so much as to root out of your nature a satirical cast? Do you love me? Can you forgive this letter? If not, it is well. God of mercy bless you.

MME.

MWA. *Addressed:* Brewer / Not Opened in her absence. *Added in pencil:* Any time from 1816–1817.

1817

To Sarah Alden Bradford

Concord   Jan. 1 1817.

While it is *yet* dark I am busy with the image of my young friend. Oh may the brightest beam of prosperity illumine her path and her declining life resemble this fair dawn. Seldom a fairer.

My dear Mother and Sister have taken their medicine and sent me off, most tenderly with their new years wish. The last, I think, I shall ever hear from my Parent. Father has gone a Journey with Mr Sewell— The Servants are quiet, and I am so well, as not to have shared in the food or physick, which has been administered; who will blame my mania for the pen? But a truce with sentiment, to one whose broad eye scans all the movements of head and heart and can analyse them in her chymicial head till they return notice and all (as indeed they too often do in the Labatory of earth) to the very dust from which Adam's body sprung. And after you awake you will have new food for discussion among the great and Learned. Do *historise* We have few subjects. You are a prominent figure—we speculate on your career and think how splendid it may be. Oh that a guiding Providence might place you sometimes where you might look up. Amid the changes and chances (apparent) of overturning Time may your Companions acquaint you with what others feel— But you will feel nothing of their complacency, unless you knew christianity as some poor ignorant men did some ages gone bye—or unless you are so excentric, as to love these superiors, as devotedly as seriously, and disinterestedly as you are beloved by

MME.

Sarah desired her love, whenever I wrote & said she wished to do the same— But I discouraged— Her cough is bad & has not left her chamber yet. Mother comfortable

MH: bMS Am 1280.226(1271). *Addressed:* Miss S. A. Bradford / Care of C. C. Emerson / Charlestown.

To Ruth Haskins Emerson

Sab Night   March. 2. [1817]

I wish I could step in, my dear Ruthy, and know how you all do—whether Edward is prepared to go on tomorrow and what Charles is doing. I found Sarah much more unwell than I expected, and under the Doctors hands. She took an emetic yesterday and it is probable will soon recruit.

How did you get to meeting today. What an immense snow. Father and myself were out a long time after service attending the funeral of Miss Barrett of whom I told you. This is the Sister (if you remember) of Mrs Frothingham.[1] A woman who always interests me. Yesterday she came here with some things for Sarah to prepare a shroud. She went into Town on business. Her grief, her efforts for decency—made a stronger impression than the most splendid appearance. I had the sattisfaction of hearing her husband preach all day. A scholar—and fine writer— He preached like a christian and philosopher— but felt like a man when he told us of the loss he sustained in this Miss B. She had been much with Mrs F— and shared her numerous cares with more than a Sister's sympathy. The late misfortunes of the family—the last days of the deceased rendered[n] by poverty (more painfull, for they refused to receive assistance) excited an interest you can easily concieve. Yet lovely and desirable was the appearance of the dead. How sweet and placid her countenance. No trace of pain,[n] care or want. Do you remember a hymn of Doctor Watts' appropos to this?[2] Mr F—'s text was, about the *great multitude which are before the throne*[3] Tho' it was not a funeral discourse, yet the association with the death of the pious was very natural. How fleeting are all earthly possesions, is a very common remark.— But you, my dear Ruthy can feel it to be a very weighty truth. We feel it at every new made grave— And perhaps more painfully at those over which time has thrown its mouldering hand— for alas the cares—the privations remain without decay.

MH: bMS Am 1280.226(1003).
rendered] ⟨pinched⟩ ↑ rendered ↓
pain,] ⟨hardship⟩ ↑ pain ↓ ,
1. Miriam Barrett, daughter of John and Experience Barrett of Concord, died 27 Feb. 1817, at the age of twenty-three. Her sister, Lois, was married to the Reverend William Frothingham of Belfast, Maine.
2. Possibly Isaac Watts's hymn on Rev. 14:13: "Hear what the Voice of Heaven Proclaims / For all the Pious Dead" (see *The Psalms and Hymns of Dr. Watts, Arranged by Dr. Rippon* [Philadelphia, 1842], number 653).
3. From Rev. 7:9.

To Sarah Alden Bradford

Wed. Noon. [1817?]

I cannot see you dearest Sarah while it rains. How do you do. You have been sick; & are well again blessed be God.

Oh dont go away—for you think this a fine world—a sweet pretty place. Neither mourn for the dead—for oh how much better is the day of death than that of birth. This breathing without going on is most painfull. This moving about has placed me below the dear notch of absolute indifference— And this house seems as more dolefull than the last as that was below B. St.[1] Surely you will say this is repining. No—all is not done within—or the worst of all diseases—⟨nerves⟩ is upon—or you have never been here—no sweet hour in Heaven or earth has marked this little building at the side of a wall, apparently. And the folly of taking it. But this is all pretence to murmur. Oh did you ever feel nothing to rest one complacent tho't on?— One congenial soul near. You—you only excite me— I can love nothing so much above me tho' I do more than any one—I believe.

Well this physick will be over and I can bid you all adeiue tomorrow. I did intend to draw out your compashion—but will not force it.

Louisa[2] speaks much of you and wants to come again with me. I shall not stir till you write.

How priviledged above me—all the emptiness[n] of this mortal, weary state you, like others, *perhaps*, will consecrate to a pious grief—and add dignity to the memory of a really worthy parent by attributing all to her loss.[3] This cannot be censured. How often in the long journey of *uninterrupted* sterillity— have I said God has denied me even a lad to weep over. But precious was the resignation— Oh dearer than prosperity, *at times*.

After all I shall not move you. But you will pardon these reflections, when I tell you, I regreted having too much solitude at Concord. With one of the loveliest spots, is connected so invaribly gloomy associations of my infant exile, by the death of a peculiarly benevolent & affectionate Parent—that I became every day more stupid. Only burn & forget this.

I came with Father thro' Walth—   & Sarah sends love to you.

I must say that unfailing joy always goes with the idea of being untied to littleness & pomposity. Take this for a caution in your setting out.

MH: bMS Am 1280.226(1275). *Addressed:* Sarah A Bradford / Charlestown. / Kind care of Mrs Elisson.

the emptiness] ⟨your sorrows⟩ ↑ the emptiness ↓

1. After their year-long residence at Beacon Street, the Emersons moved to Hancock Street in early Nov. 1816 and then to 20 Essex Street in June or July 1817, probably the address from which MME writes, probably in summer 1817.

2. Louisa Farnham.

3. SAB's mother, Elizabeth Hickling Bradford, died 19 May 1817.

To ?

Waterford   Au. 18 [1817?] Monday

I have this eveg arived, my darling friend, whose image has accompanied every scene, and hear that at the other house is a letter from you.[1] After tea I shall have it.

The why and wherefore so tardy a journey, was a wish to see Mr Hildreth at Exeter discover the road by which he had arived at so commanding a stand in old divinity to inquire into the Academy—to visit Prentiss[2]—to open a communication with a Gentlem about books at Portland—possibly visit Ann Brewer some miles beyond Portland. However I gave up the plan almost when Mr Haskins appeared with a direct conveyance. One ill rash moment fixed me at Exeter, as I was puting on my bonnet Mr H. promised after one week to take me to Dover. But I became so homesick, that I took stage on tuesday for Portland and remembering how useless you think all "contrivance" resolved to get on without any further. But at Portsmouth felt loath to give up ever seeing Prentiss and should have gone in the Packet, but the Servants of the Inn advised not. I went on to York wet and uncomfortable felt obliged to put up there till thursday. Saw my antient Cousins[3] whom I have not^n since childhood. Heard their tale of woes, was surrounded by the recollections of my family who repose hard by the walls of the house. Found the next morning present one of the pleasantest views of sombre rural life—and could not but wonder to see live geese and children on the Common, so completely had my associations been led to the grave. The day was very pleasant—there is a fine beach to ride on—a few venerable families to visit—and to hear annecdotes of Grandfather Moody. The Mother of T. Lyman[4] was an orphan Niece, brot up by my Grandfather. She is extremely aged and garrulous. She said she never "returned home without feeling her heart leap at the expectation of seeing Mr Moody". This is the best test of his character I ever heard. Thursday after a dark long night ride between a young Bigot and old Quaker got to the Stage office in Portland with an intention to take the mail carrige at 4 next morning for W. It was full, and I was perplexing myself whether to remain at the tavern or go to North Yarmouth for the week— I could not bear to set out visiting again, and would happily have kept my lodgings, but a few acquantances rendered it improper; And to my great sattisfaction, on friday afternoon a Country Gentleman was going to Norway with a good chaise. The Host set us up, and I never remember a pleasanter journey. The road was new to me—the farms richly loaded. As we ascended (ah, how ill placed this description after reading yours) the prospect opened with indiscribible effect—Sunset &c &c I dare not describe the cause, thou Ridiculer of sentiment. But to be up with you, how little the world its arts its' sciences its' languages its systems its parties and Sects! The "new Jerusalem Chh" w'h Mrs Prescot[5] tells about, covered the whole earth. "You never saw this landscape." But I am not the fair daughter of Rochelle so much as you are the Philosopher. My companion interested me greatly. A Deist. I met him on that ground, and a long evening passed in discussion. All distinctions seemed merged in one grand sentiment. The next day, when the labors & realities of life returned to memory the conversation was found to stand in need of other aids than the silent & oft equivocal voice of nature—other athority than reason—ties more strong on the first great Cause.—   and hopes more encouraging. This man a stranger to common instruction (in religion books & socity) is a gentleman of handsome manners—rapid perceptions and delicate humour. My curiosty was much excited and gratified   At home he was an accomplished husband & father *apparently*. Forgive if I have no confidence

I left Norway this afternoon and have passed the pleasant hubbub of seeing & hearing every thing in a minute. All all well & apparently prosperous. You must be the organ to my dear families—if I do not send by private opp^y which I somewhat expect tomorow mor^g. But my dear Ruthy's letter will be acceptable at any time as it is the offering due to her merit. To Charles I shall soon write. Why did none write?

Tuesday— I shall not send by post—but the Bearer cannot wait for other letters. This, tedious as it may be to the Scientific, w^d be interesting to my folks. Send it, if proper, to Concord with expressions of love & respect. Write if it is consistent with your pursuits   I shall think no postage expensive. Give much love to Louisa & her family, & I want to hear from her. Send Taylor from Boston & the Swen. book. & "Germany."[6] What a letter. Who pretend to despise fancy—but weave her loftiest flowers as by accident, and merely at the feet of investigation. Indeed, what naivete.[n]

Adieu dear & valued tho' so very heartless.

MME.

MH: bMS Am 1280.226(1297).

not] not ⟨seen⟩

naivete] *illegible in MS; left blank in T*

1. The most likely addressee for this letter is SAB. A letter dated only "friday aug 7th" from SAB to MME (at Waterford) may be the one mentioned here. Although 7 Aug. fell on Friday in 1818, not 1817, both letters refer to a time when MME has recently left Boston to return to Waterford, which was the case in 1817, not 1818. Also, SAB's letter contains a poetic description of MME's "independent solitude," to which MME may respond below (MCR-S).

2. Hosea Hildreth (1782–1835) studied theology and served as a minister for a few years before becoming professor of mathematics at Phillips Exeter Academy, Andover, Mass., where he remained until 1825; Lydia Prentiss.

3. Probably the family of MME's uncle Edward (1728–1806) and Mary Owen Emerson (m. 1749), who settled in York, Maine, where Edward was a merchant. Edward was fifteen years older than MME's father, and her cousins were between twenty-five and five years older than she.

4. Two of MME's father's siblings, Mary (1726–58; m. Rev. Daniel Little 1751) and Waldo (1735–74; m. Olive Hill 1759) settled at Wells, Maine, about ten miles from York. Waldo and Olive's daughter, Sarah (b. 1762), married Theodore Lyman in 1776. "Grandfather Moody" may refer to MME's great-grandfather, the Reverend Samuel Moody (1676–1747) of York, or to his son Joseph (1700–1740), "the famous and eccentric Father Moody" (Edward W. Emerson, *Emerson in Concord*, 3), also known as "Handkerchief Moody," the prototype for Hawthorne's Reverend Hooper in "The Minister's Black Veil."

5. Tract by Margaret Hiller Prescott, *Religion and Philosophy United; or, An Attempt to Shew . . . Philosophical Principles from the Foundation of the New Jerusalem Church, as Developed to the World in the Mission of the Honorable Emanuel Swedenborg . . .* (Boston, 1817).

6. Probably Jeremy Taylor; probably Prescott's tract (see above, n. 5); de Stael's *Germany*.

To CHARLES CHAUNCY EMERSON

Elm Vale   Oct. 14. [1817]

My dear Charles,

I thank you for the letters which I received not long since. The first written, probably, was dated the 9th of August—the very day I left Boston. This must have been a mistake. And *such* kind of mistakes are unpleasant. It is a want of punctuality which your Father disliked very much.

When it is done by Adults to cover some inattention, or forward some design, it is *contemptible*, and what is worse, is *wicked* for it is an absolute falshood. To inform you of this mistake was the errand of my present note.

To inquire after your and my friends is a sweetener to the task of mentioning a fault. How do all do? When did you see Sarah? When hear from Concord? How is Uncle Ripley? Do you go on as well as you began? Do you love & respect Mr Gould? Do you remember the pleasure we took together in your reciting the Messiah, Thompson's hymn & the dying Saint?[1] And the recital of Roman history? Whelpley[2] you were not so fond off. You will cease to be dazzled with the splendor of the Romans when you view them with *feelings* of humanity expanded and christianized. Whelpley will always be usefull (till you can read history for yourself) as a compendium, slight & easily remembered. But of all the treasures of my darling boy none gives me so much pleasure to remember, as the committment of our blessed Lord's sermon on the Mount. This divine code of morals, loved and obeyed, will be the gardian Angel of a youth of prosperity, an age of adversity, and at death, conducter to a eternal life of knowledge and benevolence! Farewell. Child of my most affectionate solicitude.

MME

Love to W. & R. & B.

MH: bMS Am 1280.226(637). *Addressed:* Master C C Emerson. *Endorsed:* M M Emerson / O T.

1. Benjamin Gould, headmaster of Boston Latin School after 1814; German poet F. G. Klopstock's *Messiah*; probably the "noble Hymn which crowns" James Thomson's *Seasons*, "the sublimest production of its kind since the days of Milton" (J. Aikin, "Essay on the Plan and Character of the Poem," in *The Seasons*, by James Thomson [London, 1811], p. li); possibly Pope's "Dying Christian to His Soul."

2. Samuel Whelpley, *A Compend of History, from the Earliest Times . . .* (1808).

To RALPH WALDO EMERSON

Elm Vale   No[v]. 4
not the 5*th* [1817]

What dull Prosaic Muse would venture from the humble dell of an unlettered district, to address a son of Harvard?[1] Son of — — — of — — poetry — — of genius—ah were it so—and I destined to stand in near consanguinity to this magical possesion! Age itself w^d throw off its' gravity for a moment—and dream that there was a vestige of fame to attach it to earth—that a name so dear was one day to leave some memorial. Vain wish. Where are the names which blazoned an admiring world! Where the Heroes so powerfull—the loftier Statsmen—the facinating talents; the wonder working powers of attracting and guiding the human mind! "We are such stuff as dreams are made off and our whole life is rounded with a little sleep."[2] A name on this flying planet, at which even the powers of higher orders are subject, is not matter of joy, when viewed by the celestial light of faith which shows us the destiny of man thro' the long vista of future ages. In that great Assembly, where human nature is purified from its' native dross & ignorance, may the name of my dear Waldo be inrolled. And while sojourning thither, may he acquire, most richly, those virtues and graces which do not pretend to dazzel, but which shed a pure and steady light, over the interests of humanity and religion—that the ear which hears him & the eye which beholds may bless him.

I want to hear more of your new life— And of William. Does his sage face wear any smiles? How does Edward? And B. & Charles? I have not time to write even to their dear Mother, as the Bearer is expected any moment. When I parted with you, it was with pain—tho' concealed— I knew, and always intended to part for a long long time. And I wished to save the pangs, by silence and indifference.[n]

May the broad hand of the Almighty cover thee, and sweet be thy[n] shelter
prays daily your affectionate Aunt
MM. Emerson.

Love to W. & your Uncle Ripley, whose book I shall soon send. Stewart.

Nov. 20 The Messenger who so hurried me came not And I intended to have written in less haste But I find another opp[y]. Last post bro't me the illness of D[r] Mckeene from S A B.[3] Alass, Genius & all the fine things which give worth to existence is, I fear, to be removed. What a loss. Among the dull, cold herd so ardent and pious a Spirit is inestimable. What sympathy, what friendship gloried and irradiated the sphere he trod! But it is for other worlds such as he seems best adapted—where no cold calculating Mortal shall approach.

E

MH: bMS Am 1280.226(815). *Addressed:* Ralph Waldo Emerson / Student at H. University / Cambridge. *Endorsed:* M. M. E X / 1818.

indifference.] ⟨levity.⟩ indifference.

thy] ⟨your⟩ thy

1. Although RWE endorsed this letter "1818," the references to his entry at Harvard and to McKean's illness date the letter to 1817.

2. Shakespeare, *The Tempest*, 4.1.156–58.

3. Joseph McKean (1776–1818), a brilliant young Congregationalist preacher, was ordained at Milton in 1797 but, because of poor health, resigned his pastorate in 1804; for two years he was Boylston Professor of Rhetoric and Oratory at Harvard. In Dec. 1817 he sailed to Saint Croix to find a climate more beneficial to his health; he died in Cuba in Mar. 1818.

1818

To Charles Chauncy Emerson
Elm Vale   Jan. 1, 1818.

A happy year to my dear Charles, if it be one of virtue. How important is every day of this new year! Tho the earth runs her wonted Journey without complaining of the idleness of her inhabitants, which she constantly carries down the stream of time, yet you know there is an account made of all the days she travels. She will continue to begin and end her journies with the same velocity, when you and all the present generation are intombed within her bosom, as now you are playing and bustling on her surface. But where will be the immortal souls of this vast multitude then? *Where will you be,* and how occupied? You, my dear boy, who have been my joy and companion for so many years, where will you be some long years hence? Who will associate with you? *The spirits of the just made happy?* Shall you so govern your temper, so cultivate generous amiable dispositions as to be admitted into a state of honor and employed in delightfull pursuits—in acts of love and charity? But how dreadfull is sin! One wrong act only in the affairs of this life has been known to throw the whole of a man's fortunes into the dark and gloomy paths of abject poverty disgrace and uselessness. But after all this, the same unfortunate man has become religious—has died happily—and in the language of scripture *forgotten his miseries as waters which pass away.* But the splendid and famous in this worlds goods have often *died without hope.* One wrong action persisted in—how inexpressible its' consequence! Who can tell that has entered the invisible world, and been denied the blessing and protection of God and the Redeemer.

I tremble while I write. God of mercy spare my dearest child from the misery which awaits the ungodly, the Proud and deceitfull.[1]

Your Aunt
MM Emerson

How much of the bible have you read since we parted—[2]

    * * * Be kind enough to procure me three quires of letter paper at Mr. Francis. *Such as your Aunt used have* like this 19 cents per quire   I cant finish your socks—but send you an apple

MH: bMS Am 1280.226(632). *Addressed:* Master Charles C. Emerson / Boston. *Endorsed:* M M Emerson / Jany 1st, 18.

    1. RHE to MME, [?] Jan. 1818, reported CCE's response to this New Year's letter: "His eyes glistened with tears & he seem puzzled how to express his feelings—after twisting in his usual way to get rid of the appearance of crying he says O Aunt writes strangely. What makes her have a prayer in her letter—but seemed delighted with his letter" (MH).

    2. MME had returned to Waterford the preceding July or Aug.

To Edward Bliss Emerson

Elm Vale   Jan. 1, 1818.

    Whether happy or not be the coming year, to My dear Bliss Boy, God grant it may be a pious year! On each of its revolving days may he impress improvement. And while the weary earth beginns anew her old course, and we rejoice that she travels the same orbit with invarible order; may his mind begin a new one—rise with yet untasted ardor to the study, the knowledge and practice of his heavenly Father's will. Then will those powers of mind, which will naturally unfold beneathe the influence of literature, be embued with a celestial complexion, never eradicated. Yes, my loved Edward (tho' I have often wounded your feelings by the severity of my criticisms, yet you were always *loved*) it is *early* piety alone can deeply and with peculiar charms tincture the whole soul—expand and ripen it's good dispositions   The habits of prayer, will instead of being a distinct and artificial part of the character, which leave no trace when over, and the whole soul returns to low, selfish or merely, at best, earthly concerns, raise and sanctify it's pursuits, whether they be literary or of the most menial kind. No, nothing is little to a soul fired with the love of true glory. It's light never fades in the darkest scenes of outward degradation; but ascends from the lowest grades of human condition to mingle with it's great Original.

When I think of your fatherless situation, I feel a stronger hope, that you will have grace to unite your fortune for time and eternity to the Father and Redeemer of your spirit. That He will mercifully conduct your path into the sacred ministry, and that you be a blessing to your poor fellow creatures. *That you live not in vain*—not *ultimately for yourself* in this world. In this hope how does the heart of your good Mother rejoice. Bless God for her life, and cultivate the minds of your younger Brothers.

I thank you for my letter and for the pleasant information that W^m is at Kenebunk[1]   I enclose you this trifle.

Let it be accepted for the sake of your Aunt
M. M. Emerson

MH: bMS Am 1280.226(749). *Addressed:* Master Edward Bliss Emerson / Student at Phillips Academy / Andover. *Endorsed:* Miss M. M. Emerson / Waterford / Maine.
1. WE[3], a Harvard senior, spent his break teaching school at Kennebunk, Maine.

To Sarah Alden Bradford

[13 Jan. 1818]

Whence this difficulty about jurisprudence where the xian religion, or Jewish, is established? It seems altogether a different question from the nature of morals or their foundation as it respects politicks. As it enters into the intricacies of law and adapted to different countries &c I lose sight of it. But that political justice, or what is *right* for a community s^d be different from what *is right* in individuals I cannot perceive. And on another observation (or what ever more important name) w'h Stewart with other Moralists are always making against *morality* that "moral distinctions are created entirely by the arbitrary and revealed will of God."—[1] And why that belief of a natural law coeval with human constitution, should be said to be in opposition—   It is the *will* of God revealed in the heart—   And why as I have before asked you is the danger of all morals originating to us from that *will*. They arise from the nature of God—revealed by creation of moral agents & revelation.

I dont understand Clarke's folio opposition to Malebr. when Stewart quotes the sentence which we have so often dwelt on & is in page 191 note bottom.[2] But the idea of Malebr that every perception of mind is the immediate effect of divine illumination has it's charms.—[3] And in some sort it's reasons. But Decartes I venerate with all his paradoxes. How could he reject final causes? And what does he mean by the abstractions of imajanation being totally distinct from those of understanding? Again, he gives to it (or by some other hand) a high degree of intellection. Without it how could we form notions of a future state? But to end all and level you my dear lovely pride inciting freind, do think of what Raynal says page 45.[4] I beg you read it again my respected scientific Oracle of Altitude at which I love to gaze. And yet to doubt that the present times are not better in a moral as well as intellectual view is, even to me, strange. It may make no odds *now* to the savage who was busy a century ago—but to the present spectator of things there seems immense choice   Corrina poor Corrina whom you would not read perhaps, possessed talent accomplishments—was not sufficient to herself—strong fine orijinal picture, (tho' polluted with daubing) of human heart.[5] But again I spare you any longer from such a jargon of epistolary stuff. But I owe you no good will in this way for I have had no letter so am not anxious to please. True in your last you deign for the first time to flatter me that the idea is melancholy of not seeing me for a long while. Yes long—never to reside there. And how I loved you all— Yet how indifferent on the whole surpassingly indifferent are cercumstances. What is lost one way gained another. If you would awaken apathy write of your *whole self*. Ah by the way did I offend your "lady Mind"? I help your holy dying— You are bound on the voayge of life. And I want you to buy some pinchusion[6] or other & say this Mary gave

I dont know why the inspiration of St John was less valueable for being in bodily vision?[7] Ezekiel's was probably of the optical sort. It does not make them Dramatists. I think. How is your family? How the charity school? Had not Louisa better visit for me? Yours dearest Sarah for ever

MME.

Would it not be pretty to add If in the melancholy shades below[n] of friends & lovers cease to glow— &c   Cold, & late— Mrs H. goes morning. Elm Vale   Jan 13

MH: bMS Am 1280.226(1276). *Addressed:* Miss S. A. Bradford / Charlestown. below] ⟨the throngs⟩ ↑ below ↓

1. Dugald Stewart, *Dissertation First: Exhibiting a General View of the Progress of Metaphysical, Ethical, and Political Philosophy*, originally published in 1815 and contained in *Collected Works*, ed. Sir William Hamilton, 11 vols. (Edinburgh, 1854), 1:38.

2. Stewart quotes Samuel Clarke, *The Evidences of Natural and Revealed Religion*: " 'The course of nature, truly and properly speaking, is nothing but the will of God producing certain effects in a continued, regular, constant, and uniform manner.'— *Clarke's Works*, vol. ii, p. 698, fol. ed." (*Dissertation*, 159).

3. Ibid., 159.

4. Stewart quotes Raynal: "Everything . . . has changed, and yet must change more. But it is a question whether the revolutions that are past, or those which must hereafter take place, have been, or can be, of any utility to the human race. Will they add to the tranquillity, to the enjoyments, and to the happiness of mankind? Can they improve our present state, or do they only change it?" (ibid., 35).

5. MME refers to the heroine of Germaine de Staël's novel *Corinne* (1807).

6. SAB to MME, n.d., indicates that MME enclosed some money for Sarah: "Your present shall purchase a Pindar, not a pin-cushion. I have long wanted him to fill a niche on my shelf of classics, but not as a token to remember a friend who has had more power and influence over me than any other being who ever trod this earth or breathed this vital air. You have sometimes been so unjust as to impute it to pride that I have so seldom protested how much I loved you, while the true cause was the incredulous smile with which the expressions of affection were repulsed." SBR's Pindar is inscribed "Sarah A. Bradford from her friend M. Emerson" ("MrsSR," 138).

7. Compare Johann Gottfried Eichhorn's theory of the Apocalypse in his *Commentary on the New Testament* (see MME to RWE, 26 June 1822, n. 5).

To Sarah Alden Bradford

Vale   May 4   1818

I have delayed writing my beloved Sarah, whether from pride or humility you will judge who know the tho'ts of my heart as well as I do. Tho' I longed to congratulate you on Your Brother's recovery. But one day I was setting the folks to *guese* who marked my stockings—   Whether it was because I had forgotten that the same question was asked before—or from some unlucky humour, Mrs H. replied that she knew too what you said about a letter I wrote to you. I was all amasement. She said you told Sister S. that you tho't you knew me but did not think I could have written so. Dear dear S. what letter did you mean? I did not press the subject—but asured her I was easy— that there was a misunderstanding on her part & Sarah R—'s. Still I believe so—only implore you to explain, if I have offended it was unwittingly.[1] What idle malignity to injure the feelings of a being the nearest my heart or rather attempt it? But the charges you close your letter with (in jest probably) of my taxing you with want of love is groundless. I always respected your non professions and loved your actions which certainly constituted my greatest comfort. It was impossible you could not then feel interested and affection for me. But I was never curious about the degree while I was supported with the effects. If it is possible that any reference is made to a letter sent to my brother *I s^d like you to see it*. I told him I was alive, eat & slept without S.A B—that in truth I was glad to find myself capable of an individual[n] existence, after so long merging myself and all that I know. Did he not feel releived *on my account*? This not the reason so much as fearing to intrude on your time by writing.

Well, D^r M'K. is gone, tho' not from his fire side. He found the place indifferent probably. I have read many a better wish from the heathen. since I entered the woods. But I do sorrow for his death, not for him, & "wish him joy of the worm." And that the mild light of Thacher has set is sad. You liked him— I the more regret his death.[2]

I believe from your explanations, that my questions did not express my meaning. Some of the first principles of abstraction I know   No Metaphiscian will as yet perhaps explain the exclusive province of imajanation. In a note in Ste. it is given an importance very high.[3] But unluckily for that Philosopher and for me his work is in "a pamphlet," and tho' you regave me some, not so much of him as I wished. Is it worth while to read Locke on understanding? He says that the doctrine of resurrection of body is a fundamental article &c— Speaks with respect of Solomon— What pity he could not have been instructed by the spruce. Preaches of the present day? But he was probably the source of much materialism and the mean stuff which attaches to it. However that is nothing to me, but, for my weakness, forbeare to speake of the German. And a stranger, Scholar, Divine, called Stewart a Deist, the other day. Pray is he not very possible for a christian in Cambridge?

How is your health and your family? Does the Spring open new delights? It will no doubt with its fragrant gales bring the mournfull remembrance of an afflictive event. My love to Martha. Where is Mr Pratt?[4]

May the richest blessings of existence be ever yours prays
MME

If you see Ruthy & she inquires I shall in the course of the month have opp.^y to write to her & all by a Neighbour. How does dear Charles?

MH: bMS Am 1280.226(1256). *Addressed:* Miss S. A. Bradford / G. Bradford Esqr. / Charlestown / Mass. *Postmarked:* Waterford May 6.th.

an individual] an dividual *in MS*

1. SAB to MME, 11 May [1818], defends herself against this attack, saying she felt no betrayal in showing the letter to MME's sister REH and that she regarded their peculiarly intellectual and speculative conversation as a mark of a friendship more elevated than that which is possible within a family (MCR-S).

2. Joseph McKean died 17 Mar. 1818, far from home at Havana; Samuel Cooper Thacher died 2 Jan. 1818 at Moulins, France, where he had gone for his health.

3. MME seems to continue a discussion with SAB. In an undated letter that refers to seeing MME the previous evening, SAB says she is reviewing Stewart's *Dissertation.* She singles out as most important his "refutation of Locke's hypothesis of the origin of our knowledge." Stewart quotes Jean d'Alembert on memory, reason, and the imagination (*Dissertation*, 6–8) and comments that d'Alembert gives the imagination "a creative and combining power" (8 n. 1).

4. MME refers to SAB's mother's death on 19 May 1817; SAB's sister Martha Bradford. Pratt was a suitor of Martha.

To Sarah Alden Bradford

Vale   May 22 —18

Dearest friend,

You have given pleasure[n] by so speedy an answer.[1] But what is surprising, at receiving your letter, I mentioned the explanation to Mrs H., and she wondered at my writing—or thinking of it. In fact, even this grave and literal lady says she only did it to try my feelings. The words from Sister S. were the same, but without an implication. All I can say in excuse, *you* are the *only* person I ever troubled with my suspicions of this kind. And I suppose you compare me to the weakly suspicious Rousseau, and your Self to the cool, decided all comprehending Hume. Well any place for me, if you dont treat me as Hume did the poor Fanciest on the alluded occasion. I have had but little till now to give, and could expect accordingly.

What a walk you must have had.[2] Oh were you old enough to "wish the hairy gown & mazy cell—how could *you* spell of stars & herbs.", or rather read without spelling. But your humble fate may be to "chronicle smale beer"—   And I sometimes am idle enough to wish that even were come, which in a poor woman's life, seems

"to end all other deeds,
Which schakels accidents and bolts up change,"[3]

and I departing with more pleasure after seeing your bolts drawn. But I do hope you will not be prisoned in heart or soul. I dont like the bordering on obstinacy of the character you mentioned. It is a proud, ugly, selfish trait whereever found in opinion—   But in the affections, in truth I should tolerate it heartily. "In loving he'll do well, in passion not." But what is best of all, he has not got the "tune of the time—   —kind of yesty collection— carrying tho' the most fond & winnowed opinions". Oh how loathed, only in recollection, it gives new zest to the grave of solitude

Who but would wish his holy lot
In calm oblivion's humble grot?[4]

Well forgive me if this is pedantry, and call it respect for the Muses, which this propitious Season awakens. Or what is as true, that the moment of receiving a letter from you brings a flavor of their magical stores to mind, and the russet clouds seem to bend on the mist clad mountains as vehicles of the Bards who sung of other times.

It is passing strange that your letter w'hich came a week this eve[g], s[d] lie in the office till this very afternoon. But the stupid lad whom I engaged to go every post neglected it. The young lady[5] whom I mentioned with some respect &c is in this Town, but some cercumstances have forbidden me any intercourse scarsly. And what I tho't uncommon 9 years past, when just budding, seems ordinary & formal, or I am jaundiced. That I have no chance even for Swift's quantum of friendship to be diffused. I have thought of boarding

in a Neighbourhood for the purpose of attending Astronymy with a Preceptor
of an Acadamy in private lessons. Now do tell me if it is probable I could have
any clear ideas of the science under an ordinary Teacher? And speake not of
the wish. I learn with regret that Galelio sacrificed truth to the fear of persecution. Oh science is this one of thy boasted lens! But Johnson's Astronomer
illustrates, perhaps, the most strongly the ineffacy of knowledge to promote
happiness[6]   But tho' I do not expect to be mad or envied for my learning, I
think the attempt will never be made.

Farewell being, most dear to my pride & affections. Does Charles *otherwise improve?* Oh tell me in secret what you predict of all?

M M Emerson.

If in a week you leave a letter and answer the above question glad. If ever you
keep my letters I need not ask you not to lay aside this "collection."

MH: bMS Am 1280.226(1277). *Addressed:* Miss S. A. Bradford / Charlestown.
pleasure] ⟨comfort⟩ ↑ pleasure ↓

1. See above, MME to SAB, 4 May 1818, esp. n. 1.
2. SAB to MME, 11 May [1818], reports a walk that day "to the pinacle of
your Malden mount" with her sister Martha, brother George, and Martha's suitor,
Mr. Bartlett (MCR-S).
3. MME responds in kind to SAB's letter, which begins with a quotation from
Shakespeare. "Wish . . . herbs": cf. Milton, *Il Penseroso*, 169–72. "Chronicle smale
beer": cf. Shakespeare, *Othello*, 2.1.160. "To end . . . change": Shakespeare, *Antony
and Cleopatra*, 5.2.5–6.
4. "In loving . . . not": Milton, *Paradise Lost*, 8:588. "Tune . . . opinions": Shakespeare, *Hamlet*, 5.2.189–93. "Who . . . grot": not identified.
5. Probably AB.
6. In Samuel Johnson's *Rasselas*, chaps. 40–44.

To Ralph Waldo Emerson

Vale   May 26 1818

On all sides surrounded with the beauty of Vertumnus, what shall I say to
my dear Waldo, whose taste I have known in his early days, somewhat morbid
to his decorations. And yet a pact[n]—surely in compliment to your profession
I must talk of the pow'rs[n] of nature. If you were plumigerous as Muses generally are, that you might visit the Vale; and hear the songs of the grove echoed
by the little tritons of Neptune, who is suspected of holding a smale court in
the neighboring Lake—if indeed his sedge crowned Majesty ever inhabits less
than the "vasty deep". If not, you could people a sylvan scene with Nymphs
or Faries; and queen Mab might send her followers after moon beams.

Hithertoo you have had no association with retirement—for you,

"the Spring may yet
Distill her dews, and from the silken gem
It's lucid leaves unfold— — —

Each passing hour sheds tribute from her wings
And still new beauties meet thy lonely walk
And loves unfelt attract thee
               All declare
For what the Eternal Maker has ordained
The powers of man. He tells the heart
He meant, He made us to behold and love
What He beholds and loves, the general orb
Of life and being; to be great like Him,
Beneficent and active." [1]

I began in jesting with poetry—end with respecting it. Could not resist pleasure of writing the above. Those who paint the primitive state of man's creation are sweet poets—those who represent human nature as sublimed by religion are better adapted to our feelings and situation; but those who point the path to the attainment of moral perfection are the gaurdian Angels. But this is no easy poetic task. The lowly vale of penitence and humility must be passed before the mount of vision—the heights of virtue are gained. Therefore we so often hear the warning voice of high toned Moralists against the seductions of the vagrant flower clad Muse. May yours if she should continue and preene her wings, be sanctified by piety and I shall not blush to decorate my age with a sprig from your garland. But let pass the flowrets of nature and art—or deck them with sepulchral dews when we think of M'Kean and Thacher. Alas, for us who knew their worth, for you whom they would have cherished, and for Society—their light is departed. Would you know the worth of earthly blessings, visit the tomb of genius learning & influence. What avails these highest sublunary gifts! Where now those strong prejudices— those ardent sensibilities which so fully attracted our attention in the celestial spirit of the Professor? All gone & useless, but his piety—his faith in the Son of God—his penitence and humility   These only pass the Ordeal of holiness in the world, where the naked character appears! Peace and honor to his memory! His family—how deprived! Yet sweet are their tears, and hallowed their sorrows for they mourn no common loss.

           Adieu dear Waldo. Love to William and many a greeting wish
                      from his & your Aunt
                      MM Emerson

MH: bMS Am 1280.226(814). *Addressed:* R. Waldo Emerson / Student at H. University / Cambridge. *Endorsed:* MME / 1821 / Nature.

pact] *possibly* poet (*JMN* 1:333)

pow'rs] *possibly* posies (*JMN* 1:333)

1. Mark Akenside, *Pleasures of the Imagination* (first form of the poem, in three books), 586–88, 591–93, 622–24, 625–29. Following "powers of man," MME omits a sentence: "We feel within ourselves / His energy divine."

To Charles Chauncy Emerson

Au. 9, Sabbath day [1818]

My dear Charles,

I thank you for the letters by Thomas; especially the one of antient date, for in that very letter, was the intelligence of your committing the 12 chap. of genesis and another which I have forgotten. Have you read the story of Elijah of late? What an astonishing history! How sublime his exit from our dark world! Could any of the prophets disbelieve the report of his favorite deciple who wittnessed this miraculous assent? They might and yet be good men for the time to bring light and immortality to light had not come. Jesus Christ who descended from God went to Heaven in the view of a great many. And to confirm his assension sent down such astonishing power on his followers, that *no good* men can disbelieve the present existence of Jesus Christ in Heaven. At some happy period, I humbly trust, you and I, my dearest object of anxiety, may see Him, and unite in the delightfull employments of eternity, *because* He hath so loved our unhappy race as to die for their good. I beg you to get often pieces from the old testament. Miss Hamilton whom I lately read with new pleasure, recommends the habit of young children being accostomed to read it as a preventative to those objections which grown children are apt to make to some of it's peculiar phrases and rites.[1] Your Mother will direct you to omit some part of leviticus   You will there find some fine specimens of sensibility in the narratives—and there is strongly expressed the duty of filial obedience, and it's rich rewards. If you were to write one copy a day it would much improve your hand and be a usefull way of passing some of your long intermissions.

Your afft Aunt
MME.

MH: bMS Am 1280.226(636). *Addressed:* Charles C. Emerson. *Endorsed:* M M Emerson / Old Times / X.

1. Elizabeth Hamilton, *Letters on the Elementary Principles of Education*, 2 vols. (London, 1801); see esp. vol. 1, letter 6.

To Robert Bulkeley Emerson

Monday   Elm Vale   Au. 24. [1818]

My dear Bullkley,

You have written me so often, I am resolved to be no longer in your debt but hasten to thank you.

I rode to your Uncle Ripley's this morning, and told your Aunt what an affectionate letter you sent me. I rode the old horse, which you well remember; and a little Dobbin was campering after us. But the old beast is resolved to take her own way[n] with me, that I had a long time to behold the beauties which surrounded me. The grasshoppers are very thick, and very troublesome to the farmer, they are not contented with the provision which nature has made them, but incroach on the grain. Their merriment and flippancy reminded me, as I passed thro' thier ranks, of a race of men and women, who dress like gentlemen and ladies, and pass all their time in frivolous amusements and empty noise. They skip about as easily as the grasshopper, and appear as much occupied. But when the first frost comes the poor insect is destroyed; he has not like the industrious Ant provided himself a shelter and food against the inclement season. So it is with the more unhappy insects of the human kind. Those who have frittered the morning of life away and laid up none of those hopes which are so delightfull, of a happy world, when there is no more, and no stores of knowledge to enable them to give and receive enjoyment; how dreadfull is their condition, when chilled by the frosty winter of age, or early sickness, or the loss of freinds & protectors! The finger of scorn is pointed at them. And when they die, people speake of them very much as the Farmer does when he is rid of the poor singing hopper. It is a joy to me, to believe that you, dear Bulkley, and my Charles will (thro' the goodness of God) be usefull members of society, respected in life and lamented at death. I could not but contrast the modesty and beauty of the yellow butterfly with the chirping Songster. These gay[n] people were in numbers, under the mountain where the watering trough stands. They hung on the purple flowers of the thistle without intruding on any prohibited land—and while the beautifull contrast of their drapery[n] to the flowers on which they fed pleased the eye, the emblem of innocence delighted the mind.

I hope you will improve in your writing; but especially in the more important duties of making your Mother and brothers happy, by your pious, obliging and amiable manners. Love to Charles, he will generously prefer, that as I could afford but one letter, it should be to you.

Your aff[t] Aunt,
MM Emerson

We were glad to see your Cousin Daniel.[1]

Wednesday. An unexpected chance to send this—there will be an opp[y] to send me W[m] performance[2] next week & again the week after. in great haste   Dear Sister I congratulate you. The day is fine—joy sits on every object.

MH: bMS Am 1280.226(963). *Addressed:* Master Bulkley Emerson / Boston / Mr [Sauer].

way] ⟨time⟩ ↑ way ↓
gay] gay ⟨and happy⟩
drapery] drapery ⟨appeared⟩
1. Probably Dàniel Farnham (1797–1824).
2. WE[3] graduated from Harvard on 26 Aug. 1818; in the commencement exercises, he participated in a conference titled "Upon Architecture, Painting, Poetry, and Music, as Tending to Produce and Perpetuate Religious Impressions."

To Sarah Alden Bradford

Sept. 26. Sat. Noon. 18

Well you have contrived by the superior influence of genius to be more romantic than if castle'd and watched by a hundred dragons— Now why not like the facinating scot be forced to W—[1] But that ever you should deserve to be so vulgar as to be happy— Spoil all—like sympathises with common contentment? The world admired an Antoniette prosperous—but unfortunate—they idolized! And after all, you were left to arbitrate. And take much merit, no doubt, for your generosity. However I am glad of the step you took, apart from jest.

As to your "prudential resources & calculations & econymy," pardon once most respected—all ways dearest—I do not understand you, I hope— But tho' I will not erase the *once* I recall it—you are ajitated and not cool. As to *assimulation* too. Forbear to alter one of the fairest works of God— Be *your self* and play no part—not that I misunderstand you—but never run of the notion that timid vain people do, that every body's happiness depends on their opinions. I mean to speake of the parish. Oh better die at once on the procustus bed. The state of the society, perhaps, better than dead rusticity or the deadlier unnui of high polished ordinary people. Open both arms to charity— And in little time you will feel interested. My family will appreciate your {   .}[2] And if I mistake not, tho' little acquainted, you will {lov   } your husband better every year. Before he is such, I ask the favor of a line to know what you refer to about "my views & sentiments being mistaken." No one suspects me of any traiterous design to Church or State I trust—and of being otherwise misunderstood by my relations, I cannot believe—they do not love—but the more I am understood, that is always the case I believe. But the creature does not live who suspects my sincerity. Pardon my egotism—pardon my style to your beloved Self— But it is among the lost excitements about you— You will apoligise to my folks if I dont write you as usual— But I shall not like to intrude on your active & happy engage[ts] I should come to the wedding *positively* without waiting for *any invitation* but that I am peculiarly fixed with health & leisure for reading— which I fear to lose and a journey thither & back without a private opp[y], would be expensive. Oh for new books. If you have a chance, send me Taylor's sermons & Yates &c &c.[3]

Adieu Sarah Bradford— I will not lose a moment in painfull recollections that the joys annexed to that name are no more— In the vast orb of existence I may again meet them. My desires are that the Owner may be great and wise like the promise of her richly budding youth.

MM Emerson.

Pardon me, is the boon I ask from one, who was wont to confer so much. I just received your letter—read it again & find your calculating system only what we mean by independance & philosophy— And how greatly wise to rely on Self.

MH: bMS Am 1280.226(1264). *Addressed:* Sarah Alden Bradford / Charlestown.

1. Since SAB to MME, 12 June [1818], tells of her engagement to SR (MCR-S), MME is probably expressing surprise at the decision not to prolong the engagement. (The year "1817" in SAB's dateline appears to me to be added by another hand: SAB's letter is addressed to MME at Waterford, where she was in June 1818, but not 1817.) The couple was married 8 Oct. 1818. The sentence following this was heavily canceled and then cut out of the MS, apparently by MME.

2. Words missing because of sentence cut out of p. 1.

3. Probably Jeremy Taylor; James Yates (1789–1871), cofounder of the Scottish Unitarian Association and author of numerous tracts, including *A Vindication of Unitarianism* (Boston, 1816).

To Ruth Haskins Emerson

Sab Eve. 18. [Oct.? 1818?]

My dear Sister,

Your sententious complaint I have this eve received, in w'h I could have sympathised in those dolerous days & months I last past in Boston. But now I cannot. Every moment carries us on (loaded with it's own rich stores from the great Source) to our high & holy destination. Oh if there is any delusion in our feeling surrounded with the agency of God Himself, let us live & die with the enrapturing sentiment. It is true much delusion attends the Great & Ambitious who feel that they are the great springs of action in the universe. But in retirement with one only object— Oh there is no delusion.

But I must not indulge myself in conversing as I write on business & have no more paper. I want "John Lelands view of deistical writers." They are in Vestry. One vol. will suffice   And the 6th vol of Lardner.[1] Now as you will not perhaps have time to send to W— why not lay my wants before your Minister. Tell him I have been to Portland & there was no circulating library of any worth—that I want Grey's Key and *Chalmers* sermons. The Key is in Vestry. I can send them home safely in first sleighing. These books are more important than Taylor & Yates.[2] Mad. DeStael on "effects of literature" I want. Br. R. has a trunk   I wd write to F.[3] but you can tell him that I am starving for books. If you can do no better do send me some of Chauncey's works w'h I believe you own. I wish the Miss Ladds would loan their Whelpy's history. But you may see Br. & Sister Ripley   I regreted the gloomy account of —— which I sent you   All will work for the best. Every thing is capable of doing the work of sanctification. I would have offered to assist him in buying this place—but he was so positive about not being able to live on it.[4] Still he has perhaps altered before this. But his dear wife is anxious that I sd say nothing of the kind to him. And I trust you have not said any thing. Indeed I am completely at a loss to judge of Br. R—'s plans or views. And of course cannot tell what to advise him. He and his will be carried on without absolute want I trust.

You could not get me any thing which I queried about. for gown or linnel.

You are very kind in attending these smale affairs. I wish whenever they are troublesome you would commission Louisa   I bought some tracts—hope to have some gratis. If I have a special opp^y to pass a day or two with you shall— but uncertain—if so well & favored with reading as at present shall not wish to move.

May every blessing best calculated to promote your highest advancement & the dear Children's be continued from the Father of mercies to those who are faithfull.

Yours in good will
MME.

Dear Charles,

You must purchase me some paper   Received your favor dear Sister of Sep 30 the day your Brother left home—& the books before

MH: bMS Am 1280.226(1008).

1. John Leland, *A View of the Principal Deistical Writers That Have Appeared in England in the Last and Present Century, in Several Letters to a Friend* (London, 1754). In 1818, the only edition of Nathaniel Lardner's *Works* available in an edition of more than five volumes was an eleven-volume edition published in 1788; the sixth volume is the *History of the Apostles and Evangelists*.

2. Robert Gray, *A Key to the Old Testament and Apocrypha* (London, 1790); possibly Thomas Chalmers, *A Series of Discourses on the Christian Revelation Viewed in Connection with the Modern Astronomy* . . . (Andover, 1818). For Taylor and Yates, see MME to SAB, 26 Sept. 1818, n. 3.

3. F.: possibly Father (i.e., EzR), or Nathaniel Frothingham (1793–1870), minister at the First Church, Boston, from 1815 to 1850.

4. A reference to Robert Haskins and difficulties concerning Elm Vale's ownership.

1819

To WILLIAM EMERSON[3]

Newburyport   Feb. 14, 1819.

My dear William,

The pleasure I took in again seeing you—or rather for the first time since you appear to me as a man—compensated me for so long a journy. It was indeed most gratefull—and I no longer felt alone (as I had done at N Y) when the well known sound of Aunt so welcome, met my ear.[1] How pleasantly you are placed—   How kindly Providence has bro't you forward—   Oh dear dear William how great a blessing you may be to your precious Mother & brothers, and to society—   My heart is full—but were I to write a volumn, I should give you perhaps no idea of religion as a system—as to it's pleasures— they pass description—and the human understanding can never in this life analyse them. I regret that you pass any part of the sabbath from your lodgings. That gift even at the creation has been much enhanced by the ruin of man, whose encroaching wants renders such a day to the majority *nessecary* and to the enlightened a priviledge of the richest kind—but like all duties & priviledges there are conditions & selfdenials. If the sabbath is not appropriate to the most serious duties—of what use is it? Does it break our association with time and sense and frivolous pursuits—does a fashionable and common mode of passing it concentrate the mind to one prospect of all that is grand? And, in slighting this institution, do we not lend our influence to rob the poor of the only day they have—they cease to value it for it's original purposes and it's highest use. Neckar "on religious opinions" has said the best things in a political and moral view on the sabbath.[2]

I write in company—therefore, pardon haste. I will give you a commission to make a call for me at the elegant Sewall Mansion,[3] with my respects & love. I intended writing by this opp^y, but find I cannot. I shall always remember their kindness, and associate with them the ideas of some of the most excellent and ornamental traits of female character.

Your affectionate Aunt & friend
M M Emerson

Mrs Frothingham wishes me to mention her to you with all due Cousinship.

MH: bMS Am 1280.226(1065). *Addressed:* Mr William Emerson / Mrs. McCulloch / Kennebunk.

1. Probably North Yarmouth, Maine. MME (at Concord) to AB (at Byfield, where she seems to be teaching in or attending the school for young ladies established by MME's cousin Joseph Emerson), 29 Sept. 1819, refers to an abortive attempt to board at "N. Y.": "Your letter discouraged me from going to By. together with the engagements w'h detained me here. . . . I wonder if Mr Emerson would think it profitable for me to board there after you had all gone? . . . You should have told me as you did Patty that I should not stay at N. Y. The gloom & expense of that disasterous Journey & missing Mr Haskins is increased by the hand your fair lady ship had in it. I hope it is not ominous of your future influence on the interests and accomodations of your friends" (MWA). Following his graduation from Harvard in Aug. 1818, WE[3] went to Kennebunk to teach school and study law with a Mr. Wallingford; by the end of Nov. he had realized he could not do both and "dissolved [his] connexion with Mr. Wallingford" (MT/EW).

2. Jacques Necker, *Of the Importance of Religious Opinions*, trans. Mary Wollstonecraft Godwin (London, 1788).

3. The mansion known as the Parsons-Bourne house, built in Kennebunk by John Usher Parsons in about 1814 and sold to Daniel Sewell the next year.

To Ruth Haskins Emerson

Sat 12. June. [1819]

My dear Sister,

I received yours with much sadness. But as you have never dreaded the event of losing your Boarders you will not be anxious. God is always present—

when He tries us with perplexity & poverty, He has the wide & boundless universe at His immediate disposal— But he withholds plenty that we may not live at ease—that we may not dress, eat & visit as do the children of the world. *Our* kingdom (blessed be God) is not of this world. Should fame with her hundred tongues blazon your name and mine it cannot recall the days of youth—cannot give us those charms which interest society and render our stay here desirable. Poverty, pain obscurity can deprive us of nothing but a few richer meals or finer clothes—but may be the effectual means of inlarging our existence forever. And for the children what lesson so adapted to humble the pride of human nature—to make them feel their own insignificance and dependance on God, and humble endeavours, to supply their own wants. The fewer those bodily wants are—the greater the wiser the more independant & noble will be my dear Charles. Still if he thinks it nessecary to support the weight of his excellent example in the sphere he occupies to have a new hat, I beg you to get it as soon as Mr R. H. pays you my money.

As to advice were I in your place—*your* advice would be the first thing I should solicit. You must be guided by circumstance—and those I trust will be directed by God. How delightfull is the idea of our keeping house in the Country. My little income should all be put into the stock. And were our children to be bro't up in the simplicity & innocence of rural life, how very pleasantly might we descend into a peacefull grave. If the world did not weep over it—we would shed the more precious tears of respect for what was pious & benevolent—and of regret & nameless sorrow for what was selfish and proud.— we would take leave of each other with the strong hope of meeting with the *general assembly and church of the first born* in the worship and service of God.

Parents & Sister send love to you & children. Sarah is not well but will soon be so we believe.

Your aff^t sister & long loving friend
M.M.E.

MH: bMS Am 1280.226(1013). *Addressed:* Mrs. Ruth Emerson / Essex Street. / Boston. *Endorsed:* Miss M. M. Emerson / June. 1819.

To Ruth Haskins Emerson

Concord   Sep 16. [1819]

Thanks dear Sister for your letter. Have you moved? And where?[1] Charlotte wrote on tuesday that you were not going to move. How is your Mother?

I have been thinking if it were not adviseable to have Charles go to Exeter? If you remember we tho't much would not be saved by Edwards going but the nessesity (of a moral kind) of seperating the boys renders it desirable. I fear the time for application is over—still I could but write to Professor Hildreth if you wished it before I go west. Can you let me have any money? Sarah is at Waltham, but she may be able to loan me she returns tomorrow probably. Sarah Alden bro't a fine girl on tuesday morning last and I had a letter this morning saying she was very well.[2] The causes for joy and sorrow suceed each other in the old way—tho' we shall not know which is for the best till we drop our own earthly hopes & fears in the grave. Should circumstances prevent your being able to let me have the money ever why I must come and eat it out.

Do send me a quire of letter paper from Francis with some little articles I left. A handkerchief at Sister H.'s. I will send her another tell her but I cannot mark, and wish for that because it has my name, and I have but one for use besides it.

Does Charles discover any taste—love or even respect for religion   If I go home, as I expect next week unless you see no prospect of money—when shall I ask such another question?

Farewell, may God himself spread his large rich hand of mercy over you.

Prays an old friend
MME.

I send these by an uncertain conveyance therefore am particular in enclosing the letter. If W returns soon send my germany   Oh *what are his prospects about a school.*[3] I say Oh because of it's importance not that I just tho't it. Rejoiced to have Ned Bliss at Medford.[4]

MH: bMS Am 1280.226(1018).

1. Despite some talk of moving, the Emersons seem to have stayed at Essex Place until the following Apr., when they moved to Franklin Place.

2. MME indicates that half sister Sarah Ripley has gone to Waltham for the birth of SBR and SR's first child. Tuesday was 14 Sept.; Elizabeth Bradford Ripley's birthdate was recorded as 15 Sept. 1819.

3. WE[3]'s Boston school for young ladies opened in Sept.; de Staël's *Germany*.

4. EBE, still waiting to enter Harvard, may have gone to Medford (where some of the Ladd relatives lived) for his health. By Oct., however, he was back in Waltham helping with the Ripleys' school.

PART 3

The 1820s

1820   Boston, Medford (Jan.); Conway, Medford, Andover, ? (Feb.–July); Northampton [Mrs. Upham's, Mrs. Lyman's] (Aug.); Belchertown, Enfield [Mrs. Field's], Hatfield (Sept.–Nov.?); Boston (Dec.).

1821   Concord (Jan.–Feb.?), visit to Newburyport (Feb.); Hamilton, with visit to Kennebunk (Mar.–July?); Boston/Federal St. (Aug.); Malden and Concord (Sept.–Nov.); Concord/ Boston? (Dec.).

1822   Concord/ Boston? (Jan.–Mar.); Newburyport and Byfield [Dr. Elijah Parish's] (Apr.–Nov.); Concord (Dec.).

1823   Concord, with visits to Waltham and Boston (Jan.–Mar.); Newburyport [Mrs. Frothingham's] (Mar.–Apr.); Waterford (May–Dec.); Bridgton (Dec.).

1824   Waterford/ Vale (all year) [RWE visits in May].

1825   Waterford/ Vale (all year).

1826   Waterford/ Vale (Jan.–Aug.); Concord, with visits to Cambridge, Waltham, Boston (Aug.–Oct.); Waterford (Nov.–Dec.).

1827   Waterford (Jan.–Dec.); Greenfield, Augusta (Dec.).

1828   Andover, Maine (Jan.–Sept.); Waterford (Sept.–Dec.).

1829   Waterford (Jan.–June)/ Newburyport (July?); Boston, Waltham, Concord (July–Oct.); Greenfield [Daniel Ripley's] (Nov.–Dec.).

At the midpoint of this decade, 25 August 1824, Mary Emerson celebrated her fiftieth birthday. A year later she recalled the significance of the date. In a letter to Waldo, memory flows ecstatically from her dateline: "Tues. August 23   The 25 of last Au. was one of the happiest—not merely that it ended half a century of my life & that it was brilliant for the Country—enough—." The sentence brings together many strands of her correspondence in these years; language entwines her life with that of her nephews and the nation. Reaching fifty years of age was indeed a milestone for a woman who had seen so much death and frequently expected her own. And the performance of one of her Emerson nephews had made the day "brilliant": at Harvard's commencement, Edward shared the platform with Lafayette, the French hero of the American Revolution, and read his oration, "The Advancement of the Age." All of these connections grow out of the moment "Tues. August 23."

Her geographical movements seem similarly entwined, and they similarly affected the shape of these letters, as she moved in and out of solitude and society, from Boston and Concord to Elm Vale and back. Forced to leave her Vale by real or imagined difficulties with her brother-in-law Robert Haskins and his family, she began in 1820 the habit of boarding in new places between visits to her other families. In 1821 she considered selling the farm for one thousand dollars (MH: 819), as she did again in 1826, when the second lease with Robert Haskins expired. From 1820 to 1823, she continued to spend part of each year with her Boston and Concord family. In 1823 she returned to Vale, where she remained (except for a month or more in Concord, Cambridge, and Boston in the fall of 1826) until late 1827. The next two years were unsettled: eight months in Andover, nine in Waterford, five in Concord, and two in Greenfield, where she began the year 1830.

From this decade survive 176 letters written to sixteen different correspondents; 125 of the letters were written to her four Emerson nephews. Other regular correspondents were Ruth Emerson, Sarah Bradford Ripley, Ezra Ripley, and Ann Gage. (Although she must have corresponded regularly with Samuel Ripley, virtually none of these letters survive.) From these I have selected 75, most of them unexcerpted. The letters are written from both "society" and "solitude." Those dated at Boston to Ann (Brewer) Sargent Gage at Waterford continue a relationship from the preceding decade and provide some details of her situation. (Few of the many other letters she must have written from Boston and Concord survive.) On the other hand, those to her nephews are most often written from her "solitude" at Waterford or an interesting place like Byfield, near Newburyport, where she boarded with the orthodox minister and historian, Dr. Elijah Parish. While telling something of her current life, many also continue conversations begun earlier, when she last saw them. All of these letters, to and from Waterford and beyond, are part of a continuing oral and written conversation—or rather, several conversations whose various threads are difficult to separate.

The metaphor of the entwined text suggests the problem of introducing these letters. Any attempt to codify or explain seems to limit and diminish them. We might approach them as Mary says she does poetry: "I must content with admiring this hidden treasure—too exquisitely fine to be analysed—a very proteus—at times to me nothing less than a Minotor & lost in labyrinths—at others like the sybiline leaves scattered at the misterious cavern by blighting simoon." But they are also philosophical texts, demanding flights of the intellect written in a poetic style that resists analysis. Each reader will have to find her or his own way to read them without robbing them of the will-o'-the-wisp quality Mary Emerson finds in poetry. My goal here is to locate them within the context of the Emerson family circle.

Although she had shed "bitter tears" at passing Vale for the last time in 1818, this five-year exile had a profound effect on Mary's relationship with her Emerson nephews, making this the great period of their correspondence, in terms of both numbers and substance. During the years when William, Waldo, Edward, and Charles were moving into adulthood, she was able to play an important role in their development, challenging their beliefs, counseling them about their careers, urging their questions, and responding to them from her always spiritual perspective. Their conversation began when she was nearby, staying with Ruth Emerson or various Ripleys for much of the period from 1818 to 1823 (between Waldo's fifteenth and twentieth birthdays). Here she enjoyed the stimulation of visiting and talking, attending lectures and reading books, even while she was occupied with caring for the sick, comforting the bereaved, and consoling the disappointed. When she would leave—to visit in Newburyport or board at Northampton or Byfield—she would continue the dialogue on paper.

Mary seems to have boarded with "strangers" for the first time in August 1820, establishing a pattern that would continue throughout her life. Like any new experience, this was scary; characteristically, she met it with fortitude. "Do not be anxious, my dear Ruthy," she wrote to her sister-in-law from Northampton; "I meet with fine accomodations & kindness among all the strangers. And if I am disappointed once & a while in a plausible freind it is made up else where" (MH: 1007). Writing from Hamilton in March 1821, she describes the town as "of all desolate places . . . the climax." But, she goes on to say, "Nothing seems easier than to get good accomodations for 9⅝" (MH: 819). Other references to the cost of boarding indicate that this was a usual weekly rate.

After returning to Vale in 1823, she rarely saw these same nephews for almost five years. There her society was made up of the Lincoln Ripleys and the Haskins (the last of their eleven surviving children was born in 1822) and Gage families (five children were born to Ann and Leander Gage, married in 1820, during this decade). Her solitude counterpointed her nephews' more worldly lives, which she was eager to hear about: in 1827 she called William's descriptive letter of busy city life "a valuable novelty to my cell" and urged him to write more. "There is nothing in the literary, social, gay & especially in the political world which will not be novel & welcome. One does love to lose oneself in somthing better." The feeling was mutual: after Mary left Boston for Newburyport in 1822, Charles wrote emotionally that "when *you* are absent—there seems a kind of void which I cannot fill up" (MT/MH).

These letters brought more than news of society, however; they also brought valuable thoughts and questions, subjects for speculation. She sums this up after rereading some letters in 1827: having "wandered over the starry letters of Waldo," she says, "I can fix on nothing. . . . Take a text from either [Waldo or de Stael] and the mind expands." Writing to Charles the next year, she admits that she thinks of her nephews more than ever and muses on "their power to excite the mind & heart—the only *power* after all." Though at another time she complains that Waldo's letter increases her desire to write but lessens her ability to do so, her nephews' letters more frequently unlock her ideas, as she takes her text (in the sense of a passage from Scripture to be expounded upon in a sermon) from their texts (their letters, conversations, lives) and expands upon it, transforming it to express her own vision.

For most of the period her particular concern was Waldo, then in the critical years of his transition from lackluster Harvard undergraduate to junior pastor of Boston's Second Church. With him she shared her disappointment in "modern Unitarianism," her enthusiasm for William Ellery Channing, and her discovery of Thomas Brown's lectures; she introduced him to Germaine de Staël, discussed the art of oratory, led him to examine the oratorical style of Edward Everett, and argued with him about Hume. She wrote amazing letters that alluded to "Merlin's cave and Homers shades," Juvenal, Johnson, Dryden, Gifford, Mosheim, and Russian poetry as well as to reading in the *North American Review*, the *Edinburgh Review*, the *Foreign Review*, the *Quarterly Review*, and the *Christian Examiner*. In 1822 she responded to Waldo's questions about the enigmas of nature, and throughout his theological training (roughly from 1825 through 1827, when he could read little because of eye problems), she continued to spar with him on questions of human nature, fate and free will, and the origin of evil. She avidly followed his early preaching career, critiquing his sermons and fertilizing his thoughts.[1] The intensity of their correspondence is suggested by the knotty and mystical letters Waldo copied into his journal. Stimulated by this dialogue, Mary Emerson raised the epistolary conversation to an art form, drawing out the best in her companion, provoking him to self-expression and then taking back

the theme and weaving it into her own vision of divine order. This process—
a mutual stimulation and fertilization of ideas—was one that both Mary and
Waldo recognized and enjoyed. On it they built their relationship.

Seventeen years old when this decade began, Waldo was ideally situated
to become his aunt's most important correspondent. She had never been as
close to Edward as she was to the other boys, and some disagreement that
occurred while she was in Boston made conversation with him difficult; by
the end of 1823 William had left for Germany, where she followed him in her
thoughts but not on paper. After his return, his theological change sparked
her intense questions, but William was an unwilling correspondent. In 1823,
fifteen-year-old Charles found the demands that his aunt placed on epistolary
conversation too great: "You ask me to send you a thought which never has
& never will have any connection with my corporeal being," he complained
in October, and in December he protested, "I cannot send themes for letters"
(MT/MH). By the end of 1828, Charles supplanted Waldo as Mary's chief
correspondent, but in 1823 she acquiesced to his preference for "commonplace
observation," even though, after writing him a letter full of ordinary gossip,
she confesses she finds her "imitations of fashibble letter writing" rather dull:
"You remember the Cat transformed to a lady who behaved well till a mouse
appeared" (MH: 652).

Waldo knew well how to play the mouse to Mary's cat, how to draw out
of her the natural, the wild, the imaginative, the repressed that her metaphor
suggests. As Mary's current "favorite," he encouraged her to play the role that
Wordsworth assigned to Nature: spiritual teacher and guide. To Waldo, Mary
was the muse, the voice of untutored wisdom, of intuition and high vision, of
his ancestors; by writing to her, he addresses Plato. To her, he is "the coset of
the Muses," her child of old, her "dearest Correspondent," an inquirer and a
seeker like herself, a young mortal who deserves Plato's rebuke. At the same
time, their correspondence is an intense intellectual exchange between equals
whose wisdom derives from wide reading.

This phase of their relationship began to develop soon after Mary left the
Boston area to board at Byfield for six months in 1822. She responded to
Waldo's request for a letter, dutifully reporting on the recent visitor from India
and her reading. But his next letter, written after a walking tour on which
he failed to find the kind of creative "intoxication" she claimed derived from
nature, prompted a spirited response from his aunt: "You do not 'ask' but impel me to speake of that Muse—so loved—so wild—so imaginative so dear
to me." She was impelled, in fact, to create a six-page paragraph that weaves
together society and solitude; philosophy and poetry; sensation, sentiment,
and unbounded Being; Caesar, Cicero, and the Medici; Eichhorn, Berkeleian
idealism, and Hindu poetry; his destiny and her situation.

This letter of 26 June 1822 from Byfield marks the real beginning of Mary
Emerson and Waldo Emerson's epistolary relationship. Waldo recognized this
when he reread the letter the following December, calling it a "most beautiful

monument of kindness and highminded but partial affection." It is also an excellent example of her method: stimulated by what he has written, she takes her texts from his letter and weaves them into her web in sentences that wind around their subjects, transforming them into something new and wonderful. His life and his thoughts become themes for her homily on his destiny and the vanity of ambition. As she plunders his letter, plucking her themes in no apparent order, she suddenly injects herself as writer into the center of her own letter: "In the zeal of writing I began with the last sentence of your letter, & have just read backwards till I am now for the first time in cool possesion of the whole." His letter has produced in her the intoxication he sought in nature.

As Mary recognized, Waldo had learned Sarah Bradford's secret to unlocking his aunt's thoughts: provoking her marvellous expression by means of letters offering interesting and challenging topics. In the fall of 1823, after her return to Vale, he initiated a new dialogue with a "catalogue of curious questions" (*L* 1:137)—rich metaphysical and moral speculations on the enigmas of the universe and human nature.

The drama is played out on a stage prepared by Waldo: the satirist of women, he remarks, accuses woman of "the love of being sought . . . & the design of being followed as the reason of retiring." Her flight has prompted his pursuit. Rambling among doubts, finding no solace in books, he seeks answers from "the pen of a living witness & faithful lover of these mysteries of Providence" (*L* 1:137). She applauds his ingenious method of breaking the spell of her silence, and the game begins. This is an intense exchange, preserved in a series of fifteen letters dating from October 1823 through December 1824, when Waldo was making his decision to enter divinity school. The Plato dialogue in the summer of 1824 epitomizes the unique nature of their relationship: through their multivoiced role-playing they provoked each other to full self-expression.

Waldo's preaching career was Mary's central concern in 1827, when his progress seemed to fulfill her hopes and dreams for her nephews and when his illness increased her anxiety. Where he preached, what he said, how he said it, how he was received: these drove her questions and responses. Meanwhile, her nephew was drawing on her letters and conversation: in 1837, while recalling those sermon-writing years and the inspiration he drew from his aunt's letters, he claimed, "I could not find any examples or treasuries of piety so high-toned, so profound, or promising such rich influence" (*JMN* 5:324).

In January 1827 she critiqued his first sermon, which she had heard in Waltham in October 1826: she found his discourse on prayer long on style and short on substance. In the summer she offered her views of the role of the preacher, the origin of evil and the Fall, and the role of Christ. As the year progressed, she continued to spar with the novice, adding to her subjects questions about immortality, the wisdom and goodness of God, scriptural authority, free will. In August Waldo summed up her role: "To *ask* questions, is what this life is for,—to answer them the next. & those intermediate people who, like my correspondent, seem to partake of both" (*L* 1:208). As Waldo's counselor and muse, Mary Emerson mediated between this world and the next.

A more detailed look at the letters of this decade indicates the interconnectedness of this family's lives. As 1820 opened, Mary was writing from Boston, happily "surrounded with new & most dear books which I cannot get else where," but before long she was on the road, traveling for the rest of the year to Conway, Medford, Andover, Northampton, Hatfield, Enfield. In December she returned to Boston, to the Emersons' house at 24 Franklin Place. She spent January 1821 in Concord before moving on to the "blessed solitude" of Hamilton and visiting in Kennebunk; by August she was back in Boston, in time for Waldo's commencement. She spent September through November 1821 in Malden and Concord, caring for Bulkeley, who had become unmanageable.

She probably passed the winter of 1822 in Concord and Boston; not until she moves to Byfield in April 1822 does the paper trail begin again. There she remained until autumn in the household of Dr. Elijah Parish, enjoying discussions of natural theology and visits to nearby Newburyport. A letter from July 1822 gives a rare glimpse of her physical state: writing to Charles Emerson, she says she has "not been as well as usual. . . . I think we resemble each other more than ever, and I am pleased with my thin pale face better than I am to hear of yours" (MH: 642). In December 1822 she returned to Concord, where she stayed for the first third of 1823. Then she visited in Newburyport on her way back to Waterford, her first stop there since 1818.

Mary was ecstatic on her return to the Elm Vale farm. Writing immediately to Charles in May 1823, she describes the "mountains w'h seem to shut out human passions," the hazy blue mist rising from the surface of the lake, and the "soft atmosphere w'h invelopes the traveller in a new & complete solitude." She rejoices to rediscover the familiar graveyard to the east and the merry brook to the west; she analogizes this scene and then suggests how the "poet's eye" might view it. Nature and solitude would provide the context of her letters for the next four and a half years. From Waterford, she continued the dialogue she had established with her nephews, especially Waldo, during her years of exile.

In 1823 the Emersons' fortunes seemed to be rising. The family had moved to the "country" (Canterbury, a section of Roxbury), from which William and Waldo commuted by foot to Boston to teach in their school. By year's end, William had left for Germany to pursue theology. In 1824 the Haskins heirs completed their thirty-five-room hotel on the family estate on Rainsford Lane in Boston and were expecting an income from their investment. Edward and Charles won distinctions at their commencements. Mary and Waldo's correspondence rose to new heights in this summer of her fiftieth birthday: in May he visited Waterford,[2] and probably in August she wrote him an eight-page "letter from Plato" in response to his "letter to Plato," composed about the time of his twenty-first birthday in May, when he was still teaching in Boston. By the end of the year Waldo had closed the school to rest at Roxbury before beginning his studies at Harvard—not Andover, his aunt's choice for one in "pursuit of greatness."

But 1825 marked the beginning of a period of sorrow and anxiety, as the letters between Waterford and Boston make clear. Within weeks after entering divinity school in February, Waldo developed eye problems that made reading—and therefore study—impossible.[3] This bitter calamity, Mary recognized, could teach the value of suffering. In February, her mother, Phebe Bliss Emerson Ripley, died at the age of eighty-four, and in April, half brother Daniel Bliss Ripley died in Alabama, leaving a widow and a small son. During the spring Mary, too, suffered from an eye condition (possibly a sympathetic illness), and in the summer, as Waldo's eyes seemed to improve, she worried that he was recovering too quickly. At the same time, Edward's health began to fail, and Waldo returned to teaching, taking over the Chelmsford school that Edward had to give up. In October, after almost two years abroad, William returned to Boston and announced that his studies had led him to reject the ministry as a profession; the next week Edward sailed for Marseilles in quest of health. Ruth had also been ill for much of the fall, and in December Bulkeley was again "deranged," requiring more care than Waldo was able to give him in Chelmsford. Writing to his aunt on 21 December 1825, Charles hoped that the coming year would prove "happier & healthier" than the past twelve months of sickness and suffering had been (MT/MH).

Though Mary considered selling Elm Vale in 1826, her sense of the Haskins family's needs led her once again to continue the arrangement, and she remained at Waterford for most of the year. She did make a four- to six-week visit to Concord in the fall, both to see Ruth (who, despite her illness, had moved twice, first from Roxbury to Cambridge in April 1825 and then to a second, smaller Cambridge house a year later) and to help care for her failing half sister Sarah Ripley (who died on 2 November, shortly after Mary returned to Maine). She arrived in Concord or Waltham before August 28, when she completed a letter begun twelve days earlier at Vale. Thus she was present for Waldo's first sermon at Waltham on 15 October and Edward's return from Europe a few days later. William had moved to New York in August, and in December, Waldo, fighting the "mouse in his chest," left to spend the winter in the warmer climate of South Carolina and Florida.

In 1827 the Emersons were forced to "hold intercourse . . . by letter," as Charles put it when writing to his aunt in February. From New York City, William explains: "When I write 'home,' " he wrote to Waldo, then in Charleston, South Carolina, "Where is it, pray? Boston, Concord, Cambridge, or Chelmsford? One of us is to board at each of those places" (MT/MH). For a short time, Mary seems the still point around which these correspondences revolve. She was happily situated at the farm at South Waterford, which she described that year as "a pleasant home & with all it's little trials . . . much better than such an old body could deserve." Her sister Rebecca Haskins was ill; eight unmarried children, from five-year-old Charlotte to twenty-two-year-old Robert, still lived at the farmhouse, and Mary hoped she might still be needed. But she seems to have felt like an unwelcome lodger and was ready "to clear out if they prefer . . . [to] rest them and change those sensations w'h irk" (VtMiM). Years later, on two occasions she recalled a September day in 1827, when, "under the immediate impulse of showing my confidence and good will," she invited Robert to *"take what he pleased"*; soon afterward, Haskins stopped by with a deed for some sixty to eighty acres for her to sign. (She explained in 1851 that she did not really own this land; it was "crowded into my deed for a cover.") She was in a hurry, however—on her way to East Andover, as she recalled—and did not bother to read what she signed, although she believed it would not be recorded. Another time she promised Robert the "Cottage land," some acreage and a small building. By year's end she was in Greenfield and Augusta, making her way to Andover, Maine, where she would spend the first eight months of 1828.

Charles compared his aunt's latest move to the sybil's removal to Cumae (MT/MH). Andover was a remote village twenty-five miles north of Waterford, where she went to board with the father-in-law of the new orthodox minister, Thomas Treadwell Stone, a young Waterford native whose "refined & philosophical" mind impressed her (though she was later put off by his coldness). Then the most northerly town in the state, Andover was an "abode of 'wolves & loons and savage wildness' . . . unfrequented but by a uncertain conveyance of mail & no church building—but the mountains are more numerous and invironing and grander than at my beloved Vale."

No letters from Waldo to his aunt survive for 1828, when he was much in demand as a supply preacher and was courting Ellen Tucker, whom he had met while preaching at Concord, New Hampshire, in December 1827. During this year Charles became Mary's primary correspondent: almost twenty-one years old, graduating with honors from Harvard and beginning his stint at teaching, leaning toward the law rather than the ministry, Charles was ripe for the instruction Mary no longer heaped on Waldo. Still, Mary avidly followed Waldo's new career. William was beginning in business and law with the firm of Ketchum and Fessenden in New York. Edward, who was ostensibly reading law in Boston when his health began to fail in April, was committed to McLean Asylum, where he remained from early July until early November of 1828.

Mary probably left Andover in mid-September 1828, returning to Waterford in search of health. She seems to have boarded in town, rather than with either her Haskins or Ripley sisters, for most of the next ten months. Though she did not attend Waldo's ordination in March 1829, she was still not rooted: that summer, after a visit to Newburyport, she suddenly showed up in Boston. On 2 July Edward reported to William his surprise at finding "our lady eremite" quietly seated in Waldo's study (MT/EW). The visit lasted several months; she celebrated the delivery of Sarah and Samuel Ripley's seventh child

(Ann Dunkin, on 12 July in Waltham) and Waldo's marriage to Ellen Tucker (on 30 September in New Hampshire). In October the newlyweds moved into their rooms on Chardon Street in Boston, but Mary had already left Boston, apparently without meeting Ellen and unsure where she would spend the rest of the year. In November, Edward, who appeared to have recovered and had passed the bar, moved to New York to begin practicing law with William. Mary's letters of November and December 1829 are written from Greenfield, a town in northwestern Massachusetts where she boarded with half cousins, the David Ripleys. Thus, by the end of the decade, with Waldo married and established at Second Church, Charles's conquest was complete: in March she mistook one of his letters for Waldo's, and in December she congratulated him on writing one of the "best letters . . . in any age."

Throughout these years, Mary Moody Emerson practiced her art, a mutual act of correspondence. She hungered for her nephews' letters; she begged them to write; and, carefully observing the economy of epistolary correspondence in which a letter puts one in debt to one's correspondent, she made their letters the condition of hearing from her and apologized when she wrote out of turn. The best of these letters—a great many of them—preserve this conversation, this process of mutual appropriation, assimilation, and transformation of high-toned speculative subjects, that weaves together the Emerson family's personal and intellectual lives. Taken together, the letters constitute a unique synthesis of old and new, as traditional Christianity becomes high romanticism, an argument for a feminized, spiritualized view of nature and human life.

NOTES

1. Evelyn Barish has begun to explore some of the connections between Mary Emerson's and Waldo Emerson's writing.

2. ASG and LG (Waterford) to Phebe and Lincoln Ripley (Greenfield), 2 June 1824, mentions that RWE has been there for a five- or six-day visit and that he enjoyed "Pleasant Hill"; the letter was probably carried to Boston by RWE to be sent on to Greenfield (MWA). RWE's visit is also mentioned in MH: 1252.

3. See Barish, *Emerson*, 158–59.

1820

To Ann Brewer

Boston   Jan 20, 1820

That you have forgotten me, dear Ann, is among the events which years teach to expect. That I am not offended is certain from my giving you the most valuable moments of life. Surrounded with new & most dear books which I cannot get else where I must ask you how you do and what are your plans? The sweetest recollections remain with the remembrance of Waterford, the

Vale and the frequent assent to the Hill offerd me a gratefull knowledge of the capacity to enjoy. Oh could I have a stomach as pure here. But dont tell the Doctor,[1] for I used to assault him with my complaints when I first went. Give him my best wishes. Is his aspect as lofty as ever? But I too much like an independant spirit to complain. True humility is consistent with true independance. I have ever thought that when the heart was most intimate with Heaven, it was most independant of earth. Mr E.[2] told me you had written him. I had a most interesting conversation with him on religious practice   He was my Confessor. I am almost a Catholic when I see him.

I am here waiting (tho' most happily situated among my dear children and excellent Sister) for cash to go on to Conway. I was at Medford and offered to accomodate Sister H.[3] with the money with which I s^d go on &c &c but situated as she is, prefers being alone. I enjoyed my visit—her good sense & piety highly interest me. I left Concord three or four weeks since. I staid so long tell your Mother[4] (whose judgment & feelings are always important to me) that they did not express a wish to detain me. Sarah must have the exercise of taking care of her family or school keeping would be still more injurious. She is blest with great strenght of constitution and able to exert that influence over her domestics by which they get on better than with me. And she is not obliged to sew, so that she goes from room to room with *constant*^n effect & more than I could give.

My affectionate remembrance to Brother & Sister for whom the above was written to mitigate anxiety, and love to Patty Sam. & Noah[5]   To Mrs Farrar & Hamlin &c &c

Adieu my dear Ann whose non appearance in this quarter last Autumn was much regreted by Mrs E. and your long interested & affectionate freind

MME.

I want to tell you of Orators, publications & my attendance on conferences in Mr Channings^n Vestry[6] and so forth &c but here is Waldo reading and I must to thursday lecture.

Sisters love to your parents   she dont hear from their Banker. Ask his acceptance of some bryon tea[7] which I hope will get safe. Will you buy my bed? Get it at your house & take it if you should settle at any rate till I can dispose of it.

MWA. *Addressed:* Miss Ann Brewer. / Waterford. / Major Monroe.
constant] *possibly canceled*
Channings] Cannings *in MS*
   1. Possibly Leander Gage, whom Ann married on 5 Oct. 1820.
   2. Probably Joseph Emerson of Byfield.
   3. Probably REH, but possibly one of RHE's sisters.
   4. Ann's adoptive mother, MME's sister PER.
   5. Noah Ripley, another adopted child of Phebe and Lincoln Ripley; "Patty" is adoptive sister Martha Bliss; "Sam." is possibly Samuel Moody Haskins, then seven years old.

Figure 11. The Reverend William Ellery Channing (1780–1842),
engraving by J. Cheney from a portrait by Washington Allston,
painted in 1811.

6. In 1817 WEC proposed the erection of a "vestry-hall, or small building," by the Federal Street Society; among its other benefits, it would be a good place for the "young ladies of the Society" to meet for instruction with their pastor (*Memoir of William Ellery Channing . . .*, ed. W. H. Channing [Boston, 1854], 2:139–40).

7. Probably abbreviation for white bryony, a European climbing vine whose leaves and dried roots have been used for medicinal purposes.

To Ralph Waldo Emerson

Medford   March 11, sat Eve [1820]

Dear Waldo,

I had an interesting visit at Andover—regreted that I could stay no longer   Found an account of Socrates (novel & the Proffessor S.[n] told me highly important) in quarterly Review for *last sep.* 1819 [1]

How have you done since giving me the wise demonstration of joy at parting? Do you remember the fable of wisdom & folly? Which do you think was the most glad at parting? No matter, it was only poetic frenzy—or joy at *event*, which gives *some* employment

To be serious, how do you, dear play Mate? Mr Ladd is going—or I have a world of chit chat. *Do write.* I am going to stay here a few weeks, till Phebe comes. Rebecca is going to N.P.[2] *Write* I say—   Colledge news—that will be literary—but above all about yourself—a very important personage to me.

Alas, that an ill star should have directed bad news to me—to lessen my pride is good—but there are times when the heart does love to have a treasure even on earth—and when they are surrounded by the learned to say within (at least) such *will be mine*—   So will his name go down, and tell on his Country's page a line which time will not blot. But if you do not study as others—if your exertions do not swell the literature of the age—a dearer part you may act—   As minister of the blessed religion of Jesus, Angels may echo your name and saints greet you where time & death are no more.

> Adieu dear dear Waldo.
> Your Aunt & friend
> MME.

MH: bMS Am 1280.226(816). *Addressed:* Mr Ralph Waldo Emerson / Student H. U. / Cambridge / Mr. W. Ladd. *Endorsed:* MME X / 1820 / College.

Proffessor S.] Proffessor ↑ S. ↓

1. Probably Moses Stuart (1780–1852), professor of sacred literature at Andover Theological Seminary, 1810–48; the only recent discussion of Socrates in the *Quarterly Review* (London, not published in September 1819) is in a review of Schlegel's *Lectures on the History of Literature, Ancient and Modern, QR* 21 (Apr. 1819): 271–320, esp. 311–20.

2. Newburyport; probably niece Phebe Ripley Haskins, but possibly sister PER; probably sister REH.

To Ann Sargent Gage

Boston   Dec. 27, 1820.

My dear Ann,

Tush "my sister's family" you regret you prevent me from. I said to Mrs Ripley, I should admire with my bad eyes, to board with her this winter as you & the doctor would be in the habits of conversation,[1] and your society induced me to wish more than usual to be in her family. But eyes are better, and I have lost my taste for W— amid the charms of Hampshire County.[2] However, first or last I shall be there—   And I strongly hope that you will live & die there—that my dust may mingle with those I love.

As to society & literature—the rapture of a few days & hours are no compensation for the evils which polite life induces—waste of feelings—time— devout habits—independance on earth—ambition—vanity—*apathy*—want of sympathy—*because* of emulation—&c   The *advantages* are some—but in the busy, peopled world of reason, truth and endless activity which lives[n] beyond this sepulcher of mortality, we can only find true genuine sentiment & "holy feast of reason & flow of soul."[3] Beware, my young friend, how you go to keeping house on this ball of dust so as to lay up treasure in Heaven. However we theorise contemptously of earth, it gets dominion & the grandure of the soul lies beneath rubbish. Pardon the caution.

Last eve. I desired Mr Sargeant to fetch me his daughter;[4] She is very sweet & accomplished—but I pitied her. A fair flower, but the thick atmosphere of wedding visits, balls theaters &—all the stirring din of life will rob it of it's freshness & flavor. I met them at Louisa's.[5] He has grown old—surprisingly fast. I longed to speake to him of another person—but I did not.

Ask the D[r] not to mention that I own the farm or at least a part of it. In haste—write to me long & particularly, and be sure to represent the state of this H. family.[6] Direct the letter to me, care of Mrs Emerson, Boston.

Commend me to yours with many good wishes

MME.

Love to Br. & Sister Ripley & Patty.

MWA. *Addressed:* Mrs Ann Gage / Waterford / Mrs Haskins. *Endorsed:* Miss M. M. Emerson.

lives] *possibly* lures

1. Sister PER; "the doctor" is ASG's husband, LG.

2. In the Berkshire area around Northampton, Mass., where MME spent about four months in 1820 boarding with a Mrs. Upham and others. MME to RHE, [16 Aug. 1820], indicates this is her first attempt at boarding by using the interest owed her by Robert Haskins (but which Haskins seems to be slow in paying) for her living expenses (MH: 1007 and 1023). Another letter [Sept.? 1820] is written from "Enfield   Mrs Fields" (MH: 1025)—possibly MME's cousin Sabra Emerson Field (1773–1837), a daughter of John Emerson of Conway, who married the Reverend Joseph Field, minister at Charlemont, Mass., or a relative of Mr. Field's.

3. Alexander Pope, *Imitations of Horace*, Hor. 2, sat. 1 (1733), "To Mr. Fortescue," line 127. The word "holy" does not appear in Pope.

4. ASG's father, Daniel Sargent, and her "legitimate" half sister Maria Osborne Sargent (1803–35), who married Thomas Buckminster Curtis on 8 Dec. 1823.

5. Niece Louisa Farnham (1794–1864) married the Reverend Orville Dewey (1794–1882) 26 Dec. 1820.

6. The Haskinses, with whom MME had purchased the Elm Vale farm.

1821

To Ralph Waldo Emerson

Wednesday [1821?] 1/2 past 11 'ok

"*Philosophical devotion,* for instance like the enthusiasm of a poet is the transitory effect of high spirits, great leisure, fine genius & a habit of study & contemplation: But notwithstanding all these circumstances, an abstract invisible object, like that which *natural* religion alone presents to us, cannot long actuate the mind, or be of any moment in life. To render the passion of continuance we must have some method of affecting the senses & imajanation, & must imbrace some *historical** as well as *philosophical* account of the divinity. Popular superstitions & observances are found to be of use in this particular."[1]

This is the finest thing that Hume himself could say—delightfull testimony to the theist & devottee. Reading it & writing it to you shared the same moment— The part before you ran in my head, & I determined to write to ask you to take leave of your hostess for tuesday as Louisa[2] will see all her friends in the eve. And in the little pageantry which will pass before us some ideas may arise from forms of beauty to light the combustibles of fancy. And fancy tho' a trull, sometimes may be converted into a ministering spirit. All doing better. Ed. poor soul, will be a victim to study—but an early death is a patent from above.

Yours with too much partiality

MME.

Historical—the xian theist glories in the tangible evidences of his religion—but he has still stronger hold on future *provisions* from the adaptation of his mind to *these*—and to commune with the Auther & supporter of his mental & moral powers. And nothing is more true than in every pursuit or object of mind or appetite, there is no real sattisfaction but in contemplating the Auther of nature & revelation and approximating to Him.

MH: bMS Am 1280.226(824). *Addressed:* Mr. R Waldo Emerson / Cambridge / Mass. *Endorsed:* MME / 1821 X.

1. David Hume, "The Sceptic," in *Essays Moral, Political, and Literary,* in *The*

Philosophical Works of David Hume . . . , 4 vols. (Edinburgh, 1826), 3:189–90; opening quotation marks missing in MS. MME's footnote is not from Hume.

2. Louisa Farnham Dewey.

To Ralph Waldo Emerson

Concord   Jan. 18   1821.

I want you, dearest Waldo, to write me whenever nothing better offers for you. Of that M.S. I find it nothing of the nature of history—highly metaphi. & boldly interspersed with my objections & queries.[1]

How is thy soul? Not that of which Paul speaks—but thy poetic? The spirits of inspiration are abroad tonight. I have rode only to go out & see the wonderous aspect of nature. Do we love poetry as we do the flowers of the field—because *they* supply not the nessecaries, but the luxuries of life—& give presentiments to the soul, so rich of an existence where all cares & labours cease. Fancy, celestial gift, is to the mind what those to earth. "Imajanation penetrates the sciences"—"they supply analogies to poetry, and history decorates it".[2] "There were of old perhaps, more intimate relations between man & nature than now exist. The mysteries of Eleusis; the religion of Egypt—the system of emanations of the Hindoo—the Persian adoration of the elements; the harmony of the Py. numbers—are vestiges of some curious attraction w'h united man with the universe."[3] Blessed is our condition—we recognize with scientific delight these attractions—but they are material—yet they are the agency of God and we value them, not as our relations, near & dear, but subservient to the great & grand relations we seek and pant after, in moral affinities & intellectual attractions from His moral influence. We love nature— to individuate ourselves in her wildest moods; to partake of her extension, & glow with her coulers & fly on her winds; but we better love to cast her off and rely on that only which is imperishable. Shakespeare has admirably described the universal influence of the infinite Spirit by that of the sun, whose light & warmth brings to maturity the healthiest plant & the most poisonous—corrupts the corruptible, & nourishes the splendid tribe of flora with the same beam.[4] What an illustration—and of what a truth! It is ours to cooperate—to imbibe—to spread forth every faculty for this influence—to open the soil tho' by the hardest labours—by martyrdom (if need be) that much may be taken— what an endless approach to the fountain of light have the pious begun! After ages of "onward and onward" assent, then you can better discourse of the history of morals. *Morals* coeval with existence—where did it's records beginn? Melchisidec[5] might have been in distant worlds a Preist of natural theology. *Right* and *wrong* have had claims prior to all rites—immutable & eternal in their nature; what connection has xianity with their primitive state, involves endless, & perhaps useless, inquiries. That this scheme seems a provision a medicine for diseased, disturbed beings is clearly discovered in all its parts.

That it places before its adherents a higher destiny than what awaits those who expect the awards of justice—that is, that the order of beings whom we call Angels are on the original plan of fullfilling their obedience, and receiving the favor covenanted by their Creator. While to the order so frail, so afflicted, and so hazardous as man, the "rewards of grace," a magnificent plan has been laid for him. But I shall weary my light haired Youth. How does Everett? May his progress be rapid to new hieghts of fame, if at every step some new {   } attend.

A little child of Mr Hoars has died today and excites the sympathy of the Villiage,[6] as tho' Evertt himself were its' parent. But it is natural to ask where the little wanderer is—to what new school—what consciousness— what loves? On the naked branch of a neighbouring tree hangs a birds nest. Cold & desolate, its melancholy appearance recalls the beauty & song which once surrounded it. Where now it's gay & fond Inhabitant, and her maternal brood? Are they basking in warmer climes, or devoured by Vultures? Or are they cowered down to sleep, & will awake some sunny morning in the form of happy peris?[7] Not so, do we view the little nest of human clay—somthing sublime is cast over it—its spirit is conscious—lives in the ever active benevolent care of its God and Saviour! In some such mansion as He prepares for those who love Him, may we hereafter meet   I am too much *beguiled by you & your imajanation* to wish to see you much—   Other ways demand me— Oh s^d I be so blest as to find you in the same paths. And there you will one day be; after the truths which God has sent down. There may all the honors & pleasures of immortality attend, & your name be a gift to your age

MME.

Love to your dear Mother & brothers. Ed was very good to me, when I was more pettish than he. W^m tolerated & entertained me to his honor. Well what a report about his engaged to Phebe B. poor things, they need not fret—for they will never find so good a husband or wife.[8] I wish the gossiping had truth.

No one knows of my writing, or else love w^d go

MH: bMS Am 1280.226(817). *Addressed:* Mr R Waldo Emerson / H. University / Cambridge. *Postmarked:* Concord MS Jan 20. *Endorsed:* M M E 1821 X / Poetry? *and* Tnamurya.

1. Possibly an early draft of RWE's 1821 Bowdoin Prize essay (see below, n. 3).

2. Loosely paraphrased from Germaine de Staël, *Germany*, trans. from the French, 3 vols. (London: John Murray, 1813), 3:166.

3. "There were . . . universe": The passage beginning with "more intimate" and continuing through "moral influence" (below) was used by RWE in his 1821 Bowdoin Prize essay, "The Present State of Ethical Philosophy," in *Ralph Waldo Emerson, Together with Two Early Essays of Emerson*, ed. Edward Everett Hale (Boston, 1899), 100; the quotation is from de Staël, *Germany* 3:159–60. De Staël reads "the Indians" where MME has written "Hindoo" and "numbers, which was the basis of the Pythagorean doctrine" where MME writes "the Py. numbers."

4. Not located in Shakespeare.

5. Old Testament king (of Salem) and priest, who blessed Abraham (Gen. 14:18–20); he came to typify the priesthood of the Messiah (Ps. 110:4; Heb. 5–7).

6. Samuel Johnson Hoar (b. 4 Feb. 1820), son of Samuel and Sarah Sherman Hoar of Concord.

7. "Peris": "In Persian Mythology, [a Peri is] one of a race of superhuman beings, originally represented as of evil or malevolent character, but subsequently as good genii, fairies, or angels, endowed with grace and beauty. Hence *transf.* 'a fair one'" (*OED*).

8. Probably niece Phebe Bliss Farnham.

To William Emerson[3]

Feb. 16, 1821.

What a character that of Visconti! "Worn with age & dreadfull disease, all antiquity present to his boundless memory"![1] What a wonderfull subject of speculation opens on the grecian art! Oh I cannot regret, tho' they *should* be preserved with religious care, that mounds are "opened or dug down" if nessecary to discover their precious relicts. Can any thing be more poetical and sublime than the figure of Minerva in the supposed grave of Achilles? Her car & horses—but in these we recognise the sentiment of religion which is implanted at the bottom of the heart! And tho' in the idolets of heathenism, we had rather find it, than find that desolate void which levels man with his "brother tenant of the shade". And vandal as, you votary of the times may call me, I am, I had rather altogether rather[n] live at the grave of these arts than when they florished. Not because they receive additional, inexpressibly so, worth from antiquity and as monuments of history, but from the attendant evils which have connected with their highest altitude. Not *nessecarily,* for it was mythology gave rise to the art—and thus adds to[n] it's charm. And how delightfull would our tempels be adorned with statues of the Apostles & martyrs? And perhaps the luxuries of the Augustan ages had no connexion with the perfection of the arts. I want, in vain, to form an idea of the genius which can give *soul* to marble! *Will the art ever be equaled to the past?* It is *impossible to surpass it, is it not?* If so, is not *this* the reason why it is not spread over Europe? and all civilized world? True it is yet, even here— But no Phidias, or even I should have heard of him. Perhaps one of the reasons or causes may be traced to the great Architect of society, who graces one portion of the mighty collossel with arts,[n] and others with intellectual trophies—that is, the genius of a Bacon Locke & Newton, Johnson & Sam. Clarke. When did the Greecians give form[n] & fashion to the whole body of science? Or to morality and religion their Alpha and Omega? With the Palleys and Stewarts and Sherlocks and Butlers[2] let us rejoice, and leave coulers and blocks to their repose! Sacred be their remains, for they point us to higher scenes where genius & virtue will find the only mede of fame. Yet I must inquire further. What was the mental, or book instruction, of these Artists? What their habits of thinking and feeling? What their moral state? Of the contemporary War-

riors & Statsmen we often form no sublime moral[n] idea   We love to adorn
these artists with pristine innocence; but peradventure, they were of all men
the most voluptuous? If you my dear Nephew, can be artist enough to shape
any ideas from an heap thrown together (because the noise prevented my
reading to profit) *you* shall have a mede of thanks, and answer me long and
learnedly. From the same source of this subject I find one more interesting—
Astronymy.[3] Wraped in mystery as is some of its' history its' light is broad
and grand as its original Creator. Afternoon. I have been looking over Evertt
on the above, and am surprised (and not a little thrown down from my love
of departed genius) to find that for the last 50 years sculpter has progressed
so far.[4] But our pure & divine religion will afford no subjects so poetical as
the fancifull mythology of pagans. As to the "glorious world" it has before—
there is nothing in it like ours since the Reformation. They had no Milton
Paridise lost—nor knowledge of natural philosophy.[n] Love love dear W[m]

Yours with interest & esteem—

M M Emerson

MH: bMS Am 1280.220(75). *Addressed:* Mr. William Emerson / Franklin P. 24 /
Boston / To the care of Mr Waldo Emerson / Cambridge / Mr Cutter. *Endorsed:*
M.M.E. / 1821 X.

rather altogether rather] rather altogether ↑ rather ↓ (*possibly incomplete alter-ation*)

adds to] ⟨derives⟩ ↑ adds to ↓

arts,] arts, ⟨and sciences⟩

form] ⟨soul⟩ form

sublime moral] sublime ↑ moral ↓

natural philosophy] natur⟨e as⟩al philosophy

1. Ennio Quirino Visconti (1751–1818), Italian professor of archaeology, cura-tor of the Capitoline Museum, Rome, and the Louvre, Paris; in 1817 he traveled to
England to examine the Elgin marbles. MME quotes loosely from Edward Everett,
"The History of Grecian Art," *North American Review* 12 (Jan. 1821): 190.

2. With MME's suggested authorities, compare the lists of Jonathan Mayhew
and Simeon Howard, in Wright, *Beginnings*, 148. The less-familiar names in MME's
reading list are Anglican bishops Thomas Sherlock (1678–1761) and Joseph Butler
(1692–1752) and the American Congregationalist-turned-Anglican Samuel Johnson
(1696–1772), first president of King's College, New York (later Columbia University),
who is considered "one of the two most important exponents of idealistic philosophy
in colonial America" (*DAB*), along with Jonathan Edwards.

3. See J. Farrar, "Bailly's History of Astronomy," *North American Review* 12 (Jan.
1821): 150–74.

4. Speaking of statuary, Everett (see above, n. 1) says that taste "sunk" fifty years
ago, but that the present generation of sculptors rivals the Greeks ("Grecian Art," 186).

To Ralph Waldo Emerson

Sat. 24 Feb. 1821

Dearest Waldo,

Has Shakes. never been translated? I rejoice in his empire as far as it is reckless of that learning which some dotards make merit off—but as held on the sensual, regret & abhorr his dominion. It is for a still brighter era to erase his deformities and possibly set a mightier Magician over the witcheries of fancy. But to me—to his old admirers nothing could supply his place. Nor always "dark the woof"—   What pseudo Byron have we here? And a better than Horace or any of him I have seen. His prototype is drawn by the eastern Sage most strikingly.

Oh yes, "an examination of the superstitions of all riegions".[1] What an endless field! Yes, and there does appear a Soul in nature. And when we clothe it in a human form its' head is lost amongst clouds—we behold—we live only in her skirts. If she raises a nation to her bosom, but a few ages, and she covers it beneathe the sod of barbarism and forbids a Mourner to trace its' history. Again she weeps over its' ashes and sends some favorite to remove the pall and bring to light its past glories. In every riegion she had alters whether ensanguined with blood or decked with flowers. If we were to continue the personification we might say she acted like a wise parent in mingling the Northern natures with the south that the hardihood of those might be softened by the refinements of these.[2] Tho' with some it might be questioned, whether the arts were always given by her in love, or as toys to children for a temporary diversion, and which often prove a bane. But to return to your letters (which has so interested me that I could not to bed without reading them tho' two of the best friends even the Frothinghams, laid without a full reading) you represent the Northerners not exactly like Ossian, whose heros are religious and tender, tho' gloomy & vengefull.[3] At any rate they were more intellectual than their effeminate Nieghbours. "Fogs & frosts appear to be the natural element of men of a lofty and vigorous imajanation." In correspondence possibly to your idea of the antients magic, the german philosophers professed "two general opinions" for guides in studying the sciences;—"one that the universe is made after the model of the human soul; the other that the analogy of every part of the universe, with it's *whole,* is so close that the same idea is constantly reflected from the whole in every part & from every part in the whole."[4] Now I confess I have no *clear* idea of this guide to the sciences, and should think it some of the correspondencies of New J. Unless it means that "nature is perfect in a hare as heart"—in a blade of grass as in a planet.— "that considers the phisical world as the basso-releivo of the moral."[5]

You should have told me it was a secret. However I hated to speake of it—but when at W. I remembered you expressed a wish to ask S.A. I might just as well avoided names. However, it is safe. The pamplet is intitled, "The history of meta[s]. and ethical philosophy," the only one I know of from D.S.[6] It is succeeded by Playfair on mechanical philosophy.[7] After all it's conclusions are seldom—it's history not prominent—of course mingled with times, men

&c   And it leaves no permanent impression (except Bacons phi. &c) than the evanesent changes of the sky. The less probably, for my large notes. But the same, nearly, observation Sarah made. She told me that when the President read your Socrates he asked why not a better Locke, Stuart & Pally Scholar?[8] They seem ambitious about you. You can see "Price on morals,"[9] & find that his theories has no more to do with the history than the *nature* of a turf has to the Different Owners from which it has passed.[10] As it is so late nothing can be gained from the state of the existing theories. I prize your letters and now forgive your writing my *name* only on Bulkleys, but I cannot in conscience urge you to take the time to read or write epistles while this is pending. May God bless my dear Nephew & freind.

MME.

I long for Everetts sermon. Rejoiced to hear that work I read with such interest is Norton's.[11] You are pretty high to tax me with bountifull letters. Tell Sib. she is an impertinent hussy. For you, sage Sir whose affectation of "sobriety" may be amused by me I say

"Thy way thou" must "not miss,
Me mine demands." *Never pay* for letters.

Didst thou not tremble at Evertts page on poetry in article of English Uni?[12] Perhaps the new born dignity of your style is indebted to his rod.

I must have Burlamaqui[13]

MH: bMS Am 1280.226(818). *Addressed:* Mr R Waldo Emerson / Har. Univ. / Cambridge. *Postmarked:* Concord Ms / Feb 26th. *Endorsed:* 1820 X / Concord.

1. This and other unidentified quotations in this letter are probably paraphrases from the letters recently received, referred to in paragraph 2, which do not survive and in which RWE discussed ideas for the essay on ethical philosophy.

2. Cf. de Stael, *Influence of Literature*, esp. chap. 8 (1:202–30).

3. Ossian was a legendary third-century Celtic bard who supposedly authored numerous poems, including *Fragments of Ancient Poetry* (1760) and the epic *Fingal* (1761), "found" and edited by James Macpherson (1736–96), who was their real author.

4. "Two . . . whole": de Staël, *Germany* 3:150.

5. New J: Church of the New Jerusalem; i.e., Swedenborgianism. "Nature . . . planet.—": unlocated; " 'that . . . moral' " is from de Staël, *Germany* 3:150.

6. W.: probably Waltham; S.A. is SBR; Dugald Stewart's *Dissertation*.

7. John Playfair (1748–1819), professor of natural philosophy at the University of Edinburgh, was best known for his contributions to the theory of uniformitarianism and was author of *Dissertation Second: General View of the Progress of Mathematical and Physical Sciences* (Boston, 1817).

8. John Thornton Kirkland, president of Harvard College, 1810–28; RWE's second-prize Bowdoin dissertation, "The Character of Socrates," 1820, in Edward Everett Hale, *Ralph Waldo Emerson, Together with Two Early Essays of Emerson* (Boston, 1899), 57–93. Probably Dugald Stewart, whose *Elements of the Philosophy*

of the Human Mind was a standard Harvard text along with Locke's *Essay Concerning the Human Understanding* (1690) and William Paley's *Principles of Moral and Political Philosophy* (1784).

9. Richard Price, *A Review of the Principal Questions in Morals* (London, 1787).

10. RWE used this simile in "The Present State of Ethical Philosophy," 110.

11. Probably Edward Everett, *A Sermon Preached at the Dedication of the First Congregational Church in New York, January 20, 1821* (New York and Boston, 1821); Andrews Norton's "Thoughts on True and False Religion" was published anonymously in *The Christian Disciple*, n.s. 2 (Sept.–Oct. 1820): 337–65, before it was separately printed (Boston, 1820).

12. Edward Everett, "The English Universities," *North American Review* 12 (Jan. 1821): 1–16, is a review of Edward Copleston's Oxford lectures on poetry; see esp. 13–15.

13. Written in margin on p. 1. Jean-Jacques Burlamaqui, *Principles of Natural and Politic Law* (1752).

To Phebe Emerson Ripley and Rebecca Emerson Haskins

[16 May 1821]

My dear Sisters,

Amid the excitement of new books literary conversation, bilious stomach and much self reproach, how soothing to forget all, but the scenes of solitary life, and dwell on the welfare of those, who we think are going an upward and onward course. There I to shall see the sun rise and go down with my bible and book in hand, and the green grave, so sweet and tranquil, in full view. Oh when will you let come? In the rich hours of contemplation ages pass away—fame, wealth and freindship itself becomes idle to the soul when standing on the brink of time— Let us hasten dear Phebe & Rebecca, to prepare every virtue for that grand & immortal stage to which we hasten.

I congratulate you in the good and excellent conduct of Rebecca[1] thro' every day & trial. May God give her grace that every motive of her heart may be as acceptable to Him, as her manners to her friends.

Farewell   Love to D[r] & Ann, after Mr Ripley. My eyes are troublesome. but by the time I leave B. expect they will be well. Adieu

MME.

MH: bMS Am 1280.226(2761) [added to RHE to PBER, dated Boston, 16 May 1821].

1. Letter is to MME's sisters PER and REH of Waterford; here she probably refers to niece Rebecca Haskins, age twenty-one.

To Sarah Bradford Ripley

Boston   Nov. 15 [1821]

How do you all do? Mr Feild talked about the babe[1] at Concord last sabbath. I never knew she walked till I went there. Oh dear Sarah, if I go as I hope to to W— next spring, may I not take her? You can come in the Autumn &

have her if you must. I do really expect you will do as you said that she might go there. I certainly depend on it while she is very little. * * *

Dear Sarah how much I want to see you. I have a deal of time & books & these school masters but I dont learn as I should with you. I dont know enough of your pursuits to say what you are about only in the german language—and as to languages I dont feel the respect perhaps I should for their knowledge. I dont see that linguists & even Mathematicians reason better than others, or have more true & genuine feeling. Besure they are not obliged to resort to the refuge, which you so kindly tax me with, of saying, well, "I shall always carry these notions to the grave". Do tell me how you and my Brother think of Woods last book—& Professor S— sermon? There is a letter of the last to the trinitarians in the New Haven Spectator, very interesting. Brown's works you know are come. I hope Br. will have them for I want to read the one on "cause"—the last I've had.[2]

Will you let me ask my best & first of friends & Sisters, how you reconciled yourself to a loss so great as Daniel's death?[3] How often you used to speake of him—what letters you had— How did you feel at first, and how veiw the subject? Did you mourn for his loss of life and its advantages? You will not need me to apologise—as you know it is a curiosty about *you*—not of the gossiping kind. I heard of his death at Malden. I knew you were superior to any assistance by way of consolation—but I could think of nothing else at first.

It is after 11 o'k—but I dont know when I have felt so miserably out of sorts with myself, and of course every thing as this day or two. So you will not wonder at this rare visit—it will make me sleep I hope.— And yet should you tell me as when in Chambers Street 1815, that this was all reasoning in a circle—all the letter to no point, I should be just as patient as then. But that severity was usefull. I shall never regret the want of all that society can give— for vigor to mind when the body is out of tune. And then what a blessing is solitude if the grave refuses to open. But I wont bore you any longer. What does Mr Farley stay so long at Concord for? Would not Sarah make us a fine hospitable lady to visit?[4] However I neither wish one thing more than another. Life seems at moments so farcical & it's best modes so indifferent— that there is nothing to hope or fear.

Waldo is about to join W^m in the school.[5] *Will it be well?* If you think it a good & respectable way for so young a man why will you not be kind enogh to write me a line.

And by burning *this* request and the rest, of course, oblige one who is seldom stupid enough, not to respect & love her Sister & friend.

Good night dearest Sarah.

MME.

Thurs. M.   Only write at any rate. And one time when we may have nothing else to say, I'll tell you why I am dull. Not that I wish to be otherwise— Oh how sweet the indifference. If any one should talk of you this very day I^d tell him that for all I care you might turn into an Oyster woman & the babe into a fish. What is prettier than a little smelt, which is gen'lly swallowed by a larger swimer? Right sorry am I for the book stuff I've lugged in to this illfated paper. The folks are wise who love "the beggars Nurse & Cesars"[6] to laugh at sentiment. To tell if one feels a gripe of it is truly rediculous.

MH: bMS Am 1280.226(1280). *Addressed:* Mrs. S. A. Ripley / Waltham / Mss. *Endorsed:* M.M. Emerson.

    1. Probably SBR's second child, Mary Emerson Ripley, born 19 Nov. 1820.

    2. Probably Leonard Woods's *Reply to Dr. Ware's Letters to Trinitarians and Calvinists* (Andover, 1821) (the exchanges between the Calvinist Woods and the liberal Unitarian Ware came to be known as the "Unitarian Controversy," or the "Wood'n Ware Debate" [Howe, 14]); Moses Stuart, *A Sermon Occasioned by the Completion of the New College Edifice for the Use of the Theological Seminary at Andover, delivered September 13, 1821* (Andover, 1821) (Stuart was aligned with Woods in the controversy and had published his own "letters" to Channing). Scottish philosopher Thomas Brown's *Lectures on the Philosophy of the Human Mind* was first published in a four-volume Edinburgh edition in 1820; for Brown on cause and effect, see MME to RWE, 19 July [1822], n. 2.

    3. SBR's brother Daniel Neil Bradford died in Mississippi on 3 Oct. 1821.

    4. Possibly Frederick A. Farley, identified by Rusk as WE^3's college classmate (*L* 1:142); probably half sister Sarah Ripley.

    5. Late in 1821 RWE began teaching in WE^3's school for young ladies in Boston.

    6. Shakespeare, *Antony and Cleopatra*, 5.2.8.

To Ralph Waldo Emerson

Friday Night [Nov.? 1821]

    Your *oracular* page may give any or no meaning—& yet I am idle enough to treat it like a sybiline leaf. Why choose to misunderstand?— Did I not say, if we met at all, it w^d be thro' Clarke & Stuart?[1] And about writing, or sublimity, I said nothing—but for the matter of that sublimity of *motive must* form *that* of character. *No implication,* I aver— Neither did I intend any on the Muse— No never was the icicle on Dian's temple chaster— But *now,* I could not seperate her nor you from your condition— No Corrina nor De Stale—not one least ray of their light is about you. *What could you mean,* by connecting those "things in your school" with Parnassus?— But if you are thus awaked write— So would Moore & Byron— But offer nothing to me. *You* may never choose to "exchange the *Lyre* for the Caduceus." And *I* will no more stop for *apples.* Before I ever knew *you,* I did not ask, even a dirge. I invoked nature, with rapture, to sweep over my grave with her roughest elements—for there would be the voice of a *strange* spirit—and there might be a *strange* light to guide the *icy worm* to his *riot.* We then feel as becoming "portions of eternity"—and ask for nothing of time. Yet I do ask the favor, to be remembered rather as dead Cassandra—not prophesying, but praying for thy welfare. Were I a Seer, I should say, that their refusing your meddling with the drama boded good. If your destiny is high—you may reform the Drama of life. You see my prophecy is not decided. And I do request you as a gentleman never to represent me as thinking your situation nessecarily degrading. Tho' I do think meanly of women, compared to men, yet you need neither the Styx nor shield. Now that I have made my peace with God, for having indulged a sort of doating pride & fondness, and come to be able, to view you as *one* among a number, who must encounter the ills & temptations, belonging to a large & incomprehensible plan, I still regret, & know that the coolest observer would do the same, that a youth of your easy & poetical habits should be placed in so easy & rhymlike circumstances. Were your veiws of your, sometime intended, profession above, far above those whom you admire—were you deeply engaged in study—or did you only enter the school from the side of a parent (whose loss for your sake I daily mourn) or from that of a Channing or Webster, you might comparitively adopt the language of Saurin, & "spread over them hands purified in the innocent blood of Jesus."[2]

Sat Night   Were it optimal[n] to get without the precincts of an infinite Being, whom *nature* proclaims the design of his moral creation to be *ultimately virtue*, and points to future rewards & punishments with almost universal consent, would it be good taste? Is it good taste to press on our companions the respect we feel for animal propensities tho' we mention only those of sleep & eating? Am I misinformed or are not these subjects the most often to say no more tolerated among scholars & such like when they would be joking & merry? A little of this with an occasional boast of *pride* is found among the best, probably, to accomodate their superior genius to the multitude of ordinary minds.

Sab M.   I have been telling Ned that I think every man has a right to sleep when & as he likes (& that the best sleep the longest) but that no man has a right to jest about sleep or times before those who consider the subject as connec[d] with morals. And he says, *you* were not laughing about it at tea time as I thought. Still let the appendix go. If I have not made a proper use of the *Caduceus* as an emblem of clerical profession, let me know.

Aunt Mary.

Tues. Eve.   Dear Waldo,   It has scarce seemed worth while to send you this—as sentiment is much to a Recluse & can be little to you. Yet to *appear* neglectfull to yours.

Well will it not be better for you to get rid of the sight of so irritable a lady? I w[d] off for your sake but my own determination is bent to stay till I conquer every regret & forget you. This distance is my wish & it will rid you of me almost wholly. The snows are coming & we may away to Waterford. *What shall I do about* W[ms] *note?* I am not glad.

MH: bMS Am 1280.226(824a). *Addressed:* Mr Waldo Emerson. *Endorsed:* X 1821.

optimal] *possibly* optional (JMN *1:195*)

1. This letter, even more obscure than usual, should be read in the context of MME's continuing dialogue with RWE, source of many of the allusions. See RWE to MME, Nov.? 1821? (*L* 1:104–5), to which she seems to respond, and his response to this letter, Dec.? 1821? (*L* 1:105), Rusk's notes to both letters, and RWE's transcriptions from MME's letters, *JMN* 1:195–96. MME may intend Dugald Stewart, the Scottish philosopher and theologian, but possibly refers to Moses Stuart of Andover Theological Seminary, where she would prefer RWE to study divinity.

2. Jacques Saurin (1677–1730), French Protestant preacher known for his rich eloquence and his clear and moving style; a six-volume English edition of his *Sermons*, translated by Robert Robinson, was published in New York in 1804; this quotation has not been located.

1822

To Charles Chauncy Emerson

Byfield   Ap. 3   1822

My beloved Charles,

* * * It is a fortnight since I left my Sister and Nephews. * * * And now I am at a loss here to fullfill my part of our intercourse. I did not ask what kind of subjects, or in what form they should come? Shall I compliment your understanding or excite your affections? That is shall the subjects be grave or gay serious or trifling? * * * If they wish me to write they must do as you have done. If they ask how far I have proceeded on my pilgrimage to Waterford, tell them to the house of Dr Parish.[1] My regards to your Uncle Farnham;[2] he well knows the old parsonage which has stood the lives of so many ministers, and where *Judge* Parsons[3] was born. The old Dummer Academy he remembers, and the full curled wig which is to be seen in the portrait of the English Govenor in that venerable Mansion. And the elegant mass of wealth which the Parson's farm exhibits.[4] Save these places, this *Byfield* seems hardly inhabited—never was solitude better personified. This old house with the aged trees thickly set in the front resemble a ruin, and when the stars shine thro' the naked branches, they remind us of these bright spirits which may be looking on the dark and wandering inhabitants of earth. If they ask how I came to turn aside to sojourn among these strangers, I can hardly say, it seemed so undesigned. I was going out to walk the day after I came to N.P. and Mr E.[5] asked me to take horse & chaise whenever I wanted   And his wife and myself called here. The D^r introduced me to his wife as Dr Ripleys daughter and the lady who 25 years agone took care of him when he was one day sick at Concord, whom he had often desired to see &c &c   All this was pretty—

Figure 12. The Reverend Elijah Parish (1762–1825), minister at Byfield.

He then spoke of D^r R—'s kindness, and then of my Brother and finally of my Nephews— There was no bigotry—and every thing was delightfull, and in one moment I forgot the prejudice I had received formerly of boarding in Byfield, and told them I was getting out of the way of east winds, what if I should adjourn my eastern route for a few weeks? Mr, Mrs & Miss Parish (who constitute the family) urged it so kindly that I almost agreed to return immediately. However, I set about sending to Kennebunk to learn the name & place of my future hostess, but a trifling circumstance prevented the letter, and I came the same day I wrote to William. The D^r forbears whether from his own or my sake, to touch on certain subjects of theology—tho' *I* should like *his* discussions. He likes better to speake with me of the pleasures of poetry and the geographical situation of Etna. Once indeed he spoke of the levity and coldness which finds or makes itself a shield under the broad wing of unitarianism. But I as feelingly regreted the mischiefs which result from the long faces & cant of some of the orthodox, which he also allowed.

Now, my dear Charles, will you write to your kind Aunt Sarah[6] and put all this page into your letter And put it in the post office with much duty to my honored Mother. If you cannot ask Waldo to. There is no post office here but you may direct to N. P. or here till you hear from your affectionate Aunt

MME.

All will write when they *feel* in the mood, and their letters will be welcome whether answered or not. You must pay no regard to my lack of answers. Direct Care of Dr P. Byfield

28. Would you, my beloved Child, see the "windy notion" of power and the *"fade"* of human glory—contemplate thrones & laurels in history—not in the phantoms which visit like dreams of wakefull life. I am reading Bacon's english kings.[7] Ap 3. I was very impressed last week with that history

MH: bMS Am 1280.226(640). *Addressed:* Master Charles C. Emerson. / Boston / Mss. *Postmarked:* NEWBURYPORT / MASS / Apr 5. *Endorsed:* M M Emerson / Apr 3^d '22.

1. Orthodox minister and historian Elijah Parish (1762–1825), MME's host at Byfield.

2. MME suggests William Farnham of Newburyport is now living in or near Boston.

3. Theophilus Parsons, born in Byfield in 1750, served as chief justice of the Massachusetts Supreme Court from 1806 until his death in 1813. His father, the Reverend Moses Parsons, minister at Byfield, 1744–83, was a friend of George Whitefield.

4. Samuel Moody (1726–95), known as Master Moody, a cousin of MME's father, served as first principal of Dummer Academy, Byfield, from 1763 to 1790. The academy was named for Lieutenant Governor William Dummer (1677–1761), who, soon after his marriage in 1714, built an elegant mansion in Byfield. He left all of his real property to found a grammar school. His portrait is reproduced opposite p. 82 of John L. Ewell's *Story of Byfield* (Boston, 1902). Eben Parsons (1746–1819), another son of

Moses Parsons (see above, n. 3), made a fortune in shipping; in 1801 he returned to Byfield and built a magnificent estate, known as Fatherland Farm.

5. Possibly cousin Samuel Emerson of Newbury or Joseph Emerson of Byfield.

6. Probably MME's half sister Sarah Ripley, but possibly SBR.

7. Paragraph written on outside, the portion dated "28" [Mar.?] probably written first, perhaps as an "Almanack" entry. The Bacon title is probably a misattribution: Francis Bacon wrote *History of the Reign of Henry VII*, first published in 1616; it was later published together with the histories of Henry VIII, Edward VI, and Queen Mary, all by Francis Godwyn, bishop of Hereford (London, 1676).

To Ralph Waldo Emerson

Byfield   May 24 [1822]

My dear Waldo,

I can truly say with the idoet, I write because *asked*. But how relate "facts or news or make extracts"? What indeed are *facts* to me? There are those who are young and learned, and enough of them too, who can creep thro' the entrails of spiders and pick over the petals of a flower, and say they are finding the way to a designing Cause. No harm—very innocent employment—if they dont make their rest with them. The dandelions are peculiar; Miss P.[1] shows me in each petal or blade being a perfect flower itself. The little children will soon amuse themselves with seeing its downy leaves fly away. Now my dear Waldo, if your imajanation wanders into riegions of *sentiment*, dont blame me. I will keep to *facts*.

And I have been fortunate this week to find a Visitor here from India, well versed in its literature & theology. He showed us some fine representations of the incarnation of Vishnoo. They are much akin to Greecian fable—and from his representation I believe the incarnations to be much like the doctrine of transmigration. At bottom of the histories of the incarnations is often the doctrine of the universal presence & agency of One God. I will send you some of those he gave me, if you have not met them. None of the ten which occupy 3 or 4 pages are equal to an incarnation of Vishnoo, I once read, but can't tell where. There was a stronge resemblance to the xian facts. Our Stranger gave the history of the conversion of *Rheumas*[n] (I *think*) a learned Hindu, to xianity from his own researches. He studied much in the Vades[2]—found that in antient times his religion was purer & better than now—however he forsook it, and adopted for a time mahometism—disgusted with that, he found an english new testament, & from that he became a believer, has since read it in all it's languages, and without any bias from education is a fixed Unitarian, and an enthusiastic admirerr of the high toned philosophy and morals of our blessed Master! But you will or have heard of him in all unitarian publications   I wish you would let me share news of him.

As to books, I've been only where you have, sometimes in Merlin's cave and Homers shades, sometimes. Was delighted with the speech made by Ulissys to the shade of his mother. Pope's—*is it better* in original? Have been surprised to find in the 10 book of Juvenal some lines very like to the concluding ones of Johnson's "vanity of human wishes." Could Johnson have borrowed from the heathen?[3] They are finely translated by Dryden, but not so fine as inlarged and inriched by the christian. And what should accompany these very lines, but a borrowed note of Gibbon's, remarking that a heathen is never consistent, sometimes all doubt, and again all resignation. No wonder a gentleman of his severe uniformity in religious faith is scandilised by the natural abberation of a heathens opinions. I speake of a note in Gifford's translation of the satires.[4]

You seem to estimate more highly Gibbon's elegance than you did, one day, when I was admiring his style.[5] As to Mosheim, you are not singular in disliking his manner,[6] tho' his introduction does not pretend to any thing more than a compend. And the facts are so interesting that I've never discovered the faults with which you so heavily tax him. What has been alluring in his plan, was the tracing events to their real or supposed causes, the philosophy of which, and it's importance, no one will dispute. If he is said, often to assign wrong or imajanary causes, it is better than to make no attempt of the kind? He leaves the Reader at liberty, and stimulated to find truer ones. But whether from associating the historian with the woes he relates or the cause to which he devoted his long & laborious life, or the renown he gained from Princes, I dont wish to think of him disrespectfully.

What am I to think of the little vol. of Russian poetry?[7] It dont make its own way as one w^d expect from it's subjects & Authers. It dont make one yearn to put forth a hand on the (invisible) wheels of the universe and pluck a purer nobler nature, or mode of existence.

It shall be just as you say about showing any thing you favor me with. Tho' I am not able to see the least danger of the same person reading or hearing the same performance repeatedly. *Webster* in his addres[8] relates the same sentiments he had in Congress or elsewhere. But dont send me any *worlds*[9] which I cannot communicate somthing of their wealth. Letters I should like for my self. And trust you will send them whether you hear from me or not, as writing is often a task. I have your class poem[10] & will send it with other things the first opp^y. If perfectly convenent do call at Mr Parson's on Dr P.[11] & ask him to a family cup of tea. I repeat this notice, not because of its' weight, but perhaps your Mother is not at home likely none of you. Can you tell me any thing of Hunts? How does Mr Dewey like being alone without Dr C.? Why did not Upham go South?[12] What is thought of him? Or rather what is it fashionable to think of him? An accident fell on my 3^d page and I have more paper probably than you time.[13] How does Charles get on in books manners & scholarship? Do you or any one read his letters to me?

Farwell, dear Waldo, may every thing good await you prays your Aunt
MME.

Please to send books in a trunk in your chamber if the Dr able to take them.

MH: bMS Am 1280.226(820). *Addressed:* Mr R. Waldo Emerson / Fed. St. 26 / Boston / Hon^d by Rev. Dr Parish. *Endorsed:* [on p. 2] 1821.X.

Rheumas] *possibly* Rheumer (T)

1. Probably Hannah Parish, a schoolteacher in Byfield and daughter of MME's host, Elijah Parish.

2. Vades] *for* Vedas, the sacred writings of Hinduism. MME's "Rheumas" seems to be an attempt to spell "Rammohun"; see *L* 1:117 n. 23, and Alan Hodder, "Emerson, Rammohan Roy, and the Unitarians," *SAR 1988*, 133–48.

3. *Odyssey*, bk. 11. RWE to MME, 10 June 1822, chides her for forgetting that Samuel Johnson's "Vanity of Human Wishes" "is professedly an Imitation of the 10th Satire of Juvenal" (*L* 1:115–16).

4. *The Satires of Decimus Junius Juvenalis: and of Aulus Persius Flaccus*, "translated into English verse by Mr. Dryden and several other hands" (London, 1754); William Gifford, trans., *The Satires of Decimus Junius Juvenalis*, 2 vols. (Philadelphia and New York, 1803); the note containing Gibbon's remark is appended to the end of satire 10, 2:137.

5. RWE read five volumes of Edward Gibbon's *History of the Decline and Fall of the Roman Empire* during this period and may have commented on his style in the lost "Wide World 5" (see below, n. 9).

6. Johann Lorenz Mosheim, *An Ecclesiastical History, Antient and Modern, from the Birth of Christ to the Beginning of the Eighteenth Century*, trans. Archibald Maclaine, 6 vols. (Philadelphia, 1797–98). RWE to MME (? June 1822) says he's "amazed at the insipidity of Mosheim" (*L* 1:118).

7. Probably John Bowring, trans., *Specimens of the Russian Poets*, 2d ed. (London, 1821–23; Boston, 1822).

8. Probably Daniel Webster's *Discourse, Delivered at Plymouth, December 22, 1820* (Boston, 1821).

9. RWE's earliest journals were each titled "Wide World." MME had borrowed "Wide World 3" and perhaps others; here she may be responding to ideas in the lost "Wide World 5" (10 Mar.–14 Apr. 1822).

10. RWE's "Valedictory Poem," read at the Harvard exhibition on 17 July 1821.

11. Possibly Theophilus Parsons, Jr. (1797–1882), who, after his graduation from Harvard in 1815, read law in Boston and began practicing law in Taunton in 1822. In 1823 he became a Swedenborgian, and in 1848 he was named Dane Professor of Law at Harvard. "Dr P." is probably Elijah Parish.

12. Hunts: unidentified. Orville Dewey served as colleague to WEC at the Federal Street Church, Boston, 1821–23. In 1821 and 1822 Channing was traveling in Europe for his health. Charles Wentworth Upham, a Harvard classmate of RWE's, had received a generous offer to serve as a private tutor in Kentucky but turned it down "as an interruption to his studies" (*L* 1:118).

13. First two pages of letter written on two sides of a single leaf; MME then began a new four-sided sheet, but wrote on only two sides.

To Ralph Waldo Emerson

Byfield June 26 —22

You do not "ask" but impel me to speake of that Muse—so loved—so wild—so imaginative so dear to me. Is she become "faint & mean"?[1] Ah well she may, and better oh far better leave you wholly than weave a gargland for one whose destiny tends to lead him to sensation rather than sentiment— Whose intervals of mentality seem to be rather spent in collecting facts than energising itself—in unfolding—incorporating its budding powers after the sure yet far distant glories of what Plato, Plotinus and such godlike worthies, who in the language of St Austin, showed "that none could be a true philosopher that was not abstracted in spirit from all the effects of the body." &c &c—more than I dare to impose. Yet it is verily most valuable to find the principles of the human constitution, the same when developed by philosophy in all ages & nations—to find that after all it's disections at bottom, is an insatiable thirst for what they well denominate "a state of mind being unable to stay, after it's highest flights, till it arive at a Being of unbounded greatness & worth"![2] Oh would the Muse forever leave you, till you had prepared for her a celestial abode. Poetry that soul of all that pleases—the *philosophy* of the world of sense—yet the Iris—the bearer of the resemblances of uncreated beauty! Yet with this gift you flag—your Muse is *mean* because the breath of fashion has not puffed her. You are not inspired, in heart, with a gift for immortality, because you are the Nursling of surrounding cercumstances— You become yourself a part of the events which make up ordinary life—even that part of the economy of living which relates in the order of things *nessecarily* to private & social affections, rather than publick & disinterested. Still there is an approaching period I dread worse than this sweet stagnation— when your Muse shall be dragged into eclat—tho' like Ceciro perhaps, your poetry will not be valued because your prose is so much better. Then will be the time when your guardian Angel will tremble. In case of failing—of becoming deceived & vain—there will yet remain a hope—that your fall may call down some uncommon effort of mercy and you may rise from the love of deceitfull good to that of the real. Had you been placed in cercumstances of hard fare for the belly—labour & solitude it does seem you would have been training for those most insidious enimees which will beset your publick life on every hand. How little you will be armed with the saying of a french divine of highest order that "it is safest for a popular character to know but part of what is said." You provoke me to prose, by ulogising Ceasar & Ceciro. True, the speech you quote is sublime, & instanced by christians.[3] But for him, for that Tyrant (whose only charm, the love of letters was not accompanied by enthusiasm) it was mere rant; or he was thinking of the egg from w'h Venus sprung (w'h was preserved by fishes & hatched by doves) to whom he was a most debauched devottee. As to Ceciro, one wants to admire him— but different accounts forbid—tho' none are favorable enough ever to place him one moment beyond the imperious controul of passing events. Defeated in adversity & without any respite from age or experience pursuing—begging other people to let him be praised. Is not this enough to neutralise those effects for the publick, as we know not their motive to be beyond emulation? His eloquence it is true is glorious—but himself remains an object of pity, & the only apology for becoming the meanest of Scavangers, is that in company with genius, is the love of fame, & *he knew* of no object hereafter to feed it. Such are the men you are more excited by than by your noble & heroic Ancestor! "Pomp of cercumstance"   Mercifull Creator, this child so young, so well born & bred—yet so wedded to sounds & places where human passions triumphed! When he knows that spots the most famous, even by thy own appearance, are swept out of record! This is one of the few whom I desired my new friend not to ask me any thing about; for I wanted to forget what I had lost. And for some time I neither read his papers nor wrote to him. And what is still worse, this portion of sentiment will probably disgust. Yet write to me, dear Waldo, give me the pictures of times & Empires gone—where? Why did you not assign the probable causes of Florence's superiority to sister states? Were they not the Medici family? Yet of that family, the last members that I remember a glimps, were Leo the tenth & Catharine who instigated the hottentot St Bar. massacre. And of Cosmo their Grand father, is it not related that he held his influence over the citizens by loans of money?[4] Not that *this* was bribery, or that the most disinterested motives did not move him to controul the people. But whoever wants power must pay for it. How unnatural—one man asks another to give him up his rights—   This is the nakedness of the trafic, & if there is ever so much fraud or violence after ages produce slaves enow to celebrate their Conquerors. As to words & languages being so important—I will have nothing of it. The images, the sweet immortal images are within us—born there, our native right, and sometimes one kind of sounding word or syllable wakens the instrument of our souls and sometimes another. But we are not slaves to sense any more than to political Usurpers, but by fashion & embicillity. Aye, if I understand you, so you think

   In the zeal of writing I began with the last sentence of your letter, & have just read backwards till I am now for the first time in cool possesion of the whole letter—   Glad to hear you complain of fine splendid expressions without proportionate fine thoughts. But not that in order to judge you must read all the pieces or rather that you intend a reform which will oblige you to go thro' such bogs & fens & sloughs of passion & crime. True one ought to sacrifice himself to the publick, but how long & poisonous the execution compared to other Martyrs. Still if by plucking up those principles of human nature w'h have made dramas agreable to the populace & w'h have been sometimes considered as drains to human vices or perventatives to worse pleasures—if you pull down old establishments w'h have found places in almost every age & nation of civilized or semibarbarous life, why may you not undertake it? To men in general it would seem gigantic. And to me who am, if possible, more ignorant on the history & character of the Drama than any other subject, it seems a less usefull exercise as it respects the *reformer* than any scientific or literary pursuit. Mathematics or languages remain with one for use and ornament. And all the universe of facts w'h are collecting will some time or other *prove* somthing. And if they dont, they are apoligies for higher exercises. The picture of a bird is better than the idle jokes & saturine gossip of ordinary socety. There is one idea of dramatic representation interesting—that of Eichorn's respecting the Apocalypse of St John. The learned German, you know, beleives all passed in Patmos in scenic order.[5] And why may not this be a key to many revelations? In the infancy of the world men were taught by signs. It would seem that the higher & last mode of instruction from Heaven applied to reason as well as sentiment. And I am glad to escape from all kind of earthly dramas.

To lessen the fatigue of so long talk I will insert a sweet morsel of Hindu poetry w'h made me think of those lines on "Idealism."[6] Their philosophy is as it respects matter the same as Berkliasm you know. Farewell your Aunt
MME.

Of dew bespangled leaves & blossoms bright
Hence! vanish from my sight!
Delusive pictures! unsubstantial shows!
My soul absorbs one only Being knows
Of all perceptions one abundant source,
Hence every object every moment flows;
Suns hence derive their force,
Hence planets learn their course
But sun & fading worlds I view no more
God only I percieve   God only I adore!

The first two verses are equally fine.

I have not read over the epistle—   Confide that it will not be condemned for fanaticism in politicks or metap.s. Wish you to read the inclosed w'h is an obligatory thing & if incorrect write it again & let it be sealed so as only to meet its object solus. When any one needs a walk they can take it. Please to get my eastern money exchanged & pay discount & send it by Mrs F.[7]

To a certain Muse.[8]

I dont love to address you ungratefully for the first time—   But I return your present   Not because I am unable to discover any merit,—not that I do not love thy favors. Yet I must bid the farewell. Thy favorite is in a situation & will be more & more so where thy gifts, unless sterner & holier, than hithertoo will only injure—perhaps he will make the fire bells known to thy

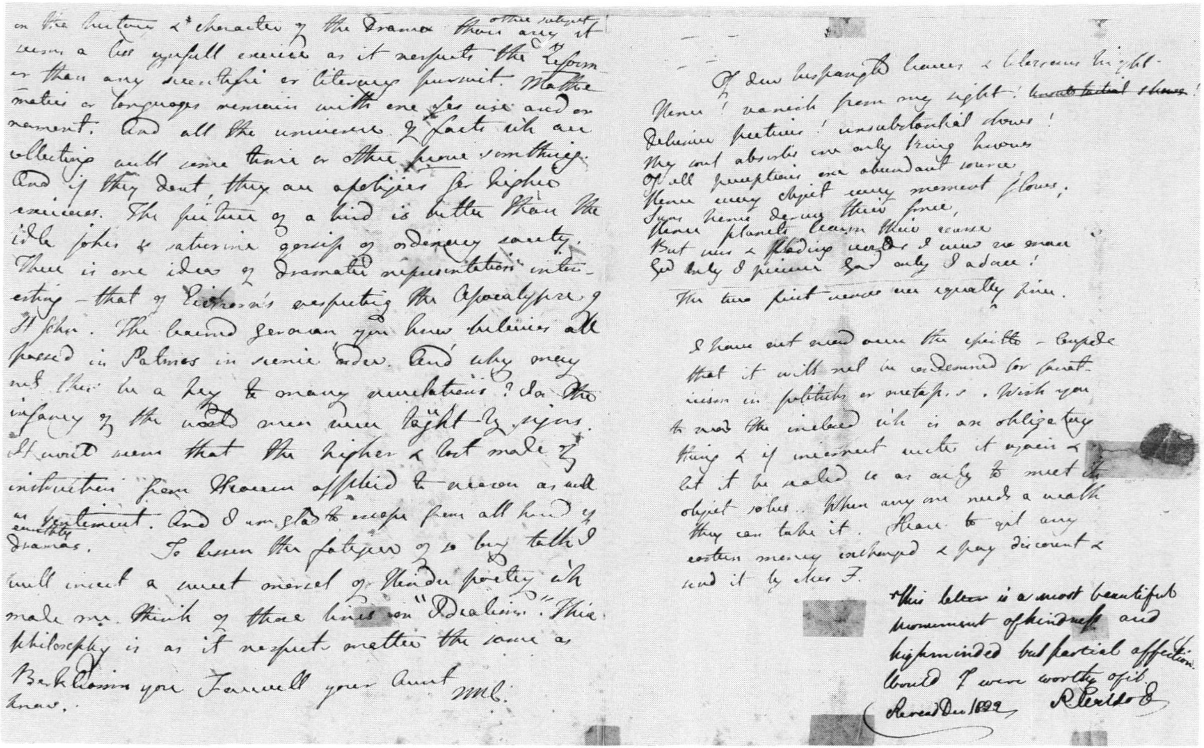

Figure 13. Letter to Ralph Waldo Emerson, 26 June 1822. Manuscript pages 6 and 7 of Mary Emerson's lengthy discussion of the "Muse"; note Waldo Emerson's comment in lower right corner. By permission of the Houghton Library, Harvard University, and the Ralph Waldo Emerson Memorial Association.

visitations— Oh let him alone—should he ever stoop to flatter or be praised. True, he appears to unusual advantage—but may be pride called forth by the prophecy of friendship—not the ripening of those germs of dignity w'h have budded amid folly & limited society. *And he may be redeemed*—from the unfavorable effects of place—a double redemption may call him to true glory—it will add to the joy of my latest pulse. And if thou art any thing but a name—a phantasy—I may converse with thee then— And thou wilt see that there is not a spark of resentment in the bottom or top of my heart about his condition— No habit of dictation—scorn it—s^d scorn to complain of my own disap^t—had I ever bro't him in debt— But it has been him who has lessend the dolorous tedium of this unwholsome air—pleased my taste— & made me a debtor. But accostomed to sacrifices, this will cost but a few more tears. Do you ask if I am fearfull of pleasure—or too proud to wish excitement? It concerns not me to answer such like gentry as thyself. I may be too proud to be willing to be told, even by S.A.^9 "that no one could feel the interest & admiration for him I did." No, so lessening an individuation of his character—I will not unite any hopes too. Only last night—the bittrest enymy of his future rise might have liked to have seen him so easily fixed in female socety. *What has* (if thou knowest anything of cause & effect)—what has done the most injury to men & women since the allegory of Adam? Sexual influence. I would not wisper it to any one but thee, but what (do I know), robbed him of the highest honors of Gov^t but the waste of hours with female socity at F. Place ^10 where the sex was not forgotten in mind. My present design is to have no intercourse, but of common mingling, unless he meet me on my ground—about those relations which unite us to a common Center. Any little extract from Clark or Stewart bestowed on decrepitude of sight will be received with gratitude. And I promise never to deride school unless it is needlessly forced on my feelings.

MH: bMS Am 1280.226(828). *Addressed:* Mr R. Waldo Emerson / Solus / Fed St No 26 / Boston. *Endorsed:* X / M. M. E. June 1822 / Poetry / Cicero / Medici / Drama / Cop.

    1. Possible allusion to RWE's letter of 10 June (*L* 1:114–19). Other references indicate she also responds to another letter from RWE, which does not survive, answering hers of 14 June (MH: 827, omitted here; mostly printed in *JMN* 1:199–200). See *JMN* 2:373 n. 67.

    2. Probably Saint Augustine; quotation not located.

    3. Rusk suggests that the speech was "the famous passage from Cicero, *De Senectute*, XXIII, 84" (*L* 6:333).

    4. MME counters RWE's praise of Florentine politics as "high minded wise & patriotic . . . far above the spirit of any other state" (10 June 1822; *L* 7:118) by reminding him of Pope Leo X (1475–1521; pope 1513–21), a son of Lorenzo de' Medici the Magnificent (1449–92); Catherine de' Medici (1519–89), daughter of the second Lorenzo de' Medici (1492–1519) and widow of the French king Henry II, has traditionally been blamed for the Saint Bartholomew's Day massacre at Paris, 23–24 Aug.

1572, when thousands of Huguenots were killed; and Cosimo de' Medici (1389–1464), grandfather of Lorenzo the Magnificent.

5. *The Christian Disciple* 4 (Mar. and Apr. 1822) printed "An Account of Eichhorn's Illustrations of the Apocalypse," which claims "it was the design of the author of the Apocalypse to give a scenical representation—an actual exhibition to the eye of the spectator" (66).

6. Probably RWE's poem "Idealism," dated 12 Feb. 1822, in "Wide World 3" (*JMN* 1:81–82). Rusk identifies the "morsel" that follows as an imitation by Sir William Jones, "A Hymn to Narayena," published in the *Asiatic Miscellany*, 1818 (*L* 1:116 and *Life of RWE*, 93).

7. Probably Mrs. Frothingham. At this point, at the bottom of the leaf, RWE writes, "This letter is a most beautiful monument of kindness and highminded but partial affection. Would I were worthy of it. Reread Dec. 1822   R. Waldo E."

8. A note in Cabot's hand states that the remainder of this letter, on a separate leaf, was found with the letter of 26 June 1822. However, it is endorsed 1821.

9. SBR; the following quotation may be from a conversation or a letter.

10. The Emersons lived at Franklin Place, Boston, from Apr. 1820 to Apr. 1821.

To Ralph Waldo Emerson

N. P.   July 19 [1822] Friday

Is it possible that you talk with so much elevation of *history of universe*— [1] How (artfully I fear) contrive to rouse me from sweet tranquility—   I keep you from that—? No that that is the glory of existence—   But in the name of truth & glory, are you well versed in *Stewart* & his host of noble predecesors—   Have you read *all* of Brown's three vols of lectures to say nothing of *Cause & effect*? [2] But what is more harrassing—with the most apparent simplicity talk of the sympathies of society—they are needed, it is true, to form the "common mind" to principles of action—   And the irritations of vanity are better concealed in a bustle—one mortification drives out the memory of another—and finally the mind looses all that vivid sensibility which nature first gave

Besides how you abuse my opinions expressed in last—are mathematics—labour at languages like draining the native soil—   No I had rather my young[n] favorite w[d] wander wild among the flowers & briars of nature— would scale the "tempel where the Genius of the Universe resides" & mew herself in the rays of distant stars, while you are getting her a home more permanent—   But adieu. I am "asked" to stay a day or two with Madam & Miss B. & she is reading me "Annals of a Parish" &c— [3]   I have no eyes— Came here monday to look for some friends in the stage & took lodgings with Cousins. [4] Found yours wednesday w'h I had sent for repeatedly. Bro't home Brown w'h finished my eyes without reading him half. Instead of flattery I tho't you found so much the reverse that you w[d] not write. Yet was prepared to retort that if I had called your fancies of mind *budding*—it was true for you were little acquainted with metaphi. &c &cc

You write sneaking short letters. Mr Farnham w^d send a packet to N P. any time

Your aff^t frind & Aunt,
MME

Love to Sister and all.

MH: bMS Am 1280.226(821). *Addressed:* Mr R Waldo Emerson.— / Federal Street. N° 26. / Boston. / Miss Lucy Searle. *Endorsed:* M M Emerson / 1821 / New-buryport.

young] ⟨old⟩ young

1. Perhaps in RWE's "Wide World 1" (1820; see esp. *JMN* 1: 5–6), but more prob-ably in a letter from RWE that does not survive, written in response to her letter dated 26 June 1822. Letter endorsement "1821" is probably incorrect: 19 July fell on Friday in 1822, not 1821; MME probably did not go to Newburyport in 1821; and "last" letter (see paragraph 2) seems to refer to 26 June 1822 (compare remarks on languages and mathematics).

2. Thomas Brown, *Lectures on the Philosophy of the Human Mind*, ed. M. New-man, 3 vols. (Andover, 1822). Like many other philosophers (including Dugald Stewart, Richard Price, Thomas Reid, George Campbell, James Oswald, and James Beattie), Brown was spurred to respond to the skeptical conclusions of Hume's philosophy. In 1804 he published *Observations on the Nature and Tendency of the Doctrine of Mr. Hume, Concerning the Relation of Cause and Effect*, revised and enlarged as *Inquiry into the Relation of Cause and Effect* (Andover, 1822).

3. The Bromfields of Newburyport; *Annals of the Parish; or, The Chronicle of Dal-mailing, during the Ministry of the Reverend Micah Balwhidder*, written by himself; arranged and edited by the "Author of the Ayrshire Legatees" (Edinburgh, 1821).

4. Probably Elizabeth, Martha (Patty), and Samuel Emerson, all of Newburyport, whose father, Bulkeley Emerson (1732–1801), was an older brother of MME's father and a Newburyport "bookseller, stationer, and publisher of pamphlets" (*IpsE*, 124). The two women conducted a private school. According to a younger cousin, MME often spent time at Newburyport with these cousins, who considered her "bookish, rather strong-minded, [and] not nice in her habits" (*IpsE*, 174).

To Ralph Waldo Emerson

25. [July] Eve [1822]

That some of the best intellects have been infidels is certain—but does that argue that the natural course of *mind* is to scepticism? Does it not rather go to prove that the legitimate direction is to it's Source? But that led astray by passion & superficial science & false philosophy, it becomes bewildered? But what else but spirit emanating from Spirit could enable those daring Infidels thus to speculate? Are they not a proof of the falshood of their own theories? All *this*, weakly conceived & illy worded, carried from the last sentence of your last but one, w'h contents I touched on in 6 or 7 pages.[1] That sentence expressed a most abhorred thought—"that instead of intellectual excellence you hoped to be a good man." Now tho' I don't believe a word of what you

say—   Yet the provocation is, that moral & intellec. grandeur are at variance—when they are nessecery to each other as you well know. They were
embodied in the character & *actions* of the great model of human nature—
and the pursuit of future glory, as connected with morals, was the object of
his mission not only for a world, but himself. Away with your offerings at
his shrine if they come not like the emblem of those laid up in the antient ark
pure gold & polished without, & celestial manna within. His cause is worthy
of master spirits, & tho' superior to the decorations of arts & sciences—yet
accepts them & immortalizes their gifts by the sign of the cross. If in heathen
ages *valour* was so often called *virtue,* it is to the credit of xian times, that
every thing grand is allied to morals.

I write because I have opp^y to send Wide worlds. I send them my dearest Correspondent, because I must send them at some time, tho loath. They
gave much interest to my companion, who read them all without rising. We
felt curiosty at the 8 page of 4 No. "*What was that thought?*[2] What could it
be—honor—letters—poetry"? I hoped—it could be nothing transient—   I
thought it must be of nothing short—nothing below those endless relations
which indissolubley bind the heart to it's Maker. Was I right?? Or you had
given the thought a clothing it did not deserve. I do not like to send them
by Mrs F^{mn} as her feelings w^d be hurt in not gratifying a curiosty somewhat
wakefull. Too delicate I can be in this way. And to account for *your tho'ts* I
never pretend. He is reserved, I've no right only to guese.

Cannot you tell me—have you not looked within the tempels of antient
idolatry—   I^n see you at the door, you might turn round, & give me (purring
without the outer porch) some notices. I say what is the cause that no alter is
there to Poets—no incense—no worship—while the Inventors of other arts
mean & only usefull, the Warriors & Butchers have their priests and nations
of devotees? And yet what everlasting sources of joy does the poetry of the
soul supply. It is at the feet of the Muses that the timbrel & harp & sackbut
should play. And what notes like these

> "He comes, he comes—
The power of philosophic melancholy—"[3]

It is for such bards to inspire presentiments like those described by a resurrection to a new Heavens.

26 July Friday   Reread yours this mor^g after writing the above, because I
could not help it, & thinking your fortnight must perform it's wonted quar-
entine (of some kind) before you wrote, I left it till I had a letter to answer.
Which letters occupy all my capasity. It is possible, pardon me, that there may
be profound thinkers among the great men who like Hobbes are not historians, and you not know them. For you *seemed* ignorant of that host of Recluses
who in solitude have neither been "peevish nor selfish." But if Ste. condemns
these "illustrations," you mention, then he condemns all reasonings *apriori* it
seems??[4] Which would forever mortify & limit certain thinkers? If *generali-*

sation is nessecary to a statsman & genius, which are surely to the man who has a patriotic soul (but I'm told statsmen are frequently mere tools & what is worse the best of them generally become disturbed in their sense of truth) then metaphysics must have early & deeply imbued their minds. Your term "mere philosopher" is so vague that I cannot reproach you for abusing the sacred name. As to the history of *universe* being vague— Oh graves of gentleness spare my temper, when he knows what I meant—when he would have felt his understanding affronted if I had explained, &—his gaity clouded if I had dwelt on, if I had touched those marvellous relations which that history imbraces. Neither would he, if frank, speake of every *tho't returning to self* when in a metaphi. sense it does not there originate & should never *descend* unless like the phoenix to *ascend* in fire. Let me ask, if history & the philosophy of mind could not be both cultured, whether the most difficult should not stand first in claim? Please to explain or reconcile the "extending an interest (to the many you see) beyond what is *general* or *romantic*"? Perhaps I ought not to be so curious about such opposite terms, when you do me the honor to feel so sleepy. I will excuse *such* frankness. It was then you entertained so ordinary views of hill & dale. You *may* find their effect *positive*. It is not the absence of competitors—it is the sight of those angelic "scales" w'h were held out among the stars—where all distinctions "kick the beam" but those of w'h you can speake better than I.

But it is the lamented Brown, if I understand the glimps I have, who will lead you to the pearly gates of philosophy. I long to know if you will not blame the looseness of his style— & the unnessecary novelties and hypotheses. I have no one's opinion—yet think it less profound & more explanatory (forgetting in my expectation that it was for youth) than I expected. But some of the last vol—some pages thro' the whole are beyond my power to praise. One of the gems w'h reminded me or rather came to mind by your "jewels." "There is an education of man continually going forward in the whole system of things around him; & what is commonly termed *education,* is nothing more than the art of skilfully guiding this natural progress, so as to form the intellectual & moral combinations in w'h wisdom & virtue consist." Vol. 2, page 167.[5] And he leads us to the gates of knowledge thro' the flowery & blissful paths of poetry. This, be sure, was unexpected—to find ourselves at home by his illustrations from old acquaintance. But we are not *always* pleased to find so much allusion to Pope, whom we did not respect the poet fully,[n] when the mind is made up for labour. Do *you* tell me what you & your Master Hallam think of the religion of middle ages?[6] He will not be of my opinion. Undoubtedly the times colour the common mind—but there were pure & bright spots in those dark nights—not merely from comparison. As we find extremely different exampels of virtue under the same cercumstances. There does appear indubitable evidences by the historian of minds making their way without winds & against tides. But what is the cause that after the sleep of ages the human mind should arouse like a giant refreshed by slumber? Here is a succesion of events which cannot be connected—surely any more than that night should be the cause of day. This indeed must be among the arbitrary connections of the Auther of socity??

Thanks many, & long remembered, dear Waldo for the vindication of your-self in regard to Ed. I can't but differ from Warren.[7] A voayge is generally the last resort of the phy. & to delay it when there is a hope is strange. He speaks of a weake cons^n.[n] Never was a healthier before that cold.

The lady who takes this is sister to Mrs Stocker in F. Place.[8] You can send me any thing, perhaps, if prefer to be obliged to Mrs. S. thro' me. As to Mrs Kast, till you are able, as you will be, to redeem yourself & throw a lustre on both sides of your house, it does seem best not be seen in connection with her. I called at Mrs. M—s anxious to see her daughter a fine woman   Mrs S. was there and asked me about my family in connection with her boarders—there were quere looks &c. I boldly mentioned the connection & not a word more was said. I was weake enough to regret that it s^d be known till you were older.

Adieu your friend & Aunt

MME

MH: bMS Am 1280.226(829). *Addressed:* Mr R Waldo Emerson / Fed St 26 / Boston / Honored by the care of / Mrs Marquand. *Endorsed:* M. M. E 1822 / X / Cop.

F^m] *probably abbreviation for* Frothingham

I] ⟨it seems as if⟩ I

respect . . . fully,] respect ↑ the poet fully ↓ ,

cons^n.] *probably abbreviation for* constitution

1. MME to RWE, 26 June 1822; see esp. n. 1.

2. On p. 8 of "Wide World 4," RWE muses that "a beautiful thought struck me suddenly, without any connection, which I could trace, with my previous trains of thought and feeling," which he does not divulge (*JMN* 1:96).

3. James Thomson, *The Seasons*, "Autumn," 1004–5.

4. Dugald Stewart's *Dissertation* begins with a critique of Jean d'Alembert's method of "mapping" the sciences and his "Encyclopedic tree" in the "Preliminary Discourse" to the *Encyclopédie*, which d'Alembert coedited with Denis Diderot. See also MME to SAB, 4 May 1818, n. 3.

5. Brown, *Philosophy of the Human Mind*.

6. Henry Hallam, *View of the State of Europe during the Middle Ages*, 4 vols. (Philadelphia, 1821). RWE's essay "Thoughts on the Religion of the Middle Ages" was published in the *Christian Disciple*, n.s. 4 (Nov.–Dec. 1822): 401–7.

7. Illness forced EBE to withdraw from Harvard in Mar. (he was in his second year); EBE to RHE, 15 May 1822, from Worcester, where he went to "recruit," boasts that he is now able to walk and feels stronger than at any time since his arrival seven weeks earlier. RWE to MME, 10 June 1822, says that Dr. Warren has advised Edward to travel for his health and that he is considering going to Germany (*L* 1:117).

8. According to the address, a Mrs. Marquand.

Figure 14. The Reverend William Emerson (1743–76), father of Mary Emerson.
Courtesy Concord Free Public Library.

To Charles Chauncy Emerson

N. P.   July 26 [1822]   Fri. P.M.

* * * I wished you were here wed. Cushing addressed the Wash. Ar. Company.[1] There was much excitement— Ministers & people of all sects attended. His youthfull & handsome[n] appearance & fine speaking, were[n] not lost on me. So far other wise that I was affected to tears— Now what could be more ridiculous—his haraunging a few sturdy soldiers— I only hoped that no one saw me. But you will soon bethink yourself that it was not the ideas of Cushing or what he said, for I did not hear much, only of the glories of 76 a little. But he reminded me of other Orators—of my prize getting boy— of that patriot so enthusiastic who was sacrificed by the events of 76. Who would now have so largely enjoyed the blessings bestowed by that liberty he so loved. When my father left me I was within 6 months of the age you were, at the loss of yours. When you came with your brothers for the last time & stood by age at his bed, his look so tender & anxious rested on your little face (which seemed to me conscious of the scene) with increased regret. Cherish the memory of scenes w'h soften the heart, and show the frailty of prospects the most flattering. I felt not half the anxiety for you when clad in that little grey tunic you turned your orphan steps from the chamber as now that you are pushing your way to the world. And whenever your idea gives me real pleasure, it is the remembrance of some few moments after going to bed last winter, you discovered symptoms of anxiety. I have no right to say of what nature—but I hoped & still hope they related to an interest more noble than any below. If you do not act altogether below the gifts of reason & affection— of the demands of Him who will not be trifled with in his requirements these moments of solicitude[n] to please Him to improve his gifts must be habitual.

Adieu dearest boy.

MME.

You may direct here or at Byfield. I am in a place more like Country than Town & made very pleasant. Waldo need not be thinking the papers lost for I dont see the need of sending them & if I cant find paper to do them up I shall not. Love love to Sister & all.

MH: bMS Am 1280.226(642). *Addressed:* Master Charles Chauncy Emerson / Fed. St. / Boston / Honored by Mrs Marquand. *Endorsed:* M M Emerson / July 26 / 1822.

handsome] ⟨beautiful⟩ ↑ handsome ↓

were] ⟨excited⟩ ↑ were ↓

solicitude] solictude *in MS; possibly* solitude *intended*

1. Caleb Cushing (1800–1879) graduated from Harvard College with honors in 1817, passed the bar in 1821, and was practicing law in Newburyport. His *Oration, Pronounced at the Request of the Washington Light Infantry Company*, in Newburyport, 24 July 1822, in commemoration of the company's twenty-second anniversary, was soon published.

1823

To Charles Chauncy Emerson

Feb. 10   1823

Dear Charles,

You ask how I like W's piece in Deciple?[1] I have not had the pleasure to see it. How do you? You have supposed me moved and so I have lost some letters—let me have one soon. I have been some how kept, and now stay while H. R.[2] goes—   And am ashamed to say how long the time looks before I am east.

What shall I say to fill up? I have met with some young men whom I thought promising—   One especially, Stearns of the sen. class in Cambridge.[3] At first I avoided him, thought he was an owlish looking gentleman—but heard him converse a little and was ashamed of prejudice. His manner then appeared the calm of a mind sattisfied in itself without notice and when called on, delivered his opinions with admirable independance, taste &c. P. Evertt[4] was one subject—and tho' he had not been like myself an admirer yet of his divinity his views seemed very correct.

S. Alden speaks in high terms of Bancroft—says that when he first came home he was pleased with his tour[5] and thought every body would be—that he received such chills as to keep him very quiet now—that after solicitation he converses with great effect—   The best test of his preaching she can give is the excitment was so great that she collected the young folks round her in walking home after Church, and talked & laughed so loud, that her husband told her she must let go his arm. The subject was the immortality of soul. This perhaps, our fine scholastic and beloved Sarah dont so often recognize in her german books, or she would not have been so elevated. Comparing B. to Evertt, why she said E. was so & so great in argument—but some how one gets tired of one. Now had Evertt been more occupied with the subjects of religion than the eloquence of display—had his hearers thought less of him and more of one in the *form of man,* would they ever have tired? Would he himself ever have left the pulpit if he had been enamoured of his subject? I shall never cease to regret it. His genius, and attended with ever wakfull good sense, is like other genius' who have left us their glory—may be played with and admired as children do their baubles—but when he shall have passed the ordeal of justice and found to be influenced by piety & benevolence how indescrible the emotions of pleasure he will afford. When you see me seeking Rousseaus Memoirs[6] & such like, it is always with an eye to contrast the meteor-light of Genius with that of a Mrs. Holloway which is like that of the dawning morning.

Hannah is going and I have no more to say, but love to your Mother and brother W^m and want to hear how B.[7] is.

Wish my Sister to burn the enclosed note which you may read if you like. You must write while I am here as correspondence is not so convenient at distance. Love love to H. St. 26.

Your aff^t Aunt
MME.

MH: bMS Am 1280.226(647). *Addressed:* Master Charles Chauncy Emerson / Miss H. B. Ripley / Boston. *Endorsed:* Feby 10 '23 / M M Emerson.

1. MME responds to an undated letter [30? Jan. 1823] from CCE (MH: 30). For RWE's article, see MME to RWE, 25 July [1822], n. 6.

2. Probably Hannah Buckminster Ripley (b. 1804), daughter of EzR's cousin David Ripley of Greenfield, Mass.

3. Samuel Horatio Stearns (1801–37) of Bedford would be ordained pastor of Boston's Old South Church in 1834, but he preached only three sermons before leaving for an extended trip to Europe, where he died.

4. Probably Professor Edward Everett, Eliot Professor of Greek Literature at Harvard from 1819 to 1824. MME to AB, 3 Sept. 1814, expressed her admiration of his preaching: "From young Everet (the Sucessor of Buckminster, the more illustrious star) I have heard sermons of late so powerfull that all the vissisitudes of life lost their power—religion alone triumphed, and the glory of the resurrection morning appeared to open in visions of blessedness on the eye of faith" (MWA).

5. S. Alden is SBR. Although CCE's recent letter was addressed to MME at Concord, MME may be writing from Waltham, where she would have stayed with the Ripleys. George Bancroft (1800–1891), who graduated from Harvard College in 1817, returned to Boston in July 1822 after five years' study in Germany.

6. Probably Rousseau's *Confessions.*

7. Nephew RBE, whom MME had cared for when he became unmanageable in the fall of 1821.

To William Emerson[3] and George Barrell Emerson

24   New^y port   March 1823

My dear W^m

You will all like to hear where & how I am.[1] I wrote to your Mother, but so many are the chances whether she gets it out of the office, or the other lady by the same name that I'll send it, or some other, when farther removed, I shall want some kinder *postings*. How do you all do? I have not thought so much of you as I shall when in those "tongue"y woods, one often tries a sort of reminiscence as well as *futurition*—if there be such a word *Sir*? Yet the full occupation of time in visiting old friends & being pleased with new, has made me forget the pleasant time I had with you all; and for you, if we differed, the mutual forbearance calls to memory the additional & most permanent of all pleasures. Mrs Frothingham reminds me time is come for me to go for my dinner—this eating medicine so much is quite inconvenient—and I vary the place almost every meal. The D^r supplies me with drugs & freinds with food.

Miss Bromfield's society is so influential that I *almost* forgive her *romantic* connection.[2] I've met with a poetess, whom you may find in N.P. herald.[3] I joined her & went to *read* the first hours acquaintance—but left her with the sage advice, that rose-buds fade & dews evaporate. But as you are not *wholly* averse to jokes, I will insert one of the epitaphs which she has written on all the young gentlemen; just premising that a lady opens the door to much satire on herself by *dispairing* of the lives of mankind.

> Lie aside all ye dead
> For in the next bed
> Reposes the body of Cushing,
> Who crouded his way
> Thro' the world as they say,
> And perhaps now he's dead he'll be *pushing*.

Give my love to 26 Hawley St. I shall write to all when I have successfully fought my stomach enymy. If any write to me direct here, be it ever so long, till you hear of me else where. If I could steer away from sea coast to W—d I s^d be willing to imitate old Esau I believe.[4] But this *duty* of dining out. Adieu dear W^m may ten thousand goods surround you says your Aunt

M M Emerson

Dear George,

As you are so destitute of attentions, I charitably bestow a bit of paper. And will entertain you by gossip. Tho' the *Cushing* fever subsides, yet I hear much of his passion for a Miss Bartlett, who shuns him with a Daphne-like zeal. But he is romantic, & says were it mere indifference he would not hope, but expects to turn hatred to love. Miserable calculation—a sin against nature. Does he not know that the probability is, that if he suceeds, much of life will be past in remembering that the *pride* of perseverance & of being *pursued* was the cause, and that the first prejudices of women are often the most lasting?

I did not say to you any of the *good bye* I felt, tho' I thought it likely we might not meet, till you were harboured in years, & could sympathise in my weather bound voayge—or in that state where I should be better furnished with arguments against your emulation system of education. *There,* my dear Geo., we shall learn the true nature of mental qualities, and whether the love of distinction can be put to purposes of high & lasting virtues. If so, I shall (tho' choosing even there a contemplative state) joy to see those youthfull spirits in whom I have been for the past year *too* absorbed, spreading a bold & enterprising sail. But for distinction in that high and unbodiless state, what a perpetual self abandonment of present interests is justly required? May you so live as that the success of that great future shall bear a happy proportion to that of the present prays your affectionate Relative

MME.

You will I hope meet with *Emily Sullivan*. A richer flower seldom blooms on our cold sterile earth.

Monday 24.

My love to Ralph. I feel so desirous to steer a due north course that if my W—d folks encourage me I shall never see K—[5] but will send his letter. Tell Bulkley to be a good boy.

MH: bMS Am 1280.220(75). *Addressed:* William Emerson A. M. / Corner of Fed. & Williams St. / 26 / Boston Mss. *Postmarked:* Newburyport / MAS. / March 25. *Endorsed:* Miss M. M. Emerson / March / 1823.

1. MME had recently left after spending four months with her families at Boston and Concord; she is boarding at Newburyport with "Cousin" Frothingham.

2. The intention of MME's friend Ann Bromfield, then in her late forties, to marry the Reverend Thomas Tracy of Biddeford, Maine, was recorded 4 May 1824.

3. Hannah Flagg Gould (1789–1865) of Newburyport, whose periodical verse was collected by her friends and published as *Poems* (1832).

4. After Esau, son of Isaac and Rebecca, was tricked out of his inheritance by his twin Jacob, he settled in the wilderness on Mount Seir (Gen. 26–32).

5. W—d: Waterford; Ralph Emerson (b. 1806) was GBE's younger brother; the family lived at Kennebunk, Maine.

To Ralph Waldo Emerson

Space & time   [23 Apr. 1823]

Dear Waldo,

Women & *inconstancy* & *caprice* you may think of at this unexpected letter from a discarded correspondent—for you did not accede to any thing *future*, I believe. But I fear you & Ed. will think me stuffy—and nothing was farther from my intention than to recall trifles w'h I could not blame you for—for surely you cant dislike me half so much as I do myself. Forgive all, & let us part at the alter peculiar to amity. I never did wisper a complaint or claim after I left your parents and applied to strangers for employt—and finally set down in their neighbourhood in ignorance & solitude unenlivend. God be praised I never envied nor blamed them. But I could not see S. A.[1] without telling *her,* who had seen my interest, that with you I had failed of sympathy.

But it is from Ed. & you inevitably born to distinction (& him wholly to a world in w'h I can take no interest) that I part & humility sanctions it—it is not from you in your present most enfeebling condition—but you who may draw a golden lot in the urn of love & honor or be led by the "precious Jewel of adversity" to a high character in religion. My sister was good enough to tell me your intentions of professing publickly your faith in xianity[2] In less liberal days it was the right of the meanest member to inquire the motives of the Noviciate. If I doubted yours, I would not use this obsolete privilege. Yet I may ask, *what you mean by this rite?* Is it a monument rendered sacred by ages, by holy martyrs who have sealed their faith by blood, at its alters to the *history* of its Founder? In this light it is important, and every one who comes to honor it with new trophies of evidence and bind himself by religious vows to strengthen & purify their weight is a welcome member—his youth his talents—his erudition render his sacrifice to its' avarice most valuable. And if his influence is ripe, no haste can be to great for this view is all that the subject demands. Or if he comes without being conscious of adding strenght to the claims of this duty finds here the only place where his devotions can be kindled and his allegiance to the great Example of all that is great & good sealed, surely he comes worthy of its aids. Or if he views the subject as some of the wisest have done—as both the historians appear to represent it, as signi-fying a sacrifice the most solemn and wonderfull—as a symbol of that scheme which "solves the enigma of human nature." That such an acknowledgment of it, in this light, seems nessecary to partaking it's benefit—that the earliest compliance with it's conditions—abjuring all the pride & frivolous pleasures of life—the strongest ties which do not accord with its meek & selfdenying spirit are alone worthy the disciple. But I cannot think that loose or crude opinions respecting it are so impious & dangerous as Divines (and in some sort Dr Clark) represent.[3] But that one suffers under a superstitious or cold & formal administration of it is certain, and they are often tempted to say, if the rite means nothing more than many teach, why pass so many hours to a vague purpose unless it be the *key* to a profession? But it does seem wise & safe to study the character of the Founder & the nature of his offices? Whether the scheme applies to the affections, & thus extends its influence; and whether human nature is required to arrive at virtues, w'h it cannot, without a super-nal assistance. It is from such worthy men as your pastor, that we learn the difficulties which attend the liberal scheme, and w'h the indolent would make us believe are nothing. Mr F.[4] regretted that W^m should appear so ignorant of the difficulties of a clerical profession. Pardon this needless tax on your time, and accept my grateful remembrance of many fond recollections of your kindness & society, & prayers for your highest good.

MME.

I am between P & W.[5] shall then write as I promised Sister. (But I have nothing to send as the very existence of this letter is needless to mention.) if ever the roads & weather permit going on.

Carry the inclosed to Geo.[6] & burn it instantly after he has has read it & may you prosper as you are silent on it's contents. Good will to Ed. Bliss—we love to quarrel   Better to me than peace with many folks. Of course you are to read the note.

MH: bMS Am 1280.226(825). *Addressed:* Mr R Waldo Emerson / Boston / Mss. *Postmarked:* Windham Me / April 23. *Endorsed:* M M E 1822X.

1. SBR.

2. Endorsement "1822" is an error: RWE's public declaration of faith at First

Church, Boston, where Nathaniel Frothingham was minister, was on 31 May 1823 (*Life of RWE*, 100).

3. Samuel Clarke.

4. Frothingham (see above, n. 2).

5. Letter posted from Windham, Maine, which is between Portland and Waterford.

6. Probably GBE.

To Charles Chauncy Emerson

W— *May 12 1823*

Here are the mountains w'h seem to shut out human passions, and tho' I love my dear Charles, they seperate one from all City sympathies, more than oceans w'h bonded one in a Metropolis. This morning was such as you love— I rode far on horseback. The mist rose from the waters & mingled with the blue haze of the mountains, and formed that soft atmosphere w'h invelopes the traveller in a new & complete solitude—while the vapoury mass ascends to pass an alembic, which will give to some gaudy bow it's richest hues from what so lately hung a withered mildewed shrub. Those who are fond of drawing analogies from the material world, would say, that thus from the discordant mass of social society will arise new combinations of beauty and order.

Do you remember any thing of this place? The grave yard (now one of the most populous establishments) on the east, and the brook on the west, were the bounds of your freedom? Well that very brook runs and lowls as merrily as tho' you were not approaching to the cares and powers of manhood. Before that time I shall see you here. The journey from Portland is fine. After 20 miles from thence, you will have the white hills in front for a number of hours. On the summit of them you may find the snow, as I did, in many a gigantic shape, and fancy the hoary forms to be the ghosts of the preAdamites, revisiting their former abode & ridiculing the dwarfish resemblance of its pristine[n] majesty— Or with a poet's eye, you may imajine them the Antient proprietors of Parnassus who again had found their own mount—but filled with ire at finding it covered with toy shops, were streching out their arms to sweep away the pictures & pozies. Or if more modern in your taste might esteem them the true descendants of the primitive Owners & that Milton himself was ("tho' blind a mighty boldness in his looks")[1] was driving into his own limbo the trash he found, and pursuing the apostate Muse of a Byron into the place of the fallen Angels?

If any remembrance clouds the pleasure of having seen you of late years, it is that of your devouring so many books of taste. I said nothing, for it w[d] have lessened your pleasure—and great names are affixed to such habits— but would not they have been greater? more original & profounder xian is hardly questionable (tho' their digestive powers were stronger than others), if they had been less voracious.

Figure 15. South Waterford, Maine: the road from Mutiny Brook (location of the Elm Vale farmhouse) to town. Courtesy Waterford Historical Society.

On the subject of xianity you may wonder, my beloved freind, at my comparative silence. It was not more from my incapasity and unworthiness as a deciple of that glorious scheme, than an intention to avoid familiarity with it, or to connect with your first impressions certain modes of faith, w'h your future investigations might reject. And how many stronge minds have, amid the flux of opinions, let go their hold on some of the highest principles, in shaking off their associations. And in these views I thought I had the sanction of your Mother. Your infant pleasures & pains were linked with the idea of an omnipresent Being. That sole idea is enough to awaken hopes & fears, which would distract the firmest mind, were they not counteracted by habit & sense. Indulge in solitude the idea of such a Being as nature teaches and what apprehensions are awakned? Does a child need any other to lead him to ask for safty? And can there be any other rational way of instruction than to consult the book which comes with an athority like the bible? If your responsibility is greater than some—so will be the virtue   For what is the religion of education, memory & an intimidated conscience, perhaps, compared to that of choice, one's own reason; love of God & his will for thier own intrinsic beauty? Tho' surrounded with every advantage, you will excuse this leave taking letter from one whose sweetest remembrance is sometimes with you.

Your aff^t Aunt—MME.

* * *

MH: bMS Am 1280.226(650). *Addressed:* Master Charles C. Emerson / City of / Boston / Massachusets. *Postmarked:* Waterford May 14. *Endorsed:* M M Emerson / May 12 '23.

pristine] ⟨former⟩ ↑ pristine ↓

1. Adapted from Pope, "The Temple of Fame," describing Homer, "Tho' blind, a boldness in his looks appears" (line 186); see *JMN* 4:437.

To Edward Bliss Emerson

Oct. 7. [1823]

The notice you gave of exhibition (whatever it meant) was not received with indifference.[1] I have often wished the few last days spent with you had been otherwise. Yet when we part with our Brutus'[2] it is best to be stout, and besides there is much danger of appearing to hang on others. Nothing could accord less with a lasting seperation than the illtimed jest I sent to *William—it meant nothing.*[3] You still recur to "a jest & a conversation"—tho' you have each so fully exculpated the other from blame. And I from having any thing to forgive. Yet I have never wished that accident undone—   I had determined to live on in the Cell, and pride was not hurt I do believe. Modesty should have made me more diffident in being seen with you, undoubtedly. And especially after you intimated being hurt at meeting with Miss Bancroft[4] when you were obliged to say, "an Aunt was a near relation." *It is very slight;* but you must never claim it again, my dear Sir, for I have avoided respectfully the name of nephews. And when called to answer any inquiries, w'h lead me to speake of the sucess of one of the best of mothers, it is very sweet to do her justice. If I have failed to do it, to her sons, it was from a strange notion that her influence was intirely calculated to make men above trifles. She was the first idol in the female line I had. But my manners were to her what one calls a "sort of crucifiction." And I passed years of solitude without seeing or *thinking* of her or her distinguished prosperity. And I loved her so well always, that I had rather find myself wrong than her—for I was never patient with the faults of the good.

But I have no claims—never, never had any since I was tow years old— *never mentioned any*— Yet was weake enough to solicit you to tell this to Waldo that *he* might not seem so *disclaiming. But I am not what I was in earlier days. Then all of dress & accomplishments was sacrificed to what I thought a xian publick should require. And lastly, what is dearest to woman the protection of a man of honor & talents, whose faith & politicks were not sound. Yet it *seems* I have not been decorous and nice, & it is very likely character may not stand very well with others, than Miss B.   But I am afraid it w^d not rise[n] if better understood. Erasmus says "one must praise themselves if no one else does." I do it always readily; at this time the more, that you may regret nothing for me. That in losing all, I lose none of those things which are offered to women who have trod the highest paths of fame & fortune. True, I shall never share the publick sympathy in the eloquence of any of you. Nor s^d I, if you had been ever so attached. In forgetting what I owed to myself, and thrusting about to see what I had never done & never should gain, it was because I was about to depart. If you love genuine honor you will not choose to live injured in the opinion of the meanest, and will turn aside from the most busy pursuits, to hear this gurrulous adieu, to find all is kind about the thoughts, & that in saying I have lost nothing of just claims I meant only that I was early familiar with the names of my sisterhood, & with those fine images of fancy; it may be I have less[n] calculated. But the *first* motive to part with relatives has been one w'h disarms age & want of every terror. To those who justly prize their existence for future ends, will laugh at receiving their *bread* from publick or private charity provided it comes not from those with whom they might have cultured a nicer frendship than alms. Nor has time given a terror to dependance of this honorable sort, but still clothes the cercumstances of extreme discipline, to one so faulty, with coulers of stronger virtue. * * *

With esteem & godswill[n]
Adieu[n]

MH: bMS Am 1280.226(751). *Addressed:* Mr E. B. Emerson / Sudbury Mss. *Post-marked:* Waterford Me   Dec 3ᵈ. / Cambridge Mˢ / Decʳ 17—forwarded. *Endorsed:* Miss M. M. Emerson / Oct. 1823 / Recᵈ Dec. 1823.

rise] rise ⟨so high as it might⟩

less] *possibly* o'er (*T*); *possibly* o'er *written over* less

godswill] *MS torn; T reads* goodwill

Adieu] *MS torn; no signature.* Large tear on p. 3 of the MS results in so many lost words as to render the final paragraph of the letter unintelligible.

1. EBE read an exhibition oration, "Encouragement of Literature, the Duty of a Patriot," at Harvard, 23 Aug. 1823. His letter does not survive.

2. "Brutus'" is MME's way of pluralizing a name that ends with *s*. Rusk cites CCE's quotation of a letter from MME written in June 1834: "'Could you see the brief letter of Waldo—the appointment to meet in some other world,—Philippi—you would say this is like the transient interests of life"; Rusk then explains, "The allusion might . . . be to the story of the appointment with the evil genius told in Plutarch's life of Brutus" (*L* 1:415). Cf. Shakespeare, *Julius Caesar*, 4.3.275–86.

3. MME to WE³, 27 May 1823, mentions that CCE describes EBE as being "so full of joy" that the "lightest bubbles dance merriest when the ocean is most troubled" (MH: 1067).

4. Probably a sister of George Bancroft.

To Ralph Waldo Emerson

Oct 24 [1823]

Dear Waldo

You surely dont insinuate that mysteries were *designed* "to puzzle all analysis." "The ordinary effect of an inexplicable enigma"¹ can do no hurt, for while it remains inexplicable it tells no bad tales of any operations of nature illusory or contradictory. Is it not wholly sattisfactory to reason, that all it discovers and *knows* indicate design & good ends? Were not the laws Newton discoverd inexplicable before his day? And did *he* ever complain that he remained as ignorant as the vulgar of any connection between what he called gravitation and solidity—or motion and thought or where the power resided? The bible theist exults in the secrets of what is called *nature,* for after finding a God (tho' it were only such as the wise heathen had) he is sattisfied, for the present, with the immutable limits of his own understanding, and finds every thing to invite hope & curiosity. Besides, he worships with new ardor at every new proof that this God of nature & the bible are the same, as *this* never offers to explain metaphysical difficulties, but the consequences of those evils w'h have arisen from these difficulties are no more to be charged on the bible, than the bigotry & sceptiscim of the Infidel on the book of nature?

That portion of misery w'h appears in slavery involves some of the most difficult questions, and by the old xian have been quieted some how or other   One thing seems certain that the state of a negro slave is not so despicable as that of the *one* of Court favor. The greater inigma may be found in the nature of the tormentors? Is it not the same constitution w'h is capable of an abstract love of God and being universal? Is this affection to virtue by process or indefinite inspiration? Is it less strange that this soul can adore the Creator, while it finds much to hate in itself & somthing in every body? Would it be folly or manicheanism to suppose there was somthing of evil in the nature of things, or laws w'h God was rather controuling than distroying? The Edwardians[2] would ridicule it? But of all the phenomena w'h exhibit this uneven fragment of creation, none perplexes so much as the case of one who believes, & has received living tokens of distinction from God, yet thinks of Him "with thoughts *cool & calm.*" It has not been the part of *reason* in the highest orders to be calm on such a subject, & the heart *cool there,* must appal the greatest admirers of genius.

I can make nothing of Channings saying "Rev. was in the order of events as much as any thing."[3] What order? matter? like the growth of apple or animal? Civil? But all such order has been to return to barbarism? And was this the cause of the new Rev. sinking into obscurity & corruption in the Dark ages? But all we have to do with rev. is its miracles as they are the foundation of our faith. Now *they* must be of a different order of things from any thing we experience in the stated order? In the order of the whole scheme of universe they may be natural and undoubtedly are provided for, tho', to us they appear wholly unconnected. And the miricle of xianity was, we are emboldened to believe, a unique in that vast order. The Jewish oracle represents it *as a stone cut out of the mountain without hands whose power should cover the earth.*[4] "An effect so singular"[5] that Hume might object to the statment of the preacher without leaning on our holy writ. Of that old scotsman you surely feign respect. He has been robed of his necromancy as a miricle enymy, & of late found shallow in metaphisics, so that curiosty to read him is blunted.

But no suspicion of D[r] C's being affected by German illumination, or in danger of humanising what should not be, has set me on my hobby of inquiries, w'h you can have no time to answer, but to show you that your ingenious mode of breaking the spell of silence has suceeded, tho' the *charm* has lost none of it's power.[6] Is it not better to be weake than wise with the show of sulleness? And before the wand of a Magician Maker it might be idle to stand.

Your Muse it seems averts her favors.[7] She may have the decernment of Diomed,[8] and dislike your keeping company with so many *mortals*— And finds your senses too "well fed" to have celestial intercourse. In turn you may spurn her youthful gifts. "Time, nurse & breeder of all good"[9]

In haste adieu   MME

MH: bMS Am 1280.226(830). *Addressed:* Mr R. W. Emerson. / Roxbury / Mr T. Haskins Jun. *Endorsed:* M.M.E. Oct. 1823. / X.

1. RWE to MME, 16 Oct. 1822, asks, "What is the good end answered in making these mysteries to puzzle all analysis? What is the ordinary effect of an inexplicable

enigma?" (*L* 1:137). MME to RWE, [23 Apr. 1823], refers to Jesus' sacrifice as "a symbol of that scheme which 'solves the enigma of human nature.'"

2. Followers of Jonathan Edwards.

3. MME loosely quotes RWE's report of WEC's sermon for 12 Oct. 1823 in his letter of 16 Oct. (*L* 1:138–39). Rusk (*L* 1:138) suggests comparing "Evidences of Christianity," WEC's *Works*, 188–220, esp. 193, 212, 213.

4. Dan. 2:45.

5. See MME to RWE, 20 Jan. [1824], n. 3.

6. See RWE's insinuation that a woman flees with the "design of being followed" (*L* 1:137) and his barrage of questions in the letter of 16 Oct.

7. RWE complained of "few visitations of my coy & coquettish muse" (*L* 1:137).

8. Also Diomedes: Homeric prince of Argos and one of the heroes at Troy.

9. Shakespeare, *Two Gentlemen of Verona*, 3.1.245.

1824

To Ralph Waldo Emerson

Jan. 20— [1824]

My interesting Correspondent has excited more curiosty to know wherein he differs in *opinion* from those "young divines," than surprise at their slender thought and easy faith.[1] These are the natural result of the times—of enervating literature, luxury & ambition, and were foreseen, when so often your patience was tried at my bitter impatience with the spell binding Evertt. He had been my idol—and I still looked forward to one who had lived free from those shackels of education & monotonous exhortations w'h hasten the youth to show his love of liberality—one who would preserve his publick vows, till his opinions of the Auther & scheme of xiainity were fixed & his affections interested. But forever adieu to recrimination. In intire solitude, minds become oblivious to care & find in the uniform & constant miracle of nature, revelation alter & priest. The cause of truth will lose nothing from the desertion of disloyal subjects—tho' very likely these gay people believe more than they acknowledge—like children make a noise in the dark to keep of spectres. One would like to have them desert openly and form a novel religion. Why cannot some of them have ingenuity to recall the antient philosophy of the Hindoos? Their Maya seven winds—their eagle fledged gods—what a delightfull machinery for poetry—true, the sublime devotion w'h these sensitive hindoos felt might not so well assort with modern views. The probability possibility[n] is that the tide of xian faith may return swelled with accessions to the calvinistic party—w'h will make some demands on our resignation, who are attached to unitarinism. But if truth should be found to preponderate there, *well*.

Did you write me on the 4 of No. besides the 11? In that you respect Newton—& speake of the divine operations being "irregular, not in the promulgation of gospel, w'h was to incompass some mighty design, but in the *moral* such as justice with injustice" &c &c   Now I did not perceive how the giving the means of salvation could be called "*material*" & the designation of other events "*moral*." And of "irregular" destinies—do you refer to the guilt & innocence w'h have promiscuously appeared & covered so much of the earth with blood, that it has been termed by divines, since the reformation, the scaffold of the divine Justice?[2] A moderate phrase yours surely. The simple biblest, however, has the key to decipher these dark characters to all the purposes of the present life. If God be infinite, he is infinitely good or evil?? The latter impossible in the nature of things, and by the testimony of facts—that of the *certainty* of moral distinctions being immutable, the greatest fact? And whenever a mind is completely anxious to attain the perfect rule of virtue, there will never be found any insuperable difficulty in matters of faith? I am reading Hume's essays—   Never was more disappointed—expected to find new mental excitement & many moments of inspired thought. You must tell me whether there are any direct answers to his epicurean argument about the universe being a "singular effect"? That this Out law, who finds every thing unconnected uncertain & illusory, and "the effect totally different from the cause,"[3] should cast such a mist that we cant get hold of his sofistry is irritating. And yet we know that if one of the least effects of nature are beyond human power it argues one superior to all visible powers? Is an effect to be equal to the Cause? But what other proof of such a Being (as natural religion teaches God to be) that the mind is so formed as to be unable to get rid of the ideas of immensity & eternity? And can such a creature surrounded on all sides with infinity be able to get out of it and compare by analogy this illimitable universe? Is it not a contradiction in terms by w'h he perplexes us? But I am not able to give up neither the argument by analogy. If we find a bird's nest we know there was a builder—and we know by the same way there was an Artist to the world—tho' we have other apriori ways w'h Hume very consistently detests. "In judging of the future without experience is taking a step" &c[4]   Why? Is it not the very constitution of the understanding—its use & design—thus to do? In morals how cold & dead? Cicero w^d have known by all the immortal gods, that such a man was never touched by the love of virtue or glory. Yet he is of use   he discovers to those, who may too often love to linger around, what they feel to be their primary relations to Deity, that however infinitly valueable, will not secure them against infidel times—that they are often weak except in the responses of conscience, against temptation & the disorders of the world, & give not sufficient assurance that the future may not resemble this, or be much more liable to ill from the suceptibility of an unbodied state. How far is he exceeded & put down by the letters to Voltaire

Good night.

MH: bMS Am 1280.226(831). *Addressed:* Mr R. W. Emerson / Roxbury / Mss. *Postmarked:* Waterford Jany 21st. *Endorsed:* Unitarianism / X / M. M. E. Jan. 1824.

probability possibility] probability ↑ possibility ↓

1. MME may be responding to lost portions of RWE's letter of 11 Nov. 1823 (*L* 7:122–24); quotations at the beginning of paragraph 2 are paraphrases of this letter. CCE to MME, 7 Dec. 1823, reports that RWE prefers WEC to Everett (MT/MH: 29).

2. Attributed to James [Jacques] Saurin in *JMN* 2:225.

3. David Hume, "Sceptical Doubts," *Philosophical Essays*, 1748 (retitled *An Enquiry Concerning Human Understanding*, the source for my citations, in 1758), *Philosophical Works* 4:37.

4. See ibid., 4:42–43, 51.

To Charles Chauncy Emerson

March 9 —24

When I saw my Nieghbour take letters for the City, this morning, I thought of you, my dear Charles, and of yours of Jan. 3, of the fine burst of patriotism w'h goes along with the character of Columbus; and resolved to write by the next opportunity, tho' its passage will be uncertain.

You tell me nothing of the sucess of your Comittee for a Greek contribution; tho' I do not doubt of it, nor of your sympathy with that suffering people. Tho publick sympathy must of all other sentiments be most liable to lose it's worth amidst a crowd of frivolous politicians and fashionists. Yet it must be owned, one needs some of their sources of information to give scope to solitary emotions. Tow or three weeks after Webster's speech (or parts of it rather) on the 19 of Jan., was out, it was given me by a stranger, whom I met by accident. And nothing else but Webster & the Greeks—the Greeks & Webster filled my head all night.[1] I had to put out the lamp—open the window—and look out on other worlds to get rid of an excitement so useless. Here in the deep blue plains, we sometimes see a little darker spot, w'h is no vapour like a cloud—and it may be the pall of a world w'h has passed from light & motion forever—where gay & joyous people have gone into further riegions of space & infinity! We thus lose every view of Country and time, and our own little world is but an undistinguished speck.

Still if what W. had said, has possessed the interest it ought to, who w^d have wished to free one's self from their own Country or others? Complete ignorance, father Confessor, will plead for every thing in my ennui. But what an epoch in the xian world—what a time for a xian Orator to make a deep & eternal impression on socity. True, the times are not dependant on orators as in days of comparative darkness—but yet the populace are immensely influenced, & the history of our times might from the voice of a Wilberforce[2] have gained an imperishable lustre. A cause w'h is so free from all selfish political policy, or ought to be—yet he names our danger from the *exampel* of republicanism, the least approach to w'h, from our peculiar & lofty condition, is to me a mere bugbear. If there is any thing to be feared, it must be from those mentioned by Randolph.[3] But it is a cause of humanity & freedom, to say no more, & opens a feild so great & glorious for eloquence, that the best calculation of home policy degrades it. To the xian philanthropist it opens an endless interest. It is a war between what is properly *called* a xian nation and Infidels. And it may be the means of destroying Islamism! The hope of this is enough to jeopard every interest the world can bring to its' aid. And the better hope to those, who love Greeks in distinction from their kind, is that *their* religion, no better now than Mahometanism, will become real xianity. With such a prospect there are those who are now dead, and some who are alive, who would throw the "brand into the Porte" and perish in the flames, to hasten the event. It is not desirable to return to the middle ages—but how much better the heros & Orators of those days to mingle religion with every thing, than to exclude it from every thing, except to give it a poetic garb? Webster loses not the fine opportunity of recalling the Grecian arts and love of freedom. To those who know little of them, the miseries & cruelties suffered by their slaves disgrace their goverment & names. And as to their arts, they hastened their destruction— Hastened, perhaps, the mere speculatist might say, the adversity of their descendants— And the reverie might go on to those periods of revolution, w'h the stoics foretell, in w'h all the generations of men inhabit again the same scenes & suffer a retribution. And when one thinks of our own great Land—of those whose principles & virtues gave it existence, and of those who redeemed it at the Revolution, how infinitely dearer than all Grecian[n] & Roman fame is our glory! Of this Country, should you, my ever loved Boy, become an ornament—the idea of it would in death endear it to me, as in life has the memory of one, whose love of liberty & honor is escutehoned in more desirable characters than the earth could ingrave.

Love to sister and sons. I shall do myself the honor of writing to the Ar.bP of C.[4] the first opportunity. But the subjects of his letter are ever interesting and can never be old.

Your Aff[t] Aunt
MME.

MH: bMS Am 1280.226(653). *Addressed:* Master Charles C. Emerson / Roxbury / Mr Greenough. *Endorsed:* M M Emerson / 1823.

Grecian] ⟨Egerian⟩ Grecian

1. The *Christian Register* of 26 Dec. 1823 reported a meeting in Boston held on 19 Dec. to "consider and carry into effect the best measures for affording effectual aid to the oppressed inhabitants of Greece in their present struggle for liberty and independence [against the] Turkish yoke." Those present at the Exchange Coffee House resolved to form a committee of twelve to bring the issue before the United States Congress. CCE does not seem to have been a member of this committee. On 19 Jan. 1824, Daniel Webster delivered his speech, "The Revolution in Greece," before the House of Representatives.

2. William Wilberforce.

3. Probably Edmond Randolph (1753–1813), sponsor, at the Constitutional Con-

vention of 1787, of the Virginia (or Randolph) plan of union, which favored large states; the upper house would be chosen from nominees proposed by state assemblies and the executive by the legislature.

4. Probably abbreviation for "Archbishop of Canterbury" (the Emersons were then living in the Canterbury section of Roxbury); apparently a reference to RWE. MME to RWE, 9 Mar. 1824, mentions "Sir Canterbury" (MH: 1044); and RWE to SBR, 1 Aug. 1824, describes his family as "the whole Archbishopric of them" (*L* 1:148).

To Ralph Waldo Emerson

Ap. 13   1824

Imajanation, my dear Waldo, will always revolt at the loss of the butterfly's beauty and the rude waste of the rich dew of the welkin from its own azure cups, but be patient—there are many who are forced to creep thro' the entrails of reptiles & roots to find an infinite Designer. Never dislike these little "lobes" & livers and all their capasities to enjoy the rapture of sense for they afford so much comfort to those who seek for analogies & who are otherwise related to the amiable instincts of animals than to the lofty relations of reason & principle in higher orders. The longer you live the more you will have to endure the elementary existence of society, and your premature wisdom will dictate quiesence, when the old^n become gay & the young queer at the portrature of a fly & the Gallen dissection of a flower[1]

Then you find no nesecery sacredness in the Country. Nor did Milton— but his mind and his spirits wove^n their own place & came when he called them in the solitude of darkness. Solitude w'h to people, not talented to deviate from the beaten track (w'h is the safe gaurd of mediocrity) without offending, is to learning & talents the only sure labyrinth (tho' sometimes gloomy) to form the eagle wings w'h will bear one farther than suns and stars. Byron & Wordsworth have there best and only intensely burnished their pens. Would to Providence your unfoldings might be there—that it were not a wild & fruitless wish, that you could be disunited from travelling with the souls of other men, of living & breathing, reading & writing with one vital time fated^n idea *their opinions*. So close was this conjunction, that a certain pilgrim lived for some months in an eclipse so monotonous as scarsly to discern the disk of her own particular star.[2] Could a mind return to its first fortunate seclusion, when it opened with its own peculiar coulers & spread^n them out on its own rhymy^n palette, with its added stock, and spread them beneathe the cross, what a mercy to the age. That religion so poetical and philosophical, so adapted to unfold the understanding, when studied, "whose sublime sentiments and actions spring from the desire w'h Genius always posseses of breaking those bounds which cercumscribe the imajanation. The heroism of morals, the enthusiasm of eloqunce, the love of an eternal fame are supernatural enjoyments alotted only to minds which are at once exalted and melancholy, and wearied and disgusted with every thing transitory and bounded. This disposition of mind is the source of every generous passion and every philosophical discovery."[3] Would this description of character, w'h I have copied from a glorious Auther, suit even our boasted Evertt? Is he not completely inveloped in foreign matters and an artificial character? I am glad that his notice has fallen on Edward, who will be for flinging his light on a civil profession, than on another destiny. If Virgils shades still lingered in curiosty about their old world, I may have it about these "gospels of thought and erudition"[4] which you find so gossamar?—when two or three old books contain every thing grand for me. Yet you call this age the ripest. Is it in virtue? Where are its Martyrs? Where was an age, since xianity, when the publick mind had less hold of the strongest of all truths? The Mass will ever be in swaddlings, and there ever have been great minds—so I cannot see clearly the comparison betwen infancy & age. The arts not equalled—and even Milton casting an eye toward Ovid and Virgil w'h seems less bearable than towards Homer?

Your letter of the 1. of Feb.[5] gratified me for its' time of coming, and its stately subjects & style— And I was for answering it so fully, that you would have thought of nothing but the Wizards inundation,[6] till I read it again, and supposed the *Humism* merely assumed for the purposes of amusing, to have been certain either way would have given life to writing Alas many a Bishop has thus thought perhaps. And now I would remind your Grace, tho' but an Abbess of a humble Vale, that the triple bow *was never* seen before the deluge. Nor it is a legend. There were no rains in those reigions, or none heavy enow, to give the binding of that flowery verge before the alteration w'h the flood caused. St Pierre's theory favors this, if I remember.[7] Rich as is the triple bow of promise (and it has been seen reflecting on the grave of long buried friendship) it would lose its best beauty, even if the Commentators restoring it as a *covenant bow* were just. I am glad to show out a scrap of learning to your scienceship in revenge for your speaking of my "moral scrools and sybiline *scraps*". In truth I have nothing of the old Eld but as many sands w'h I fear. The better part of the flattery of the letter, I receive as a token of kindness. It was ingenously done to write so well on my old almanacks—and I never reject handsome compliments, for the only thing would occur to you, *what possible interest* can one have in flattering me? Yet in solitude it is not nessecary, as in society, where even the oars of life can hardly be kept in motion without it.

But if you were to tax me with any payment in the course of this letter, why take it as a debt or a due to merit—it is always passable in the best society. Thanks for news from William.[8] Many a kind & sad thought have followed him. Yet it is a pleasant route, and he will become a better companion and gentleman for shaking off the dust of domestic cares. Love to my Sister & Nephews but say not of W.m to her. Your affectionate Aunt

MME.

This must go to office if no chance offers I must send it by stage & not be able to pay for it. In haste

MH: bMS Am 1280.226(832). *Addressed:* Mr R. Waldo Emerson / Roxbury / Mss. *Postmarked:* Waterford Me   April 17. *Endorsed:* X M. M. Emerson. *and on* *p. 2:* 1824 X.

old] ⟨grave⟩ ↑ old ↓

wove] *possibly* were (*JMN* 2:380)

fated] sated *in JMN*; first letter does not look like MME's usual *f* or *s*

spread] ⟨painted⟩ ↑ spread ↓

rhymy] ⟨grotesque⟩ ↑ rhymy ↓

     1. The Greek physician Galen (ca. A.D. 130–200) practiced dissection of animals; RWE to MME, 21 Mar. 1824, complained that nature (the flower, butterfly, and rainbow) loses its charms when subjected to the scrutiny of science (*L* 7:125–26).

     2. The "pilgrim" seems to be MME.

     3. Unlocated.

     4. In his letter of 21 Mar., RWE confessed his disappointment upon opening the "accepted gospels of thought & learning" in the "rich library of [inherited] knowledge" (*L* 7:125).

     5. No letter of 1 Feb. survives. Rusk (*L* 1:140) suggests a passage printed in *JMN* 2:378–79 may be part of this letter.

     6. In *Germany* 1:357–58, de Staël retells Goethe's story of the sorcerer's pupil and the magical broomstick that continued to draw water "at the risk of inundating" the house.

     7. The unorthodox geological theory of Jacques-Henri Bernardin de St. Pierre (1727–1814), in his *Studies of Nature* (1784) and its sequel, *Harmonies of Nature* (1815), hypothesized that the earth was elongated at the poles, where the alternate fusion and melting of ices produced ocean currents, tides, and the motion of the earth. The deluge resulted from a "total effusion of the polar ices" (*Studies of Nature . . .*, ed. the Reverend E. Clarke, 3 vols. [London, 1836], 1:126) as a result of the sun's deviation from the ecliptic, which shifted the poles from their previous position, producing (among other catastrophes and reversals) vapors in the atmosphere and universal rain. Since the rainbow is a product of reflection and refraction, impossible until this cataclysm had released frozen water into the air, it would follow (as MME seems to conclude) that no rainbow occurred before the deluge (*Studies of Nature* 1:xxvi–xxxix, 1:122–37, and *Harmonies of Nature . . .*, ed. Louis Aimé-Martin, 3 vols. [London, 1815], 2:49–51, 57, 65–67). MME's source not identified.

     8. WE[3] was traveling in Germany.

To Sarah Ripley and Phebe Ripley

W   July 6 [1824]

Dear Sister

     Mr H says you would have come here if you could have seen your Phisian and had his leave— We all say—would that you had—for it is probable that a few weeks here would complete your cure. He says you appear nicely and are getting better. And you have every thing to encourage you from past experience of the divine goodness. Why cannot you and Sister Emerson come together. Waldo staid but so little[1] I was glad she did not come with him, for I had not time for both. It is growing dark and I want to send this by tommorow morning. You could not be where you could give & receive more pleasure. Remember a great many messages to parents & sister Phebe. I was never so glad that she was absent before now   Tell her how often *November* is talked off.

Accept this written at the desire of your Sisters R & M.

& Neice

Brother just got home to dinner. There is nothing needed for an invalid but what can be procured at P. by stage twice a week.

Dear Phebe   I must add tho it is dusk that your letter was gratefull. and shall be noticed in November   Rebecca pays you thro' me—if you need it before coming present the order

A lamp & glasses enable me to add that I would adopt the style of Mrs Grant who was so modest (tho' she had herself to offer) in inviting her freinds to visit because she had so few accomodations.[2] But if the mountain air & a rich scenery can please you it will greatly please me and I do want to see Sister E much. Letter called for

Write soon

MH: bMS Am 1280.226(1252). *Addressed:* Miss Sarah Ripley / Care of Mr R W Emerson / Roxbury Ms.

1. Reference to RWE's visit to MME at Waterford in May. MME to CCE, n.d. [1824?], states, "If any thing could have added to seeing Waldo, it would have been you. But you did right—tis a dull place—   A parcle of dolts who dont distinguish a Genius. And those who may, will be so stupid as to think there is no nessecary connection between happiness & *thot*—are confident (stupid) that there is none with *that* and *virtue* (MH: 837). MME to RWE, 18 Oct. [1824], notes that RWE advised CCE not to visit: "No wonder—you who came as it seemed to my modesty, only for a solitary walk & found a poor cryselis writhing into life from the ill humours of the spring . . . could say nothing in favor of his journey" (MH: 834).

2. Anne MacVicar Grant, *Letters from the Mountains*.

To Ralph Waldo Emerson

[Aug. 1824]

The letter addressed to Plato[1] was made known to him at a moment when he emerged from a rainbow pavillion, where he had been holding converse with some who had first attained the imperial robes of martyrdom—there too had been spirits of later days—such as Fennelon, William Law, Eliot and other herors of the Magnalia. After assorting with such, there is sometimes a shade of regret on the luminous brow of the Sage—but it was accompanied with a prophetic smile at the mundane epistle—an instant—and he resumed his lofty aspect—and signified rebuke at it's familiar style by appointing (thro his numerous attendants w'h form a connection with the inferior spirits of earth and air) one of his most ignorant admirers to announce his notice

"You introduce yourself young Mortal, under the auspices of the historic Muse—but the once proud names of Greece & Rome and Plato's earthly praise are to one, who has past the compages of matter, like the dreams of Indiots. Of the names of those and other Empires—and their great men, mention is sometimes made at the arival of some virtuous souls from oppression and obscurity. I do remember now to have listened to the exploits & the virtues of Ceasar—and even sought his ghost—but in vain— It is said the Corsican[2] has found him surrounded with fallen crowns, but that the Roman spurned his offered homage.

The woes of the place of my cradle I know—and that there has been a winding sheet seen at which the spirits of *dread eternity* shook their raven wings and shouted a horrid joy.[3]

You proceed to speake of your own times—to boast them—yet own— ah you might have owned the whole sad truth—of nations untold of your vaunted revelation, as yet, to any purpose—of slaves—more miserable than ever my Country made, under xian skies! But what is it you *know,* in these fine times, of my metaphysicks—my theology and of my theories, which would put them to shame? The very Scotsman,[4] so eminent, will take his place with his predesessors. What *did* he *know* or *prove* to vanquish my universals— my innate ideas independent on *perception*—forms existing orignally in the divine mind—and impossible to explain the production of them, if they were not independant on experience. Aristotle thought otherwise—he was practical and prepared the inductive method for the illfated Chancellor[5]—but I prefered—I exulted that my ideas—my existence, had been one of the divine ideas. In my "formation of the universe" there was nothing to blush at even here. Surrounded with nature, which I was capable of studying and loving— yet it was filled with phenomena—with mystery—with some that spoke of terror & pain My Demiurgus—the stars inhabited by Genii—could *you then* have imajined better? In my theology, was not the unity—the absolute perfection of the first Cause? True, in my explanations of that unity, many *xians* have found whereon to build a tritheism. In my Republick (apart from the woman kind and the neglect of the ignorant) what can you object? The truth is it was to pure—too desinterested for the place—it's prototypes were in Heaven. It's principle of prefering *truth* & *justice* to *utility* might not please some of the early *xian writers* and some of the *last*—and the object of perfecting the leaders of society by the profoundest piety may, at all times, be rather irksome The proscribing Homer—the representation of the Cavern—its shawdows—it's illusions were never acceptable to the gladiator of pleasure & honor.

But all that I have said, you know. My "travels in the land of souls"[6] are not so easily learnt. You remember I departed suddenly from health, and from a marriage festival. To find my shackels gone—my self—my soul—for-

ever freed—awakning from dreams, feverish & confused, to the most joyous
& tranquil of mornings, that should fain linger—without any day pleasures,
resembles what I was— Every law of my existence seemed to me tending
nessecarily to harmony. The objects and forms of intelligent beings, which
passed & repassed, disturbed not my reverie—and whether ever I should
voluntarily have aroused? But at the coming of the sphered souls of Anaxagoras, Thales, Pythagoras and my loved Master—at the recalled associations
of active virtue—*origin of evil*—character—divine goverment I sprung into
another state of existence— No mortal can judge of what the soul of Plato
passed—his exalted imajanations—his high perogatives—what he had called
merit—not permitted to approach—to do homage to the Ineffable—but thro
His visible Son—that "only begotten" so unlike what I had formed—a being
so august & perfect—yet who had in mighty perspective assumed human
nature—was destined to humiliation—to death—accursed death—not for
the higher ranks only, but for the poorest! The proud Plato revolted at the
scheme— I knew morals were universal—eternal—my relations to the first
Cause by the attributes of intellect as well as sentiment—what I called virtue—
what *was was*[n] virtue—but not all—not its purest—its humility—not in any
point fullfilling that irrepealable law which became God to give. What I suffered at such discoveries—let it pass— I was able to endure— I choose to
leave these sainted friends—once so valued—they were changed—less speculative, more of sanctity. In my wanderings I saw the abodes of misery—some
resembled those in your world, who are wretched—others were surrounded
with remembrances of former pleasures and ensigns of what seemed to them
endless sorrow—but to me these dire omens did not appear to be forever— I
was visited by some, as I often changed the scene, of those who had ministered
to man from his birth—among them were those who had bore the telescope of
prophecy—the lost oracles of which, I had heard some echoes—these knew
with what dilligence I had sought to hear a divine voice—how often I did have
some more than human instruction—and they were commissioned to tell me,
I was at liberty to *seek*—to join some other order than my own—to search
for the highest interpreters of the ever during nature of divine laws and of
created beings. I took the wings of light—and finally found admittance into
the abode of those sons of God who shouted at the creation of our world—
of others—here were monuments of some which had long been changed into
other forms. There I found what the visible world (tho' I fancied it eternal)
could never supply—"a property which it never could receive—*eternity*—
the essential attribute of the intellectual world of w'h the visible was not
susceptible" That spherical figure—I had imajined—how meanly—here a
measureless dial—it's dread gnomes—pointing to dreader numbers—and not
all of these alike veiled in countless waves of light—some, and some of those
which were marked with human destinies were covered with blackness—interminable—the wheels within wheels w'h gave motion, if it were motion, to
this terrific circle *appeared* to be impelled by living beings—others whirled

beyond created agency—their height & depth and numbers extended beyond the ken of these select seraphim devoted to knowledge. The soul, or whatever it might be which seemed to lose it's hold on identity, shuddered at this heirogliphic—that infinity—so easily I had talked off—poetised—and thought. I believed! Was I sure of happiness—even of safty? Could I be allowed to join these strange spirits? Their looks—their very courtesy was appalling to my high spirit—they indicated some invincible detriment in my constitution, whether from contact with my former body or not, I could never bring myself to inquire. They were heard to foretell a period when the intermediate scheme would be absorbed—when God should be all and all—but they knew not the consequences to those who had refused the new dispensation. Yet I felt no desire for hazard—I repaired to the mercy seat—it was the only way to the Father—and the great Hierophant initiated me into the glories of xianity. My being seemed new with knowledge—hope & love—where their objects are immortal. Am I certain of the highest success—   —advancment like to those who have borne an active part in this suffering econmy

Silence thou lisping Inquisitor—know *I* possess the same gifts—these affections which give the xian soul to rejoice when defeated of some attainments—able to sympathise in the higher success of others. I wittnessed the *Resurrection*—I saw the first fruits of it—and at times wished I were a fisherman of Gallilee—but the speedy corruptions—even the Reformation never found me regreting my age. Know too for thy persuming questions, that at some high Jubilees, pagan Plato whom thou darest to pity is found nearer the Head of principalities, powers, virtues & dominions, than many of those who have assumed his name and ministered at his alters.

Farewell—   We may meet.

Au. 10.   Very doubtfull whether my first assay at pening *imajanings* will not be ridiculed—& know my theology will be disliked but the train of thot has pleased me[n] & you call for a letter. Is it likely Scot would apologise for crimes as "it is said" he wrote a piece in E. paper about Byron?[7]

MH: bMS Am 1280.226(833). *Addressed:* Mr R. W. Emerson / Roxbury / Mr. T. W. Haskins. *Endorsed:* M. M. Emerson / Plato 1824.

was was] *repetition at page break, but may be intentional*

me] ⟨MME⟩ ↑ me ↓

1. See *JMN* 2:246–49, 250–52, for RWE's "letter to Plato" written between May and July 1824 and possibly shown to MME during his visit in May. In his "letter," RWE addressses "the Spirit of Plato in a new language but . . . one whereinto has long been transfused all the wealth of ancient thought" (*JMN* 2:246). No separate letter survives. See also RWE's and Rusk's comments on MME's "Plato" letter, *L* 1:160.

2. Probably Napoleon.

3. Allusion to Greek war against the Turks and probably Byron's death on 19 Apr.

4. The "eminent" Scot is most likely Dugald Stewart.

5. Francis Bacon (1561–1626) advanced from knight to chancellor under James I

but in 1621 pleaded guilty to accepting bribes and was barred from office. Bacon is credited with formulating the inductive method of modern experimental science.

6. Loosely quoted from RWE's letter.

7. Sir Walter Scott published two reviews of Byron in the *Quarterly Review* (London; "E." may stand for "English" paper): "*Childe Harold*, Canto 3, and Other Poems by Byron," *QR* 16 (Oct. 1816): 172–208, and "*Childe Harold*, Canto 4," *QR* 19 (Apr. 1818): 215–32.

To Ralph Waldo Emerson

Elm Vale   Sep 15. [1824] Wed.

Thy wand dear Waldo called forth holier and higher spirits than Prospero's,[1] for they came in the garb of primeval truth followed by prophets apostles and Another—but their humble scribe has lain bye their verdict on perceiving that it was intimated that the chasms[n] were closed. Since, so much of life's moving beating fleshy panorama has been—that it the connection[n] would be obsolete indeed. Well it has been a proud period for our Country and not much otherwise for a certain name.[2] Why have you not made visible by pen the interest w'h youth takes in these things. It would have awakned no regret that I did not wittness— Nothing less than that—but more. Yet the very waters of the tarn waved pleasanter at the approach of La. to A. one of the few living monuments of another race—of other palms—which like those same waves suceed each other and are forgotten forever in the mighty immensity. You have not had time to feel that this huge "globe was but a web drawn around us" that the light—the skies the mountains are but the painted vissisitudes of the soul. But it is the happier power of bodiless souls, perhaps, to estimate the beauty[n] of such a description and to love the offerings of a mortal imajanation.

I asked for your disertation—wherefore did it fail? And if you will not think it demeaned send Edward's oration.[3] What can it be? I know it must be good after all you have said of him, were there not a less partial ordeal, yet to my dim sense, human perfectibility is among firm *human institutions,* the dreams of enthusiasts with Godwin[4] & D'Stale. If the divine law—if that scheme (in w'h you find a mixture of clay—but w'h has none any more than the original law) so perfect fails and becomes weak thro' the corruption of the means to w'h it is committed—what can human institutions do? What have they done in our own blessed land to keep an Adams from calumy & the people from intestine war? Were you gratified with the mention of your father? It might be as well, as it is a protestant Country, to let the dead slumber. A long disease— many brilliant youths—perhaps eclipsed— And happier those who will rise with more lustre in the world than was expected at the time of their exist. The eclat of name—of fame is often present to my thought, when I see some beauteous cloud impress it's image on the tranquil lake, and as it passes to mingle in the vast vault it's *shawdow* climbs the sides of the mountain over bog & brake & tree and suddenly disappears at the instant of ariving at it's summit. But if shadows add to the beauty of fleeting scenes how much more the aspirants of other mounts to the interest of life. Where were *some* of the *present* joys of solitude had not genius spoke & wrote? This richly laden season, whose every leaf begins its own mystic story, which soothes the soul & dwells upon the soul, & blends itself into the soul derives a zest from the tale of other days & from prophecy of those who are rising into honor. Your affectionate Aunt, who sends

love to Mother & Sons.
MME

MH: bMS Am 1280.226(835). *Endorsed:* 1825.
chasms] *possibly* charms (*T*)
it the connection] it ↑ the connection ↓
beauty] ⟨power⟩ ↑ beauty ↓
   1. Probably a response to a recent letter from RWE (possibly dated ca. 1 Sept.; *L* 1:147) that does not survive; unidentified quotations and allusions may be from this letter.
   2. Despite the 1825 endorsement, these allusions to Lafayette's visit to America ("La. to A.," below) and Edward's oration at the Harvard commencement, 25 Aug. 1824 (where he shared the stage with Lafayette), place the letter in 1824.
   3. EBE's dissertation on China took a Bowdoin Prize at Harvard in 1824 (*L* 1:147 n. 30); MME may err in thinking RWE has written a "dissertation," or she may refer to an unfinished journal essay; EBE's oration on 25 Aug. was entitled "The Advancement of the Age."
   4. William Godwin (1756–1836), radical English political theorist who believed in human perfectibility.

To CHARLES CHAUNCY EMERSON

Sab. Night 17 [Oct.? 1824]

Welcome, dearest Charles, your own dear letter and your present.[1] Never was so splendid a drawing of our own blessed Country— Happy are the old—willing to depart without seeing—any other millenum of intellect than the promise of the E—s.[2] And were they to live forever—what could be higher—better wiser—sweeter than the old rolling world hath already turned out? Ever honored be the talents of Edward Evertt—and his ideas—his love (for surely it is genuine) of freedom—not for Country only, but kind.

You will not say any thing again of respect for the decapitated Charles— A single strip of velvet would have made him a tyrant.[3]

But if such a one as I might speake of what I do not know—I should ask if the Orator did not describe the effects of liberty on literature exclusively as a politician? The philosopher might suggest that the Muses were fettered by other chains than the tyrants—that the same causes w'h degraded a nation relaxed *their* power? And the saint would say—that the sands of destiny which bounded a nations progress—said to the arts hithertoo and no farther— Never were the Jewish harps (from w'h it is said sometimes the Grecians had their lyre) nobler, than when hung on the willows of a strange land—nor ever were loftier notes from the prophets, than in the dungeons of Babylon. But I have put an extreme case— And have I not imitated the Professor in some one or more of his references?[4]

But I am about to enter serious complaints to you, my dear friend (for I have no one to ask, even if they have read the oration). Religion has, whether good or bad given her inspiration to arts and especially to that of the Muse. Christianity has done more for learning than ever learning can do for her—and to goverments of all kinds it has been the basis. What moments did the Orator omit of adding to his laurels an amyranthine leaf. He touched once & again on the accostomed name of Providence—but when owning that the speculation of phisical causes were elevating—then to have traced thier connections with *His will* who raises every mountain and coulers every marble for means of carrying on the great theocracy of the world! What else can solve that problem, which all nations present of civil government, in w'h the strenght of the many submit to the few? The Spirit that goes now abroad on the earth asks not only for political freedom—but for immortality—it is breathing an ardor of inquiry—of eager prophecy—and in some forms looks for the completion of that glorious scheme which will consolidate all the nations and all their honors into one perfect fabrick—their awakning energies will not be soothed by the present eloquence—if they are sounding only of the visible frame of things. If that was not the time to inspire the holiest visions—why pardon my incurable ignorance. But think—our nation had her nativity cast beneathe the influence of the cross as no other nation—and the most ignorant of her xians will say—that without the prophetic eye of genius they foresee the hatefull time, when if she loses her orbit—if she wander (as some of her sons) into the havenless and heavenless chaos of deism, the graves of our sainted fathers and their sons will be trodden by despots & slaves—or if there be no worse retribution. And after all—the impression of liberty and sucess to the *soul,* which at first reading was so vivid, dwindles into the slavery of climbing the literary mount—of being excited by the crouded hour—of effort and event. Pardon me, my dear Nephew—but the moral impression is nothing to Cicero's. Could he (with sincerity) but once, if only once, have raised his gifted voice to the aegis of our salvation? He would then better resembled Burke who descended from a higher sphere, when he would influence human affairs. I have not forgotten, for one who is to build with the Professor (but on other principles I trust) read to me the review of poor Butler[5]—and I respect the close of it—but there was nothing to lessen my regret of the omissions of this pamplet.

Yes Byron is gone[6]—and it *did* excite the Valley. I could not but grudge for the cause of religion the showy virtues w'h were gathering around his vices—Could not but *feel* that he had left none who would give life to those mysterious and profound sentiments of the soul as he had given— None who could so call^n the voice of nature from her dreadest heights or deepest caverns. Nor can I part with his ghost—it often appears to me wandering in scenes like to his own "darkness"[7]—and amidst his stygian journey the golden branch is forbidden—no chaste Sybil warns him of Cocytus—of death & death's half brother sleep.

Farewell—the night gets on—the blast descends moaning from the mountain—the leaves murmur as they fall—but all unite to speake of the future happiness of man in w'h may you have a large share trusts your

aff^t Aunt
MME.

MH: bMS Am 1280.226(654). *Endorsed:* 1825X.

call] ↑ call ⟨awake⟩ ↓

1. CCE's letter does not survive; his "present" was probably Everett's *Oration Pronounced at Cambridge before the Society of Phi Beta Kappa, August 26, 1824* (Boston, 1824), discussed below, on the progress of literature in America. MME to RWE, 18 Oct. [1824], requests his "review of the Professors oration" (MH: 834).

2. Probably a reference, not to MME's Emerson nephews, but to the Everett brothers, three of whom were then distinguishing themselves: Alexander Hill Everett (1792–1847) graduated with highest honors from Harvard in 1806 and was currently U.S. minister to the Netherlands; Edward Everett (1794–1865), an honor graduate in 1811, served as professor of Greek at Harvard while editing the *North American Review* and was elected to Congress in 1824; and John Everett (1801–26), Harvard, 1818, studied with Daniel Webster, served in the American legation at Brussels and The Hague, and delivered an oration in Boston on 4 July 1824.

3. Charles I of England, decapitated in 1649.

4. "Harps . . . Babylon": allusion to Ps. 137:1–2; comparison is to Everett in his oration.

5. See the review of Frederick Butler, *A Complete History of the United States of America, Embracing the Whole Period from the Discovery of North America down to the Year 1820*, 3 vols., in the *North American Review* 16 (Jan. 1823): 156–63. The reviewer essentially says that printing this work was a waste of paper.

6. Byron died in Greece on 19 Apr. 1824. MME responds to RWE's indirect question in his letter of 26 July 1824: "I suppose it jarred no chord in the Vale when Byron died" (*L* 7:130).

7. Title of poem by Byron.

To Ralph Waldo Emerson

Dec. 6 [1824]

The inclosed[1] was written with the pen taken for the old almanack at the moment of reading yours of antidiluvian date. Then you do not go to Stuart[2]—you, who are no fop, might like him, tho' he makes mouths at the heartless strainings of kindnesses w'h tickel, not benefit the weak world. He thinks, a man in pursuit of greatness feels no little wants. Why did you not study under the wing of Channing—w'h was never preened^n at Cambridge.

If he advised C.,[3] he did not know your capasity to think for yourself—or he is not able or good enough to be willing to jut out alone tho' he avows dissent in some points. Alas that you are there. There is a tide in the affairs of men, w'h connect the soul to the future, taken at the moment bears on to fortune— omitted the rest may be shallows.[4] Do we repine that so much is dependant on mortal life? The reason we ca'nt determine,—yet that this dread responsibility is not extended—is not lenghtened to the unknown world is matter of constant gratitude to those, who find terrors in the divine law & gov^t— and in His natural attributes.— Were this probation to be extended, as the liberal believe, to those who have heard of the gospel—of what reason was that astonishing apparatus given? Did xianity, even as much as the good Ware allows (w'h seems to leave more difficulties tho' not so frightfull as Calvin & the improvements of Woods) not imply much war with human nature, why do its professed deciples run into atheism so often, rather than deism? Diluted as it is, it demands too much lofty & serious virtue—and as it humanitarianism opens the door[n] to conclusions most forbidden, they make them. Price, so eminent, yet so flouted,[n] says xianity cannot be *credible* in Lardners scheme— neither does it seem more so, if nessicarily connected with the trinitarian. Blessed be God for the history (whether its penmen were inspired or not) of primitive religion in the old & new testament. A descended being, the Companion of God before time, living & suffering as he did— —giving not an intimation that he provided for any earthly comfort to his deciples—leaving if but a few of the precepts & engagments w'h he did, contains enow to demand constant martyrdom of speculation or interest—gives & does enable it's devoted children to look at death & hell with sovereignty—to call God, tho' so tremendously holy, to wittness that while he sustains their fullfillment of His conditions—while they love Him thus—He himself can do nothing against them. This deep & high theolgy will prevail—and German madness may be cured—the publick ear weary of the artifices of eloquence will ask for the wants of the soul to be sattisfied. May you dear Youth be among others who will prove a pharos to your Country & times. But I wander, because it is a penance, from the designs of writing. It is to say that the years of levity & pride &c &c (w'h some of them you have wittnessed & w'h render me unworthy to speake of the heights of religion) I can not but think were in some measure owing to the atmosphere of theology—to my own speculations—to what is worse & certain the sore of human nature— Could years of penitence restore me the last 20 years— It was pretty—it seemed best to tell children how good they were—the time of illusion & childhood is past—and you will find mysteries in man w'h baffles genius. The other is to request your opinion of Chalmers sermons (illy called "commercial"[n]) Appleton's lectures and Wilbeforce.[5] It is a year since I wanted to ask you to read them, but I thought of the king who despised the stream of Jordan. I want { } to read the vol. of sermons thro'[n] For yourself, were you a stranger, I could with more confidence intreat you to gather up yourself in solitude with the scriptures—

to forget the world and that profession w'h is to connect you with its duties before you enter Cambridge. It would, I am persuaded open a new field of thought & self knowledge—but never was there more quixotism in advice—whether you are already at C. or have some weeks on your hand. Yet hithertoo I have had my say in your movements & have not regreted it.

May the God of your Fathers bless you beyond your projentors to the utmost bounds of your undying existence prays

MME.

Sab. Main   Nov 7

He talks of the Holy Ghost—   God of mercy what a subject—and tho' Thou hast gifted him with an inquiring ghost—and besides other gifts—yet he dont seem to like thy dispensations.—   "Holy ghost given to every man in Eden"[6]—it was lost in the great contest going on in the vast universe it was lost—stifled—it was regiven—embodied in the assumed humanity of the son of God—and since—the reward of prayer—agency—self immolation! Dost not like the faith & the means?—   —take thy own—or rather the dictates of fashion—let those who love the voice of uncorrupt nature seek for supernal aid—for an alliance with the most powerfull of spirits—the holy Ghost—such was the ambition of Paul—of holy martyrs—it burnt up every earthly element and would not stoop to ask an angels record nor an angels wreath. Would to God thou wert ambitious—respected thyself more & the world less. Thou wouldst not to Cambridge—true they use the name *Christo*—but that venerable institution it is thought[n] has become but a feeble ornamented arch in the great tempel w'h the xian world maintains to the honor of his name. It is but a garnished sepulchre where may be found some relics of the *body* of Jesus—some grosser parts w'h he took not at his ascent, and w'h will be forgotten and buried forever beneathe the flowerets of genius and learning if the master spirits of such as Appleton Chalmers and Stewart and the consecrated Channing do not rescue it by a crusade of faith & lofty devotion.—   The nature & limits of human virtue[n]—its dangers—it's origin—"questions answered at Cambridge—easily"—   God forgive thy favored child his levity—subjects veiled with somthing of thine own awfull incomprehensibility—soothed only by the faith w'h reason loves but can never describe—w'h rests in solemn delight on Him who not once calculated it for earthly[n] emolument.

MH: bMS Am 1280.226(836 & 879). *Addressed:* Mr R. W. Emerson / Care of Mr E. B. Emerson / Roxbury / Mr. T. W. Haskins / Boston. *Endorsed:* X / M. M. E. 1824 *and (on Almanack leaf)* M. ME *and (added in pencil)* ⟨1827?⟩ 1830?
    preened] pruned *in* JMN 2:383
    it . . . door] it ↑ humanitarianism ↓ opens the door ⟨perhaps⟩
    flouted,] ⟨forgotten⟩ ↑ flouted ↓,
    "commercial"] "⟨mercantile⟩ ↑ commercial ↓"

read] *apparently canceled in MS;* thro'] *followed by three unrecovered canceled words*

thought] ⟨said⟩ ↑ thought ↓
virtue] virtue ⟨ ↑ & dedication ↓ ⟩
earthly] ⟨human⟩ earthly

1. Probably the Almanack leaf dated 7 Nov. (MH: 879) that follows. RWE's letter on his plan of study for the ministry that prompted this response does not survive.

2. *Possibly* Stewart *in MS;* Moses Stuart, professor of sacred literature at Andover Theological Seminary.

3. WEC's theological training while at Cambridge was "largely self-directed," according to David P. Edgell, *William Ellery Channing: An Intellectual Portrait* (Boston, 1955; Westport, Conn.: Greenwood Press, 1983), 21.

4. Loosely quoted from Shakespeare, *Julius Caesar,* 4.3.218–21.

5. Thomas Chalmers, *The Application of Christianity to the Commercial and Ordinary Affairs of Life* (Glasgow, 1820); Jesse Appleton (1772–1819), *Lectures, Delivered at Bowdoin College, and Occasional Sermons* (Brunswick, Maine, 1822); possibly William Wilberforce's *Practical View of . . . Christianity* or *An Appeal to the Religion, Justice, and Humanity of the Inhabitants of the British Empire, in Behalf of the Negro Slaves in the West Indies* (London, 1823).

6. Probably quoted from RWE's letter, which does not survive (see n. 1 above).

1825

To Ezra Ripley and Sarah Ripley

Waterford   June 3d   1825

What can I say my dear Father & Sister to comfort you—   I can only say God will console support and most fully bless you[1]—that son & brother so justly beloved & so affectionate, are remembrances which while they embitter your feelings will soothe them—   What could you ever have done more than you have done to make him happy? O when I think of his genius, his virtue, his sympathy in all the sorrows and joys of his family & friends my heart aches—but the thousand things I have to say, cannot be said by the hand of a stranger—   To you my dear father I have been hoping to write for many weeks, to speak of your kind letter & of my mother—to comfort myself & you by speaking of that world to which we go—where we shall meet with those we have lost & love—but I can't write and I need not—you who have been successful in leading so many to the source of light & comfort—who have so often been the happy instrument of binding up the broken heart—will draw largely yourself—and may God continue your life a blessing to your family—and to the people with whom you have been so uncommonly happy—prays your affectionate friend—and dutiful

Daughter M.M.E.

Do not weep my dear Sarah, pray do not continue to weep—think of God—think of those divine attributes—the thought of which alone can support you—and make you forget every bitterness— O what could we do with our own afflictions & those of others if it were not for this tho't— Be comforted dear Sarah—you have loved as few sisters have loved—you have nothing to reflect on—live and be happy & make others so— As I have no use for my eyes shall I rise at the[2]

I want to say a great deal to our only brother but cant—give him & my beloved Sarah[3] my remembrance

O Sarah you can easily think how much Waldo's eyes[4] afflict me—I never have been heard to say much about mine since—however I meant to *attempt* to journey next week, but shall not till the week after—possibly before that I shall hear you & father are coming here, which will glad me more than any thing else— Farewell dear Sarah—your sister in sympathy & love—

M. M. E.

MH: bMS Am 1280.220(76). *Addressed:* Rev. E. Ripley D. D. / Concord / Mss. *Postmarked:* Waterford Me / June 6.

1. Half brother Daniel Bliss Emerson died 20 Apr. 1825 at Saint Stephens, Ala. The remainder of this letter is written by another hand.

2. The top quarter of the next leaf is missing; about seven lines are lost.

3. SBR.

4. In Mar. 1825, soon after he began theological studies at Harvard, RWE developed eye trouble, which made reading impossible; between Mar. and Sept. he underwent an eye operation and left Cambridge; in Sept. he began teaching in a boys' school at Chelmsford; in the fall he had a second eye operation; and on 31 Dec. he closed the Chelmsford school. See Evelyn Barish, "The Moonless Night: Emerson's Crisis of Health, 1825–1827," in *Emerson Centenary Essays,* ed. Joel Myerson (Carbondale: Southern Ill. University Press, 1982), 1–16.

To Ralph Waldo Emerson

Tues.   August 23 [1825] The

25 of last Au. was one of the happiest—not merely that it ended half a century of my life & that it was brilliant for the Country[1]—enough— Dear dear Waldo I could not write to you till I heard you were better[2]—the object[n] of my hopes & prayers—but now that it is come I say you are getting well too soon—before you have seen[n] the mystic visions w'h visit the soul—before *thought* (oh wonderfull mysterious power w'h allies us to Him who passes wonder) has dispelled those mists w'h rested on some of your speculations—*natural religion* so connected with revealed—would you follow her thro' her glimmerings—would lead you like a good schoolmaster— But tell me, like a true man, your feelings. I have *thought* (while the hand of Him I adore has

pressed so heavily on my eyes & health) that I had read where in a storm at sea the master & pilot had looked down & cheered the obscure passenger with a halloo at least. But *you* cant write, perhaps yet. No one mind has met mine in sympathy—for, alas, they might say I had nothing to lose—sweet consolation truly—but its real worth few are willing to know. Were you to have continued blind I would have told you, what others can better tell—how we hunger & thirst for the celestial dews & fragrance[n] of new & orignal poetry—then I'd hardly blame your school & Roxbury fasts w'h have been the immediate means of your defection in health of optics— But God (whose sharpest arrows are welcome when directed by Himself) forgive me for blaming your industry—there is, as George Douglas says, "a destiny &c—"[3] your opportunity for virtue & glory is equal to the severity of the trial.— Destiny allows of much freedom.

Adieu   This is the first letter but of business & written amid constant applications to the eyes—still hope to be better tho the appearance is of fixed sore eyes. Yet it is so good to speake of virtue & glory—and resignation—w'h seems to me sacriledge to pronounce to most people[n]—or to those who are so orthodox as to back every thing with a pious proviso—if you believe aright

If I hear from you, I may write by Martha—about the monument—   I told Mrs R. that it could be of no possible consequence to us—to his grandsons it might possibly—   Alas could E.E had known the character of your Ancestor he might have given him somthing better than a marble.[4] Of this, if I see what you have written, in future. Love to Mother & brothers. Yours as ever & most truly

                                                                MME

Had I been able to await Sib's return I believe I should have had a fine visit—   She is much approved in that q[t]   After reading this—I hardly send it—yet to this heterogenous mass I may add that tho' I met with much kindness in the journey I found no family more amiable than the one in the Vale. Will you come & see us? & when—tell beforehand. I s[d] have urged my interest but tho't that the best diet[n] & socity were most medical—except that of solitude for the refitting the soul.

MH: bMS Am 1280.226(838). *Addressed:* Mr. R. W. Emerson / Cambridge / Mr T.W. Haskins. *Endorsed:* 1825 / X.

object] ⟨subject⟩ ↑ object ↓
seen] ⟨tasted⟩ seen
fragrance] ⟨invisible⟩ fragrance
most people] ⟨strangers⟩ ↑ most people ↓
diet] ⟨living⟩ diet
1. See MME to RWE, 15 Sept. [1824], esp. n. 2.
2. See MME to EzR and Sarah Ripley, 3 June 1825, n. 3.
3. A character in Sir Walter Scott, *The Abbot* (1822). Following the death of the

villainous Jasper Dryfesdale, a fatalist who tried to poison Queen Mary, Douglas says, "There is an overruling destiny above us, though not in the sense in which it was viewed by that wretched man, who, beguiled by some foreign mystagogue, used the awful word as the ready apology for whatever he chose to do" (chap. 33).

4. For the monument for WE[1], see MME to Sarah Ripley, Apr.? 1826. Reference to Edward Everett's possible connection with this monument is unclear.

To Ralph Waldo Emerson

Elm V.   Sep 27 — 25

Just received yours—feel anew the dreadfull blow which has so misteriously stricken us thro' you.[1] Yet it is not misterious—should not be lamented perhaps—for there are no accidents—contingences—but they resemble those clouds w'h so often adorn & sometimes obscure the planets and are so much parts of the design of the whole as the sun itself. "What is glory, virtue"—? why not even the "beneficence" w'hich haunts every young Seeker of fame & virtue, like that unappalled going forward in sickness & discourgment which you maintain. "Beneficence"—fine words deceive—"*glory*"?—it is contending with genius' the very reverse of those which Webster surrounds Adams with.[2] Poverty, obscurity & calumy have been among the smale armory of the martyrs to true immortality. But of this *future,* there prevails such a variety of doubts of its existence—more abundantly of its requisites—   "Certainty"?— oh, then where the nature of that high virtue, faith? Religion is pillared on it—and is there not more worth in a sacrifice to duty where the excitment is least? "The meshes of the human web are thickly woven"—and many of its threads tie evil to evil across a thousand ages—millions—perhaps. We see and hear but a few throes of the shuttle—but the thunders of Siria—the groans of misery are in it's echoes—and black and bloody clouds mingle with its' fairest figures—yet we know from the records which revelation bears, that when completed, it will not be soiled by a drop of blood from the meanest slave.

In the letter of last Dec. 24, which I have now *read* as for the first moment—you dissent from these long "ties." It would then seem only to bring nearer difficulties—and narrow the objects of our faith & imajanation. Besides if nessesity were the sole condition of man—what imports it how it came, whether by a daily decree or by joining our day of life to the past eternity? If you remembered that page I should say much of it. You seem to feel anxious to direct your own destiny to earn your rewards. Is happiness lessened by being a gift of that Being who can only bestow it? It seems inhanced. To learn the nature of man & of the origin & nature of evil the liberal school is not sufficent—the weakest part of their system appears then. But it can never be sattisfactorily known here. The scriptures are misterioss there—always the same light & darkness appear on almost every page where the subject of nessicity and source of evil are mentioned. Perhaps it is this feeling which leads us on with unwearied curiosty to search it's meaning, as we should follow some supernal vision that was always the same yet never the same. There stands the account—man has deeply fallen— An Enymy *hath sown tares*. A friend is plucking them up—is renovating the fallen & guilty. To dislike such an interference savors of pride, & is hazardous. The history of human misery calls for it. You say science finds the provisions of nature simple—nothing winding & fantastic I dont know what it finds—but that the *how*—the arcana of matter remains undiscovered I rejoice to know. That vision is not inspired, but passes thro' many cercuitous means I am told—that many of the *laws* of nature (*as called*) are justly denominated "compensatory" may be analogous to more interesting parts of the divine econymy

Yet for simplicity of an account, which pictures the destiny of a whole race, what but an inspired writer could give it? *As by means of Adam* sin *entered and death so* by *means of a divine* man *death & sin are destroyed!*[3] Ah, my dear Waldo, prepare (sight or no sight) to preach this divine medicine to a thoughtless ambitious world. Describe to it, in characters of a style so peculiar & rich as yours, that high Being, who best of all created ones, knew the value of true glory and sought it in the most sucesfull and humblest of all human paths—who poured the most ample contempt on human glory of condition—yet who loved true honor which comes from God, better than other being.

William writes that you are somewhat encourged about eyes— I have not touched this paper since the day of receiving your last—tho' I am well enough But the fear of your not writing—and B. can never read me. How is he? What your occupation & society? Alas for Edwards health? Tell me what you think of it. For your sake whom he loves so well, I hope, & for all of us he will do well. But dont expect it. What do you think of W^m's change of profession?

Write soon to your aff^t Aunt
MME.

Dec. 18,[4] Sab. day 1825 Tommor morning this goes or it might get a more correct appearance than the present haste allows. I have quoted your last letter also.

MH: bMS Am 1280.226(839). *Addressed:* Mr R. Waldo Emerson / Chelmsford, Mss / Care of / Mr. W Emerson. *Endorsed:* M M E / 1825 X.

1. See MME to EzR and Sarah Ripley, 3 June 1825, n. 4. Neither the recent letter that MME quotes from throughout nor that of 24 Dec. 1824, mentioned below, survives.

2. Possibly "The Election of 1825," Daniel Webster's speech at Faneuil Hall, Boston, 3 Apr. 1825, before the general election, supporting the candidacy of John Quincy Adams for president.

3. Cf. 1 Cor. 15:21.

4. Date looks more like "13," but in 1825 18 Dec. fell on a Sunday.

To Charles Chauncy Emerson

Elm Vale   Oct 2 —25
Sab Morn

Your letter dear Charles was what it should be in point of frendship—none genuine without egotism—could not have interested me so much as to hear your queries of future character.[1] Why think misery attends illusion about *distinction*? Is it not because you are on the contrary way to real greatness? That glory w'h attends true greatness is very far out of sight of mortal distinction—some even of the wise heathen, thought it beneath them. And tho' in those days of darkness we read of Cesars & Catalines who had unquestionably great talents & even great souls, yet since the sun of true grandeur has risen, we never feel or confess any King or Conquerer great who is at variance with the will of God—the order of the universe—nay more we involuntarily shrink from the fame of our beloved Fayette, when we find his virtues so handled—so mauled as it were by every body—the secret—the ineffable charm of virtue w'h alone allies us to God, seems sullied. And, it may be an erroneous notion, that the love of distinction is incompatible with fame in a world of durability—of high event—of tremendous worth of internal character. True, were it not for this principle we should want theatric pleasures & characters & Orators & statsmen—therefore I respect them as led on by the constitution w'h thier Creator gave them & by w'h he conducts this shadowy scene. But the puppets w'h are waked to the effect will always be pitied by those who view the hazards of human virtue & the nature of xianity in a deeply serious light. You speake with good sense & modesty of your talents—less than your family & the world think perhaps—   But that you will arrive at greatness—at even worldly greatness is doubtfull—there have been so many ship wrecks—there is a charm—an underpining (as it were) a postponing—a universality of soul—of sympathy—an habitual—as well as constitutive superiority to trifles in fame & self love—what the stoics called a generous surrender of ones self to the order of events—which seem the requisites to greatness & sucess even in this unweeded garden. You have at these times—this nascent greatness—   But (tho' it is well—it is releaving to find the common prudence and selfishness of man lose its' hold for a moment) these spasms are not foundations for respect even among things rank and gross—they are termed excentric & affected—they resemble the religion of some the[n] present calvinists—whose characters & hourly conduct bear no part with what is grand & common to xianity, and to their pious moments. To be plainer—you seem more deeply wedded to every thing w'h concerns your self—to the external events w'h pass about you than is consistent with your talents—but I may be mistaken, as I know your late years so little. And I can illustrate my meaning but illy. Yet the memory of your jests about that poor Man (whose name I have lost, and who left the house without my being informed of it, till by accident a week afterwards) made an unpleasant impression on *me*. You are able to be witty—but avoid it on fellow creatures—it is the uniting social bond of empty minds—and it has cankered the most noble. To be serious, you, my beloved friend, who still bind me to earth, are defective in those parts w'h religion can only remydy. Not its holiest faith—its praying forms & modes—& its burning verities[n]—but its indwelling love of the Au- ther—its transforming power—w'h nothing but God can give to the efforts of your soul—to the obedience he demands. He has constituted man never to be good & grand, but as he is in communion with Himself. Glorious nature— tho' sadly fallen   This principle will like the ethereal fire w'h penetrates the world of matter diffuse light over your *habitual* character & you may leave a track w'h after times may point out. I write with trembling—for *at twenty the character is said to be formed.* How rapidly you approch it. Amidst those too, who call in question, by their non existence only in the present, our very faith in the immortality of souls—   It is, it is an enervating thing to live in a croud—to hear first scholarship called grand—but there is a magnet true & omnipotent in piety w'h will give you to enjoy talents learning & fame in their proper place   Alas alas, you will not listen to its stern requirement its sacrifices are great—for its prize is immortal. MME

Monday   I am unable to write more clearly. Besides what matters just the kind of letter—   Surely it was a trifling in you to defraud me of those you wrote first   You had been in debt from May. If my letter displease—be frank & manly enow to say it[2]

MH: bMS Am 1280.226(655). *Addressed:* Mr C. C. Emerson / H. U. / Cambridge / Mr C. U. Sheperd. *Endorsed:* M M Emerson / X / Oct 2[d] '25 / 1825.
 some the] ↑ some ↓ the
 verities] { }ties *in MS; supplied from T*
 1. CCE to MME, 12 Sept. 1825, says he's been preoccupied with the question, " 'What is the character I am to sustain, the part I am to act, in my future life' " (MT/ MH). MME picks up several ideas from his discussion.
 2. Paragraph written on outside. CCE to MME, 12 Sept., apologizes for not writ- ing sooner, saying "letter after letter, has been begun or written, and then committed in disgust to the fire"; he also mentions his own recent sickness and EBE's severe illness, topics MME ignores (MT/MH).

To William Emerson[3]

Elm Vale   Dec. 11. —25

I received yours with interest, my dear Nephew, and should have told of it before but I could not but think I should hear again from you or of you, and about the restoration of your excellent Mother who was then convalesent— for w'h blessing I thank God with her children. Your letter[1] was eloquent— but it is not easy to sattisfy a mind if it is awakned to a subject. I want to know of the German literature—how connected with theology and morals? What impulse your character heart & mind recieved from letters society &

the grander scenes of nature. What is most of all—your change of profession. The roman women were fond of calling themselves Mothers to the youth— Think if I have no smack of their patriotism—no right to call you to account? Was I silent at Evertt's change?[2] Do you doubt of the origin of xianity? Dislike its purpose—perplexed with it's wonders—at a loss about it's nature? Then you do well to avoid teaching. But if all or any of these causes operate—if you are a theist and are immortal their importance you well know is the same to you as tho' you were to take the high & holy office of priest & minister—tho' less hazardous.

Tell me truly, and I will respect your confidence. Is it matter of doubts caused by novel views? Let me have a history of the nature & progress of your opinions, if it be not asking too much. For consider, that the subject forms exclusively my existence—of my feeble^n visions—my unalterable faith—tho' for evidences I would now hardly look—so limited has always been my means & intercourse with the external world. Yet a new difficulty—wh would give a new source of thought would be valuable. Do you seek honors more tangible—read the history of the ambitious. You know it. Is it pleasures more^n lax—virtues less self denying and lofty? To choose a less degree of virtue you know is not possible to a lover of virtue. Its' nature is lost. But I meant not to preach, tho' it is sabbath day. And of great virtues to one in my situation may not be becoming to talk. And that were you now a candidate for another change, and I could elect it I would not dare to persuade. Lawyers are usefull nessecary—& somtimes the best of men.

I wish you had been particular in speaking of Edward.[3] When shall you hear of him? What a change in your family, dear William, but all that is dark at present will at the fittest moment become bright and more welcome for the passing cloud. I want to hear from my favorite correspondent and trust his eyes are and will be restored. How are his own hopes and Charles   I send love & thanks for his letter & want to know why he did not write by his Uncle.[4] Thomas can find conveyances. Adieu (tho' I am forgetting to say that health is good & eyes well not stronge) may God richly bless you prays one whom you must love if you can

MME.

MH: bMS Am 1280.220(75). *Addressed:* Mr William Emerson / Cambridge / Mss / Mr J. Hale / to care of Mr. T. W. Haskins. *Endorsed:* Miss M. M. Emerson / 11 Dec. 25.
feeble] ⟨growing⟩ ↑ feeble ↓
more] ⟨less⟩ ↑ more ↓

1. WE[3] to MME, 27 Oct. 1825, contains a poetic account of his voyage and thoughts while crossing the Atlantic. He arrived at Boston on 18 Oct., after almost two years in Europe (MT/EW).

2. As a result of his experiences in Germany, WE[3] decided to "renounce" his plan to study for the ministry and to take up law instead (*Life of RWE*, 113). Edward Everett, who had succeeded Buckminster as pastor of the Brattle Street Church, gave

up his Harvard professorship when he was elected to the United States Congress in Nov. 1824.

3. EBE, overtaxed by his combination of legal studies with school teaching, had been forced to give up his school at Roxbury in the summer of 1825. On 23 Oct. he sailed for Europe for his health, landing at Gibraltar in Nov.

4. RHE's brother Thomas Haskins.

1826

To Charles Chauncy Emerson

Elm Vale   Feb. 4   1826

Your interesting letters, especially the one of Autumn, my dear Charles, are before me. Your short vacation up and I fear no time to remember me, unless I ask it—no leisure to tell me of the whirl of empires[n] and the cradle of freedom. But we will neither forget that the year has been a jubilee in the calender of nations. That society has made rapid strides to that "perfectibility w'h is the declamation of the Orator"[1] is scarsly a question. For the ideas of perfect society of the man who is merely attached to his own present interest may not rise above very low degrees of virtue—and that "state of civilisation which generally arives at an epoch when all the beauties of the soul are mouldering to dust,"[2] may be his millenium. God be praised, there is a higher order going forward to encompass the perfection of virtue—by means probably, beyond human exertion and prophecy. There is one consideration w'h revolts all sympathy with these theorists—that the very first of all sciences which has been moulded into a system by man lies cumbered[n] in the rubbish of barbarous ages, and is so loaded with them and with artificial (and I fear fraudulent) apparatus that it takes years of the flower of life to pass thro' their dadalian volumns; and that often the rights of an individual are lost in their involutions. The Bar will excuse my warmth if they knew I was thinking of my nephews. Fifty years hence and the improvements may regenerate[n] the practice of law to those few grand principles, w'h are at all times & places sufficent for the largest and most difficult judicatories, an unlearned person believes.

Your subject of the G. O.[3] is among the most curious—and w'h I write now to tell you that I want you to send the disser. to me by the bearer of this who will be at Boston & Thomas[4] will take charge of your packet. Do not fail me. I want to trace their history, w'h will carry us to those wastes of time, when man travelling from Ararat lost the memory of all traditionary revelation, and allied himself to the harmonies of the material world—   When the flowers of the valley was the record of his time, and their melody the expression of his affections—when the terrific and lovely forms[n] of nature unfolded the instincts of his immortality & imaged to him the authers of his destiny, whom he called to his birth, his festivals & funeral. It was the same instinct w'h bore such high characters in the abstractions of Anaxagoras and his followers. But your object has led you to scenes where fraud and superstition have corrupted the primitive sentiments of the heart. Of the '*nature*' of these oracles, can there be a doubt? Tho' brass & marble have recorded the prodigies of hero gods[n] in tempels devoted to their apotheosis and Socrates sent to the tripod, we believe & know with an intuitive kind of certainty[n] that miracles are never in the power of any agent, but by the ordination of God and thro' his influence *alone*[n] for the ark of revelation. And tho' there may be a fallen spirit, who is compared to Monus,[5] & expelled from his cart, because of the satirical humour, who was supposed to sport with the delusions of idolaters, we know that the wretched priestess of Delphi was the victim of the fumes of the cliff & the cruelty of her masters. Yet these responses are vouchers for the Jewish prophecies, w'h they no doubt imitated—tho' useless & dim amidst the stronge proofs we have of the past & present existence & fullfillment of prophecy. There appears a resemblance in the certainty of the prediction, and the subject never fails of his fate, whether doomed to the caverns of the earth or the constellations of Heaven. You will not fail to let me have yours. And if I were less ashamed to ask for Edwards com[t] oration,[6] I would again desire it. You were kind enough to say I should hear of him whenever news came, w'h I do most daily expect. And I have hoped to have had an answer from your brother W[m] of mine of the eleventh of Dec.[7] But I fear me that he thinks me undeserving—and if that be the case I should grieve to know I was unworthy of his friendship, from any cause, tho' in ignorance of what.

Thanks, dear friend, for your wishes—because they are yours—to me all times are alike—my gnomon points to numbers w'h confuses imajanation—but given by a redeeming hand—therefore mine—tho' my life, of unsucessful efforts streched ever so long, would never merit one of those smalest figures w'h glow on the chart of our faith. To you on whose rosy pinions revolve novelty & knowledge, may each day of the year mark your progress upward & onward. The successive waves of time bring nothing to age (except to cross the ferry) only as they promise to bear the names of the youth it loves *to the other side*. Farewell, and tell me of Waldo, of whom I think much, and hope much to hear of his good eyes.[8]

Your Aunt   MME.

Pardon the whim if such it be, to ask you not to compare me to any wierd woman.[9] I who live so as to try never to offend by one singular word—whose whole time is devoted to one & the same object, pray you spare my age & vocation.

I do not speake of my Sister[10] because I intend writing a few lines. Never stop a letter for postage sake—and have you not a bill of charity w'h we talked off? Ask W[m] if he received a packet from me by post first of Jan.? I think it has taken the rounds w'h one of my letters did last summer.

MH: bMS Am 1280.226(656). *Addressed:* Mr Charles Chauncey Emerson / H. University / Cambridge, Mss. *Postmarked:* PORTLAND ME. / Feb 10. *Endorsed:* M M Emerson / Oracles &c. / Feby 4th '26.

empires] ⟨nations⟩ ↑ empires ↓
cumbered] ⟨buried⟩ ↑ cumbered ↓
regenerate] ⟨restore⟩ ↑ regenerate ↓
forms] *possibly* poems (*T*)
hero gods] ↑ hero ↓ gods
believe . . . certainty] believe ↑ & know with an intuitive kind of certainty ↓
God . . . *alone*] God ↑ and thro' his influence ↓ ⟨&⟩ *alone*

1. Freely quoted from CCE to MME, 21 Dec. 1825: "Society has been advancing with gigantic strides, so at least say the orators of the day, towards that perfectability wh. has so long been the theme of declamation" (MT/MH).

2. Unlocated. CCE to MME, 30 Jan. 1826 (MT/MH), complains that compared to Milton's age, the present state of society tends to hinder devotion to learning.

3. CCE to MME, 21 Dec. 1825, states, "One of the questions for a prize dissertation is 'the Nature of the Grecian Oracles'" (MT/MH) and solicits her advice.

4. Thomas Haskins.

5. Monus: *probably* Momus *intended:* according to Hesiod, Momus, son of Nox, was the god of "pleasantry"; as a result of his satire and ridicule of the gods, he was driven from heaven (*LCD*).

6. EBE's 1824 oration, "The Advancement of the Age."

7. See MME to WE[3], 11 Dec. 1825, n. 3.

8. Reference to improvement in RWE's eye condition that allowed him to begin teaching at Roxbury in Jan. 1826. MME to RWE, 26 Feb. and 22 Mar. [1826], was ambivalent about the news: "That you do not feel as on the tide of full sucess seems apparent from a little chilliness of style. What can you want more in this world than sight? You have not suffered enogh to make you estimate its value—to turn your soul to it's native & great objects." She also regretted his school teaching: "Solitude might have given you the Nymph Egeria or the white hind" (MH: 840).

9. In his "Wide World" journal entry for 7 Feb. 1821, which MME probably read, RWE called her "the Weird-woman of her religion [who] conceives herself always bound to walk in narrow but exalted paths which lead onward to interminable regions of rapturous & sublime glory" (*JMN* 1:49). Charles's use of the expression is unlocated; in his letter of 21 Dec. he calls himself "the suppliant at your tripod" (MT/MH).

10. Probably RHE.

To WILLIAM EMERSON[3]

W   March 21 [1826], Tuesday

With an interest (I've no eyes to speake off) I just received yours my dear Nephew, with no common degree of gratitude. I receive your manly confidence and with equal secrecy solicit you to answer the queries w'h press on my solitary mind at the rehearing of Eichhorn opinions.[1] Does *that original* gos. *give proof* of *any miracles?* Of *a divine mission* to this "Moral teacher"? *What does that gospel* w'h he *allows original* (& *true* perhaps) what does it report of Jesus? *Is it unconnected with judaism & prophecy?* If it denies or does not report of miraculous birth or resurrection, does it give an ever living and active soul distinct from matter in the reported Saviour, and that it went to God? Or does he say with Paul, if no resurrection—no faith? It is not nessecary? Yet again I beseech you tell me of what athority E. esteems this mutalated gospel? And of what athority Judaism? I will own to your own self, that at times and of late years I have felt tenderness to pure Patriarcal deism— and have said if the bible were proved useless, and the attributes of God the same which they are there represented, and such as I ever believed, and the soul immortal, it (the loss of bible) would leave me the same motives & hopes & joys. But without the facts w'h that book reveals where are we to find this God? The book of nature has more inexplicable pages, if not explained or in some degree by the supposed revelation,[n] than xianity. The providence—the terrible inequalities of nations, like the sufferings we mourn in Greece, are left in darkness. The unparrelled men like Plato & Aristote & others leave us so utterly at a loss for the nature & destiny of man—of the origin & athority of virtue; that if this "simpel and natural story" have no indubitable proofs of miracle (which a revelation must, in some way, be what *we* call miracu- lous, because beyond the usual course of nature & above all human power) that is, of revealing somthing of an invisible Being and immortal state, what is the value of the story? This is what I am anxious to know. You must go all lenghts to compleat your generosity—and tell me not only what you dont believe—but what you do. I respect heartily your renouncement of ministry.[2] It is a proof that those who leave it for *doubts*—have *doubts* that it may be true—and fear to have preached what they did not believe. Would the worthy Historian (Robertson) had done the same with his doubts, for his own sake.[3] The history of the world is a sad school for the xian, who has not those pecu- liar views w'h have been known to survive[n] the darkest views of providence. Robertson was facinated by imerging from obscurity, probably, and uniting with Hume & Gibbon. Neither of whom when considering their education & habits, have ever said any thing to startle even my poor intellects—   Hume has appeared so well answered by Campbell & of late by Channing (tho' in a single half page of a sermon) and in some measure by Brown, who tho' on the whole, I am not able to discern that he has done any service to real philosophy or xiainity.[4] These observations are to ask your attention to them & opin- ion—for of all, I have not retained the memory of their *arguments*. For I was never startled on the difficulty of miracles—it is the account of them. I admit your Critics, & your own conclusion, that "miracles cannot make falsehood truth &c—cannot affect the nature of moral truth." But is it not begging the question of those who believe that there are no miracles but by the power of God? Moreover, they were not wro't (if wro't at all) by Jesus in proof of any moral truth but of the reality of his divine mission, we say. I regret, dear friend, that you had not more time to consult the orthodox Critics. I respect the German literature, & love the glimpses I've seen, but think their excitment for novelty & rage of innovation may influence their critisms & couler even facts beyond my limited comprehension   And may I not be countenanced in scepticism[n] when even the doubts w'h rest on so much of the Roman history and the contrary opinions disturb the litteratie themselves? I wish I were worthy to offer myself the companion of your search in one pursuit[n] in which we have a mutual interest. I would say of the history of xiainity as Butler says of it's doctrines, if there is illusion let them in the name of God be given up.[5] But how shall we use and appropriate the name and attributes of this Being, if He is seen only in the cold and uniform laws of matter??

I write amidst the pain of blisters & the sweet regimen of a bilious stomach—but I want another letter from you. It costs you but little time, & the more pages you send by the post the more cheerfully I shall pay it. I send no messages as nothing should be more confined than our correspondence except to Waldo. Does he know your opinions? It is impossible he should not? Will you tell me however.

I did not know that you would think it worth while to give any mortage on that Hotel[6]—but as you have let it remain till I send for it & the interest. If in the interesting[n] page of information you can find time to speake of Charles' character—do. Of Waldo's eyes & what sources of pleasure he finds. I fear to trouble his eyes with any thing I can write. Your obliged and

aff[t] Aunt MME

* * *

MH: bMS Am 1280.220(75). *Addressed:* Mr William Emerson / Cambridge Mss / Care of Mr T. W. Haskins. *Endorsed:* Miss M. M. Emerson, Mar. 21 —26.

the supposed revelation] ↑ the supposed ↓ revelation

survive] ⟨live in⟩ ↑ survive ↓

countenanced in scepticism] ⟨excused⟩ countenanced ↑ in scepticism ↓

pursuit] ⟨interest⟩ ↑ pursuit ↓

interesting] ⟨more⟩ interesting (*heavily canceled*)

1. Johann Gottfried Eichhorn (1757–1828), known for his "higher criticism" of the Bible, wrote historical and critical introductions to the Old and New Testaments and challenged notions of Mosaic and Pauline authorship. WE[3] had met Eichhorn in Germany and purchased his five-volume introduction to the New Testament for Harvard College (MT/EW). No letter to MME on this subject survives. For WE[3]'s account of Eichhorn, written in the fall of 1824, see *L* 1:160–62 n. 12; RWE to WE[3], 20 Nov. 1824, mentions WE[3]'s letter of 8 Aug. 1824 to John Fessenden, regarding Eichhorn (*L* 1:155).

2. See MME to WE[3], 11 Dec. 1825, n. 2.

3. Scottish historian William Robertson (1721–93), an ordained minister, gained personal wealth and preferment in the Scottish church partly as a result of his extremely successful histories, *Scotland during the Reigns of Queen Mary and of King James VI . . .* (1759) and *The Reign of the Emperor Charles V* (1770). Also an active politician and debator, Robertson published only one sermon.

4. George Campbell (1719–96), Scottish "divine," whose *Dissertation on Miracles* (1762) is considered one of the "chief answers" to Hume's "Of Miracles" (*DNB*);

probably WEC's Dudleian lecture, "Evidences of Revealed Religion," 14 Mar. 1821 (*The Works of William Ellery Channing, D. D.*, new ed. [Boston: American Unitarian Association, 1875], esp. 224–26); see MME's comments on Thomas Brown in 1822.

5. Bishop Joseph Butler, *The Analogy of Religion to the Constitution and Course of Nature*, first published in 1736.

6. See introduction to part 3, p. 130.

To Ralph Waldo Emerson

Vale   Ap 27 [1826] thursday

My dear Waldo,

You must err about Humes fame.[1] May be that I know nothing & fear nothing. That he is not profound is acknowledged. Where is the danger of miracles being violations of those events we call laws? They are arbitrary— do not exist in the nature of things as laws of mind & morals—for in beleving the future in phisics to resemble the past "we take a step &c."[2] Yet the mind (unless strangely perverted) is constituted to receive & love miracles—and does not need the gratuitous assumption of Brown that they are no violations and that there is a new antecedent to every new sequence.[3] I cant see where the advantage is of thrusting in a new antecedent to changing the nature of the old or the effect? And perhaps we are just as much in the dark about 'relation' as ever. It is a secret far less interesting than some which affect the destiny of the world. It seems Brown puts a monstrous miracle, w'h would tend to let every thing go to rack, on the same footing with a phisical one—when he rates *that* of the false testimony of an apostle, or all of them, at the same as any miracle in the laws of &c   You will pardon so obsolete[n] a subject as Cause & effect—but I am just reading it—and he does admirably else where about miracles—   It surely must be nothing short of atheism knowingly to deny their possibility as does Geniseus—probably Eichorn and others. Still I do not see with a late divine that calling them 'violations' is intended to impugn the divine rectitude.[4] But when I trembled *of late,* at the name of Eichorn, I remember he is said by his admirers to be excessive fond of hypotheses & ingeniously able to support them. I call to mind Michaelis and Euler and Leibnitz[5] and others—   But for xianity I should not tremble if they should take away every written gospel if they left one epistle of Paul genuine I should find that *Jesus had risen*—if they were to take away all the miracles he performed, but that of his assension (as on that was founded the faith of the apostles & first martyrs) and leave what they cant take—the prophecies w'h have and are verifying, we should be stronge enough. But Michaelis proves the genuiness of all the gospels—tho' in *doubt* of the two first chap's of Mat.[6] The account of the resurrection is discrepant, & when I was young, I used to collect the harmonies—but since I learned that the revelation, tho' divine was cast into human circumstances and to pass thro' human hands I dont want any more natural account of the event than terrified men & women running back

& forth would give. And that the tempel of Adonis[n] kept charge of the spot recorded the place in history as faithfully as when Helena built a chh.[7] But for poor me, who never learned, I see the history of xianity on every barbarous age w'h it survived—those very ages bro't together nations to hear of this story—in all that is great refined & good in the whole world w'h is sweeping before us. I want to say more on the letter of 8 of Jan. but am obliged by Sister Phebe to send by this mail— And shall venture to send a scrawl w'h your last occasioned. Pardon all prosing & repetition.

MH: bMS Am 1280.226(841). *Endorsed:* 1825 x.

obsolete] *possibly* absolute (*T*)

Adonis] ⟨Venus⟩ ↑ Adonis ↓

1. 1825 endorsement incorrect: MME responds to RWE's letter of 8 Jan. 1826, in which he anticipates increased fame for Hume, whom he calls "one of those great limitary angels to whom power is given for a season . . . to cast . . . another weight into the *contrary scale*" in the great system of "good & evil" (*L* 7:140).

2. Central to Hume's skeptical argument is the idea that, "in all reasonings from experience, there is a step taken by the mind, which is not supported by any argument or process of the understanding" (*Works* 4:51).

3. Thomas Brown, *Relation of Cause and Effect*, esp. 61–66 and note E, 219–33. RWE responds to Brown on cause and effect in Nov. 1824 (*JMN* 2:402–3).

4. Probably Wilhelm Gesenius (1786–1842), German orientalist and biblical critic; Brown (see above, n. 3) located Hume's major error in his "false definition of a miracle . . . as 'a violation of the laws of Nature' " (Brown, *Cause and Effect*, 220; Hume, *Works* 4:133).

5. John David Michaelis (1717–91), German "higher" critic of the Bible; Leonard Euler (1707–83) and Gottfried Wilhelm Leibniz (1646–1716), both mathematicians who followed the rationalist tradition of Descartes.

6. John David Michaelis, *Introduction to the New Testament*, 6 vols., trans. Herbert Marsh (London, 1802), discusses at length the question of the authenticity of the New Testament and at one point concludes it is impossible that the first two chapters of the first Gospel "proceeded from the pen of St. Matthew" (1:165–69).

7. Saint Helena (ca. 248–328?), mother of Constantine the Great, was converted to Christianity in 313 and is said to have gone to Jerusalem, where she found the True Cross and the Holy Sepulcher and was responsible for having churches built on the supposed sites of the Nativity and Ascension.

To Sarah Ripley

[Apr.? 1826?][1]

and the passing earth can do nothing worth mentioning for us or against us if we be immortal—*relative* to that destiny they do much. I shall never cease to think of my Father—but as to his name or memorial it can be of no importance to any but his grandsons & they might have raised a stone if they wanted one. hereafter. I dont intend any shall tell where or when I rotted. Tho' I am not indifferent to the inscription and was glad to find you did not like

Waldo's. I inclose one which I hope will meet Father's & your approbation, and as it may need modeling I have sent a copy to Waldo. I know very much of my father's childhood. The *simplicity* and *enthusiasm* was remarkable of his character.

Farewell dear Sister, that you may soon recover & long enjoy health & usefullness is the daily wish of your sister & frind

MME.

Erected by this Town in memory of their Pastor Rev. W. E. who was born 1743 graduated at H. U. 1761 ordained 1767, died 1776 in the A. A. where he was appointed chaplin.

> Truth charity and enthusiasm distinguished him from the dawn till the close of life; exalted by profound peity. He passed the ordeal of afflic-tion uninjured. He loved his office and filled it with the eloquence of the soul. He loved his family and was to it as a good Angel. He loved our blessed revolution better and would minister to it he said, tho' it should cost his life.

Our Sisters dont like enthusiasm—but you will & it is true & good quality. Without it dear Sarah what all our hopes in future? (I omit the word better[2] to please them)   It gives life to reason & faith

MH: bMS Am 1280.226(1254). *Addressed:* Miss Sarah Ripley / Concord / Mss. *En-dorsed:* Fathers epitath *and* (*in RWE's hand*): M. M. Emerson / Inscription for her Fathers tomb.

1. MME sent another, slightly different, version of this inscription for the memo-rial for WE[1] to Sarah Ripley; the fragmentary letter is postmarked "Waterford, Me. April 28" (MH: 1253).

2. In the last sentence of the epitaph, MME crossed out the word "better" but then interlined it above. The inscription on the monument in Concord reads, "Erected by this Town / in Memory of their Pastor / Rev. William Emerson / who died at Rutland, Vt., 1776 / aet. 33, / On his Return from the American Army, / of which he was a Chaplain. / Enthusiastic, Eloquent, / Affectionate and Pious. / He loved his Family, his People, / His God and his Country / And to this Last he yielded / the Cheerful Sacrifice / of his Life."

To William Emerson[3] and Ruth Haskins Emerson

Vale   May 20 [1826] Sat Eve.

I just received your very interesting letter my dear Nephew and will not let the post go out without a line.[1] Do you think the professors of xianity so exclusive as to view their friends with altered eyes who dont believe with them? In your case I do—for till my fears were confirmed by the 1[t] letter I knew not how much I valued you—knew not that I should so regret what I esteem unhappy. I thought of your past character w'h had attracted the re-gards of society—of your future prospects—surrounded with beauty worth

Figure 16. Monument for William Emerson (1743–76), Old Hill Burying Ground,
Concord. Notice Mary Emerson's word "enthusiastic."
Photograph by Nancy Craig Simmons.

& wealth perhaps—of the wife the children and extended connections. But you are not be treated with bug bears—nor do the liberties of friendship, w'h you kindly allow me, excuse the least approach to cant. I am very desirous, being very unacquainted, to learn all that can be offered against my faith. Without evidence it has no charms—tho' I sacrificed the little all I had in youth—I would not be deceived. Alas, it has done little for me—but the defect is in my constitution. It has given by connecting me with the will of God to rejoice in the eagles of the race who sun themselves in its' orb. *Would* that all of the better order were willing to accept of a system w'h professes to provide for the low & helpless—and divest themselves of the littlenesses w'h attaches to the undergrowth. Am I uncharitable to ask if a report that the Son of God had been on the earth to enlighten the Platos and Ciceros it would not have been thought the most glorious of plans—the 'chivalry'—the heroism the philosophy & poetry of the universe? The calvinists hold to a kind of aristocry and they are more attached to xianity than my order of unitarians. I am obliged by the *information* on the 3^d page. If E.[2] reports this—it *is well*— *his conclusions* are nothing   Surely not if he can work himself into a belief that an uninspired Peasant could be "inspired with & teach a lofty morality and a pure philosphy"—   This is a miracle—an effect w'h violates all laws & reason. On the other hand, this morality this philosophy—bears the strongest evidence of being almost wholly prospective—look at it—who would in their reason be persuaded to practice it if this were the only world? Not that it does not naturally produce contentment & peace when habitual—not that it is not fitted for the natural seriousness and forecast of the immortal race— but it militates against so many artificial wants and darling propensities that it has lived & thriven in a continual warfare. I would not speake of the power and price of that which I believed you would not one possess. * * *

sab Morning 21

     I rejoice to find that you have not yet woven a web of deistical sophistry— or things worse—rejoice to find you cannot tell what you *do* believe. It must be a bold sailor on the abyss of infidelity that can do that—   It has not been known that a believer educated in xianity has been ever able to adopt a consistent scheme of deism. And it is to the honor of that imperishable law of virtue which cannot be fullfilled by man in his present unaccountable state. I confess I deceved you by coolness in my answer—   I wanted to know your course—what coulers—what compass—? But I gladly give up female curiosty—   You will return my dear William if not soon—later. If you do not feel the wants of the soul now you will get rid of the opiate by the wholesomness of pain. God, in whom I believe, take you into the arms of his mercy, prays fervently

MME

* * *

My dear Sister, Thomas writes you are still confined. I grieve for you—   I pray for your restoration as sincerely as I do for my own happiness   And much as I hate journeying should be at your side if Betsy was not. What a favor it is she can be with. She is indeed an excellent Nurse better surely better than your aff[t]

Sister MME

MH: bMS Am 1280.220(75). *Addressed:* Mr William Emerson / Cambridge / Mss. *Postmarked:* Waterford Me   May 29. *Endorsed:* Miss M. M. Emerson / May 20 — 26.

1. WE[3] probably tried to answer questions posed in MME's letter of 21 Mar.; his letter does not survive.

2. Probably Eichhorn; MME seems to debate ideas in WE[3]'s letter.

To Ralph Waldo Emerson

Sab M. 21 May [1826]

I know the value of your letters, dear W sufficently to have them all restored—enough to excite a lively gratitude[n]—they generalise—concentrate—and panoramise (if that is right word) the misterious tides of human life—they swell at times—at others lessen the little puddle stream[n] that is hastening one on. They give me a great deal to say—but lessen my ability to do it. * * *

Have you thriven under evil? The oak is grander stript of foilage. How is it possible you can divest your self of faith to write as in the 10 date?[1] I believe it to be only as an intellectual exercise—so let it pass—   Such would decorate the grand tempel w'h is building in the universe to the honor of God—but you would not like to be absent at the laying the corner stones—the supporting pillars in your section of the Country—   You would like, may hap, distinction among the stately orders in solemn worlds of grandure—it will be the benefactors of their race—who have purged the system—led them to the means—the faith w'h purifys. Oh I do rejoice that you have been kept from launching till your anchor is stronger than I suspect it is—till the tide w'h you imajine is sweeping away old beliefs will ebb & return with full bearings of truth—if you prefer socity to the solitude of an Abdiel.

In haste—I fear I write the same things over—for some ideas possess me so much. "Why am I anxius about C."[2] Curious only perhaps—why about you & others   A cat may look out for a king.

Adieu dear & valued Correspondent. Write for every letter shall be numbered so that you cannot lose one when the heart is cold which they have agitated.

MH: bMS Am 1280.226(842). *Addressed:* Mr R W Emerson. *Endorsed:* 1826.
gratitude] gratitude ⟨for the gifts of [*illegible*] they contain⟩ (*heavily canceled*)
puddle stream] puddle ↑ stream ↓

1. Probable reference to RWE to MME, 10 Apr. 1826 (*L* 7:143–44), and possibly 10? Feb.? (*L* 7:141–42).

2. CCE; see MME to WE[3], 21 Mar. 1826, and RWE to MME, 6 Apr. 1826 (*L* 1:169).

To Ralph Waldo Emerson

Tuesday   Vale   June 13 [1826]

My dear Waldo

It is vain to draw nearer to the living—nothing so "weary and wasting" —the anatomy of one carcase ("pah! how it smells") answers for a thousand to him who can see. As to your divination, if by those who had seen the Allwise, you mean like the priestess of Ob to recall the Jewish prophets, my allusion to the Pythoness is smale implication.[1] The legislator and his succesors were inspired—and their code embraced the honor of the Creator and the safty of the creatures to the very beasts. It is true that the Inspirer intended a more perfect dispensation—and in the fullness of time he came to add the ineffable charms of sympathy and benvolence to a system w'h (like that of the antient philosophers) recognised only the immutable principles of justice. He came not as some ill fated Germans insinuate to connect xianity with Judaism and its'ⁿ abuses—*but* he *opposed all of them* at the expense of a bitter persecution— & took away the whole fabrick of ceremonies. Yet he fullfilled its prophecies that the universe might be convinced of his mission. What else he accomplished—it becomes me not to dare to touch at this time—with you to—who have not introduced those controverted doctrines. Respecting his vouchers in letter (Jan. 8—26) you query "whether were the external evidences given up it's internal would convince."[2] If prophecy & miracle were none, what proof of a revelation that would come with athority to the multitude? It's worth & fittness would only attest & include natural religion? As to what are usually called internal evidences seem to be an essential part of the revelation? Your sort of commercial ideas of Heaven remind me of a young man in Boston, who asked another young man (tho' the questioned was less gifted) if commerce would not answer the same good purposes of xianity? It may be (for scripture dont affirm absolutely) that those who have had no advantages here may find a purgatory and an education. But it seems that the nature of spirit is to imbibe knowledge of the Great Spirit as naturally as the bodily senses do their elements—that the genuine lover of virtue cannot sustain any painfull discipline where the providence of God will not be clouded by that veil of matter w'h He has intercepted between His throne and our present perplext state. The *"within"* you do not mention—there and there alone will exist *that* which will forever prevent any irking of inferior condition. The martyrs may have the palms if they want to—palms—there are none in that broad spacedⁿ reigion to him who only wants the virtue to love perfectly his God—and lose every sense of deficiency in that ocean of wonders. But should our revelation prove only one of those events wh take place without cause law or Design— like a delightfull vision of the poet—w'h has had its effect—merely to occupy the deceived and make up the force of life, till some other mythology takes its' turn—then *indeed* the future may resemble the present—   Exist we must— not a shrub lifts its' head but bears the impression of passing & repassing— And whether nature offers any certainty that it's Auther will afford us any thing better is hardly questionable—rather the spirit may wander in scenes more unpleasant than any here—with more dread certainty of change and hasard—or if that we call spirit depends on a transmutation & collection of matter again to act—the Genius & the king may take their turn in the mines and dungeons.

What is there, apart from the effects of xianity, to give any rational prospect of that perfectibility they talk off? The fine arts have been stationary for ages?—the phiscal sciences advance—but what are they?—politicks progress—but most "spirally"—and thier *natural* progress is very questionable? Surely while man remains what he has been? My interrogations are put when there is not the form of a question—but indeed I feel^n a diffidence in shaping my tho'ts to you—and should never write but you make it the condition of letters from you   And soon as the good news came of your improved health I wrote as rapidly as four bad pens in exchange can blot the paper. Suffer one query more if each have a "solitary law, universe" &c^3 what will be the conclusion? That opinion is innocent if it lead to idolatry and all its foul breed? The colours of the bow are more vivid to your eye—but essentially the same to all—or where would be laws? "The priests of God, says De Stale, should be able to tell us what they suffer and what they hope; how they have modified their characters by certain thoughts, in a word we expect from them the secret memoirs of the soul in it's relations with the Deity"^{4}

If I needed any other excuse for wanting letters I would not name it after this eminent sentiment. Farewell dear Waldo—I will not add what keeps beating adieu

Your Aunt
MME

Still I persume not to pry into that sanctuary of memoirs tho' your expressions of frendship are as gratefull as honoring. Would to God you were not at Cambridge.

MH: bMS Am 1280.226(843). *Addressed:* Mr R Waldo Emerson / Cambridge. *Endorsed:* 1826 / X.

and its'] and ⟨tolerate⟩ its'
spaced] *possibly* spread
feel] ⟨express⟩ feel

1. The opening sentences echo RWE's letter of 6 Apr. 1826 (*L* 1:167–69). See also *JMN* 3:19–20; cf. Shakespeare, *Hamlet*, 5.1.219: "And smelt so? Pah!" The priestess of Ob is unidentified; "Pythoness" is a term used for the priestess of Apollo at Delphi, that is, a prophetess.

2. See *L* 7:141–42. MME's comment suggests that the letter Tilton dates Feb.? 10? was part of the letter of 8 Jan.

3. Freely quoted from RWE's letter of 8 Jan. (*L* 7:140).

4. de Stael, *Germany* 3:333.

To WILLIAM EMERSON[3]

Vale   June 21 Wed. —'26

Your triply welcome confirmation of the restoration of your Mother & brothers my dear Nephew renders me your debtor in the epistolary way very desirable. And I was very glad to hear of my old friend Bulkley being in tolerable care.

Thanks also for the courteous manner of saying you had altered the epitaph.[1] So long since I sent it that it was almost unexpected to hear it. I gave it to you to shape & 'lick' into "usage". And you have done it handsomely. And the confidence you have reposed in me by sending it to the Committee before sending it here is a compliment to my freindship for you, which I hope will prosper and increase. You understand me, that it could be of no importance to any but yourselves. As it is done—and I have a space here I would submit my opinion or rather *feelings* w'h often purblind judgment. As the love of God was at the bottom of all his affections—does it hold a discriminating place in the epitaph? Is it not a repetition of "piety"? When I first received it I dreamt (and dreams are nothing) that you appeared with your brothers in advanced life—when a sort of speculative interest in ancestry attends liesure—that you were visiting this very stone with some highly interesting woman, the wife of some of you—that she had a great share (too much) of family pride—and besides, one of the very "claws" with which Johnson used to criticize epitaphs of the more gifted poets. And with a very severe smile, she observed that many a man might return from the quiet office of priest in an Army, and die by the way without having intended any sacrifice of life. But you assured her that his constitution was such, that he little expected to return. She appeared sattisfied—was silent at least—read it again—looked at the little boy beside her thought of those who absent were entering an Evertt's career, and seemed more curious to learn the character of their Ancestor—asked if as 'affectionate' was expressed in "loving" whether there was no other quality to have been named—whether he was not generous—full of truth & honor? I wanted to tell her yes yes!—that the very last thing he did in publick at home was the representative of heavenly. When he was watching the filling up the ranks one day, and found a deficency, he instantly gave liberty to a dutchman, whom he had purchased, and whom for some time, he had been training to the care of a family that was to be deserted. I wanted to tell her listening ear the story of his afflictions—that amidst a party counsel, raised by the enmity of an individual, he had sustained himself by the consciousness of integrity without the interference of a single clergyman—that they had deserted him in some cases—in others[n] he asked not their aid. While I stood thus—the venerable form of a minister who had told me the story—who had stood forth the first to exchange pulpits—who had known him always—who forsaw that the cloud would leave him more luminous—this very man (whose ashes lie in the woods w'h are seen from the City) seemed to me clothed with his wonted garb—and as he read your inscription—he said it *was enough*—

the record was elsewhere! that the love of our revolution was the love of God & liberty and humanity.

Pardon, dear Nephew, the dream—the dreamer has no faith in hereditary virtues—or she would not have told it. Indulge her in preserving it and showing it to your brothers. They know only one branch of your grandfather's family. My very aged Uncle.[2] Nothing could form a greater contrast than he to his brother. One capacity he has enjoyed uniformly—that of admiring loving & respecting the brother & patriot.

Your aff^t Aunt
MM Emerson

MH: bMS Am 1280.220(75). *Addressed:* Mr William Emerson / Cambridge. *Endorsed:* Miss M. M. Emerson / 21 June (26.

others] *possibly* ethics

1. For her father's monument (see MME to Sarah Ripley, Apr.? 1826). MME to WE[3], 16 Aug. 1826, seems to respond to a recent letter in which he must have apologized for further revising her epitaph. She claims she is "sattisfied—that no female pen shall inscribe it—*him* over whose grave the honors of our revolutionary war were heard & seen. That the grandsons of other patriots are at this moment employed in doing honor to their names" (MH: 220[75]).

2. Uncle John Emerson of Conway died 26 Jan. 1826 at the age of eighty-one.

To Ralph Waldo Emerson

July 18 [1826]

"What is poetry?"[1] The eye sees not its own lustre. To me it is an ingoing— And like the shepard who lost his pleasures in inquiring after the Naid, I must content with admiring this hidden treasure—too exquisitely fine to be analysed—a very proteus—at times to me nothing less than a Minotor & lost in labyrinths—at others like the sybiline leaves scattered at the misterious cavern by blighting simoon.[n] —Like a will of the wisp, and in the form of it's own darling Will. carries us one bog & brake at once dazzeling & tormenting—the very 'mouth piece' of bawds & swaggerers—yet like Vulcan able to forge armory for kings & Gods—and throwing off sparks worthy of the skies. True, alas, its drapery floats to every common eye with the insignia of all nations & climes—it comes mournfull & terrible in the clouds of the north— gorgeous & defying in tournaments & conquest—winning & voluptuous in Asian splendor. Amazed I gaze—and it is lost in the tomb of nations—it rises with empires—and blood & pestilence & woe have brot their trophies to its aid—the dust of antient urns make rich the laurels of modern bards. Not so with him to whom this celestial Guest has appeared in a garb w'h is conjectured to be original and native. She has come not with sword & fire and dragons & gorgons—nor even with sylphs & faries (tho she would not have disdained the chamber where King Richard died) nor bows & arrows—but bearing the olive and palm—decked with the humblest flowers w'h grow wild in the mountains—often with the staff of the wanderer—sometimes in rain-bows &[n] the loftiest gifts of nature and asks no other "epoch of thought—no point in actual history"[2] to concentrate around her alter the *souls* of men. She has constituted her priest—and he alone of poets, since Milton,[3] deserves to be called *a hermit in the fields of thought*[n]—(the philosophers may take um-brage)—she has enticed him into the sanctom santorium of nature—where there is a perpetual millennium—yet she has her festivals and arrays herself in magical vestments—when the seer & yellow leaf of Autumn lies motion-less—when the aged trees lift their naked arms to the dun & mellow clouds—when the sun seems to tarry in the Heavens & take no note of earth—marks no sign on the dial—gives no form to the shawdow of man—then[4]

MH: bMS Am 1280.226(844).
blighting simoon.] blighting ⟨monsoons⟩ ↑ simoon ↓ . ⟨True, its' drapery⟩
sometimes . . . &] sometimes ⟨decked with⟩ ↑ in rainbows & ↓
thought] *underlined twice*
    1. "What is poetry?": RWE to MME, 30 June 1826 (*L* 7:148–50), asks for her thoughts on the "nature & value" (148) of poetry, a question he then explores at length; his conclusion begins "What is Poetry?" (150).
    2. Cf. RWE to MME, 1 Aug. 1826 (*L* 1:169–71): "or doubtful if some moral epoch is not just now fulfilled in its history" (170).
    3. The "priest" of poets is probably Wordsworth, who is discussed in RWE's letter.
    4. Letter is incomplete.

To Ezra Ripley

July 25   Thurs. 1826

Honored Father,
    The letters I *hear* about that you favor our Brother[1] with have interested me so much that I cannot but take the liberty to write to you. I think of you very often—*but I hate to write*—and never do it but as the means to do busi-ness or get letters. But when I heard that the venerable House which had so long been filled with the voices of my Fathers had a neighbour of the sort I sus-pect, I was for puting forth at once—   I grew cooler (and wiser perhaps) and waited to congratulate you on the sight of the little Daniel & his Mother.[2] God grant they may prove comforts. And indeed the more I considered the matter the less cause of regret I found in the schismatic Church. To be rid of fanatical narrow minded christians is a blessing. *Offences must come.* There must—there is surely a large class of people so formed, as a link in the great social chain, as that the high rational and extended views of the divine goverment make no impression on—the sole clue to their feelings and understanding is—"the chh I belong to is the only true one." They never read (and it were pity they should—for it would be a kind of sacriledge to give them the sayings of Whichcote)—"that the only seperation between the world and the church is

that which is made by innocence and virtue."[3] Oh I am sick to the very heart when I see long faces and high orthodoxy, where it is united with exclusive salvation and canting declamation—and often times with a most sad gripe of the hand when obscure charity calls. But I forbear—you will hardly think, my dear Sir, I have grown wiser than at the first *pious* and *liberal* intelligence conveyed by the Recorder.[4] Let us talk of higher and brighter matters—tho' while on the subject (as you *may* hear I am a methodist) I would observe that for these two years I have scarsly attended Mr D.[5] not less from weariness of his cant, than want of health—that want of eyes and so forth, led me to wish for "some publick worship" & that of late I have attended in the little Chaple, which stands in a near wood, of the Methodist—that to my surprise I found the Fabricator of pails & tubs[6] a very sensible & interesting preacher—and that I have gone there for some weeks constantly. I hope you will not dislike it. I wrote for your opinion before I had bad eyes—but I must say dear Sir, you are rather close about answering letters. I told Mr Douglas that I had written to you on the subject. Mr & Mrs Ripley dont seem to relish it. And of all things I have shunned the groaning religionists— But I have found nothing so exclusive and grating as at the old meeting House.

I was going to speake of the singular coincidences of event on the glorious 4th![7] It was indeed an auspicious day to our pious Adams—to be released from earth and care and exhausted powers—and to have such a memory! I thought of my native state—and could almost hear the tolling of the bells and firing of guns—& eulogies of oraters. Of Jefferson, I know nothing—but respect for his talents & scholarship. What was his prevailing character? If he was not a good patriot & man I would throw up all the rest.

Of the interesting state of my sister[8] I would speake—but it is said I am peculiar in not estimating life— Yet for your sake[n] and her little orphan Nephew and others I hope she will live. It is my prevailing opinion (and you were wont to allow me some skill) *she will,* and slowly recover a degree of health. God we know will order life or death for the best.

Adieu, dear Sir, Yours with respect
M.M.E.

28[9] In reading over this—it sounds severe— But you, dear Sir, will understand—I mean no disrespect to any sect—nor to the good genuine calvinists of which were our fathers— The trinitarian may be right— But it is this seperation from orthodox unitarians I dislike when I trouble myself to dislike any thing which occurs in the great whole.[n] I have not thanked you for the letter of february. But I felt pleased, & should have written but for eyes. at that time

It would be a gratification to me, Sir, if you could let me hear of the subjects—or points which have seperated the members who have left their Fathers house.[10]

MH: bMS Am 1280.220(76). *Addressed:* Rev. E. Ripley D. D. / Concord / Mss. *Endorsed:* M. M. Emerson / Answered Augt 8th. *Postmarked:* Boston / Mas. / Aug 5.

sake] sake ⟨& mine⟩ ⟨*heavily canceled*⟩

whole.] ⟨plan⟩ whole.

1. EzR's brother and MME's brother-in-law, the Reverend Lincoln Ripley.

2. Son and widow (Susan Fitts Ripley) of MME's half brother Daniel B. Ripley.

3. Numerous editions of sermons and sayings of Benjamin Whichcote (1609–83), a Cambridge Platonist, were printed from transcriptions made by his admirers; not located in *Select Notions* (1685) or *Moral and Religious Aphorisms* . . ., republished by Samuel Salter (1753).

4. An article titled "Encouraging Prospects," in the Boston *Recorder* for 9 June 1826, reported the organization at Concord on 5 June of a new church "professing the primitive faith of the New England pilgrims"; ten of the sixteen new members had been dismissed from EzR's First Church for this purpose; the organizing minister was the Reverend A. Rand, and Lyman Beecher of Boston preached the sermon.

5. The Reverend John Abbott Douglass (1798–1878), Waterford's Congregational minister since 1821.

6. Probably the deacon of the Methodist chapel.

7. The deaths of the second and third presidents, John Adams and Thomas Jefferson, which coincided with the fiftieth anniversary of the signing of the Declaration of Independence.

8. MME traveled to Concord in Aug. to be with her half sister Sarah Ripley, but she returned to Waterford before Sarah's death on 2 Nov. 1826. MME to WE[3], 16 Aug. [1826], was "resigned" to her death: "For Sarah own self no one can mourn—her ardent & affectionate spirit has run it's course." But she added her wish that "Sarah should live if she can be well. The only friend I have in single blessedness and she would have taken an interest in me which my own sisters cannot" (MH: 220[75]).

9. Dateline reading "July 25 Thurs." is an error: 25 July fell on Tuesday in 1826. This second date suggests MME probably began the letter on Thursday, 27 July.

10. See above, n. 4. RHE to MME, 15 and 18 Feb. 1827, reports that Ripley has "lately been afflicted by several persons leaving his church, & among them, his good friend, & neighbour Deacon White, & joining the other society" (MH).

To Ralph Waldo Emerson

Monday   Sep 11 [1826]

Dearest of Writers

I got by sheer stealth yesterday to the 12 page—[1]   Set down sattisfied to marvel & admire at the developing so new to me the principles of arts in every body—fine—but the "shell" is finer—because of the comparison— Oh what a wonder is man—& how glorious the career of him who is able to tell man what is in him—you will you must kindle as you go forward like the light of morning—   A glance this morning at pages 36 & thereabout has resusitated me—shall I find sermonising in every deed? That is what Im after. I looked for later dates than I find. What I now want is (if wholly convenient) a letter now & then by mail—   It will keep me along & you cannot excuse me on score of mail cost. I want the long letter you mention in the one you gave me. Indeed *we* can only commune by pen. You are more sensitive than ever—that dolefull shake of head & grim look I had when you interested me thursday in parlour disgusts you so that you wont talk—all the way going you said nothing that you might. That destiny of which the freedom of our wills seems but an obedient member, forbids me to enter fine society at the peril of constant & hopeless disgrace from the ebullition of vanity & confidence w'h lies so dead in solitude— Therefore write I say if you can & I will write to remember that I have self existence of some sort.

You wanted to converse of your mother— I should—but you began wrong by excluding some of my first friends from any share in *her* virtues. There is a family singleness of heart and goodness of temper in some of them w'h nothing can equal in the social life. True, when she first grew up, I knew her to be without any comparison— I knew her, as none can, in all the purity of obscurity & characterised by a fervid calvinistic piety. At about 17 she worshiped at Malden one sabbath in an Autumnal season—her manners & looks riveted the attention of grey hairs— I continued to see for some years & thought her looks words & actions the sweetest wisest fittest chastest of all others—she conversed on riligion from the heart & I loved every accent— of Young, Cowper & such like with calm & stedfast degree of confidence in her own opinions—the rage of literature had not injured the sentiments of the heart in those days—& the best of all virtues *humility* gave an independence which is *now* the effect of frivolous accomplishments in women. She married one of the finest of men—but their rural Eden was not stocked with fruit enow for him—& the little I saw of the innocent Eve did not answer my expectations of her. Their removal w'h I attended for some months showed her in a more improved light. She met the demands of socity with honor to herself and approbation of that. In a new situation, w'h tempted the ambition of the Adam she sustained any occasional trial of temper with a dignity firmness & good sense that I shall ever respect—and obtained a greater influence than is common over one of the best of husbands. At his death (w'h was preceded by a lingering disease of long endurance & of a kind w'h deadened almost every affection) she behaved with that same dignity above noticed. Since, in the trials of boarders the most I could say would not be too much. *But*—always a but—whether the indulgence of her sons' frivolous ambition for fame—her intercourse with their mirth & latidenaism (what is it)[2] has not altered her?? Not at this moment for she is scarsly recovered from the rod of chastening, but whether had they treated her like a being whose kingdom was not here—had they spoken of that world to w'h she goes—had it been possible to restore that tone & feelings w'h she naturally possesed—she would more have resembled what she once did, the vessel laid up before the Lord full of heavenly mana within & without like pure polished gold. I have run a risque perhaps—but I've nothing to lose. Yet I do think you wished to speake on the subject. Tell me *I request,* if I pain or please. That I can write better, than speake of one of the most favored of women who excites envy, is certain.[n] Mrs R & Sarah send love to my Sister & you & Charels. Susan has made a just remark in giving you all manner of advantage over G. R.[3] She is a sensible woman. Adieu.

MME

I write by snatches. Sarah talks of your Mothers visit   I lot on it.

MH: bMS Am 1280.226(845). *Addressed:* Mr. R. Waldo Emerson / Cambridge / Mss. *Postmarked:* Concord Ms / Sept 11. *Endorsed:* 1826 X / M M E.

certain.] certain. ⟨That if there were no literature & effo⟩

1. Probably RWE's untitled journal of 1826 (*JMN* 3:3–41); see mention of the "shell of Clio," on which MME comments below, on RWE's p. 10 (*JMN* 3:7).

2. Probably an attempt to spell "latitudinarianism."

3. Susan Fitts Ripley; George Ripley.

To Ralph Waldo Emerson and Ruth Haskins Emerson
Concord   25 Sep [1826] Monday

My dear Waldo

Oh I never wondered at your preaching! But the marvel is *that* feeling *how stronge*[n] *the sentiments of moral beauty are*—love of final causes—these are all we dream—*know* of God—   —Yet marvelous—"your feelings of piety cold"—![1] and to the desert the letters came with the cold speculations of Humism. Yet I never said I wondered you preached.

But I do say I sometimes wonder—always regret your measure of books & men when I venture to place them by my standard? When you rate them up—& more seldom prize them lower. Now this pamplet of Sampson's—why there is[n] enow unique to redeem its triteness obscurity & swedenishness?[2] —Besides all that is rare is culled from the rich field of Wordsworth—who is no sweendborgh. Tell about fiction—why that itself is in the creative power of the first Cause—and *I* dont want any Baconian rules for the witchery of the souls musick. But I have only looked thro' the pages—some are admirable. Some such as you would invent with more athority.

G. R. is indeed a fine man—popolar & interesting—eloquent tongued—& at times & sentences brings Evertt to one's ear very strongly.[3] He had no place for originality if he had chosen.

Adieu—   Oh if you see him & lack talk—say that the conversation w'h we *touched* on returns with fuller force—viz my opinion that a mind like Byrons would never be sattisfied with modern unitariasm—that the fiery depths of calvinism—its high & misterious elections to eternal bliss beyond Angels—and all its attendant wonders would alone been calculated to fire his imajanation—   Moreover had he been there schooled he might have been a flaming minister of the gospel??

In haste   Write with anxiety   I've been absent so long from Sarah[4]

Monday 25

It is time you heard, dear Sister, from the house of care & sickness. If any alteration it is to more suffering of our poor Sister. She lies whole days in bed—tho now & then her vital strenght seems equal to rising as she tries it—but feels better in bed. It is likely she has much & long to suffer. The dependance on your visit while I was here & we could have Mrs S—'s chamber we have not been able to bring about. Harriet has kept stairs a week tomorrow eve.—better now—   And as Mrs S. returns (*this* week at my request) Sarah & I concluded it might be agreeable to you to come in chaise when I go down—as I shall go to Boston for a few days. And your presence would comfort & benefit her & gratify all. Change of objects & friends is the best medicine oftentimes. We did hear Phebe was coming—which is still possible—tho' she will not be glad I think.

Can you come if I should within ten days be at your door? We can say nothing decided. You may hear again from your afft Sister

MME

Sister Susan[5] sends love who is sitting by sitting room fire.

MH: bMS Am 1280.226(846). *Addressed:* Mr R. Waldo Emerson / Cambridge / Mss. *Postmarked:* Concord Ms / Sept 25. *Endorsed:* M M E 1826 X.

strenge] *possibly* strange (*T*)

there is] is there is *in MS*

1. RWE to MME, 1 Aug. 1826, announces he will be approbated to preach in the fall (*L* 1:170); for other ideas in this paragraph, see RWE to MME, 23 Sept., on philosophy and feeling (*L* 1:174–75).

2. Probably RWE sent MME a copy of the New England druggist and Swedenborgian Sampson Reed's *Observations on the Growth of the Mind* (Boston, 1826), which he praised highly in his journal entry for 10 Sept. (*JMN* 3:45) and in a letter to WE[3], 13 Sept. (*L* 1:173). Reed (1800–1880) graduated from Harvard in 1818 and, in 1821, delivered a master's oration, "On Genius," that profoundly affected RWE and his contemporaries (*TR*, 49–50). Swedish philosopher and theologian Emanuel Swedenborg (1688–1772) believed that scripture reveals laws of correspondence: natural objects express spiritual causes.

3. George Ripley completed his studies at Harvard Divinity School in 1826 and was immediately called to the new church on Purchase Street. MME probably refers to his master's oration at Harvard's commencement on 30 Aug., "The Claims of the Age on the Young Men of America" (*L* 1:173 n. 20).

4. Sarah Ripley died 2 Nov. 1826.

5. Susan Fitts Ripley.

1827

To Charles Chauncy Emerson and Edward Bliss Emerson

Jan 1. Vale 1827.

Howl winds—roar tempest—thou carriest us on thy preened wings to scenes where we shall defy thy whole magazines—tho' contending with unquencable flames— Pass on old giant—thou but goest to meet the warm & gorgeous spring—where thou llt melt like Hercules in the arms of beauty. How many a stout heart who blenches before thee today will not beat when thy urn is decked with flowers—would I need not tarry—but take a wreath from thy hoar hand—gladly coil beneath thy shroud—& see the spirits which bind and bend thy course. But oh to him whose budding honors ask for suns and dews to ripen—for storms and clouds to discipline let springs suceed to winters summers to autumns—carry him to the last stage in kindness—if he gives to thy fleeting course the imperishable character of growing piety & benevolence. But if his young[n] sucesses are but the growth of hot house[n] culture—if they will not florish amid the frost of disappointment & the neglect of society—oh may he not be destined to journey thro' the calm season of age.— so chilling to earthly spirits—gently may he be forgiven and quietly dismissed from the field of toil & honor into which he has entered. Oh no, my dear Charles, let us quit poetry—there is no real honor in the race for scholarship (only as a means of virtue) than there was in the bouncing gladiator of barbarous times. Alas, that it should so absorb the mind—so quench the soul oftentimes. How often I see you bending your ear down with the most vivid attention—with an interest I had seen on no subject—to the relation which Edward Bliss gave you of his conversation with Hayward.[1] The memory of that smale moment clings to me spite of my self.

Did star eyed genius wander thus to bring tidings of Hayward? It was well in him, E. B., and you all mean that your scholaring shall be *usefull* subserve the purposes of *utility*—virtue. But is it only secondary? Do you not feel a higher interest in gaining a lesson than in prayer? in contemplating & adoring the Source of all beauty. Pardon me. I never catechised you before. But in the year 1825 Jan. 4 or 5 you spoke of devotion as enthusiasm—meaning illusion I suppose—for enthusiasm in all that is great is the best idea we have of Heaven.[2] I made no answer—how I felt I am loath to say—for I dared not say how high that act of the soul was, having been so little raised by it. But it is for the great Spirits of the heathen and xian world to say how great and glorious is a devotion which raises the soul to all that is magnamious & pure. Consult Plato, Antoninus Newton & Locke, who represent others.

But—my sole errand was to inquire after Waldo.[3] And now I can't but believe that had you occasionally prayed for your solitary Aunt, you would have reached out the hand of charity to inform her of one who is an invalid, far from Mother & brothers. One whom we would fain have retained in good N. E. Tell me where to direct a letter to him.

"What will the *post Master* think"? that I am becoming so poor that I have no bill.

3 Wed. eve. As I have no letter from you dear Edward which I had flattered myself with the hope of since I began to Charles I recollect that I know not where he is, if at C. I *would not* have this letter read there by Grand papa[4] I take the liberty to trouble you again with the request to hear of our dear Traveller. If half a score of Edwards journey we imagine them at home—but this Coset of the Muses & home—he is in my very dreams a stranger—   And I ask again to hear of yourself. I know I am not of any importance—but let obscuity enhance your kindness. I did not express the interest I felt in your arrangments—sentiment is not the order of the day

   May God abundantly bless you dear Edward prays Aunt MME * * * Ah my dear E. you will smile at my ignorance—will smile or scorn only write to me of all that is interesting in the gay & fluctuating world.

MH: bMS Am 1280.226(659). *Addressed:* Mr. Edward Bliss Emerson / Care of Mr. T. W. Haskins / City of / Boston / Mss. *Endorsed:* X   M.M. Emerson / Jany 18 '27. *Postmarked:* Waterford / Me / Jan'y 4.

   young] ⟨virtue &⟩ ↑ young ↓
   hot house] hot ⟨bed⟩ ↑ house ↓
   1. Probably James Hayward (1798?–1866) tutor at Harvard, 1820–26, and professor of mathematics and natural philosophy, 1826–27.
   2. CCE visited MME in Waterford in Jan. 1825.
   3. RWE left for Charleston, S.C., on 25 Nov., arriving there on 7 Dec.
   4. EzR.

To Ralph Waldo Emerson

Jan. 15 1827   Elm Vale

My dear Waldo,

   You have no time to write to me—nor to read how much I think of you— your health—pursuits—the house you inhabit—the people—thier character. You who never wandered from the wing of the Muses w'h visited your study— you, whom we hoped to keep on consecrated ground—are you far away— How did the sea beat—did the skies tell better tales than where the evening star so holy shines? Did strange faces beget new ideas—what is the state of society & religion? These & many more—more precious—the thoughts of the magic cell I want—if consistent with ease. How do you look? What do folks say to you   what do they think of you? Is there genius to find you out? Good lack! good lack! They have been cold & stupid about intelligence of you to me at home—tho' they are interested enough themselves in your welfare. They have never said whether you preach. How long you stay or where you end travelling—whether you are glad you went. Your complaint hangs on in some form or other it seems. I thought it so easily moved that it would escape at the first change of climate. Never mind—it comes from a freind and will not depart till it's errand is accomplished—till it has fixed your eye more stedfastly on the skies—that it may leave you a better Consoler of human ill—a better director to human ignorance. There seems a certain portion of suffering to be sustained in our part of the creation—and it comes heavily on those who appear destined to decorate rather to bear the burdens of life. Indeed so heavily do the sorrows of the great, wise & good weigh against faith in a benevolent Providence, that were it not for the miraculous messages of Heaven they would disturb the whole morrality of man. The gospel w'h you have so wisely called the chivalry of the universe explains every thing—and gives interest to every thing & every moment. Would it ever have come if man had not been made naturally immortal? If there were not nessecarily some inexplicable terrors—some endless loss to those who were not made holy? Materialism—humanitarian plan—leaves every thing either low & little— or unexplained. Those who love virtue as it may & can be loved for its own sake might need no terrors to allure them—but the multitude would brave the pains of purgatory and the disgrace of appearing in their naked deformity to the world of higher beings, with the same kind of bravery as they meet the punishments of this probably?? Now my beloved Nephew all this plain trite page you'll say comes a great many miles. Well it is because I can think of nothing else but the sermons you may be preaching. How often I live over the day at Waltham—the enthuseasm of Mrs Ripley—the admiration she felt.[1] But where the miracle power of the name of the Savior? The athority of the Founder? The wonders He performed? The self devotion—the contempt of honor—the tenderness of benevolence.[2] Your kindness will pardon—your extent of thought will do it. You know I want you to leave the fragrance of an elevated piety—of talents devoted to the good of every being you meet. Your manner so peculiarly happy in impressing what you said in the pulpit excited a desire that the unction of a higher order should go with you. That which we feel but cannot describe when we read the new testament. Live on it—and it will give you to honor here & hereafter.

     May the God of the stranger protect you and return you happily
               daily prays your afft Aunt

                                                        MME.

     It is dusk & letter goes tomorrow so I cant even read what I have wrote if there is a mail do do write   I forgot wholly that I had a 100# in Father's hands when I was with you—probably because he had written in the summer that he could not pay his brother. I believe it likely you might hire that or more in this nieghbourhood of a gentleman who wd ask me no more than 6 per cent without any security

     Farwel dear Wald   Write if you wont pay postage

MH: bMS Am 1280.226(848). *Addressed:* Mr. Ralph Waldo Emerson / Charleston / S Carolina. *Postmarked:* BOSTON MS / Jan 27.

1. MME and SBR heard RWE preach his first sermon in Waltham on 15 Oct. MME to WE[3], 5 Nov. 1826, reported on her recent visit to her "Middlesex friends—of the attainment of so many desired objects of seeing the travellers & hearing the minister among my Nephews . . . —highly gratified in the serious simple dignified *manner* of Waldo in pulpit. —of his *thoughts*—style &c you know my feelings." She admitted, however, that much of the pleasure was "lost . . . in apprehensions for his health" (MH: 220[75]).

2. RWE to MME, 23? Feb.? 1827, responds to her critique of his sermon (*L* 7:157–58). Tilton, it seems, overlooked MME's letter (see *L* 7:157 n. 10).

To CHARLES CHAUNCY EMERSON

Please to ask your Mother for the key of sec. has a green ribbon. The one she sent is not the right.

[May 1827]

My dear Charles,

I felt & still feel indebted for your two last letters, in no very common degree. They were written in those moments w'h lift & purify the heart—& give it to diffuse itself over others. The good sense with w'h you rate your talents *may* be just. But those gifts like the embryo in the shell of the eagle depend on culture. The impulse of a lofty faith & far streched benevolence give a wing to talent w'h nothing else can. A soul intense on great objects, and the calm indifference with w'h it holds at bay temporary ones, create the finest effect of genius.

You kindly speake of my wishes & opinion about your profession of theology.[1] If I had advice it would not have slept—scarsly wishes I indulge—not a whisper have I communicated of your intentions since I returned. I advise—no—I who can remember my devotion to your childhood with a pleasure, like no other, that leaves me (faulty as I may have been to almost every body else) nothing to regret in affection, I would not influence if I might—but I am persuaded—I know I cannot. My means of judging are too limited. I advise a man to place himself as a sort of mediator between God and his fellows—take an office so essential to the welfare of his Country & the salvation of immortal souls—till I know how supremely his soul is devoted to that cause—to that God—how superior to the fear & love of man! Till I knew with what emotions he dwelt on the inspired history of the revelation. A revelation w'h discovers its' Auther as working by means of human agency the great gov[t] of the world—making man essential to the comfort & improvement of man—and showing a responsibility that makes one tremble. With views like these it is difficult to find an excuse for any benevolent man of mind who *dont* preach—   And with these views too, are many excuses for a man at all sensible of the reality of his accounting hereafter for his conduct, to[n] adopt the instruction of society. The extreme in opinions respecting the doctrines taught in the bible, present the most interesting (and sometimes painfull) and endless sources for speculation. That unity in opinions[n] is not the design of Providence is pretty certain—and the benefits of keeping alive the publick mind obvious. But when the loose latitudinarism of some unitarians has opened the way to infidelity, there is cause for certain denial of its having a foundation in natural or revealed religion—is there not? Coarse damnatory calvinism has often the same results when offered to mental people. Truth lies, as the old saying, in a medium. But who will be so unfashionable—so modest—so moderate as to go to Clarke Paley and Price?—[2] They need not—the scriptures in every page almost recognise the unworthiness of man—they coincide with the voice within—with the history of the world—they come to man on account of his disasters—to bring him news of salvation by the interposition of a great & benevolent being—even the son of God—they proclaim an original law— the very same which Cecero so marvelously describes—they describe means of assistance besides the personal ministry of Jesus, to be had from God by prayer, which coincides to the voice of nature and to the testimony of Plato and all true philosophy. And indeed much as one dislikes the whole of Calvinism, there are to be found some of its best & high tones in the revelation.

Now if I had the dearest son I would not advise him to preach, tho' every drop of my blood were to suffer martyrdom, till I was persuaded of his own connections with God. Then whether he defended the genuine gospel or not, I should know his life w[d] influence the cause—and such a life could not be far from the truth. But he had better know what he intended to preach before he resolved? If man is not a sinner and in a highly dangerous state why did Jesus come?

Why need any man preach? There are publick theaters where talent may be displayed—and much better means of geting a living than preaching, if it imply no more than many teach. Those who teach what they dont believe run an amazing risk of disgrace in a future world, even if in that future world (which must be the destiny of every immortal soul if reason is not given as a mere illusion) xianity should prove a fable—a glorious vision which had miraculously deceived. But I know you believe the truth of an authentic revelation. At your age, few become so infatuated as to reject evidences so obvious, "that the rejection goes to sacrifice[n] most of the admitted premises of all reasoning and speculation"—and with Hume to dissolve the human character. One thing I beg you consider whether you can hope for final sucess if you take a profession w'h is but secondary in it's object for the publick, that is decidedly less a means, to say the least, for your own virtue and salvation? Even Cecero united the priestly character to the law. Oh could you enter with *your* voice—*your* whole soul and fine capasity into this sacred office—so as to forget yourself & make others forget you in the object you present—but I hold myself unworthy to paint your destiny. God himself guide you far from the curse of ambitious & selfish accomodations daily prays M M E.
for you speake of literary ease &c w'h must terminate in those??

I had letter this week from our dear Waldo. Congratulate you & your dear Mother & Edward & myself on his expected return. Dont give him my letter till he is rested from better things— Unless the mention of some trifling business should call for it. What is W^m doing?? He wrote me a fine letter last winter. But writing is my aversion or I s^d to him. Yes, I feel as tho' every letter from me was opened with weariness—as I never write but on one subject. I read of nothing else, and every day & thought of health & spirits is employed on it. It is the joy of reason & sensibility as C. says.[3] C. could never have so warmly painted the worth of unitarianism if he had not early embued his mind with a severer theology than prevails at present. I knew him when he was more orthodox. And cannot but wish he had thought more of the *facts*— of the pure & spiritual worship of the high & heroic virtues of the trinitarian, rather than of the possible conclusions of their system. Nor can I see the nessecary connection of a belief in the Unity with piety. More argument and scripture athority would have done our cause more good?? But how are you to judge of it if you dont examin the best works of the other side?

You find I have run down unintentionly—& so will fill up for it seems I shall live a great while before teasing you again with a homily. A homily indeed for I have carefully avoided speaking of you with any thing that approached discussion of talent & merit, tho' the subject led to it. No my want of athority of fashion & influence prevents it— And I dont like to say what would appear of course—and indeed what would not flatter unless it could pass some pretty silver trumpet.

Adieu affectionately.

If Waldo unexpectedly tarries please to send the inclosed & charge it to me.

MH: bMS Am 1280.226(660). *Addressed:* C. C. Emerson / 24. Holworthy / Cambridge. *Endorsed:* M. M. Emerson / 1828 / In college—as to Profession / of minister.

to] ⟨not⟩ to (not *possibly not canceled*)

sacrifice] ⟨unsettle⟩ ↑ sacrifice ↓

unity in opinions] unity ↑ in opinions ↓

1. CCE to MME, 11 Feb. 1827, states, "You seem to wish me to be a minister," argues instead for the law, and asks for her advice (MT/MH).

2. Three favorite theologians considered safe at Harvard (Barish, *Emerson*, 101–5).

3. WEC, "Unitarian Christianity Most Favorable to Piety" (1826): The soul acts joyfully when "thought & feeling, reason & sensibility conspire" (*Works*, 399).

To Ralph Waldo Emerson

Sab   8 July —27

My dear Waldo,

It is worse than idle to ridicule the fall—unless you can account for the origin of evil to demonstration. It is evident the races of men have arisen by generation—from one pair, or pairs in different parts of the earth. There must have been a first pair created. And they had a sense of right & wrong—

and what object must develop this principle? The apple may be allegorical—but if it were real it answered for a sign, an arbitrary one, be sure, of a goverment disciplinary & perspective. The principle of obedience is the first in education—and the more trifling the object the more important the danger of defection. That *literal* apple might have been (for all the most *venerable* & *learned* theologian can tell) the *seed* of a gov^t w'h has dug for men the hell of sin and extends to the highest rewards of Heaven. Not that it is possible in the nature of things to have sin or virtue *imputed transfered*.[n] But evil exists. Whence? Among more daring spirits than men for ought any can tell. And a higher temptation. And there is nothing in the united reason of all this world to disprove that it was some connection with the Son of God (whom scripture says that the Angels were commanded to worship) that caused their defection. Evil must have a beginning. If it were eternal—! What should we infer—that eternal right was coeval with—& implied in it's opposite? Would not Gnosticism (one of its principles) be probable? And that evil should some how result from matter is possible. We may speake more freely of this enigmatical matter as Milton thought it eternal & Channing speaks of its intimate[n] relations.[1] But old Jenyns makes the most of it—and perhaps he is righter than his modern Reviewer.[2] You never read that little book? But think how it was taken from Plato about origin of evil. Well, one & all have the subject in the dark where God intended. And I never talk of the fall nor think of it—for the difficulties are too great. A holy being could not sin—an ignorant & innocent one might eat an interdicted fruit—but if that were sin in it's absolute sense it could no more corrupt his race than an holy act could redeem it, in the view of reason. The old Calvinistic view of the fall is as unscriptural as horrible. That there are ultimate facts in the divine gov^t is certain, & happy to rest on, tho' clouds & darkness are about them. We need only think enough of our nessecary moral difficulties to estimate & judge of that part of the gov^t w'h is made tangible to us by Jesus Christ. That it's connections are beyond human ken, the faith it teaches rejoices in. That his sufferings (for his history attests perfect virtue) are vicarious—   —and interwoven with the miseries of man can not be doubted by the bibleist & those who have entered on no party. That its' main design was & is & will be accomplished to reunite the immortal soul, w'h sojourns in clay, to it's Creator—   He who by exacting the whole affections, does it not by right so much as by benevolence—by the nature of things & their primitive fitness to produce the highest happiness.

I have written on this antidiluvian subject of our lapse[3]

MH: bMS Am 1280.226(850). *Endorsed:* 1827 M. M. E.

imputed transfered.] imputed ↑ transfered ↓ .

intimate] ⟨wonderful⟩ ↑ intimate ↓

1. In "Remarks on . . . John Milton," WEC discusses Milton's belief that "the world was formed out of a pre-existent matter, . . . an 'efflux of the Deity,' " and goes on to say that matter "is still wrapped in mystery. We know it only by its relation

to mind. . . . Of its relation to God we may be said to know nothing" (*Christian Examiner* 3 [Jan.–Feb. 1826]: 63–65).

2. Review of Soame Jenyns, *A View of the Internal Evidence of the Christian Religion,* in *Christian Examiner* 3 (Mar.–Apr. 1826): 136–57; the reviewer objects to Jenyns's hypothesis of the "pre-existence of the human soul" to explain human misery (137–38); MME probably read Jenyns's *Free Enquiry into the Nature and Origin of Evil in Six Letters to—* (1757).

3. Remainder of letter missing.

To Ralph Waldo Emerson

Vale early
on the 23^d
morn of July [1827]

Walking & riding before breakfast gives the poor stomach a sinking— Yet so cloudy—so exquisitely cloudy. If these coulers and forms be not material— real—they are^n like uncreated beauty—the beau ideal of their Creator? Oh no prophane I fear me— Besides it is not on this polluted speck of universe that such a thought can be allowed any truth.

Noon If it is certain that sensitive experience furnishes evidence, of a kind less certain & indubitable, than that, which is seen by mental inspection then we are more certain of this beauty than if it were real? Apart from this conclusion, so questionable, the above is a notion^n full of perspective—tho' it was bro't to prove that if we are only a chain of ideas & exercises, & not the cause & agent of the changes w'h we effect then are weakned if not destroyed the evidence by w'h we prove the being of God."[1] Pho, if it so pleased God to have one set of beings or apparent beings who existed by this chain— & might forever exist where is the contradiction? One of the fundamental links is the perception of a Creator. Were as the Doctor says ideas only events & created perpetually how delightfull to derive an existence from its Auther fresh & inspired with love to Him such as some feel! Old Hume was a morbid hermit in the vast of being & came to different inferences like this systemising divine

Wed 15 Au. You called for poetry to divert me (I suspected) from theology— obedient as usual I wrote immediately.[2] In the last meagre letter you call for answers to your other kind—most of them torn—these I roll up— & in look- ing for the letter you request of yours on "succession" I have read with high interest those of last summer & fall—but do not *know* if the one I send is the intended one.[3] Could I find my comment in a day Alma. I would send that & should know if this is the one you want. I have not written since these lose papers— & *today* am intirely at a loss to know if they are worth sending. This is always true that it cannot affect me & if you will but write why I can send any thing I choose in return. The mail today has bro't me nothing no more than late ones. Have you received mine directed to Cambridge? It was poor but I did not care. No books—no nothing. What do you mean about Channing streching &c &c[4] I only see that he irradiates our old & loved images.

Adieu dear dear Waldo   I long to hear of your bodily & mental state. Your Aunt H. is sick but there is a persuasion in me that she will get about tho' the Doctors wife told me not to have health probably.[5] Your aff^t Aunt

MME

Pray restore me this letter of yours.[6]

MH: bMS Am 1280.226(851). *Addressed:* Mr R. W. Emerson. *Endorsed:* X M M E / Aug. 1827.

are] ⟨seem⟩ ↑ are ↓

notion] ⟨rich⟩ notion

1. Opening quotation marks missing; source unlocated.

2. See RWE to MME, 15 May 1827 (*L* 1:197–200).

3. RWE to MME, 17 and 22 Aug. 1827, indicates he has received and copied what she sent (*L* 1:206–9). Since the "Almanack" passage at the beginning of this letter is not on a "loose" (or separate) sheet, she must have sent others that RWE returned.

4. EBE to RWE, 9 Apr. 1827, reports hearing WEC preach on the "certainty of future judgment" on 8 Apr. (MT/MH); cf. RWE to MME, 15 May 1827 (*L* 1:200).

5. REH; ASG.

6. Written on outside, upside down below address.

To Ralph Waldo Emerson

To be returned   Sep. 4 [1827]

Let all the Angels laugh, if so pure beings can be frivolous, "at the days of epic if there are those fine episodes to high & soft recollections."[1] Those periods when the soul feels as tho' it were an epoch—when some revelation is about to be made"   They may show a Newton as an Ape of their *knowledge*[2]—but those sublime feelings are of their very *nature*.

Tis' then the mind percives the harmony of the works & word of God. No fear—no apprehension of those errors & interpretations which surely exist—but of no importance except to the mere caviller of words—to the digging mole.[3] His eyes are *designed* for their place & that is of use in the great whole   Indeed it is the very office of the worthy ants who bring their grain to the heap of erudition to confirm the faith of the xian world. On the very athority of their contentions we may rest assured that disputed texts have an antiquity of indisputable athority, and they were early begun & have stood the test of almost the whole age of xianity. Such as refer to the nature of the mission of Jesus—of an expiatory kind. The pride of philosophy was as much opposed to any thing in the way of implicit faith—of any thing inexplicable as the modern monopolisers of knowledge. Yet their heresies^n were not able to expunge those texts from the early records w'h represent the death of Christ as somthing more than martyr & teacher. But it were credulity to take insulated texts as guides. It is the whole history of man as described in the revelations—the types[n] which appear under every form of worship instituted by Partriarchs & prophets—the divine oracles of prediction which are stiled *the testimony of Jesus*—of a suffering Messiah. Now if he were no more than man & his sufferings only of the short continuance of his ministry & crucifiction—and of no more meaning than a great inspired prophet, what fittness is there between the apparatus and the end? If we attend only to his institution of the supper (believing its' athority according to our theory) and the exact, but more full repetition[n] of St Paul is there not strong evidence to believe that the voice w'h proclaimed, in the infancy of man respecting his ceremonial sins, that without shedding of blood there was no remission, was typical of that same voice which proclaimed the same to man in his fuller growth? Was not the world prepared for the development which the fullness of time gave by the first acts in the great drama—and by the exhibition of judaism exposed to all nations? And is it not the succession of the acts and scenes of Providence which are connected thro the whole series that gives the very "portion of truth bright and sublime"—(brighter & sublimer for every improvment of individual genius) "that lives in every moment."[4] But here we verge by this series to nessecarianism. Well on the absolute conclusions of that there is no other resource than "the publick", to the whole universe, "execution of a *"god"—of the creator and govonor of the fallen beings.[5] If it revolts the sense of the eternal fittness of things—if indeed imputation—sattisfaction in their full bearings appear absolutely impossible & the calvinist & humanitarian nessecarian give us a scheme that cannot stand, must we not adopt the middle one of Butler and Price? The extremes of the others meet? Channing, of whom you spoke in a former letter, talks most eloquently of nature in this and the Gannet sermon.[6] But how lose a term. Moral nature retains as many secrets as at the advent of Him who commanded the phiscal. The hottentot—the Savage the tyrant born to a mitre or a crown cultivate the seeds of every vice—which comes to advantage—and tho' those of every virtue are likwis indigenous, yet in the whole race how few spring and less are cultured? Now what "analogy", to use his word, has the pure forbearing self denying spirit of the gospel with moral nature of man? With Plato and Socrates and Aristides it would have assorted with little difficulty—but it came adapted to their *wants*[n] to call sinners. And here we get back to somthing of a *fall*? Christianity appears as we have often talked like a regimen—a compensation to the original plan which was disturbed by the greatest of all secrets the freedom of moral agents (higher than man probably and man himself) and the prescience of God. If the text w'h represents the Angels as beholding the wisdom of God in a new & higher light by the ministry of Jesus, be genuine & authentic, there must be somthing more in it than teaching and bringing futurity to clearer light? And to the German divines who believe nothing of inspiration (so besotted) the meaning of the old & new testament to some of them is clearly that of a certain indefinite expiation—so says Stewart.[7]

*I have not the sermon of Channings but it was written with a great G? an infinite difference.[8]

MH: bMS Am 1280.226(852). *Endorsed:* 1827.
heresies] heresies ⟨(if such they were)⟩
types] types ⟨of the early⟩
repetition] ⟨explanation⟩ ↑ repetition ↓
came . . . *wants*] came ↑ adapted to their *wants* ↓
    1. RWE to MME, 17 and 22 Aug. 1827, says, "Men's seasons of thinking answer to the divisions. . . . One day is a ballad, another day is an epic" (*L* 1:209).
    2. Cf. RWE to MME, 11 Nov. 1823 (*L* 7:124).
    3. RWE to MME, 17 and 22 Aug. 1827, says the mole can distinguish colored from pure light (*L* 1:209).
    4. Quoted from RWE's letter of 17 and 22 Aug.
    5. Cf. WEC, "Unitarian Christianity Most Favorable to Piety" (1826), in *Works*, 397–98.
    6. WEC, *The Demands of the Age on the Ministry, Discourse at the Ordination of the Reverend E. S. Gannett, Boston* (1824); *Works*, 269–78.
    7. Probably Dugald Stewart, but possibly Moses Stuart.
    8. See above, n. 5; written at bottom of p. 3. WEC wrote "a God" (397).

To Ralph Waldo Emerson

Sep. 9 [1827]   Sabbath

    Would I could die today that this aching sense of immortality might be satisfied or cease to ache. The difficulty remains the same when I struggle with the extension of never never never—just as I repeated the exercise in childhood—cant form an idea—cant strech myself to that which has no end—it may be owing to the limits of childhood repeating the idea & wishing to come at an end in vain. If so—unhappy instructions w'h have bound my intellect, fated to be always smale. This smalness is the will of God & the most absolute resignation is with it. But this inexplicable eternity! Oh how vanishes the difficulties of a Deity simple or complex—no matter—of the madness of the understanding in fanaticism—of bigotry and persecution—of dungeons & racks. Is it because of these lumps of matter w'h move with us & above us—of their perpetual changes and influences that we cannot form an idea of the identical immortal substance which is to remain essentially & absolutely the same without end—had it a beginning?—or was it always an idea of God like Platos notion—after ages of individuality will it be reabsorbed? New orders rise—   In those orders will transmigrate this immortal (but what is immortal)—this identical essence—principle within this coffined case—these excrements of the inhabitant—   I'll go the woods—but there I shall see a sort of immortal matter—a reproduction of seeds— Well but I shall not think—dont think only feel pleasantly abroad.— rather dont try—cant never think—there's this crazy yeast like matter which makes the bark un'holsom'. P.M. It is this impossibility of losing ones self, tho' ages pass over the change that argues immortality—yet clouds & darkness rest upon its nature—i e endlessness   Again "Philosophy in G. has defended by abstract reasonings all the fine affections of soul."[1] De Stale throws a rich halo of sentiment round the words *infinite feeling*—but it dont explain anything. She felt the subject of an indefinite future with enthusiasm—but had no leisure to travel with it in untraveled depths—for she never sacrificed the charms of fame & pleasure to obscure motives. She was heroic & noble[n] in sacrific-ing to friendship. But no one should dispute, but forever respect her faith in the suceeding chap. on Protestism. That the "*feeling infinite* is an attribute of mind"[2] is certain & like the principles of all the sciences, w'h are there, but seldom developed. 10. M. Were not God, whether simple or complex, *per-sonal* how much more vague & how terrific might be this never never ending nessesity of existing?— Perhaps not—if his influence is certain, as it does appear, on our otherwise inexplicable existence and delight, what matters—tho' we are now incapable of finding any links to attach our faith to? Jesus the emanated—created (on what polemics please it matters not) god, has a tan-gible visible personal existence—loves, angers—knows what virtue & glory mean—pursued them as perhaps none other could? Of these things reason can be only acquiesent? not revolted? Her instruments are experience—and of that world she can have none—the intuitions of the soul supercede those—and more readily link themselves to what are only objects of faith. Priestley and Belsham and other materialists[3] have no soul—and they tame away reve-lation till tis not worth excepting. For if it reveals nothing beyond our every day reason what is it? 11. Did the tragedy, or somthing like it, in Eden give type to the whole world of tragic poets? To the terrible mythologies of barba-rous ages not yet exploded? Did not these become more bloody & dark after the antediluvian revelations were lost—or Noahic? Did not the confusion of languages multiply pernicious idolatries? Yet it was—it seems—a design of utility to mankind? To prevent an overwhelming monarchy? One language will never absorb others. What a strange notion was Evertts about the great-ness of a nation literature[n] promoted by one language?[4] Burke says no one can do greatly that cant suffer greatly"—bodily? How idle—how absolutely false. And my Burke gives more in that letter to matter than beseems him. As to old Burke he has lost (perhaps erroneously) with me his *wisdom* by finding him so slanderously opposing Price & freedom—who is my Priest philosopher and politician.[5] But to day I have wandered over the starry letters of Waldo and I can fix on nothing—as it is sometimes with reading too much of De Stale. Take a text from either and the mind expands.[6] And tho' I felt too much at begining this Almanack to think of sending it—yet tomorrow I may. And if he instead of answering queries says, I ask why night is night day day, time

time? why those very questions can be answered—can be speculated now as Shakes. could not.[7] Return these—or a blank in my Al. And it is strange—but the same feelings return not. However feeble they are a part of ourselves.

MH: bMS Am 1280.226(853).

noble] ⟨romantic⟩ ↑ noble ↓

nation literature] nation ↑ literature ↓

1. de Staël, *Germany* 3:93.

2. See de Staël, *Germany* 3:269–72.

3. Joseph Priestley (1733–1804), Unitarian theologian and scientist; Thomas Belsham (1750–1829), defender of Unitarianism, was professor of divinity and resident tutor at Hackney College, where Priestley was lecturer on history and philosophy, and Belsham was offered this post when Priestley emigrated to the U.S. in 1794 (*DNB*).

4. Edward Everett's Phi Beta Kappa address, 26 Aug. 1824, "The Circumstances Favorable to the Progress of Literature in America."

5. "no one . . . suffer greatly": passage from Burke's "Letters on a Regicide Peace," letter 1, quoted in RWE to MME, 15 June 1826 (*L* 7:147; see n. 24). Reading Dr. Richard Price's sermon before the Revolutionary Society in London ("Discourse on the Love of Our Country," 4 Nov. 1789) led Burke to his vigorous attack on Price and the revolution in *Reflections on the Revolution in France* (1790).

6. Despite its poetic, mystical tone, this "Almanack"-letter is a direct response to RWE's letter of 17 and 22 Aug. 1827 (*L* 1:206–9), a good example of the mind-expanding power of his texts. Compare also de Staël's description of the effects of contemplating "the starry heaven," *Germany* 3:270.

7. Shakespeare, *Hamlet*, 2.2.88.

To CHARLES CHAUNCY EMERSON

Elm Vale   Wed 12 [Sept.] 1827.

Ah, my dear Charles, and you think nothing brilliant belongs to old ears & eyes—   Your praises forsooth must pass thro' lips wet with castelian dews, or dyed in celestial roses? No account of Edwards performance[1] neither—did not know, till last sat. by T. W. H. to his Mother, that this year was his graduation—tho' I always paint him to my vision as taking degrees in the ascending scale.[n] Nothing can make up with me the loss of sympathising in that day & yours but the things themselves.

Yet one cannot quarrel with any losses[n] this fine season—when nature throws her wand binding spell round us. And as Byron says, we live on a tomb stone[2]—and the Danes told their posterity, that the gods made the earth of the skull of Ymir and the clouds of his brains, and the mountains of his bones[3]—we cannot stop to inquire into causes when effects are so full of thought. Not another word for I had no idea of bringing you more into debt. Write or not just as it may please. I can hear of my nephews from Salem if no more— Write or not

it is always right with your afft friend & Aunt

MME

MH: bMS Am 1280.226(661). *Addressed:* Mr C.C. Emerson. *Endorsed:* M M Emerson / May 12 '27.

scale.] ⟨order⟩ scale.

losses] ⟨event⟩ losses

1. EBE delivered his oration for his master's degree, "The Importance of Efforts and Institutions for the Diffusion of Knowledge," on 29 Aug. 1827.

2. Byron, "Churchill's Grave": "The Architect of all on which we tread, / For earth is but a tombstone, did essay."

3. According to a Norse creation legend, in the beginning was *Niflheim*, "a world of mist and ice." Warmer air gradually "melted the frost of the North, and out of the clouds that resulted sprang the giant Ymir and a whole race of other giants." The gods Odin, Veli, and Ve slew Ymir and "out of his body formed the heavens and the earth: from his flesh the earth, from his blood the sea, from his bones the mountains, from his hair the trees, and from his skull the sky" (Max J. Herzberg, *Classical Myths* [Boston and New York, 1946], 396).

1828

To Ezra Ripley

Andover Me, Feb. 1 1828.

Honored Father,

I received your interesting letter of the 18 of Dec. at Augusta, from which place you asked me to write. I immediately informed you of the two # overplus of interest by my nephew,[1] but thought you might like to hear from me at my arival at this abode of "wolves & loons and savage wildness."[2] Indeed Sir, your eloquence excited my young friends, whose opinion leaned very much to yours. But how any one (besides my Waterford nieghbours, who advised me against *retirement*) can think one place more wild than another in the interior of Me I dont understand. It is true, the place is unfrequented but by a uncertain conveyance of mail & no church building—but the mountains are more numerous and invironing and grander than at my beloved Vale. And the people probably less corrupted with the desire of ornament than most places. But it was the wish for society led me *here*—and I expect to find a considerable improvement in other respects. But I came only wednesday. The journey across the Country takes time. It is but 40 miles from Augusta to Paris—but it is a week from that day till the stage comes to Bethel. In that week I heard the stage run again from Waterford to Bethel & I went over to see them who were all well. From Bethel it is but 20 miles here but the snow was so drifted that with a single horse it was difficult to get here. I came from Augusta with my friend Mr Stone far as Winthrop (his wife being with him)   I remained there some days for the stage which rises by night in Augusta—and had a very pleasant visit at Mr Lee's lodgings & at Mr Thurston's.[3] You were often mentioned in our theological conversations. I desired Mr T. to read your sermon in the L. P.[4] He said he would—he remembered you with respect. That is a fine florishing town, with new handsome churches one of Mr T—'s, a baptist & Methodist. The latter is shared by the unitarian party and Mr Evertt of Hallowell is about to exchange with the methodist. With the calvinists, as in other places in Maine, there seemed to me to dwell a heavy and exclusive cloud which often obscured the native benevolence of character. It is not so with Mr Stone. If he is one, it is of the refined & philosophical cast, and leaves his mind unfettered from system   He is fervid in piety & devoted to study. He resides with his father in law, where I am, and is free from care.[n]

From the little observation I have made in the winter, it appeared that if Calvinism & unitarianism do not have better advocates, in Maine universalism will prevail over both.

My sister & nephews will hear from me thro' this letter—and will be glad to know that my health & eyes are good—better for being bro't into action by moving. For yourself my dear Father, accept the reciprocation of those wishes & affectionate expressions which I found in your letter. If my brother & Sister remember one who always loves them—I am glad—if they have forgotten me—please to speake a good word for

your & their affectionate daughter & Sister

M. M. Emerson

I hope dear Waldo's charity will hold out in writing to his obliged Aunt.

MH: bMS Am 1280.226(1237). *Addressed:* Rev. Ezra Ripley D. D. / Concord / Mss. *Postmarked:* Andover Me / Feby 1st. *Endorsed:* Miss M. M. Emerson / Feb 1828.

care.] ⟨all⟩ care. ⟨as I am⟩. (*heavily canceled*)

1. EzR to MME, 18 Dec. 1827, sent eight dollars in interest via EBE, but EzR admitted he did not remember the amount of the principal, which MME seems to have loaned him (MH).

2. EzR regretted MME's plan to move to "New Andover" rather than "the place of your nativity & the land of your ancestors. . . . Surely it cannot add to your happiness or improvements to hear the screaming of loons, the hooting of owls, & the howling of wolves. The wildness & simplicity of nature you may see & enjoy, without being surrounded by that in her which is savage, terrible, & unsocial" (MH).

3. Thomas Treadwell Stone (1801–1895), son of a Waterford farmer, began his study of theology after graduation from Bowdoin College in 1820. In 1824 he became pastor of the Orthodox Congregational Society in Andover, Me., where he remained until 1830. The Reverend David Thurston (1779–1865) was the Congregational minister at Winthrop, Me.

4. Ripley's sermon, "On the Bible Method of Becoming Religious," *Liberal Preacher* 1, no. 1 (July 1827): 63–72.

To CHARLES CHAUNCY EMERSON

Andover Me   April 25 [1828]   thurs eve

Will you my dear Charles forward this pecuniary business immediately? And will he have time to read the invelop? You sometimes urge me to write— but I hate to think after a letter is gone that it is gone. For all I want is to hear from you & that is not in your leisure." I love to think of you all—and to you this summer is not like any other. When the sun first steals to light over these blue mountains wreathed with the poet's mist—it is pleasant to think of the youth springing forward to join in the opening course of manhood   "So life's young hour enchanting smiles, with sparkling health & hope & joy & fancy's fairy wiles."[1] And does she strow your path with flowers & hang the laurels on your brow? Make me a sharer in her painted dreams. And shall I hold the telescope of prophecy—be her interpreter? No—and let me ask you never to talk even of the best of the Sybils to me. It is unpleasant. But your last letter was well worth the having, except that.[2] But of your plans—do you propose to be *sufficient to yourself*? It is the only security—but requires an uncommon deal of virtue. You will of course choose a more splendid & generous way of enjoyment—and visions of friendship & influence be cherished. And it does seem most goodly to play a large game in life—to hazard much & hold many cards—and when one loses or gains to work himself up to something that will *tell*. But these become like a *tale that is told*. And after all it is those constant and silent sands w'h run thro a man's whole life, whose echo is heard beyond & above this earth—where the horoscopes of human fortune assume a divine aspect—whether under the influence of phisical connected with moral causes—or arbitrary—matters not to him who connects himself irrevocably with the first Cause. But to you who are capable of enthusiasm— who only need oppurtunities of having it excited beyond the bee hive of a College—to you, to whom I can seldom speake, I will use plainess. If it needs apology, read the description of the interest w'h one would feel in the rudest savage who loved him beyond any possibility of seeing him, by the admirable Brown.[3] Why have you never told me of his lectures? To me his intellectual theory is nothing as no use of it for *me*—but the golden apples of his Hesperides are the intimate relations w'h he brings to view of the other world with our souls and of the nature of virtue. If you have forgotten this work amid the flux of books, I will tell you what I mean   "—That by the medium of the internal states of mind, the discoverers also of that infinite Being who framed every thing, and who without acting directly on any organs of sense, is yet present to our intellect with as bright a reality of perception, as the planets to our corporeal vision." "His presence when virtue is admitted into it, is at once Joy & immortality."[4] This is not new to the bible theist—but when without any other athority but what philosophy gives him a man is able to bring such truths forward, they make the miraculous revelation more precious as showing it's adaptation to human nature. And at sight of man, almost as much at the plough as in the frivolous pursuits of mere science[n] and drawing room accomplishments, how difficult it is to believe in his future destiny? And to the sceptic, in the whole unmutilated bible, how slight is his hold on the scheme it opens—then is it not most precious to find the philosopher convinced of truths from the nature of them? I read Brown the more as he is so great an antidote to old Hume, who lies on my table tho' he confutes himself as soon as we get out of the insideious mazes he fishes with. You see the effects of age— how I have wandered from the plainess I was to venture on. It was to say *are you pious?* Why not? Love of the world? How much better might you love it & enjoy it if you loved its Auther. Neglect of your excellent parent tho' you had every other virtue could be a kind of parricide—yet you neglect, I fear, the worship—the adoration of your real & only Parent. Excuse me. But when you were at the Vale you spoke of devotion as delusion.[5] I could not answer— but it has weighed on me some what like the punishment of being tied to a corpse. The embodying of one's feelings in solemn prayer[n] is as nessecarily connected with all virtue as any cause & effect. Ah how daily do I desire to be worthy to pray for you—yet it is my habit—& when I think there may be some high office for you to fill in a future state this little world appears less than ever. Little it must, as yet, appear to one of your understanding, as you have scarsly been but a pasive recipient of it's hopes & pleasures & advantages. God grant you be one of its benefactors

How do Waldo & Edward? I think much & love them much & desire to hear of their health above any thing of this world. My love to your Mother whose letter has been sent from W. but never reached me as it came by a private conveyance only to Albany. My friend is a complete Domini[6] & I have the same solitude as ever—and most content—for health is fine. But how a man can *write* so fine sermons & possess & diffuse so little *character* is a novelty to me. My nephews I have thought of more since here than in any other Cell. Their power to excite the mind & heart—the only *power* after all. Farwell dearest Charles—   I hope the mail w'h takes this will bring me one from you as I requested the business some weeks since to be inclosed in a family letter. Tho' I shall not be at com[t] yet I lot on the pleasures of that day[7]

The one of Edwards[8] is still dear to me. Your affectionate Aunt & friend

MME

MH: bMS Am 1280.226(664). *Addressed:* Charles C. Emerson / Cambridge / Care of / Mr T.W. Haskins. *Endorsed:* M M Emerson / Apr 25 X / '28 / Brown's lectures / T. T. Stone / Nephews.

    leisure] ⟨line⟩ ↑ leisure ↓

    science] ⟨literature⟩ science

    prayer] ⟨forms of⟩ prayer

    1. Not identified.

    2. CCE to MME, 12 and 28 Jan. 1828, compares her recent move to Andover to the Sibyl's moving from Cumae (MT/MH).

3. Thomas Brown, *Lectures on the Philosophy of the Human Mind*, 2 vols. (Hallowell, Maine, 1828), 1:103.

4. Ibid., 1:323.

5. Cf. MME to CCE, 1 Jan. 1827. CCE's last visit to Waterford seems to have been in Jan. 1825; CCE to MME, 18 May 1828, denies he ever said this (MT/MH).

6. "Domini": "dominie" is a Scottish term for a pedagogue or clergyman; in Sir Walter Scott's *Guy Mannering*, Dominie Sampson, tutor to Henry and Lucy Bertram, is a poor, modest, humble scholar. MME probably refers to T. T. Stone (see MME to EzR, 27 Aug. 1828).

7. CCE graduated from Harvard on 27 Aug. 1828.

8. EBE's commencement in 1824, when he shared the platform with Lafayette.

To Ralph Waldo Emerson

Andover   Ap. 26 [1828] Sat.

This morning my dear Waldo I received yours—in w'h you seem the magician of nature and art   Your eastern blasts[n] thrill the nerves—your castle towers—but rather too antient for the light of the present—and what does no honor to the genius of the place (w'h was capable of placing the idea of God) old Hume peeps out thro' the grim lattices with his doubts—not respecting that impregnable fortress the existence of one's thought and its Auther (no with *these,* it is perfectly indifferent whether there be matter or not. It brings the Creator of every illusion, rather *reality,* more strongly) but thro' the first page & the notion "that life is emberrassed with prudential considerations." [1] This is new for the friend & lover of virtue! Duty & interest often clash, and disturb to the fanatic & hypocrite, the harmony between virtue & sucess. But the believer in this eternal connection is never at a stand—it is the steps of the Angelic ladder w'h he can alone mount by the habitual & persevering sacrifice. Where were the sweet secrets of moral science to be evolved but by the inward devotion w'hose wand seperates the fogs of sophists and temporary[n] interest? Had your duty led you to missionizing with the humble Tuckerman,[2] or schoolkeeping, you would have done it I trust. A harder task—a deeper hazard attends your way—to be humble with success—to look beyond the vapouring breath of poor fellow feeble mortals—to rise from the mean fears of want & dependance, fears w'h are connected with the constitution (& a good constitution) of human nature—but above all to quit the doubts of epicurian theology w'h is insensible to the dangers of man's nature, in its present state, and to the nature of the wonderous remedy. Your reading Hume when young has rendered you, I cannot but think, so imbued with his manner of thinking, that you cannot shake him off. There seems, or I am stupid, so much of his *manner,* tho' *better,* in this letter that I feel as I do when reading him. But to *my old* frame his arguments, if such they can be called, make no more impression than the spray of a child's squirt. And in *painting* the astounding difficulties of the abstract sciences he has opened the eye to dispel those of moral.[3] Now[n] would there be any doubt that virtue (rather piety) was it's own reward in a good tempered constitution, were one capable of acting & feeling to the extent of it's demands? It is not in man—& the hero who has made the most renowned sacrifices is found the victim of unnui & discontent in the shade of solitude, or of a fresher patriot. And can there be a provision more adapted for these defects of our nature than the resignation & self devotion annihilation[n] of the xian doctrine? Would not this be among its' strongest proofs of the internal kind?

Sab 27.[4]   No I would not have xianiaty as a means of political or earthly good—and only that—   It has been given for such high purposes to our faith that if I was to lose that faith it would still seem sacrelidgious to use its' hithertoo cherished object as a mere secular good. This looks like holy nonsense perhaps—but the Lover would not use a symbol of his friend to ordinary purposes. Convinced it were nessecary, to the comfort of a transcient world one must submit—   But whether it would make a good or practicable code? It dont, as now related, need the secular arm. Common rules of justice & publick utility seem better fitted for this earth than the pure & perspective *vision* (in the above case) of xianity. Old Almanac.

Noon—   "interfere with the culture of intellect?"!!
Were it to suspend it *at times*—it would be wise were there one chance to a million of that retributive day w'h rev. promises   But it is in the earthly Eden of xianity that the intellect gathers most effectually the fruit from the tree of knowledge. It gains that refinement and strenght w'h gives it to discern the fine links of the moral chain that hangs on its infinite Auther. Illimitable prospects can best apply euphrasy to the understanding—and to him whose feelings are not given to tumult, abstraction can best & only supply the apparent want of enthusiasm. "Doubts" will then sink to the fens from whence they came, w'h so often glitter like the beams of intellect. This Castle rises with delight on a longer view. How holy & "inaccessible"! The soul—and the sole idea of God—at the alter of w'h every thought should come from its cell to minister—and he would there learn to dedecipher many a portentous and hopefull hieroglyphick—or with more mystic delight prepare to realize *these* when the scenes of the waring & agitating drama are transferred to another stage. Only multiply these "moral epochs in a man's condition" when he feels in correspondence with an eventfull agency. It is then the hero in virtue not merely the doer of duty, feels "that present and future time are" no longer "rivals."[5] There is a subject of doubt, w'h true phi. may never dare to decide— the complexity or unity of God, since xianity has left it dubious. Ignorantly or rashly to reject any office or attribute of the Messiah is a poor use of reason? Farewell. May God render you superior to "popularity" as you have been to adverse sickness. Pray for me what I daily do that the freedom of death may be granted. Tho' fine health & content[t] are your aff[t] Aunt's.

May 2 friday Morn. Tho' you dont ask me to write I send you these scraps. I cannot but write when I see you the head of that house & Society my father loved so well.[6] It looks to imajination as it did in his day. Write me from thence, if you wont take my postage out my hands.

My thanks for the sensibility you express at my being hurt to be tho't by you distraught. But after *all* I *do appear so* to other folks, when under the influence of the indifference I feel to society (or somthing worse) with the extreme pleasure of wittnessing their fine things. The fears w'h I read in the countenance of my family lead me to act more independently than I should, if I were coaxed with their confidence. And in fact, you said in the 16 of Nov. last that "doubts of — or *the adjustment between reason and feeling have they not discoulered the mind of my Aunt thro' the whole of her life?*"[7] I have erased the sentence from among my jewels—that the two or three first words I cannot copy—these are indellible. You have borne with my outre manners and protected them better than any youth. Only forgive me greater & worser defects of character—and these w'h pass away with the discordant humours of the body are of no import.

I wish you would read the Portland mirrow of today or next week. My Domini has writen in it after reading my xian E a piece signed T*.[8] Tho he is no talent at controversy

MH: bMS Am 1280.226(857). *Endorsed:* May 1828 / X.

blasts] blasts ⟨w'h you summon⟩

temporary] ⟨self⟩ ↑ temporary ↓

Now] *possibly* How (T)

devotion annihilation] devotion ↑ annihilation ↓

1. This and other unidentified quotations in this letter are probably from RWE's letter of 16? Nov. 1827 (see below, n. 7).

2. Joseph Tuckerman (1778–1840), minister at large, Boston, 1826–40, was concerned with problems of poverty, administration of charity, and philanthropy.

3. Hume, in *An Enquiry Concerning Human Understanding*, contrasts "easy and obvious" moral philosophy with the "accurate and abstract" metaphysics (*Works* 4:4, 8).

4. Two paragraphs beginning here are "scraps" of MME's "Almanack," written on a separate leaf; on 2 May, MME continued her letter in space left on the center of the "Almanack" leaf, verso.

5. Attributed to Sir Joshua Reynolds in MME to CCE [Mar. or Apr.? 1835?].

6. RWE preached for EzR at Concord's First Church for four weeks in April and May.

7. Not included in RWE to MME, 20 [16?] Nov. [1827?] (*L* 7:166–68; see n. 35). MME to RWE, 23 Mar. 1828, also deals with the question of "adjusting life between reason & feeling"; she responds, "Oh no—reason sanctions feelings of the utmost rapture when their excitment is of the right order—and feeling keeps the sacred fire of reason always bright" (MH: 855).

8. "Xian E": the *Christian Examiner*. "T*" is probably T. T. Stone. An article by "T*" (as distinguished from another writer, "T") entitled "Christianity Adapted to

Man, and Incapable of Improvement," on the first page of the *Christian Mirror* (Portland), 2 May 1828, sought to expose Unitarians' "visionary conceptions" concerning the progress of mind and Christianity.

To RALPH WALDO EMERSON AND CHARLES CHAUNCY EMERSON
                                    Andover   July 15 [1828]   Mondy
     My dear dear Waldo & Charles,
          I write not to comfort you—this bitter calamity must be lessened only by time[1]   And what that may do for him we mourn—is it vain to hope—to pray? Is it possible—it seems a dreadfull dream that the most affectionate of Sons & brothers lives—but without life—that the sun—the earth—the friend (how dearly he has loved you Waldo from his infancy) are nothing to him— That God is nothing to him! But I meant not this—   I write because I have but one thought and that is of Edward—one companion & he a maniac— And I want either of you to tell me first how he is. Does he suffer? Does he eat & sleep like others? Who has the care of him? I am totally ignorant of that place. I have wanted to inquire about Bullkey—but hated to name *that* place.[2] But now I beg for distinct knowledge. Suppose the patient alone & reason returning—my God how frightfull the conviction of such a place   Will it not be lost forever? It is not possible I suppose for a *friend* to intrude on their practice. Oh how gladly would I spend the rest of weary wasted life in watching in his cell—in seeing there was no severity used by Nurses—or whatever they have. When such establishments are first made they profess and indeed practise great mildness probably. I would not put one there owing to my prejudice & ignorance. It has cured some—confirmed others. Good place for the confirmed if they are mild. What do you both lose? You have been too proud of him to be told. You lose besides, Waldo. His manners character set off yours by contrast—tho' he lost nothing. Your precious Mother—I cant say any thing to comfort her—therefore I forbear to send the letter which I wrote last week. Tell her my heart ackes for her. It *was* a sorrow that you have not written me dear W. but how could I expect it—and now every thing looks so altered that I dont seem to care. I believe I pestered you with a very silly letter last time. My Brother tells a great many fine things of you—but their value is less since Edward knows nothing of them. His first expressions of admiration were of your young muse. In most of the letters which his kindness (never to be thought off but with emotion) induced him to write of my affairs, were you & Charles the theme. I forget— & only afflict you. Remember I cant talk of[n] him to any—how could they understand the loss. I might have suspected this from an intimation last winter—but nothing was imajined—but desires for his life. Is he deprived of the blessing of an early & lamented grave that his brothers might learn a solemn lesson—become superior to the little fleeting honors of time—of a world that is a hospital[n] & Lazar house—or many worse abodes. Yet bear up—minister to it's woes & wants till the last gasp.

My dear Charels your last letter[3] was every thing. Go forward with such views— Your useless ambition of scholarship I do not mean. The dreadfull event gives no forboding of insanity to others—tis not hereditary—but let it give a strenght of higher & holier pursuits than eminence in college. How many a character date their fortune from some affliction. Bury it not—but mingle the sorrow in all your pursuits. No it is disease & over exertion that has bro't this on E. His *ancestors* on my nor his Mothers side were never tainted in the least. Some of my Cousins have been so[n]—and an Aunt—but it was an embicillity rather in *those*

I direct to you as Waldo may be absent. I need not repeat the request for *immediate* & *particular* intelligence. I did not mean that you ever represented devotion to God as illusion.[4] It is the received opinion that seclusion for that purpose degenerates into superstition. It may be. I can say little for it's effects within a few days, perhaps never. Adieu with love & sadness

MME.

Thank your grandfather & Uncle for their letters. particular remembrance to William when he comes. Well for him & Waldo they have done all for Edwards health & welfare they possibly could—this is the only alleviation you can all have

19. I have read Waldo's "bubble" letter to Ed. Bliss who was so "proud" of it. How does so frigid tho lofty a philosophy operate now on the writer? Yet it meets in it's extreme the extreme of xian faith. I've read more of your letters—and today it seems that I should most greatly prize a letter from you of the old sort—after all the particulars of your beloved Edward. And if you can *send me Charles' dis. on poetry.*[5] Your aff[t] & grateful Aunt—

MH: bMS Am 1280.226(858). *Addressed:* Mr Charles Chauncy Emerson / H. University / Cambridge / Mss. *Postmarked:* Andover / July 19. *Endorsed:* M M Emerson / July 19 / 1828.

cant talk of] cant ⟨mention⟩ ↑ talk of ↓

hospital] ⟨sort of⟩ hospital

so] so ⟨from their Mothers⟩

1. In late June EBE became "deranged," and on 30 June RWE took him to McLean Asylum at Charlestown. RWE to WE[3], 3 July 1828, describes EBE's situation (*L* 7:172–74).

2. MME's retarded nephew, RBE, had become unmanageable and was also at the Charlestown asylum at this time. WE[3] paid his board.

3. CCE's most recent surviving letter is his response, written 18 May, to her letter of 25 Apr. (MH).

4. This letter is part of a continuing "conversation" on the subject of "devotion" as "delusion": MME to CCE, 25 Apr.; CCE to MME, 18 May (MT/MH); MME to CCE, May/June (MH: 665). Cf. MME to CCE, 1 Jan. 1827.

5. In 1828 CCE received the Bowdoin Prize for his dissertation "Whether the Moral Influence of Poetry Has Been on the Whole Beneficial to Mankind."

To Ezra Ripley

Andover   Au. 27. 1828

Honored Father,

* * * Another favor I want of you Sir, and trust I need make no apology, in getting you to procure me a favorite object. I borrowed a dozen books of Mr Cabot,[1] when I was last at Cambridge, for a year. It has not been in my power to return them—nor have I wished to. He has a great many which are of no more use to him than to an owl. And these would not be valued at a dollar a piece. Some are only in boards. If you were to ask him to give them to me I have no doubt he would—especially as his Governess is dead, who is thought to have fettered his gifts. I have left them safely locked in my book case at the Vale and if I may own them I want to have them here. I am poorly off for reading. Mr Stone has gone to housekeeping at some distance from my lodgings—and I was disappointed in him as to society so do not regret his absence. It was speculative to see a man live so destitute of the sympathies & influence of a man. If a new book came we could talk—but that seldom came. He lent me an old worn sermon preached at Belfast 9 years since[2]—and this very week I read it without expecting to correspond with it's Auther—if I were not exhausted of thought at this time of day should have somthing to say—and still would ask if the tide of liberality has not lessened the opinions expressed in the 18 page * * *   One circumstance to which I had not been used at Waterford strikes me unpleasantly here. They rise when the doxology is sung—this seems an impropriety even for trinitarians—and tho' I dont like to appear singular yet I do not rise. Is it well?

My pen is very bad as you perceive—but I have laboured not to pester you by illegible

My dear Sister must read it if it proves so.

My love to her. She must write me. There will be a man from here at T. W Haskin's 3 weeks hence. And I depend on Charles' oration[3] and other good things.

Good Evening my dear Sir and pray for your friend & daughter

M M Emerson

* * *

MH: bMS Am 1280.226(1238). *Addressed:* Rev. E. Ripley D. D. / Concord / Mss. / Mr Strickland. *Endorsed:* Miss M. M. Emerson— / Aug. '27 1828.

1. Possibly Joseph Cabot (Harvard, 1788) or Charles George Cabot (Harvard, 1796).

2. Ezra Ripley, *A Sermon at the Installation of the Reverend William Frothingham to the Pastoral Charge of the Congregational Society in Belfast, Maine, July 21, 1819* (Cambridge, 1819). Title: "The Peculiar Work of Christian Ministers Explained," on a text from 2 Cor. 4:5.

3. CCE's commencement oration, delivered 27 Aug. 1828, was titled "Publick Opinion."

To Ralph Waldo Emerson

Oct. 7 [1828]   Vale

I have just received yours of the 6 of sep. from Andover—for w'h I am very thankfull—   It is indeed kind of you to narrate the things I so much want to know.[1] Poor dear Edward—is he going to suffer like Cowper?[2] He is still in a deplorable state if he must not see you—it would greatly refresh my reason to have that vision. I have written a few lines—but there is little likelihood of your giving it him. Such sentiments however from a higher source w^d be good—they are too simple & common to excite old associations.

Glad if Charles discerns & feels the blessed power of freindship. *But* age is incredulous about the durance—or the principle of ambitious youth. A little a little while & coldness jealousy or mishap suceed.

I received the trunk containing yours of July 24, a sketch of "intellec. biog." which I appreciate with thankfullness. "Evidences of nat. religion stronger than xianity." True the existence—eternity of God—but what he *is* or *demands* nature is silent in her storms & calmms—and rational nature presents a history that libels it's Cause. True again, the account of it in Romans is grand—but that it ever affected what it might, we dont learn—it was traditionary or Jewish revelation passing from Asia that gave the roman code of laws w'h xians revert to? But *now* my dear & respected Waldo, what does it do? How distinguish it from *revealed*? w'h is first taught—which halos the lamp to traverse the dim, tho' starry, way of nature? If you mean the conscience of man—again I ask what that has done in the history of crimes? You preach "the beauty of virtue". Aye, so did Noah & Socrates & what was the contempt they met! But the times are better now & you meet with applause—but ask the sacrifices the great antients did & the liberal and the orthodox would find other than applause. And unfortunately religious controversy is enlisting the bad passions on both sides, that eagerness for nominal religion will rage? But pardon so trite a digression—   And inform (for I ask it) what principle of morals has been established by what is called natural religion? And what its athority? To us, as xians or theists, it is *every thing*—it is what makes man capable of revelation—the reason the all glorious cause of receiving revelation—what makes man an agent—an immortal being—relates him to God & rendered him worthy of redemption by the divine man—the Son of God. In the sense implied of the existence of an immortal immaterial substance w'h implies a relation to God, tho' of a nature incomprehensible & indefinable (thank God *at present*) natural religion is a glorious existence—it is—it may be called in platonic language an emanation from eternity of the divinity! Its light has been smothered^n   Jesus came to reluime it—arts & science never did it—they are like pictures w'h reflect the power of the artist—but have no vitals. Does he use the means of illumination under the aspect of a series of causes, & their nessecary effects, existing far beyond human ken? Why we rejoice—in that web of destiny are the freedom & conscience—(natural religion) of man. But *were* that "nessesity said" as it respects our present condition—give us the God of the bible & we defy fear—ages may pass—but blind nessicity can do us eventually no harm. Yet *that* is a most fancifull specter. That God governs by what we call decrees is certain— Without a plan what were a man? we decree—but cannot accomplish. God has decreed to perfect & restore human nature (w'h "an enemy injured") by means of a misterious being— And because he has wro't by means so slowly—and so corrupt—so natural and cercuitous we say he has done nothing—& will do nothing? But to closer & dearer view of this marvellous subject—in case of your affliction for Ed Bliss—was the cause phisical—no lawless particle exists—moral—no event without its law—design beatifys every thing.

Write if you can—the dews & lights shed over a fat society one day would refresh me a long while—but I cannot be selfish enogh to urge away any of your time. You will of course withhold letter & MS. from Mr Dewey— I shall write him with the return of his reviews today. Your Price & Hume are safe—you progress—& look back on these old affairs with indifference & as the opp^y is cercuitous I shall not send them. I want some No's of xian Examiner. I was disappointed in finding my little Calvinist no companion.—^{n}

Yours affectionately & admiringly,

MME

a cold little thing who lives in society alone & is looked up to is a poor specimen of genius. I performed a mission in secretly undermining his vanity or trying to—alas, never done but by mortifying affliction. Love to Sister & Charles

MH: bMS Am 1280.226(867). *Addressed:* Mr R. Waldo Emerson / Cambridge / Mss / Care of Mr T. W. Haskins / Boston. *Endorsed:* X / 1829X.

smothered] ⟨quenched almost⟩ smothered

companion.—] companion.— ⟨timid cold & wary—superficial & vain.⟩

1. RWE's letter of 6 Sept. and another of 24 July (see below) do not survive. Although Rusk accepts the endorsement date (1829) for MME's letter and thus places both letters in 1829 (*L* 1:282, 274), internal evidence indicates that MME wrote this letter in 1828. Below, she refers to RWE's sermon 23, on a text from Rom. 1:20 and on innate belief, which he first preached on 28 Sept. 1828 (*CS* 1:203–7).

2. Poet William Cowper (1731–1800) suffered his first serious depression in about 1752, during his study of the law; ten years later, while experiencing violent symptoms of madness and delusions, he attempted suicide, and in Dec. 1763 he was confined in an asylum, where he suffered "religious terrors" (*DNB*). Released eighteen months later, for the rest of his life Cowper continued to experience depression and mania. MME to EBE, 5 Oct. [1828], preached on Christian acceptance of affliction (MH: 220[71])—as she does later in this letter.

To Edward Bliss Emerson

Waterford   Dec. 23   1828

Nothing but ill health prevented me dear dear Edward, from thanking you a thousand times for your ever welcome letter—more welcome than any other even you ever wrote me—for your vision is clearer—stronger—   You speake of those things which are great—tho' the subjects were only touched—there is light over them—   "Repentance"—how reasonable—and how dearer than honors & pleasures the sense of pardon—a foretaste of Heaven—but more desirable as a partaking of virtue. You feel too—yes I am sure you feel a calm superiority to the impetus of that useless bustle of ambition for knowing & doing & being every thing. Oh what dreams I had on my bed after your letter—of those gaurdian spirits w'h watch with more than human sympathy the cares of man—how they regret the toil of the puppet show—how they commune of those who return to the tranquil pursuit of duty to God—whose minds resemble the deep & transparent Lake which reflects not merely the beauties which rise from it's banks but the dark blue sky and the stars and the sun itself—while the noisy streamlets hasten to reach the ocean w'h covers them with oblivion and the traveler is forever ignorant which was the *first* who gained the goal. Your mind my estimable Nephew will not only restore to society its acquisitions but leave I trust original pictures of itself—what is more—will embody the ideas of those skies (for w'h the xian hopes) by an eminent piety. Well serious as is the subject I can't but smile to find myself running my image into such lenght—   And I want you to smile whenever you can. "*Rejoice always.*" Not so much that you have returned to the world— alas it is but a hospital—where those who are truest to it's spirit are in the true sense of the word insane—where the most innocent affections become by self exaggeration the means of vanity & "illusion"—& wither like other "plumes."

Appropos. Is not Moore's Epicurean very fine?[1] But the only mere book (if it is human & not an antisapation of the divine philosophy of the divine Saviour) I kept near me in inability to read a page, was the maxims of M. Antoninus. If you should like so obscure & obsolete a thing it is in C. Library—but some what different in it's translation from mine. It has not I believe the following sentence. "Ask yourself every morning if it be of importance whether a good action is performed by you or another?"[2] Is not this a wonderfull counterpart to *his* who assigned to the labourer of an hour the same as to the one of a whole day?[3]

Farewell—as I hear you are gone to N.H.[4] I direct this to Charles care. Write me I pray   And tell me your opinion of every thing but speake of that w'h will interest me most—*yourself*—   Again farewell. May the spirit of Him who best understood and loved glory rest on you—his—who in view of real, cast contempt on all earthly glory.

Your affectionate Aunt
M.M.E.

MH: bMS Am 1280.220(71). *Endorsed:* Miss M. M. Emerson / 23 Dec. 1828 / ans^d.

1. Thomas Moore, *The Epicurean: A Tale* (Boston, 1827).
2. Unlocated in the meditations of Antoninus (the emperor Marcus Aurelius).
3. Parable of the laborers in the vineyard, Matt. 20:1–16.
4. CCE to WE[3], 9 Nov. [1828], tells of RWE's plan to remove EBE from McLean Asylum and take him with him when he travels to New Hampshire to preach; on 18 Dec. he writes that EBE and RWE are still in New Hampshire but are due to return on the following Monday (22 Dec.) (MT/MH).

To Ann Sargent Gage

[1828?]

There have been compunctions that the D^r & you should find their aged friend so excited against a well meaning Preacher— But physicians know that a complaint long restrained gets latitude. Let us my xian fellow travellers pray for him—for ourselves that the peculiar dearth in w'h we live may render us more assiduous to inhale that celestial dew which may give increase to our fleece more surely than the highest means of external excitment without it. I spend all the little sight I have on the subject of theology, & read other things^n for repose. And sometimes feel a great desire to converse—but mere theory can do no good in conversation unless there is liesure to throw light on each others mind. I see, I think, the want of this intercourse in our Pastor— & feel it in myself. I hope you will both give me your opinion on D^r C—'s sermon as soon as I can get it from Susan.[1] Why will not the D^r bring it & a No. of Examiner? For myself I feel that they (Unitarians) are going far far from Clarke my old orthodox Master—they seem to forget that xiainity was founded in sorrow & that repentance & an ever wakefull warfare with sin & error must be kept up.

I mentioned to Dr E. the care of my books— You will please to see to Germany—it is my darling & one of the q^t R. is torn apart—w'h I intended to have sewn.

I dont know when I shall see you if you dont come. I took cold tho' your work of almost superogratory kindness. And I am always glad when such whimsical care of my self fails—leaves me better.

Adieu God bless you all.
MME.

MWA. *Addressed:* Mrs. A.S. Gage. *Added in pencil:* 1828–32?
things] ⟨trifles⟩ ↑ things ↓

1. Letter is undated; possibly a reference to WEC's controversial sermon, "Likeness to God," delivered at Providence on 10 Sept. 1828, the reason for placing this letter in 1828.

1829

To Ellen Louisa Tucker and Ralph Waldo Emerson

Sab. 24 Jan. 1829.

As soon as I read your character—"*stronge religious feelings*" lovely Louisa I could do nothing but commend you to God—and pray that you might be a lasting blessing to him, whom it is your favored lot to attach.[1] Yes highly favored I may well say, not because he is a relative—(that is distant and less than ever I expect any intercourse with him) but I know his temper & the world tell of his talents. But why are you in the City? They will buz to you of musick—of literature of chemistry—of every thing that will disturb the culture of your *character*—every thing averse to that enthusiasm of piety— of extensive benvolence—of high minded principles which can alone support devotion to God & love to th{   }[2]   A fine lady talks of these things— but is almost alway{s des}titute of deep feeling—of every thing to assuage {   } & age. They will pester the world with tales of their love to parents children & forget, that unless there has been some great sacrifices there is no more merit than puss loving her kittens. The moment of merit in loving near relations in common cases destroys every thing flattering. *Do not read every thing.* Let Laws "serious call" be ever on your table and "*night-tho'ts.*"[3] Those will inevitably form you to rational & fervent religion—do you love works of fiction—let Flora MacIvor, Jenny Deans, Corrina and the full portrait of Moore's Alethe[4] be before you. The man that God has blest you with is devoted to the highest & most urgent office. Lean not on him for resources— but urge him on to aid in the work of moral improvement which is going on for Heaven. Be yourself a ministering angel to him and society. You no more than others can ever love virtue practically till it costs you somthing

Jenny Deans is a master piece for illustrating the *morals* of religion. I hope you dont paint nor talk french. Hope you'll be a unique. And *love* poetry— that musick of the soul.

Waterford[5]

me the letter already begun I intreat. And say *how* & *where* is dear Edward. *The sermons I want* and every thing else interesting can come by J. Chamberlain who is going to Concord soon.[6] You will of course see that Louisa's education is admirably directed by me. Fudge you'll say. Oh why is she in Boston? Dont let her sing.

Adieu most affectionately.

M.M.E.

* * *

MH: bMS Am 1280.226(758). *Addressed:* Mr R. Waldo Emerson. / Cambridge / Mss. *Postmarked:* Waterford Me Jan—8th. *Endorsed:* M M E / To Ellen X / Jan. 1829.

1. RWE and ET became engaged on 17 Dec. 1828. CCE to MME, 1 Jan. 1829, describes ET as a "beautiful, sensible, religious, girl [who] is rich too. Though this seems to be forgotten in her loveliness & excellence" (MT/MH).

2. MS torn by seal; several words lost.

3. William Law, *A Serious Call to a Devout and Holy Life Adapted to the State and Condition of All Orders of Christians* (1729); Edward Young, *The Complaint; or, Night-Thoughts on Life, Death, and Immortality* (London, 1742).

4. Flora MacIvor is the sister of Fergus in Sir Walter Scott's *Waverley*; Jeanie Deans appears in Scott's *Heart of Midlothian*; Corrina is a misspelling for the heroine of de Staël's novel *Corinne*; Alethe is a young Egyptian princess in Moore's *Epicurean*.

5. The remainder of the letter is written upside down at the bottom of the outside leaf, below the address, and seems to continue another letter (to RWE) with which this portion was enclosed.

6. John Chamberlain of Waterford married MME's niece Phebe Haskins in 1824.

To RALPH WALDO EMERSON

Jan 28 [1829]   Thurs.

My dear Waldo

Well I always hoped events would bring forth religious *feeling*. And, if I remember the interference of the gods was more celebrated by antient heros when the gifted were prosperous.[1] Then thier names were echoed in tempels— and natures noble self gave symbols that they were in harmony with the great *designs* of the universe. No lawless atom—no luckless disease crossed thier path to obscure & sullenize their views when the horizon shone for them. To continue my porcupine humour—   You do exaggerate (notwithstanding the modest & gracious stole of moderation is thrown so gracefully on) your success—   It is *common* for such as *you*—& thousands less deserving. Your poverty (tho' to you, *disproportionate* to your merit) was natural—the fate of both your families. Till sickness & sightlessness attacked you—every thing was joyous & hopefull. One would think to hear you all vapour about your changes that the contrast was to be as poetic as the fisherman's of Gallilee— and that the world was to bear the marks of your destiny to the end of time. You can readily account for my spleen on this head—as I never remember an hour in my life when the change of events promised me any thing *I* wanted and the utmost delight ever known has been in bounding on without *any thing*. The most society that ever I enjoyed was the year I staid with *Bullkey* after you all grew up.[2] For the last time said I hope. Now I sympathise most warmly with those whose golden spoke the white fates have turned up—and would fain hail your ascent—were it such. But as you are too wise not to see that such a society will hang on your intellec. flight as the fogs on the beams of the morning—that after all—the appointments of *enjoyment* are fixed beyond the power of circumstances—that indeed its preponderance belongs to a mediocrity of talent and virtue while virtue is in an exiled state. In this gaity of heart—of my returning health & fine accomodations, of your busy *dove* like condition, I avoid all theological views. And as the modern faith renders your profession a mere sinecure in comparison of the religion of the heart, I forbear to speak of those eagle *flights* which the deciples of a rigid & suffering faith can attain. Well I may now descend to the humble truth & own that week after week I looked with desire to hear of this call—that I inquired of Edward & Charles why you went to Concord (in vain) nothing was said. And the pleasure was inhanced by your attention in a speedy communication. A solitude, such as genius would like, could not be yours. The old world must go on. Torches must light it. I never compared nor thought till last night, and then not *compared* the story which my Aunt used to dwell on of her brother Waldo.[3] Sickness & disappointment follow him in every trial to subsist till he was free as they called it two or three years—then merchandise suceeded & his increase knew no diminution. In those days the similarity of your names would have nothing short of marvellous. As to Ellens—it is handsome—but my Louisa[4] was your first admirer after your old Aunt, & is a fine woman. & I wanted Ellen to drop her first name as you had done.

If you are ever questioned about the rev. John Emerson of Topsfield (Mss) say he was the only brother of J.E. of Malden, but as he was a musty miser there was no tie between them—that his descendants are miserable creatures spread over Essex & some in Maine I suppose belong to him. The ministers in Salem & Reading & of Baldwin (Me) are a swarthy race—connected with the grandfather of G.B.E. probably—& will claim us tho' needlessly I suspect.[5] The only sister of J.E. of Malden married an Edwards & her poetic history never failed of awakening delight in my childhood.[6] She became so poor thro' liberality, that she was reduced to make ginger bread to sell—but calling in children to give it away finished her last resource. I have sought the sacred spot which contained her hut in Newburyport of late years in vain. Farewell. God will sustain you, and I hope render you superior to fortune. Yours in love.

M.M.E.

Do tell of the beau clergy—S.R. &c   And my old idol Channing.[n]

MH: bMS Am 1280.226(872). *Addressed:* Mr R. Waldo Emerson / Cambridge / Mss. / Care of T.W. Haskins. *Endorsed:* 1829.

Channing] Channig *in MS; T reads* Chauncey

1. In a note attached to the MS, Rusk argues that this letter, despite the endorsement "1829," belongs to 1830 (because 28 Jan. fell on Thursday in 1830). However, MME refers to two important events: RWE's engagement to Ellen Tucker in Dec. 1828 and his becoming junior pastor at the Second Church in Jan. 1829. CCE to MME, 1 Jan. 1829, remarks on the year's propitious beginnings: "Edward's restoration, & Waldo's happy . . . prospects" (MT/MH).

2. Probably Sept. through Nov. 1821.

3. Waldo Emerson (1735–74), older brother of WE[1], was a merchant in the West Indies trade at Wells (now Kennebunk), Maine (*IpsE*, 75, 125).

4. For a while, MME insisted on calling ET by her middle name; she may also be thinking of niece Louisa Farnham Dewey.

5. The Reverend John Emerson (1706–74) of Topsfield was the younger brother of MME's grandfather Joseph Emerson (1700–1767) of Malden. He married Elizabeth Pratt in 1729; they had sixteen children, twelve of whom reached adulthood, but MME seems to have had no relationship with them. George Barrell Emerson (1797–1881) was the grandson of MME's aunt Hannah Emerson (1722–1812), the oldest sister of MME's father and the wife of a distant cousin, Daniel Emerson (1716–1801).

6. "*Newbury (Mass.) Records.* 4 February, 1724. Abraham Edwards and Elizabeth Emerson intend marriage" (*IpsE*, 418).

To Charles Chauncy Emerson

March 1. Sab 4 'ok 1829

My dear Charles,

This moment I've read yours.[1] And never suspected but it was Waldo's hand till you named him. This just & large view of nature & society—this philosophical *confession* which might be made where Rosseau's was daring profanity—all these I own delighted more coming from him in his situation (tho' I doubted their permanency or reality) than from any other. These convictions of the soul—this holy homesickness was strange in him now—but most valuable qualifications for his office & pledges for his growth. With you, dear Charles they might be the effect of nerves finely attuned and rising like the mercury. Still they are buds of high promise—for they will often revisit you—and give a "caste" for immortality. You can no where solve the enigma of man's nature—the variance of his will with his affections—his self love & self contempt, far nobler, his benevolence & his malevolence but in the revelation which Jesus made. Without this aegis of human nature man is the most unaccountable & unfortunate of all animals. And here only can great virtues be acquired—tho' they may never be able in this life to eradicate the hereditary & educatory disadvantages of a cautious and too discreet prudence & respect for the world—& the *utile* of virtue—(all of which articles, so seemly, I think you must have refered to in the noble burstings of the confession) yet this faith will purify[n] them. Ah study it—preach it. In the study of the divine attributes—in those abysses of thought—lose thy poorer self—& become a new—an angelic man. It is certain that not any Emerson is capable of deep investigation—long continued thought— What has only study done for deranging[n] dear Edward? his[n] last letters—not his they seem. Tell me immediately what I am to think of him. But I was going to say religion that "home of genius" will strenghten the mind as it does the character—there abstraction becomes habitual & gains power with the affections. The simple history of Jesus unfolds marvels. How completely is the interests of time abandoned— the very miseries of the dark ages & of persecution are wittnesses that it's design was not to improve the present. And what are a few centuries blotted out in the tale of eternity? Were it only as a reformer of man—would it not do more for him in these better days? Is there not much more in the plan than Ware & his school perceive?[2] Is there not an expiation for the immutable law

w'h no mere man has kept? Enter the nature & history of man & you may not give yourself to that study which seems the most worthy of a man. I am glad you dislike the present state of metaphysicks. They can never be explained fully—never improved but by a divine as well as philosopher. Brown's[3] holy theory of morals loses its worth by the slimness of his metaphysicks? Or I am too old to leave old opinions. If there is nothing but phenomena & they to be analyzed like matter—will not the sceptic gain strenght? If there is only the *principle* of *thought* (w'h I know not what he means by), if there is no *essence* no *substance* (immaterial) in w'h the attributes of mind ad or inhere[n]—what is soul—mind—immortality? True, where this the case by Gods will—were it possible to conceive of such a phenomenon, why I should beleive that this chain of ideas might exist forever—it does not nessecarily lead to atheism— but it contradicts the elementary belief of such a Being as we are wont to consider *God*! We believe in an infinite Essence—a somthing which consti- tutes Personality—resembling a soul. And he does not enlighten the *relation* of cause & effect. If not *nessecary* by divine constitution—we lose one of the grandest truths in nature. But I have not read it some years. Apart from it's theory do we not continually meet the doctrine of nessesity in this warfare of our own characters? And do we feel less humble that we fail in greatness? Surely not—tho' more resigned & more eager for the unknown future. I could not but write after such a letter— And I did it now—to ask you when you send the money to send a review of Channings sermon[4] and the reasons why S. A. says he lost his reckoning. Never was a more *glorious* sermon tho' his view of human nature is too bright for truth. The money may be inconvenient to send— Alas that I need it.
March 13.

You were always my confidante—dont *in mercy* think from my wishing the money I ever expect to want— No nor be dependant for a cent. It w[d] spoil all my intercourse of friendship.

Yet I do not indulge the infirmities of age with even a glass of wine—the *secondary* cause is expense—the first is exclusion of all tonics. Farewell dear friend & Nephew. May those blessings which you can most enjoy & influence others be yours

MME.

Who is Mrs Lyman that ranks you so high? Do you ever see Charlotte F.?[5] How does she *wear*?

MH: bMS Am 1280.226(667). *Addressed:* Mr Charles C. Emerson / Care of Rev. R. Waldo Emerson / City of Boston, Mss. *Postmarked:* Waterford. Me March 19. *En- dorsed:* M M Emerson / March 19 / 1829 / C's letter mistaken for / Waldo's / Edward B. E. / Brown's lectures.
purify] ⟨sanctify⟩ purify
has . . . deranging] has ⟨scholarship⟩ ↑ only study ↓ done for ↑ deranging ↓
his] ⟨How weake⟩ his
ad or inhere] ad ↑ or in ↓ here

1. CCE to MME, 21 Feb. [1829], discusses "the enigma of man's nature" (MT/MH).

2. Probably Henry Ware, Sr. (1764–1845), Hollis Professor of Divinity at Harvard, 1805–45; possibly his son Henry Ware, Jr. (1794–1843), RWE's senior colleague at the Second Church.

3. Thomas Brown.

4. WEC's Providence sermon, "Likeness to God," preached at the ordination of the Reverend F. A. Farley, Providence, R.I., 10 Sept. 1828. CCE to MME, 1 Jan. 1829, asks whether she's read it and adds, "Mrs Ripley thinks he is clean out of his reckoning—" (MT/MH). MME to [EBE], 11 Jan. 1829, expresses her fear of "modern" Unitarianism: "All that is sublime, earnest—infinite seems to have no place in their faith. . . . I am the more afraid of it since hearing of Channings P. sermon. . . . Should he fall—it will be because he has departed from old fashioned unitarianism, such as Paul preached" (VtMiM).

5. Anne Robbins Lyman, wife of Judge Joseph Lyman of Northampton and mother of CCE's college classmate and roommate Joseph Lyman. CCE visited the Lymans in Aug. 1828 (*L* 1:244 n. 73). Charlotte Farnham.

To RALPH WALDO EMERSON

Wed night   March 11— [1829]

Rev. R. W. Emerson.

It is a finer night than even the day—the moon has not filled her horns—good sign my dear Waldo for your inaguration.[1] And may all happy constellations reign over you long after the heart which has prayed for you today ceases to beat. It is well you were not ordained *last* Wednesday—that ill ides for our Country.[2] Long may you influence human weal and ever may retain that gift of instructing without ostentation. I have been more uncomfortable for some dull weeks of confinement, from Ellen's illness. As the Naturalist loves to see the flower perfect—so the Naturalist of the universe loves to image perfect happiness—or the means of it even here. And of this Ellen I had a singular opportunity of hearing from an impartial hand one dreary evening. My hostess[3] persuaded me to send for a young physician as I had not been well. He came and after his medicining, asked if I had relations in N.C.[4] to which I modestly replied in the negative. He then read or rather translated from french a letter from his Sister giving a most brilliant account of Miss E.T. & your sucess—but more important of her worth & being in fine—an Angel. The physick man himself had seen her—and could describe her. In this remotest of all corners the circumstance was noticable & I did not grudge my 50 cents a visit. After all that influence and fame can do or may it is domestic love makes happiness. But you will not answer De Stale's criterion of love "know not why."[5] In general—any absorbing passion has a noble effect—to deliver from the little coils & cares of every day—   And as "old dogmas in religion", some of which had a commanding power, and "holy nonsense" are exploded (and much is improved age owns) it is well that your affections should be engaged—that while you mingle with your society—duty & benevolence should motivize

Figure 17. Ellen Louisa Tucker (1811?–31) and Ralph Waldo Emerson, from photographs of the miniatures painted by Sarah Goodridge, 1829. Courtesy the Ralph Waldo Emerson Memorial Association.

rather than pleasure. *How is it?* Have you supplanted *H. Ware??*[6] Father says, "Ware has asked a dissmission knowing their attachment to you   But they are loath to part with him"   To part with Ware I suppose. This is all I ever heard. Another subject of higher curiosty is to read Stewarts Hebrews.[7] It is expected here. And to know if unitarians do not like Channing's P. Sermon?[8] Did you send that note to Wm? he has sent a quarters interest instead of a third of a year. * * *

MH: bMS Am 1280.226(861). *Endorsed:* 1829X.
   1. RWE was ordained on 11 Mar. 1829.
   2. "Last Wednesday" was 4 Mar., the date originally established by Congress for the inauguration of the president in 1789. In that year, lack of a quorum prevented the vote count until 6 Apr., and Washington did not take the oath of office until 20 Apr. 1789. All subsequent presidential terms until 1933 began on 4 Mar.
   3. Still in Maine, MME seems to have left Vale and boarded in several different places between Jan. and May 1829 (MH: 670).
   4. Probably "New" Concord, N.H., where Ellen Tucker grew up.
   5. de Staël, *Germany* 3:18.
   6. Henry Ware, Jr.
   7. Moses Stuart, *A Commentary on the Epistle to the Hebrews* (Andover, 1827).
   8. WEC's Providence sermon (see MME to CCE, 1 Mar. 1829, n. 4).

To Charles Chauncy Emerson

[? Apr. 1829]

   It was kind to speake of ordination and of the dear pastor's sermon. It bro't back that of Everetts on the same occasion[n] & the same text—   And the idea of Waldo to whom I said truly there is nothing to be ashamed of in this gospel.[1] The arts and sciences have bro't their honors to the cause & xianity has mingled with every thing good & splendid. It seemed that those whose horoscopes were cast beneathe the influences of the cross in it's first ages were to be the beacons of the world. Yet there are wreaths for early piety—there are yet palms in the celestial plains for those who are able to rise above the imperious calls of fashion & ambition—calls w'h demand a longer & sometimes more trying martyrdom than fire & gibbet. In the wanderings of your imajanation, dear Charles can you find a world where it is likely there are such differences in theology? None where the subjects of dispute are greater? Tho' here it cannot be decided whether the Deity's existence be complex or simple—Reason could never decide—but revelation & the ministry of Jesus seem to determine that the doctrine of trinity is not a subject of our belief— and that if it exists—Jesus Christ is an individual—sent of God—His son— as no other being. This old exploded faith w'h stands in a humble medium florished in the augustan age of the Chh. If it has difficulties they are only the trial of faith. If it is not so plausible & polished as modern unitarianism— why one single page of fiction w'h represents human nature—not to speake of the history of one nation or age, brings objections w'h tarnish the beautifull theory. True, these facts, tho' facts of difficulty, do not contradict our first revelation—*reason*—as do the calvinist dogmas. Yet why s^d you & I care—I at my grave—& you no publick teacher   As long as these are better than their faith—have ranked among the noblest heros in practical virtue. And that they are perhaps labouring with their opponents to do away the rubbish left by the reformation. Yet you may be a teacher—and a man capable of influence as you are will not publickly profess a religion in ignorance of its' founder's character and pretentions. If there were no other world it would be glorious to unite one's fleeting existence with the felt presence of the first Cause—then deism would do—but as we are going where our connection with God is boundless it is important to adopt His own method of getting there with safty. If our own reason could devise a better way than that by the revelation—would it not be persumption? This plan of the bible promises to do more than human wisdom can comprehend. With humanatarianism has usually been connected the belief of materialism—that belief w'h has done so much degradation— and how cold & slight is it's hold on the affections. If the Lindseys & Priest-leys sacrificed to it—their characters were early embued by a loftier faith.[2] If xianity were a development of human nature—it must be owned a very fine thing—but that *nature* itself denies such an ofspring—and did *it* not in that case the bible would lose its' athority. May an old friend, who never troubled you with catechisms in childhood, ask why this haste in "joining the chh in a few months"?[3] If Jesus were only a man—and you would honor him—why not wait till you had drank deeper into his lofty philosophy—and had more laurels to lay on his table? If a god—and holding the keys of life & death— if the only medium of communicating with the self Existent—if his death were an "ensign" to prove that w'h had been typified by sacrifices thro'ut the world—which had been foretold by prophecy—which had been reasoned on by Apostles—and w'h the researches of the profound Germans argue— if you hasten to celebrate such a death—to receive an admission into a king-dom too grand to be purchased by mortal merit you cannot be too speedy in gaining veiws worthy of such an inheritance. You will of course study the whole bible—and a few of those divines who consider the shedding of blood for the remission of sins as an inevitable principle of the divine econymy. Is this inscrutable?—what more so than the most incontestible truth—the self Existence of God? Have you read Erschine's "internal evidence"? Chalmers (merchantile) sermons?[4] I am the bolder in these requests—as the intreaty I once used and uselessly I know, to an interesting youth, has since lessened my own sorrow at his loss of faith. He is too correct to celebrate the sacrament (willingly) as its existence tells of & *proves* to us the very resurrection w'h this gentleman disbelieves. This resurrection so important, you may say, "argues the nessesity of a publick death—& nothing more in those sufferings." Could there not have been a publick ascension without the cross—Elijah's fiery chariot told of an hereafter. A divinity thus showing it were stronger still—

but those who believe in the preexistence of Christ rationally infer—('induct') that his death had other purposes—they think it deciphers—or redeems the enigma of man's nature—attones for the origin of evil. Not all—there are a few in this Country who seem to hang on the old fashioned doctrine of the divinity of the Messiah and renounce his vicarious mission. How do they do it with any consistency? Their motives may be innocent—long habits of ortho-doxy—wishes to remain—and the politick adherance to those who are more liberal?? Probably motives for the good of the ignorant. Ah dear Charles give your bright gifts & days to the study of theology. You will be glad in old age. And if you become an Arian may you (if consistent with truth) conceal the treasure till the times & full conviction enable you to come forward with a strong influence—shed a light w'h long rest on your name when your dust shall have mingled with its elements. A few years will do much—it is a period of wonderfull revolutions. I am never asked & obliged to give opinions—as I am very very ignorant & ever shall be an inquirer. Father Riply who is easily sattisfied with one's theology (if not calvin) I say nothing to on the subject of attonement. He says it is not in ('the bond') the bible. Jesus signified it enough—he gave himself like a god—   T'was for ages to develop—   And the more enlightened may better be understood that his sacrifice was the high-est ulogium of virtue—the cement of morals thro' the universe. The helpless sinner may rank among scenes where those spirits who never erred would not could not sustain otherwise the admission. Farewell. dearer to me, when thinking of these

immortal things than at any time.
MME

Please to inclose the money from T. as soon as possible

Sat 4.   I w^d ask Waldo & you to write—but cannot think of taxing *his* charity—& your lines are few & far between   *How is Ellen & Edward?* I send this in haste—were I to tarry, a sense how little this blessed religion has done for me might render it painfull to communicate even with you.

MH: bMS Am 1280.226(668). *Addressed:* Mr C. C. Emerson / Care of Rev. R. Waldo Emerson / Boston / MS. *Postmarked:* Waterford Me April 6. *Endorsed:* M M. Emerson / April 1829 / Christianity / Joining the Church.
    occasion] occasion ↑ ⟨I believe⟩ ↓
    1. SR preached the sermon at RWE's ordination (*Life*, 137); CCE to MME, 14–17 Mar. 1829, states that the text of one of Waldo's first sermons to his new congregation on the following Monday was " 'I am not ashamed of the Gospel of Christ for it is the power of God unto the salvation of every one who believeth' " (Rom. 1:16) (MT/MH); see CS 1:231–37.
    2. Theophilus Lindsey (1723–1808) and Joseph Priestley, early Unitarians and materialists.
    3. CCE to MME, 14–17 Mar., says CCE plans to attend RWE's "meeting regu-larly" and in a few months to join the church (MT/MH).

4. Thomas Erskine, *Remarks on the Internal Evidence for the Truth of Revealed Religion* (Philadelphia, 1821); Thomas Chalmers, *The Application of Christianity.* . . .

To Ralph Waldo Emerson

Sunday Morn. [July 1829]

This moment I read yours—and the craving after Kantism is gratified for the day.[1] You give as great notions of God—or Intelligence, as any of them as far as you go—   And probably find "shadows" only as they do for want of an intimacy or faith in revelation. This docile revelation faith likes to part company at the time your clouds gather—he rejoices & harmonises with the evolvings of your natural religion—for he has dispelled their anthromorphisms and dropsical phantoms in the mountainous air of plain scripture. He has become so familiar with the idea of the agency & personality of the Infinite Spirit—that so far from Fichtes loss of God with his consciousness—that if he were losing his own existence he would find consolation in the faith that his Creator was eternal.[2] But is it possible for a man to divest himself of hope in some portion of eternity who thus believes & idolisies the belief of God?[n] Another anchor to the vulgar belief in the old english version[3] is that its adherent finds no difficulty about liberty. He is so reliant on this Revelation that whether nessesity is the order or freedom it is all one to the true heart—   But he feels certain they both exist, in a degree, & in so fine a union, that nothing short of disencumbered spirit can value and know the connection of divine & human agency. And he rejects Price's idea that man must be either wholly free or bound.[4] He is neither terrified were this infinite Being Himself to be under some indefinable nessesity in respect to matter as old Jenyns hypothesis' about.[5] Jesus has assumed flesh[n]   He would plunge into that nessesity himself. If matter is it's origin—Jesus has assumed it—and Jesus diciple loves material world and it's vast & sublime analogies. Can they exist with idealism? They may it is true—   But idealism, grand as it is in some views, leads to atheism in others. It is an ignis fatuus—leads from the high way—removes old land marks—and somtimes like Byrons darkness[6] stagnates all the old laws around which we love to swing. When viewed as giving us certainty in the existence of *spirit*—and as opposed to the heresies of materialism in theology we are led away to wish nothing better for this life than confirmation in it—above—and beyond all it seems at first sight to bring the Deity into immediate contact. But experience shows it has not this effect—but pantheism perhaps—   And that in losing hold on old notions—this very soul w'h we have beleived naturally immortal is only one of the immediate creations of Deity—to play its' part in the wonderful panorama.

Farewell   may God continue to bless you & Ellen & long prolong your health & lives daily prays affectionately

MME

MH: bMS Am 1280.226(862). *Endorsed:* M.M.E. / July 1829 X.

God?] God? ⟨is questionable⟩

Jesus . . . flesh] *heavily smudged; possibly rubbed out with a finger (cancellation)*

1. Probably a response to a letter from RWE that does not survive; possibly to a recent sermon (such as sermon 29, 14 June 1829, CS 1:296–300).

2. A probable source for MME's comparison of Fichte and Kant is [A. H. Everett], "History of Intellectual Philosophy," *North American Review* 29 (July 1829): 67–123; see esp. 104–6, a lengthy quotation from Cousin's *Cours de philosophie*, one of four books reviewed in this article.

3. Probably the empiricist school of Bacon, Newton, and Locke; Everett (see above, n. 2) quotes from Cousin a long passage pointing out that Locke did not "wholly overlook the internal part of our nature, that is, liberty and intelligence" (ibid., 83), although MME goes beyond what she could have learned from her reading of Everett's review.

4. Richard Price's best-known work, *A Review of the Principal Questions in Morals.*

5. Soame Jenyns, *A Free Enquiry into the Nature and Origin of Evil in Six Letters*; see esp. letter 4, "On Moral Evil."

6. "Darkness": title of a poem by Byron.

To Charles Chauncy Emerson

[? Aug. 1829]

I have been looking for some dab of paper to imitate your scraps— But as I can't get so *much* into a whole sheet as one of those "savings" of yours contain I here take a common-piece. However, were it not for the "Queen's"[1] renouncings yours would have had no grace—no explanation to have put them in the pale of wit. And humour it seems now is the soul of every thing. Till this very last winter I lived in ignorance—and thought *it* only to be tolerated as a companiable thing. But it seems that with Germanism we are to be guided. And J. P. F. Richter had humour as the sole & soul inspirer of every talent & work. But you had rather be C C E than all those other letters. We dont love monsters— And his very midnight description so exquisite, is too vast or bloated for my unpoetic ear—except when he says "about this hour 1794 Mars went down in the west, & the moon rose in the east; & my soul &c"[2] No it is your spirit I like—looking thro' plain style rather^n than obscurity or novelty of phrase w'h the Germans use^n— But why do I talk of your writing—for in truth I know nothing of it—and of original ideas—you are stingy enough when no more excited than writing to me. And you dont send the last Com. oration.[3] One fact I must sympathize with—the ebbs of thought & feeling you describe—but you need not trouble yourself to send those lines of Byron alluded to—I have long admired them as describing the doleful "prison" of his reflections.[4] Happy for you no baleful star has watched behind the house of your destiny to influence or gall the hours of depression. And may none cause you to escape from the worst of torpor by means of too much humour. For after all I shall never believe that Richters was of the kind which Yankees call by that homely name— Your Grandfather was a humourist & Mimick—but the fervor of a high minded piety cast his lighter qualities into silence the last years of his short life.

> Adieu dearest Charles   To hear of your ample sucess will always, even after death, be acceptable to
>
> Aunt Mary.

Tues. 18.   Your letter last eve. disappointed us about seeing William as soon as we hoped.

MH: bMS Am 1280.226(674).
looking . . . rather] ↑ looking thro' plain style ↓ rather
phrase . . . use] phrase ↑ w'h the Germans use ↓
1. RWE's name for ET; see *L* 1:282.
2. Quoted by Carlyle in "Jean Paul F. Richter," *Edinburgh Review* 46 (June 1827): 194.
3. See MME to EzR, 27 Aug. 1828.
4. Possibly a passage from Byron's "Prophecy of Dante," which describes the "moral morn, too long with clouds defaced / And noxious vapours from Avernus risen, / Such as all they must breathe who are debased / By servitude, and have the mind in prison" (3.58–61).

To Ralph Waldo Emerson

[Aug.? 1829]

I saw Bulkly yesterday and the affection he has for you seems to be the effect of more than mere care. It seems you have been tender. This dear Waldo will outlive all your other doings—love & fame often resides with the worm— & last no longer than forage is afforded. "Surely not the love of Ellen!"—"if any thing is immortal this is." It may be so. God grant it may—and that every thing of health & its most bright & joyous attendants be given. It is weakness (for my views) to wish this so much. Her devotional *feelings*, if they are no more, sheild you in times of skepticism: view them as idle—still they will be a kind of gaurdian Angel to both. If you want to feel the power & worth of revelation converse with William & such like and the superficial knowledge & philosophy veiled in sometimes lofty langue will make any one hug their faith & think a whole life well spent in strenghtening it. Nay—that the feelings with w'h one contemplates a mortal who feels no relation nor has any reference in his actions to the God he believes in—has no faith in a revelation of His will, are so revolting, that till this sad experience I knew not that one could feel towards a relative in whose welfare I was interested. I keep bleting & muring—know not how to express myself. S.A.R. is still more culpable— her society to be shunned whenever she touches on religion—and how can I love her?[n] Total Atheism is more excusable than belief in a God who has cast off his offspring & is not expected to remunerate the slave. If they would make a God of fate—it would be somthing— And to follow them up they run into atheism. Let us not complain of calvinism—its' most terrible points are better than nothing. If the bible is a fable I would cherish it now in age with undying zeal— It may have a truth of infinite weight like other fables wh have a little. But it is not a fable I know It answers to the living consciousness of Gods impress on the soul. It develops the divinity within. Not the poetic *gospelless* divinity of German idealism—whose baseless fabrick will vanish into thin pestiferous air. The night is spending— And you will have no time to read this. W[m] has obliged me by his frankness—he attaches no infamy to his situation—thinks Humes argument against miracles never answered—does not yet know that the old bloated gentleman has ceased to interest this enlightened age. Is this strange apathy in the sceptics of this period wonderfull—argument of no care of God—or no Personal & all pervading Being? No—their case is provided against—warned—threatned—& the natural consequences will follow. In the large number of these worlds which are showing their starry[n] faces at this moment, may be one prepared for those who have been born under so terrible an influence as to enjoy existence without a God. That Limbo where anomalies & untimely births and monstrous contradictions cohabit.

In presence of that "universe whh you intend to use in preaching" [1]—of its ever active Auther I bid you affectionately God speed in all that will unite you to the will and agency of this Being

MME.

If W[m] converses with Charles, please show him this & burn it. Please not to fail send the "law utility" by Madam Emerson [2]

MH: bMS Am 1280.226(864). *Endorsed* (*inside*): 1830; (*outside*): M M E X / Aug 1829.

her?] her ⟨as I do⟩?
starry] *possibly* stormy (*T*)
1. Probably a quotation from RWE.
2. Written on outside. Unidentified.

To Charles Chauncy Emerson

Keene   Oct. 10 —29

Dear Charles,

Your philosophy contacts with my thermometer. I have devised this union. But the morphisian stone no more moved. Such is the "wither"ing cast of changing life. One thing is sure A portion of good & ill—come how it will. And its' way is marked—its' design great as a future life. "Your light quenched." Never—if you adhere to it's Source. Your strech of overlooking the present nothing less than sublime. Yet why am I a moment deceived into admiration! At your writing it—that very instant might have been sanguine and—pardon the garullity of age. It is true you have a real good portion of indifference—could it be but of this little life alone—but it may obtrude on affection & devotion of self. Yet you are not developed Some fair—some gifted Ellen may enter the secret avenues of your soul & give a holy cast to this *sang froid*— And convert it to an abstracted unearthly temper—while the heart was beating—burning to the idea of "good done by others" Of late years there has been a mania among females to do good—& it has done much for those who needed such a stimulus. But when one hears the men talk & wish about it—it gingles like other toys. To leave the shadow of a duty undone is sacriligious to talent & faith—but character formed—and eternity has means enow to make one forget that in one of the atoms of space he was forgotten. Virtue in this state has none of the self denials wh'h Channing describes—it is one with pleasure—with rapture—with the idea of Gods presence—then tho' we cannot "sympathise" with the supreme object of 'affection'—yet we are absorbed in love—and sympathise with his lofty works of mind. So I feel different about his review of Fennelon—[1] Let literature take care of itself as Smith says of commerce.[2] When writers affect to sanction their pages with it they lose their peculiar genius & irreverence[n] the divine ark. In Homer Virgil and even Byron the pietist finds food for his faith & joy— But the cant of sentiment whh runs thro poetry & sames it to disgust. Let the infidels paint their anomalies in their own coulers & shapes—the true theist can discover the ruins of a Lucifer. But in the secreted infidel—the mongrel theist—we find a "moral at whh his satanic majesty laughs"[3] But why should I coute Young— Christianity needs not the aids of arts—they existed better before than since—tho' that loves to use them at the foot of its alter. Well it is time to say adieu—this has given me solace amidst the chit chat of one single fire to whh a number of boarders are absolutely confined. I shall soon depart—but among a number of places have not determined where Love to all & congratulations to the pair imparadised. You are not a Richardson—no miniture[4]

If this is difficult to read—you would not have had it but for this conveyance & letters of—&c

Yours aff^t MME

MH: bMS Am 1280.226(676). *Addressed:* Mr C. C. Emerson / J Prentiss Esqr / Cambridge / Mss. *Endorsed:* M M. Emerson / Oct. 1829 Keene.

irreverence] ⟨mar⟩ ↑ irreverence ↓

1. In his "Remarks on the Character and Writings of Fenelon," *Christian Examiner* 6 (Mar. 1829): 1–35, WEC focuses on "self-renunciation," or "self-sacrifice," or "self-crucifixion" as one major element in Fenelon's thought and then turns to the other side, "that strong, deep, supreme affection towards the Supreme Being with which Fenelon's book overflows" (25).

2. Adam Smith's economic theory of laissez-faire, as articulated in *The Wealth of Nations.*

3. Possibly a misquotation from night 9 of Edward Young's *Night-Thoughts*: "SATAN, instructed, o'er their *Morals* smiles" (line 1814).

4. MME seems to say that CCE lacks novelist Samuel Richardson's skill in depicting affairs of the heart.

To RALPH WALDO EMERSON

Greenfield   No[v]. 10 [1829]

Dear Waldo,

Your *knee—how does it*? I would it were well—the picture I would fain have no shades in but such as mortality absolutely imposes—and which give lustre to the whole. How came it *philosophically*? Was it one of a series of events inevitable—or provided for as a means of virtue? Either reposes the mind that excludes blind chance? All your head winds I hoped over—and this is nothing, if it be only a winter's job. With Ellen beside you a knee more or less is trifling. Yet but for the lameness w'h confines you, I should hardly have written—for I want you to tell me in your leisure about this "man who is to tell of God in truer, that is, nearer statments than ever any did." [1] Who is to tell us "what xianity has left untold"? How is it to be *one*—and is it to be a revelation from Heaven, when the "universe is so full of religion"—? and the development of the learned mind is so astonishing—that we are going to be gods ourselves? I am serious—I live & breathe with no other wish but to learn what you (plural) mean. What is "the new & mighty want of knowledge"? Is the only "outline to be illuminated by knowledge how distinct personality may exist with the infinity of the devine mind? To my simplicity—*personality—identity—consciousness* (w'h form our idea of personality) in their grandest significance belong naturally to infinity. As to this "personality consistent with a nature that must be described by negatives" I believe in no such Being—but consider these negations as spawns of infidelity & bastards of metaphisiks   But here is not my inquiry now—but what it is expected about *understanding* the revelation w'h some of you admit (for the mode of the divine existence *it* does not pretend to treat) to be from a superior power? And why not inquire once & for all, beloved[n] & estimable—gifted & favored—tell me without qualification if you believe with the Germans (who are high & enlightened) that what we have called a revelation has no divine athority? I have never pressed this for your judgment is as in case of Review "reserved," probably, till the concessions of opinion give more light & your researches have more scope. Then if I am not asking too much, give me your suspensions. Frothingham is a radical—fixed in un*belief*—so is S.A.R. [2] but she says there must be a God tho' He may be as distinct from his work as a basket from its maker.[n] Now if there is one, and we hope to live again, what is our best way—if we are not to live again what connection is it likely we have with Him? But these questions will be cold to you who are hoping so much for the new light? What grounds have you to expect it—and apart from your metaphisical distinctions and personalities you have expressed nothing to reform the world.

I thank you for offering to send Ed Review.[3] I met it in book store in Concord read the introduction with disgust—the rest with admiration—& finally discovered the writer, I thought, to be a no God man—and wrote you by Charles the dangers of idealism. His account of "art" was new—I asked S.A. for an explanation w'h she did not or could not give—find it gloriously explained by Novalis—and I shall love *art* if it be the power of picturing the interior of one's own mind. Novalis himself is a fine vision.[4] I thought of *one* all the time who may be a kindred genius. Cole. never wrote it. (Review). I was ashamed to be so interested in it till Sarah told how Channing was &c. I do want to know when you first read it—that *now* you offer it. I cant get the "aids to reflection" and the "Friend" is an unconnected mass of {great}ness & little egotisms.[5] But why do I dally on an errand so absorbing. The rationalists you say are growing better— But you (for I dont know what you did read) antisapated them to me some years since. And I want your doubts— I meant only to say I breathed one wish to know the state of mind of those who represent the Deity in a seperate relation to each individual—it is called 'false & partial'—but it's existence in a good sense is the all in all. Give us the God we love & the sceptic may take his own way. That distant ages & nations have had different means is a fact. But I have learnt to affix no distinct meaning to the terminology of the unitarians (so called) or the idealists, for some years. I read with great expectation that Novalis was about to do away the hostility about the divine omnipresence by asserting with some other Idealists that He existed not in space; but was baulked. In that view is removed one of the strongest arguments of unity—for there may be millions of infinites. If you can send me any thing of this sort do—but what is far better your own waking balm. I am boarding very pleasantly at Mr D Ripleys.[6] Please to send remembrances once. I should say much to the beau ideal of my imajanation— but she must not see a line. Thanks for your "welcome days"—but nothing can be farther from my plans or feelings. Write soon & tell good news of the knee. *Write soon* and to one whose hopes & presentiments bode that you will not always write to her corporeal power

MME

Dont let Charles see this if he should inquire after me

But the worse inference of this nonexistence of God in space is no existence? Ah dear good old Clarke! I have not left thy Demonstration[7] tho' I have wandered.[n]

Cousin send me of him[8]

MH: bMS Am 1280.226(868). *Addressed:* Rev. R. Waldo Emerson. / Boston / Mss. *Postmarked:* GREENFIELD MS. / NOV 12. *Endorsed:* MME X / Greenfield / 1829.

beloved] ⟨most⟩ beloved

God . . . maker.] God ↑ tho' . . . maker ↓ .

wandered] *possibly* wondered

1. Several unidentified quotations and paraphrases in this letter are probably from a letter from RWE to MME that does not survive (see headnote to letter of 15 Nov. 1829, *L* 1:287). Possibly RWE described his role as a new kind of preacher within the context of new German thought. RWE and ET were married on 30 Sept. 1829.

2. Nathaniel Frothingham, minister of Boston's First Church; like the reviewer of his sermon *A Plea against Religious Controversy* (8 Feb. 1829), MME would have objected that controversy is both necessary and useful (*Christian Examiner* 6 [May 1829]: 241), although she probably had other reasons for considering him an "unbeliever." Another reference to SBR's "unbelief."

3. Further comments indicate that the article she has read is Carlyle's review of two works by Franz Horn in "The State of German Literature," *Edinburgh Review* 46 (June 1827): 304–51; the discussion of art begins on p. 327.

4. Probably in another of Carlyle's reviews, "Novalis," *Foreign Review and Continental Miscellany* 4, no. 1 (1829): 97–141. Carlyle quotes Novalis's definition of art as "self-viewing, self-imitating, self-fashioning Nature" (130).

5. Samuel Taylor Coleridge's *Aids to Reflection*, ed. James Marsh (Burlington, Vt., 1819), and *The Friend*, 3 vols. (London, 1818).

6. David Ripley (1768–1838) of Greenfield, Mass., was a cousin of Ezra Ripley.

7. Samuel Clarke, *A Demonstration of the Being and Attributes of God*, in *Works*, 4 vols. (London, 1738), 2:521–77.

8. Written on outside. MME may be asking for Sir William Hamilton's review of Cousin's *Course of Philosophy* in the *Edinburgh Review* 50 (Oct. 1829): 194–221; CCE to WE[3], 3 Mar. 1830, calls it "a key to the whole German system" (MT/EW).

To CHARLES CHAUNCY EMERSON

Dec 27   Greenfield   —29

As your time, dear Charles, is so full I dont hasten to answer one of the best letters written (I believe) in any age.[1] Yet it is shaded with "doubts". But of what kind I pray? They ought & must exist about many exigesis' of scripture—that the hero of faith (and faith itself were not that courageous virtue it is, were there no inquiries & doubts) may come forth in the brightness of his steps. But till you have time to search, wherefore doubt? Of what, in this dawn of *your* day, *can* you sceptisize—when all is hope and *conscious*ness of existence? The sole persuasion of the Cartesian is enough to fill the young aspirant of immortality. Your embodying so much of the German idea was good. But it is not literature w'h gives these "glimpses of the divine idea"— and the description belongs with little modification to the xian philosopher of a more antient time. It is this borrowed language of the idealists which throws so rich a charm about their Babel fabrick. And after all, it is bricks & mortar for matter exists relatively they say—   And this relative extends itself to the existence of God with all Fichtians, probably. The Hindoo creation of matter, or appearance of it, immediately by God was altogether more sublime and emblematical of our future Heaven. And the apotheosis of man's ideas were far better imajined by Malebranche.[2] Their intellectual Cob house cannot stand—but it may lead from baser materialism and aid by its very illusions[n] in that reaction of opinion which is coming forward to the glory of uncorrupted xianity   If we had this very fine pencil to create all we see, we might still ask, if to be inspired to vision at once, without our telescopic eyes, were not better? But so munificent is the Creator that He has made every material thing to our senses—and gave us the use of our high powers for higher objects—to paint characters & existences beyond the fading canvass of matter & time.

But I wander far from my particular star. Of what do you doubt? Of the conscious presence of God? Your intellectual—& moral nature—(conscience) prove it—and as they are enlightened, prove the adaptations of our old out of fashion, Bible to be divine. "Why then not universal & coeval with man?" Who has ever been left without wittnesses of God & conscience? And a few ages of darkness & barbarism will only serve to inhance the worth of the hidden treasure—as its propagation by human hands will tend to increase virtue. It's sometimes trackless existence—its often calumniated state, is but like the infancy youth & earthly career of it's Messiah—and alike before their mission is ended, will be owned and honored by the universe. It has been a wonderfull source of virtue & opinion & knowledge to ages & sects—each of which is laden with some tribute to it's worth. The ethereal & often noble Idealist, who seems in his excentric orbit to lose sight of it's light, is bringing new plumage to the wings of a spiritual faith. And even the *grub* existing materialist has his weights to throw into the scale of truth—and the bibleist often looks to the revolution in our little world when it's fires will master all other elements &, perhaps, by a natural process restore the purified body to it's spiritual inmate.

But Klopstock has that w'h no other man has—w'h every good theist will love on every belief.

"Joy thee of thy death, oh body;
  Where thou dost corrupt beneathe
  There will he
  The eternal be
  Joy of thy death, oh body; in the deeps,
  In the hieghts of creation, will thy wrack blow away;
  There also where thou wilt anew decay,
  There where it's dust in sightless ruin sweeps,
  There will he
  The eternal be"[3]

Farewell dear Charles. May your spirit beginn to look out with a somewhat more earnest manner, not on the gew gause of events, but on existence, that the very "outward shape may imbibe its east" and throw off the non chalance which is sometimes taken for better than it is. *Write* if you can to your

afft Aunt
MME

MH: bMS Am 1280.226(678). *Addressed:* Mr Charles C. Emerson / Cambridge / Mss. *Endorsed (twice):* M. M. E. / Dec. 1829.

aid . . . illusions] aid ↑ by its very illusions ↓

1. CCE to MME, 14 Nov. 1829, explores the German "division of men into two classes," the "literary man, who has caught glimpses of the Divine idea which pervades the world," and the "mere practical man," and then CCE confesses he often has "doubts" (MT/MH). In several places, MME quotes or paraphrases from this letter.

2. French philosopher Nicolas de Malebranche (1638–1715). MME's source is probably Dugald Stewart, who explained that Malebranche concluded "*that we see all things in God* . . . that every *perception* of the mind is the immediate effect of the divine illumination," which led him to "transfer the seat of our *ideas* from our own minds to that of the Creator" (*Dissertation First*, in *Works* 1:159).

3. From "The Omnipresent," quoted in "Klopstock's *Life and Odes*," *Foreign Review and Continental Miscellany* 3 (1829):373. In the source, the first line begins, "Oh, body!" and the second line reads "wilt" rather than "dost."

To Sarah Bradford Ripley and Samuel Ripley

Greenfield   Dec. 31— '29

I say to myself what a fool—weake—dependant to ask Sarah to write— And till today have always hearkened to the good demon—but this is the last day of the year—and hope beckons on that many a folly & error will be buried & better days come—   And that I shall not commit my self again to neglect. Besides I have so little time that this desire to question[n] a mind—to hear from living responses rarely finds admission. Coleridge—& a few relations of his idealism I pick up & sit late & rise early to question of a truth which can be of no consequence to me in the grave. Instead of truth I might say illusion—sophistry—for the truth of *objective* matter is to me immovable as yet. That the inward senses perceive—have the power to paint external nature in delightfull or dolefull coulers as the mood happens is all the idealism I understand. And this old pencil has done grandly for me this winter—shut up in a little box of a chamber always alone. If I reflect how you talked of the "wicker basket"[1]—& so on & so on I am glad—well I write to ask what you think & feel—what new books—men or women you deign to notice— whether Coleridge is yet in Boston   I have not his aids—no Edin. Review. You spoke of Dwights travels[2] & I read them—should suppose he was ignorant of the Kantian mania w'h has revived within tow or three years?? But to me Kant like his modifying followers are nothing short of spinozaism. As to the divine Personality? Some of them say this Being does not exist in "space and time"—which tends to bewilder & leaves the good old Clarke out of all reckoning. He & I will never part. If you will not initiate me—tell me of husband & ofspring. Does the little Ann grow? And grand pa'pa—is his health good. How do they all do at Concord & Boston? I fear yes really suffer fear ("old & bare" and as one w^d think beyond all fears) that Ellen is sick— Waldo has not written so long.[3]

And how does Charles get on in his Uncle's & your view? Has he not too much ease in manner?? Your brother George I heard well off in N.[4] & would have gone to hear him but no horse. Is he there now? I may have thought of so strange a being as you from the joke of getting rid of a long call yesterday from a lady whom I understood to say she did not think you handsome— I was going straight out—when she exclaimed she had never seen you.

Adieu in haste haste

days short eyes weake so haste & love

MME

Dear Brother

I can never beleive you grown so out of the fashion of the old mansion feelings as not to be glad to know that a pilgrim (tho' early a wanderer from that dear old house) is well & hopes & prays for all you can need in this & a better world & begs you to use your spousal influence on my most neglectfull Sister

to write to yours in love
MME.

I dont beg but of one at a time—so if you dont notice me—let it alone. Love to Molly & tell her I sent to Aunt Phebe to sell her last springs wool.

Write now or never

MH: bMS Am 1280.226(1281). *Addressed:* Mrs Sarah Alden Ripley / Rev. Mr Ripleys / Waltham / Mss. *Postmarked:* Greenfield / Ms. / Jan 1.

question] ⟨speak⟩ question

1. For SBR's view of God, see MME to RWE, 10 Nov. 1829.

2. Henry Edwin Dwight, *Travels in the North of Germany* (New York, 1829).

3. MME indicates that she has not received RWE's letter of 10 and 13 Dec. (*L* 7:188–89).

4. MME probably heard of SBR's brother George Bradford in Newburyport.

PART 4

The 1830s

1830   Greenfield, Mass. [David Ripley's] (Jan.); Amherst, Brookfield (Feb.); Hartford and Wethersfield, Conn. [Joseph Emerson's] (Mar.); Hartford (Apr.); Springfield, Conn. [Dr. Howard's] with visits to Keene, N.H.?, Phillipstown, Mass.? (Apr.–Dec.); Waltham, Boston, Concord (late Dec.).

1831   Concord (Jan.–Apr?); Boston (Apr.); New Bedford (May); Boston, Concord (June); Malden, Andover, Mass. [Prof. Ralph Emerson's], Newburyport, Portland (July); Vale (Aug.–Dec.).

1832   Vale (Jan.–June) [RWE and CCE visit, June–July]; Fryeburg, Maine [Dr. Griswold's], Conway, N.H. (and possibly Crawford's Notch) [with RWE] (June, July); Vale (Aug.–Nov.); Fryeburg [Dr. Griswold's] (Nov.–Dec.).

1833   Fryeburg (Jan.–July?); Paris, Maine (July); Augusta, Hallowell, Maine (Aug.); Saco, Maine (Sept.); Vale, with visit to New Bedford? (Oct.–Dec.).

1834   Vale (Jan.–Aug.); Boston, Concord [Mrs. Persis Woodward's], with visits to Newton, Waltham? (Sept.–Dec.).

1835   Concord all year, with visits to Plymouth, Watertown? (Mar.), Plymouth, Boston [Mrs. Beach's], Andover?, Lexington (June), Acton, Waltham? (Oct.).

1836   Concord (Jan.–Feb.); Waltham (Feb.–May); Portland (May); Vale (June?–Dec.).

1837   Waterford (Vale) all year, with visit to Sweden, Maine (July) [EH and RHE visit in Aug.].

1838   Vale (Jan.–June?); Portland (June); Gorham, Kennebunk, Maine (July); Windham, Maine [Dr. Charles Parsons's] (Aug.–Oct.); Augusta, Maine (Oct.); Belfast, Maine [Mrs. Lidian Frothingham's] (Oct.?–Dec.).

1839   Belfast (Jan.–May); ?? (June–July); Vale (Aug.–Dec.).

A persistent motif in Mary Moody Emerson's correspondence from the 1830s is the idea of "wandering." Whereas in 1795 she had claimed that she seldom wandered from home "without loosing ground in my spiritual Journey," by 1830 she had relocated that "home": "I send you an Almanack! 'Catch me'— Soberly—I will not till you return the others. They are my *home*—the only images of having existed." "Home" was no longer rooted in any particular place, nor did wandering threaten her "spiritual Journey." In this decade she "wandered" more than ever, both in terms of the number of different places where she lived and the intellectual ideas she explored.

This continued, open-minded quest for knowledge is the intellectual center of the letters she wrote and received in the 1830s, a period rich in correspondence in the Emerson family circle. They wrote, read, begged for, treasured, shared, and reread letters that served to communicate, counsel and console, inspire and bind them together over the miles and the years. Hundreds of these letters survive; many contain, for the first time, particulars of the physical realities that underlay her quest for the "metaphysical truths" she called the "soul of existence." Her 211 letters are addressed to twenty correspondents— primarily Charles Emerson (80), Waldo Emerson (30), and Elizabeth Hoar (30). They include details about where she boarded, with whom and for how long, why she went there, her expenses and connections. Her health, reading, responses to family events (including many tragic deaths) are all recorded. From these I have selected 71 for this edition. At least 150 letters to her survive, providing another side to these conversations. Letters between the nephews document regular payments of interest on investments and comment on her in various other ways.

These documents reveal Mary's remarkable ability to soar above physical circumstances. Though they grew in soil that was often rocky and hostile, her letters and conversation have an opposite effect. "How rich the world is!" Waldo exclaimed after reading a letter that she had written to Elizabeth Hoar during the first six months of 1838 and that he considered a "scripture" (*JMN* 7:22). Whatever her physical condition, "she speaks," as Charles said when she arrived weak and ill in Concord in 1834, "& the light inward irradiates" (MT/MH). The many comments that survive indicate that it was not so much what she said that mattered, but an effect that must be called inspirational. She conveyed what Wordsworth called "intimations of immortality." Waldo's response in his journal, cited above, indicates she "gave" neither wisdom nor poetry. Her letter was not a product, a contained literary work; instead, it was a process. Through her they always heard "a sort of argument for the immortality of the soul, . . . a fragment [that] only affirms that it came from [wisdom and poetry]" (*JMN* 7:22). All of her correspondents felt this effect; it expressed her version of transcendentalism.

The calendar of her residences in the 1830s traces a complex path that wound through Maine, Massachusetts, Connecticut, and New Hampshire and that continued to zig-zag with some regularity between Elm Vale at Waterford and places beyond Vale. In these years she changed her residence at least forty-five times. All of 1830 was spent away from Vale, boarding at numerous places and ending the year in Concord, where she stayed until spring; afterward, she boarded at several places in the summer of 1831 before settling down at Vale for more than a year.

Problems with the lease with Robert Haskins resurfaced, and in 1832 Mary Emerson was outraged that she had not been consulted about an offer of twenty-two hundred dollars (which she considered "miraculous") for the property; nephew Charles Emerson turned the offer down, partly because Haskins had exaggerated his investment. During his visit (with Waldo) to Vale in June 1832, Charles researched the records with a local lawyer and revealed that the property was indeed legally hers—to which Mary retorted "it was no discovery & . . . in selling I should give up my right to their wants." Though she was willing to continue the arrangement to help the Haskinses, tempers must have flared, and by the end of the year she had moved to nearby Fryeburg, where she remained for eight months. In the summer and early fall of 1833, she traveled to various Maine towns before returning to Vale for almost a year. In the fall of 1834, she left to board in Concord, where she remained until February 1836—the occasion of the major disagreement with Waldo that ended in her vowing never to return to his house "except bro't there on a liter." By June 1836, she was back at Vale, where she remained for a full two years. She then spent a year boarding mainly in Windham and Belfast, Maine, before returning to Vale in August 1839, where she remained for another two years.

All of this traveling was accomplished by a physically aging woman who turned sixty in 1834. During the decade she suffered several periods of prolonged but undiagnosed illness, which left her weak in "eyes & mouth" and head, or with stomach problems, unable to travel or read, even with the glasses she increasingly depended on. Still, she displayed tremendous stamina, moving every six months or so, boarding and visiting, reading, writing, talking, attending lectures and church, and taking exercise by walking and riding horseback.

Her wandering path continued to move between the familiar poles of solitude and society. But this is no simple, romantic valorization of nature or solitude (represented by Vale, home for more than four years) over modern commercial society (the larger towns in which she boarded); the background sketched by these movements is far more complicated. Each pole offered advantages as well as traps. Not only was she often driven away from Vale by difficulties with Robert Haskins and their continuing lease, but the driving force for her quest, as her letters make clear, was also excitement. Her moves were often her way of "regulating" the excitement she found in both social conversation and solitary communion.

Mary recognized the therapeutic value of a change of scene to her own mental and physical health. In a letter to Charles, who frequently lamented his own bipolar, manic-depressive swings, she prescribed a method of regulating and using emotional highs and lows. Since "our senses administer to the virtues," she preached, "we can so manage them that when they depress we can use them as organs of xian humility & patience—when they exalt— as means & messengers of praise & diffusion. They are the instruments of Providence indisputably." To Edward, whom she foresaw would never resume the life of a New England businessman, she suggested rural retirement was "safest" for one "not born nor destined to possess the hardihood of an inflexible constitution." "Temporary seclusion" could lead to a "return to society & with a soul grown . . . above the feverous excitements of fame & fortune."

Society bred ambition, envy, and "the depression of disappointment" (MH: 727); yet in the first half of the decade she went to society to gain health. Excitement was not "feverous," but a tonic, taken for its "strengthening" effects. Writing to Waldo in 1838, Mary recalled she had gone to Concord in the fall of 1834 seeking the "rhapsodies of the idealists." Her reading in the "Germans" and other "new" thinkers had made her eager to be where she could discuss these ideas. As she explained, "No famished beggar ever craved food so needy—these I had felt in situations of famine & effort and darkness—to get athority—to acquire new blood in old veins was an object to w'h I felt no pains & sacrifices too mortifying. But I was either obtuse or my oracles were not magnitised." Her metaphors join physical health and metaphysical quest. Though in later letters from Waltham and Vale she alluded to a dinnertable quarrel with Charles and differences with Waldo as reasons for leaving Concord, the home of her fathers, the exact nature of this disagreement remains unclear. But the separation was probably inspired more by the need to put a physical distance between herself and her "relations" and her constitutional propensity to wander than by any specific intellectual disagreement with Waldo, whose ideas she continued to share and debate.

The first six years of the decade were marked by tragedy and disappointment that forced new consideration of the grand Miltonic questions of fate, free will, and destiny, which were at the heart of her intellectual and metaphysical quest. She shared in the death of Waldo's wife Ellen in 1831 as well as his resignation from his pulpit in 1832 and subsequent struggle to regain his strength and direction; Edward's bouts with insanity and fevers, which led to his permanent residence in the Caribbean from 1831 until his death in 1834; Charles's illness, which forced a trip to Puerto Rico by the end of 1831,

followed by his repeated struggles with depression and finally death, probably from tuberculosis, after a severe cold in 1836; Bulkeley's increasingly
frequent "violent" periods, which caused delusions, temporary hospitaliza-
tions at McLean Asylum in Charlestown, and the need to find farmers who
would board him; separation from Waldo during his European trip in 1832–
33; the lingering illness of both mother and child after the birth of the first
Emerson grand-nephew, "William the fourth" in 1835; the severe hemorrhage
and near death of Sarah Bradford Ripley in 1835; the death of George Barrell
Emerson's wife, Olivia, in 1832, two months after the birth of their fourth
child; the deaths of several Haskins and Farnham "children" or their spouses
or children. In the midst of this tangle of birth, marriage, and death, it is no
wonder that Mary greeted the arrival of Waldo and Lidian's first child in 1836
with foreboding: "You are pleased with the little boy of Waldo's," she wrote
to Elizabeth Hoar early in 1837. "How could I hail his entrance on a stage of
so much danger? How often I had done it & the child had scarsly budded or
the man promised before they were passed!" (MH: 1098).

The Concord-Waterford movement of 1834–36 epitomizes her complicated
path through society and solitude. In September 1834, she had arrived in Concord feeble and ill, hoping to board "in Waldo['s] neighborhood an hour or
two a week w^d be great excitment for one who has had none these two years"
(MH: 744). Soon she was getting about: by late November, Waldo claimed
she kept "a surprizingly good understanding with the people of this world
considering her transcendental way of living," and he went on to tell a story
of her arriving at his house in a shabby gig borrowed from a stranger in town
(L 1:423–24). Writing to Lidian the following spring, Waldo tried to prepare
his fiancée for meeting his aunt: "Now she will respond [to any] sentiment you
utter, with the s[implicity of] a c[hild] but Rousseau would not detect so quick
the slightest error in sentiment. And so though we flout her, & contradict her,
& compassionate her whims, we all stand in awe of her penetration, her indignant eloquent conscience, her poetic & commanding Reason" (L 1:444).
(Charles Emerson, however, warned his fiancée not to exhaust herself with
"Aunt's insatiate roaming after metaphysics and illuminati" [MT/MH].)

Concord offered a great deal of excitement, but not always the kind she had
sought. Boarding on Main Street with a Mrs. Persis Woodward, Mary was
there when news arrived of Edward's death, of Waldo and Lidian's engagement in January 1835 (though she was too ill to meet Lidian during her first
visit to Concord in March), and of the couple's marriage and settlement at
Coolidge Castle the following September. Mary was there for visits from
William when he stopped at Concord on his way between Portsmouth, New
Hampshire (where he visited the family of Susan Haven, whom he married in
1833), and New York, where his legal career was flourishing; for Harriet Martineau's visit in 1835; for hearing Waldo's "Historical Address" at Concord's
bicentennial in October 1835 and for following his burgeoning lecture career
(his winter 1835–36 series in Boston was on English literature) and his early

friendship with Alcott (though she had left Concord before the real beginning of the transcendental movement in September 1836). She was there to witness the heated reactions to antislavery activities in Boston and the founding of the Middlesex Antislavery Society in 1835 (during which she was converted to the antislavery position by such people as the Peabodys, Charles Burleigh, Samuel May, and George Thompson) as well as Sarah Bradford Ripley's illness and the prolonged engagement of Charles and Elizabeth, while he worked in Samuel Hoar's law office and his health declined. About two months before Charles's death she had taken off in a huff to Waltham.

Charles's death on 9 May 1836 was a devastating blow. Within a few weeks she was on her way back to Waterford, a typically romantic flight to nature. Writing to William a year later, she admitted that her only desire in returning to Vale had been "to wrap myself from all intercourse in that intire solitude w'h was ordained from childhood for me." Even writing a letter "seemed like breaking open the web, w'h caterpillar like, should remain till the final liberation." Only rereading some of William's letters, found, during the week of the anniversaries of Charles's death and her brother's, when she went back to those Charles had written to her, had broken the "crust w'h had gathered round the heart"; finally, after a year, she felt "resucitated" and "extended," liberated from her cocoon of mourning. The "unvaried solitude" of Vale, she soon realized, led one to appreciate the "uninteresting circumstances of the outward man (the inner containing it's own excitments w'h oftener burst out in a prison, than ordinary life)."

In that year, however, Elizabeth Hoar had already broken into that cocoon, addressing Mary as "Aunt" in her first letter to Vale on 7 June 1836 and urging her not to "separate" herself from her Concord family even if absent and to write of "yourself, of Charles" ("EH L" 1985, 142). Mary's response three weeks later began an immense correspondence with the woman Mary came to call her "human Angel," a record of their friendship rooted in their shared love for Charles (150 letters to Elizabeth survive). In the summer of 1837, Elizabeth visited at Vale for the first time.

Mary Emerson's movements from one residence to another were dictated by her constitutional desire for excitement and were limited by her resources. She was drawn to both Springfield, Connecticut, in 1830 and Fryeburg, Maine (ten miles west of Waterford), in 1832–33 by the controversial preaching of two men named Whitman and Harding. "If necessity didn't impell," she explained in 1833, she would choose a place like Andover, Massachusetts, where "I could learn instead of living with ignorance" (MH: 730). Often, however, she was disappointed in her quest. Responding to a letter from Charles while at Springfield in 1830, she admitted that his letter was far more stimulating than anything she had found in this town: "Your very dreams are more to me than all the realities I meet. This place is the most destitute of mind that I ever found. The men are fond of putting together painted timbers & bricks in elegant forms & the women of sewing together bits of lace & stuffs" (MH:

681). After almost eight months at Fryeburg, she complained that the house was full of teenaged girls, a teatime assemblage of "beauty wit & alas too much levity," and that the village was full of Universalists who were less than receptive to restorationist preaching. Her situation made her long for the "hereafter"—and admire the actress Mrs. Siddons, "for she lived off the stage in a grand, ideal world" (MH: 727). Mary was constrained, she recognized, by the difficulty of "getting places of low board for a lady." [1]

Finding affordable lodging was only one of the conditions that influenced her winding path. In 1833 Charles described Aunt Mary as a "wandering star" after hearing from her at Saco, Maine (south of Portland). She had first gone to Augusta intending to spend three weeks with niece Sybil Farnham Lambard, but soon she was boarding elsewhere. Sybil's husband, Allen Lambard, owned a successful distillery, but also Sybil had become so "orthodox" that communication was impossible. Mary claimed she never voiced the big question, "Can religion exist where rum is sold?" "You may wonder at this 'dodging correspondence' being extended to Saco," she mused, adding that she was "at a loss to account for it." Restored to health by her travels, she had planned to go to Paris, Maine, to retrieve her winter clothes, before she moved on "to hide in some place to take the joy of the season alone." But, while making arrangements to travel west, she ran into an old friend, Dr. Deane, who offered lodging at Saco. "Two minutes while the stageman was calling [Deane] left me time to think or I could not have given up my hopes of finding a place in the dear woods," she explained. And, she added, "this family are pleasant" (MH: 736).

On another occasion (in 1838), Mary explained to Elizabeth Hoar how she happened to be in Augusta: she had left Windham, a three-month "oasis" in her nomadic life, and had headed for Waterford; but, having discovered that her room at Vale was taken and having decided against a visit at Kennebunk, she received a letter "from my old friend (& sometime daughter) Lidian Frothingham of Belfast offering to board me & make trial of a lost home. I set off the next day and have been detained here [Augusta] thus long thro' hospitality & weather" (MH: 1108). Attraction and repulsion conspired in her moves: her stay at Windham was an "oasis" not only in the nomadic life of "passing from one boarding place to another" but also in "what is worse the dread of *visiting*—the more attentive the friends—the more irksome to put myself about—when it may well be tho't 'impertinent to live so long' " (MH: 1108). In 1833 she tells how a chance meeting with a Reverend Mr. Miles led her to Hallowell: "Every intelligent & worthy object—every bright & famous event seems to lessen the lenght of the journey" (MH: 735). It is not difficult to read that "journey" allegorically, as a metaphor for her life, and her quest for "intelligent & worthy objects" as her way of living that life most fully.

As she did on her physical path, in her mental life Mary Emerson, with many of Waldo's generation of thinkers, "wandered" in these years into the mists of transcendental thought. Stimulated by reading in the "Germans" and other "new" thinkers, she was both fascinated and disturbed by the "ends & orts of Kantism" that she picked up along the way: the "mistifications" of transcendentalism, she recognized, often led to a "chaos of doubts & dreams," to pantheism and infidelity. At the same time she praised Cousin's "*enthusiasm* and his refutation of dear old Locke" and foresaw that "when the fogs are cleared some true light of human nature may arise from Germanism." By 1837, her appetite for the leading doctrines of transcendentalism had been temporarily satisfied, and she claimed that the great questions of "personal divinity and man's relations" were better answered by the "plain dealing Scotch school": Thomas Reid, Dugald Stewart, and Thomas Brown, plus her "old favorite," Samuel Clarke.[2] But her language indicates that, for Mary Emerson, mental, like physical, wandering had a tonic effect; her quest for excitement was a means of keeping the soul open to new influences, which she assimilated into the matrix of her thought.

The letters show that Mary Emerson continued to beg for, borrow, and buy reading matter and to attend the sermons or lectures of those who looked promising. More than in the earlier periods, we can follow here the course of her reading: novels, poetry, the lives of John Adams, Byron, and Scott; philosophy, theology, the sermons and lectures of Waldo Emerson, Channing, and Dewey; Martineau, Mackintosh, deGerando, and others' reviews, both religious and secular. Mary's reading in these years recalled earlier favorites, especially Wordsworth, de Stael, Clarke, and Stewart. Most important is her intense interest in the "over sea folk" (she had first responded to Kant as early as 1827), especially as mediated by Coleridge, Carlyle, George Ripley, Frederic Henry Hedge, Charles Follen, and the eclectic philosophy of Victor Cousin. She responded immediately to Coleridge's distinction between Reason and understanding, which she found an adequate weapon against the sensational philosophy of Locke, using it repeatedly, as early as June 1830, in her analyses of character and situation. The language, not the idea, was new to her. Her faith continued to rest on "a pure domaine of Reason" and its God-given "spark" as the means to metaphysical truth, which she easily distinguished from the more practical reason that Coleridge and others called "understanding." She distrusted these ideas as misleading to "common folk": after reading something by the German mystic Jakob Böhme in 1835, she confessed that a "plain header" like herself had difficulty with such "mazes of genius" (MH: 774), but she had no problem with interpretations of the "German" idea that imaged Reason as the sun that reveals truth.

Her avid reading of *Aids to Reflection*, *The Friend*, and the *Biographia Literaria* (and probably other works) indicates that she was not at all "bewildered by Coleridge," as Rusk claimed (*Life of RWE*, 143–44). Though she frequently objected to Coleridge's misty language and fragmentary method, his Trinitarian position and pantheistic tendencies, he fed her mind and soul, as documented in her intense exploration of and frequent allusions to his ideas. She was more ambivalent about Carlyle, whose essays on German literature in the *Edinburgh Review* and *Foreign Review*, and then *Sartor Resartus*, exasperated her, but again he was almost godlike in his ability to kindle her mind. Through Carlyle she came to know Novalis, Schiller, Jean Paul Richter, and Goethe, among others discussed in Carlyle's reviews of German literature and ideas. She appreciated Hedge's review of Coleridge, which explained the "transcendental philosophy" in terms of Kantian origins, and she eagerly read and responded to Cousin and to the introductions and notes in C. S. Henry's and George Ripley's translations of Cousin's works. Many of her letters to her nephews, Sarah Bradford Ripley, and especially the two addressed to Hedge contain deeply speculative theological inquiries that suggest how she was synthesizing the new thought with her New England theology to produce her own version of transcendentalism.

In his review of Coleridge's literary character, Hedge claimed that the "key to the whole transcendental philosophy" lay in the Kantian relocation of the source of the creation of one's personal reality, from the Lockean world of sense impressions to a "transcendental" consciousness or intuition: the "transcendental point of view" distinguishes "interior consciousness" from "common consciousness" and assumes that "the objects without us are determined by our cognitions."[3] Though the idea threatened, because it seemed to deny any sure "authority" beyond the individual self, it offered much, and Mary appropriated what she could. Her exploration of these writers led to her transformation of transcendental Reason into a Miltonic God within. Rather than being a "determined foe" and "sworn enemy" (Rusk, *Life of RWE*, 229, 230) of Waldo's transcendentalism, in these years Mary Emerson was an active student and seeker, genuinely interested in discovering and considering its main ideas.

A wonderful statement of her transcendentalist position occurs in a letter to Charles in 1833: "What a ponderous & astonishing thing it is to be on this mighty planet! It is for faith & fervid peity to live beyond & above circumstances—to create a world within to w'h the outward bows as far as it is permitted by it's Auther." This was her transcendental solution of the great questions of philosophical liberty and necessity that continued to excite her. As Waldo would conclude in "Fate," many years later, "circumstances" (which she often equated with the "Emersonian constitution" that led to the defeat of her hopes for her nephews) often determine "what you may do"— in Mary's language, what is "permitted by it's Auther." She sees "constitution," the whole inherited complex of physical and mental tendencies, as a kind of fate, which, like a theatergoer, she watched as it worked itself out on the stage of her family's life. Still, she never lost sight of the possibilities of the "within," of living life "beyond & above circumstances."

In his response to Mary's letter to Elizabeth Hoar, written in his journal, Waldo Emerson focused on the shimmering quality that made the letter a "scripture," an affirmative "fragment of wisdom & poetry," "a sort of argument for the immortality of the soul." And he wondered whether life were "long enough to study out the tendency & idea which subterraneously shines, sparkles, & glows in these sybilline leaves" (*JMN* 7:22). These letters offer many glimpses of the "tendency & idea" that guided her and spoke through her conversation as she wandered through the 1830s.

NOTES

1. As they became older and skilled in law and business, CCE and, later, WE[3] took on the task of dealing with MME's legal problems with Robert Haskins and the deed to the Vale farm, which often prevented her return to Vale, as well as other financial matters. Numerous letters between the two brothers and their aunt indicate that they handled her quarterly interest on her investment of the remainder of her inheritance with her brother-in-law Thomas W. Haskins, which amounted to $18.00 per quarter, and in about 1834 helped her to set up an annuity arrangement that paid $90 per annum on her $900. Many other facts about her financial circumstances, none of which are very clear, can be found in this correspondence.

2. Scottish "commonsense philosophy" accepted Locke's emphasis on observation as the basis of knowledge but stressed consciousness as a "medium of observation" containing ordering "principles . . . independent of experience" (Howe, 30).

3. Frederic Henry Hedge, "Coleridge's Literary Character," *Christian Examiner* 14 (Mar. 1833): 124, 119, 124.

1830

To Edward Bliss Emerson
Hartford   March 15   Monday [1830]

Dear Edward,

Thanks for the letter—beg you to write again by Waldo—if it is possible when he & Ellen are casting about the light of thier path. I like her better better than I dreamt—but not near so handsome—genius & loveliness are enough. How do you & W^m? Tell me if you are as fond of the chapel in the great work shop of N Y as in the lovely sanctuary of Concord?[1] Return to Concord— but if not—live amid noise as in a corner from which you aspire to get out thro' the golden gate of death. "How did I like our minister yesterday?"[2] Well & heartily his voice manner. Wonderfully good—"why wonderfull?" True a natural orator in his boyhood—but got chilled you know—& now to find it warm & unostentatious (family fault) is delightfull. His inferences spiritual & highly poetical—but the family heir loom—not logical—too many golden apples to find his way straightly to the essence of his argument—but perhaps the difficulty lies in his shallow theology—highest views & principles not bottomed on the facts of man's true nature & the revelation adapted to that riddle—unfolding it here & there—promising to open its' lantern at the end of the race when faith shall yield up pretty much to vision—not always— the long career of eternity opens vistas of hope & curiosty. And (tho' I was

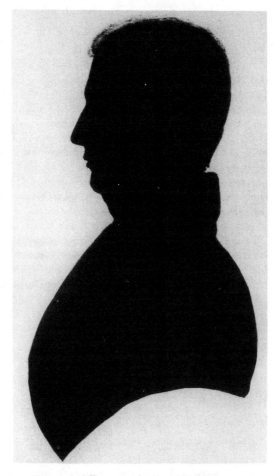

Figure 18. Silhouette of Edward Bliss Emerson
(1805–34), nephew of Mary Emerson.

stupid beyond measure owing to the craziness of pleasure saturday) I *thought* *felt* there was not climax to the eloquence &c—an apex as Coleridge *might* say—but Coleridge is as far from logic & argument as twilight from noon. But keep his 'aids to reflection' always on your table with Paskel [3]

MH: bMS Am 1280.226(755). *Addressed:* Edward B. Emerson Esq / New York. *Endorsed:* Miss M. M. Emerson / Hartford. March 15. 1830 / Ell., R. W., Coleridge &c. / Ans^d March 30—.

1. In Nov. 1829, EBE moved to New York, where he shared lodgings with WE³ and began to practice law.

2. RWE to Abel Adams, New Haven, 16 Mar. 1830, reports he "preached in Hartford three times on Sunday [the 14th] to a small but attentive congregation" (*L* 1:293). He and ETE were traveling to New York and Philadelphia.

3. Probably Blaise Pascal, whose *Pensées*, published in an abridged form in 1670 and in its entirety in 1844, are comparable to Coleridge's aphoristic *Aids to Reflection*.

To Charles Chauncy Emerson

Weathsfield   March 26 —30

Thank you for the new years wish.[1] And is time a proser unless he reveals events? *No* then his very bold face grins at the play of children. It is when he seems to drop his wings & they lie motionless without reflecting the azure & purple & golden toys of love & fame & wealth—it is then the soul assumes the car—the reins—and makes the path to the Center of minds by its own gravitation. Did not the gaurdian Angel of Webster blush at times in the last speech?[2]—   Apologize to some sociable spirit to find an immortal so bent on a mole hill? Again he smiled for he saw the wires w'h agitate the puppet show.

Well I've seen dear Ellen—not so beautifull—but more attractive than expected. How does she now? Do do write. I have nothing else to say—so send an old page to make up talk.[3] Waldo preached to head & heart—it was an era to me.[4] Give him my love & ask him to write thro' you or by himself by next mail for I am about moving from this house—perhaps Town as school &c &c   He & all tells good stories about dear Charles—the darling object of my hopes. Waldo if at home will send the *business* matter if he can by next tuesday. I've had much good talk with my learned Cousin[5]—but learning is poor stuff for happiness.

Adieu   May hope & joy attend thee
MME.

Greenfield   Dec 28—'29[6]

Were Plato & Shakespear to meet! Could the distance of so high an intellect as the former & the long ages of a preceding education render it possible for him to notice the plebian poet there might be affinities of one kind stampted on their original nature w'h even ages would not obliterate—that of *method*— the one in arranging according to Coleridge the pure innate ideas—the other of portraying them thro' the gross medium of human actions & high wrought passion.[7] Were it congruous among the strange things of the other world to find old Shakes. holding a pencil there—and Plato etherealising the images— more—sketching the eternal forms of beauty, w'h his Country sought to embody, and rendering them objects of the naked vision of souls. Ah what an education awaits the hungry & thirsty who sojourn in this dreamy[n] waste— to whom knowledge exists only as a beau ideal—or more truly an ignus fatus to lead from the only Absolute existing Being—and dispell the charms of mystic wonder & adoration by a wearisome accumulation of material phenomena. Old Bacon made a good use of *these* with his *methodical* head— and as Cole[e]. says was to *nature* in it's tangible forms what Plato was in its spiritual.[8] Whether the sublime Phi. will as easily notice the sensual one as he may the poetic one is doubtfull—or rather not—for the Chancellor led away by false notions knew not to esteem the platonic phi. And mean in his ambition gave no credit to the noble stagirite or his Master for opening to him the way to science, Old theif. No he Bacon[n] knew not to love—to bow down with rapture & reverence to the form of knowledge if she beckoned him on while hooded from influence & fame—and in truth he was incapable of those naturally invisible prospects w'h light & enfold the divinity of the soul. An excellent medium to conduct the student of higher aims. Yet Coleridge (blockhead) places his intellect among the divinities of Plato & Milton. & adds Demosthenes & Shakspeare[9]—sad grouping—the two first are in the horizon like the loftiest stars with care descried by telescope while the others regulate human affairs as the pale moon born only for earth & unknown among primary planets. Forgive me bard of nature—but thy gold & gorgeous wing if plumed at some particular star or raised to nobleity in some aereal vision—thou hadst but a locality & domicile on old mother earth, or couldst never have painted her antics & gloated shapes so apeishly.

MH: bMS Am 1280.226(680 & 869). *Addressed:* Mr Charles C. Emerson / Cambridge / Mss. *Postmarked:* Weth[fd] CT / Mar 26. *Endorsed:* M. M. E. / Dec. 19, 1829.

dreamy] sic *in MS; possibly* dreary *intended*

he Bacon] he ↑ Bacon ↓

1. CCE to MME, 9 Jan. 1830, wishes her a happy new year and remarks that "old Time must begin to be pretty tedious to you" (MT/MH).

2. Probably Daniel Webster's "Second Speech on Foot's Resolution" (concerned with the possibility of limiting the sale of public lands), delivered in the U.S. Senate on 26 Jan. 1830.

3. Leaf from "Almanack" dated 28 Dec. 1829 and printed following this letter.

4. See MME to EBE, 15 Mar. 1830.

5. At Wethersfield, MME boarded with "Tutor" Joseph Emerson (1777–1833), son of her cousin Daniel Emerson (1746–1820); a pioneer in the education of women, he opened a seminary for young women in Wethersfield in 1824 (*DAB*).

6. Both Rusk (*L* 1:286) and Tilton (*L* 7:188) misread the month in this dateline as "Oct" and both assume (as does the MH assessions listing) that the "Almanack"

was sent to RWE. CCE to MME, 30 Mar. 1830, responds directly to her "grouping" of "Plato & Milton—Bacon & Shakespeare" (MT/MH).

7. See Coleridge's "Essays on the Principles of Method," in the third volume of *The Friend* (*The Collected Works of Samuel Taylor Coleridge: The Friend*, ed. Barbara E. Rooke [Princeton: Princeton University Press, 1969], 1:448–524, esp. 448–63, 472).

8. See Coleridge, *The Friend* 1:467 (Coleridge's note), 492.

9. See Coleridge's "Answer to Mathetes" (actually written by Wordsworth) in the introduction to the third volume of *The Friend* 1:392.

To Ralph Waldo Emerson

Springfield   June 7   Monday [1830]

My dear Waldo,

Yours 1^t of May containing Ellen's poetry[1] I answered sab 2 of May— & sent it by one, who without fault, returned it last sat. I opened it today find it a tissue of theology natural & conjectural—of human gratitude to Ellen— too warm to be sent in cool blood. Besides the theology is designed for comments—of w'h you favor me none since you wedded—always the case when mortals were enamoured with super mortals—notwithstanding the 'elevation' described in the Steam boat of that affection. And in truth what time or incli. for speculation when the heart is full? I send you an Almanack! 'Catch me'—   Soberly—I will not till you return the others. They are my *home*— the only images of having existed—   And the Andover The.^{n} life was to be remembered. While I was pleased with the sweet flattery of your keeping it, I forgot how much I should need the chasm w'h it makes in my *eventfull* life. But you need not send it now—nor any books *unless it be* 'history of enthusiasm'—or some German phi. or Cousins.[2] Cant read but little—just returning to life & the vistas of faith overwhelm. "Aids to reflection" awaken new interests. But this letter is not for them. It is one w'h I want burnt among many others. How could you be so icy as not to say you were coupled with Channing on Elec. day? Register told me.[3] How is his sermon liked? I run over it in company   Dr H.[4] says it is not severe enough to the Legis. for the times. To me he is becoming cantish about liberty of mind?? Facts seem against this grand effect. If it were complete philosophical liberty that man possesses or *could* how would the virtuous strech forth into perfection! What did freedom of opinion do for Voltaire & Hume? True, she was in a strumpet condition then. But what has it done for German sceptics—bewildered & bankrupt *thier* "reason." Yet if there must be grotesque figures in the human portrait (as a whole) oh give me their dreams in philosophy—their very pantheism can be turned to account—for it exists in a sublime sense—and it may be this with certain minds, w'h operates against a distinct Agent & Saviour— Channing's, for instance   Yet it is thro' means the great first Cause has ever discovered Himself. What Bolingbr. says of '*causation*'—& what Cole. says of the impossibility of knowing the absolute ground of any thing[5] (I believe, is

somthing or just like it but the book is down stairs) opens a vast field of faith
& "reason" & truths in dim perspective—among w'h appears the redemptive act—plan &c!?!? How many virtuous aspirants miss of great objects &
good, by not understanding the direct road? But how unexpectdly you have
got me into this strain? You must write me longly. Tell your Mother & queen
& Chas I shall send them a packet (ribbon too to my sister) next thursday by
C.M.E. *if* I can get it to H—.[6] He sends me word he will take any thing to or
from Boston & returns this way. I wish Charlotte or any one would buy me 8
or 9 y^{ds} of black silk for a summer gown.[7] It will please your mother as it does
my friend Howard that I have it. I want the silk figured^n—I shall be pleased
with the sprigs—there will be hundreds in one gown. —but for all of them
I hope to give but this 5# if needfull loan it—but I dont like to send a ten.
I admire at our namesake's bold stroke—why M. I thot—if not ensky'd, a
thing remote—a vestal—I liked her.[8] And think if she likes to wed she would
have found a gentleman, intelligent & upright in E. They speake well of him
here. *M* must not expect to be as fortunate as Ellen—even if the "building"
were as fine (w'h indeed I think perfectly gracefull & "the windows painted"
in the very style of the folks above) as hers.[9] Ellen *herself* (whose beauty is not
any thing as it will be) appears to me remarkably favored. But I want the rest
of the poetry. adieu most dear friend

MME

* * *

MH: bMS Am 1280.226(876). *Addressed:* Rev. Ralph W. Emerson / Boston /
Mss. *Endorsed:* 1830.
   The.] *abbreviation for* Theological (Andover Theological Seminary)
   figured] fifurged *in MS*
   1. RWE's letter does not survive (*L* 1:301); for ETE's poetry, see the "Philadelphia
Journal" (*OFL*, 115–23).
   2. Isaac Taylor, *Natural History of Enthusiasm* (London, 1829). MME seems to
want to read anything available about the French eclectic philosopher, Victor Cousin,
author of *Cours de l'histoire de la philosophie*, 3 vols. (Paris, 1828). No English translations of Cousin were available in 1830; she may be asking for Sir William Hamilton's
1829 review.
   3. The *Christian Register*, 29 May 1830, reports that WEC preached the annual
election sermon before the Massachusetts legislature on 26 May: "Devotional exercises were performed by Rev. Mr. Emerson of the 2d Church in this city."
   4. The Reverend Bezaliel Howard (1783–1837), MME's host at Springfield.
Howard was pastor of Springfield's First Church from 1784 until he retired because of
poor health in 1803; when the Unitarian Church was organized in 1819, with William
Bourn Oliver Peabody (1799–1847) as its pastor, Howard became his associate. "My
friend Howard," below, is probably his wife, Prudence Howard.
   5. Henry St. John, Viscount Bolingbroke (1678–1751), questioned the human
capacity to know "real causality" because "to know it in its first principles . . . would
be to know as God himself knows" (*Essays on Human Knowledge*, in *Works of*

Lord Bolingbroke . . ., 4 vols. [London, 1844], 3:199–200). See Coleridge, *Aids to Reflection: "There is nothing, the absolute ground of which is not a Mystery"* (90).

6. Charles Milton Emerson (1802–81), son of Reuben Emerson (1771–1860), the minister at South Reading and a distant cousin of MME's. H—: *possibly* Hartford.

7. On 2 July, MME wrote anxiously to RWE concerning the gown she had sent for "to attend a splendid party at 4th." But, she adds, "if I had it—might not go" (MH: 877).

8. MME seems to refer to another Mary Emerson soon to marry "E."

9. A reference to ETE's verse account of her meeting with MME at Hartford: Waldo returned from Wethersfield, "& by his side / Aunt Mary's eyes her niece did scan / Compared it with her previous plan, / The building was not half so fine / Nor did the painted windows shine / As her fond fancy nursed his lies, / But hard enough to like she tries / To faults determined closed her eyes" (*OFL*, 116–17).

To CHARLES CHAUNCY EMERSON

Springfield   Sat Night
June 19   [1830]

Dear Charles,

I read this week your letter of 1t of April.[1] It was—it will remain very——how stale are^n epithets. But the worth of the letter was peculiar at the time & place. Cousin J. E. has fine boys—but his notable wife drills them beyond measure.[2] One of the most likely is 7 or 8— He has more history & geo. & such like than many youth. To spare their minds from this parrot knowledge I often spoke to Mr E. of you—your unlearned childhood &c. The letter interested him much—he expressed a strong desire to be acquainted &c. You'll say fugde. But show a man of so varied knowledge—of so logical & phi. a head. True his weake & ridiculous side is as obvious. He is a mass of disease—yet clings to a name & influence in life—talks of his engagments—when he has nothing to do but lie abed or read—very little about the seminary. But the worst of all is (besides his dogmatism) he is dying (tho' much better than to prolong the illusion) with a greater opinion of his talents &c than any one else. This may be owing to want of superior society—or a complete retirement. He says his brother R. E.[3] is the greatest Emerson that ever lived except R. Waldo. Good night. Is it possible my dearest friend I have spent all this time on that Skeleton? The clock is about to strike—it is a noble bell. How the air trembles—as if it was the prophet of man. I've heard Peabody—or rather his companion J. Walker talk this afternoon with the excellent doctor H.[4] but tho' I liked the time—yet this fine reverbation of sounds is not the same as in the morning—Coleridge—Dick[5] & Fennelon—the—the— Well we must (& I have said before to you?) give up to Coleridge about the *name* of "reason"—it is what we in that dear walk termed *under*. The *distinction* is what we defined.[6] And how many good understandings without the inspiration of "reason"—that gift by w'h communion with the nature of things—

the interior—& their Auther!? Is it not possible that S. A. R's talents are of the former? Baconian? Paleyian? She is not so superficial a scholar as to lose her faith in religion—in immortality from German scepticism, were there no constitutional defect in those qualities w'h seek a spiritual existence?? Give me her character.[7] I have been dazzeled with it's scholastic attainments & have been flattered by her attentions. With what have I been captured? Shame on me. A meteor—passing away like the shadow of the cloud w'h climbs the mountain top & is seen no more—& the cloud itself changes it's form & is seen no more on the mountain—or in the valley. Nothing more are talents— acquisitions—w'h rest on earth—w'h climb the mount to be seen   True, that strong sense (under.) w'h has led her to convert all of what usually appears under the form of vanity—into pride—to conceal egotism—tho' may be for want of sympathy—all these facinate without giving us a wish to penetrate the cause. And tho' I want your opinions in this new direction, could not have given my own a form but for long forgettfulness between us. Now Cole. is an egotist[8] & I like it the better—not *him*—but the exampel to shelter ones own private character of ego. And this fullness of existence in one's self, however ridiculous it may appear here, where appearances are all in all yet prophecies well for a full partaking of existence hereafter. But you & your brothers can hardly know what I mean—you are so remote from it—& so your family connections on both sides. Well if one needs[n] praise, it is better to give it to one's self—of two evils choose the least—or the comfort w'h is nearest & surest

Write soon by mail (tho' you may by C M E.)[9] & write as silly & idly as your affect

Aunt MME

if you can.

MH: bMS Am 1280.226(682). *Endorsed:* M. M. E / June 19, 1830.
are] ⟨grow⟩ ↑ are ↓
needs] ⟨asks⟩ ↑ needs ↓

1. Possibly CCE to MME, 30 Mar. 1830, which responds directly to her letter of 26 Mar., especially the Plato and Shakespeare "Almanack." In closing, CCE appeals to MME for her wisdom: "I need a great deal of spiritual influence, I live in so Earthly a place" (MT/MH).

2. Joseph Emerson was father of three sons: Alfred (b. 1812), Edwin (b. 1821), and John (b. 1823); "notable": "4. b. Of women: Capable, managing, bustling; clever and industrious in household management or occupations" (*OED*).

3. Ralph Emerson (1787–1863), professor of ecclesiastical history and pastor at Andover Theological Seminary, 1829–53, was a brother of Joseph Emerson.

4. W. B. O. Peabody; possibly James Walker (1794–1874), minister at Charlestown, 1818–39; Dr. Howard.

5. Probably Thomas Dick (1774–1857), author of *The Christian Philosopher; or, The Connexion of Science and Philosophy with Religion* (New York, 1826), and *The Philosophy of a Future State* (Brookfield, Mass., 1829).

6. MME uses terms borrowed from the "German" distinction between Reason and understanding (as explained by Carlyle and Coleridge) to express her concern about SBR's rather stoic philosophy.

7. CCE to MME, 29 June 1830, refuses to send the requested "character," reminding MME she taught him "it is not safe to trust one's self to write characters of the little or the great. . . . But I judge her over-harshly . . . for I do not know her in her worst moods; & she redeems herself by the severe yet cheerful performance of her daily returning duties—making no murmur & seeking no praise" (MT/MH).

8. CCE to MME, 29 June 1830, discusses different kinds of egotism, from self-interest to benevolence.

9. Charles Milton Emerson.

To Ralph Waldo Emerson/"Almanack"?

Sab July 1— [1830]

First pages of the "history of enthu." on providence[1]— Well it is well if I never calculated in obedience & respect to the uniformity & disuniformity— happy release to be permitted to meditate the larger features of Providence in the order of things w'h is to last forever—connected by invisible eternal ties to the Cause. I suspect I shall not like it. 7. DeStale in her well known remark that formerly man was more intimately connected with nature may not have foreseen even with her argus eyed genius that these relations drawn improperly intangle the mind—fatal as the web of—(of—what her name) whom Minerva destined to spin forever.[2] When the mind like the insect entangled becomes the victim of pantheism. No—nature in her largest works presents but emblems of the Infinite—those globes of fire, w'h run such constant rounds, are but signs of his immutability. Hereafter the soul may have senses to percieve the divine mind more clearly tho' analogous, than bodily ones do material.

Yea—those eternal abstractions from w'h creations—time & all possible existences drew their modes—their persons—their subsistence—their ideal—or real being— Powers[n] of thought!—by what new names can the gasping soul call thee! These & those it cannot name will receive life & light & shape like the invisible flower[n] when blown on by torch light. This shapeless speechless figure I am never weary off. It takes place in philos. of mind of the principle of life in an egg (my earliest[n] theory)—it is in the Soul the emblem of that vital germ of benevolence—without w'h all superinduced principles or habits—outward acts—are lifeless like a body without spirit—are acts of *prudence* mere calculation whether they relate to this or a future state. And whenever the good actions are performed without a correspondent feeling— love of virtue—they are in truth filthy rags as to the individual, compared to the love of virtue & God for their own sakes

MH: bMS Am 1280.226(849). *Endorsed:* Nat Hist Enthusiasm.
Powers] *possibly* Forms (T)

invisible flower] ↑ invisible ↓ flower ⟨at torch time⟩
earliest] ⟨youngest⟩ ↑ earliest ↓
    1. 1 July fell on Sunday in 1827 and 1832; however, Isaac Taylor's *Natural History of Enthusiasm* (see endorsement) was not published until 1829. Written on ivory paper with a distinctive G & C⁰ watermark, used by MME for only two other letters, both dated July 1830. Possibly MME meant to write "11," which was Sunday in 1830.
    2. In Greek mythology, Arachne (the Greek counterpart to the Roman Minerva) challenged Athena at needlework and was punished by being turned into a spider, "ever [weaving] a web of marvelous design" (Herzberg, *Classical Myths*, 72).

To WILLIAM EMERSON[3]

Springfield   Sep 4   Sat. [1830]

My dear William,
        I never had a letter that more interested—your affectionate frankness—
& above all your *complaints*—they bespeake a living state of the soul—
it's immortal appetites—not sattisfied—tho' your mind evidently progresses.
Nothing that can sattisfy it! The simple reason w'h your granmothers have
echoed from their infancy to the grave   'A preparatory—disciplinary state.'
And nature bears its' testimony to this theology in all its' analogies & emblems. It is rebellion to that ever transmuting—yet ever permanent nature in
some forms—and to higher nature within to seek for a good home w'h is only
hereafter. That in the wonderous whole of human kind there are lower orders
who appear and are sattisfied does not militate against the grand acknowledged truth.
    What you so eloquently represent as to practical application applies to the
Emersonian blood more than any I have met. Their views & principles are
high—feelings sensitive—& alass their reason or understanding or perceptions beyond their practice. This this makes calamity of living here. Better
to suffer liesure than want these gerons of future glory—indispensable seeds
of greatness & virtue. But without piety—without a pole star to concentrate
their power they resemble in the present life a total loss as the seed w'h is
never sown—or the rich promise of fruit blasted. They must exist again as
they inhere in an immortal substance—but unprovided here with suteable affinities how useless they may be hereafter or worse no mere mortal can only
conjecture—and believe from the revelations. *Revelation!* What an ark for
the tossed vessel. And are you in earnest about being a calvinist? Would you
were. Tho' I can never be one I respect those eminent minds who have reached
"the far off lofty summit of virtue & wisdom" on that ground. Errors in opinion w'h do not injure the mind or heart are not frightfull as the eternal ice of
sceptiscim. I rejoice in Sybill's conversion to religion.[1] Some strong excitment
was nessecary for her. Let her *feel*—and let her *act*. After all *action* of soul
is the main point. If every thing like the Germans about the Emersons is be
more of strenght of understanding than *character* let them prepare to *act* (w'h
is said to be the test of greatness) in a higher & purer world. It is possible

to love such a God as Calvinism in it's early[n] days represented. Its advocates triumphed in their love & confidence amidst flames. If they followed their system to some of its conclusions they probably believed or *felt* that if such was the case of the non elect there were reasons w'h rendered Gods conduct just & in a certain sense nessecary tho' they could not comprehend them. Soame Jennyns has somthing of this, if I remember, in his origin of evil.[2] If any sect were without difficulties there would be more apology for the bitterness with which the illumenated unitarians scorn this orthodoxy. It was supported by the bible tho' never with legitimate argument probably. The revolutions of mind and event are so rapid in the hot beds of cultivation that a spectator has only to suspend his judgment for the present—and hope every thing from the better state of Germany and its foster children.

You had not heard of the French affairs[3] when you wrote? Or you would have thrown me some clue to your opinions I hope. My good Doctor is at a stage of marvelment as yet. And we have no telescopes in S.

Adieu. "Attempt things impossible in your Lord's[n] stile, and do them"— be a self devoted servant of God—and I need not add you will be a xian. It is singular to see the orthodox pour out a thousand when Mr P—s[4] seldom arrive at the 5th of that. Religion made too easy is not exciting for an immortal. He tells them they are free free—he has not sounded the human mind. A portion of freedom most tremendously important is ours—   But

"in the sacred book
Where leaves or white or dusky never change"

are promises w'h give courage to do every thing.

That line from Dante makes me think how often I want to ask some one why he is not more read? Do read him. If old David Humes opinions are not yet obsolete and shamed I would mention one w'h occurs while reading Dante—that all mythology may be realised some time or other. Pardonne glorious Poet me[n] for this comparison—thou inspirest faith & the present morality! Thy wanderings are plumed by the mystic spirit of devine love! and many such as we antisapate.

Adieu dear William   May God give you to *prepare* for that great busy scene where *action* will alone be sucesfull and naturally flow from the character.

MME.

* * *

MH: bMS Am 1280.226(1072). *Addressed:* William Emerson Esqr. / Wall Street / New York / By the kindness of Mrs Pynchon. *Postmarked:* NEW YORK / Sep 9. *Endorsed:* Miss M. M. Emerson / Sept 4 / 30.

early] ⟨ancient⟩ ↑ early ↓
Lord's] *possibly* Shah's (*quotation unidentified*)
Poet me] Poet ↑ me ↓
1. Sybil Farnham Lambard.

2. Soame Jenyns, *A Free Enquiry into the Nature and Origin of Evil in Six Letters*; see esp. letter 4, "On Moral Evil."

3. Events in the revolution of 1830, which on 30 July resulted in the restoration of the Bourbon line in a constitutional monarchy.

4. Probably W. B. O. Peabody.

To CHARLES CHAUNCY EMERSON

Springfield   No[v]. 2 —30

Dear Charles,

Yours of the 18 spoke of pills & blisters. *What was the matter?* Do not labour too hard. The last letter described a state of mind peculiar to your organisation.[1] One w'h promises better things than common contentment— but is wanting in those common excitments that make up so much of life. Could you but once get awake in your affections t'would be a fine sight to see you engaged in some object like those w'h have sent so many names to Heaven. And there are so many objects & whole nations who need help! Do you ever view the bright & true sides of orthodoxy? Their deciples have a most desirable zeal. Look at their labours. Ministers of all that is great—to tell of God—& his will. But your vocation & constitution forbid missionising to those *reputed* heathen. Yet you would fain awaken the charm of sympa- thy—as it is "not weakness" in an active character. Hear them talk of the nessecary connecttion between means & ends, antecedents with consequents as Leibnitz—and the theologian adds that certain influence of moral motives, as the natural & sufficient means whereby human actions & tho'ts are bro't into that continued chain of causes & effects, w'h taking it's beginning in the operation of the infinite mind—   Thus they place the glorious doctrines of absolute foreknowledge & universal providence upon a firm & philosophial base. And their minds & hearts bound forward to labour with God himself with a sterness of purpose w'h leaves behind the more easy unitarian. Some of their biography paints them as so ingrained with the high & burning mag- nificence of the gospel phenomena as to have lost all that "chaffing" of human nature with its mighty projects & destiny.

I am picking up ends & orts of Kantism. What a chaos—what[n] a miser- able paradox—contradiction the auther—he who dwelt of the capasities of apriori proofs of a supreme mind—of the high power of an abstract idea of morality to this proof yet he so much of an athiest? To deny objective proofs when our very sensations prove a power superior to nature—of an agency seperate from all causes and effects known. Now for a real or pretended ideal- ist to deny such a proof (w'h perhaps rises to demonstration) is idiocy? How transcendently better is Berkley who admitted reality in the cause—& the antient Hindoos who admitted nothing the divine agency? If you ever specu- late on these favor me by them   But whether you speculate or feel or act may a strenght & beauty superior to human nature be accorded. The provision is made—and a man never acts so greatly as when he feels a supernal aid. Your complaints are a mystic musick—betokening that your horoscope is cast for better scenes.

Give thanks to your mother for her attention to the shawl—more & lasting ones for her truly gratefull welcome of my bodily approach to her vicinity. But it may not occur if I can help it. When feeble in health I want to mew up in my native nest—& flatter myself it will aid father in the solitude he regrets since Mrs E. left him[2]—tho' I can never hope to make her place good—& hope to go to W. in the spring.

How do Waldo & Ellen. He & I have a little coquetry I believe in our correspondence—& I look forward to his starry letters some fortunate time. As to visiting Ellen I should be afraid of being a bore—she is so ethereal—   Yet she was delightfull—& seemed wholly undisturbed by my oddities. Louisa[3] is daily expecting me. What an object I am!!

Your Aunt in love & prayer
MME

How is father? If he s^d be sick let me know it. Tell him thanks for his letter—he did not ask an answer & I tho't I might be there in past weeks of debility.

MH: bMS Am 1280.226(686). *Addressed:* Mr Charles C. Emerson / Cambridge / Mss. *Postmarked:* SPRFD MS / Nov 2. *Endorsed:* M. M. E. / Nov. 2, 1830.

what] *possibly* & what

1. No letter from CCE dated the 18th (of Oct.?) survives; however, CCE to MME, 12 Sept. 1830, reflects a melancholy state of mind (MT/MH).

2. CCE to WE[3], 15 Apr. 1830, says RHE would soon leave Concord (where she had been keeping house for EzR) because Ripley's brother Noah and his daughters were moving in. About 22 May, the Emersons moved into the Aspinwall house in Brookline.

3. Louisa Dewey.

To Ralph Waldo Emerson

Sp^d No[v.] 9   [1830]

Dear Aspirant,

Many of your years have come & gone since we commenced—   Yet tidings have come by a higher medium than formerly—that is higher in rank of business—have sympathy with the potent geni called fortune—and in truth I was not displeased at the favors w'h have been lavished on you from the illimatable. It is amusing to see mortals swiming in their joyous elements—& love is akin to those above—however disturbed with fears & clouds. But at this season, in your specky orb where every leaf tells it's tale, there appeared in one of my visions (for I oft descend from those w'h make my best bliss) the same tinny genius w'h belongs to the class thro' w'h we corresponded   It had the form of inquiry—was thinking that my theory of the divine existence in my mortal shell was not only more solid (as well as musickal) than many better educated. True, my demiurgus—my Psyche might be but a prophecy of that last best gift to man. How correspondent to the two first orignal emanations of the nessecary Being? And when my liliputian admirer finds the best theory of my friend & favorite S. Clarke wholly at fault in his proof of the *Unity* tho' not of a God she occurs to my antient revelation. When mortals attempt to say that before God determined to exercise his several attributes in producing somthing distinct from Him self^n then & not before is it probable that *time, sucession & increase* began—that a perfect Being could be supposed alone in nature without any sucession of ideas—alteration in his essence and knowledge— — —compared to this how much better my eternal abstract ideas—*not* (oh no dare not child make me blush) independent of this Being. Those ideas whether they existed alone in one mind or more were essential to Deity—constituted what mortals call the knowledge of sucession—duration and all the high modes by w'h they frame an idea or notion of the mode of His existence. It was from the school of "a point"—of a standing now— w'h gave one of the forms—atheistical notion of every thing being God— of proposing mind to "make Him."[1] Ah could your Germans but know thier true relation to some of those archetypal ideas which have in the course of ages been realized they would lose their fancied greatness—would learn that if the creation of this world were in any sense nessecary it was connected with another of dire and mysterious character—that had no intermediate scheme been in operation their fate had been like the shadow of darkness.

Dec. 2 —30

Dear Waldo,

Reduced to this only paper and what is worse a bankrupt for this long time in thought—I send it only to say that I am packing up to remove— that letters may not be sent here. I think of going to thro' Phillipstown^n possibly may creep into a deeper solitude than here—have been disappointed in a place w'h invited when I wrote Charles. A great sense of weariness (has^n prevented any attempt to answer yours) of every thing relative to myself—so very very long is life. I pray God you, wife and mother & Charles are well & duely appreciate your appointed tasks and enjoyments—but can scarsly sympathize in any thing that is not enclayed.^{n} Thank you for invitation—& hour glass—when your own sands are running low may they be brighter for all your kindness—but you know how distasteful it is to reappear when one wants to sleep.

Adieu   Affectionately
Aunt Mary.

That eve§ you & Charles went to hear Taylor[2] was indeed a glorious time. Plato would not have written so tamely & see saw under the influence of such tidings

MH: bMS Am 1280.226(880). *Addressed:* Rev. Ralph W. Emerson / Boston. / Mss. *Postmarked:* Phillipstown. *Endorsed:* M.M. Emerson / 1830.

Him self] *possibly* Himself (*unhyphenated at line break*)

to thro' Phillipstown] to ↑ thro' ↓ Phillipstown

has] has ⟨I believe⟩

not enclayed] ↑ not ↓ enclayed

1. Cf. de Staël's discussion of the creative power of the *ego* in Fichte, who "makes the whole universe consist of the activity of mind" and scandalized the world by saying "he should create God" (*Germany* 3:110).

2. CCE to MME, 16 Nov. 1830, reports his visit with RWE to "Father" Edward Taylor's Seaman's Bethel in Boston (MT/MH).

1831

To CHARLES CHAUNCY EMERSON

Wed Jan 12 Noon [1831]

Dear Charles,

This moment received your welcome letter & pens— And from the interest of the Spinoza & Kant *subjects* should have gone today to hear Waldo tonight & staid over saturday—but I had just concluded not to go.[1] Should not have demurred about the highest lectures on earth if the old carcase had not run down—but a little of the crash cloth & exercise gave me to stay. Nevertheless if these lectures can't be obtained in any way I shall come & take lodgings every saturday. Will they be printed? Dont answer me uncertainly. No one would think you in exile—thirsting after invisibles who sees you in a Country resting place for body & mind. It is a fine time to hear of your discontent. Repose is the gift of wisdom in age. When you can have power to distribute faith & consolation & any thing else of lesser import—this appetite for losing oneself in lofty services like the prophets will be inlarged & sattisfied— Still the beau ideal w'h is impressed on real immortal souls—and re-given as a command in the divine law can not here be possessed— Oh no—it's too too celestial—but like a delightfull vision it is sent to beckon onwards thro' all the weary wasting desert—if at times its' golden wings are folded & its' spotless form almost hidden by murky heavy human passions—it again appears with most illusive invitation— Always however when viewed by sane minds as wearing a cross—the emblem of his life who sent it on earth—but near this are stars—sometimes to youth more or less—telling his fortunes. Cherish the vision with devoted zeal. A few hasty years and rest & weariness & hope will alone surround it— True competition ceases—& benevolence is more pure if less active—but the goal is only to be gained by death—& one omen of his is more exciting than any pursuit. The *experience* (for so it may & ought to

be called) of a spiritual world w'h we carry about—& the *experience* of its'
Author, in all we see & feel—& *reason* about, is enough to fill the appetite—
to burn on with contempt for cercumstances. If the leaders of our Community felt this *certainty,* could they turn aside to controversy? Would not each
sect be left to his own faith? How desirable to find a variety of opinions in
travellers on the same road? You will weary of truisms   Not so much as I
off this bold & virulent Whitman letter[2]   There is infatuation in the rage for
prosyletism on the orthodox side—& too much on ours. Step forth, as on
one of your mounting stones, and throw the balmy oil of sentiments grafted
on the gospel palm[n] & take your companions to Olivet & Calvary and show
them the land to which these scenes ministered. You remember the sublime
spectacle Italy gave in the beginning of the 14 cent., At persuasion of the approaching day of Judgment—their quarrels were forgotten as tho' they had
never been, and the States clothed in white visited each other in love. Would
the same kind minister who might have spread this glorious report visit our
fighting men & women. It is so the dictate of *reason* as well as intimation of
scripture that the universe is full of spirits (mortal & others) that we allow it
without any definite ideas of their agency or if there be any. When we think of
the varied ills that are gathered in this world it seems no happy spirit would
choose to visit it. Yet you find me anxious to pursue the inquiry of Follen.
Wherever there is a moral dug up there is a direct history of its' Original. Yet
I would not Waldo should invite me—I should know that he knew I was an
anomaly—or somthing I cannot always define—   But for health occasionally renewed & these lectures I might go—   And had rather do it on the
persumption of hospitality than being deceived with invites. Keep my secret. I
look forward to a correspond with him unsullied by obligation when I remove
into the Vale. My first design in this long talk was to request Wallenstein &
Dejarando's other work[3] or somthing grander. Your mother will send me a
bundle by Saturday. Tell me of your spirits flights & forever oblige

MME

All are pleased with your remembrance. Never omit it.[4]

MH: bMS Am 1280.226(689). *Addressed:* Mr Charles C. Emerson / Cambridge /
Politeness of Mr Fulsom. *Endorsed:* M. M. E. / Jan. 1831.
    palm] ⟨stock⟩ ↑ palm ↓
    1. CCE to MME, 1 Jan. and 7–8 Jan. 1831, mentions a series of Saturday lectures
by Charles Follen (1796–1840), who in 1831 became professor of German language
and law at Harvard. On the 8th he writes that he will definitely go "tonight . . . for we
are to have Spinoza & Kant" (MT/MH).
    2. Bernard Whitman (1796–1834), pastor of the Second Church at Waltham, be-
came involved in a Calvinist-Unitarian controversy that split his parish. He defended
his Unitarian position in *A Letter to an Orthodox Minister on Revivals of Religion*
(1831), *Two Letters to the Reverend Moses Stuart on the Subject of Religious Liberty*
(1831), and a reply to a review of the latter in the *Spirit of the Pilgrims* (1831).

3. Johann Christoph Friedrich von Schiller, *Wallenstein: A Drama in Two Parts*, trans. S. T. Coleridge (London, 1800); the Emersons were reading Marie Joseph de Gérando, *Histoire comparée des systèmes de philosophie*, 4 vols. (Paris, 1822–23); the "other work" is probably *Self-Education; or, The Means and Art of Moral Progress*, trans. Elizabeth Palmer Peabody (Boston, 1830).

4. Written upside down at bottom of outside leaf.

To Ellen Tucker Emerson and Ralph Waldo Emerson

Jan. 14 —30 [1831]   Concord

This starry evening I had yours dear Ellen[1]   If your pensive style of character suits the taste of your friends (which it does me surely and is such a treat from the general style of women) why do you seem at war with it & call it by ill names? Is it that celestial resignation which such a style intimates? It is allotted you by Him who distributes his gifts & graces as seems most wise & kind. Those "threads of thought" you weave with the sweet fingers of taste & fancy are better than the imported stuffs of learned lore which our young females are loaded with and expose to the highest bidder of admiration. And now I am schooling you I will say that the only moment in which you did not appear lovely, was at the intimation[n] you wanted more variety or was not accostomed to have two days alike. There lives not a being who could less sympathise with such a want or whose days are so exactly alike. But it is a want attendent on human nature—but never sattisfied,—the more indulged by outward motion—the more insatiable it becomes—till in some cases it lays waste the finest flowers of imajanation—and withers the affections of the heart—even when that heart has an object on earth which is able to supply the richest variety. But this appetite for novelty we must not contend with— it is to be sattisfied only in the spiritual world. And it is sent to beckon on the exiles, who in change of scene are taught the completest lesson that can be learnt—that the wants of the soul can be sattisfied only by the *action* of it on it's natural objects. It was this idea I intended when I answered that if you were in health to be employed in arduous delightfull duties you would not feel any wish for variety in externals. If there is any place where Gods agency is not in all its' magnificence—and in the event of every possible motion of matter & mind then may we ask for variety of objects—or if disease of body or mind render us unable to perceive that agency (as I know by experience) then may we ask for the play things of time in a new direction.

Good night dear Ellen   May the tenderest hand of mercy cover you ever with love & grace prays

MME

My love to your Mother, for whose indisposition I am truly sorry, & to Marg.[2] whose way of dreaming is very pleasant & whose mention of me is gratefull

So you think I want more crimson than I'm willing to pay for—indeed! I am able to pay for all I want & for a calico as red as blood & can get it for 17 cents[3]

Dont read this medley my dear Waldo. A writer that dont know that the jews had the decalogue that fountain of light & im^tn to them, *tho'* now it is denied that they had any ideas of immortality. There is nothing that is new but what tends to chill the blood, even when disbelieved by the reader & when he knows he is forever connected with God even if the xian rev. is striped of its' miracles & its' Auther of that glory w'h prophesy '*his witness*' & God in a variety of other ways declared belonged to him. * * * I am delighted with your publick views of benevolence— Beg you to practise them in giving me some new ideas—this divine principle can best be developed in obscurity—where there is no tie but charity—no motive—no interest but what is invisible & future. wed 19 * * * I may be on my way to the Vale before long if they desire it in lieu off—if not does Ellen intend my visit after you are both at Phi.?[4] I am glad you will also have the exercise &c &c of the route. I have been writing in great haste—a funeral of an infant of a day at Carlisle calls for father & I need the ride. That particle of dust gives the old horse to dine in haste at 12! Well—the immaterial spark may have mingled with the soul of the world & bloom in fire or flowers till it's unconscious existence became ripe for wings & then it may fly thro' worlds. Unite every thing with your principle & it becomes a sermon & a tongue   Tell Charles I continued to write him—but his continued little letters make me afraid to send so long a one. And hearing father read & admire Degarando (who has so much detailed porridge with but few plumbs) scared me from the writing any more words. Yours in haste as the bundle goes

MH: bMS Am 1280.226(871).
intimation] ⟨expression⟩ ↑ intimation ↓
im^t] *probably abbreviation for* immortality
    1. See ETE to MME, [Jan. 1831] (*OFL*, 137–38), which Gregg presumes is the "last of Ellen's letters" (138). This indicates MME's letter is misdated and belongs to 1831.
    2. ETE to MME, [Jan. 1831], states that her mother, Margaret Tucker Kent, has "raised blood" and that her sister Margaret "is well and still dreams on—tho' occasionally starting in slumber—speaks of you" (*OFL*, 137–38).
    3. ETE to MME, [Jan. 1831], reports, "Mother has been looking for a gown for you but how can you expect to be clothed in scarlet or crimson without paying for it."
    4. ETE to MME, [Jan. 1831], says she is looking forward to going to "North Phila[delphia] in 6 weeks" (*OFL*, 138), a journey she did not live to make.

To Charles Chauncy Emerson

Jan. 14 [1831]

Do you perceive so clearly this beau ideal of a perfect moral?[1] Happy gift—tho' like the wheels of the promethean chariot will never in mortal durance reach the goal. Cherish your mitigated nessecity—by entering the designs—by uniting your soul to the plans of the Infinite Planner as a "flame is united to flame" Oh how happy to concentrate the diverging rays of genius (w'h are attracted by the seductive love of whatever is dazzling—by all the illusions of power & pleasure to feverish efforts) to one simple invisible object—one so little understood by the world—w'h must ripen in the hidden vine till the appointed event brings it to action. This divine power you know was called an influx by all the good antients—(except by the epicureans & democritians) and was better reverenced than by many who profess to believe in it's assuming a real form in the Mediator to be administered in material miracle while he was present and afterward in a richer manner on the spiritual. Well I hear you say here is Aunts cartel or cartouch—the same strain. In uniting one's self to this origin they whose sensibility is not yet so apparent as their intellectual power can find this union, perhaps, more absorbing as an exercise of mind than others and may suceed in *moral principle* till the germ of sympathy shall receive its' culture in a richer soil. Here that amaranthyne is sadly exposed, and yet will ever seek to gratify itself—often at the expense of sterner beauties.

But to our late favorite subject as a healthfull faith. If nessecity or fatalism as is intimated thro' bible be certain what need of religion?[2] Oh it is her patrimony to give it—reveal it in its' perfect accordance with a *liberty,* w'h tho' very like a go cart, in w'h poor man tottles round, yet with such sure effect that the circle widens forever within the devine decrees, w'h like an infinite ocean surrounds & absorbs the human bubbles.[n] Does it ever seem to you that this liberty is illusive answering & serving the purposes of virtue? Surely not. But the mighty problem can only be understood by an infinite Giver—who (Himself embraces moral nessecity in all its infinitude of a natural attribute) can alone send forth this seraph to attend created beings shrouded in mists w'h reach his throne. If we exercise our *understandings merely* we lose sight of it—but never in consciousness Hume had not the gift of "reason" & he was a nessecarian of the lowest order. Degerando is slight indeed as a philosopher. Calls it a primative law of thinking beings you know. It is a law—and nothing but a law as any other phenomena *perhaps* of matter. What is a law? Will it operate without agency—cause? no but invaribly under certain cercumstances. Then where the boasted self determining power? Influenced by nothing? A cause without effect? Who would covet such a power? D. continues to say "that there exists no antisapated certainty of the action of a moral being". Not in the divine mind, is it possible he means? Were this liberty as full as the demagougs of moral or civil liberty would have it it would still be a limited gift surrounded with the divine prescience, yet not affected by it. And any thing out of that glorious {orb}^{n} would be dark to the adorers of the divine attributes. True, we generate our own *motives* by virtue & vice— & the chain of causes & effects are always reacting w'h constitute our little orbit of liberty

But after all the gifts of birth & those w'h are received by promise at application of the supernatural religion are the only realities for the present.

May your heavenly father supply you with more than all you have needed by being left to form your religious character alone prays

MME

Feb. 2   Dear Charles, how is Ellen? Do write that she continues better— Every week I expect a letter if ever so short while I am so near—   And now I want them on her account   When you hear & write of Edward let the letter be to Grandfather   Why do you think of sending Degerando when he is un-translated? The first book is here. As to Follen's lecture som one can get the whole for me.[3] How did you get on Monday night in Town meeting?[4]

You know how I love to see you—"but am no one to write"   And unless you take bed & straight jacket, w'h are very usefull to me, think any other place at this season better for your exercise. If there is nothing in B. to read why I am in no straght am reading Edwards against Chauncy.[5] I shall look for you as the best of Springs gifts

MH: bMS Am 1280.226(691). *Addressed:* Mr C. C. Emerson / Cambridge / Mss. *Endorsed:* M.M.E. / Feb. 1831 / Liberty & necessity.

bubbles.] ⟨circles⟩ bubbles.

{orb}] *torn by seal; supplied from MH:690*

1. CCE to MME, 7 Jan. 1831, describes his increasing belief in a "qualified Fatal-ism. So different are we from what we wish to become—   So hard do we struggle, day by day, & year by year, to fashion ourselves after the Ideal which we seem directly to conceive"; yet he also finds himself unable to change the direction of the innate individual character as it develops (MT/MH). In a draft version of her letter, MME called this "moral" the "grand archetype of one of the first in worth ideas of God!" (MH: 690).

2. MME probably alludes to conversations on this subject with CCE during their week together at Concord during CCE's Christmas vacation; CCE includes these ideas in his letter of 7 Jan.

3. See MME to CCE, 12 Jan. [1831], esp. n. 1.

4. In CCE to WE[3], 30 Jan. 1831, CCE is extremely upset about the United States government's mistreatment of the Indians and indicates that he plans to attend a citizens meeting in Cambridge the next night to "remonstrate" (MT/EW).

5. Jonathan Edwards's *Some Thoughts Concerning the Present Revival of Religion in New England* (1743) responds to antirevival forces, led by Charles Chauncy (1705–87), one of the ministers of Boston's First Church. Chauncy's sermon *Enthusiasm Described and Cautioned Against* (1742) and other publications "vilified the revival as 'the effect of enthusiastic heat' " (*The Great Awakening*, ed. C. C. Goen, in vol. 4 of *The Works of Jonathan Edwards*, ed. Perry Miller, Sydney E. Ahlstrom, John E. Smith,

et al., 7 vols. to date [New Haven: Yale University Press, 1957–], 62–63). Edwards's vindication of the revival in *Some Thoughts* further polarized the religious community in New England into "New Lights" (followers of Edwards) and "Old Lights" (headed by Chauncy) and prompted yet another attack by Chauncy in *Seasonable Thoughts on the State of Religion in New England* (1743).

To Ralph Waldo Emerson and Charles Chauncy Emerson

Concord Sat. night   Jan 22 [1831]

The winds sweep over the winding sheet of nature as tho' they were the dirge of her children—   A dim corpse light hides moon & stars. No one starry watch tower where spirits halt—not even one black curtain w'h might bear the genius of dreams to the unconscious dwellers of this lone house. One unvoiced wail[n]—nothing to figure the dread past—and more wondrous future— No melancholy ghost of dead renown to wisper ought of thy sunless realms. And thou old time Server who art blabbing the same hour that thou didst when liberty first fired on thy countrymen—how forever the same—how forever tuned to the present.[1] Tho' thy first notes bore to thy master demands on fortitude rarely so sustained— & as soon as inde[sn] war waxed[n] he watched thy every measure with burning patriotism—   Yet there was a happy cradle w'h he carressed—   Oh couldst thou have been its' knell—'twere *notice enough* to have told thy pointing at its' exit & appointed its restoration to the sleep of kings.[n] It lived—but heard thee not when thou wast wittness to the grief which forever prostrated the widows heart—thou kept it on & numbered the hours of the school *boy*—but the change that had arrested his rosy progress could not be regained—rekindled—   Yet he is vital in worth & beauty & talent. He paused—but thou kept on—nor, like thy spruce brother of the City, so much as stoped thy pausing paw[n] *at 15 minutes past 8*

And now thou art as obedient to the relentless hand of female order as when her namesake wound thee up— & would have given thy wheels to move by the living spirits of love & fame   So like the hoary handed[n] chronicler thou wilt date his death whose praise is in Churches—and with the same sad dignity thou hast always worn wilt number the hours in which thy future Mistress[2] will be hoarding classic lore and with the subtilty *of understanding*[n] of her German friends translating their "sandy" metaphysicks—or dissecting the problems of mathematics—   To her scientific eye thy *mechanism* may have no mystery—but the *power* by which *that* plays is beyond the faith of material philosophy—thou art thyself a living proof of powers beyond visible matter. Canst tell & tell—but even *that Influence* cannot make thee live in the hour[n] which has past—time itself to w'h thou pointest cannot be that w'h has gone bye! My sole purpose was to inquire about your letter dear Waldo—I rarely comprehend them at first & tonight I had speculations—but the storm has scattered them & a slave to the horologue I go to bed— & the moon & stars have come—but not in poetry

Do do purchase this clock— We want it at W.—but it is too good to be moved—& we do not deserve for our short space so valued a relict.

Wed. Jan 26 Eve

Dear Charles

How is Ellen? Do let me know our Synosure is better surely. But still I dont want to say any thing to poor Waldo till I know how she is   How is your health & thermometer of soul—this most arid weather. I could not cower down in a better place. God shelters or tempers all conditions

May He preside over you all & hear prayer for the invalid   How does Mrs Kent? Her illness is most undesirable and now especially. Love to my kind Sister & thanks.

Yours in hope & waiting
MME

& I dare not write long to you least you should fear them & not continue these precious dots of paper   Do keep my money till I need it & charge me with a quire of letter paper— Tis 2⅝ here

MH: bMS Am 1280.226(692). *Addressed:* Mr C. C. Emerson / Care of Rev. R. W. Emerson / Boston. *Endorsed:* 1831.
  unvoiced wail] *possibly* unvaried vail (*T*)
  inde^s] *probably abbreviation for* independence's; *possibly* isicled
  waxed] *possibly* ceased
  kings.] kings ⟨by thy movements⟩.
  stoped . . . paw] ⟨kept⟩ ↑ stoped ↓ thy pausing paw ⟨quiet⟩
  handed] *probably altered from* headed
  subtilty *of understanding*] subtilty ↑ *of understanding* ↓
  live . . . hour] ⟨number⟩ ↑ live in ↓ the ⟨same⟩ hour
  1. As becomes clearer near the end of the letter, MME refers to a family heirloom, the clock in the Manse at Concord. In his diary entry for 10 Dec. 1767, WE[1] reported buying an eight-day clock, in Boston, for twenty dollars ("good Bargain"). The clock remains in the dining room of the Manse (*Diaries and Letters of William Emerson, 1743–1776*, ed. Amelia Forbes Emerson [Privately printed, 1972], 37–38). CCE to MME, 4 and 5 Feb. 1831, calls the "ancient clock . . . the pregnant theme" of her letter (MT/MH).
  2. MME suggests that SBR is to become the new owner of the clock; her "namesake" (one who shared her name) is MME's half sister Sarah Ripley.

To Ralph Waldo Emerson

C^d Feb 16 Wed Night [1831]

The high noon of night comes on— Not the hour in which the antient Egyptians figured their great god as visiting happy souls—but the xians is always with the disembodied—not always alike. Once of late, the young saint appeared under the guardianship of a lofty spirit who seemed more interested in her than others   He knew her—he was on earth remarkably fond of childhood & for a long time had not received his mortal reminisences with weak delight.[n] "Love beauty song & all he had here guesed of Heaven" shone sweetly in Ellen.[1] T'was his to lead her first to the Messiah—there she first saw the emblems w'h she had seen dimly decyphered in Patmos—and there too was the cross—in coulers so deep and grand—such as she never had seen or imajined in fancys highest mood—   She made a sign, for as yet she has not learnt the language of spirits, with her fine vehicle, for her gaurdian to pray—he smiled & pointed to Him who is himself the Preist—a moments contemplation and Ellen felt above all offices of prayer. Why at this great time her thoughts should have reverted to the image she bore in her heart of hearts is not told—but that for some days her blest condition—so surprising—so full of wonder and amazement had excluded every past event of joy and pain—that this perfect tranquility might have restored to fuller view her husband is not improbable. It was him she coupled with her soul—and she was understood by her Antient—he well knew what it was to have loved—if a pause of bliss came over him it was not of disapprobation of her—no he forsaw the time when she would also lose earthly love and *resign with* him—   She was anxious to understand the meaning—& might have made too minute inquiries for his Euridice had not a select band of spirits called him to join them in an embassy of high behest in a distant world. She imajined some military insignia—somthing denoting a patmotic mission—but all was conjecture—and a benevolent minister conducted to her a young & beautifull soul whom she knew to be her own loved Sister—and then indeed they will commune of those they have loved—so commune as no *lonely* scribe can sympathize. The clock has spoken one. Oh how do they measure time beyond the peristiles of matter? By accesions of knowledge—by new forms of poetry & praise—by of all other modes, that of active soul virtue. Why is it, dear Waldo, that we give a reality—permanence to the spiritual world which we do not to the visible? when that alike hangs on the creative Being. *Does it*? Has He not given a natural immortality to it—spiritual substances may not possibly depend like material ones? Aye, look on it as we may it is all triumph & wonder.

But you dear friend have a most heavy loss—& many a bitter day to struggle with. God only can comfort you—   He is wont to try his best works in the hottest fires. 21   Charles again says, write to Waldo—   This vision is imperfect for your affection perhaps pride—but visions must be only described—not finished. When your Meta appears again, she may be with Klopstocks—   And if they talk of his ode on the omnipresence I will surely be scribe.[2]

Adieu. Love to your Mothers & Margaret.
MME.

Write if you find time.

MH: bMS Am 1280.226(881). *Addressed:* Rev. R. Waldo Emerson / Boston / Mss. *Endorsed:* 1831.

delight.] delight ⟨as now⟩.

1. Ellen died on 8 Feb. 1831.

2. Reference to "Ode on the Omnipresent," by the German poet Friedrich Gottlieb Klopstock (1724–1823). "Klopstock's *Life and Odes," Foreign Review and Continental Miscellany* 3 (1829): 340–77, prints the full text of this ode, which it notes is the "only Ode written in 1758—the year in which Meta [nickname for Margaret] Klopstock died [after four years of marriage]. It may, perhaps, be considered as her husband's tribute to her memory" (375).

To SARAH BRADFORD RIPLEY

Cd   March 10   Wed [1831?][1]

It is delightfull to find you removed from the epicurian liberty—to believe in a nessisity that effects *events*—all but the doing wrong—that irks & torments—then there could be no absolute nessesity in it—and there must be a liberty absolutely essential to the virtue of an immortal creature or conscience would not exist—would be stifled amidst the toils & fumes of arid speculation. What a link in a great chain of your existence was that scrap of an S. E.?[2] It was so smale too that you abhor the failure—*why not others?* Whose standard is high but has a warfare with hosts? Think you that speck, w'h agitated no ambition, is the only barrier to your consummation? Oh when you have passed the stygian pool of doubt—when you, who are able to solve scientific problems, shall find the only true liberty of belief and connection with God thro' His own institutions—will rejoice in that grandest of all problems—the liberty of the creature & the agency of Creator—   You will with the lofty spirits above delight to find your self subject to the same high destiny which embraces secrets w'h dwell in the abyss of the individual divine[n] nature. My God! I bow before thee in view of those elections w'h give to some an intellectual power to approach Thee so nearly by the relations of mind when their hearts receive[n] thy moral image! Till then cannot, dear S., the character—mind, or whatever, be said to be built on one side only? But could such an anomaly exist now in the virtuous were it not for some modification of German idealism—the essence of w'h is to believe in mind without individuality? Is not this the seed of all the old thinking infidels of past time? Yesterday—*you* only gave me ideas of the dramatic kind—a strange enigma

But of yourself I meant not to intrude—   Do tell me some new things—we said nothing. Try to explain this last affair—"how mind—the substance or essence can exist independently of an individual—and this they call God himself"—or rather say if you can have a notion of such an essence—or principle or existence? I like their use of substance-essence—because it at once gives me the Individual-substance w'h is the substratum & cause of all others—& all things. You can, if you are willing to be a martyr in charity, let me into the metaphisks of these teeming novelists—tho' probably the same speculations have been set to brewing ages ago? There is somthing to take hold off w'h gives the old jaded mind a spring in this ger. phi. after it has purred over the analizings & cercuits of the Scot[n] school—a sort of meteor[n] to the inquirer— But when we inquire of nessity, that same old school oracles forth the truth that the scheme of moral nessisity proceeds on the idea that there is a nesse- cary connection between means & ends antecedants & consequents   Now you weary of our New England ancestors. Shame on your want of respect for Gov. Bradford.[3] Leibnitz said the same as well as Horsley.[4] And this was their chain (w'h you are glad enough to get hold off in your own way) of causes & effects w'h took it's beginning in the operation of the Infinite mind. We exist—how overwhelming the consciousness at times—   You will be old— Oh what sort of woman—   Can you be old—or die? Your present worship- ers all dead or lost in palsies or somthing worse—   Your children—but they cant be companions nor husband for one whose fame is *strechy*. You seem to admire wealth.—   Happy you are not gilded with it—   The prospect would be mighty fine from the very top of the ladder—   Yours lies in discipline & when you have encompassed the ends of being—   I am unable to describe my feelings of respect for you as a xian! the vision of your spiritual state in the homes of knowledge—   How natural & sure these scenes—w'h make them- selves familiar even to the imajination always finds its own place obscure— but wittnessing what will forever delight—& excite hope & love—there the solitudes will be filled with views of an eternal providence—& absolute fore- knowledge on the true philosophy of your own links—w'h to me is in sublime union with the Liebnitz[n] & Horsley nessicity & the most glorious liberty to love & choose & practice right. You speake nobly (& long shall it stimulate) of xian "motive". Is it not righter to embrace a high one if we can't act up to it than take the responsibility of rejecting what does appear in theory so great? It seems good for the ignorant & "young ones." Oh but is it for the higher to embody it—to build thier eyiree beyond the clouds & lights of earth—then they fullfill the design of their being by bettering this poor old weary state.

Take my poor tedious declamations as you will—or come not near me to absorb my little orb of thought. 'Tis vain to try to bid you adieu as I feel. Write me somthing of Kantism & oblige

Sister MME

This hankering after Kant may seem ridiculous—but some early fondness for Male Bra[5] leads me to find a resemblance w'h I like to trace & see the delusion of the former man

MH: bMS Am 1280.226(1289). *Addressed:* Mrs S. A Ripley / Waltham.
the . . . divine] ↑ the individual ↓ divine
receive] *possibly* revive
Scot] ⟨english⟩ Scot
meteor] met ↑ e ↓ or *in MS; possibly* meter *intended*
Liebnitz] ⟨German⟩ ↑ Liebnitz ↓

1. 10 Mar. fell on Wednesday in 1824, 1830, and 1841, but in none of these years was MME at Concord in March; in 1831 she was in Concord and much interested in "Kantism" and other "German" ideas.

2. Possibly "Struggle for existence"; see RWE's transcription of MME to SAR [26 May 1827], in which MME exclaims, "'Struggle for existence'—what a phrase for one like you about the bubble life!" (*JMN* 2:391).

3. SBR was a sixth-generation descendant of William Bradford, governor of the Plymouth Colony.

4. Both Leibniz and Samuel Horsley (1733–1806) defended belief in human freedom; Horsley, an English bishop and scientist, is best known for his attack on Joseph Priestley's materialist, necessitarian position.

5. Malebranche.

To Hannah Adams

Ap. 25 [1831]   Chardon Street

My dear friend,

Ever since I had the pleasure of seeing you it has been matter of regret that I expressed so stronge an interest in what seems to me the only priviledge of those who have been distinguished for their character and literary usefullness—that they should be called home before the infirmities of age render life wearisome.[1]

You think life may yet be desirable & preparatory. May your heavenly Father render yours so to the last moment. He has blest you—your principles & feelings lead you to the highest of all hopes—may they continue to brighten & shed comfort on the path of others. And whether this or its reverse be the case, any ways which do not effect the soul itself and the xian triumphs   He knows no moment of duration whether past on the bed of langour & prostration of mind or in the circles of fame & fashion is lost when his motive & pursuit is to realise his high destiny of moral perfection, and tho' ages were to intervene between his admission to the vision[n] of God, his perfect resignation would know no failure. This idea of an interruption to our consciousness, you remember, was the subject which Priestley introduced, and one which we were wont to discuss.[2] That dark & unphilosophical opinion has given way to juster ones—and returned in one view[n] the antient faith of the gospel. We should rejoice—and we do—but with the evolutions of speculation much of dubious and artificial arises—amid the stars & rainbows of modern spirituality is much of misty & cloudy. Let us be glad that our years are fast numbering—that while novelty and hope beckon forward the young, we have the old sure words of revelation to give us allready a sort of fruition in the world of spirits—that we were initiated into a faith which instructs us rather more in the faults than the perfections of our nature—but richly provides an inheritance which no created being could merit by his own agency. With these hopes with this confidence I bid you my xian fellow traveller an affectionate farewell. I expected to have called again but I cannot. I will tell Mr & Mrs Dewey about your respect for this life & faith in a better.[n]

Remember in your prayers
M. M. Emerson

MH: bMS Am 1280.226(620). *Addressed:* Miss Adams / Boston / Care of Mr C. C. Emerson. *Endorsed:* M. M. Emerson / to H. Adams. / April 1831.

vision] ⟨divine⟩ vision

returned . . . view] returned ↑ in one view ↓

better] *possibly* letter

1. Hannah Adams (b. 1755) was a prolific writer of history (or, as the *DAB* somewhat uncharitably labels her, a "compiler of historical information"); she died 15 Dec. 1831. CCE to MME, 12–28 Jan. [1828], reported, "I went to see Miss Hannah Adams the other day. She is well & looks well & talks well—her memory is as vigorous & retentive as ever. She asked eagerly after you & longs to have the pleasure again to talk metaphysics with you" (MT/MH). MME to CCE, 9 Feb. 1828, responded by asking him to write about "every body in greener life than my friend Miss A. What a bore" (MH: 663).

2. Possibly in *The Doctrine of Philosophical Necessity*, section 5, "Of the Supposed Consciousness of Liberty, and the Use of the Term Agent."

To Edward Bliss Emerson

[June? 1831]

My dear Edward

As we still sojourn on the same changing blowing trying planet, it is soothing to meet if only to say how changable the winds—how bleak the clouds—how weary the sense of mortality! How delightfull to meet (tho' on this pale paper) & say how grand is existence—how inexpressibly rich to exist *in* God—to be surrounded with eternity! To be in that state of health w'h places one on the verge of a holier state is far richer. Then the child holds out it's hands & raises it's eyes as tho' its real Parent were present and about to raise it to the embraces of pure reason—active intelligence and real virtue— by w'h we mean wisdom & love. But the *name* of *virtue* answers to our poor ideas of wisdom & benevolence—when we come to see them as they exist in the divine Mind we may be ashamed of our poor copies   Yet there is One who has suffered for us—whose sympathies will extend long long beyond this embryo state—even perhaps—not wholly improbable, after his offices shall close—when God becomes all in all—when we are thro' his ministry restored to absolute communion with the Infinite—even then his intercourse may continue and tho' we shall no longer be ashamed of our poor efforts in the body, we shall love the being who has enabled us to go on—forward & forward with those who have never tasted the bitter woe of sin

Adieu, dear Edward, I am hasting to solitude—   Daily have my prayers accompanied your voayge—   I pass the pain I suffered in your illness—and the useless regrets of your removal.[1]

All transient wills are lost in the ocean of events to which we run.

Farewell till better health restore you—if you wandered in affection from the school of Christ in pursuing earthly subsistence you must play the truant no more

Your affectionate Aunt
& sympathising friend
MME

MH: bMS Am 1280.226(756). *Addressed:* Mr Edwd. B. Emerson / Care of Mr Geo. Barnard / Santa Croix. *Endorsed:* M. M. Emerson / 21 Dec^r / 1831 / A 11 March—.

1. EBE, in very poor health, sailed for Saint Croix 14 Dec. 1830 (*L* 1: 313).

To Ralph Waldo Emerson

Vale   Sep. 23 31

You wrote,[n] some few years since, my dear Waldo you prefered nat. to revealed religion. And I do not tease to *know* your opinions—probably un-fixed   In your last (welcome to the very heart) you seem still looking beyond the bounds of pure reason or naturalism so I shall write in the old loose strain—always hoping to find you beyond what mere human virtues can af-ford. True—if we could have but one—'twere best to adhere to the immortal principles of our own constitution—unless we were as confident of the re-vealed—but no Plato has been a perfect character. But in my limited notions, 'twere as hard to seperate the first from the influence of the last as to seperate the all surrounding electric fluid from its' effects on the elements.

Your preference arises chiefly from the difficulties of nat. to revealed—for except some deductions common to all—its' voice is indistinct dark & often uninterpretable—   And Genius loves to stand gazing into the clouds, or like the worshipers of Baal expect to find thier gods *napping* while the secret of the *"law of laws"* is contained in the *"mighty Compensation,"*[1] who has been typified thro' most of the earth and shadowed forth on its most antient alters, and at lenght has come into the hands and mouths of men so tangibly that the supernaturalist, in faith, becomes as clear a mirrow to the facts of xianity as the mind of sense is to those of the material world. They find, that, as man is said to give his idea to his age—so in the cycle of infinite existence, God may be said to give his peculiar idea (respecting so mysterious a race) in the person & ministry of Jesus to the ages w'h compose the mortal race of man. Do you want *"principles"* beyond what this ministry teaches? penetrate like the Newtons of nat. phi. far higher than the common traveller—and you will find the origin of the light of revelation w'h is shed so—so—like every day things—will find the curtain w'h conceals the invisible world to have been drawn enough—oh enough—to rouse the *thinker* to increasing wakefullness were there but a millioneth chance of the realities of that glorious world.

"The dead speake not"— No they rest from mortal cares—'tis your high office to explore and interpret the living voices of the wittnesses of Jesus—the spirit of prophecy.— The Angels who testified of him are still living & burning in other offices of benvolence—for their friend is risen and active—'tis yours to carry on their & his work—to apply the remedy to the poorest of the miserable—the meaner—the more respect to the Donor of all. True, the higher gifts of explaining the gospel in its advanced stages seems allotted to you & your time & place. Suffer the remembrance of Beza's[2] caution—that "the most dangerous temptation to pride is the inventing new methods of explaining or treating a subject"[n] This is as far from you as darkness from light. Your poetic visions—your early philsophisings in a bright & particular orbit account for your wanderings from the Central sun.

Well well when I come to read over this declamatory homily I wish it otherwise—but I cannot write a better now— And I've been reading again & again yours of 30 of Au. and if you could see it with my eyes[n]—you would pardon all my faded truisms

And now how many rich & happy thoughts crowd to my idea of you—and as the long benefactor of many a weary hour—of your own hopes & prospects how fully I share And sympathise in the illness of your Mother & Sister.[3] It is hard for you—very hard to trace the same dark way which left you bereft of one of the loveliest beings that ever graced our world. My love to M. and tell I hope she will live. Tell me more of where you go & what you feel. I've just read J. Adams' bio. What a noble career! Yet of all the contests he endured what real advantage to his Country? Could we be worse if we had remained? The *Country* surely made a few herors—but what they did for *that* seems a problem. The German writers never meddle with politicks— Monarchies have given Homers & Archimedes & Newtons & Isaiahs & Pauls!

My love to C C E & will do just as he says when I can send the papers—He is my patron of patrons in sending me some pens. One failed of any use—& the 2[d] in two or 3 days—but I hope by keeping this 3[d] out of ink to preserve it? Love to my Sister. Write write to your most truly

MME

Sad disapp[t] last eve to hear W. H. is not coming with letters & books. I dont know how to send R. E—'s pamplets[4] to Andover.

I referred to a few expressions in yours which are not of the grave stern cast that even occasional speculations require from a man of your cast.

MH: bMS Am 1280.226(883). *Addressed:* Rev. R. Waldo Emerson / Boston / Mss. *Endorsed:* M.M.E. / Sept. 1831.

wrote] ⟨said⟩ ↑ wrote ↓

subject"] subject" ⟨The truth becomes obscured or diverted and the path of safty rendered misty.⟩

see . . . eyes] see it ↑ with my eyes ↓

1. Cf. RWE's statement that "*Compensations* is one of the watchwords of my spiritual world," 15 Aug. 1831 (*L* 1:330).

2. Theodore Beza (1519–1605), French Calvinist theologian.

3. ETE's mother, Margaret Tucker Kent, and sister Margaret both died of tuberculosis within the next two years.

4. Possibly RWE's cousin, William Haskins (see *L* 1:299 n. 31); probably tracts borrowed from Ralph Emerson of Andover.

To Sarah Bradford Ripley

Nov. 8 [1831]   Vale

I long to hear from your body & mind, dear Sarah, you were not well in the summer. And how is Margaret?[1] Very happy? Give her and all your folks my love— And send me some cake & a letter by Mr Haskins.

I often think of you in these 4 times 40 meetings—and find an apology for their running to get religion poured in—when I remember that you have lost your confidence in the mind—in the moral constitution. And I am not able to see but that it is better to have an immediate change take place than to expect every bad body[n] to be happy *if* they exist hereafter. There may be some very obstinate affinities in the moral nature that need the discipline of body & certain means w'h may not be at hand there. "How silly". Well it may go—for theres nothing too wild when we leave revelation—nor too terrible—for you say "there must be a God"—now were wrath an element of His infinite nature what but calvinism might we antisapate? Pardon me—but I was induced to say, & thought of nothing more, how much I think of you when the little Chapel of methodists[2] is light up amidst the beautifull woods and your commanding figure—your eyes & nose & mouth bending, at the same time with my freinds, to hear of the glad tydings from another world— Oh you seem but a future Angel. And you must take your children—for if I understand you, education relates but to the present life virtues[n]—then the love of the Auther of all virtue must be supernatural? Your friends Fitche & Shelling[3] talk of preparing the mind for the idea of God. They are very condescending—tho' I meant not to carp—for, as the old saw, if they never said any thing more paradoxical. But indeed I had rather imajine you with those than with me in the methodist Chh, where I sometimes go of a sunday. How readily would your mind react— & see at once that because the primitive philosophy was universal they had proudly sought to undermine it— You so capable of finding its' relations to revealed religion—you have travelled with the analogies of nature from childhood—told me of "the perfect system in the humble dandelion" have mounted from the simplest numbers (w'h were enough to convince you of a spiritual nature) to some of their hieghts—who have known the wonders of language—how soon would you be converted to faith—unless there is a real insanity resting on some part of your organisation—w'h is possible. Then you are innocent. You have been unfortunate in your connections with men who seek to please you and to gather strenght for thier speculations & non inspiration. But were they to know of your pining after the great & ineffable truths would it not benefit them? I am not able to see that speculations here would not exercise your powers. You could unfold the wonders of the half handkercheif with more effect than you did to me in the old sitting room, for you would find immutable truths in your learned stuff.

But I weary you and am *very* much so. Your letter I just read, after Ellen's death, and find it a most elegant thing. "There is *method* in it. Mine," if it be sane in matter, wrote every thing else. So it is humble to send it.

God bless you your husband & children

And give me a kindness in your heart prays
MME.

Mrs Dr Bradford[4] told me the very day I bid her adieu that you told her you had a train of thought for an hour w'h led you to believe in a future state. Oh what would I give for to know that train. Probably some stronge conviction of your capasity for endless improvement?? Good night dear Sister & give love to my Brother.

MH: bMS Am 1280.226(1282). *Addressed:* Mrs S. A. Ripley / Waltham / Mss.
every bad body] every ↑ bad ↓ body
present life virtues] present ↑ life ↓ virtues
Mine,] M⟨y⟩ine ⟨manner⟩,
  1. SBR's sister Margaret Bradford Ames (1804–47).
  2. In 1818 a small Methodist church was built at Mutiny Corner, a mile west of the town of Waterford, on land that adjoined MME's property and that had originally been part of the parcel she bought from Ralph Haskins. MME's warm feelings about this meetinghouse contrast with T. H. Gage's description of the "uncomfortable house [where] hardy, devout worshippers" gathered: it was a "low wooden structure, with a rather flat roof, its exterior unclapboarded, blackened, and weatherbeaten; its interior cheerless and bare, with hard plank benches, no adornment of any kind" (*Notes*, 66–67).
  3. German thinkers Fichte and Friedrich Wilhelm Joseph von Schelling.
  4. Sophia Rice Bradford, wife of SBR's brother, Dr. Gamaliel Bradford (1795–1839) of Boston.

1832

To Ralph Waldo Emerson

Vale   Feb   [1832]

And is it possible that one nurtured by the happiest institutions whose rich seeds have been bedewed by them—should be parrisidical![1] Or is it only the great *one* w'h lies at the root you reject? You most beloved of ministers, who seemed formed by face manner & pen to copy & illustrate the noblest of all institutions, are you at war with that angelic office? What a problem your existence   Love of truth (& practice of it w'h has always commanded my uncommon respect) leads you to sin against what is believed by the highest men to be truth in it's origin to man & leading to all others. It was at that fountain your infant mind imbibed the development of your moral nature! Oh why not seek it again with simplicity & intense exclusion. If truth can't be found as your preaching demands, then the sacrifice to it of all comfort & fame demands your attention. For the relation between your Creator if you have one, remains paramount. On what footing you are to treat with Him excites the deepest curiosty. But I take not the liberty to inquire. What you commit to me is enough. And I may ask—what you mean by speaking of "a great truth whose athority you would feel is its own"? In the letter of Dec 25 you "whether the heart were not the Creator." [2] Now if this withering Lucifer doctrine of pantheism be true, what moral truth can you preach or by what athority should you feel it? Without a personal God you are on an ocean mast^n unrigged for any port or object. Then why *not* continue to preach—& pray too? Where is the truth, so infinitely weighty with the true theist, injured? Some body must keep up these idle institutions & they may keep men from jail and gallows. What better scope for the intellectual reservoir? And such has been your integrity, whenever I have been indulged with hearing or reading, that St Paul, who had the fullest convictions of Jesus being the only medium of communication with the Incomprehensible, would not tax your sincerity, tho' he would regret the different character you assigned. Pardon me if I declaim with the garrulity of age. But it was you—so constituted— & placed with the benevolence of these institutions, without the bustle & detail whom I expected would rise to an eminence from w'h you would have as strong convictions of the only true phi.—the divine personal agency as of your own consciousness—God within the heart but not the heart. And how was your correspondence to brighten & renew my wrinkled mind! Another, & perhaps childish antisapation. That an old venerable pastor in the most delightfull spot, you could point to your grand children that within a few miles reposed the ashes of your pious ancestors—who preached the gospel—and that the very place w'h gave you birth & contains your father should wittness your last aspirations after the sovereign Good. It may be that the short lives of those most dear to me have given couler to the hopes of one minister remaining to be enrolled with the Mathers & Sewells of that venerable City. But it is rather idle to name hopes. It is, however, images of virtue, truth, & success w'h cheers the patriotic heart at it's own dissolution. As a man, were you a stranger, the unique trait in your history of having "no intimate friend" would excite interest. If it has disadvantages they are infinitely surpassed by the preservation of one's own magninimity—one of the greatest in this weary wasting world of effort. Charles 5th's motto is good in all cases "*not yet.*" [3] Time enogh when your faith shall be decided and your opinions vital with it's warmth.

Your study of nat. his. & phi. I suspect has been among the "senses" writers. Decartes, Malbra. & Clarke[4] studied the *Cause.* Fixed there the student resembles the noble Abdiel while the mechanists & rationals the busy & dainty Ariel.   23.   I wrote on having yours to send by a neighbour—he dont go for some time. This is too much to burn—too little to send—to lie bye is unsafe—   The Spectre, clothed with beauty at my curtain by night & table by day, forbids. I venture not on argument—& you can't be offended with *me* poor me. The hope of learning your process is tempting to my wish for excitment   The intellectual diseases of the day I cannot otherwise find. Do tell me of EBE. CC did not name the other members of your own le doute most noble *institution*[5]   Did you ever read Fosters sermon on the nullity of friendship to perfection of character?[6] I used to exult in that when young. Did I understand rightly Coleridge leaning to pantheism when he talks of human nature being subsumed in the divine?[7] Perhaps Channing got disturbed[n] by his adherence to the complications of this mystic, who is taxed I believe with the disease. Farewell

Your obliged & affectionate
MME

I've learnt to speake of you as Mr E.   It is proper to youth & strangers
Ive a mania for talking today

MH: bMS Am 1280.226(888). *Addressed:* Rev. R. Waldo Emerson / Boston / Mss. / *Endorsed:* Miss M. M. Emerson / Feb. 1832. / Concerning Second Church. *Postmarked:* So. Waterford / Feby 24, 1832.

mast] *possibly* most

disturbed] ⟨spirited⟩ disturbed

1. A response to early signs of RWE's dissatisfaction with his ministry at the Second Church, Boston, although he did not resign until the following August.

2. See L 7:200–201; RWE asks, "What from the interior Creation, if what is within be not the Creator"?

3. William Robertson, *History of the Reign of the Emperor Charles V, with a View of the Progress of Society from the Subversion of the Roman Empire to the Beginning of the Sixteenth Century* (1770).

4. The French philosopher Malebranche followed the rationalist philosophy of Descartes, as did Clarke, "the great English representative of the *a priori* method" of theology, who made Cartesian doctrines palatable to English taste (Leslie Stephen, *History of English Thought in the Eighteenth Century,* 3d ed., 2 vols. [New York: Peter Smith, 1947], 1:119). The material world is "an Eternal Effect of an Eternal Cause, which is God" (Clarke, *Works* 2:536).

5. EBE and CCE, both in Puerto Rico; MME seems to mean that a recent letter from CCE contained no news about EBE. In MME's lexicon, "le doute" probably means *sans doute,* ("without doubt" or "doubtless").

6. See James Foster, *Sermons,* 4 vols. (London, 1755), vol. 1, esp. sermons 2 and 3, "The Characters of the Righteous and Good Man Compared; or, Benevolence: The Noblest Branch of Social Virtue," and "The Perfection of the Christian Scheme of Benevolence."

7. Coleridge, *The Friend*: "But I speak of man in his idea, and as subsumed in the divine humanity" (1:516).

To Charles Chauncy Emerson

June 7 [1832]   Vale

My dear Charles,

Your letters recall to me an interest, that is of no use, to this crazy going world—w'h would vote me so without doubt. Were it not for you & such like I should be a perfect optimist about all its' jars—   Yet it is hard to think how much God did for it & our Settlers did for him, now that his countenance *seems* changed. But do you shrink at the mere shadow of death—"getting over"!—   And do you want to "*do*"?[1] These are common & indispensable to Gods plan   And why should I sadden? The prisoner of Chillon got over both & his unearthly picture is sublime—but who would him? The Tasso so restless? —tho he reached the future to live in.[2] But did ever any reach the ackme of his immortal nature who was not old enough to look back on defeat in the noblest purposes with more than resignation? But you are not the man to speake of these—   Your temperment is destined to taste the varied sweets of sucess. That the sails are furled occasionally & you feel above ambition, is good. You know too well that the puffs of dame fortune will fill them too gaily for grandeur. Few are so stern as not to live a puppet life—unless they get into a den.

I respect your respect for our hallowed institutions & the ties w'h bind selfish man to man—tho' I admire the extravagance of Waldo and the truth of that excess—[3]   But the truth w'h lies in such visions of virtue & freedom can only find strong hold in the xian plan whose outlines are alone so grand as to give foretaste of this perfect liberty and transcendant virtue. And to such, I cannot but think, there is not one too many sands in the banks w'h girdle human knowledge. In removing them by lawless speculation one might reap more sorrow than the peasant who sought the source of his stream. Not that there is not a perfect & infinite and personal God like to the revelation—but his design is to lead man by faith thro' many a cloud   And did we know the full consequences of every wrong thought & action, till we find them absolved in a better state, perhaps human virtue would despond. How often I rejoice that amidst the novelties w'h have corrupted the age you keep to the ark of testimony. And the sensitive well cargoed bark w'h you have piloted so well in orphan youth will have an open & abundant entrance into harbour, where you may enter new tracks of speculation without danger of those wrecks w'h have been so often caused by charterless voaygers.

Why does Waldo journey this way without you?[4] You seem to forget how I depended on both. True he would not have the taste of solitude nor with "the restraints of Uncles & Aunts"—tho' their labours would deny their time— nor do they covet the best of gifts. I alone should interrupt him—   Yet you mention my meeting him. It would be of all things my pleasure—& I was going in a fortnight to Dr Griswolds at Fryburgh[5] for two or 3 weeks—or if I did not stay there at Conway where solitude more deep & scenery more beautifull cannot be had. If he should like Conway I should hope to see him some times at F. 2 or 3 miles distant—where I am urged to visit. If he comes here & looks round a little & then follows me why their feelings can't be hurt as they shall know nothing of your letter & my proposal. I am very timid about them finding it so difficult to please. Does T. W. H. think I meant to remove for good? His Father said when he returned the place would be purchased   I merely assented—& had expressed in his absence once a wish to board else where as the noise of Phebe's family was bro't on me without the least consultation of my comfort or knowledge.[6] But she has lately moved. And tho I should like the interest to feed myself instead of boarding with them I care little about it—but if you could learn their expectations without my appearing to wish it I should be glad. Could I not have a ratable life annuity? I never noticed your kind invitations because I never dreamt of going. Whatever attends my nest[n] it is safe from the ills of wandering. I am getting stronge & love to be out of sight—but not so well as when in low health—yet as I need a change & perhaps a future home am going to F. It would be a relief to Sister to be alone she *thinks* I do believe. It would to me if I were her. I told T. W. if he had ever mentioned any thing to your house to show you the few lines I sent him when you last went. He is like to the Reed planter. They are all good natured now   And I found Phebe very clever.

I expect an answer to this w'h will govern my movements about the minister. Some years since I boarded very well at Conway for him & am sure of finding space any[n] where among the mountains or Vallies if I were not a little like the old prisoner. But this *must* be a secret. Let them do as they like

MH: bMS Am 1280.226(708). *Addressed:* Mr Charles C Emerson / Boston / Mss. *Postmarked:* 1832.

nest] *possibly* rest
any] *possibly* every

1. CCE to MME, 30–31 May 1832, writes that he is distressed by recent political events (probably the triumph of Jacksonianism at the first national Democratic convention plus continued dubious actions concerning Native Americans) and meditated on "being ferried over 'that grim flood which poets talk of,' " but he also desired to "*do*" something "before that human consummation" (MT/MH).

2. In Byron's poem, the prisoner of Chillon (François de Bonnivard) suffered years of imprisonment in a lightless cell for his religious beliefs before his release; Italian poet Torquato Tasso (1544–95) suffered in an asylum for seven years. See [W. H. Prescott], "Italian Narrative Poetry," *North American Review* 19 (Oct. 1824): 337–89.

3. CCE to MME, 30–31 May, reports RWE's response to problems of the "commonwealth moral or political": " 'I will not enter into a compact with any body that I will not steal.' He would shake the yoke of Institutions and venerable forms, from the mind, as hindering it from seeing & fulfilling its own duties" (MT/MH).

4. No mention of RWE's planned journey in CCE to MME, 30–31 May (last page missing); CCE to WE[3], 18 June [1832], says RWE plans to leave for Waterford on Friday (22 June) and that CCE has not decided whether he will accompany him.

5. Oliver Griswold, M.D., practiced in Fryeburg, Maine, from 1798 until his death in 1833; he married a daughter of William Fessenden, the Congregational minister in Fryeburg. MME boarded with the Griswolds for the first half of 1833.

6. Possibly the family of niece Phebe Haskins Chamberlain, married in 1824.

To Ralph Waldo Emerson

Sab Noon 15 [July 1832]

I have done wrong to speake as tho' it were possible in your present state of opinion & "aversion" you could (tho' the people knew them) break that emblem of life & nurture. I was dazzled by your presence—degraded by the love of your office & situation— My solitude opens far distant views—& would see you climbing the hieghts of salvation thro' the lonely roads of what appears to you truth & duty. If truth has demanded this exposure of your sentiments—will she not a thousand times stronger for the publick demand adherance? Yet hope faints that time may meet you in socratism &&cc & finding all insuficient return you to truth in the arbitrary appointments dogmat. theology[n] as well as in the natural voice of Jesus. "Why this opinion? The first w'h is retracted was as gratuitous as the last." It was my fate to err— tis mine to retract—'tis yours to pardon. T'was Charles, who knows how to state questions, who led me from my right simple path, by saying this was tenable ground. I then thought it ground w'h laid beyond my ken— It may— & if I hear of your holding it with all it's priviledges of place & tithe shall not grapple—but queitly wait till we meet in stronger vision

Have the kindness to show this to CC. I came on as I hoped to get to F. & found the last statment of invite at Mrs —[1] to be the truth rather than the first. And they did right.

Farwell if for aye—never will the belief of your defeat in the best attainments finally, forsake the affectionate & now more than ever disinterested Aunt

MME

Pray dont have any thing said to Thomas but of peace. *Let them place themselves without a direction.*

MH: bMS Am 1280.226(889). *Addressed:* Rev. R. Waldo Emerson / Expected at N Conway / Should this be forgotten please to have / it sent me to Fryeburgh. / Care of Miss S. A Hanover. *Endorsed:* Miss M M Emerson / X July 1832 / On Second Church.

appointments dogmat. theology] appointments ↑ dogmat. theology ↓

1. Probably Mrs. Griswold.

To Ezra Ripley

Vale   Waterford   July 31 [1832]

Honored & Dear Sir,

Your letter, of May last, was gratifying—so much of interesting narration that I favored our friends with it at the Hill,[1] and cannot recur to it as I now wish. But other subjects induce me to write by an opportunity which gives me but a very little time. I have been looking for a letter from you on the situation of our beloved Waldo. I am grieved at the step he has taken—tho' I respect, in no common measure, the fidelity to his conscience which induced it. And if in a temporal view he should have long cause to feel it's privations, we know that every sacrifice to truth and one's convictions will be amply rewarded. What will he do? What is best? I have not heard from him since he returned as they do not know that I have finished my little routes—and I have not had time to write—besides we expect Ralph Haskins with letters this week. Mr Emerson of Baldwin carried me from Fryeburgh to his house where I found a pleasant hostess, and him a sensible man.[2] He honors Waldo's conduct and thinks that many others would do the same if their consciences were as tender. I maintained that the unitarians of the old school were the only xians who could best commemorate the ministry of Jesus—and that I could see no possible objection to the mere humanitarian doing it with the utmost respect— He thinks it invidious to select *one man* for such long continued honor as this rite implies. I only wished that I could have given what I believed your opinions & respect for this ordinance better than I did. In any questions of the present day I prefer giving others views than my own, as well for the athority as to keep mine to myself. Yet on this ritual subject I have no doubt.[n] That it is abused by protestants sometimes for a cloak and by others for a test of xianianity is no argument against its' importance if considered only as a invaluable evidence of the historical kind.

How is your health this season and that of all our Concord friends? Have there been any expectation or fears of the Cholera in the Town? If it comes it's errand will be eventually good if it comes from the Auther of all causes and effects which are beyond human controul. Your gout Sir will produce a certificate against all other diseases— And to me it will become the long desired friend which is to exchange ignorance for knowledge and frailty & sin for strenght & virtue, thro' the rich mercy of our great Provider. How ·do my Brother & Sister and their children? My love to them, Deacon and Miss Ripley and any who may remember their and your affectionate & your dutious

M M Emerson.

I have no time to send the respects &c &c in their order

MH: bMS Am 1280.220(76). *Addressed:* Rev. E. Ripley D. D. / Concord / Mss. *Postmarked:* South Waterford / August 3, 1832. *Endorsed:* Miss M. M. Emerson July 31 / answered Augt 6th.

doubt.] *possibly* doubts

1. Rydal Mount (named for Wordsworth's home), or the Hill, home of the Gages in South Waterford; according to tradition, it was named by MME.

2. Noah Emerson (1787–1860) was a younger brother of Reuben Emerson. A graduate of Middlebury College (1814) and Andover Theological Seminary (1817), he served as Congregational minister at Baldwin, Maine, from 1825 to 1850. According to the family genealogy, he "dissipated his own estate and his wife's fortune in a mission to the negroes in Jamaica"; he then separated from his wife and became a missionary to the Indians on the Shinnacook Reservation on Long Island, New York (*IpsE*, 212–13).

To Charles Chauncy Emerson

Vale   Au. 5 [1832] Sab M.

I long to hear from you my dear Charles & from Waldo.

For the first time I seem to apprehend that by the lines of Wordsworth

For adoration Thou endurest; endure,
For *consciousness the motions of thy will*
For apprehension These transcendant truths &c[1]

indicate those motions to constitute our consciousness. Glorious beam of light—but I fear I'm not intelligible—but 'tis to you—or if you get at my feeling—perhaps I mistake my poets mysticism for the real high romance of our existence! This *consciousness* w'h is our all & all—the agency—the seed of immortality to be but the *motions* of His will—! and our own will & virtue free as we wish it carrying on His plans whether in spreading light from youthfull genius or nothing in adoring age! And how can any scepticism lurk—? And of a bible w'h meets all our wants & describes every sin & woe?

I wrote after the absence of a month on returning—& of you & W— & impressions suceeded[n] by W. Erving[n] at Fryburgh & of all such gossip—but hearing of Olivia's death & business like such letter would not have met my respect for your sympathy with poor dear George nor the loss of a personal friend as she was to you all.[2] Happy woman in life—happier to escape its' stale & weary ills. In those sunless realms how like the shawdow of the butterfly will be all the objects in w'h she ever took an intense interest—   Yet there how colossal appear the consequence of all our insect winged pursuits. But emotions are fading while the tremor attends the pen—   So I'll quiet all down by going to the Chapel in the wood   Night. Yours by R.H. came this morn. Grieved to hear that Waldo has lost the fine health & even bloom w'h he had in the mountains—& before I had his history by you of the rest of a journey w'h interested so many mountaneers & myself. Yes, likely he leaves the pulpit. And what is best for the cause of xianity—for the whole is best for him   Torches not light for themselves.[3] Others may be led to prize more the symbols of an everlasting feast—may learn to disrobe the institution of remaining corruptions w'h prevail among the ignorant. And he himself free from ties to forms & instruction may find the Angel who can best unite him to the Infinite—may find in the religion of a solitary imajanation that nearer to the heart. without bating but adding to the respect of his reason   But your observation is best & needed no more. That you may both have health is my desire. Your return to "prospects" is gladning. Go onward in the love of God & rejoice

MME

MH: bMS Am 1280.226(710).

suceeded] *illegible; T reads* made (*but too many strokes present*)

Erving] *illegible*; serving *or* being *possible alternative readings*

1. Wordsworth, *The Excursion*, book 4 (1814): "Despondency Corrected," lines 94–96.

2. Olivia Buckminster Emerson, wife of GBE, died 10 July 1832.

3. Cf. Shakespeare, *Measure for Measure*, 1.1.32–33.

To Charles Chauncy Emerson

Vale   Au 7 [1832]

Why my dear Charles (whose fine eyes & life have performed some of the disgust of Walter's children if ever you got my last) I did not dream of mentioning 1100# to any one—but in answer to your saying Whitman & you found the place mine I felt it was no discovery & that in selling I should give up my right to their wants.[1] But never dreamt of doing it without nessesity. I gave for the Pollard place what another man was to, for the sake of housing a destitute family   loath enough to—just so mean then—   And I wished to be benefited—and took an engag^t from Br. R. that I should share the profits of its future sale—this I tore up at his first discontent—but knew the farm to be mine as justly as my shoes. The lease you found gave me doubts—that was given probably for some pieces of land w'h did not belong to Mr Ralph—and have proved to be those I gave a quit claim off. With my convictions I was surprised to hear as by accident that the place had been put to sale & refused 2200. Sure enough I said without my wishes. H—h said you proposed it— I only said I did not remember wishing for any thing but the interest to board myself or at Fryburgh but it was perfectly well and that the offer was beyond my expectation. Indeed it is a miraculous offer & if Mr H. had been sane or wished to sell he would have taken it. For me it is better as I had no roof tree provided in the sale and it w^d irk my little mind to give 1200 to one who is no otherwise. To lose is one thing—to throw away voluntarily is worse. Then your letter unriddled the cause of Thomas' urging the sale. But the disgust was on my part. What has your "discovery" done? Riveted in the possesors mind & Chamberlains that it is only as a mortage & the latter wished H—h said to move in & help pay it off. There is a fine possesion—   Can niether sell nor improve it. Now my dear dear Charles allow me this retort—   And be convinced that where there is such insanity, w'h his wife so speaks of to H—h, there can be no use in conviction." Providence can only assort the thing. Let it rest—and he said yesterday when I was hoping Chamberlain would go to Mr Ladds, that he was to stay here—spoke with disdain of selling—that in the spring Mr Perly of B.[2] was to let him have the money & take mortage. That I replied was time enough. Nothing more has ever passed. It is very natural for him to forget the different tone he used the first years—how pleased that I did not assume the name of Owner & how pleased at my gift of the land   And that now he only dwells on his purchase of the Pollard farm for w'h he gave 2500 & for which his brother paid I believe & will not sell till he can get the same. To argue would be to rob him like the Athenian. The place is not so good as when I bo't it, & can not, till great changes, be expected to fetch the above sum. I gave up the wood lot & a farm is not estimated much without one. Some future years when experience & athority shall enable you to force a sale it would be well to do if they would be benefited for I question if ever Perly takes it—and at least it will be a good place for me to rot in.

When I see you I hate to interrupt a reverie or lose a thought so I've never explained myself. If you have thought me more forgetfull of the cents than I am—tis well to be endured for if we are immortal you would read the deceit if ever you stooped to converse with the obscure—if not what avails *character*?

Do do come here if sickness prevails.[3] I shall forget that I ever repine at losing any toly" sacrifice to others who are so embarressed that nothing lifts"

Adieu this dolorous epistle sickens me only that I am in better spirits in body & that I only repeat what I told you both that I was easy. privations" are my element—& less than I deserve probably   Adieu

most affectionately MME

I told you the *why* Judge White undertook to look after annuity some time agone. I beg you to say nothing to T.W.   *Time* will convince them best that it was a mistake of yours to lessen my claims & that I must have a roof or consideration

Roberts Lucretia comes next week[4]   Do send my MMS & letter from you   You will not understand that I do not wish to sell to my advantage—but it can't be now

MH: bMS Am 1280.226(711). *Addressed:* Mr Charles C. Emerson / Boston, Mss / Care of Rev. R. W. Emerson. *Postmarked:* South Waterford / August 8 1832. *Endorsed (outside):* Aug. 1832 / Respecting Farm &c. (*inside*): M.M.E. / Aug 7 / 1832.

conviction.] ⟨doubt⟩ ↑ conviction ↓.

toly] *possibly* ⟨to⟩ by

lifts] lifts ⟨up.⟩ (up. *possibly smeared rather than canceled*)

privations] ⟨Trials⟩ privations

1. This is one of several letters written during the spring and summer of 1832 on the subject of MME's ownership of the Elm Vale property. Charles Whitman practiced law in Waterford and nearby Norway from 1817 to 1837 and often served as town clerk.

2. Possibly Thomas Perley of Bridgton, who married Charlotte Hale.

3. CCE to MME, 16 Aug. 1832, responds to her invitation with details about the cholera outbreak in Boston (MT/MH); CCE to EzR, 9 Aug. 1832, mentions RWE's illness along with the "general indisposition" and outbreaks of "sudden distempers," which "seem to indicate that we are breathing the same infected atmosphere that has carried disease round the globe" (MT/MH).

4. Nephew Robert Haskins married Lucretia Childs in May 1833.

To Charles Chauncy Emerson

Sep 29 [1832] Sat   Vale

I hope to get better by writing w'h a want of my glasses urges. Please hasten Ralph H. to send them—he was to fix the rims & said he could send them any week. And ask his bill. Hope you will have better offices—not more charitable ones perhaps. Tonight my dear Charles I hope a letter from you—the best remedy for the palsy bro't on by reading Byrons life this afternoon.[1] Take it up ever so well it depresses. E. Peabody sent me a long long letter some time since—mostly of the history of breaking up care of her family &c   I never read it but once & cant find out well the name to whose care I must direct. * * * I was provoked at her apoligies & thinking I had urged her to write. I would not do it for the sake of gaining more than she appears able to give. She also thinks that finding a freshness of existence in my age has influenced her to get rid of many cares &ccc   A letter of interest from S.A.R. the answer to w'h I hardly think worth while to send—   So stale & profitless is all externals but the sight of nature in her solemn altitudes." To hear from Waldo would invite other thoughts—tho congenial to her prophecies. Do tell of Sarah's health. Your Mother I rejoice to hear from   Father is better. He wrote an almost complete duplicate of what he had written some weeks before—chiefly about Waldo. I wish he would send his letters to your care instead of post.

Sab. Morn. 30. Art thou well—thine eye is in its' full orb & thy bones well moistened?[2] I trust it. And that as yet canst say nought of the brother— And shall you ever say he is an heresiarch? Surely he was not formed for one. Waldo his name sake[3] was not. The various orders we hear off in other worlds are none. His name will already go with Chh history? Would it were your lot to innovate—to curtail the corruptions of your profession—to uncowl the mendicant class of your order. And when every thing is done by way of probation what will man exist for? Or why these means? Perfection of existence? Oh why not at first? Is it to give zest to the future—or was there somthing like nessecity in the nature of things in some part of universe w'h needed all these means to give beings the sole desirable possession of life—knowing God? If I remember D. Stewart thinks fatalism the same whether existing with or without a Deity. Was there ever so gross & ungodlike a thought in so good a man! Did he ever know the consciousness of believing in the divine presence? Decrees (w'h end the same as fatalism) of God are at the root of all faith— such as connect virtue & happiness finally—of limiting virtue itself & human knowledge. And were we mortal by such decree how grand to that of atoms. But this is deceptive—we never could feel this grandeur were we not related to Him beyond the present. Could we arrive at the ultimate (or *chief* as Edwards would say) end of our being[4] without so many subordinate ones! Not ask with the traders what is the use—the *utilities*—but know by experimental philosphy that to admire the beautifull & love the good is enough.

I shall send this by chance tomorrow—for you never refuse to give when I ask. And besides church affairs tell if every man is not insane who believes in a personal God & doubts his immortality?

May that portion of the holy Ghost w'h is accorded you diffuse over you an increase of wisdom & joy prays

ME

I had yours a fortnight since & the bill   Have committed your account of Waldos sermon[5] to memory by repeating it to those who saw you. E B E must leave me a letter & when he is alone I'll do the same

MH: bMS Am 1280.226(714). *Addressed:* Charles C. Emerson / Care of Rev R. W. Emerson / Boston / Mss / Forward by / Mr Paine. *Postmarked:* LOWELL, MASS. / Oct. 5.

altitudes] sic *in MS; possibly* attitudes *intended*

1. Probably *Letters and Journals of Lord Byron: With Notices of His Life*, ed. Thomas Moore (London, 1830), which was widely reviewed and extensively quoted.

2. Possible allusion to Ezek. 37:4, "O ye dry bones, hear the word."

3. Cornelius Waldo, father of Rebecca Waldo who married Edward Emerson of Newbury in the seventeenth century (great-grandparents of MME).

4. Possibly Jonathan Edwards's "Dissertation on the End for Which God Created the World," *Works*, 10 vols. (New York, 1830), 3:93–157.

5. CCE to MME, 13 Sept. 1832, reports RWE's preaching his "opinions" (on the Last Supper) to his congregation on 9 Sept. and his letter to the church asking "a dismission" (MT/MH).

To CHARLES CHAUNCY EMERSON

Vale   Oct. 3 [1832] Wed.

After a long visit from the pseudo C.C. & conning over the resemblance to the dear C.C., I can't but say *how do you* do? Else I don't seem to have much to say—tho' this patmos season,[1] which would make a soul out of the very ribs of desolation—is soothing—& dwelling on the soul—& yet so blending with the soul that to give it a local habitation were to dispell the charm. "All this to me who say as fine things, as even the poets & philosophers, about nature & solitude, who have come so brave thro' ages"?[2] Yes Sir, for your last letter was posing the subtleties &c &c of going into socity this winter—that is the close of it—& to find the letter itself, amid the ransacking of putting up & burning papers, I can't at this hour. Else I should find so redeeming things as to lose the scent of stuffed drawing rooms—effeminate beaus & displaying bells—images which at some weary descending suns attend the leaden visage of time—tis in vain his grisly finger points me to the withered leaves w'h whirl in his path, and to the changed course of the planets— I beheld him but closing a season w'h is to bring one of artificial scenes & characters in lieu of natural delights & pursuits. Yet what has the past season to boast in the genial climes of the South? Alas, his wings[n] are folded & he is shrouded in gloom & mystery—& on the skirts of his robe are the red traces of woe from afar and nigh. Where & when would you visit—the selfish—the gay, in exterior—the literary, in mouthing?— These are surely visible in the ominous Allegory—hardly have a sustenance in his lower parts. Yet associate—fasten the human ties on rare spirits—if it be possible—add to Waldo, others who shall bring forward Time, such as he appears in some bright thrilling morning. His wings are unfurled—liberty & peace & plenty are on them—genius in all its wide dominions hover on his plumes—nations surround him from every wind of Heaven—the laughing African & the stern savage shelter at his feathery feet—and feel the one great influence from the morning star, who has descended & overshadowed the collosius with an halo that beckons on to a perfect day.

But to some triter things w'h apply generally but particularly to the Emersonian constitution. In society you are tempted to a contempt of others—with the excitment of the scene you lose the philosophical veiws w'h show the whole drama filled with the same nature in different habits—and so far from dispising—one becomes like a leaf of the forest a part of the whole—can constantly behold ignorance bigotry & deformity without sympathy or contempt—but with pity & faith. Besides & more than this—your sense of the ludicrous—your wit impels a wish to entertain—*to please* (the universal law) but dangerous—if you would do all or any thing you kindle at in menial hours. Let the tough hided youth go & be as superior to the sensitive as he likes—this assertiveness is related to morals & it grows & blooms in proper places till ripe for better ones.[n] I respect *their* hides—also suppose Webster to be one. Oh probably a more nice & effeminate ambition? Did you *respect* him on the late publick occasion you were kind enough to mention?

In looking for your lost letter I read one of Waldo's which is very true in the following "How do men's seasons of thinking answer the division of Parnassus. One day is a ballad another an epic with many an episode to high & soft recollections, a third a dull commentary on the poets 1827"[3]

Farewell dear Charles & write soon & long

to the *most solitary*[n] MME

MH: bMS Am 1280.226(715). *Addressed:* Mr C. C. Emerson / Boston / If absent Rev R W Emerson.

wings] ⟨leaden⟩ wings

ones.] ⟨occupations⟩ ↑ ones ↓ .

solitary] underlined twice

1. Patmos is the Aegean island where Saint John experienced the vision recorded in *Revelation*; hence, transferred epithet meaning "divine" or "heavenly."

2. Unlocated in CCE to MME, 13 and 20 Sept. 1832; other allusions indicate MME is responding to a letter written about 27 Sept., which does not survive.

3. See RWE to MME, 17 and 22 Aug. 1827 (*L* 1:209); MME's transcription fills in several lacunae in the Rusk text.

To Charles Chauncy Emerson

Sat. Night   Oct 13 '32

And is it so my dear Charles, have you taken station as a man of business?[1] To me, how little besides the change of seasons has taken place, since you were toddling thro Court St with as calm and superior an eye as tho' the busy world were only a path way. Oh happy reckless childhood. Here lies Schillers Ideal[2]—it is ever with me when I enter the young mans career. War! what do I think of it—why in your ear I think it is so much better than oppression that if it were ravaging the whole monarchial world it would be an omen of high & glorious import. Channing paints it's miseries[3]—but does he know those of a worser war—private animosities—pinching bitter warfare of the human heart—the cruel oppression of the poor by the rich w'h corrupts old worlds   How much better are blood & conflagration. They are but the letting blood which corrupts. What would the popolare nations have been had there been no outlets? Be sure had some visible Angel descended & swept away the nuisances it might have saved the corruptions w'h follow war among the morals of a people. But then there would have been no Adams' or Washingtons. What sublime & generous victims has war br't forth in private & publick. What would history be but a pale faced monotony—the publick mind a stagnant pool & the earth a dung yard. A war trump would be harmony to the jars of theologians & statsmen such as the papers bring. It was the glory of the chosen people—nay it is said there was war in Heaven. So good night & burn burn this scrool which shall presently reach you or I shall burn it over & over   15   I could do nothing but write the eve. I had yours   And gave my word it should go. And tho' this war is a terrible argument against conscience' divinity—yet it is not so violated as in private. And if you tell me of the miseries of the field with the sensitive Channing (of whose love of life I am ashamed) why what of a few days of agony—& what of a Vulture being the bier tomb & parson of a hero, compared to the long years of stiking on a bed & wished away! Of the widows & orphans—   Oh I could give facts of the long drawn years of imprisoned minds & hearts w'h uneducated orphans endure. But it is among the means of discipline and no worse than other warfare with poverty and ill & ignorance.

This "Characteristics"—this morbid diseased writer gives me to suffer more than the expectation of the wars of Gog and May Gog—[4] Here there is niether rest in Heaven earth or hell—hope or dispair. A terrible caricature of the enigmatical style of Richter & Coleridge & German rant. Besides it is just as you are setting out this daubing of the age. And is it in any sense true? And your civil & paper *war* is to be maintained thro' the brightest days of youth! Why I had read of nothing but the enlightenings of the age & improvements? But if times were ten times darker those who believe in the bible God are firm—they expect trial—the very thing man is here for. They judge from what they know of the divine character—from "His noble conceptions of nature & redemption" that a winding sheet of glory will intomb the virtuous—that every accident will find its' use in the prescience of the Planner and every evil but what is voluntary terminate well at the denoument of the whole. A comet in the east has preceded your commenced career.[n] And may your course be as bright and your object more distant than his. Commend me to Waldo. His position so novel—why do I not hear more of him? Sarah talks about him as[n] the bird of Jove at w'h the crows craw[5]—& the apostle of the eternal reason. But what she means I know not by this reason. She is on a chaos without pilot or helm. If she is well, as God grant, send her my letter after sealing. And rectify the 66 my mistake to MRE[n] if you have not paid her. There were but 4/ 2⅝. Love to my Sister & that her health will be every way improved & Waldo's by this temporary loss. Write soon. I talk of boarding else where as family arrangments desire but I shall let you know when

Your aff[t] MME

If I need not acknowledge that paper called a will I may sign it.[6] I forget Edwards remembrance & seem to dislike no mention of William so exclusive. Better take E B's & put to the unappropriated 100? He is full of busines?

MH: bMS Am 1280.226(716 & 738). *Addressed:* Charles Chauncy Emerson Esq[r]. *Endorsed:* MME / to / CCE / "Characteristics."

preceded . . . career] ⟨announced⟩ ↑ preceded ↓ your ↑ commenced ↓ career
talks about him as] ⟨calls⟩ ↑ talks about ↓ him ↑ as ↓
MRE] *possibly* MER (*written over undeciphered word*)

1. Possibly a response to CCE to MME, 8 and 10 Oct. 1832 (MH), although neither this comment about business nor anything about war appears in the letter as it survives; the top and bottom thirds of the second leaf have been torn away.

2. Title of Schiller's poem on "the loss of youth . . . of that enthusiasm and innocent purity of thought peculiar to early age" (de Staël, *Germany* 1:345).

3. WEC's first discourse "War" (*Works*, 642–53), preached in Boston in 1816. South Carolina's "nullifiers" saw the new tarrifl bill passed by Congress in the summer of 1832 as a deliberate challenge to states' rights; in Nov. South Carolina declared the act null and void and threatened to secede from the Union; President Jackson responded with military preparations at Forts Moultrie and Sumter.

4. Thomas Carlyle, "Characteristics," a review of Thomas Hope, *An Essay on the Origin and Prospect of Man* (London, 1831), and Friedrich Schlegel, *Philosophische Vorlesungen* (Vienna, 1830), *Edinburgh Review* 54 (Dec. 1831): 351–83. Carlyle sees the scientific and analytical habit of the modern mind as a symptom of disease. Ezek. 38–39 prophesies that the leader Gog will come from the land of Magog and attack Israel; Rev. 20:8 also warns of Gog and Magog.

5. SBR to MME, 4 Sept. 183[2], says of RWE that, though "we regard him still

more than ever as the apostle of the eternal reason, . . . we do not like to hear the crows, as Pindar says, caw at the bird of Jove" (MCR-S).

6. CCE to MME, 20 Sept. 1832, states that he is sending a new will he has drawn up for her and instructs her to sign it in the presence of three witnesses (MT/MH).

To Sarah Bradford Ripley

Oct 15. '32   Vale.

I did not say how frightened I was to hear of your illness dear Sarah for I feel that you have a sort of immortality w'h sickness can't make head against.[1] And by this time you are well as Charles has erased his lament and Father wrote lately to the Hill. No, you will live I hope & trust, many years— Long enough surely to settle your great question about the original nature of conscience.[2] And I will venture to give you the answer of unlearned nature, to w'h the great *seem* fond of recurring. Why it seems almost insane to doubt it to those who believe in spiritualism. Unless every thing is artificial—or foreign & the divine agency causes the moral as well as the material elements to *appear*. And then the fanatical conversions would be allowed, w'h would sadly disturb the mystic delights of the mere recipients of the phenomena, and how otherwise, if conscience is raised on transient scaffoldings and not a divine turnpike to its' Auther? I believe your very Germans hold the contrary, tho' they have lost the compass w'h directs it's source. "Sir James leans" indeed, and will fall as a moralist—for his very arguments of the unity & universality of conscience make against him. And when he opens the door to light, it is like a child who fears a spirit and hopes some grown person will come & finish the business by opening it wide.

You like his praising the good David.[3] I like him for exposing his crimes, after w'h he ought to call him a cold hearted Frog who cast up a deal of dirt with some fine ways of speculating. How farcical the disinterested affections and all else without an Original author. "And how futile your complaints & trite remarks"   Well they can't offend one of your attitude. Nor is it from fear of Hume, for he shows the fallacy of reason in a way to neutralize all his religious harlotery. His old name Sake[4] never caused so foul adultery. But I forbear Hume, & do respect Sir James memory with for others respect. But what can a historian of ethics mean, if he dont revert to the immutable nature of truth? And where is the pledge to be found if not innate in man. Revelation doubted—devotion itself (grown on that by its' likeness[n]) fitfull & weather bound—where would every thing civil & humane be but for the stern divinity w'h keeps on the throne against wind & tide? Is it not as "eternal" as the "reason" you thus name? Tho for my life I dont know what you mean by the term—as you say nothing sattisfies imajanation but conceptions of the Soul of the universe. Is it Plato's plastic nature—christianed by Cudworth?[5] But was this the Being on whom the pious heathen reposed himself in awfull admiration? Surely not—nor that which your noble nature aspires to, when you say how can finite conceive of infinite. Now hear the simple query. Have I not clear consciousness of a few numbers w'h you can carry beyond my dazzled view—& your own imajanation. Are these less real than those?

This Soul w'h is to sattisfy so inferior a power in *you* as imajanation must be of a very *subjective* nature? I like better the antient mythology of the Germans w'h was so fancifull, and yet had real objects & palaces, than the present so full of Fitchianism. Persuaded that revelation of the oral or action, and that within gives us to know there are affections exclusively for a God I believe all other parts of our econymy are but subordinate to this first relation. And you my female idol & oracle in the great world of intellect, will find at some happy day, your relation to Him thro the medium of your humblest virtues better than all high abstractions or bold generalisations. To show the inefficacy of these, your torch may have been light for a time on places to w'h the humble can only reach an admiring gaze.

I have rid myself of the ill effects of the "characterists"[6] a little—but I may not perceive that he is orthodox for old truths. I only run it thro' last eveg. And he seemed like a lunatic in a lazar house knocking every one down that retained any "consciousness" or pretention of any kind. If indeed our poor planet is running wild he can never regulate its time? Love to my brother & the children and your whole original stock. It is good to hear Dr B[7] is returning to his proper element. Your Sister

MME

MH: bMS Am 1280.226(1284). *Addressed:* Mrs S. Alden Ripley / Waltham / Miss S. R. Haskins.

likeness] *illegible; possibly* heresies, Reviews, *or* Powers

1. CCE to MME, 20 Sept. 1832, reports that SBR had been "attacked with hemmorhage some three weeks since" and, though she remained far from well, was recovering (MT/MH). SBR to MME, 4 Sept. 183[2], minimizes her illness as a "slight cough attended with a little spitting of blood" (MCR-S). Throughout her letter, MME quotes from and refers to SBR's letter.

2. SBR to MME, 4 Sept. 183[2], expresses her disappointment in "Sir James, [as] the only question to me of philosophical interest in Ethics is whether the moral element be original or acquired"—a question he does not answer, "though it is evident to which side he leans" (MCR-S). Sir James Mackintosh, *A General View of the Progress of Ethical Philosophy, Chiefly during the Seventeenth and Eighteenth Centuries* (Philadelphia, 1832), rpt. in Mackintosh's *Miscellaneous Works* (New York, 1873) as "A Dissertation on the Progress . . ." (94–198), the source for my citations.

3. Mackintosh discusses Hume in the "Dissertation" (*Miscellaneous Works*, 139).

4. Probably Old Testament King David (cf. similar use of "namesake" to mean the person for whom one is named in MME to CCE, 29 Sept. 1832).

5. For " 'eternal' . . . name?" see MME to CCE, 13 Oct. 1832, n. 5. Ralph Cudworth (1617–88), professor of Hebrew at Emmanuel College, Cambridge, was a leading Cambridge Platonist. In *The True Intellectual System of the Universe*, Cudworth de-

scribes the position of the "Platonic Christian" and argues for the "independence of the intellect upon sense." His most original theory concerns a " 'plastic nature,' [which] provoked a famous controversy. The doctrine, which has some resemblance to modern philosophies of the 'Unconscious' was intended to meet the dilemma of mere chance on one hand, or a constant divine interference on the other" (*DNB*). RWE owned the four-volume London edition (1820); my quotations are from the two-volume Andover edition (1838).

6. See MME to CCE, 13 Oct. 1832, n. 4.
7. Probably Dr. Josiah Bartlett of Concord, SBR's physician and brother-in-law.

1833

To Charles Chauncy Emerson

Fryeburgh   Jan 8 1833.

My dear Charles,

The "coming" year will be one of uncommon importance to you I should think. To judge by the events of your family there is much to fear. But if you are designed for the promotion of good to others your success will be inevitable. As well might the flight of the eagle be arrested by the vapour beneath his feet—or the ocean stayed by the grains of sand on its shores as the soul devoted to God be defeated of it's sucess.

Still I am sad while I write. It is like—it is far sader than the translation of a soul by death of the body to lose Waldo as I have lost him. And now that he is far far away I can complain.[1] I do believe he has no fixed faith in a personal God! His letters have been confused & dark—a mixture of heathen greatness—of worse than antient good heathenism—pantheism—Swedenborganism—hypothesies of nature & german rationalism. And *yet yet* you talk of his being a "*reformer* & needing good health." A reformer! and beginn at the wrong end? annuling a simple rite w'h has bound the followers of Jesus together for ages & announced his resurrection! A reformer—who on earth with his genius is less able to cope with opposition? Who with his good sense less *force* of mind—and while it invents new universes is lost in the surrounding halo of his own imajanation. No. He never loved his holy offices—and it is well he has left them. Yet hope points to his conversion & return to his pen. These complaints are not merely for their own sake. You who can so well state questions and see with the eyes of society—and have adhered to the only sure revelation—*why* did you not become his counsellor & influence his destiny? *You*, who would hasten to that ordinance have you lost all respect for it—cease to see in it the "*utility*" to the vulgar (to speake of its baser purposes) and the weight of historical evidence to the inquirer? It is unfortunate for Waldo if we consider him as taking a higher ground for truth

& spirituality than the Channings & Lowels & Wares.[2] He has been called to give no test of possessing the capasity for great virtues more than others who live in the bosom of peace & plenty. But I forbear & crave pardon— had other feelings & brighter possessed me I had written before. But I follow your precious Mother driven from her sweet home— I see the vendue—the "breakfast table" itself sold & the house filled with the hollow and frivolous. But these partial sights are lost some times in painfull & greater ones. I hear the papers read & the ominous voice of Mr Hurd relating the miseries of man. Tell me of your feelings & pursuits. Glad you are with George.[3] Tell me the names & characters of your competitors in law & of all great things. Judge Danna often inquires the character &c of City folks I can give no answer. Miss Danna told Mrs G. that at Concord N. H. she heard Waldo had sued for Ellen's property.[4] I thought not. Will he get it? *When is William wedding?*[5] How is E Bli. in his *no world*? How are the Haskins? Commend me kindly to Hannah (not exclusively) & tell her to write me. * * * Every day I use less of fire & somthing than is pleasant—so that I feel strange^n in demanding all dues from debtors. It is enough if I continue to struggle with the journey of life with patience without any other accomplishment. *How* can you send me C—s sermons?[6] I want them *very* much but more to hear of your prosperity, prospects, private & publick—most of all the faith & fervor of your heart w'h is indeed included in private & publick prospects

Farewell dear dear Charles left alone in your own native place may God accord you to benefit as well as ornament it prays night & day

MME.

MH: bMS Am 1280.226(721). *Addressed:* Charles C. Emerson Esqr. / 17 Court Street / Boston / Mss. *Postmarked:* Fryeburg Me / Jan 9th. *Endorsed:* M. M. E. / X Jan. 1833. / Waldo.

strange] *possibly* stronge

1. RWE resigned his pastorate in Oct.; in search of health, on 25 Dec. he sailed for Malta, where he arrived on 2 Feb. 1833. MME to WE[3], 16 Feb. 1833, summed up her losses: "Waldo's misfortune in the death of Ellen—his leaving—his people—and now his land have been sad sad disappointments to me" (MH: 1073).

2. Three well-known Boston ministers: WEC, at Federal Street Church, 1803–42; Charles Lowell, at West Church, 1806–61; Henry Ware, Jr., at Second Church, 1817–30.

3. CCE to MME, 10 Dec. [1832], tells of the Emerson family's breaking up house-keeping at the Chardon Street house, where RWE and RHE had remained since Ellen's death: RHE went to Newton to stay with her sister Mary Ladd; RWE traveled to Europe; and CCE went to GBE's, a "melancholy" "abode," following the deaths of GBE's wife and infant son (CCE to WE[3], 19 Jan. [1833], MT/MH). Other letters in Jan. 1833 tell of the auction of the family "chattels"—furniture, glass, brass, and so forth. MME seems to connect these events with the period when RHE was forced to move from the Summer Street parsonage following her husband's death.

4. Judge Judah Dana (d. 1845) of Fryeburg; probably Mrs. Oliver Griswold. What

MME has heard rumored is old news: RWE's problems with gaining his share of the
Tucker estate are recorded in family correspondence beginning in May 1831 (*L* 1:323).

5. CCE to MME, 16 Aug. 1832, told of WE[3]'s recent engagement to Susan Woodward Haven, daughter of a Portsmouth, N.H., merchant. "The family are highly
respectable & the father . . . is wealthy— . . . Susan is very good . . . — but not
handsome" (MT/MH).

6. Probably WEC's *Discourses* (Boston, 1832).

To CHARLES CHAUNCY EMERSON

Frye   Feb. 10   Sab.   '33

My dear Charles

Your dear letter [1] was written in one of the holiest attitudes of w'h youthfull human nature is able to ascend—   Oh if they are illusive—thus let us live
& die & rise where illusion is no more. The love of others better now seems
the criterion of true virtue—loving God for his own sake.

Have you time or taste for theolo. reading? The July & Oct. No's of Biblical. R. are well worth your time. In one of them is contained—"that we
shrink at human nature being a partaker of the throne of the U."[2] Now this
to me argues against their trinitarism. The Arian shrinks not that the God
of the universe is able to delegate a power w'h is astonishing (not like some
other articles of theism) but not contradictory to our "*reason*." It is not human
nature like our fallen—but it is the Great Antitype of our wonderfull nature.
The voluntary creator & naturally its Redeemer and Guide to its perfection.
True the mind is constituted to press on to the first & original Cause—and
perhaps might have recognized no relation to the second had it been perfect—
its' pride perhaps is still active to present itself there. The lustre of the Son
was so veiled that a crucified unlearned Founder of religion, is at war with
gentile as Jew. But since he has revealed himself in Patmos (tho' the rev. is
obscured and symbolical like what we must expect, if faith have her triumphs)
yet there are indubitable marks of the same Prophet Priest & King prefigured
by Judaism & foretold & described by prophets and promised by the Messiah
himself. This scheme of raising a fallen race (which might have been under
some nessesity to bear the burden of that inexplicable origin of evil) this compensatory plan may well be called "the transcendental philosophy"   May be
called with reverent gratitude the philosophy of the Origin of all good—who
is counteracting that principle of evil w'h might have "been (inevitable) in
the nature of things"—? but this, Richard Watson says would nessesitate all
creatures—& no virtue could exist—this prin. w[d] go on from the moment
of creation till all good were extinguished."[3] Why? Then why not the good
princ. do the same & under the divine assistance triumph? I want you to write
a sermon on the text in Gal. 3 & 21—where it is said like this—"there could
be no law given w'h could give life"—   Our nature dont admit of obeying
a perfect law—and none other surely would be honorable to give? Hereafter

we shall cease from the vicarious econymy & obey perfectly. Dont dislike a reference to Revelations of St John. You admired them when you first read it at 5 years. Michaelis believes in its' canonical rights, as do some other great scholars.[4] Nothing seems grander than that the divine book should be closed with a prophetic voice w'h embraces the consummation of all the nations on earth & describes some lines of their history. With this subject dear Waldo is ever connected. But I can write him nothing if I could send you any letters. But I do wish to hear from him most sadly. Tell him so & that I dont see a star in the nightly Heavens with out often thinking he is standing on deck & reading their fates.[5] May nature & its Auther shed the best influence on him say for me. Yes he loves the flowers of the sky & the earth & the religion of the imajanation. But I think he has never been led from his peculiar good temper to feel the need that a contrite heart has of the religion of Jesus. And there is no lustre—no hieghts of tho't and depths of feeling caused by common humanitarianism. Channing if, as it is said, he is one sublimes it by deep poetic sentiment. and pious enthuseasm. The take off from all they preach is the want of their *faith in bible* athority.[n] The heathen said better things than these popular scholars but they had no unction from a particular specific revelator. And it is the like when we hear our modern orators   True, they awaken & delight the xian somtimes, because the sentiments are common to xian morals. I'm glad of my prison for it gives me time to read the scriptures—& when inlarged by their truths think I shall never read else. Stewarts commentaries are a great matter to me.[6] Do you read them? *A bible lawyer!* What a gift to your age dear Charles! * * *

Ask Father to write me by mail. I winced at having two letters in that way & both the *same* contents & telling of his belief in Waldo's insanity. My answer keeps him cold & silent. To tax him with an unpleasant duplicate! In reading over this—doubt if it goes. *Arianism*—that faith so deserted on all hands that it seems more like a solitary column amidst ruins. It may—but its summit is among the high ones—who admire its wonders—& who look forward to the end when it shall restore all beings to means of virtue.

Why Charles what has the high strained thoughts of the Channings done for the last 20 years? Humanitarianism—what has it done to lessen slavery—to convince the obdurate persecutors of man—to promote publick good & lofty private virtue? On the contrary has it not indirectly as connected with shearing the bible or doubting of its inspiration chilled the faith of the very expectants of immortality? Take away the supernal character of xian[t] & it becomes like a straw before a tempest. Raise man ever so high by high flown language like Channing's Pro. ser.[7] and after a few efforts his waxen wings fall—   The only eagle wing is that preened & strenghtened in the divine Sun. And has not infidelity grown in greater proportion among unitarians than in any other denomination? If Calvinism has dug the dark ravine—*that* has filled it with victims. If that vindictive creed makes sin appear in its odious truth—it too often renders its deciples antinomians but the dour baked humanitarian affords no compunction and gives no Judgment day—no consummation of this passing world!

Tow things I want your answer to. If the Bible is not to be relied on as inspired what prospect is that our future existence (for that is inevitable) will be better than the present? If there be these impersonal principles, and more affinities are as operative as they may be after disinterment—may influence by all powerfull nessesity—may we not fare worse than here? If there be a nessesity in our sins of any kind does it prevent the nature of sin. At any rate we fall & are unworthy as Dewey says "the scriptures every where represent." Has there ever any lived who acted up to his full convictions of right? Does not this last fact prove that xianity as a medicine is desirable? And this leads to the high stronge meat of perfection

And is Waldo to administer only the milk—be the pedegoge? The man who can break up the great foundations of the immortal mind may prepare it for the seed of eternal life. But Waldo with his poetic eye sees nothing but the race immortal here—tho' stars have vanished—& new systems forever rising else where, yet he & S. Reed[8] (poor theologuge) deny all passing of the old earth. What a fall since Pistorius scanned Hartly. That a good thing on nessesity? "Repentance changes the cercumstances—the same evolve the same effects." But you cannot read these things. The world Waldo says loves you. There you must be & hide your capasity of certain kinds—keep any spice of orthodoxy secret. Well do it—till time shall come when your athority of opinion will gain weight—when like a river suppressed before now rolls its fertilising waves. One single question more only one & I promise to leave. Is there any thing more strange in arianism (whatever good Lardner may say of amazement)[9] than the contradictory nature of man & the existence of sin & woe? Tow vicarous facts—beyond limited experience   At any rate orthodoxy has made of the same materials stronger marked & *acting* characters than its' opposors. Novel & strechy speculation dazzles—but dont influence their inventors—dont touch the heart by their poetry—often but masses of voilets & clouds and bodily forms & sentimental conceits.

17. Sab Eve. Unexpectedly I've a chance to send—   And as you seem weary of writing this long stuff may part us.[10] * * *

In solitude (Lucia studying Spanish)[11] these pages have served for soceity to your aff^t Aunt

MME

Is my sister at Newton? No money have I.

MH: bMS Am 1280.226(723). *Endorsed:* M. M. E. / Feb. 1833 / Christianity / Calvinism, Humanitarianism / Waldo & Reed.

their faith . . . athority] ↑ their *faith in bible* ↓ athority

1. CCE to MME, 26 Jan. 1833, compares his life, "consumed in vulgar cares & toils," to MME's, "so rapt & penetential—with every vital pulse beating in unison with the sweet cadences of Nature, & the Eternal Moral law." At times he foresees an

early death for himself and feels his "appointed" "task" might lie in "other spheres—'Whom the gods love, die young'— Let me be still a learner. . . . God will have some to glorify Him by simply receiving & contemplating" (MT/MH).

2. The *Biblical Repository* was an Andover Theological Seminary publication begun in 1831; quotation not located.

3. Bishop Richard Watson, *An Apology for Christianity* . . . (1776), and *An Apology for the Bible* . . . (1796), responses to contemporary Deists.

4. John David Michaelis, *Introduction to the New Testament*, trans. Herbert Marsh, 2d ed., 4 vols. (London, 1802), discusses the authenticity of Revelation or the Apocalypse, though he seems to conclude it is a "spurious production" (4:487).

5. See MME to CCE, 8 Jan. 1833 n. 1.

6. Probably Moses Stuart's published commentaries on the Epistles to the Hebrews and the Romans (1827).

7. WEC's "Likeness to God" (*Works*, 291–302), stresses that the preacher's role is to raise and quicken men with "affection, confidence, respect, and freedom," not debase them with terror (301).

8. Sampson Reed.

9. Nathaniel Lardner, *The Credibility of the Gospel History* (1727).

10. Written on both sides of a large folded letter sheet plus another half sheet, thus making a full six pages, this is MME's longest letter to CCE. The order of the unnumbered pages is confusing.

11. Lucia Wadsworth Griswold (b. 1813) was a daughter of the Griswolds, with whom MME was boarding.

To Charles Chauncy Emerson

Frye. March 13, 33

No seek not to "penetrate the curtain w'h covers the infinite mechanism."[1] Its web involves eternity   Thence arose the long woven scheme of man's creation & redemption. If we can feel some of its leading threads—follow along the wonderfull track of our divine Model—whose glory (higher in those places than we can estimate) is inhanced by suffering—by assuming "*a body*" wh was a link nessecary to privation—enough   Enough—to find for the exercise of our powers but one prophecy thrown down from above & obscured in the rust of conserving[n] ages, w'h he fulfilled by suffering. Oh how greater wiser generous than to have spent his ministry in explaining expiation—left it for the wants & history of misery to adapt. No your question of his "*august Soul* tortured with agony*" is the question valued by the Arrian—the mount of transfiguration where they find the low humanitarian fogs dispersed. A mere Carpenter was a gainer by his followers & hosannas—& popular by his censures & opposition. And what did this son of Joseph & Mary teach? More than our rationalists affect from nature? More sublime morals than Plato & Soc.? Unless some monopolist in matrimony might object? Did he even in any divine light teach a greater commandment than love supreme to God? They affect to boast of his bringing the doctrine of immortality. That great commandment taught it—besides how slightly his athority and predictions of a judgment rest on these kind of believers you will know—how often we find them at the death of their friends (Mrs G. Lee[2] one of the *sincerest* seekers) hunting in the reigions of nature material for proofs—picking up weeds & pebbles on the sandy shores of time—when the vast ocean of eternity is spread *before* them & the Son of God shining on its ceaseless waves. It seems he was not "the type of our instinctive dread" of bathing in its lustrous abysses— for when you get a glimps of the vast duration of God's past & future exis- tence—all other instincts are lost—you have existed in him—"made one of his eternal ideas"

But I want plain questions stated by you as you have a clearer head than other E—s   And you would naturally start the difficulty of this August soul giving us always the idea of sorrows & grief when possesing such divine powers & the aproval of his Father—w'h is hardly accounted for by vicarious assumption. Did you ever think how much you must suffer to have taken the dancing & menial organization of those blacks, w'h use to annoy you—what a melancholy solitude would you exist in to have retained the perception of all your former refined enjoyments? Is there no sober resemblance to the loss of all the active ineffable pursuits of Heaven? And—perhaps—besides—the astonishing plan he was operating was to lose as it were—surely for many bloody ages—it's grand desired effect—it was given in its outlines to be man- aged by that inexplicable gift w'h none but Omnipotence could give—the *will of man*—'twas to be met (as a still greater wonder) by his agency and their limits never known—   Yet all would sometimes fail—he saw that those who boasted of being touched by the sole principle of generosity—full gift of sal- vation & freedom—and those who could produce revealed vouchers also for what they esteemed a still richer gift—a power to comply with his conditions and make divine bounty a debt—that each would often pervert thier good faith & use these celestial gifts to cover the inherent fiend—or keep company with the foreign deceiver. He saw that those who would call him An example merely & teacher would despise his unlearned[n] & lowly character—and re- ject him virtually because the poor & ignorant were the first objects of his mission.

This shall go that is, sattisfy my appetite into my day book, if I have a letter from my dear dear Correspondent next mail that may turn the direction of thought. A while he sits occupied with great things—   Anon and he's busy with care & strife   Ah it was sometimes pleasant to think of having a friend guiding the helm of state—   But now in these times it sickens. Who comes out from Congress pure? The principles of corruption seem to resemble some elemental part of the air—and the cell & cowl are far safer. I've lost the dream by hearing a scrap of newspaper now & then. You "do not take" to a cer- tain correspondent of mine. She does to you—hopes you will call. My devout wish is that you might take so strongly to some strong character of the sex as will give your life new interest & your death brighter charms. Whatever you are I shall rejoice that I did not incubate this favorite faith on your mind. It will be the result of your own research—nor that your brothers who reject it will have received any prejudice to it from an antiquated woman. It's morals your excellent Mother & her unworthy coadjutor strove to teach   And thus God bound you to their observance by irrevokable bonds. And now if you put forth your hand & live & grow rich in the great Vine from w'h these flow! And with Coleridge administer this spiritual sacrament! What does he say of original sin? I scarsly retain—but 'twas not satisfactory. Do send me his lit. life of Waldos.[3] *When*[n] will you hear from him??

Thurs Eve. 14   Are you well? I want to hear and tho' this is the trite old faith of your poor Aunt yet it goes with love & all hope in you

MME

MH: bMS Am 1280.226(724). *Addressed:* Charles Chauncy Emerson Esq[r] / 17 Court Street / Boston / Mss. *Postmarked:* Fryeburg Me / March 15th. *Endorsed:* M. M. E. / March 13— 1833.

conserving] *possibly* consuming (*T*)
unlearned] ⟨obsure⟩ ↑ unlearned ↓
When] *underlined twice*

1. Several unidentified quotations in this letter do not appear in CCE's most recent letter to MME, 6 Mar. 1833, to which she seems to respond in other respects.

2. Following the death of her husband (about 1816), Hannah Farnham Sawyer Lee began writing to support herself and her three daughters; she published a novel, *Grace Seymour* (1830), and a continuation of Joseph Tuckerman's *Life of Hannah Adams* (1832). Between 1837 and 1854 she published over twenty novels (*AWW*).

3. Coleridge, *Aids to Reflection*, "Aphorisms on Spiritual Religion," aphorism 10, "On Original Sin" (159–78). CCE to MME, 7 Mar. 1833 (MT/MH), recommends FHH's "Coleridge's Literary Character," in the *Christian Examiner* for Mar. 1833; in his reply, CCE to MME, 20 Mar. [1833], says RWE did not own the *Biographia*: "It is the rarest of all C's works in this country" (MT/MH).

To Ann Sargent Gage

Sat   Frye.   March 30 '33

Yours much touched my heart. The same mail bro't a letter from Miss Peabody of Boston, whose history I have often wanted to relate had your time afforded. She is a gifted mind—pupil & inmate of Dr C.[1] Becoming an Autheress. Her letter was also frought with the natural complainings of genius and disappointed aspirations—w'h in this exile state attend talents & virtue as the most beautiful body has it's shadow. Happy condition of immortal instincts. Still it runs down the finest tuned mind when the round of actions compose always the same ideas. Religion itself then follows instead of guiding. The orthodox and their opposites fall into this morbid state alike. That the latter should repose on their oars when every hour is a billow w'h wafts them over the stagnate pool of time is not so strange. That those who think the compact is made by others it is natural also. But that those who are happily placed between the extremes who expect to reap as they sow—to maintain a constant warfare with every unholy affection—when they seem to lose sight of the Heaven w'h has been promised by a divine Sufferer—to drag instead of soaring—then we wonder at the mysteries w'h surround human nature. Oh when they are dispelled—when higher & holier ones expand the inlarged mind and kindle new & newer curiosty—*these* shall be understood to have formed the discipline ordained. Yes I was fully awake that eve. by your letters. Your first page as it was of the same cast lost nothing by it's companion— And my old affections roused with a life w'h my new young freind failed to effect. I began to write her & you but pen failed—however it must try again as the question you desired answered shall go whether you read any more— And by the time I get to the close a better pen will come w'h I've sent for. My new freind (again?) wrote also much & most sweetly enthusiasticly, on Dr S.[2] but of his system is ignorant. If it can develop character (native) it must influence education. But the modern is bad in my opinion. I am sick of scholarship—to find a mind un*formed*[n] with elementary literature is a treat. Some great minds can bear a great deal. I have my old opinions strenghtened. A moral discipline w'h instills the most complete obedience to parental athority lays the foundation for religion & happiness. Some exceptions we find who are neither obstinate nor overbearing in indulgence. Man is born with conscience & disinterested affections—swerve they will for there is a moral taint of dreadfull & inexplicable power—but the direction given in childhood rarely fails—the effect is nessecarily connected with Cause? In some of those pious epochs w'h visit every xian more or less his mind dilates and strenghtens—and the impulse he is then able to give is unquestionable. Why not maintain the celestial commerce and make traffic for posterity! Forgive dear freind this didactic style—but if you discuss the education subject I get running. "What I observe?" I think, as when my Brother tho't different—and reflect with gratitude on keeping C.C. from learning early—he carried away more prizes in his between 12 & 14 years than any latin scholar. I had long before left him. Tranquil childhood strenghtens the mind. A certain quantum of animal spirits all possess—when too soon expended age becomes stupid. What little connection there is often found between the academy learning and the natural taste for poetry and intellectual research in all thier delightfull relations to devotion. How often the elements of the future Angel—a moral sympathy & sensibility—are checked. It seems you are doing well to give them habits of attention and cultivating *memory*—   Any thing that *disciplines* mind—*subdues* the growth of selfish passions. Theres the point that presses itself daily on my observation. These good Mothers are predestinarian in education—perhaps have little or no *tact* that way. The object of your inquiry has *captivated* me. Tact in the most gracefull & correct conduct. A good Scholar & *Instructor* and better for imitation than most in this reigion. But sabbath keeping except teaching at School Sab. & heart religion seems un-happily distant from. The state of society here is probably unfavorable. And many young girls together render them frivolous without the slightest dis-courgment from age. Burn this instantly as I cut out the question. Her time has been so taken up with spainish &c, & now absent at P. that I have never got near enough. Who is the pupil? You must write again. "It pumps up thought." The Ladies send love & desire with me to see you & the D^r here & Mr & Mrs R.³ It would delight me   Channings Discourses I will send you if you wish them   T'will excite a host of ideas. An hour a day with new veiws will furnish any capable mind that is in action it seems. I have opened this letter since last eve. to ask a favor of you   I hear of an article in the last Examiner on "Coleridge & German metaphysicks" and you will need to read it.⁴ If you can get it of my friend Whitman & send it by Mail it *will gratify*—and one or two more Nos. Col. is orthodox. You can put a letter in it. Please to be carefull to remember me to Whitman & acknowledge his favor.

I had no time to write more to the Vale & now cannot alter it tho' the book is come by Mr H.⁵ How is his eye? Love to Mrs Farrar & Hamlin if you see them. I wish you could have more neighbourhood to inlarge the affections of the children—yet how precious is their solitude compared to frivolous ones or what cankers the young heart party spirit. Frances must send her letter & the rest must not forget their affectionate and much interested freind

MME

* * *

MWA. *Addressed:* Mrs Ann S. Gage / Waterford / Maine. *Postmarked:* Fryeburg Me / April 1ˢᵗ.

un*formed*] *possibly* un*tamed*

1. EPP and WEC; in the 1820s, their acquaintance "evolved into a close mentor-student relationship" (Bruce Ronda, ed., *The Letters of Elizabeth Palmer Peabody* [Middletown, Conn.: Wesleyan University Press, 1984], 51).

2. Probably Johann Casper Spurzheim, a German phrenologist who died during his U.S. lecture tour in 1832. EPP mentions him in a letter dated 8–11 Nov. 1832 (*Letters*, 105); and CCE to MME, 11–12 Apr. [1833], promises to buy her "Follen's Eulogy on Dr Spurzheim," but asks, "What can make you wish it? He (Sp.) was a shrewd observer & a pleasant lecturer, & no doubt a very benevolent schemer" (MT/MH).

3. LG and PER and LR.

4. Hedge, "Coleridge's Literary Character," 108–29.

5. Probably Haskins; other persons mentioned are Waterford neighbors.

To Charles Chauncy Emerson

Vale   July 9 '33

Thanks, dear Charles, for the last letters & the kindness of copying the travellers.¹ So sweet is good tidings from afar! And does our well beloved Waldo go to bed the *wiser* for what he sees & dreams? The more knowing—

inlarged & happier besure. Oh it is fine to live in those arts w'h refer to the past—w'h antisapate the future & forget the little present of w'h you speake so *bubbly*. See the force of cercumstances. When you are at Home this world may appear the very mart of wisdom. Or when teased with clients & pressed for publick services what a ponderous & astonishing thing it is to be on this mighty planet! It is for faith & fervid peity to live beyond & above cercumstances—to create a world within to w'h the outward bows as far as it is permitted by its' Auther. In resigning to events as our medicine we fullfill His high purposes. Like all others I suppose you are too much at liesure for a profession. *Burke* spent ten of the best years of life in literary obscurity & at 36 made his first publick entrance, you know.[2] His admirers say it was his eagle genius scorned to court the mole like course of popularity. The theist thinks it was the ordained way to establish his pious & patriotic character—   And says or thinks that Pope was an envious libeller. But not the brightest blaze of flame from publick life ever appears with the power & charm celestial, as literary retirement—it's benevolent designs spread like the dew of Heaven & purify the sultry vapours of bustling men. A man of "moods" (like the many of genius) which you profess should covet this best estate more earnestly than other men. I rejoice in Waldo's accession of property that he may live in Eden.[3] And hope points to the same for you after less years of toil & disappointment. A few may give you a sterner mood than to yield to all. Bear with this—for your late letters have implied all but the transcendental & devout—or write not those wh bear so high a tone. Tell Waldo that I did not think he would altogether neglect me. But add—it is well with me—and with the former child of my pride & affections. Did you give the letter to E. P.?[4] So plain truth dont get any notice. What delusion has got hold of Charlotte F. (one so free from moods) to edit a paper??[5] You see that I want information of folks & things—& admired as well as others the witty letter—but want the swelling thoughts w'h picture out the wonderfull divinity within—the conception of perfect virtue—to feed[n] it—to give life to the coulers by every effort is all we can here do—'tis but a faint picture of the real future soul. And yet she sojourns in mists—these fine cloudy days give the Vale to be an enchanting symbol of the saints pilgrimage—its beauties are shadowy—flitting—but in every form a permanent beauty. And bye & bye the Autumn will come like the Angel of consumption to translate the fancy to other worlds—and the seer leaf will "hang light and hang high." Yet Cole. should not have touched that single leaf w'h was the boon of more solitary minds—those who watch it from day to day—who see its shawdow thro' the dim light w'h visits their cell like some beckoning ghost. The pure mind of a Cowper could better have told the tale of the withered leaf destined to glow in the rainbow after a few migrations, & shame the Smith theory w'h represents talent virtues as only valueable or rewardable by God not society.[6] Again you see your letter (of w'h I complained) recognized on this high ground.

Farewell dear dear Charles—it seems long since & far longer before we

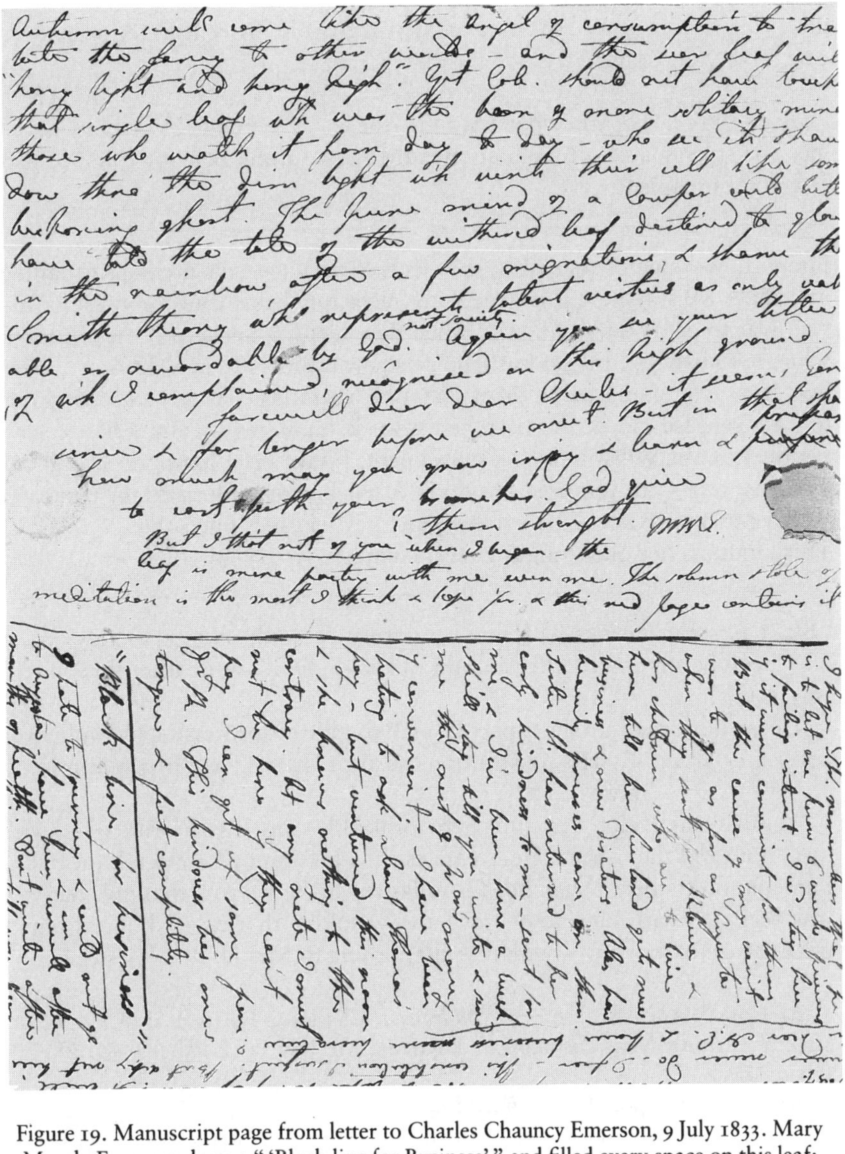

Figure 19. Manuscript page from letter to Charles Chauncy Emerson, 9 July 1833. Mary Moody Emerson drew a " 'Black line for Business' " and filled every space on this leaf; tear caused by breaking seal. By permission of the Houghton Library, Harvard University, and the Ralph Waldo Emerson Memorial Association.

meet. But in that space how much may you grow in joy & learn & prepare to cast forth your branches. God give them strenght.

MME.

But I tho't not of you when I began—the leaf is mere poetry with me, even me. The solemn stole of meditation is the most I think & hope for.   & this red page contains it.

I hope T. W. remembers that he is to let me know 6 weeks previous to failing interest. I w^d stay here if it were convenient for them   But the cause of my visit was to go as far as Augusta when they sent for Rebecca & her children who are to live here till her husband gets new business & new disasters.[7] Alas how heavily presses care on them. Sister H. has returned to her early kindness to me—sent for me, & I've been here a week. Shall stay till you write & send me the next of W^m's money if convenient. I have been hating to ask about Thomas' pay—but ventured this noon & she knows nothing to the contrary. At any rate I must not be here if they can't pay   I can get up some from Dr R.[8] This kindness ties ones tongue & feet completely.

"*Black line for business*"[9] I hate to journey & could not go to Augusta— have been & am unwell after months of health. Don't write after this one till you hear.

Does your dear Mother expect E B E[10] to take his profession? It will never never do—I fear—   His constitution I suspect. But why not live in dear N. E. & have business more lucrative?

Your Cousin Ralph is coming here for health soon. If you write to him you need not send the money. He is careless like his Aunt M. & send not but 5. I am ignorant where I shall be. Yesterday my hostess wrote that my chamber was occupied with Lads to board. I always told in that case I'd quit. I regret the expense of moving—but have said nothing to Mrs H. It w^d pester her

MH: bMS Am 1280.226(729). *Addressed:* Charles C Emerson Esqr / 17 Court Street / Boston / Mss. *Postmarked:* Raymond Me July 12. *Endorsed:* M. M. E. / July 9, 1833.

feed] sic *in MS; possibly* feel *intended*

1. CCE probably sent copies of letters from RWE (in Paris) and EBE (in Puerto Rico).

2. Born in 1729, Edmund Burke was thirty-seven years old when he became a member of Parliament in 1766; his first important speech, on 27 Jan., argued that Parliament should acknowledge a petition from the American Congress, and a week later he made two additional speeches on the Stamp Act (*DNB*).

3. CCE to RWE (in Paris), 27 June 1833, reports that Judge Shaw has just ruled in RWE's favor on most points regarding his inheritance from the Tucker-Kent estate (MT/MH).

4. Several of CCE's letters to MME during this period indicate that she enclosed letters to EPP (which do not survive) in those she wrote to CCE.

5. EBE (Puerto Rico?) to Charlotte Farnham in Boston, 6 Oct. 1833, refers to her review or *Ladies Gazette,* for which he's written a letter he's happy to have published if it's "fit to print" (MT/MH). Possibly the *Ladies Magazine,* founded at Boston in 1828 by Sarah Josepha Hale, who advocated professional female teacher preparation and the establishment of seminaries for women. Contributors included Lydia Sigourney, Lydia Maria Child, Hannah Flagg Gould, and Catharine Maria Sedgwick. The magazine continued until 1836.

6. See Coleridge, *The Friend* (appendix A, no. 13, 16 Nov. 1809), the story of Maria Schoning. Coleridge describes Maria's sinking into solitude: "As when a withered Leaf, that has been long whirled about by the gusts of Autumn, is blown into a Cave or hollow Tree, it stops suddenly, and all at once looks the very image of quiet" (*Collected Works* 2:178); quoted by Hedge in "Coleridge's Literary Character," 113; MME to CCE, 13 Aug. [1833] (MH: 733) uses the image again. Here she seems to say that poet William Cowper, who stresses the need for "religious truth as a fresh subject for exhausted poetry and futile social chatter" (Ricardo Quintana and Alvin Whitley, eds., *English Poetry of the Mid- and Late Eighteenth Century* [New York: Knopf, 1967], 225), would have treated the subject of the solitary leaf better than did Coleridge. Adam Smith, *Theory of Moral Sentiments* (1759).

7. Niece Rebecca Haskins married Dr. Costillo Hamlin of Waterford in 1826; CCE to EBE, 30 Apr. 1834, writes, "Do you know that Dr Hamlin,—who married Rebecca Haskins, lately moved from poverty & debts to Rhode Island the town of Portsmouth & was there doing well in the world,—has just died of a fever? He leaves to his widow the treasure & the anxiety of two children" (MT/MH).

8. Probably EzR.

9. "I hope . . . completely" is written sideways at the bottom of the leaf and is completely set off from the rest of the letter by heavy lines on all four sides of the passage. CCE to MME, 22 May 1833, responds to a complaint about his failure to attend to some business, saying that her business request got lost in the text of her letter. "If you are so nervous about mixing business & sentiment," he suggests, "the best plan will be to draw a long black line at the bottom of the letter & write BUSINESS in large characters—& then give your orders, subscribing them like the Chinese Emperor's proclamations, 'Tremble at this.—' " (MH: 220 [17]).

10. E B C *in MS;* however, CCE to MME, 22–24 June [1833], contained news that "Edward remains another year in Porto Rico—whereat his mother looks grave" (MT/MH).

To Charles Chauncy Emerson

Sab. P. M.   28 July. [1833]

I this moment had your dear letter—tho' its feelings are not of the order w'h will soon prevail.[1] As Rouchefoucald says "the humours of body have a regular stated course."[2] This is too true—the most severe part of a wise & inscrutable destiny. Yet that our phisical power—our senses administer to the virtues is good—& we can so manage them that when they depress we can use them as organs of xian humility & patience—when they exalt—as means & messengers of praise & diffusion. They are the instruments of Providence indisputably. But Channing sometimes expressed the delights of immediate revelation. Yet was not the infant state of these Patriarchs every way inferior? How little unfolded the glory of conscience—*think of their deciet!!!* True, Abraham & others as interpreters of divine will—as mediums of communion—as possessing the noble disinterestedness of benevlence as in the case of interfering about the destruction of certain Cities or persons—why it is the very embodying of all that God has carried on in earth thro' his heroes!— The type of the Great Restorer—influencer! My narrow circle perhaps has prevented doubt. Are you unwilling in the great career of an immortal to hazard anxiety & responsibility? Surely not. The voice of conscience instructed by rev. leaves you generally[n] certain of the final result of all you do. Intimate with God, by this vicegerant[3] you can appeal to his Omniscience that you prefer His will to your own—there cannot be a failure tho' the genius of evil (w'h pervades the universe in so sure yet misterious a manner) should assault your fortunes with as much power as ever it did the greatest saint. The Nemisis of the heathen is the adversary of Jesus—of whom he spoke. You have not read DeStale of late. She felt as genius is wont to, in all its memoirs, the power of nessesity & the certainty of freedom. Oh what a glory hereafter to understand that the great Purposer and Finisher of fates could *give liberty enough*—liberty to do as He pleases the great orthodox writers have it, if we unveil them. But it is of a higher kind than that—*it is real*—   And He weaves it for perfect justice & benefit to the whole. Were it like the flattering selfish systems— how meagre our condition—how impossible for a benevolent Creator to have given. I've read again your letter & find you have said the best about your faith that I have spread out. Still you are cloudy about your orbit. Doubt you of your profession being good? No I rarely feel that I could have benefited or adorned "the garden."[4] If I had been in ought but dreary deserts I s[d] have idolised the objects of my affection—despised the world & been haughty. I never expected connections & matrimony. My taste was formed in romance & knew I was not destined to please. I love God & his creation as I never else could. I scarsly feel the sympathises of this life enough to agitate the pool. This is general & interest in one or so excepted. Even this is a relation to God thro' you 'twas so in my happiest earthly days when you were at my side.

July 28   Sab Eve[5]

* * * The books you mention do not appear. Strange to send them when you did not know where I was. They may be safer in boat I suppose. I blundering asked about money. I've been waiting for it—hired it—wish you to send me every dollar remaining. after 10 or more days to Augusta[6] * * * Could W[m] E who wrote me a *very* good & kind letter pay me I would get Judge White to buy me a life insurance immedeately.[7] The difficulty of getting

places of low board for a lady is obvious. And at moments I'm tired out—
Yet how independent—how better than to hang on freinds. And sometimes
I fancy that I am emptied & peeled to carry some seed to the ignorant w'h
no idler wind can so well disperse. Surely if nessecity did not impell I should
choose places like Andover where I could learn instead of being with ignorance. But my old stomach dont always agree to their diet & this makes me
so expensive for what is the college term of additions. Well what a mess I've
written but this change of weather has withered me. And the idea of dressing
a garden contrasts so well with my desires only for meat & lodging. And the
effort to live takes off all factitious desires or ennui. So good night dearest
freind & forget large duties & "expensive interests" in pure sympathy with
less & greater pleasures. Ah is E. E. running down with his large & expensive
interests?

MME

MH: bMS Am 1280.226(731 and 730). *Addressed:* Charles C. Emerson Esqr. / 17
Court Street / Boston / Politeness of Doctor Houghton / To the Care of Mr T. W.
Haskins. *Endorsed:* X M.M.E.— / July 28 1833.

generally] *possibly canceled*

1. CCE to MME, 22 and 23 July 1833, discusses his religious beliefs and admits
difficulties with the concept of freedom. "How can I be sure that each day & hour
of my present occupations, manners, fellowships, is not holding me back, pulling me
aside, from the orbit I was ordained to 'circle rejoicing—'" (MH: 220 [117]).

2. François, duc de La Rochefoucauld, *Maximes suivies des reflexions diverses*,
maxim 297 (edition of 1678).

3. Cf. Whichcote, *Moral and Religious Aphorisms* (1753): "*Conscience* is God's
Vice-gerent; . . . the God, dwelling within us" (aphorism 1058).

4. CCE admitted his problem was too much leisure and insufficient duties: "Yes
you know—you in your private and lonely sphere must all your life have had to wrestle
with the same uneasiness of mind. You must from the nook into which you had with-
drawn, have thought with a transient pang of the garden of beauty you once believed
you were destined to dress" (MH: 220 [117]).

5. MH: 730 begins here. In the 23 July portion of his letter, CCE mentions MME's
need for money, lists some books he is sending in lieu of the Coleridge and Wordsworth
she requested (which were unavailable), asks whether she knows that "Edw Everett has
been shaking good mens' confidence in him by going over to the Anti-Masonic Party,"
and tells her of the "treasure" gotten recently from Charlotte Farnham: "a profile of
your face, cut by Williams many years since" (probably the silhouette reproduced as
the frontispiece for this volume), now hanging in his room.

6. Niece Sybil Farnham Lambard was living in Augusta.

7. MME to DAW, 5 May 1832, seeks advice from her old friend on an annuity
(MH-AH).

To Charles Chauncy Emerson

Wed 14 Au. 1833

The date of the happiest news I believe I ever heard! Blessed be God for it. Genius temper & piety He has granted. If you never have the letter I sent yesterday it was wholly on this subject.[1] And I thought of Elizabeth Hoar and felt sincere regret that I had heard you say nothing of her. And often have I regreted that a crazy mood w'h generally attends a *visit* in the world rendered me so mad with ambition as to be blind to your mutual attachment or insensible to its advantages. Her family! Roger Sherman a signer! Her father so good & influential— Her mother excellent pious & charitable & sincere.[2] Herself beautifull & what is incomparably better *ardent*. I estimate this beyond price of all kinds as it's agency on your tendency to nonchalance apathy stupidity or whatever name—no matter—I could beat you for not telling me before. Tho' it has roused me from the saddest mood w'h fatigue of visiting & little disappointments could inflict. Yet I would have known of your doubts fears & hopes—ah is there more pleasure in the chase than——? I was willing your affections shuld be so received that you would forever be a converted man from apathy. But romance apart this early & incog attachment far better than the most splendid adventures. And thro' the sober years you have to earn will thrive a better   True, in those years so fine a girl may give your jealousy a little exercise. This will discipline you for past years of scape the rod. Now I have stirred your ire—and dared impeach the immaculate constancy of one Eve. Well after a nights sleep gained by reading late of the pure & holy friendship of Darcie & Alan,[3] think you I can be as impassioned as at the moment of receiving your little god's triumph? Calm as the dun cloud w'h rests between heaven & earth—image of patience that no attraction carries it either above or below— I am thinking how less I shall write either to amuse the waiting for clients or my own imprisonment. Surely tho' the event I esteem the happiest you could have met. And if any object to long engagments say "pash". It is the rich flowering time of life— And it will be your fault if Elizabeth does not lay in a better stock of wisdom than she could unengaged. Say a hearty welcome to E. I could not write without congratulating her—& she may not understand me. I am not beloved by her.* A good omen for earthly prosperity—as I am not its child. Love to her parents   I could not have desired better alliance tell them or any thing—my heart is as full of delight in every event of others as it is at low ebb in immediate cercumstances. And the pen is not in tune.

Most affectionately farewell
MME

*I forgot it till this moment & remember only a stronge preference for such as your Mother. I've taken revenge in talking of jealousy. It was mere jest I seriously aver

MH: bMS Am 1280.226(734). *Addressed:* Charles C. Emerson Esqr / 17 Court Street / Boston / Mss. *Endorsed:* M. M. E. / Aug. 14 / E. H.

1. CCE to MME, 10 Aug. 1833, announces his engagement to Elizabeth Hoar (MT/MH). MME to CCE, 13 Aug. 1833, tells of reading "Flints translation of Droz" (*The Art of Being Happy*, trans. Timothy Flint [Boston, 1832]), a true picture of human nature that represents "*home* as the only seat of comfort," though she found its "picture of matrimony" "sad but too true." Then she writes, "By the way in one of your spring letters you were in so fond a mood of sociality that I dreamt you were about to be in love. I fear it will be but a dream! Were your whole heart united to genius & *temper* & piety, what an Eden you might find in this wilderness of bogs & fens!" (MH: 733).

2. EH's grandfather, Roger Sherman, "was a signer of the Declaration of Independence, Governor of Connecticut, and Senator to the first Congress of the United States"; her father, "Squire Samuel Hoar, town lawyer, judge of the Circuit Court, always active in Massachusetts and national politics, was considered the leading citizen of Concord" ("EH L," *SAR 1984*: 230).

3. At the beginning of Sir Walter Scott's *Redgauntlet*, Darsie Latimer (later, Sir Arthur Darsie Redgauntlet) is corresponding with his favorite schoolmate, Alan Fairford.

To Edward Bliss Emerson

Elm Vale   No[v]. 10, Sabbath '33

My dear Edward,

I want to hear from your own pen of your health—your occupations of mind & heart. You are, like me, alone.[1] Do you have any of the advantages of solitude? Can you sit on the mount of transfiguration, w'h faith casts up, and hear the stirrings & see the whirlings of the puppet show world with tender pity—with wholesome sympathy? And while you look at the pageantry does your eye mount the eagle wing w'h shows you the real & unfading world? The hope that your temporary seclusion from scenes in w'h you had shone with distinguished light—scenes w'h you gave promise to administer to with no common effort & effect will correct your youthfull impetuosity—will discipline you far better than an uninterrupted course of health & prosperity. You will return to society & labour with a soul grown, in some good measure, above the feverous excitements of fame & fortune. In the present state of speculative theology (from the glimps w'h visit the Cell) the coldest & most distant retirement is safest for youth, even age, who are not born nor destined to possess the hardihood of an inflexible constitution. False philosophy rears her crest with plausible theories & seduces the inquirer before he is aware of her Circeian power. Read the bible more than ever my dear xian fellow traveller. And tho' it sometimes sojourns in a cloudy pillar—it gives sufficient light to make your path straight to the perfect day. There are true metaphysicks for your intellectual taste—the glorious secret of which lies in finding God in all things—   This the only legitimate philosophy—   And this ground fact—

w'h makes us what we are—agents—free to all purposes of virtue & vice is there found in every history private or publick—in every judgment & mercy dealt immediately or thro' human hands. Yes, dear Edward, read by the light of day & by the stars and by the storm & by the shine and you will find the ultimate *good*. A hallowed sentiment of the Invisible Leader as distinct from the pantheism of the false philosopher as Heaven from earth. One of the wonders of our being is there explained & no where else. That capasity to go on & endure defeat in happiness & perfection & yet go on with hope however chastised. It is the immortal God within. And xianity reveals the secret—does infinitely more—prepares an influence—embodies it in the divine person of the wonderfull Redeemer to counteract the miseries & guilt of human nature. It would seem at times that the whole race—the whole revolution existed but to reveal this Marvel of the whole universe—this Son of God. But it was rather for the sake of a fallen race that he existed—surely as incarnate   Ah, dear Edward, time is bringing on, however slow, the fullness of this revelation. All sects—all errors all hydra headed infidelity is but hastening the vindication of Providence and the manifestation too of the Messiah. There may be many a severe & bloody contest before, between the powers w'h have been at work so many ages—(eternal ones *perhaps*) and which Jesus is to conquer. May you be preparing to take part beneathe his banners—to act[n] manfully & soberly the deciple of the cross. Even should humanitarianism, in it's lowest forms, be the fact there approaches it is probable a crisis. Certainly the disorders of the present scene are to be regulated—and while they prove sucesfull to the trial of a few heroic spirits oppress the mass with doubts which are too heavy for their virtue.

You have sympathised with the joy of Waldo's return—with William in his happy prospects and Charles in his love & lovely condition. I have no acquaintance with his beautifull Flame—but rejoice in his engagment for his sake. You may be at Portsmouth.[2] What delight it would give to see you here   Here I do hope to see you in the coming summer.

Adieu & write soon to your ever fond Aunt
MME

I have a fine flower in the wilderness w'h began to cast forth its blossoms & awaken the tones of pleasure & poetry in my fancy. But disease has come on it—   And tho' checked—is not conquered. Do you remember H. U. H.?[3]

MH: bMS Am 1280.226(757). *Addressed:* Edward Bliss Emerson Esq[r]. *Endorsed:* M. M. E. / Nov 10 1833 / R March 4 1834 / A. April 5 ".

act] ⟨play⟩ ↑ act ↓

1. Since CCE's return from Puerto Rico in late May 1832, EBE had seen little of his family.

2. MME suggests EBE might return to New England for WE[3]'s wedding in December.

3. Niece Hannah Upham Haskins.

1834

To Charles Chauncy Emerson

9 April [1834?] thurs.[1]

Dear Charles,

So you are not like Marc Antoninus who said "what matters it by whom good is done?" You want an influence to go out as your sun ascends". Very fine sublime. And it is right—but expect not the superior comforts—little hopes & fears & joys must enter into such a web—woven on the fluctuations of earth. And a lover has all his cares doubled & thribled— "Haste then to cleave the waves"[2]

Thanks for you offer of advice. Had I needed any but my feelings[n] I would have taken a strangers. Cherish your relatives & employers with benefits w'h you cannot me. You have done enough for me in rendering so many years of your childhood soothing to me. And if you forget, Mrs Quickly dont, that the only moment in w'h I refered to disposal of farm was one evening at the vale in my chamber   You had come from Whitman's[3] & said the place *was mine*. I pointed to the thin partition & Waldo, who stood at the south west window, checked you & spoke of the friends you w[d] injure. I added that the farm *was mine* but should take but the 1100 if they needed it. Now you will have no thought about it. It would be an unaccountable phenomenon that you should have understood me so as to offer it, but that I consider such trifling events as a part of the whole chain of Provi. My, perhaps, sneaking hope was that as it w[d] rise & the family might be better off, I s[d] recieve profit & home. It is not so—and it is right. They do well to take it now at the offer they suppose I made officially—   And to have acted up to the standard of my youthfull hopes I s[d] not ask a "roof tree" w'h has *surprised & disgusted*. *This* happened[n] the day I wrote to Waldo—it was wholly new to me that Ripley was coming &c— but I at once consented to your offer—and since Tho. came and I made him understand very easily that the reputed state of the farm at the time of pur- chase (however exagerated) was such that Uncle Ral. was going to sell it to a stranger at 1500—that I took an engag[t] from his father for the rise of the farm—burnt it at the expiration of the lease to give content—that after I had got them a good home they w[d] let me live there—   Mr Robert still thought[n] he had given 600—but at any rate whether he gave even 4 the patrimony or vestige he had which he relinquished to Ral. induced the latter to destroy a note of large amount—   So you see how easy it is to talk large & act smale. I numbered over all the benefits of the farm & the ease with w'h the interest had been paid. The morning of that day, when writing to Waldo I could not dream of such calculations. Yet the circumstances bro't it on   The boys[n] had tho't it their father's—feared I s[d] will it away Thomas says. So I trumped up in a few words *my doings*   We find the world full of children—and that w'h in our hearts we take no merit in—blush that it is no more generous—we expose to the weake as justification. They will let Riply take it & in a year we shall conclude if I take a compensation or roof tree. I consider it due to their comfort to go—shall put myself in the way of finding some solitary home— but where I can go to Chh & a book store. These are nessceary to debilitated health & inactive life. It is so universal with all classes to avoid contact with me that I blame none. The fact has generally[n] increased peity & self love. My Sister suffers as the cold & slow always do from the quick & warm. I respect her & think I ought to leave till she s[d] as in former times, wish me. A mother s[d] always be the first & highest among her family—know most & love most. But I must be in solitude to hide the pride & egotism w'h has prevailed in character & the infirmities of age. I have a forlorn hope of such a place in the vicinity of N. P. or in that. In a large place one's existence can be a secret with God more than a smale. This secret may remain forever & I be blest transcendently.

I may add that your Uncle was sattisfied and told his son no one would aid him in the return to the Vale but me. And I fancy he has little objection to my living there. And I have found it much better than I feared to be connected with him in property. T. says he will have resources in the farm after I'm paid beside the 60 acres of wood I gave him w'h did not belong originally to Ralph. As I may get a home & make my host my heir it is uncertain if ever I buy an annuity—

On a visit at Hill.[4] T. goes tomorrow

MH: bMS Am 1280.226(669).
feelings] ⟨conscience⟩ ↑ feelings ↓
happened] ⟨arrangement⟩ happened
still thought] ⟨avoweded⟩ still thought
boys] ⟨children⟩ ↑ boys ↓
generally] ⟨sometimes⟩ ↑ generally ↓

1. Dating uncertain: 9 Apr. fell on Thursday in 1829 and 1835, but in Apr. 1835 MME was not at Vale, and the event MME describes must have occurred during CCE and RWE's visit in July 1832. MME's reference to a lover's "cares" in the first paragraph suggests that the letter was written after CCE's engagement in Aug. 1833. Other principals in this continuing drama over the ownership of Elm Vale are RHE's brother Ralph Haskins ("Ral."), MME's brother-in-law Robert Haskins, nephews Thomas and Ripley Haskins, and "Sister" Rebecca Haskins.

2. Somewhat misquoted from Goethe's "The Salutation of a Spirit," printed in "The Life and Genius of Goethe," *North American Review* 19 (1824); the last stanza reads, "Restless through half of life I ran, / In half have sought for ease; / What then? Thou bark! that sails with man, / Haste, haste to cleave the seas" (306).

3. Lawyer Charles Whitman.

4. The Gage family home at South Waterford.

To William Emerson[3]

Vale   Apr. 10 '34

Dear Nephew,[n]

I have not thanked you for the letter of last May—tho' it gave me sattis-faction— I loved the handsome flattery—and was instructed by its' infor-mation. On the eve of your marriage I felt a wish to offer the gratulations so due—but I needed a health more in tone with your sucess. I heard by a clergy-man from P. of the excellencies of your bride—and from Charles a warm approbation.[1]

Still the shade which the tomb of Ellen has given to these events checks antisapation. She was the lovliest Maddona of my imajanation. Age lives on the side of the mountain as to this world[n] w'h lies in shadows—in ascending it in the morning of health the lowest shrub is brilliant—at eve. "infirm of purpose"—the loftiest tree throws the deepest gloom. Yet the wishes—the prayers formed in the Cell may argue as favorably, perhaps more so, as those from the dazzling abodes of prosperity & tempels of dedication. You are well aware that a limited portion of happiness & that often interrupted—never pure & unmixed is the lot of the most successfull. I feel sure that Mrs Emerson will find you a sympathising freind & protector in every scene—if I may judge by the qualities and conduct of the Son and brother. That she will prove all you expect there is no question. A good temper is the first & last requisite for domestic tranquility. But after all I can form no distinct idea of her character as I know not of her religion. This is a central point from w'h I can alone figure the radiations & measure the extent of the influence of character. This relation between the soul & its' Maker when recognized and made the oracle of conduct gives us a tie to those we never did and never may see w'h nothing else can give & w'h no time or distance can loosen.

Pardon me if I lugg in old fashioned opinions and obsolete notions—and thank your stars they come only on paper.

Do you remember little Hannah[2] to whom your Mother was so kind in Essex St.? She had become a gay & darling companion rather constituted all my soceity. She has been withering for many months on the brink of a consumption— And I apprehend is still in danger.

I can say nothing of your annuity[3] (as it is not likely I shall take it) till the change of my property here is effected, w'h your Uncle wishes soon to take place. Accept for yourself and wife my love & good will.

MM Emerson

MH: bMS Am 1280.220(75). *Addressed:* William Emerson Esq[r]. *Endorsed:* Mary M. Emerson / Apr. 10 / 34 / Rec'd Apr. 23.— / Ans[d] " 27/ Wrote also once during the winter / & sent per C. C. E. / Wrote again May 30—.
Dear Nephew] ⟨Dear Mr & Mrs Emerson⟩ Dear Nephew
mountain . . . world] mountain ↑ as to this world ↓
1. WE[3] married Susan Haven of Portsmouth, N.H., on 3 Dec. 1833. CCE to MME,

26 Jan. 1833, describes her as "a woman of manners, virtue, & religious principle," who was sure to be "a most sensible amiable & proper wife" (MT/MH).

2. Niece Hannah Upham Haskins.

3. CCE to MME, 10 Aug. 1833, tells of WE[3]'s plan to arrange an annuity for MME if she will learn from Judge White what yearly income nine hundred dollars should bring (MT/MH).

To Elizabeth Hoar

12 o'k Sab [19 Oct. 1834]

I am so weake in body (I believe) that every thing affects me. Your cypress leaves gave me mournfull pleasure—the first time of your leaving the dear home attire—of openly adopting another family.[1] I have often *felt* to write you welcome into ours which have so gladly received you— And it is no ill omen that I do it at this day sacred to religion. If tears mingle—'tis a religion founded in suffering   Its' sorrows are richer—sweeter than the joys of mere earth. Oh who would forge[n] them—& mingled with human sympathies— with hopes of friendship transfered to a holy state.—

You dear Girl will comfort the Mother for a most valued Son— You do—& will help us to regret not always the sainted Ellen. You will shed I hope the constant light of faith & charity round the arduous path of Charles—will always be fitting each other for a union after the tears of love & respect have watered your urns, by your family & society. Yes *if* you are worthy of your patriot grandfathers—socity will long embalm your memories.

God grant it prays
MME

MH: bMS Am 1280.226(1086). *Addressed:* Elizabeth Hoar.
forge] *possibly* forgo *intended*
1. Reference to EBE's death on 1 Oct. See MME to CCE, 23 Oct. 1834.

To Charles Chauncy Emerson

Thurs. 23 Oct '34

You never say "write" but I do it without the least motive besides. Yet I think of you—now as connected with Edwards life & death.[1] T'was for you more than any in the great web of w'h his meteoric existence made a flash that he lived—aspired—struggled—suffered—failed of all hope and died to gain what virtue not fame could give. Oh yes dear Edward thou art not walking among the haggard forms of eclipsed—dead renown—bending to earth looks of ire & disappointment— No thy sorrows & toils are weaving into thy shekinah unfading flowers—thro his influence I once knew thee to love. And you dear Charles will go forward with new strenght to all the labours & weariness of life—labours & duties w'h not the brightest star of love can always gild or always soften. No the magic of nature cannot exorcise them—

Figure 20. Concord in the 1830s. Drawing by J. W. Barber.

for depraved man must abide his condition & pass the ordeal of virtue thro
the fire & water if he would be a true soldier of the cross. Often may the
wasted darkned form of his life & fortunes attend your side to point your
brighter way or raise your head above the mists & storms of life.

Mother's parlour   Noon. 23

Here are letters of much interest. I tho't Sister might want to put a line in
mine. "Not now—Charles asked you what a man owed society." Did he   I
forgot it—pho ask me. He owes nothing—every sacrifice he makes of religion
& elevation is lost to it & he is no better but falls—but when he lives as he
should—after a while the poor world finds somthing to stare at & groping
about after some clue to the cause it is bettered. This the econymy of Providence in all ages? This St Paul did by different means in his—he was actually
obliged to become foolish to assort with children. Oh you owe the world
yourself—only give it thro' the infinite—   Or rather let Him give it—use you
as His instrument—his torch—or meanest tool. * * *

And now I look for next Wed. with desire. Yours in love
MME

E.[2] called Wed. & yesterday but I was out yes. On tuesday at seeing her I
felt Ed's death. To the young what a companion might he have proved!

No papers come. *Mothers love!*

I am pleased with lodgings[3]   they have neither the excitment of palace
or tub

MH: bMS Am 1280.226(745). *Addressed:* Charles C. Emerson Esq[r] / 17 Court
Street / Boston. *Postmarked:* Concord / Mas. / Oct / 23.
    1. EBE died 1 Oct. 1834 in Puerto Rico. On 18 Oct. CCE received the news from
WE[3], and the next day he told his mother (MT/EW).
    2. EH.
    3. RWE to EzR, 20 Sept. 1834, says, "Aunt Mary is here [Newton], & is desirous
of boarding somewhere in Concord. Mother thought perhaps Mr Prescott's would
be a good place, if they would accomodate her" (*L* 1:421); CCE to RWE, 29 Oct.
[1834], says MME is boarding at Mrs. Woodward's in Concord (MT/MH). Mrs. Persis Adams Davis married widower Ebenezer Woodward in 1817; they lived next door
to the Hoars on Main Street.

To Sarah Sherman Hoar

Sat Night   29 [1834?]

Dear Mrs Hoar,
    It would be well to visit if one could often hear conversations like yours
with our amiable young pastor—[1]   He conversed well—but you had the
most interesting view of the subject.
    But do you not find, my xian friend, that the longer you reason and medi-
tate on the subject of human liberty the less you can define it—but when we

consult conscience we have no doubts, that a certain degree (in perfect harmony with the divine purposes) sufficent to all the means & ends of virtue & religion exists within us? And should we desire to possess any freedom—or indeed any power or priviledge independent of this divine agency?

Another important subject you started[n]—of the highest indeed—speaking of lying & a "liar being different from a lie." This frightfull subverter of all morals is well "illustrated" by Mrs Opie.[2] Have you seen her book? It should be recommended by all who like yourself sustain an influential part in the active duties of life.

MH: bMS Am 1280.226(1218).

started] *possibly* stated

1. Probably the Reverend Hersey Bradford Goodwin, EzR's colleague at Concord from 1830 to 1836.

2. Amelia Opie, English novelist and poet, and author of the very popular *Illustrations of Lying, in All Its Branches*, first published in 1825.

1835

To ?

Sab. Feb. 1 '35

Fain, my dearest Child,[1] would I view all the events few & smale (from my bereaved cradle) indeed they are personally as nothing but in thier relation to God. Oh therefore how dear is solitude complete with health to give the soul but one idea—the divine presence. If one is accostomed to constant *strenghtening* society the habits of the soul rise superior to those excitments w'h occur to such as have gennerally existed alone. Thus this hour I heard after Ch of the engagment of Waldo to a woman of high character & I *hear* of nothing else as yet to attract.[2] This is very good news to me. Again Mr G.[3] gave me offence by a *kind* of toleration of slavery. He had the best motives I trust to check the excitment w'h Mr Thompson gave last week. I would go to hear Mr Wilder with whom I have formed some intimacy but to go today (as from temper for I've been so zealous in Thompson's cause) wont do.[4] Therefore I would concentrate all the emotions of religion, of social sympathy with the *free* or *inslaved* in thinking of you and speaking of the great goal to which we tend. Your note by M. R.[5] gives scope to much. Your feelings & veiws are just what they should be and the contest between theory & practice what has been endured by the pilgrims of many an age. Alas! how many of them failed of reaching the noble summit of virtue, w'h they saw rise before their youthfull eyes crowned with rainbows and stars and suns which never fade—never eclipse—for their light is from the throne of God and the Lamb. Failed! They had not perseverance to tread the steep & rugged ascent—patience enough to bear the cross—to be of *the same mind* with Him who despised ease & glory & power to set an exampel to the poor & humble of his brethen. But multitudes have suceeded—there in the high roads of immortality are gathered of all nations those who loved God better than any thing—who loved labour & poverty & ignorance because they were appointed by Him—& indeed they felt & experienced the adaptation of *these* to lessen vanity & self love—to raise the soul above pleasure & fame & all the host of mean & selfish fears & death itself.

Yet what is extraordinary in the condition of mankind (and in a sense will lessen my argument for the power of xianity) we find the nearer we approach those who are the

MH: bMS Am 1280.220(78).

1. Salutation suggests the addressee was a younger woman, possibly SBR, SBR's sister Martha Bartlett, or EH. Letter is incomplete.

2. RWE proposed to Lydia Jackson in a letter she received 27 Jan., and three days later they were engaged.

3. Probably Hersey B. Goodwin.

4. George Thompson (1804–78), English abolitionist; John Wilder, Trinitarian minister at Concord. MME indicates she attended the meeting of the Middlesex County Antislavery Society at EzR's Concord meetinghouse on 27 Jan. 1835.

5. Possibly niece Mary Emerson Ripley (1820–1907), then fourteen years old.

To Charles Chauncy Emerson

Sab Morn   [Mar. or Apr.? 1835?]

How many events & agitations have rolled over the universe since I saw thee! What contests between the hunger of the mind & body on this poor running tossed ball. Carlyle has finely traced their course in his second part of Schiller w'h I just read—yet injured the side of "letters"?[1] Ah could he have had his spiritual eye opened he would not have made the publick the god of his hero—letters w^d have been the ladder to happiness & Heaven. God send the German a pious biographer. What is knowledge & the godly gift of genius if fame is paramount^n—anything short of immortal. "Time present & future always rivals" said J. Reynolds.   Noon.   The hour w'h was skirted with gold & purple faded into emotions like those caused by a climax given to the Cook to boil beets *potatoes* & *carrots!*^n Yet it was the weakness of my own mind that could not divest itself of sounds & associations w'h had led it's youth thro' the thorny paths of arid yet wholesome struggles—w'h may have broken it in to the weary wasting waitings of age. Nor do I the more excuse your impatience under the holy zeal of that true Nazzarene—Gannett.[2] I began the note by liking to recurr to the little apology (you made on the last sacred rest) of *thinking* about it. I *understood* it—& was pleased—not that you'll ever *think* of it. for what I said   Ah we shall one day *think*. & *what thoughts*! Shall I repent that the numbering up the good[n] virtues of xianity could be tedious because in a poor style.

I hear there is a note from you—thank you. I have had better hours with Elis. this week than ever— Somthing escaped her w'h I'll tell you.

MME

VtMiM. *Addressed:* C C Emerson Esq[r].
paramount] para ⟨is but a secondary⟩ mount
potatoes & *carrots*] *underlined twice*
good] ⟨best⟩ ↑ good ↓

1. Carlyle's essay "Schiller," *Fraser's Magazine* 3 (Mar. 1831): 127–52, begins with a general discussion of the letters between Schiller and Goethe under review, then discusses Schiller's life, and ends with extracts from several of his works.

2. According to *DAB*, the Reverend Ezra Stiles Gannett (1801–71) "lived a life of unselfish, enthusiastic activity." Ordained in 1824, he served as WEC's colleague at Boston's Federal Street Church (later Arlington Street Church).

To Frederic Henry Hedge

Concord   Ap. 10, '35

Dear Sir,

I regret that you are going to leave this vicinity for myself and Mr Emerson more   The fear of not seeing you induces me to ask a favor w'h you will of course be at perfect liberty to refuse with propriety. It is nothing less than your reasons for believing that the Deity is progressive.[1] Whether in natural[n] or moral *attributes* (if *this* term may be used—in truth I shall find it difficult on so new a subject to shape any terms) or both?—whether by self instruction or experience—free or nessecarily by a succession or accession of ideas? If these questions can apply to an infinite Being—but they can't—however vague & imperfect the word infinite be it has a hold on the mind w'h renders them useless. Giving up the ideas or states of mind caused by the old fashioned reason & revelation I would with reverence for the subject & respect for you ask what can be predicated of this finite God. The first idea of improvement is of a moral kind? We have from Moses & Plato no progress of the kind till Jesus—and this was prepared for & foretold if he came at all. To allow of the perfection of his morals—and that of the first law in the heart w'h finds it's adaptations there—to feel as has been felt by noble souls in all time the identity of this moral beauty & power is to acknowledge we need no higher—can conceive of no higher as worthy of God to give. Now if there is progress in the divine mind why are there none proposed for man—why is he made so as to tremble at the possibility of changing the moral law w'h he believes[n] binds the creator & creature? If you seek for arguments in the material world or a world subjected to the creations of our minds, there is a perpetual recurrence to the same events—the same sad storms the same imperfect senses to suffer them or enjoy the same sunshine. Nothing can exceed the identity of the race tho' his situation is very varying. Surely it must be from the revelations of the new J. Chh that different modes of existence may give these new ideas. Pardon me, Sir, I meant not to be other than serious & humble; besides I have no right to speake of a sect of w'h I know nothing. And that recognizes the divinity of a revelation, w'h I could not refer to in these questions, w'h arise only from—are[n] athorised only on the rejection of the inspiration of that. I mean that my reason—an ultimate fact in human mind or whatever termed—rejects the belief of a progressive mind in the Creator—first Cause or moral govonor. That this kind provision is of the utmost consequence to virtue & happiness. That if the Deity were changable the one would be without immutable law and rule—the other exposed to dread the future. Change in a Being so great (if not infinite for the term in it's limits to my poor limits is impossible & contradictory to change) must induce changes of tremendous import—if it respects Himself from happiness to the reverse?—for if change be nessecary why not eternal revolutions? What can be predicated of his foreknowledge? How can it exist but by calculations & how those infallible? Even the new dress w'h the Sartor gives the *eternal* Yea would lose it's strong power to please.[2] And the sublime Plato who loved to dwell on the eternal ideas of God would find them but the changing decorations of a panarama. That there will forever be new displays—developments of these eternal ideas or elements or modes of the divine existence is a glorious article in reasons store house of vistas—but that they can alter, increase, & of course decay, or cease to operate (as those of the created) she[n] rejects without the power to do otherwise—as the condition of her existence leads her to a self existent and uncreated God. Yet that there are appearances of nessesity—that optimism does not seem the order of the present she allows—but if there are temporary obstructions to virtues success by the inexplicable enigmas of the human heart and the problems of it's condition in nature or artificial institutions she does not love & reverence the all perfect Being less—she perceives—feels—has faith that eventually the labyrinths w'h compose the created web will be cleared of evil to all the intents & purposes of Justice   With this belief she is or thinks the universal interests safe, with an immutable & infinite Governor were there no revelation like the bible—for if this ark of her covenant were as infallible as *some* are educated to believe, were the Giver & Revelator liable to new ideas where would be her security?[n] There would be no little or great thread of nessesity drawn round the orb of man's destiny to heighten the lustre of it's center—his portion of freedom—there would be no fixed[n] sun towards which to point his quadrant for observations w'h sustain him tho' clouds may now & then obscure that sun.

If you, Sir, will pardon the liberties of 60 years athority and accept the respect with w'h I entertain my remembrance of your preaching and the fame of your talents it will be gratefull to

M Emerson

M.M.E's liberty never extends to repeating the speculations of the young philosophers. She rejoices to believe they will return from their comet like wanderings to the center of a *Personal* Divinity—leaving which has caused their unnatural eclipse and eccentricity. This eve. gave me, by a sort of accident, your opinion and with the midnight hour I would dream it away with the goblins of fancy.

MH: bMS Am 1280.226(1083). *Addressed:* Rev. F. H. Hedge / Cambridge. *Endorsed:* April 1834 / From Miss Mary Moody Emerson.
natural] natural ⟨or acquired⟩
w'h he believes] w'h ↑ he believes ↓
are] ⟨the natural⟩ are
she] ⟨he⟩ ↑ she ↓
security?] seurity? *in MS; possibly* surity? *intended*
fixed] *possibly* fired
  1. Despite the "1834" endorsement, this letter belongs to 1835. (The last number in MME's dateline could be either "4" or "5.") Hedge settled at Bangor, Maine, about 30 Apr. 1835 (*L* 1:416). RWE to FHH, 12 Apr. 1835, explains that he is sending a long letter to a stranger from "our Sibyl whom so hardly her own friends can bring to unclose her lips." The letter was prompted, RWE says, by his quotation of Hedge's "Thursday remark to her" (*L* 1:443)—probably the idea of a "progressive" Deity. MME also recalls ideas from Hedge's articles on Coleridge and Swedenborg (*Christian Examiner* 14 [1833]: 192–218).
  2. The Emersons were reading Carlyle's *Sartor Resartus* (*Fraser's Magazine*, 1834).

To Lidian Jackson

Ap. 22, 1835[n]

I throw by writing to our friend (your admirer E.P.P.) to thank you, my dear Lidian, for your letter—to own a new & delightfull gratification in exciting your heart by my note. 'Tis indeed more than I did expect.

You give me matter for pages—but it were almost idiocy to take, or attempt to, your time when Waldo is there.

You gave me a full confidence in your sincerity—so I take full hold of all you profess—and joy to hail you on my way as a believer (in the bible sense) of our blessed Master. You go farther in your dependence on Him than myself in some respects probably—for if I lost[n] his mission or attoning ministry, if I retained my relation to God there would be nothing to fear—if He is the bible God. But as He has, I believe, contrived this medium of communion & manifestation (and of all grand & generous plans the greatest minds could imajine, it is beyond in beauty & wisdom) it seems persumption & arrogance to neglect it in those who cannot attach or embody their religious sentiments to it. Yet there have been among the gifted & honest such[n]—therefore we can not must not reprobate—but respect—. Now dont think I include your frind Gothe—for woe was him—he seemed destitute of the common gifts of nature in religious feeling. I thank you for a new instance of his insane superstition—

and believe that as you go on in mental & moral progress you will come to the best conclusions of him—one of which will be that he was designed to show the possibility of a great intellect w'h existed as a machine—cut off from its Maker apparently.

As to metaphisical speculations I understand you as you must us—that with certain explanations we admire a witty jest—any thing w'h partakes of wit. Mere speculations w'h do not touch the heart are barren—but metaphisial truths are the soul of existence—vital to reason & the condition of its operations—are they not? They throw light on our consciousness—the link between God & us—the torch by w'h we look into the vistas of the future— the security of our faith the charm of our poetic existence in the prologue of the drama^n of life— & the star w'h points us to the sun^n of science in its' progress. You have awakned me—you I was thinking of in the midnight hour for this sincerity of character last night after getting a little nub of another cast. God bless you dear Lidian

MME

MH: bMS Am 1280.226(772). *Addressed:* Miss Lidian Jackson.
1835] *possibly added by another hand*
for . . . lost] ⟨as⟩ ↑ for ↓ if I ⟨doubted of⟩ ↑ lost ↓
gifted & honest such] ⟨wise⟩ gifted & honest such ⟨ ↑ perhaps ↓ ⟩
prologue . . . drama] ⟨unfinished⟩ ↑ prologue of the ↓ drama
sun] *possibly* sum

To Elizabeth Hoar

Mrs. Beachs. S. Court.[1]
Tues. 11 ok [June? 1835?]

Bulletins dear Elis. ought to be issued. Health better than expected—but pain confines me to a fire with my hostess. Mary P. all kindness goes & seeks out Charlotte—so does G. B. She is expected every day—but I do not feel able to remain—I walked toward Mrs Howards after getting here last eve. but took Hack & pursued my object—without telling the Hackman I was in quest of one who had weatherd more days & nights with me than yesterday. I expect to see her at P. or B. Mrs G. Lee out of Town alas! But we shall meet some time or other—for we have been intimate. Garrison & Childs I cant see but Mr May whom M. P. brot to breakfast has given me much encourgement about abolition. I'm looked on^n as too proud—a little of this element strained when May asked if Mr CCE would engage to lecture or be agent a few months. I said he would do every thing he could I knew not what time he had as he was settled at C. & had an office. M. will write him. We dropt Mrs G. in Cambridge St. & Mr G. racketed over the City to land me here. 'Tis a good place Mr & Mrs Alcot are here—as I laid down in a room next theirs I heard the managment of her two little children. I regreted the ordinary complaints &cc w'h I heard—conjectured the union—& the every day disasters of posterity. After tea Miss P. invited them to see me. Behold he had carried his child of 4 years & had a tooth out without knowing she was to have it out. I objected. But they all justified it as no deception. The *behold* is now He is a spiritualist of the platonic & new school. I wondered at nothing then— but referred to plain truths of Dr S. Clarke w'h excited George's risibles. No I don't know where to find the spiritualists of the present days—reminiscnces he talked much off—of the idealism—& that of Jesus I know not what they get the Christ to be—talked of the infinite with much ease. Well he's a goodly man & much celebrated teacher.— so the hour is up & I'm to prepare my gaurdian says. I do believe young folks are designed to gaurd age. Mary is worthy to fill your place. Love to Sister & Waldo

Yours truly & very much
MME.

Miss P—s love to you

Mrs Alcot is sister to S. May

Oh the job of getting to P.

Perhaps tis not best to say any thing but as short a time as is convenient for me to leave H & then he need not remember it. Mrs W^2 expects me to stay till I get a place tho' I would^n rather remove at once. If you know of any other you can tell me.

MH: bMS Am 1280:226(1088).

on] me *in MS*

would] woul *in MS; possibly* now

1. *The Journals of Bronson Alcott*, ed. Odell Shepard (Port Washington, N.Y., 1938), 1:57–58, includes MME among the group the Alcotts entertained at their rooms at Mrs. Beach's boarding house, 3 Somerset Court, Boston, in early July 1835. This letter indicates MME also boarded there for a time. MME to ?, 1 Feb. 1835, indicates MME's interest in antislavery activities before the early April meeting with Charles Burleigh (see Gougeon, 24–25); mention of going to "P" (Plymouth?) suggests this letter was written before 30 June 1835. Other references are probably to Charlotte Farnham, Mary Peabody, George Bradford or GBE; "B.": possibly Byfield; Hannah Sawyer Lee, William Lloyd Garrison, probably David L. Child, husband of Lydia Maria Child; Samuel J. May (1797–1871), brother of Abba (Mrs. Bronson) Alcott, general agent and secretary for the Massachusetts Antislavery Society; CCE; the Bronson Alcotts. I appreciate Phyllis Cole's pointing out the importance of this letter and help with illuminating its obscurities.

2. Mrs. Persis Woodward, with whom MME boarded in 1834 and 1835.

To Elizabeth Hoar

Plymouth   Tues. 30 June [1835]

If we carry the image of those we last associate with into another state as we do here at change of season,^{n} it behooves to mingle in our last days with the good. No 'tis low perhaps worse, to think that mortal objects however good can accompany us at the first entrance into an unbodied state. 'Tis natural that the very strongest affections of earth should lose their influence tho' they may return when the amazement—the novelty—the escape—the hopes & prospects of the real great state first open on us. The only element of our existence w'h will find its own dear affinities and make us feel at home in any comfort will be that habit of existing for & in & with reference to the fountain of our existence—there where we shall realise our stream of life seperate yet united—responsible yet dependant in a clearer & higher way than we could by living & talking here of the infinite & beautifull—of correspondences & laws forever. All this has come parenthesis like (as old folks talk) to say that I have talked with you ever since I left you standing at the door with a look of sympathy for the feeble pilgrim so taking to the fancy & heart too. For so long time you have been my outlet for all things—have been my receiver more than all others—for the visits of the gentlemen have been oft but rapid as the Angels to the semi barbarians of old.

And I've thought of you for the future   Lidian & you will make a fine time of it. She is intellectual & poetic as I did not suspect at Concord. The every day cares will arrange & balance her mind—while your logical head & controuled affections (affections & knowledge I must in justice say are veiled with a modesty & self forgetfullness—utter absence of all egotism) may form the empyrean of your domestic circle.

Phebe Bliss[1] writes that she expects to be confined every day &c &c. I shall go to Boston on Saturday or Monday & may not feel like going to Andover. Kind & hospitable as they have been I long for a corner of solitude & if sickness—well. Mrs B.[2] is a kind affectionate woman. Lidian's best love. Mine to your Mother & *father* & S. I hope she returns 'fancy free.' You understood what I meant about Mary P—'s being worthy to minister the wine of comfort to a traveler beset with infirmities. The Counseller[3] was sensitive about my demands on your labours I found on monday. I want to see him for all all.

Yours most gratefully
MME

If convenient & in cog you may speak to Deacon H. but I can stay at Mrs W—[4] longer or shorter as I named to her.

Please seal & if no opp^y, put in office the enclosed[5]

MH: bMS Am 1280.226(1090). *Addressed:* Miss Elis. Hoar. / Concord / Rev. H. B. Goodwin.

season] *possibly* scene (T)

1. Niece Phebe Bliss Farnham married Matthew Cobb of Barnstable, a widower with four children, in Dec. 1831.
2. Probably Lidian Jackson's sister, Lucy Jackson Brown.
3. "S." is EH's sister Sarah Hoar; possibly Mary Peabody; "the Counseller" is probably CCE, but possibly EH's father, Samuel Hoar.

4. "Deacon H.": Probably Isaac Hurd, Jr., who sometimes boarded MME at his house on Main Street, Concord; Mrs. Woodward's.

5. Written on outside.

To Sarah Bradford Ripley

Sab Noon   26 July [1835?][1]

Dearest of women & (one day before I breathe my last useless breath) one of the highest if faith & you argue aright. And do you read good books the last thing at night? Are you about to enter on the real paths to God & his Son— are you to be a jewel in the crown of him who has redeemed a fallen race— What a trophy to that plan which baffles all human wisdom to apprehend it's depths & heights! What numbers will your conversion lead to virtue here & safty hereafter—   A sight to rejoice the Angels literally. Let the drudgers of this mean world pass other scenes of education where their senses & little learned stuff will not dazzel their weake minds—but gifted souls hasten to dwell with the spirit of Jesus in the vital unspeakable atmosphere of an all surounding influencing God—   Oh I've been afraid of your superiorty to speake out of this scheme—afraid to hear you speake lightly of Him by whom God has made the great manifestation of Himself—whether by the nessisity of his attributes—or to honor the law w'h the fallen race can never fullfill—it matters not. This medium of interaction with the absolutely infinite exists— has died & redeemed the Platos & prophets. & lights of every age to the glory of God the Father of *his father & our father*. Oh Sarah your peculiar path & arduous was allotted that you might find peace. & glory & love in none but the infinite. Of that path you so openly speake & your generous husband is so famed for hearing it with smiles that I refer to it. But from the first moment I knew you I tho't you among than off society & family. You have been sett apart to show forth the true power of mind & heart I ca'nt but hope. As the world runs so wild in speculation & so hollow in devotion even it's higher sort that were you in liesure to pursue it with its trumpery of languages could any thing arrest you but miracle—   Now the happy miracles w'h will open the infinite & unite it to its auther have all been wro't for your special benefit by means so interwoven with the ordinary course of life that indirectly they influence you to climb the summit of reason & truth. When there may you resemble the emblem of a sanctified soul "the vessel laid up before the Lord full of heavenly manna within and without of pure polished gold." prays most prostrately

MME

If you speake of this letter as of one from Sister Phebe—no matter   It would'nt move a pain of humility I could not feel. But should not have had courage to have written what I felt about your kind of reading were I not in a regenerating hour thro Gannetts sermon on prayer—   —that only true ladder to faith & virtue.

Elisabeth[2] could have nothing to repeat to her father improper—if she misunderstood my long complaint of his careing nothing for me I would rectify it—if there was ought unhandsome I would with sorrow retract. But I guess he was only sportive— Hope her pond or canal is better

MH: bMS Am 1280.226(1286). *Addressed:* Mrs S. A Ripley.
1. Dating uncertain. 26 July fell on Sunday in 1835, and MME seems to write from the Concord area, where she was in July of this year. Below she mentions Gannett on prayer: Ezra Stiles Gannett, "A Life of Prayer," was printed in the *Liberal Preacher,* n.s., 6 (1836): 1–18; MME may have heard him preach in Boston.
2. Probably SBR's eldest daughter, then fifteen years old.

To Lidian Jackson Emerson

[9 Oct. 1835]

Now I am serious in being glad that the first note I send to your house, Lidian, should be to occasion your doors to open to the pirates of the humane cause.[1] Would I were to be as often, as I shall seldom, your Almoner.

The case is in plain prose I met, at Acton, Mr May & Thompson the latter gave a fine address on abolition. At the first joy of seeing *May* so unexpectedly I asked him to call on yours & you & dine—he would call but must dine in City—afterwards he proposed breakfasting with you—then before parting found it might be inconvenient—but in cool blood I believed it w^d be very pleasant to Mr E. & he confessed a wish to see Mrs E. so he comes & Mr T. before 8 o'k expecting to breakfast at 8. Have I done you a favor? It would do me one if *you* could see the subject w'h agitates the Country as some do. At any rate I was right glad to lose every little sinister concern in it. And believe you might be led to a sympathy so congenial to the gospel spirit. Oh 'tis good if it be only a dream to indulge it— Oh it is good to ponder over the prophecies w'h bring the visions of liberty & salvation to nations who sit in darkness & chains. If as some predict, the state between death & the general consummation of the plan of redemption of the soul is like dreaming— tho reasoning more clearly than ever, then perhaps the history & progress of man's nature & destiny will be the subjects— And—and the part each has acted towards the completion of that plan—!

What a thought! May God help us!—those who are torpid now a while may resemble (before the day of rest) the river whose current has been obstructed, but let loose overflows & fertilizes its banks—its far off country.

I tho't of asking you to go with me if the morning had begun fine—wished for you there

Good night in love &c
MME

MH: bMS Am 1280.226(776). *Addressed:* Mrs R W Emerson.
1. For MME's inviting the abolitionists to breakfast on 10 Oct. 1835 with the newly married Emersons, see *LJE L,* 43 and nn., and *JMN* 5:90. Samuel J. May, author of *A*

Figure 21. Coolidge Castle, Concord, home of Ralph Waldo Emerson and Lidian Jackson Emerson.

Discourse on Slavery in the United States (Boston, 1832), resigned as minister to the
Chauncy Place Church, Boston, in 1835 to become general agent for the Massachusetts
Antislavery Society. He and George Thompson addressed the Middlesex Antislavery
Society at its quarterly meeting in Acton on 9 Oct. 1835. Thompson spoke both in the
afternoon and evening, and May was the first evening speaker (MS Records of the
Middlesex Antislavery Society, Concord Free Public Library).

1836

To LIDIAN JACKSON EMERSON

Waltham   March. 11 '36

You write, dear Lydia, that we will speake of "high & deep things." Let
us commune of those w'h *deserve* the name—w'h put to silence the mys-
tifications of philosophy & piety, of sectarian dogmatism (to w'h the aged
are tempted) & to the hollow abstractions & latitudinarisms w'h colour the
young speculatist.

I should rejoice to meet you on a ground w'h would give my imajanation
some life—and my heart more of that warmth w'h some moments of our
speech of Jesus afforded. Will you do me the favor to read Wm Goodel's
speech? w'h I send least it might be forgotten & wish it returned. If you take
his ground about sin—I shall know where we can meet—   Besides it will
give you my ideas on the subject of *censuring* Col. Shattuck's[1] conduct w'h
you might think was uncharitable—w'h indeed you did oppose and I warmly
tried to refute. The subjects w'h this "Report" includes are *deep* & *high* as an
interest in God—practical—indispensable to that part of our nature—that
moral constitution w'h our divine Saviour directed all his ministry—and for
the fullfillment of w'h the present times seem preparing. Only think that the
revolutions of only half a century concentrate the great idea of man's greatness *as a man*—   That the old Countries w'h have literally breathed the air
impregnated with the ashes of the Aristocratic oppressor and the oppressed
are about to be purged—that the *Heavens will hear the earth*—and man shall
not thrive on the miseries of his brother! These are the broad & deep things,
my dear Mrs Emerson, to w'h I would hail your devotion—to w'h I would
(as fellow traveller) consecrate your growing influence in a place sacred to
the memory of Ancestors eminently spiritlised—in the bible & Godly sense
of that term (now so often desecrated by the poet & pantheist) eminently
devoted to the interests of liberty & general philantrophy! These and *thier*
holy alliances would well become—would find a way to the heroes of my
sleepy Town graced by the mild & sweetly serious manners of your ladyship.
Another book may reconcile the quarrel we had about Mrs Huntington. Read
the last pages of Mrs Judson's memoirs[2]—and I hope we shall agree in admiration—why Even the heroic Paul if on earth, would not ask *why* the book

was written & *what had* his imitator *done?* Is there any American biography of woman equal?

Thank Charles for his letter & sympathy in the restoration of Sarah.[3] God grant her to live till she knows the high truth "between the "paste boards"— and till her grave shall be honoured by the tears of the coulered man. I ca'nt write him, if I had any thing worth his notice, as I expect to send this at noon to Miss Whiting. Of Sarah Alden I see nothing as I can't see her when she can talk without nurse or children   My love to Mrs Brown—could I entertain her by a letter I would—this is a family one & carrys love to your husband & Mary Brooks[4]—especially E. Peabody if with you let her have her part of the letter—for it is on the abolition principle & she is not a convert I fear. D[r] Ripley & Neice &c &c

Yours in the hopes of the gospel
MM Emerson

MH: bMS Am 1280.226(779). *Addressed:* Mrs Emerson / Concord.

1. The Reverend William Goodell (1792–1878), of Providence, R.I., a reformer, addressed the Massachusetts Antislavery Society at its annual meeting in Boston, 20 Jan. 1836, in behalf of a resolution commending William Lloyd Garrison and his antislavery newspaper the *Liberator.* In his address (printed in the *Fourth Annual Report . . . of the Massachusetts Antislavery Society*, Boston, 1836, 54–61), he attacked the "fastidious decorum of the age [that] shelters vice from deserved and necessary rebuke" (55). MME suggests that "Colonel" Daniel Shattuck (1790–1867), one of Concord's most aggressive businessmen from 1812 until the Civil War, is among those who hide behind "decorum."

2. James D. Knowles, *Memoir of Mrs. Ann H. Judson, Late Missionary to Burmah . . .*, 2d ed. (Boston, 1829). The life of Mrs. Susan Huntington (1791–1823), another missionary, was included in *Female Biography, Containing Memoirs of Mrs. A. Judson, Mrs. S. Huntington, Mrs. H. Newell, Miss A. J. Linnard* (Boston, n.d.).

3. CCE to MME, 5 Mar. [1836], mentions that SBR was now considered out of danger, after suffering a severe hemorrhage in Feb. (MT/MH); MME seems now to be at the Ripleys' in Waltham.

4. Probably Jane Whiting of Concord, a member of LJE's Sunday school class in Concord (*LJE L*); Lucy Jackson Brown; Mary Merrick Brooks (b. 1801) was a founding member of the Middlesex Antislavery Society.

To Ralph Waldo Emerson

Waltham   March 31 '36

Dear Waldo,

I begin to see Sarah Alden alone and is it in any keeping with our years of confidence not to speake of my seperation from your house? Will she not easily see how the cause must be all in me? That the fact of your early antipathy was not voluntary? How rapidly will she run over the romance of my early admiration of your genius—which I love to hover over as like to some admirable Sculpter—like to some vision of nature w'h haunted me in youth and gave itself away to my imajanation. I remember it now a sad quarrel we had in Fed St.—but like Undine herself I *forgot* it—and when your sucess in love & office happened I well remember the look of the sky was finer & the earth less stale.[1] Forgive, dear Waldo, that I have wearied you so long. It was not—indeed it was not designed. About this very time last year I told a truth about my opinion & taste opposed to yours—and I felt sure that our intercourse must end. I afterwards grew wiser on that subject—and was curious to know more—& love more—   And foreseeable time & health might have added to the *delight* w'h it has ever been my gift to enjoy from superior merit to my own.

I dont know that I should forgive myself for protracting a connection after losing you in the chaos of modern speculation—   I knew not on what ground you did any thing—nor where to find your principles—they were an enigma. When Sarah[n] spoke of sin & *looked* to you for sympathy—I wondered how either could be found—each might be an atom turned out by the Whirl of nessisty. I could not love in the true sense—yet credulous to the last—to your complaints & contrasts[n] I answered by the long tried efforts I had made "to live"—it was the ban of society that was on me—and the excuse for you might be infered.[n] I do not regret the tedious history. I feel glad that I released you finally by my promise. I did not *promise* to write no more. And quere as it may be—it is true that I shall hear & meet you with pleasure I believe. My determination was the same & the "storm" only made it vocal   But to the business— it is giving a wrong impression to others as well as Sarah—'tis receiving perhaps, attention for your sake—and as I may repeat my journies 'tis truth to say our usual intercourse is ended. If I appeared or was sad—still there would be no implication on the favorite of society. Oh no I could not shade a leaf of laurel—   And I shall not disturb for a moment the flowers w'h grow in your path. The sorrow w'h seems an element in all sensible men is not in you. And the debt of light & comfort I've always owned to you & CC will throw only suspicion on me. If I am silent at Mr Francis[2] strain of speaking 'tis attributed to my bible philosophy. He & Sarah vindicate Newton—I poor Flamsteed— & think the Newton faults but proof of depravity[n] in human nature.[3] Ages are hastening when its' redemption will be consummated & you, I hope, an able minister in its kingdom. If I could have a message in this letter to Lydia I *would* say that I believe we shall then find I did nothing to deserve complaint in her house—except two or three jokes for w'h I grieve. Whether the tenor of good will is to be corrected for sometimes failing must depend on the principles & known character. However it is true the more I'm understood the less tolerated—& the prophecy I made to your youth that you would like me better is not fullfilled. Now dont laugh & apply my disappointment to certain other prophecies.[n]

Adieu   I will cherish the memory of your attention as sweet as the dew of Heaven. Your aff[t] Aunt

MME

May I tell CC what you repeated of his censure of my hit at Jackson extravagance. I was answerd in following suit—but he must know my sorrow at his censure.

VtMiM. *Addressed:* Mr R Waldo Emerson / Concord / Mss. *Endorsed:* M M. Emerson / March 1836.

Sarah] Sarah ⟨and you⟩
contrasts] *possibly* contracts
infered] *possibly* injured
depravity] ⟨truth⟩ ↑ depravity ↓
prophecies.] *bottom fifth of p. 3 missing; some letter fragments remain at torn edge; remainder of letter written on outside*

1. 26 Federal Street, Boston, was the Emerson home from Apr. 1821 to May 1823 (*Life of RWE*, 86, 97), but the quarrel alluded to is not mentioned elsewhere; the water sprite Undine appears in a tale by Friedrich von Fouqué (1777–1843), translated in 1818 by George Soame as *Undine: A Fairy Romance*.

2. Probably Convers Francis (1795–1863), minister of the First Church at Watertown. His wife was SBR's close girlhood friend, Abba Bradford Allyn.

3. Reference to the derogatory picture of Sir Isaac Newton suggested by letters and other documents in Francis Baily's *Account of the Reverend John Flamsteed, the First Astronomer Royal* (London, 1835). Her source is probably the review in the *Quarterly Review* (London) 55 (Dec. 1835): 96–128, or a review of William Whewell's pamphlet *Newton and Flamsteed, Quarterly Review* 55 (Feb. 1836): 306–8.

To WILLIAM EMERSON[3] AND CHARLES CHAUNCY EMERSON

Waltham   May 1.   36

My dear Nephew,

My nieghbour is going to your City, and tho' I have nothing to say but what you know—yet I add if it is not too much incroaching on your time I should like to hear from your own pen how Charles gets on.[1] Waldo saw Brother Ripley a few moments & spoke well of him last thursday. I have heard nothing since. The sattisfaction of knowing him to be with you & your Mother & Susan has taken a load of ugly stuff off my old heart that indeed grows a weary of disappointment. & bodily infirmity w'h has visited me the last weeks. But does not deprive me of the pleasure of remembering how much I enjoyed of Charles & Waldo the last year. I have taken part in your cares & prosperity & daily commit you to the best of all Beings.

In haste Your Aunt
MME

Dear Charels,

I will not feel anxious for you if you dont get well as fast as I want you to. I know your faith—your views of the great things of existence (I believe a little) and soon as the disease lets your spirit operate you will be stronge to get well or endure longer privation.

My faith & philosophy so narrow at present that I want you well right
away. Poor decrepit Aunte. Want any thing fear any thing hope for any
thing—

Well well I dont habitually beat my own rebase.[n]

Goodnight think of Elizabeth fine in look & spirit & be thankfull. Think of
her God & your God and rejoice in his present gifts & magnificent promises.

His hand is over & under & about you & I say hail to your course

MME

MH: bMS Am 1280.226(1075). *Addressed:* William Emerson Esq[r]. / Wall Street
60 / New York. / Rev Mr Harding. *Endorsed:* M. M Emerson / May 1 / 36 / Ans[d] "
7— / Wrote again—10th.

rebase] sic *in MS; possibly* rebeck (*a medieval stringed instrument*) *intended*

1. On 22 Apr. RWE set out for New York City with CCE, who was severely ill
with a persistent cough and too ill to travel alone, in the hope that a warmer climate
would restore him to health. He left CCE in the care of WE[3] and by 30 Apr. was back
in Concord. The note to CCE that follows is her last to this nephew.

To Ralph Waldo Emerson

Waltham   Monday 16 [May 1836]

My dear Waldo,

Your loss is unspeakable—& I see its' shadow over the longest path
you may tread—tis over all your books & pens—but it must not retard the
spirit—it would in olden days of faith give it to unite itself more than life's
intercourse with him.[1] But I can by searching find nothing in our loved S. A.
transcendentalism to give her an idea of the consciousness & identity of the
soul that I mourn having gone—   But blessed be God I follow him with an
intensity unfelt before—   Alas & with a sorrow unfelt. His kind of faith I
could understand—his views were to influence others—his sucess to gratify
family pride. If I'd loved him better I should be glader of his escape. I suffer
bitterly from the coldness w'h I parted with him at Boston—from the letter
I wrote him. Verily I feel to be pitied. To have buried him after parting with
you was only losing half of him & in prospect was not without those consolations w'h often attend certain feelings. And I am about to leave with intire
acquiesence that all times & places shall be alike indifferent. His last year of
kindnesses will too often recur—but never mind. I had expected to give him
some token of my gratitude—   And that I should in my last letter send for
those 3 or 4# gives me to groan in the silence of midnight as makes me pity
myself. I send no message to his bereaved Mother & Elis. I shall come up with
Sarah & see them in a day or two or 3. Mrs Hoar wrote me that Elis. was
"composed & thinks every thing has happened in mercy & love to him" She
herself invites me to visit her & D[r] R. also. But I have concluded nothing of
the kind—'tis possible I may & take stage for Boston to w'h I go this week

or first of next for Maine. Thank Lydian for a letter w'h not be exceeded in beauty & worth to my feelings— But that I would be just as I am I was designed to be alone & I never failed to realize all I put in your letter. 'Tis nothing now. The mourned appears all—when Sarah was going I bid Charles & Elis. adieu in a note w'h I hope she has forgiven.

He has nothing to forgive if he knows me I believe. If any thing unknown prevents my going to Concord & seeing you repeatedly while there remember how earnestly I desire your & L—s good

Your aff^t Aunt
MME

To lose him or any such mind & have no testimony to his sick thoughts is sad indeed. I will see Ruthy & follow his last days of whatever kind.

MH: bMS AM 1280.226(896). *Addressed:* Rev. R. W. Emerson / Concord / Mss. *Postmarked:* WALTHAM / MAS / May 17. *Endorsed:* M M Emerson / May 1836.
  1. CCE died in New York on 9 May.

To Elizabeth Hoar

Elm Vale   Au. 16— '36

You are not well I fear, my dear Child, from what Sister says in her letter. You must look to your health—must change the scene—however full of precious remembrances. I tho't of nothing better than our mountain air and in the stronge desire to have you here forgot so far the obstacels as to begin arrangements—much to the delight of Hannah's[1] gay & kind heart. But I dont forego the hope of your coming next summer with your Mother. I want you to see the place where Charles first saw nature in her wilderness of beauty—no science unveiled her—but her grand & silent figure points to other powers than hers. She is here no teacher of pantheism—or of airy idealism. Do you remember the sab. Eve. afterⁿ the last moon had filled her horns? It was remarkably— dont know what to call it—it happened that I heard by a youth from Cambridge of our good Hearsy's following passage.[2] This moon hung over the lake (whose waters were still as the neighbouring graves)—she looked sadly on her image w'h was passing into the shadow of the mountain as tho' she felt it an emblem of beauty & genius resigning this shadowy state—the air from the south west moved the leaves to a murmur—it seemed to inshroud one like an invisible substance and to a strong imajanation might have revealed the secret of its existence. The tho'ts of the dead & living needed none—yet there was one single image arose—'twas that of a flower—beautifull as the scene w'h gave it growth—'twas shaded by the cypress—'twas wet with its dews— the light but faintly breathed on it—but it bid fair to thrive—and after some days & nights I learnt that the light from an invisible Star had penetrated it's bosom as no sun could reach—and it's mission was to dispell all useless unwholsome dews—to consume all vapours w'h partook too much of the

Figure 22. Elizabeth Hoar (1814–78) in the 1830s.
Courtesy Joel Myerson.

ground—to rear it after longer & stronger efforts of its gifts, to become an amaranthine.[3]

I find dear Elis. by a few lines in your previous letter, that you are solving one of the problemns w'h meet us so often—that of loving better the Hand that has afflicted. There is a deeper one, w'h I hope you may avoid in some good degree—that of age retrospecting the shades w'h the darker sides of human nature & conditions have stained their course—yet they are able to love (while they "abhor themselves") their Creator—and to unite the sentiment of finite misery with infinite perfection. May your life be prolonged & "your age clear as the noon & forget your sorrows as waters that have passed away"[4]

"Do I like memoirs"? Nothing less. Except those w'h are connected with science & religion—w'h are nessecary to mark the progress of the race. Are they to be but tributes of affection? Who would wish to transfer the image of a beloved object to paper? to an oblivious & criticising world? Pride & affection forbids—*what has* been *done*? And is this the last office the press is ever to do for a name we hoped to stand by the side of the high interests of our beloved Country. Remember how impatiently we put aside those of Buckminster & Thacher[5] if we are seeking but an almanak. Publish the virtues of the dead? Were they martyrs? Virtue it's very nature is soiled—is contradicted—who does not feel (I should imagine believe)[n] their best actions to lose their best charm when sounded? What memorial like to that of immortal memory—where he has implanted a principle—done a favor—there it will live— Besides what is equal—what can sattisfy love holy ambitious love like meeting him in another state with unexpected virtue[n]—hidden before—but there bro't into life—some pure & generous capasity developed as none could here. Had he a peculiar mind and tis well unfold it on paper? Why spring a mine whose wealth was not for this riegion? There are many inactive Miltons & Newtons (the last name most unfortunate if one fact of poor Flamsteed's is known hereafter) in the famed Chh yard.[6] A greater truth remains that the peculiarities of genius live where & for always they will be known & used—there they will live in their own indeviently when the scrool of man's history may be forgotten, unless some pilgrim Angel carry it to new worlds for their wonder & advertisment. It is possible that Waldos pen may give a picture that will survive—surely that will be above criticism & delight taste. And so indifferent am I to my own feelings that I would ask you not to show this if it were possible any influence could arise from my opinions to retard a moment the artist.

Yes my dear Niece, I am glad to find those "three friends"[7] w'h make light every ill & disappointment. I had surrendered myself from ill health & eyes so long to live by others kindness & wisdom that I was glad to find myself (poor & limited as it is) again with old books & memoranda that spake of life and old truths before my nephews were born. How idle it was in me to try to keep sight of their progress. I will some time tell you of this attempt

at Waltham. Do write—and write of other things—your letter brings tears—
Tell me what your father thinks and says of publick affairs—of new books—
of Miss Fullers[8] visit—and when you are well we will write about your own
Charles & how I expect you here—tho' I shall be less excited probably than
when I was so dependant on you the more I saw you. Affectionate regards to
your parents—& all blessings on them & theirs wishes

Your loving Aunt
MM Emerson

MH: bMS Am 1280.226(1093). *Addressed:* Hon. Samuel Hoar / M. C. / For
Miss Elizabeth Hoar / Concord / Massachusetts. *Postmarked:* So Waterford / Me—
Aug 17th.

after] ⟨before⟩ ↑ after ↓
imagine believe)] ↑ imagine ↓ believe)
virtue] ⟨advantage⟩ ↑ virtue ↓

1. EH's response to the death of her fiancé, CCE; Hannah Upham Haskins.
2. "Hearsy's" allusion unclear. Possibly a reference to Hersey B. Goodwin; or the
passage that follows may be a paraphrase from Goodwin or from Freeman Hearsey,
Miscellaneous Pieces in Verse, n.d. [1799? 1805?].
3. Adjective form used by MME as a substantive, to refer to the amaranth, an
imaginary flower that never fades. Cf. Milton, *Paradise Lost*, 3:352–53 and 11:78.
4. Cf. Job 11:16–17.
5. Samuel Cooper Thacher's memoir of his friend, Joseph Stevens Buckminster,
was published with the first collection of Buckminster's sermons in 1814. A memoir of
Thacher by F. W. P. Greenwood was published with Thacher's sermons in 1824.
6. Allusion to Baily's *Account of the Reverend John Flamsteed* (see MME to RWE,
31 Mar. 1836, n. 3); possible allusion to Thomas Gray's "Elegy in a Country Church-
yard": "Some mute inglorious Milton here may rest" (line 59).
7. Coleridge, "The Good Great Man": "And three firm friends, more sure than
day and night, / HIMSELF, his MAKER, and the angel DEATH" (*The Friend* 1:529).
8. Margaret Fuller first visited the Emersons between 21 July and 11 Aug. 1836.

To LIDIAN JACKSON EMERSON

Elm Vale   29 Sep. [1836]

Many thanks, dear Lidian, for your valuable present[1] w'h has come but
now— Some of it is invaluable to the lover of nature— Yet the solitary
admirer of the Auther's youngest pen little thought that when his plumes were
grown he would like some other classical kind set fire to his gentle nest—but
he has saved so much more than this & other destroyers that the old nestlers
will not complain—nor burn a straw of the eyrie. We will never—for 'twere
ingratitude to change the costume or terms of our faith after travelling in it
so comfortably & having but a few more steps, before we realise the extent
of that kind gift w'h has ingraven on the very essence of the soul one of the
signs—*proofs* of the infinite and nessecary Divinity.

When in the last weeks of sorrow past at Waltham, the transcendentalists use to talk how Sarah A. had got rid of space & time and such like subjects—oh how impotent were all to lessen one anxiety. And at all places I believe that this *time* will revolve on them tho' discipline of age & infirmity w'h will naturally & graciously lead them to experience more of the nobility of their relations to God thro' the plain stale & obscure duties of every day than in all the creations of ideal beauty w'h belong to the imajanation. Yet I quarrel not with them. Whatever high claims they assume—how much better than those of calvinism, w'h I've lived with. And there is no danger of these disturbing the peace of the world. It is permitted very kindly to rainbow the cloudy earth w'h else might seem but one place of graves or institutions to lessen its miseries.

But the object of this page was to express my love in return for your kind remembrance and those wishes w'h your situation can better shape in lovlier forms than I can. Yes dear Niece, we shall be freinds forever—like your Goethe & my Schiller we have in the first steps of our journey presented repellent poles—but after all we have loved the same great principles and the great remedial plan—& in some future age may minister in it together. And before that you & Waldo must visit the Vale. You (who have so much imajanation) would have been in extacies one morning last week (monday) at the beauty w'h burst from the skies—the breaking light on the rich blue mist of the mountains and the stars riding high to crown them. But when I found what I had not expected—that these very stars were those I saw in the gloomy spring—whom I emblamised for those who had light my way for the year past—and saw the Jupiter leave his companion—when she met me here on the verge of eve. tues with so sad a look—but I knew she was to appear with new beams in the forehead of the day—and had watched her approach—but was surprised to find close to her him who I thought bent on distant travel. He has since left her side—but you will sympathise in my coincidences and pray with me that the deserted one may long continue to beautify & improve the earth. If there should be any thing done in memory of my absent star you will hasten it.

  With love to your husband, Mother & Sister I bid you an affectionate adieeu

                MM Emerson

  Please give the other page to E. Hoar.

MH: bMS Am 1280.226(782).

 1. Probably RWE's *Nature*, published 9 Sept. MME was more critical of *Nature* in an undated note (1837?) to ASG, sent with a fictional work for the Gage girls that she considered "excellent. As to 'Nature' I hope they will not read it—tho' poetic 'tis obscure & does its Auther no justice" (MWA).

1837

To Elizabeth Hoar

Ap. 13. [1837]

Many as the months are, since I wrote, my dear Elis., I have not been un-gratefull for your letter   And have hoped to hear from your health & return to our good old soil—   How your father is since his return and if he has accepted his appointment? How my friend your Mother—& last tho' not least, *Sarah*—for of her I think—of the gay preperations w'h are going on probably for her wedding.[1] And of your own heart of hearts where dwells the grief, w'h I trust, time has given in reality what the poets call the joy of grief. And it is no dream—there is a joy in enduring even the ordinary ills of life—but when beatified by love can you call it less? And without deception you will add to the cheerfullness of the domestic scene.

The old winter is folding up his robes, tho' here, sullen & grim, yet there are promises of those celestial emblemns w'h recall in fairer images those we love—who are changing their scenery with every progress—and say in every mystic breeze *weep no more for me*.

Have you a thought to spare for the humble Vale? An idea of visiting it? What are your plans for the summer—to travel perhaps with the bride. Could you with that "dear Ma'ma" have a journey here? You would see the stars as I saw them at midnight and say with Wordsworth "theres nothing finite in solitude." Oh that man reads well here—& I found many a page of him among some old papers w'h I copied when he first appeared—before every or any body liked him. And as children think their horizon the end of the world so I always think he had such a mount & lake in view as mine, when he described the peasant.

Thank you for the scrap book of Alcot,[2] & intend to do more than *hear* it read now I am well—but you know how worse than sceptical I am about all he does. If ever he preexisted it was in the Limbo of vanity beneathe some dreaming poppy. If he would really dream about some race of whose experience we know nothing, & never saw a bloody malignant trace of their history! I hear fine things about the little boy Waldo from Waltham, and that he must go & be a pupil of Mr A's probably. It was that very amiable gentleman I warned the young stranger against in a long epistle I framed at his first entrance.[3] I apologised for not welcoming him by the tale of human life I told   And shall wait to send till I know more of his character. To his parents & Grandmother my love, & say that when I bless our Father for all the gifts bestowed on his favored children they have a well worn trace in my memory.

That was a beautifull letter to them from the excellent Martinuea—how consistent with her avowed materialism it matters not to me.[4] What ideas does she attach to phi. *nessisity*? As Hartley & Priestly? *That* w'h nature &

scripture induce soothes criticism & ingrafts the blessed precept judge not before that time when secrets are to be open. It seems to me she is destitute of the finest grace of human nature—sensibility—but it was only as a grace one missed it in her narrations of herself—and I admired the confiding frankness—but looked in vain for the after reflection w'h makes the fibres of the soul cringe & writh to review any thing *like* egotism. But now that I find her tearing up the ashes w'h time & affection have consecrated & destroying our earliest respect for a Mather as she did for a Moore and the whole priesthood if she could, I revolt.[5] Why my dear Elisabeth if such a habit were universal the human mass must return to savage life—all confidence in biography weakened—all admiration destroyed. With what a clamor & terrible energy she dispells the sweet slumbers of the dead before the time—   And if they are to rise together surely there will not be chance for secrecy—but we shall see if she dont let her clan repose. After all I want the other vol. shall return this next month. And "by the bye" (how could Orville ding at this homely phrase amid the grandeurs of nature & art w'h would do very well on ordinary occasions, as our cow bell in common pastures but with a soul so deeply & richly attuned as his to apply this discordant note!)[6] I do want you or some one to send me Jackson's memoirs by Ralph H. the first of next month. It is of a use only to a phisian save the obituary. If there is no immediate prospect of the return of either from N. Y. please to ask Mr & Mrs Ripley to beg one of Dr J. for a worthy brother of the craft.[7] And by the bye, I want it to give him—the more as I have seperated from him only as a phy. His wife was cold & insensible to the departure of genius & the sorrow of beauty last summer & I tho't I could never feel as if she had a heart—tho' in her early life I had been somewhat in the state of Pope towards a poet insisted it was the best in the world—and we draged on—this winter I employed accidentally at first a young D^r but afterwards Gage. It was the only hours of conversation since I returned. A man so sensitive—sensible & imperial in skill *here* 'twas worth while to sacrifice a little peace for the variety of quarreling. Trenk had his mouse[8] I my doctors. Jesting apart, 'tis best, dear Elisath, to seperate as to the *usages* of friendship whenever the vitals are diseased—amputation I assure you is easy when the humours are morbid & been long inactive. But as I learn my bills have been slacker than I knew I wish to give a book he wants. And our intercourse is very polite

In return for my somewhat tedious communications I expect very very fine ones. I rarely have passed before a year in this place without one hour of literary or theol. interest. And somewhat like Virgils shades I like to hear of the living world. tho' prize the dead one

If any one asks of me that one give my love to. Did you show the note to M. B.?"[9]

Farwel dear Child of love & sorrow and be happy prays your aff^t Aunt

M M Emerson

My girls ask to send their love to you & S. S.

My dear watch gains 5^n minutes in an hour. I asked you if you ever heard of it's rapid motions. I have sent it to Boston in vain.

Thursday   13 Ap.   Vale

MH: bMS Am 1280.226(1099). *Addressed:* Miss Elisabeth Hoar / If absent Mrs R. Emerson / Care of Hon. S. Hoar, M. C. / Concord / Massachusetts.

M. B.? ⟨Tell her to write me of abolitionism. I ask nothing for I received nothing.⟩ ⟨*heavily canceled*⟩

5] *possibly* 50

1. Samuel Hoar was elected to the U.S. House of Representatives for 1835–36 but was defeated in his reelection bid in Nov. 1836; the possible appointment not identified. On 15 June, EH's sister Sarah and Robert Boyd Storer of Boston were married in Concord.

2. Probably Alcott's *Conversations with Children on the Gospels*, published in Dec. 1836, although the reference to "scraps" suggests EH may have transcribed portions of Alcott's "Psyche" manuscript, which RWE critiqued in Feb. 1836 but still had in his possession on 24 Mar. 1837 (*L* 2:4–6, 62).

3. MME to EH, 22 Jan. 1837, contains MME's gloomy response to the news of Waldo's birth on 30 Oct. 1836 (MH: 1098).

4. Rusk notes a letter to RWE concerning CCE's death and written by Harriet Martineau from Stockbridge, Mass., 21 May 1836 (*L* 2:24); a review of her *Miscellanies*, in *Christian Examiner* 20 (May 1836): 251–64, points out her materialism.

5. Harriet Martineau, *Miscellanies*, 2 vols. (Boston, 1836); in "On Witchcraft," a review of Charles W. Upham's *Lectures on Witchcraft* (Boston, 1831), Martineau calls Cotton Mather a man prone "to all the vices which beset the priestly vocation . . . fanatical and deeply cunning; vain and credulous, with a great outward show of humility; inordinately ambitious of temporal power, while ostentatious of his disinterested piety" (2:399). No comment on (poet Thomas?) Moore located.

6. In Jan., MME was reading Orville Dewey's sermons, probably *Discourses on Various Subjects* (1835); Dewey's Dudleian lecture, "A Discourse on Miracles," 16 May 1836, was printed in the *Christian Examiner* 21 (Sept. 1836): 99–119.

7. James Jackson, Sr., *Memoir of James Jackson, Jr., M.D., Written by His Father, with Extracts from His Letters and Reminiscences of a Fellow Student* (Boston, 1836). This new edition of the *Memoir* contained CCE's obituary of Jackson and a note on CCE's death ("EH L," *SAR 1985:* 147–48). The senior Jackson served as one of the Emerson family's physicians during the illnesses of EBE and ETE. MME seems to want to give the book to Dr. Gage.

8. Friedrich Trenck (1726–94), *The Life [and Adventures] of Baron Frederic Trenck,* trans. Thomas Holcroft (London, 1789–93); describing one of the worst dungeons in which he was imprisoned by the tyrannical Frederick the Great, Trenck emphasizes the "great obscurity" of his cell, lit only by a small, semicircular opening into a fortification. Yet, in time, his eyes became so used to "the glimmering that I could see a mouse run" (176).

9. Probably Mary Merrick Brooks.

To Ralph Waldo Emerson

Vale   Thurs. 4 May. [1837]

Dear Waldo,

I should never have heart to look up my treasures & feel so much my loss, if you had not asked for Charles' letters. Those of 13 years old & on—how fond—all full of food for me. I wish I could send many for all your sakes—and Lidian would understand what our connection had been to me—And then these thoughts of his sent to obscurity tells a true tale. How rich from their truth—yet their expressions of beauty & light resemble the bow of promise tinged with gloom—& reflected from our mountain on the green graves of the valley. But I do not regret the melancholy as you do. No xian, I thought, but enters the tempel of sorrow often—for it is not built with hands—but fitted to one of the elements of human nature—and the longer the worshiper threads its labyrinths the plainer it becomes in solution of mans great problemn. Had he whom we mourn, lived long enough—how nobly would he ascended such eminences as sometimes rise there as to lose the sense of individual defeat, in perfection, in the love of the universal plan & Planner. He would see the common lot of xians to resemble the heaving mole hill w'h opens on its struggling inmate & is soon overthrown—but he would have met the uncommon who like himself have mighty strife with the still dubious *nessesity* w'h seems at so frequent war with the lofty standard of the cross. But I forget myself—that you are looking out from higher planes—robed in resemblance to Plato, your early patron, tho' not with his reputed pride of drapery, ministering with eloquence (I know) at the alter where nature & man receive their antisapated apotheosis. Happy election—to lose the sad retinue w'h exist in time & space—happy allottment—may be that light may shine with new power on the path of the weary, wherever it shall become reflected. I speake soberly & respectfully tho' I may have been suspected of some spite against the high school— Surely it has been my day & night wish to learn it's first lessons—for I had believed that some how I myself (*poor & ignorant as I consider it*) had arrived at what they call *ontology* without any of the bridges w'h the material or inductive or learned would afford—or ignorant of what I owed them—but alas neither at Concord nor Waltham would they admit so messilanious and staid a pupil. I forget again—but I have been reading a few of your letters and they were full of your own *thoughts*!—but now I can't expect you to have time for me—and if you had I should not respond—yet you seem to wish a letter and I was pleased with yours of Oct 29—the information was desirable of the boy & of the life & health of the mother.[1] God will preserve them I believe among your other good gifts—your mothers home with you among your best. To them my loving remembrance. To Elis. also & that these later letters bring her before me in full life. None to send   I have just finished and hasten to say that there are 6 or 7 w'h would honor any collection—but when R.T.H.[2] will return who is expected next week is uncertain as his dear Mother remains sick tho' perhaps recovering slowly from severe illness. Will these precious relics be *safe* in mail? Shall they go thus? One contains the truest & most novel (to me) picture of Shakespear.

Till now I had subdued the regret w'h had mingled with the memory of the time past at your house with Charles. *There was a coldness towards me. I must have been* in *fault*—and I only want to know *what*

But you would not sattisfy me or surely would have answered that letter of grief I sent from Waltham.³ So many letters I have as future food from you— of so much kindness in writing them you would not fail if I know *any* thing of you. He might have thought me mean spirited to hang on so much. I felt a sort of hardihood w'h often nessesities had induced of body or mind or condition. But I did right at last—and when I read the power in letter you have had, I approve my magnimity. Never regreted it in days of darkness since *that could be felt* by confinement & ill health. No I ought to have done it before.

I hear much of your lectures—wish to see them without the hope—trust they exceed in all shapes those of the sublime Herder under the same title.⁴ Tell Miss Pea. she really coaxed me out of my silence and now neglects to notice my letter. Oh you must be gratified with her & Miss Fuller's visit— when the visitors can add by their talents & learning to the domestic pleasures I should think there would be real comfort.⁵

Who would have tho't I should be so like the Sorcerers broom stick?⁶ I who thought when you so often spoke of the tedious style of those I love (as oracles) that I should ever have patience or courage to write again. Farewell dear Waldo & go on prosperously, says

Aunt Mary

You will oblige me by expressing my love & mention of my Brothers attention & letters. Tell E. B. R.⁷ thanks for hers. I wish I had Coleridge⁸

MH: bMS Am 1280.226(897). *Addressed:* Mr. R. Waldo Emerson / Concord / Mass. *Postmarked:* South Waterford / Me May 5th. *Endorsed:* M. M. Emerson / May, 1837.

1. Since Waldo, RWE and LJE's first child, was born late at night on 30 Oct., at least part of RWE's letter (which does not survive) must have been written after 29 Oct. (*L* 2:45).

2. Ralph T. Haskins.

3. See MME to RWE, 31 Mar. 1836.

4. RWE's 1836–37 Boston lecture series was titled "The Philosophy of History." German philosopher and critic Johann Gottfried Herder published *Another Philosophy of History* (1774) and *Ideas for the Philosophy of the History of Mankind* (1784–91).

5. Margaret Fuller visited the Emersons in late Apr.; no record of EPP's visit has been located.

6. De Stael tells the story of the magician's broomstick in *Germany* 1:357–58.

7. Elizabeth Bradford Ripley.

8. MME's renewed interest in Coleridge probably results from reading C. S.

Henry's edition of Cousin's *Elements of Psychology* (see MME to WE³, 11 May 1837); his notes frequently cite *Biographia Literaria*, *Aids to Reflection*, and *The Friend*.

To William Emerson³

May 11. '37　Vale

My dear Nephew,

I have been in your house so much on this sad anniversary¹—have watched your steps—seen the mother—the sympathising Susan—*felt* the moment when she met poor Elisabeth—(would I could know how that mourner *felt*)—all pass before me—far heavier than then—*then* the sober certainty of his rising to the natural priviledges of a spirit—the known presence of his God—the knowledge of his redemption—the nature of virtue—no more to be at strife with it's high standard w'h the interred soul cannot reach—the happy cercumstances w'h surrounded—the quick passage—my escape from wittnessing—all brightened a loss w'h I knew solitude & age would increase. The past week has been used in reading his letters from earliest writing to the last—sad dear relics of joy & grief. Singular how often he recurs to his death—& welcoming it—yet I never looked to it. And is it not strange that he did not talk of it at last? Had he no conviction of his disease? Oh could a spirit born & living for the intellectual world—grasping after the infinite but have left a last bright legacy from his approaching wealth! *What was the state of his mind?*—disease had been wont to close its radiance as those bright flowers shut up when night comes down. Had he thro' life a presentiment & felt nothing new? In the few sad painfull moments of parting with your Mother I could never never inquier　And afterwards I desired to wrap myself from all intercourse in that intire solitude w'h was ordained from childhood for me—and even writing to Elisabeth seemed like breaking open the web, w'h caterpillar like, should remain till the final liberation—if in its' bleached texture there were no coulers of the bow of promise on earth—far better & safer—its' oblivion from all hope & fear & pursuit—one idea—of the first Cause is the only suffcent support of happiness. Finding some of your letters when looking for his, their expressions of affection broke away many a crust w'h had gathered round the heart—their sentiment resucitated me—their information on general subjects extended my thoughts—and I said I would write once more to so indulgent a friend—but I did not think this funeral day so near. To you, who live amidst the great wheels of this whirling world and do your part to turn them, the subject of my letter may have passed & received it's apotheosis—to me who part with the year as a precious companion of the dear past & dearer future it has now gathered new interest.

But no more—your house does not always appear to me clothed in somber weeds—but as I love to view *William Emersons*—the abode of manly talent integrity—& female lovliness and worth. Such as my own loved Louisa² represents it　God grant it may long continue thus—and a force of piety &

patriotism. I love the idea of Susan—more since Charles was there— And tho' I have never dreamt of seeing her— Yet 'tis possible when you are at Plymouth with *William the fourth*[3] you may like to wander into Maine & see the white hills. Of all things I should like it. Thank Louisa & Mr Dewey for their spirit stirring epistle. If S.M.H.[4] should see you & mention his mother's sickness tell him she is fast recovering.

Have you seen Miss Martinau? or read her essays? Some are excellent. They are more valuable for the plainess—as the transcendental school leave one at their wits' ends. I lost Sarah A. & Waldo, almost, in their priestly office in those misty reigions. But tho' these mistifications may be well for them & such like, they ill befit common minds who have the common warfare of xianity to maintain— And this getting rid of time & space & matter (or fancying it) has opened the road to pantheism at best—often infidelity—the same by w'h poor Hume arived at a state described by himself in w'h his "brain became heated and a chaos of doubts & dreams"[5] However when the fogs are cleared some true light of human nature may arise from Germanism. I love the *enthusiam* of Cousin and his refutation of dear old Locke—but can't believe his "absolute reason" to be applicable to the human consciousness & the general truths of philosophy—[6] And I return to the plain dealing Scotch school with respect—however cercuitous & inconclusive—there are the great facts of a personal Divinity & man's relations.

But I forget the agitations of commerce w'h may involve your professional cares.

I will no longer detain you but affectionately say farewell dear Wm

Aunt

M M Emerson

My questions involve a request & that you will answer when time allows

MH: bMS Am 1280.226(1076). *Addressed:* William Emerson Esqʳ / Office in Wall Str. / City of New York. *Postmarked:* South Waterford / (Me) May 12th. *Endorsed:* M. M. Emerson / May 11 / 37. / Rec'd " 15 / Ans'd — 28.

1. CCE had died at WE[3]'s home on 9 May 1836; MME had long set aside 12 May, the day of her brother WE[2]'s death, for mourning.

2. Louisa Farnham Dewey; her husband, Orville, had begun his pastorate at the Second Congregational Church, New York City, in 1836.

3. Son of WE[3] and Susan Emerson, born 18 June 1835.

4. Samuel Moody Haskins, then studying for a doctorate in divinity at Union College in New York; in 1839 he became rector of Saint Mark's (Episcopal) Church, Williamsburgh, Long Island, where he remained for fifty years.

5. Not located.

6. MME is probably responding to Victor Cousin, *Elements of Psychology: Included in a Critical Examination of Locke's Essay on the Human Understanding*, trans. C. S. Henry (Hartford, 1834). Chap. 9 (*Leçon* 24) attacks Locke's limitation of enthusiasm to "folly" and asserts the absolute authority of (the intuitive) reason (233–34).

To Samuel Ripley

Vale   Nov. 8 '37

My dear Brother,

From an unvaried solitude & uninteresting circumstances of the outward man (the inner containing it's own excitments w'h oftener burst out in
a prison, than in ordinary life) I would fain take a look into your abode of
ever wakefull vital moving existence. But I dare not urge any of you to take
pictures and speake any of your (often) unknown languages to my dull senses.
And I content myself with believing that all is well—and too full of progress
& pleasure to think of the lonely Aunt. God continue to bless them all.

It is longer than usual, however, since I have heard from the west. Hope
Waldo is well & will not work himself too hard. It seems very long since I've
talked of Charles. Ruthy (dear form of acquiesence) told me that there was a
letter taken out of administering on his estate & clothes prized and she dwelt
on the old organ w'h was a goodly part of the estate![1] Alas could not Mr Hoar
have averted that obedience to the old laws? Had Charles not respected them
& laboured over them to get his bread enough to have escaped their dryest
coldest grasp. Could not a life of honorable poverty suffice—but he must appear after the grave (alas, they have already buried him in the earth untombed
that sweet & silent form) had done it's office, in a few tidy garments with an
attendant organ, w'h once belonged to life & beauty.

Now his gaurdianship his dear Mother said demanded this—and it might.
And I have not spoken of it but a moment to Sister Haskins who could have
no sympathy on the subject of pitying poverty. But I would fain know if it is
in your view a fancifull disgust that I feel? And why did not those kind & best
of brothers bring up his bones to our dear native sod?

Well the time of repose "blessed Sleep" is come before I can close the letter.
But I will add the dislike I have to Martineue's religious veiws.[2] That superstition and spiritual pride may fatten on the forms of administering our holy
religion is true—but to deprive it of priest and prayer is to loosen some of^n the
surest^n ties w'h support age and the instruction of the populace. Should this
excellent philanthropist out live her politicks—should the trumpet give uncertain sounds—& no echo of society—how will she need those land marks
of faith & staff of age. But I have just put down her books while they are done
with every where I suppose. Whatever you sent me in the beaureau remains
there for as yet it is not come here but is on the way. * * *

Here is a chance to send to the office & this must go now or I shall need
the money as I've been out some time

Please send 10# I was going to trade about M—'s wool but Aunt Ripley
cant stay a moment & I must ride & she is so so & send love & all well & I
must say your

afft & obliged Sister
MME.

Thurs. 9

MH: bMS Am 1280.226(1246). *Addressed:* Rev. Mr Ripley / Waltham / Mss. *Post-marked:* S Waterford / Novr 10. *Endorsed:* M. M. E. / 1837.

some of] ⟨all⟩ ↑ some of ↓

surest] *possibly* sweet

1. RWE to WE[3], 23 Oct. 1836, mentions the recent appraisal of CCE's property, valued at $886, including the organ, valued at $300, which had not yet sold (*L* 2:42).

2. Harriet Martineau; see MME to EH, 13 Apr. [1837], esp. nn. 4, 5.

To Elizabeth Hoar

Vale   Sab Morn   17 Dec. [1837]

The only transition from finite to Infinite is the "limitations" w'h God condescends to set to Himself in nature & rev.s—in the very personality (if we dare so to speake) he, as it were, assumes? All we can grasp of infinite is somthing like losing self in transition? Yet we dont lose self subsistence—that immense gift of God's image—that charter of our own free personality—& of our Maker's!—that invincible sense of freedom—so opposed to Cousin's theory of the absolute reason as impersonal—while the elements are so—& universal—how marvelous different it's modifications?[1] And when minds who have scaped the bounds of common life how opposite the theories? That each tends to truth may resemble the material phenomena, when the spider, in his cunning den, is pulling at the stars. That there is a pure domaine of reason is our shield of faith in God & that He has given a spark of it to all—but that it is bewildered in physicks—in mathematics is a grand result to show the ineffacy of science—and of late of transcendentalism—that it is an holier inspiration—intuition itself w'h places the mind in communion with Reason w'h may be said "to be identical with God." Is my dear Elisabeth willing to enter my cave where the "obscura" is so very dim?—then a page for the Almanack shall go. Had I your capasity for metaph.s I need not "roam"—but with that internal "lamp" better far than the garish day or luscious "fruits" of Eve's paradise get into high places—one truth from thence strengthens faith beyond the power of jaring moralists & poor practical xians to obscure. Abstract—& they abstract from a world of vanity & selfishness   Oh the eclipse you describe is from Him who observes by an agency all His own the skyey worlds that they may be brighter & keep his order most exactly. If the benevolent affections kindle without these meditative kind of intuitions (more I am not permitted to speake of) they are liable to be chilled & soured. Yes in this *dimmed* light you do so *brightly* describe you will sojourn into those deeper affections w'h are given alone to the mysteries of xianity—w'h accord so well—w'h envelop" so effectively those of the human heart—that while philosophy unveils these—religion takes them under the golden wings of the holy dove.

And have I not answered querly calling at the first invitation—hoping I shall have a return call as soon   Here you will find a welcome from every one. I've met none where you are not remembered & make a part of our talk. And it is so good to be able to embody an idea where we would refine or raise. "The stars glisten as there"—but tonight I loved my twilight walk better for seeing none—   Oh they have known me so long—& are so overwhelming & oft reproach that this dark pall over the skeleton earth is more congenial— 'tis being alone indeed—and the woman & her little ones[2] are absent that I have a dear good time and as I have not been to Chh these six sundays a walk is like excitment. I am well—very—*how do you* do? Why not in City to hear those *very* lectures?[3] Surely you are going when the Mother returns? Glad she left her love—why not the oaken majesty of the father ever send his? As to Rockwood,[4] I'm not in grace I suspect—well I wont say "hang him"—for if all were to be swung of my acquaintance & kindred who dont like me wood might be more difficult to get than ever. "What can you do for me?" Why write & give me the newest ideas—what is the argument of the Lockites? E.P.P. said her party were provoked &c. She proposed a "brisk correspondence", & we have written two or three times—'tis best—& then let it rest—for in the lapse of months we lose sight of each other—'tis disinterested in her—thinking how alone I am I believe. But to my saying she must write "objectively" she pretends not to understand   And in fact she is for free masonry about the "party" 's opinions I believe—or like others thinks me unteachable. Well I'll be the humbler for my ignorance in this as in every thing—it is desirable to hear how much is knowable—rather to peep out from the way side & see the throng assembling in the tempels of genius & learning while we live at the pool—or the gate. Tell me about the lectures.—does the Lecturer ever think to send love & Lidian? Tell her I bide my time to renew the intercourse begun in your parlour

I was glad to hear of S.A.R. and of less excitment internally—surely there is nothing in this poor world to raise a temperture of so stern an intellect to the height w'h she at times discovers—it looks like a want of the heart— unsattisfied—w'h grasps at the shows of being—well I meant no slur at idealism. God give her realities that her light may shine forever & aye. It is nearing to the witching time of night and I go to bed

Tues. 19.   At looking over this so cramed, & perhaps darkly expressed, I would not send it—but what matters if you can't read it—I've no pen nor time   And it may bring me another while you have the house to yourself. Write & if I dont answer why write again   "Be not weary." You ask for Mrs R's[5] health. She dont go out—but is much the same   I dined there Thanksgiving by nessecity—for I had agreed that the other house would let me keep chamber—as the last one—telling them I had not dined socially since dear Charles went away &c—but the snow went off & I tarried till eve.

   Mrs H. well. Hannah often unwell[6]   Except a day past last week I scarsly

see her. Sarah is keeping school for Charlotte & the Chamberlains[7]—so a
call on my part is most of our intercourse. Adieu dear Neice may the lowly &
rich gifts of Heaven ever await you prays your aff^t Aunt

                                                                    MME.
I am glad you enjoy little Waldos society   Shakespear I have for my meals
company.

MH: bMS Am 1280.226(1104). *Addressed:* Miss Elisabeth Hoar / Care of Hon.
S. Hoar / Concord.

envelop] evelop *in MS; possibly* develop *intended*

  1. Cousin, *Elements of Psychology,* esp. pp. 266–67, 235.

  2. Comments about seeing various Haskins relatives indicate that MME may have
been boarding elsewhere in Waterford, despite the dateline "Vale."

  3. On 6 Dec. RWE began his winter course of Boston lectures, "Human Culture."
Elizabeth Maxfield-Miller speculates that EH heard them read aloud at the Emersons'
before their public delivery ("EH L," *SAR 1985:* 148; see also *LJE L,* 18 Dec. 1837).

  4. EH's brother Ebenezer Rockwood Hoar graduated from Harvard in 1835 and
received the LL.B. degree in 1839.

  5. PER, who died in 1839.

  6. REH; Hannah Upham Haskins.

  7. Phebe Haskins married John Chamberlain in 1824.

1838

To Leander Gage

                                                          [23 Apr.? 1838?]
Dear Lee,

   I delight to find your active mind on the wing of inquiry into reigions
beyond sense & time.

   But I cannot at this time give you any eccleseastical information about that
text. The little (alas for eyes & want of your energy) I have been able to see
of Commentaries thro my long journey has never thrown any light on scripture—   They alas, so often dilute & spread out the text without bringing to
our aid the lights of antiquity or the researches of modern reason that we are
often times better with the bible alone   That text never alarmed me before—
Glad you mentioned it and in the course of reading a very important history
of the various copies and MSS whh are of the earliest date I may give you
some clue to that mistaken text & to others.[1] But I wish for your opinion. I
was never startled at it, because I have found many dark sayings in our bible,
whh must be attributed to the mistakes of the Copiest. I know Jesus Christ
was sent of the Father and believing in that single fact and from the whole
tenor of his doctrines, I should feel persuaded that he never gave that selfish
worldly maxim as it stands in our common translation. Point to this in an

interpretation acknowledged by most of trinitarians, antient and modern of the learned, of 1 epis. of St John 5 chap. & 7 verse. Yet those who see cause from the tenor of scripture to believe in the self existent and infinite Being exists in three distinctions to which they can affix no *distinct* ideas, do not give up an inch of ground they say when they give up this long contested text, and some few give up others which the Athanasians held on to the very death. These different opinions, blessed be God (as they do not nessecarily affect morals) keep alive biblical criticism—and may be among the means of strenghtening the evidences for xianity against its' deistical enimies. As to this individual doctrine, I have no objections— It is that many spurious teachers of it connect it (for their own interest) with those doctrines of Calvin so fatal to morals and to the character of that Being whom to love & obey is the joy and glory of the rational creature. Whatever dust the Controversalists throw around his garment[n] and whatever real difficulties attend the discovery of the antient MSS the heart that has been disciplined and consoled & nourished by faith in this Being, will say with one of the antient Fathers, amidst the perplexities attending the original copy of the history of Christ whether it was verbal or written—he exclaimed *"Christ is my manuscript and testament!"* [2]

May God crown your youthfull exertions with no common blessings that you and my dear Ann may be a lights in this wilderness prays

MME

Write your answer if you like

Monday 23

I envelop this in a brown paper—as a correspondence might make questions.

MWA. *Addressed:* D[r] Gage.

garment] gar / ment *or* gov / ment (*at line break*); *possibly* gov[ern]ment *intended*

1. Unfortunately, the biblical text Gage wishes MME to explicate cannot be determined from her response. Nevertheless, I include this both because it is one of only two surviving letters addressed to Dr. Gage and because it suggests why, in Waterford, MME acquired the reputation of being a "great theologian." The other letter to Gage (MWA, n.d. [1836?]) is a similarly obscure continuation of a conversation; apparently MME sends something she has tried to write on the question of slavery and also discusses other antislavery texts and ideas.

2. Possibly the early Christian philosopher Origen (185?–254?).

To Elizabeth Hoar

Please read the last page before looking at first the 2[d] unreadable I guese[1]

What a blessing is the dramatic art— The mind finds in it the prototype of it's immortality. If a Lear can awaken so deep an interest—whose sorrows were the effect of transient & puerile interests what should the martyr at the stake, for a principle, excite? Yet childish as those interests were, even when they ripped up the parental heart, we would not give up a moment of mortal agony in him—in Ophelia—let her drown—let reason abandon her post to the affections—this boasted reason of man totters & falls when the immutable sentiments—the elements of human nature are roused—disgusted—torn away from their objects either divine or human. And we read—we see the immortality of the soul's essence in the very wrecks w'h float & flounder & go down on the boisterous treacherous ocean of time. It is this instinct w'h only can account for dramatic pleasures & pains. How desirable to lose real wearing life in their atmosphere—where imajanation, that prophet of the future, lives in it's finest coulers with the milk of human love & the sovereign ambition, when reason is palled. But look again—the grave may quench those organs w'h kindle imajanation—w'h support love freindship & ambition—hope & fear—but *reason* then regains her power—then the essence of life from God is disemcumbered of it's vapourous coulered bowes—its' flaming passions—its' worser subtleties—   Oh how naturally it's affinities find their connections—and if pure & godly what a resurrection from the chains of fancy & appetite

Feb. 14.   Reason in it's last altitude[n] can never unveil the divine agency in matter & mind—the affections are too holy—too far within the veil of the inward tempel (where the wings of some ethereal creation cover the worshiper) to be analysed *by the reason*, tho that godlike spark kindles into larger beauty when warmed by the affections, yet that it is ordained to thread it's way to the first Cause—to find it's origin—to build it's faith by it's own sternest laws is true oh how grandly true! If natures darker sterner darker ordanance throw clouds before it—if the moral world still heavier—yet it keeps it's footing—and when revelations w'h apply to the senses & experience of the wants of human nature groove in with the dictates of understanding then faith becomes justified of her children & reason is like the sun w'h gives truth to the dial hand of revelation—rather *shows* it. If man's reason keeps true to that & facts w'h prove the truth of rev. 'tis folly to ask for a wittness to the truth of reason—'tis self evident & ca'nt be proved—'tis the *condition* of man's existence & can be no more illusive than sensation—that it becomes a mere ignis fatuus in the hands of a Hume & sometimes a[n]

Portland   June 13 '38

My dear Elisabeth,

I can't go out to get any paper—and I have nothing to say this hot day & very sad spirits but the immediate object of my writing. It occured to me yesterday that at the moment of receiving your request for those letters I felt they must go & I had neither means nor time to envelop them and that a sentence w'h I asked you to let me blot was not noticed by you—viz "that S—s conscience had lost its virgin purity."[2] Now what *shall I think* or *suffer?*—for of course I did not mention their being secret—nor were they any more than one Angel speaking to another. Does honor dictate not looking at them? *Get them.* I am anxious to know your stronger higher judgment. Those letters had strenghtened & consoled me in sadest confinement. And my only tho't was the loss of them. I had not read them for stupid months. was just about it. Alas, what am I to suffer? Write & direct to care of Rufus Emerson Esqr Portland^3 not forgetting to pay as I may be off in some part of Country. Health *obliges* me to the dire task of moving.

But at nothing weary or painfull but your letter has come over me like the sweet sad musick of the soul. I felt your silence—but could not complain. I number your attentions in the record where they are most durable. You need not read the Almanak pages.— but as they calendar the few moments of existence in winter.^{n} I tho't you were to be in City last winter. I cant answer any of your letter, left at Vale, but that I hope Sarah's health is better.^{4} God grant each of your family and your dearer Self all He loves for his favorites. Yet indelibibly is great part of that letter precious with trembly dews on my heart. To the "Mama" & brother & Sister & boy of your adopted affections all love & good wishes from your ever aff^t Aunt & friend

MM Emerson

MH: bMS Am 1280.226(1105). *Addressed:* Miss Elisabeth Hoar / Care of Hon. S. Hoar / Concord. *Postmarked:* Portland / Me. / Jun 14.

altitude] sic *in MS*; *possibly* attitude *intended*

sometimes a] sometimes a ⟨self [styled] transcendentalist is pretty evident⟩ ⟨*heavily canceled*; styled *illegible, supplied from T*⟩

winter.] winter ⟨return them when convenient⟩. ⟨*heavily canceled*⟩

1. Written on outside. The first two pages (preceding the "Portland June 13" date-line) are from MME's "Almanack."

2. Reference to a sentence (possibly describing SBR) in one of CCE's letters, which she has recently returned to EH at her request; the letter is possibly CCE to MME, 29 June [1830], in which the name of someone MME has asked about and some comments have been cut out. CCE writes, "But I judge her over-harshly— You will forgive me, for I do not know her in her best moods; & she redeems herself by the severe yet cheerful performance of her returning duties—making no murmur & seeking no praise. I will not say {manuscript cut}" (MT/MH). In 1836 and 1837, EH and RWE considered using CCE's letters in a memoir, and MME reports her own rereading in a letter to WE^3, 11 May 1837. The earlier request is in MME to EH, 26 Sept. 1837: "This letter, like old women, full of privacies. I read that our sainted Charles says one whose conscience has lost its' virgin purity &c. Now had this sentence better be erased by me? Think what an eclipse comes over the brightest talents & virtues (*if virtues can exist?*) when we lost confidence in the essence of the soul—the god within the only indissoluble tie between the soul & God! I never could have pronounced— much less writen the fear—yet with bold speculations—pantheistic transcendentalism—departure from the primitive xianity—love of Goethe & his clan how natural how inevitable allmost such a soil? And 'tis proof of the wholeness and absoluteness of the demands of faith & childlike obedience to the revelations. That it is not always the case—theres Lidian has only a confused notion of Goethe & trans.^{n} There was Kant

who was a miracle of truth & morals! But the observation of Charles shows at once the integrity & purity of his own" (MH: 1101).

3. Not identified in *IpsE*.

4. Probably Sarah Hoar Storer. In her letter of 24 Aug. 1838 to EH (passage omitted), MME asks about Sarah's improvement and adds, "Heaven grant it—for how loath the mind is to see the young flower fade before it has fully blown" (MH).

To Elizabeth Hoar

Windham   Au. 24 '38

My dear Elisabeth,

In taking leave of this year of olden life, in w'h I have had occasion so often to think of you & your benevolent pilgrimage (& regreted it was no better accomodated & indulged) I am visiting that little space w'h bears you from one home to another.[1] And do long to hear from each of you—   Where are you all? * * *

So you prefer "my self" than to hear of my Almanak scraps w'h love to wander—[2] Why I yearn to hear some response to those excoria of metaphysicks—knowing your ability to indulge. Well of my pursuit—   I have been indulged with places of the pleasantest kind—but in vain searched for one object of beauty & genius to offer my homage and restore my admiration of those gifts of the infinite Potter. I tho't of coasting to Wiscasset Machias (where is T. T. Stone who had an article in Wood's literary[3] &c that even Sarah admired) Thomaston & any place where acquaintance was[n]—but all places & times are alike & the one want of the soul can be supplied from above with no local movements. So I made a zig zag move a month since to Gorham a most beautifull Village where I found a Cousinite of former acquaintance,[4] worth talking with & he lent me the volumes—but finding a younger & more enthusiastic friend, who lives here (& tired of their examination preparations for Seminary) I joined myself to his family who are glad of accession—but these cottage chambers however beautifull & large the lower part of the house & the shrubbery, I may not long occupy, perhaps—but stere for the "dark shadow of stones" w'h I found at Sweden whose waters benefited. Do you remember this embowered place when you stopped at the tavern?

But it was at Madam Storer's mansion at Kennebunk[5] I wanted you. The voice of the ocean was heard at times & we rode on the beach—& the house was full of antient aristocracy—gentility. And I may return there at any time. Next summer I expect to—& dream of persuading you & Waldo & Lidian to come—for them there is a fine Hotel—you must be with me. Her trees & grounds, once laid out with elegance, prevent heat. I feel sure of her sincerity for at parting she reduced my board very agreably—had I known it in season. What a sublime calculation! No one will complain of sentimentality in this letter. And my stupid health has buried what little I had. Happy that debility w'h fosters it I say.

And now will my ever forbearing Niece who wishes to mention the connection for the sole sake, I do know, of comforting me, let me object to her views of the "tender downⁿ of conscience" being worn away? Why this tenderness with every accession of light to irradiate the slightest gossamer is the very thing for w'h we remain in this heavy atmosphere—for w'h perhaps Angels are disciplined—for w'h Jesus came—as to wipe out it's blots from the infinite law. For wh the very "jostle" of the world is designed—the whole economy of trial prepared? In your ingenious defence of another I may have misunderstood your apology and thought you were at peace with the fact. A sin—an error—a fault in constitution may be forgiven—but the obtusenessⁿ of that heavenly tablet—it's sensitiveness cannot be restored like a fault exorcised?

* * * Farewell, dear Elisabeth, now & hence forth faire in all prosperity.

MME.

MH: bMS Am 1280.226(1106). *Addressed:* Miss Elizabeth Hoar / or Mrs W Emerson / Care of Hon. S. Hoar / Concord Massachusetts.

place . . . was] place ↑ where acquaintance was ↓

down] *possibly* dawn

obtuseness] ⟨erasure⟩ ↑ obtuseness ↓

1. MME's birthday was 25 Aug.; EH visited MME in Waterford, 4–20 Aug. 1837.

2. See MME to EH, [?] and 14 Feb., enclosed with 13 June 1838.

3. Wiscasset, Machias, and Thomaston are towns on the Maine coast; T. T. Stone had been minister at East Machias since 1832. His article "The True Utility" was published in the *Literary and Theological Review* 4 (Mar. 1837): 21–32; the review was edited by Leonard Woods, Jr. (1807–78), from 1834 through 1839.

4. Possibly Rufus Emerson. Gorham is about ten miles west of Portland.

5. The Storer mansion was one of the great homes of Kennebunk. Built in the mid-eighteenth century by Colonel Joseph Storer, the house was enlarged by his son, Joseph Storer, about the time of his marriage in 1808. MME's "hostess," "Madam" Storer, was probably the widow of the younger Joseph Storer.

To RALPH WALDO EMERSON AND LIDIAN JACKSON EMERSON

Windham [? Sept. 1838]

My dear Waldo,

I had your letter & addresses & offer of gift and loan with gratitude.[1] And am going to interrupt you tho' with diffidence (for it is after all the pleasure benvolence affords us irksome to be so often receiving) to request you would send them by the stage to Portland or boat—if they come surely   Should T.W. *know* of a chance—good—but to trust them at store or to the bringing of Ralph questionable. And I do wish you would add some lectures of your last winters such as 'the holy' and that on 'man' which Dr P. heard & tells about.[2] R. Emerson of Portland w^d take care of them. His insurance office in Exchange St. In that case they must be paid. I am very famished for books like those you offer. And I beg for another D. address. Just as I had run thro' it, it was needed by a young solitary genius, and when returned, before I had half read it T.T. Stone called, and I knew it's value to him & loved to please my favorite, gave it—tho' it left me somewhat like the Cambridge one as ignorance gazing at the stars unconscious of their course or intent. The cause however I thought might be very much in my own minds limits & isolation. Yet I love to gaze after the illuminati—for who would give the couler of the age or rather its possibilities—its prophecy like them? Yet believe with Burke that no improvement can be expected in the great truths & institutions of morality & religion. And I lost my inquiries in thinking of the fabled Urah, who belonging to the coterie of Plato, was sent down by that high person (before he was initiated into the arcana of the last^n science) to reform a certain district and give it some utopian ornaments—but the bright ambassador found every thing so slow in movement—so dully progressive so sober & stale that in his disgust he breathed a fire w'h consumed every old land mark—tore up the moss covered mounds and the very alters w'h had been the refuge of the poor & sinfull & decripid instead of being bettered were almost demolished—and in the destruction it is said the wings of the spiritual vehicle were so scorched that he was forced to ask aid of a deciple of the old reforming Patriarch who was buried on some old loved spot, and he, tho' looked on as a very plodder, constructed a chariot of clouds w'h conveyed the messenger home to new fledge his wings. And the story goes, that when they were in action again he visited the same place & found it overrun with barbarism & governed by an ugly Radicale. But how came I to use that ugly word of the legend when speaking to one whom fame, fortune & family love, place above the sight of vice & woe & the dream of radicleism. Your favorite Goethe choose a kind of heaven w'h no ills could reach.

I liked your calling Cousin "somewhat spectral"[3]—why the generalities & abstractions, from w'h he sometimes takes departure from common apprehensions remind one of the gasses of the balloon w'h goes up to the clouds & descends empty & exhausted. No I've not read him as yet but little

My love to Dr R. &c   To my dear Ruthy & the little boy whom I have become fond off, and hope his teething will be safely over. Gore[4] has gone to Cambridge and I want to answer a letter of his written soon after my leaving W. What shall I say? I liked but dont know him. How is William & his family? How his affairs? You have been good to him. And after all you did not ask me to write. Yet I needed books. Cant send my key very well for those you loaned in spring. Farewell dear Waldo and if you can love & forget the faults of

Aunt Mary

17 Sep. [1838]

My dear Lidian,

The last letter I used the word adulation—pardon me it does not apply to you of all others[5]   Yet I do not easily forgive extravagant expressions—

And did you once feel what I daily suffer from the memory of ill desert you would pity & think that situated peculiarly as I am from one long year to another that your representations were like mockery tho not intended. "The best friends have somthing to forgive". You & I have—I less—but when dependant for attention little coldnesses resemble iron—but we shall meet most lovingly. Could you see the heart of heart desirous of the glory of your husband & Son & yours you would never remember trifles. You are very peculiar— and in truth & duty I trust not common I know. Write me of the state of your heart—it's faith & prayer & progress—in that heart were feelings so like my own as I never before met. It was ordered for my trial that we could not cement a union—our faults & virtues were opposed. Write me of your views of Cousin—*his* of the trinity—of the preeminence of xianity are good?[6] Your husband reminds me of the poetical "harp of the universe"—some of whose chords he is tuning—but our atmosphere as yet too gross to vibrate to them. There may be a solitary songster that responds but the Jubilee may come & will in it's appointed time.

Good night, dear Lidian, and if consistent with your pursuits write—pray at least for your afft friend and Aunt

MME

MH: bMS Am 1280.226(898). *Addressed:* Rev R Waldo Emerson / Concord / Mass. *Postmarked:* Windham / Sept 19. *Endorsed:* M.M.E. / Windham, Sept 1838.

last] *possibly* best (*T*) *or* least

1. RWE to MME, 1 Sept. 1838 (*L* 2:153–54), states he is sending the Divinity School and Dartmouth addresses and offers a volume of Lockhart's life of Sir Walter Scott and his two volumes of Carlyle's *Miscellanies*.

2. MME probably boarded at Windham with the family of Dr. Charles Grandison Parsons (1807–64), an 1837 graduate of Maine Medical School, later a lecturer and writer. RWE's 1837–38 winter lecture series was titled "Human Culture"; no. 9, "Holiness," was delivered in Boston on 31 Jan. 1838 and, again, in Roxbury on 20 Feb., when it was called "Heroism, or Holiness" (*L* 2:115). Charvat's list of RWE's lectures does not include the title "Man," although the whole series concerns this subject; MME may have in mind "Heroism" or "Being and Seeming."

3. See "Divinity School Address," *CW* 1:85: "The snowstorm was real; the preacher merely spectral." MME's reference to "Cousin" here suggests she assumes that RWE has in mind her second cousin Joseph Emerson of Byfield and Wethersfield (compare her response to Joseph Emerson, in MME to CCE, 19 June 1830), whereas *JMN* 5:324–25 (7 May 1837, Waldo's baptism) identifies the preacher RWE was objecting to as EzR's colleague (beginning in 1837), Barzillai Frost (1804–58), as do modern editions of the address. The problem is compounded by MME's admission, at the end of this paragraph, that she's "not read him as yet but little" and her question in the LJE portion of the letter, clearly a reference to the French eclectic philosopher, Victor Cousin. What she has not yet read is possibly Ralph Emerson's *Life of Joseph Emerson* (Boston, 1834).

4. Nephew Christopher Gore Ripley (b. 1822), third child of SR and SBR, was in his second year at Harvard College.

5. See RWE to MME, 1 Sept. 1838 (*L* 2:154).

6. In his introductory notice to a selection of the writings of Victor Cousin, George Ripley points out that the congruence between Cousin's philosophy and the broad spiritual elements of Christianity is likely to gain him American followers (36–37); Cousin's "system" stresses the "triplicity of consciousness" as an "ontological unity"; the ideas of "man, nature, and God"; the "True, the Beautiful, the Good"; the soul, matter, and Supreme Being; and other "trinities" (*Philosophical Miscellanies, from the French of Cousin, Jouffroy, and Benjamin Constant*, vol. 1 of *Specimens of Foreign Standard Literature* [Boston, 1838], 144–46, 166, 177).

To William Emerson[3]

Sep 30   Sabbath [1838]

My dear William,

* * * How have you enjoyed the splendid summer? You must have been finely situated—and the little boy have streched away in growth.[1] Will he resemble Charles at all? I dont love to have the seasons w'h bring him to mind go quite so fast on that account—the flowers—the birds he so cherished and took knowledge of have lost some of thier beauty since they were his companions. And I do welcome this part of the old earths orbit when nature is so full of misterious voices and visions—like kind spirits beckoning us to places where interpretation shall take place of symbols and the realities of philosophy for many of it's dreams. If even in the spiritual state there should be theorists of eccentric kinds, they will not annoy the conservators, who will have such newer methods of attaining truth—and probably their virtue become superior to the dangers w'h so continually occur from the very elements of our constitution while in the limits of our probation. I do desire very seriously to know the state of your faith and feelings on these subjects. I see you the child of many hopes the growing boy—the matured man—candid and faithfull to conscience, while at a time departing from that light of revelation which alone could fully develop reason and sanction conscience— all other sanctions being the mere children of graceless utility or boasted independence. And I hoped your return—and have believed it in some good measure,—without venturing too "curiously to inquire." Good faith without a holy consciousness is a sacriliege—but the latter cannot exist seperate from its voluntary union to the infinite Personality. But pardon my dear Nephew, this approach to old see saws of Aunt Mary.

Have you read our Waldo's addresses[2]—he sent them with a kind letter w'h was very gratefull to my isolated life. And they bro't back many a gone bye year, when his young Muse was wont to wander into strange "universes" and find idealised people and alas, "new laws." There is no affectation in him—and his novelties are at home—while they gather somthing of the mists & coruscations of light from Germany and transcendentalism. And it may be that in the whirl of antagonist principles & views & theories w'h alarm some friends to virtue & encourage others, this new school may be a wheel within a wheel moving under the Great Mover to give some apprehension of the relation to Himself that the philosophical could not otherwise so highly attain. God in mercy give wisdom to dear Waldo that he may be a real & eminent aid to the cause of virtue.

Give my affectionate remembrance to Susan to hear from you will give me great pleasure. My health has decayed so low the year past that I have been moving around the City of Portland. Boarded with Mrs Storer at Kennebunk some weeks   Found you were not forgotten there. Expect to be able soon to resume my tree like stationary life—far more desirable to me than the little variety w'h I can obtain by moving—except a new book or so.

Adieu dear William   The God of our pious ancestors bless & build you in every thing good prays

> your friend & Aunt
> MME.

Perhaps I should never trouble any one to read—for I cannot have a good pen & make trial of numbers in one sheet.

MH: bMS Am 1280.226(1078). *Addressed:* William Emerson, Esqr. / New York / Mr S. M. Haskins. *Endorsed:* M. M Emerson / Sept. 30 / 38 / Rec'd Oct. 8 / Ans^d Jany 5 / 40.
 1. WE[4].
 2. For RWE's addresses, see MME to RWE and LJE, [?] and 17 Sept. [1838], n. 1.

To Ralph Waldo Emerson

Belfast   Nov 16 '38

Dear Waldo,

Why is "the ideal to be only a dream & never a step to realize the vision—   —without misgivings within & wildest ridicule abroad?"[1] Is it not because "nature" that word of reservoir^n—(so vague) resists it, with those "laws & forces" w'h are the hithertoo of nature's Cause—the fiat w'h prescribes the bounds of our present knowledge & discipline and gives us to rear the standard of *faith* on the moving sand banks & changing seas. If any man has bridged over "the gulf between poetry & prose" it is yourself—or rather one of natures poems who have no mechanical labour of bridging—who belong also to a school that is superior to method *theory* (in its old style) and the dingy lamp of old reason—whose rockets fly thro' our dun^n world and make its' people stare and wonder if the "moon be in its' place". They can understand the heroes of antient faith & of xian who spilled their blood for some opinion or truth sacred to the good of the publick—but they cannot understand to what tends the problems or dogmatism of the new doctrines. But let patience work—there will be some light thrown over the muddiness of man— some warmth to the ice—   Not by imitating the "contempt of the Ceasars & Cleopatras" who became so pitiable, but by modifying^n thier new ideas to the xians humility & charity—of *doing* more than others. The first sacrifice they make—the first step they take beyond the pale of common faith—we will proclaim it from the house tops—from the valley of ignorance—the bed of triumphant death. "The rhapsodies of the idealists"! For these I watched month after month—for these I longed & looked at Concord & Waltham. No famished beggar ever craved food so needy—these I had felt in situations of famine & effort and darkness—to get athority—to acquire new blood in old veins was an object to w'h I felt no pains & sacrifices too mortifying. But I was either obtuse or my oracles were not magnitised. And they left me to the invariable conviction that God manifests Himself thro' the medium of our humblest virtues rather than our loftiest speculations. Yet the rapture will always be in union with some intellectual capasity and accompanies every new idea of our relations to Him. Of these relations we do find glimpses among you and the over sea folk. For this I still hang on the skirts of your garment & would kiss its' hem for one step in the path of brightened vision with the mystery of nature. You "*will faithfully answer* my letters"   But now you are busy with lecturing—well give me a page of one—or its object and argument—and lie down with the sattisfaction (nobler than all the ambition of the Ceasars) of having cheered a solitude w'h must have its' tax of unawakened hours— of hearing of business & parochial interests w'h are merely professional. I write by this opp^y wholly & solely to save the longer route—   And know of nothing to say but to inquire after Lidian & the boy and Elisabeth & if Sister got well before going to N. York   On reading yours I was "forced" by the law w'h has guided me to urge an inquiry. If like Sarah A you ever get back to trees and take shelter under the common shade of common nature let me know of your inspirations as I listened to hers when in the Vale.[2]

Your approval of E. Palmer[3] carried me back to the times when Edward & Charles would amuse themselves with your candour. Palmer is a native of this place & his various opinions & pursuits have never impeached his morals but his sanity. Yet his herald opposes all human goverments—   And I hope he will never prove their validity by tresspass—but history notes the disgrace of many an unnatural contemner of gold w'h like many an abstract principle falls lifeless. But such are not the abstractions of your school—for where there is no *Personal goverment in the Infinite, virtue will be practised from its' disinterested love whenever so proteus an ideal meets with no opposition. Now what a sublime & amiable theory Furness has made about Jesus—so beautifull that one would be willing to have it true & wish it were more consistent with itself, were it not that facts of revelation oppose it, and represent God who (must of nessisity forseen Mr Furness & his pencil) chose to construct the nature of man so complex that from the same elements is educated a Voltaire & Fitche—both without faith—yet one a shame & the other an honor to *nature*—(that the term becomes undefinable) and to redeem & solve it's enigmas by one of a superhuman nature.[4] Yet how truly the writer catches some glimpses—and when he describes Jesus as superior to systematic instruction

&c the thought of one who has been my pride & joy came over my soul like light over darkness and who is still the affectionate Aunt

MME

*The present state of your phantasmagoria of the universe or nature I do not refer to—but some talk in the Woodward chamber.[5] And I have not a doubt but this winters lectures[6] will silence the portion of[n] publick who are disaffected and increase the admiration of friends. Would there could be such here to rouse the dead famished mind to w'h there seems no exception!

MH: bMS Am 1280.226(899). *Addressed:* Rev. R Waldo Emerson / Concord / Mass. / Mr W. Frothingham. *Postmarked:* BOSTON / MAS. / NOV 20. *Endorsed:* M.M.E. / Belfast, Nov. 1838.

reservoir] *illegible; supplied from T (where it is bracketed and written in pencil)*

dun] ⟨old⟩ dun

modifying] ⟨condensing⟩ ↑ modifying ↓

silence . . . of] ⟨redeem⟩ ↑ silence ↓ the ↑ portion of ↓

1. This and other quotations come from RWE to MME, 21 Oct. 1838 (*L* 7:323–24).

2. Several references in MME's letters and "Almanack" indicate that SBR visited Waterford in June 1838.

3. Edward Palmer, publisher of a series of tracts titled *Heralds of Holiness*, who visited RWE in Concord, 14–16 Oct.; Rusk calls him a "religious enthusiast and the mildest of communists" (*JMN* 7:xix; *L* 2:170).

4. William Henry Furness (1802–96), boyhood friend of RWE, was an important connection at Philadelphia when RWE and ETE stayed there in 1830 (*Life of RWE*, 145). His "passion" was the quest for the historical Jesus; in 1836 he published *Remarks on the Four Gospels*, called by Perry Miller "a prosaic *Nature*" in the "guise of Biblical criticism," which "endorses Christianity only because Christ adhered to the universal teaching . . . [and] makes short work of the miracles. . . . Nature is seen as itself divine" (*TR*, 124).

5. Mrs. Woodward's, where MME boarded in Concord in 1834–35.

6. RWE's 1838–39 lecture series, "Human Life," was announced in the Boston *Daily Advertiser* on 22 and 26 Oct.; the first lecture was delivered on 5 Dec.

To Elizabeth Hoar

Nov. 18   Sabbath   38

You say, dear 'Lisbeth, that I must write of my new abode.[1] The most prominent feature in the scene arises from the fine bay w'h approaches within a few rods of the house. There dance on the waves many a gay skiff—and there too is every day a little scathed one so smale so dingy so sailless that it moves as by some unseen impulse & again seems grounded—   But happy for the emblem of age it finally goes—and is seen no more with the better barges. Now & then the clouds and waters make but one huge mass—and some fair sail is seen as if in sorrow—but the wind springs up and she spreads a bolder pinion and goes to prove new scenes of larger prospect. And of whom do I think but of one whose letters remind me that I still have interests & pleasures. And it is good to find you in health & to hear of it's fine effects (from Waltham) at the said party. Is it this or your apparent introduction to the tempel of truth & light w'h you describe so vividly. The Appollo of that sect has a sweet harp & charms with a mellow voice & "cunning hand." And no wonder you feel thier power. And you dwell very eloquently on the sleep of the Church. This very musick may awaken it. And will you say (for thy head was wont to be clear) to what are they to awake—to any thing better than that xianity w'h I have long believed to be old as the creation of spirits? Or would you have it dressed in some new & airy forms w'h would put off some very hard truisms—some very sombre usages w'h come most ungenticly in the way of poetry and luxuries and high novelties in speculation? So they do—their obligations too are so far reaching & bend down the aspiring head so "meek & lowly" that there must be regeneration for the pure & lofty souls who happen now to tread this dim speck. And they must build them an ark till the old inhabitants & obsolete opinions are gone to the dust. Pardon, dearest Child, when I began to write nothing was farther from my intention. You know how I love & respect their talents. But I have so little fear of any harm that I can scarsly be serious on the subject. And now I have watched your progress & hope to find some principle—some leading idea to trans.s, if you will excuse the abreviation.[2] And as you are not a leader you will not be responsible for the want of a rigorous or scientific method of explanation. Most hierophants invelop themselves in some mystery—those of this sect exceed others and bewilder us more than any bible arcana. If there be any new motive to virtue—any influence w'h will have a tendency to improve the state of the suffering serf in Russia and over the world in Gods name let it be avowed! If clearer vision of the Infinite agency than the bible gives—oh publish it in the name of all that is grand and mercifull. No there can be nothing! Angels could do nothing of the same adaptation—of equal value. If like Elijah you think there are no true worshippers in the world of the "divine *essence*"[n] you like him may be too jealous. Unless you mean by that Essence somthing different from the personality of scripture. The pantheist unless a complete idealist makes to himself images in nature, or some limbo of it, w'h renders him an idolater. Idealism may be the true theory of the universe and exempt from those hydra monsters w'h attach to Spinoza's. But it surely does not unveil one secret of nature—adds to the wonderfull mystery of existence—lessens no terror of death to the believer of it—for when the very Minerva of the folk[3] was going aboard a single boat last summer her anxiety was extreme. And Furness has amongst much of beauty and force in his theory of miracles[4] incumbered it with mystery beyond its' literal history—besides injuring facts. The correspondence in consequence, I believe, of that work between Norton & Ripley[5] I want & have written to my brother this morning expecting the packet to sail then. If he has it not have you at either house? A bundle can be sent by water at any time by young Frothingham thro' T. W. H. at Boston. And do not fail (if you care for me) to write as long as possible consistent with your pleasures & duties. Let Belinda[6] know I remember her with interest and would like to know what you converse about. We have nothing new to read or literatie to hear. The years of domestic duties & of parochial attentions have withered the fine fancy of my hostess—but her good feelings & lively character remain. The minister never converses—rarely speaks is in study[n] and I guess respects my solitary habits w'h better health & eyes enable one to maintain. There you have all I can say for my condition   And now dear 'lisbeth to whom I fear so oft writing will intrude good winter & all seasons ever attend you with new requisitions. Your aff[t] Aunt

M M Emerson

* * *

That is F. denies some miracles of equal athority one thinks, to some admitted.[7]

MH: bMS Am 1280.226(1109). *Addressed:* Miss Elizabeth Hoar / Care of Hon. S. Hoar / Concord.

worshippers . . . *essence*"] worshippers ⟨about you⟩ ↑ in the world ↓ of the " ↑ divine ↓ *essence*" ⟨of the⟩

speaks . . . study] speaks ↑ is in study ↓

1. MME to EH, Augusta, 17 Oct. 1838, says she plans to board at Belfast, Maine, with "Lydian" Frothingham, the wife of Belfast's minister, the Reverend William Frothingham (MH: 1108). Frothingham's first wife, Lois Barrett of Concord, died in 1819; in 1821 he married MME's old friend Lydia Prentiss of Dover, N.H.

2. For "transcendentalism."

3. Probably SBR (see MME to RWE, 16 Nov. 1838, n. 2).

4. For Furness's theory of miracles, see MME to RWE, 16 Nov. 1838, n. 4.

5. George Ripley, minister of the Purchase Street Church, Boston, is usually credited with the opening volley in the "miracles controversy" with Andrews Norton, former Dexter Professor of Sacred Literature at Harvard, in his review of James Martineau, *The Rationale of Religious Enquiry*, in the *Christian Examiner* 21 (Nov. 1836): 225–54. Ripley questioned the need for miracles as evidence for the truths of Christianity. Norton counterattacked in an open letter to Ripley, printed in the Boston *Daily Advertiser*, 5 Nov. 1836; he affirmed the necessity for miracles and suggested that Ripley was unqualified to speak on the subject. Ripley came back four days later with his own open letter in the *Advertiser*. The controversy continued for several years via reviews of such works as Ripley's *Specimens of Foreign Literature* and RWE's "American Scholar" (1837) and "Address Delivered before the Senior Class in Divinity College" (15 July 1838), which was attacked by Norton in the *Advertiser*, 27 Aug. 1838. MME seems to be asking for some of the materials in this "correspondence."

6. EH's friend Belinda Randall (1816–97) of Boston.

7. Written on outside below address; reference is to Furness (see above, n. 4).

To Frederic Henry Hedge

Belfast   Dec 20 '38

Dear Sir,

It is not likely you remember me nor the letter you wrote me in answer to some inquiries into an opinion of yours. But I have often thought of you and when I hear of you remember that you offered to answer any more letters.[1] I was then among my own kith—and since—affliction has made me feel wholly divided from the bright & litterary—except some intercourse with Waldo whose opinions I too often & too ignorantly oppose. Yet those concerning the new school I have an insatiable desire to understand if I were capable. I am obtuse by reason of age as ignorance—and Waldo is no explainer. I have since being in your vicinity often wished to ask you for what may be the leading principles of transcendental philosphy—to what it tends—whether any new relation—any nearer apprehension of God's agency may be gained? This the sole ground for happiness if not for virtue. And to those who live only for the reality of this relation 'tis in fact the all. My doubts of this sect arise from some of them complaining that they cannot bridge over the finite to the infinite—this one would think the last they would make—for the simple biblist—or mere theist finds, or believes, the one in the other and this in that. And my impression remains (tho' against my inclination) that a sublime kind of pantheism results from many of their propositions and from their spontaneous expressions. Nor can I find it possible to get any clearer notions or beliefs or faith in the presence and agency of the all surrounding Infinite than I find in the revelations so accordant to our consciousness and reason. And as to our reason not being personal is out of my way of feeling—and inconsistent with human agency? Would you hold a light to my inquiries I would carry my gratitude where it could give you a pleasure w'h can never be felt so fully here. However desirous I am for this subject I should not have intruded on your multiplied engagments this season, but for the *matter*[n] of phrenology wh has occurred in this Village for the last evenings. I have a great aversion to it without any curiosty to know of its pretensions, as I have always had in the way of philosophy to that of the venerated Locke's. And always feel obliged to speake of it's bad tendency. And my arguements are always drawn from an article you inserted in the Examiner 4 years since.[2] This article is all I ever read on the subject. And last night they were produced & read by Mr F.[3] (who with my friend his wife lean towards the Lecturer) when I felt my cause to be successfull. But the preceptor with whom I like to speake (as far as I am able) of transcendentalism in a favorable way, observed that Cousin[4] was in favor of phrenology. I doubted it—as being the very antagonist of his theories—I determined to refer the question to some one—& have taken this liberty with you. It seems to me that Cousin is far from directness—and so bold in his generalisations that I am often at a loss what to understand of the little I have read—but that he embraces in any way this vagrant intruder into philosophy seems out of the question. This young gentleman's athority was some foreign journals.

And if you can spare time tell me if the page 147 of Cousin's Introduction means more than that consciousness of the Infinite I have refered to?[5] True, it ca'nt be explained—eludes deduction—yet so sure & invincible it mocks at proof—thus with that inspiration w'h even now is allowed to be natural we say with the prophets Thou *hast* wrot *all our works*   Whether by mechanical or moral agency?? Now my dear Sir, dont answer me as if I were a timid old woman & would boast of your sayings or be alarmed. My host & his seem averse to metaphysicks and I shall preserve all I get for other ears. It is a dearth of books here & even Wares sermon[6] & such like that were sent me are lost. Have you felt anxious about the stir against Waldo? God grant it do good. And wherever it may be that this new school aid the cause of philosophy & religion may it's pioneers share it's glory. You I believe are considered it's Moses—if you still veil your knowledge from common eyes your progress in all noble truth will ever give that best of all enjoyments sympathy for the love of virtue to one who respects and admires

M. M. Emerson

MH-AH. *Addressed:* Rev. Mr. Hedge / Bangor / Me. *Postmarked:* Belfast / ME / Dec 21.

matter] ⟨subject⟩ *matter*

1. See MME to FHH, 10 Apr. 1835. Hedge's reply does not survive.

2. Probably Hedge, "Coleridge's Literary Character"; he explains "transcendental philosophy" on pp. 125–29.

3. William Frothingham.

4. Victor Cousin; see below, n. 5.

5. A passage on p. 147 of Ripley's edition of Cousin, in *Philosophical Miscellanies*, reads, "If every fact of consciousness contains all the human faculties, sensibility, free activity, and reason, the me, the not-me, and their absolute identity; and if every fact of consciousness be equal to itself, it follows that every man who has the consciousness of himself possesses and cannot but possess all the ideas that are necessarily contained in consciousness. Thus every man, if he knows himself, knows all the rest, nature and God at the same time with himself" (from Cousin's preface to "Tennemann's Outlines of the History of Philosophy").

6. Henry Ware, Jr., *The Personality of the Deity: A Sermon, Preached in the Chapel of Harvard University, September 23, 1838. . . .* (Boston, 1838). Published "at the Request of the Members of the Divinity School," the sermon (Rusk indicates) was Ware's attempt to exonerate the divinity school of "any blame for Transcendental heresy" (*Life of RWE*, 270–71).

1839

To Ralph Waldo Emerson

[1839?][1]

I dont feel sattisfied with the cold glimps I have given of one whose early acquaintance was marked with so so partial a kindness to poor me.[2] But after his marriage I had very little chance of seeing him. The few months I past in Boston was badly past by one of my odd ways & disgust with society as it then was. But the letter goes written in haste as I always write—more so to you, whose time I fear tresspassing on—and my own has its aged claims. But in reading yours tonight I am surprised to find debts incurred & money freely spent. In youth he was very generous of money & always honorable but after marriage how he could willingly run in debt & yet spend money is unaccountable. That he was in debt the last two years of invalidity & a very expensive kitchen was natural & excusable. As to the wood day his journal w'h I had occasion to mention to some gentlemen who were asking after his Harvard life I named a sentence of his journal, about wood & that "he was no happier for all that" as a kind of moral jest—or representation of Harvard. Whatever indifference I discover in reminiscences my own Journal of early days disclose the warmest admiration & if "he could come to sucess I should rejoice tho' never to see him"   In the years I lived with the Waits from 28 to 34 I never visited him but in passing thro Boston or when he was sick in 1809 when the house was building. He came for me in health repeatedly once to attend Cambridge exhibition when S. R. was to speake. But strange as it now seems I had no inclination to go. I was sheltered & loved the homely seclusion   I forgot every body—hardly ever remembered his being at Boston. Our religious sympathies were frozen. But when we meet hereafter—when memory renews every moment & affection when the glowing generous traits of his character shall appear in their identity with the lustre w'h that place alone can give what a reunion—whether (if I am worthy) lasting longer or shorter—whether new views & education will unite us forever is of no consequence—while one great principle unites us to happiness & virtue. "Dont speake of Channing." When I first saw C. your father asked me what I felt & saw I said there was a cold vein in his face. I well recall his surprise &c   But he never was close with C. & when the latter came to see him on the sickness of 1809 so patronising & pastor like a visit was not very acceptable. The only minister I remember coming. Williams conversation one day when he could sit up was interesting with me   He said "why if we all rise together at the resurrection will it not be pleasanter than to be divided by ages?"

The night wears & I resolve to send as you will expect. One consolation always remains. Of immortal—how rich the joy of that aspiring soul whose competitions find him higher than earthly hopes. If "*not to be*" how like the bells of a fool the trump of fame. But what renders this idle—the spirit is framed for endless happiness in its Origin without one other object or pursuit. "The night," you use to say, "comes down"—

So may it bless you

MH: bMS Am 1280.226(900). *Addressed: Only* and *alone* to RWE.
1. This undated letter may belong to 1838 or 1839.
2. The "character" that follows is of MME's brother WE[2], RWE's father.

To Ralph Waldo Emerson and Ruth Haskins Emerson
Elm Vale   Sep. 26 '39

Dear Waldo,

You did not ask me to write in your letter of July. And now that the very man of men may be with you[1] that I should dare intrude. Well write I do—it may be in very spite. Besides this "unity"—why not the humblest of beings a part of your genius and consciousness? The dimest solitude so frought with indefinable excitment becomes a partner with the glowing interests of the beautifull & famed. We do not love the smile w'h savors of the sardonic in the "french revolution"—but the auther you have taught us to respect   And I do want you to picture his conversations & bestow some of it's wealth. I dont know what he *does* believe & say about the interior world & its divine Source. Therefore can feel not much interest. What would be his theory of a single human being forever alone with the Infinite? What his virtue? His reason & happiness immeasurably great, of course.

I write I believe (if I have a distinct purpose at this sleepy hour) to thank you for the 2 last volumes of "Misselanies"[2] received last sunday from Ralph at Portland. Looked in vain for a line—a word of a name. Why I said to my self when I give a bone to the dog if I pat or speake him how much more he relishes his bit. And the very cat sits more gracefully at her meal when called poor puss.

But I shall value the books and often bless you—hope not to find what seems to me an affectation of thunder & lightning in the parts w'h belong to Carlyle's style.

Is your Mother & Elisabeth at Concord? My love to them & Lidian & the children. Tell my Sister our Invalid[3] continues in the old spot tho' at times so feeble as to be fast going from it. Death has visited our circle in his milder forms & taken the two boys of Rebecca,[4] who she may remember. Their Mother is consoled by the hope of their better provision. But as yet she has not time to realize her own loss, or recover from the fatigue of an anxious attendance   Of disease I will say nothing more as "you do not like to discriminate." Let us fancy there is no disease—that the cauldron of woe & sin exists only in the morbid imajanations of ascetics. And it is grand in the unity of the Infinite Personality to lose every discordant fact—to live in a Utopian of our own. How you could approve of Stone's theory. Why to say that "all philosophy originated in love and goodness". That there is an infinity of truth & goodness in all true philosophy—and a philosophy arising from reflection— (consciousness) in every thought and every fact is true—　But I am too bad to prose over you at such a time. Well take the blessing of the aged and long may your virtue & happiness continue to irradiate the old earth & rise with new beams in a better prays your aff^t Aunt

MME

My dear Ruthy　I have unfolded this to say that I know you will wish to hear more of Sister Phebe. She is an anxious and fearfull subject of the future—submissive humble & gratefull　Her peculiar constitution & confused views of faith are the cause of her fears. She wrote in answer to messages from Waldo & Elis. a gratefull note some weeks since but I had closed my letter to Elis. Rebecca you will pity—but she will take a school & be able to get on tho' not so cheerfully poor woman　You may have heard from Thomas that our Sister was emerged—she made an effort of cheerfullness at parting with Ralph. *I love facts*

MH: bMS Am 1280.226(901). *Addressed:* Rev. R Waldo Emerson / Concord / Mass. / Favored by Mr Clarke. *Endorsed:* M.M.E. Apr. 1839 *and* M.M.E. / 1839.

　1. Thomas Carlyle, who RWE once hoped would visit and even move to the Boston area and edit a magazine such as the *Dial*.

　2. RWE edited and arranged for the American printing of a four-volume edition of Carlyle's *Critical and Miscellaneous Essays* (Boston: James Munroe, 1838–39).

　3. PER died on 11 Dec. 1839. MME to SR, 12 Dec. 1839, describes her death and the funeral arrangements (MH: 1248).

　4. Two sons of Rebecca Haskins Hamlin had recently died at Waterford: Lincoln R. Hamlin, age eight, on 7 Sept., and Henry C. Hamlin, age five, on 21 Sept. 1839.

PART 5

1840–1851

1840   Vale (all year) with visit to Portland? (Oct.) [EH visits in Aug.].

1841   Vale (Jan.–June?); Sweden Spring [hotel] (July); Windham, Portland, Waterville (Aug.); Augusta (?), Newburyport (Oct.); Concord [Howe's Tavern] (Nov.); Salem, Newburyport? (Nov.); Vale (Dec.).

1842   Vale, N. Waterford (Jan.–Aug.?); Portland (Oct.); Vale? (Nov.–Dec.).

1843   Vale (Jan.–July?); Newburyport [Capt. Hodge's, Brown Square] (Aug.–Oct.); Salem, Portland, Vale (mid-Oct.–Dec.).

1844   Vale (Jan.–Aug.); Waltham, with visits to Roxbury and Concord, Portland (Sept.–Oct.); Vale (Nov.–Dec.).

1845   Vale? (Jan.–June); Andover, Waltham, Concord, Malden, Boston (July–Aug.); Lancaster (Sept.–Oct.); with trip to New York (Sept.); Concord [Mr. Goodnow's], Boston [Mrs. Cobb's] (Oct.); Boston, S. Reading (Nov.); Newburyport, Vale (Dec.).

1846   Vale (all year) with visit to Newburyport (Jan. or June?) [EPP visits in Aug.].

1847   Vale (Jan.–May); Portland (June); Vale? [EPP visits Gages in July; LJE and EH visit in late Aug.–Sept.], with trips to Portland, Harrison and Bridgton (July–Oct.); S. Paris (Nov.); Waterford (Dec.).

1848   Waterford (Jan.); S. Paris (Feb.–Mar.); Newburyport? (with Charlotte Haskins), Paris, Norway, S. Waterford (Apr.); Vale (May–Oct.) with trip to Portland (June); Concord (Nov.–Dec.).

1849   Vale and Waterford (all year) with trips to Portland and ? [boarding at cottage in Dec.].

1850   S. Waterford? [Calvin Farrar's] and Vale? (Jan.–June); Vale? [EH visits, late Aug.–early Sept.] (June–Aug.); Belfast (Sept.), Kennebunkport, Augusta, Winthrop, Portland, Concord (Oct.–Nov.?); Vale (Nov.–Dec.).

1851   Vale (Jan.–Feb.); ? (Mar.); S. Waterford (Apr.–June?); Concord (July); Springfield, Newburyport, Harvard, Portland?, Stow (Aug.); Bolton [Dr. Bigelow's] (Sept.); Lancaster (Oct.); Concord (Oct.–Dec.).

In 1840 Mary Emerson retorted sharply to Elizabeth Hoar's request that she tell of her " 'external life.' " She had delayed answering: "As I had nothing," she explains, "I tho't it hard that the hand, rich in all things, should ask to uncover the little crypt where age & oft nervous debility seeks to hide its wormy aspect." She much preferred, as she makes clear, to rise above these mean cares of "external life," which she does in a lengthy and bewildering meditation from her solitude, where "the dial of time is marked by none of it's events" (MH: 1114).

During this period, she had to uncover that "crypt" of age, debility, and events. In 1849 she quoted her new favorite, Isaac Taylor, on the " 'strange incongruity . . . when the heirs of immortality are seen involved in sordid cares & the perplexities of a moment,' " which she knew well as a result of illness, aging, and problems related to the disposition of her earthly "estate," especially the Elm Vale farm, which was sold in 1850. But she also shared Taylor's belief that, seen from a higher point of view, these cares are part of the "process of preparation" for immortality (MWA).[1] The dialogue in these years is less between society and solitude, or "excitement" without and within, and more between physical and spiritual self, the claims of the momentary present balanced against those of eternity.

Though the decade ended with her permanent removal from Vale, Miss Emerson lived a more rooted life in the years from 1840 from 1851, spending nine to ten months of each year at the farm or boarding in nearby Waterford. Her pattern in these years is to winter for six or more months at Vale, making short excursions for a few weeks or months, usually in the summer, to visit, take cures, or do business at Concord, Waltham, Boston, Newburyport, Sweden Spring, Portland, Paris, Bridgton, East Lancaster, and other places. In 1843 Waldo and Elizabeth Hoar took a train to Newburyport after receiving a message that her present illness could "terminate fatally." Mary, too, began to use the train to move more rapidly, and in these years she traveled farther than ever before, leaving New England for the first time to go to New York City in 1845. As the calendar of her residences indicates, it is often difficult to determine her location when not at "home."

For 1840–51, some 250 letters to twenty correspondents (two-thirds to women) survive, although it is clear that many others have been lost. One wishes especially for more of her correspondence with Elizabeth Peabody, whom, Mary told Elizabeth in 1842, "I write often . . . as her case is so interesting" (MH: 1137)—but only two letters to Miss Peabody survive, and Ronda prints only one of Peabody's letters (from 1845 or 1846, not 1843) to Miss Emerson. At least sixty-five letters deal, wholly or in part, with business matters, primarily the disposal of the farm. While many others reveal her usual zest for theological discussion, these letters also contain numerous incisive comments on more worldly events, reading, and people: Waldo's career, lectures, and publications (the series on New England, representative men, and the conduct of life; college orations; public addresses; *Poems*, the *Dial*; first and second *Essays*; the *Massachusetts Quarterly Review*); the weddings of young relatives and friends; Hawthorne's *Mosses*; Bremer's and G. P. R. James's novels; Charlotte Brontë's *Jane Eyre*; Sylvester Judd's *Margaret*; Margaret Fuller's *Summer on the Lakes* and *Woman in the Nineteenth Century*; collections of letters and sermons, lectures, reviews, and philosophical works; Millerism and the antislavery movement; the Mexican war and the fugitive slave bill; the lives and, often, deaths of people such as William Ellery Channing, Elizabeth Fry, Leander Gage, Margaret Fuller, the Alcotts, Harriet Martineau, and Daniel Webster. Her comments often suggest a new confidence to speak out, gained from increased age and experience, as well as a desire to assent to the wishes of her primary correspondent, Elizabeth Hoar (recipient of eighty-two letters), who wanted to hear "particulars."[2]

Less often do her letters turn out to be sermons. Instead, they take many forms, from brief apothegms and statements of proverbial wisdom to imaginary conversations, journalistic reportage, apologies, eulogies, epitaphs, farewells, "characters," literary criticism, "Almanack" leaves, and sentimental, romantic, and theatrical performances. The many very lengthy and dense letters to Elizabeth (sometimes written almost weekly for several months) indicate her important role as chief correspondent, even though Mary never fully created the kind of intellectual dialogue here that she desired. With some of her new, younger correspondents—the children of her "children"—auntly counsel still prevails.

Often her comments are somewhat like the "plumbs" in the pudding for which Miss Emerson faulted Alcott, which has led me to prune and select more carefully than in the earlier periods. Still, as the seventy letters chosen to represent this twelve-year period reveal, even in her seventies, Mary Emerson remained fully capable of using her pen like an artist, drawing together the temporal and eternal through imaginative vision and language.

From this period survive two wonderful portraits, among many other partial descriptions. One comes from sister-in-law Sarah Ripley, whom Mary visited for two weeks in the fall of 1844, soon after her seventieth birthday; the second is from Elizabeth Peabody, who visited Waterford in 1846. In Sarah's account, Mary Emerson "still retains all the oddities and enthusiasms of her youth." She is "a person at war with society as to all its decorums; she eats and drinks what others do not, and when they do not; dresses in a white robe such days as these; enters into conversation with everybody, and talks on every subject; is sharp as a razor in her satire, and sees you through and through in a moment." She then describes Mary's "insatiable" appetite for metaphysics and recalls her earliest encounter (at age sixteen) with this woman who "enchained me entirely to her magic circle."[3]

Sarah's description preserves the oracular and eccentric Mary Moody Emerson in the white "shroud" who flew down like a north wind bearing tidings of another world, still an important voice in 1840–51, alongside the sharp conversationalist. To nephew William, in 1840 she still dwelt "on the lofty mountains of contemplation," as opposed to the plains of practical life where he lived (MT/EW), while for Waldo she remained a "lover of nature & the great heart & subtle mind—who has so woven her presence into the best threads & texture of my life" (*L* 3:64). He realized "how much spur" he had lost through their "separation" since 1836 (*L* 3:211). In November 1851, two hours of provocative conversation with Miss Emerson spurred Henry Thoreau to pronounce her "the wittiest & most vivacious woman that I know—   Certainly that woman among my acquaintance whom it is most profitable to meet."[4]

Her war with society appears in Elizabeth Peabody's letters during a some-what disastrous summer vacation. Mary's stormy behavior so strained their relationship that Peabody almost wished she had not gone to Waterford: Miss Emerson declared herself much disappointed in "Miss Pea.," whom she found "frivolous, irreligious, and without love for her"; was jealous of Peabody's friendship with niece Hannah Haskins; and childishly refused and then in-sisted on a mountain walk. In this last change of plan Peabody felt Miss Emerson had "*been redeemed* by some more gracious thoughts from her bit-ter Self." Her bitter self was rampant in a mock epic "affair of the Spectacles," when Mary returned from the walk and could not find her glasses. She was in such "wild excitement," Peabody reported, and so blamed others for the loss that "one would have thought there had never been another pair of spectacles in the universe" (MWA).

Though she felt sorry for her, Peabody could not but admire this woman with whom she could not get along: "She is an extraordinary creature. I think I never received a greater impression of her genius: the ploughshare of Ex-perience never seems to have broken the wild beauty of her character—which like a wild country of great natural sublimity of feature—retains its untamed rocks & woods & cataracts telling of the creative power of God—but not of the redeeming power of Christ. Now this last would shock her who has such a passionate love of *his name*—& so fine & fresh an idea of the necessity of his redemption." Later in this same letter she returned to this metaphor: "I enjoyed after all more from her—notwithstanding all—than you can imag-ine perhaps as you have heard of these storms. . . . She is so original—& then I like mountains & valleys—cataracts & wild woods—in characters as well as nature. I love her though she does stick hard things into all tender places" (MWA).

Other comments deepen the shadows in this picture. Waldo Emerson began to see his aunt as a suffering "victim," a querulous and rather disagreeable figure to be more pitied than praised. When he learned her plan to travel to New York with Peabody and Christopher Cranch in 1845, Waldo warned his brother about "how utterly unskilful she will be—a mere victim to every imposture & discomfort in your city." He advised William to treat her as though she were a child, arranging every detail of money handling, "conveyance & boarding &c.," and explained how he managed her recent visits to Boston and Concord, now that she refused to sleep in his house, by making "private terms with her landladies." (In 1841 she reminded him of her vow never to stay in his home "unless bro't there in a liter.") Despite all, however, he assured William he would not regret doing what he could, when he came to recognize "how many sad hours & days this susceptible over-excited & lonely invalid passes, both when travelling, & when at her now comfortless home" (*L* 3:302–3).

Waldo saw Mary as a victim also of illness. After her near-fatal attack of erysipelas (a painful inflammatory condition of the skin and subcutaneous tissue caused by a streptococcus bacterium) in 1843, Waldo remarked that, despite her "originality and wit," she seemed to "[suffer] more than she enjoys" (*L* 3:211). Two years later he called her "her own daily victim, unstable & whimsical & self tormenting and so tormenting those about her, in the most extraordinary & painful degree. . . . Her friends have only to keep as cool & as kindly as they can manage it, towards this gifted but most unhappy woman" (*L* 3:292–93).

Certainly illness was a problem, though her letters complain and whine less than Emerson's comment might suggest. An 1846 letter to Elizabeth Hoar runs the seriocomic gamut that perhaps best describes her situation: "I have been as stupid as infirmitys self—'weary in all the functions of stale useless life'—confined by bad roads & this head confusion. . . . I dont believe such half way diseases would ever weary so were it not for occasional hours when existence is so very rich. . . . Dont [know] when & how much to use the nux. vom. opium & pur. . . . If there should be chance for Waldo to send any more (w'h he may by Express with somthing to read) ask L. to send acon. & bry. & belladona if convenent. I have taken up a vial of each moity & sleep the better tho' the genius of dreams sends them thro' a gate hidious with war & cruel oppression" (MH: 1157). Other letters, however, remark on her decision not to use wine or other tonics or to forego medicines.

In contrast to her somewhat abstract and perennial fascination with the "worm" and other "night thoughts," by 1844 Mary was clearly grappling with the very real fact of her own mortality, as her concern about disposing of her earthly "estate" makes clear. During an attack of erysipelas she even claimed "my writing letter days are almost over" (MH: 1221). Less than a year after her brush with death in 1843, she describes the disfiguring effects of erysipelas and her worries about insanity, permanent decrepitude, and the prospect of lingering helplessly and burdening her family; she feels new love and gratitude for a home she hopes never to leave and orders a "thin flannel dress" in case she's taken "unconsciously sick." However, after receiving a heavy, lined robe from Elizabeth, she separated the lining from the coat (which she gave away) and wore it "daily in the same form"—seemingly the original of the many "shrouds" she is reputed to have worn out in her last twenty years. Perhaps it was these thoughts that prompted the anonymous publication, in the Portland *Register* in June 1846, of a brief "fragment of 1830" entitled "A Meeting of Two Friends after Death." She sought health at nearby spas and watercures, wrote at least one letter during a session with a phlebotomist, suffered some injury in a fall from a sleigh, and ventured forth from Vale primarily in search of the health that came from contact with people and ideas.

To the effects of illness must be added the impact that certain loved ones' deaths had on her psyche. " 'But come he slow or come he fast, / Death will surely come at last,' " she quipped, but each additional death drove her to ponder (and hope for) her own end: stepfather Ezra Ripley died in 1841; little Waldo, Leander Gage, and W. E. Channing died in 1842; sister Rebecca died in 1845; and half brother Samuel Ripley died on the eve of Thanksgiving in 1847. Samuel's death, when Mary was seventy-three years old, left her the sole surviving child of the two marriages of her mother, Phebe Bliss Emerson Ripley. She even had very definite ideas about where her body should rest for eternity, which she spelled out after a young woman who was boarding with the Gages died suddenly in 1849. The woman could not have her chosen spot, "w'h was large & might possibly lead some inquirer to my grave w'h was always to be stoneless."

Somewhere in and between the bemused toleration, the adulation, and the pity of the typical responses lies the Mary Moody Emerson of these letters. While her outer life was dominated by her related quests for health and home (the other side of illness, loneliness, penury, and dependence), neither her mind nor her spirit had diminished. She did not see herself as eccentric, willful, or victimized; instead, she embraced the life she had been given by that Author of her being in whose Design she continued to believe. "Nothing has so delighted me thro' life as to find in nature symbols of character, human & divine," she wrote in 1842, referring to the metaphor that closes her notice of Leander Gage's death, printed in the *Christian Witness*.

For Waldo, the story of his aunt at Elm Vale—"her dealings and vexations about it, her joys and raptures of religion and Nature"—was material for a "romance" (*W* 10:401). The true story that emerged in 1845, of her "sacrifice" and secret ownership of the property and the "irksome connection" with her shiftless brother-in-law Robert Haskins (much like an unsuccessful marriage), is indeed matter for a sentimental novel. For over thirty years Mary Emerson played the role of poor relation in her sister's household while "boarding" in the home she had purchased with her patrimony. Some people did know that she was the owner (witness her request in 1820 that Dr. Gage not mention the fact to anyone). However, after her "agents" Gore Ripley and Levi Brown threatened Robert with legal action in 1846 if he did not relinquish his "false claims," the sense of outrage among the Haskins children indicates that they, like their mother, Rebecca, had never recognized their aunt's "sacrifice." As late as 1855, she was still pleading her case, arguing her legal and moral rights to dispose of the property and somewhat obsessively telling the "truth" of her relationship with Robert.

In January 1840 Waldo told Mary he hoped she would soon make Concord her home, now that her sister Phebe Ripley's death had cut one more tie to Waterford. Believing that "God *will* preserve from dependence on kindred" (MH: 1077), Mary Emerson had her own plan: to remain at Elm Vale, the home she hoped never to leave, as a paying member of a family who would see to her needs in her old age and to whom she would will the property. Alternatively, she was willing to sell with the stipulation that she be allowed to stay on as a boarder in the two front rooms she had long occupied when at Vale. However, in April 1850, the Elm Vale farm was sold to a "stranger," and about a year later she left Waterford, never to return.

The Elm Vale saga that began in 1805 climaxed in 1845, when Mary for the first time seriously considered selling the property—in effect, "divorcing" Robert. The story is tangled and confused by a number of factors in addition to illness and age: in 1848 she admitted her alarm at "forgetting household names! & to spell common words" (MH: 235[664]). Her admitted ignorance about legal questions results in confused syntax and an impatience with details concerning mortgages and rents, leases, bonds, claims, deeds, quitclaims, interest, and notes. In her blithe inattention to details, she had made casual purchases of additional parcels of land over the years which she gave away, with equal insouciance, while signing documents she did not read or understand or bother to record. What's more, she changed her mind frequently, as reflected in various wills and other statements of her wishes.[5] She was torn in her painful dealings with Robert, the ostensible owner of the property, who, though incompetent (and, she often suspected, "insane"), still claimed her sympathy as a good produce farmer, a "helpless father," and a "poor broken man." And she disliked "manouvering," which she believed was "as dangerous to grandeur of soul for this as for another high state" (MH: 225[31]).

The raptures of Vale continue to infuse the letters of the 1840s: there the "dial of time is marked by none of its events," a "very standing still of exterior things [so] that the interior Joshua may proceed" (MH: 1114). Fall at Vale was a "season one with consciousness," when she felt "alone with the infinite." She praised its "unvaried solitude" in 1843, and the next year she wrote warmly about the home she hoped never to leave. That fall, however, she wrote that "nothing but some old cunning spiders & a few vagrant flies with my shawdow are the expected companions of the winter" (MH: 918).

By 1845 the situation was worse: none of the boys was interested in the property, Rebecca had died, and Robert's increasing debts and inability to keep up his side of the bargain continued. When at Vale, she took the interest ($80 per year) due on her investment ($1,100) in the form of board, figured at $70 per year. When she chose to board elsewhere, she expected the interest to support her travels. (She also received $80 a year from her life insurance annuity.) But Robert was often unable to pay anything, and several times she paid delinquent taxes for him so that the property would not be seized. Other letters point to how he had taken advantage of their arrangement. He sold off several small parcels of land without her signature. At least once she dated a letter from "Desolate Vale"—desolate because, during her absence, Robert had cut down most of her beloved elms. The farm was run down: when the barn roof fell in about 1843, Mary confessed surprise that the house had not collapsed instead (but also faith that, since "every particle is held by an absolute Power," she need not move). Ann Gage's complaint, in 1848, that her own farm was beginning to look "Haskinsy . . . everything patched and hammered & stowed for the present" (MWA) gives us some idea of the condition of Elm Vale. As a result, Mary refused Robert yet another lease. Still, throughout her attempt to negotiate a sale that would give her living privileges, she insisted on treating this poor man fairly, asking for no more than she had originally invested and hoping that the farm would fetch more so that Robert would have something to live on, in addition to a cottage and some surrounding acreage she had already given him.

Well aware that "unprotected women are constantly imposed on" (MH: 1183), Miss Emerson sought advice from an array of (mostly male) counselors, lawyers, agents, family, and friends, to whose wiser judgment she attempted to defer, probably more often than she should have. After obtaining the "release" from Robert Haskins in 1846, she gave him the "Cottage" and its land to live on, as well as the sixty acres she had promised. Finally freed of this connection, she explored a jumble of possibilities. Talk of a steamboat to Waterford and the establishment of a watercure fueled hope that land values would rise. She sought a better tenant for her property. But the next year she had to give up her ideal scenario: an arrangement with her niece Hannah, who had married a local farmer, Augustus Parsons, in 1845. Though the couple leased the farm for a year in 1846–47, they could not afford to buy, and by 1849 they had moved to Williamsburgh on Long Island (where Hannah's brother Samuel Moody Haskins was rector of Saint Mark's Episcopal Church).

The last two years before the sale were filled with "unusual perplexities" that reconciled Mary to her loss. She continued to seek a family, a home, to "adopt someone for life" (MH: 1182). Another potential sale—to close neighbor Oliver Hale, who planned to rent the property—fell through, partly, it seems, because Mary insisted that consideration of her needs be included in the deal. "To have a smale clever family for my life time is a motive better than money," she explained in 1848, after she had turned down Hale's offer of $1,600 (MH: 1232). But by this time, the nieces to whom she wanted to leave the farm had "scattered," and she complained of "dreary moments among strangers." Despite her continued faith that "Providence" would provide a home, her anxieties leak through such expressions as "scarecrows in my glimmering eyes about expenses" (MH: 235[664]) and "I grow bluer & nervous what a page for the 76th year. The Almshouse never alarmed—" (MH: 937). Meanwhile, despite Waldo Emerson's repeated efforts to reestablish their broken relationship, she steadfastly refused to stay at her nephew's ("the less I see of him the better"), though she was tired of the "tedious remedy of wandering" (MH: 1183). Her alternatives seemed few.

When the question of selling had come up in the 1830s, she had explained what she considered her legal rights: she wanted either "compensation or roof tree." By compensation, she meant full return of her original investment plus a profit; she expected to receive $1,500 if the farm was sold outright, because, as she maintained, the $1,100 she had paid Ralph Haskins was not a loan but an investment. She had gambled that the value of farms would rise. She hoped the farm would bring even more, so that Robert, too, would profit. She would prefer the "roof tree"—a permanent "home" as a paying boarder with a family—for which she would reduce the price to $1,100. She was content at Vale: "I eat of the produce & live better than so idle a lady deserves," she wrote in 1837. Even the arrangement with Robert Haskins had turned out better than she had hoped. "Compensation" or "roof tree" remained her terms as she negotiated the sale of the farm in the 1840s.

In 1848 Mary admitted she was tenantless and destitute; if she could not get someone to live in the house with her, to pay rent and help with taxes, to see to wood and fires and other needs, and to be there when she was ill, she could not spend another winter at Vale. Her reputation for disagreeable behavior probably contributed to her inability to realize this ideal. Instead of an "unvaried solitude," Vale now offered the frightening prospect of "unaided solitude" (MH: 1187). Thus, by October 1849, she was ready to sell for less than she had hoped, and she wondered how to invest the few hundred dollars she would have left after paying off obligations to Waldo, Robert Haskins, and Augustus Parsons (who had repaid debt on the barn owed by his father-in-law). The buyer was a stranger whom she did not like, though his wife seemed pleasant enough, who seemed willing to lease the two rooms to her; on Thanksgiving day, she wrote to Elizabeth Hoar, "My farm has been sold for taxes & the sooner I redeem if Hale intends to cheat as he is the most notorious Swindler, the better folks say" (MH: 1194).

The transaction, arranged by Gore Ripley, was completed the following April: the buyer was John Howe from nearby Norway; Mary Emerson received $1,450, with a mortgage of $325 to Waldo paid off.[6] Although she negotiated some sort of "roof-tree" arrangement with the Howes, by February 1851 this had become unsatisfactory, and by July she had left Waterford for the last time. Still, the matter was not over: she continued to deal with additional claims on the property and to write lengthy letters explaining and justifying her position to the men who had never understood her. These letters are terribly confused, as she outlines her "rights," both "moral" and "legal," while walking the difficult path between securing her own future and dealing "honestly" with the human family whose living was so entwined with her own. She felt her advisors "never perceived or saw the affair as I did"—that is, recognized that more than a "legal" right to $1,500 was operating in her search for a permanent home.

Mary Emerson's continuing effort to exonerate herself in her dealings about the farm reaffirms her commitment to laws higher than those governing human property. According to the "grand laws of benevolence," she wrote in 1831, it is "more honorable to do generous deeds with fradulent ones than to rust under that dolerous nessesty of unremitting parsimony" (MH: 700), and, despite various forms of bad faith (dishonesty, deception, and broken promises) on the part of the men she had to deal with, she never yielded on the question of "moral" rights. Still concerned, as late as 1855, with misunderstandings about the sale, she strongly maintained her fidelity to these "higher laws": "I would rather die with the stain of drunkeness or profanity or infidelity if it could be voluntary than forgoing my work, w'h would injure others besides irrevocably myself. . . . What is right to be done I shall do if within lifes power or deaths" (MH: 950). This desire to do the right thing for her sister's family as well as herself is a prominent theme in the "romance" of the Elm Vale farm.

Whatever happened, Mary Emerson always found meaning in the plot of her life as it unfolded. She compared her frequent moves to "the good old pilgrims who never staid but a month in one place" (MWA), and, like the tough old pilgrims, she profited from the stimulation of hardship. An 1851 letter to Waldo Emerson sums up much of what she learned from this chapter in her life about the connections between present self, external circumstances, and future glory: "Alas my will is a poor thing till roused for executorship. In wealth & ease & friendship how unable to controul—how much poorer & vainer & prouder would you have found the future character of your poor Aunte." Viewed from Isaac Taylor's perspective, as part of the "process of preparation" for immortality, even absence or lack gains meaning and purpose. But this is no irrelevantly pietistic retreat from human experience: in this same letter she goes on to criticize her nephew's more worldly position in his new lecture "Wealth." The maneuver is characteristic: much of the interest in the letters for this period lies in their specific attention to contemporary life and literature, the "external life" about which Mary Emerson claimed she had "nothing" to tell.

NOTES

1. Although she did read Isaac Taylor's *Natural History of Enthusiasm*, this quotation (which she later calls a "long forgotten sentence") probably comes from another of the many works by Taylor she read over the years.

2. Curiously, no comments survive concerning Samuel Hoar's and EH's narrow

escape from mob attack in Charleston, S.C., in 1844 or HDT's experiment at Walden, 1845–47.

3. SBR to George Simmons, 6 Oct. 1844 (MCR-S; "MrsSR," 175).

4. PJ 4:183.

5. See *L* 3:371–73, 8:63–65.

6. Oxford County, Maine, Registry of Deeds, book 88, p. 173; cf. RWE to WE[3], 6 May 1850 (*L* 4:202). In constructing this narrative, I have drawn on information spread across hundreds of letters. In this edition, the letters for ? Feb. 1851 and 14 Aug. 1851 most fully express Mary Emerson's position. See also MME to CCE, 7 Aug. [1832], and 9 Apr. [1834?].

1840

To Phebe Gage

Vale   March 2 [1840]

Phebe, (a name[n] almost sacred to my early remembrance from my Granmother Bliss whose saintly life will never be effaced from me) I cant think you will—can go away so away very far from your native mountains & all thier delightfull scenery to that state I do so hate.[1] But if you do go—God will gaurd, guide & bless. And in that very land of slaves & slavery you may plant, thro' His agency, some of those seeds w'h are destined to cover our wretched land with the glory of thier freedom. You love mental philosophy and if you increase in it's knowledge you will find the elements of liberty and equality coessential with the attributes of a spiritual nature—your induction will be easy to find the design of the Auther of human nature! And that this nature in all her departments of "reason, sensibility and will" echoing the voice of humanity and pleading for equal rights to breathe—to possess one's limbs & labour and kindred. Not for equal talents rank & wealth. Were all alike where the great liberal bouncing eloquent perogatives of the gifted? And where those sublimer virtues of love & resignation to God and benvolence to men w'h are the higher boon of the lower classes and w'h demonstrate the agency of an infinite Giver and prove the immortality of the soul!—prove too the design of God and of the revelation by His blessed Son our Redeemer, that the claims to freedom are indisputable. His ministry to the lost—the poor & despised preach beyond all other arguments the *rescue* of *the captive*. Is it objected that not a word is specified? Did that wonderfull being give any sumptuary laws? Did he not disclaim any Judicial athority? Think a little of that treasure of wisdom w'h his silence displayed. Had he, the founder of a religion w'h was destined from eternity to cover the world with it's universality, and embrace the different character of distant nations & ages, regulated the economy of politicks and the regal state of courts—what a descent from a commission w'h was to purify the moral world and reunite it to the Infinite!

I dread to think how you will feel when you see my brethren & Sisters of couler degraded. You will almost doubt their immortality or wonder why Providence has permitted their condition. Are not God's ways in the deep and clouds & darkness around his steps? Have not men in all ages degraded themselves and others? It is by human instruments—by their progress in light & the humanities of religion that man is to be restored   And the laws of the mind w'h are developed by xianity are in constant progress however spiral. There is an under current whose power is invisible—but sure and invincible and the gates of hell will not always prevail. Wonderfull current—w'h fanaticism priest craft and all the other brood of sins w'h are their relations parents or ofspring cannot finally prevent from it's purpose of delivering the slaves to superstition and self interest into the liberty w'h Christ ordained for spirits. The struggle will be hard—but the victory immense. Put too your youthfull strenght—perfect as far as possible your own conversion and you will effectually aid others.

I am glad you go to one who is warm & enthusiastic in feeling—whose house and purse will ever be open to hospitality. May you be to her like the flowers of spring whose *fruits* will be fragrant with the prudence & descretion of wisdom. Not the cold hollow hearted prudence of the world. Farewell my dear Child   I need not have said a word on slavery for I send *Channings* letter[2]—but if you go soon I shall not have a chance to see you long. As soon as you know the time of going I wish to know it and whether you lodge at dear Newbury Port? Can you take to Boston 2 or 3 books large as Carlyle's misellanies? And where can you stow them—in trunk? *Dont be pestered with them.*

Your affectionate & aged friend
MME

Cousin M. Bliss wished me to give her the ring I design for I Bliss.[3] Now if I.B. prefers a fashionable one to this & M. will send one at the price of 5# why she may have it. to oblige Irene but M. can suit herself to rings & so I fully & honestly refused her

MWA. *Addressed:* Miss Phebe Gage. *Added in pencil:* [1840].
name] name ⟨first⟩

1. Phebe Hovey Gage (1821–80), first child of ASG and LG, was leaving for Louisville, Ky., where she either attended or taught school for about a year.

2. WEC stated his antislavery position in several published "letters": the *Letter . . . to James G. Birney* (Boston, 1836), *A Letter to the Honorable Henry Clay, on the Annexation of Texas to the United States* (Boston, 1837), and *Remarks on the Slavery Question, in a Letter to Jonathan Phillips, Esq.* (Boston, 1840).

3. Probably Martha Bliss and Irene Bliss Gage.

To William Emerson[3]

Elm Vale   Sat Eve 13 June '40

My dear Nephew,

I received with gratefull pleasure yours of Dec. It's occasion was the death of our relative.[1] Mine is of the life of your excellent wife and the gift of a son. God bless you all—and may John Haven[2] be as delightfull as William. Waldo let me know of your addition   Of this same beloved man there is no smale excitment I find by the papers w'h by accident sometimes come to me.

Alas for the speculations of the day! Your old professor Norton & young Ripley have been unpleasantly engaged.[3] Do you read these things? Waldo speaks not of them but my brother is loud for Ripley—but soon as I have read with attention shall give him my opinion, w'h rather is, and in respect of Spinoza altogether with Norton. Tho' an amiable & powerfull man, he was in the very first but a scholar of the Saducees—well prepared for infidelity as to all positive religion. And from my earliest reading, and by no controversialist, has he been represented, at best, a pantheist—suspected of a tendency to insanity in some points of his character, tho' not inconsistent with logical acumen. Now this pantheism, tho' sometimes as in case of Coleridge & others, may be of a religious kind—& often give a sublime cast to the imajanation, is of a most dangerous tendency. Opposite as a whole calvinism is to the scriptures, and to that reason and those intuitive perceptions of God, w'h are our blessed inheritance—and low and unphilosophical as the materialism of the Lockeites & Priestleys, they are far better than the transcendental pantheism. Aye, and so is the catholic—any form of religion w'h secures the divine Personality and the immutable nature of moral obligation. If it should deny us the consolations of a particular Providence (the nessecary connection w'h some believe[n] with the immortality of the soul, I have never seen) and throw us on the stern laws of undeviating "*nature*" (as they are called) why those laws originating in an infinitely good Being are the best mode of our discipline and of strenghtening our faith. Take every thing w'h we have rested on or hoped for but the conscious designing Being whom we exist in & bye & for! Is the chasm between infinite & finite impassible? Surely in the one we find the other—tho' we comprehend neither. Yet there is a wonderous kind provision by w'h we have been made acquainted—and even united in sentiment with this infinite Being—the ground & nessecary cause of all finite existence—even by the founder of the xian faith   Oh were these bewildered & amiable speculatists to commit a crime, or be called to some great sacrifice for virtue, how speedily would they recognise the primative elements of their souls and feel the irresistable conviction of thier own and the absolute personality. Of all the fantastic flights of imajanation none seem to rebel against the divine revelations of reason & scripture more so than that of theorising about the selfishness of an individual immortality. Yet it cannot be altogether attached to the airy dreams of the germans, for S. J. Mackingtosh touches it with respect. But he was at a loss about the *inherent* nature of *conscience*—therefore can be of no athority with the self styled spiritualists.[4] May God in mercy to our Country & kind grant they be religious as well as philosophical spiritualists. Of the politicks of this agitated Country how much you could tell me—but I can hardly expect you to look from more important engagements to speake to one whose unvaried solitude (scarsly interrupted by an hours absence from her cell in a day) hardly places her among the living. But that you & yours may be blessings to this world and richly prepared for the more real & future one is a frequent prayer and daily desire of your afft Aunt & friend

MM Emerson

My love to that ever dear & estimable Sister, your Mother and to Susan. I began to write at dusk not knowing of the chance before, and now tis bed time. I had much to say of dear dear Charles whose profile came this week in a cast.[5] Alas that it dont do him justice. But not a word of this to Concord for Elisabeth's gift is precious. I have been reading all the sad letters and obituaries of that period since receiving the madallion—and nothing was farther from my intention than writing on the subject I have. I was writing to Louisa & not knowing where she is, wished you to send the inclosed to S.[6] or if she is gone with Orville your Mother may read & destroy. So you have my excuse for a few of the thoughts w'h this (new to me) controversy excited. I wrote solely to hear of our beloved Elisabeths health some days since to Concord

MH: bMS Am 1280.226(1079). *Addressed:* William Emerson Esqr. / Wall Street / New York / Mr R.T. Haskins. *Postmarked:* NEW-YORK / Jun 20. *Endorsed:* M. M. Emerson / June 13 / 40 / Rec'd 20th.

connection . . . believe] connection ↑ w'h some believe ↓

1. MME's sister PER, who died 11 Dec. 1839.

2. WE[3] and Susan Haven Emerson's second son, John Haven Emerson, born 15 Apr. 1840.

3. The "excitment" was caused by continuing reverberations from RWE's "Divinity School Address." In 1839 and 1840 George Ripley responded to Andrews Norton's *Discourse on the Latest Form of Infidelity* (Cambridge, 1839) in a series of three pamphlet *Letters*, beginning with *The Latest Form of Infidelity Examined* (Boston, 1839). Norton's work, ostensibly a continuation of the miracles controversy, was also an "old-line Unitarian . . . reply" to RWE's "Divinity School Address" (*TR*, 210), while Ripley's was a defense of a new, " 'free and generous theology' " (quoted in *TR*, 214). WE[3] to MME, 16 Sept. 1840, admits he lacks her zeal for theological controversy, spoken from the lofty mountains of contemplation (MT/EW).

4. Mackintosh, *Progress of Ethical Philosophy*, esp. 151, 181–88.

5. A portrait medallion of CCE made by Sophia Peabody (figure 23).

6. Possibly Sheffield, Mass., Orville Dewey's hometown, where MME seems to suspect they may be (the Deweys were then living in New York).

Figure 23. Charles Chauncy Emerson (1808–36), represented
in a medallion made by Sophia Peabody in 1840. Courtesy the
Ralph Waldo Emerson Memorial Association.

To Elizabeth Hoar

Vale   Monday   Oct. 6   40

I trust my dear Niece is enjoying this season w'h becomes one with the consciousness almost. I see you walking to Waldo's—and tho the scene can never be like the solemn tranquility of the wilderness—yet you hear the musick of the falling leaf and its' fortune telling notes and live in as for the future. When thus alone with the Infinite how idle the theories w'h would take from personal virtues—   Were there no other beings what a full & mighty power have they in relation to the Absolute. Are there others—'tis of the first importance to perfect one's self for their sake—'tho they may not come in contact yet. But are not their worth more in the first case than the latter—where superficial virtues answer?

But looking at the theory & waiting for the chaise have made me forget that I am liable to weary—for our opinions have diverged. But my interest cannot fail for ever & aye. Your kind words of course "to write soon" I remember— but uncertain whether T.T. Stone would visit here, w'h would bring me home, I could not ask you where to direct. He came & I arrived a day after. And be sure I have been excited at 3 sermons two lectures on slavery & a visit in my study more than beseems my age & vocation. But to hear his deep & calm eloquence awakning the sleep w'h the formulas of creeds & the trivial denunciations of partial truths had so long lasted, was more than stronger minds have with equnimity. But the lectures presented novel & higher views than any I had seen—reason was prominent & fancy & poetic art were not wanting. Speaking of man being the property of man—why he averred in the most solemn & devout manner, man was not the property of God in respect to freedom. This seperation was much better than giving the idea of man as a universal—   The distinction of right & wrong was lost by the mass. in one of the sermons. The description of the man devoted to the cause of humanity was a voice—a light w'h had never reached the desert   "And there was light—" and there were tears of joy & conversion of the Gages completed. But in all I saw the state of transition—the state of mind in a new development. He states his opinions like Waldo not explains or argues. He was by nature prepared for the present movement. But as yet an unsafe guide. In his letter (w'h I want to send to Concord sympathies) he speaks of the philosophic era as to give place to a higher—a spontaneous life.[1] Now I have believed philosophy an element of mind ever & ever to go on & on to the consciousness of the Absolute. But he says the origin is not intellect—tis within the intellect as life within the body—what the scriptures call the holy Ghost & thus he thinks he finds the problemn solution[n]—   —the holy Spirit is a "divine reality within" &c &c

If I have not spoken of H. T. I've of T. T. And now of Louisa Payson[2]   I sent for her when at Thompson's[3] and she interested me much—besides her modern learning & reading all of Schlermacher's system she has read my old folks in theology. I sent saying Waldo would thank her if she paid me attention & you must remind him so to do. She liked to talk of him & inquire about you. She was communicative & spoke of the variety of moods to w'h she was subject— Some of them probably lovely & some otherwise. She shrunk from Stone's idea of inspiration & objected to some else of this said letter. And if she had been here at his sermons would have thriled with delight at his pictures—that "if the vital spark were to be extinguished at death yet it s^d be devoted to God." Young aspirants when detached from the world often exclaim that touched with the divine influence they should yield existence with rapture. But what foundation in the nature of man? A miracle to annihilate it could only produce such a resignation. And when he put aside athority & the sanctity of the Chh—why the love of God & the inward power to become his son was all very elevating to the established—but the consequence w^d be infidelity and anarchy to the mass. Divine athority—*the will of God!*—say what they have all said for ages is the grand pilot—& to that will—rather *nature* 'tis joy & glory to yield. And T. T. says he loves to hear the old woman methodist express her piety. He has lived a flowery life & his paradoxes & kind of sublime pantheism grew out. But as to this feeling of losing existence 'tis never lost—when looking to the future under the feeling, 'tis in operation—that in some form or other *live* we shall—the shawdow of a possibility controuls the conscience and throws the present into vapours—darken & confuse the evidences of revelation as the sceptic may—the revelation within burns & finds reason sattisfied alone by xianity. But (if you can bear with me) this feeling of love & service to God—'tis not the God of the bible—'tis not the facts of human nature w'h T. T *now* recognizes—but the "musick of life" w'h his letter describes—a life of letters, fame & poetry may well pay itself in this fleeting state some w^d think. But the grandeur of man's destiny the sinfullness—the mystery—the many problemns {   } with the present philosophic theories[4]

Love to my sister & Nephew & Niece & little ones. And your family   *Where & how is Edward?*[5] The folks you saw when you were here were interested about your visit to W. I assured them it w^d have extended here had your Charge been here. The Genius[n] never ceased to feel your absence. Tell me all all. I am anxious to hear of my brother's health & parochial state, and of your own health w'h I believe good. I told my folks that I s^d tell you how glad they *spontaniously* received me

Your afft Aunt
MME

Tuesday 6.[6]

MH: bMS Am 1280.226(1117). *Addressed:* Miss Elisabeth Hoar / or / Care of Rev. R W Emerson / Concord / Mass.

problemn solution] problemn ↑ solution ↓

Genius] *possibly* Graves; *T reads* G——

1. These ideas do not appear in the portion of TTS's letter to MME that RWE printed in the *Dial* 2 (Jan. 1842): 382–83, as a "Calvinist's" letter. MME to EH, 14 Sept. 1841, mentions she has sent a letter by TTS to RWE (MH: 1123).

2. H. T. is possibly Henry Thoreau (MME refers later to Edward Hoar, EH's brother and HDT's friend). Louisa Payson (1812–62), daughter of a Rindge, N.H., clergyman, was known for her "passion" for knowledge; she had mastered the classical, Hebrew, and modern languages, German metaphysics, and theology. She studied in Boston before teaching in New York (beginning in 1830); later she gave up her school and wrote reviews, magazine essays, and children's books. In 1835 she published *The Pastor's Daughter; or, The Way of Salvation Explained to a Young Inquirer*. MME suggests that the Paysons had moved back to Portland by 1840; in 1841 Louisa married the Reverend Albert Hopkins, a professor at Williams College, but failing health prevented her from living up to her promise (*The Life and Letters of Elizabeth Prentiss, Author of "Stepping Homeward,"* ed. George L. Prentiss [New York, 1882]).

3. A hotel in Portland (see figure 24).

4. Bottom of leaf cut and torn away; about three lines missing.

5. EH's brother Edward, who ran off to California in Mar. 1840 ("EH L," *SAR* 1984: 251).

6. Bottom cut away, leaving remnants of writing at cut edge; about three lines lost. 6 Oct. fell on Tuesday in 1840, indicating the first part of the letter was probably written on 5 Oct.

To Ralph Waldo Emerson

Vale   Nov. 5   40

Dear Waldo,

The first moment after hearing that you do not lecture is to hail it with welcome. Your star has wandered fearfully—   And tho' it might continue to shed stronge rays & strange—yet it is well for you that the admirers should gaze in regret than grow too familiar. Besides—to be your own le doute man— steer your proud bark from quick sands—live as in young days & say as when Mother & Aunt were asking you "where was Rollin" [1] you were *thinking*—& they were quiet. If they restrained from urging you to their circle of thought (w'h might be smaler, yet nearer the Central light) it might have been well and it might have been otherwise? Your health also—but that secondary to those who love family fame without interest. This solitude will do more than all other means to refit your sails to catch the holy breeze of inspiration—to feel the consciousness of the Absolute more strongly than your own—identical— as the perceptions of reason and as irrefutable—or instinct or sentiment. No matter if there be a spirit within   If the high & fancifull theory of Jouffroys pantheism [2] were true what an immortal gift to get ideas of god as to constitute one's own. While that is bottomless the fact of divine inlargement lives and extends itself in defiance of scepticism and time and death & the somnamblism of age itself.

One good about this pan representation—brings into view the nature & value, somewhat, of personal virtues—w'h some theories degrade—   They —why they (when not under the influence of mere skill prudence & such like) are the foundation of all the great & benvolent publicities—and what is infinitely better—the reserve of all divine relations & realities

Well this see sawing will disgust you. But I said I would write and tho' our dear Elisabeth mistook me that I had I catch the chance of the possibility of your being alone without the dazzling coterie   And yet I dwelt with pleased curiosty on her description of an elegant party you gave where cut glass & silver were all the style of the table. I had heard with pleasure from Waltham of E.B.s[3] being domesticated before hand. When I returned and remembered your very wise caution about "useless expenses & fashion" in a lecture[4] I conjectured how many ladies would pinch the poor or their families to imitate the exquisite taste of Lidian. * * *

God in infinite love bless you and each prays affectionately your Aunt

MME

Chaise waits & I take this scrawl. In the lecture on religion[5] I refer to strange wanderings

MH: bMS Am 1280.226(902). *Addressed:* Mr R. Waldo Emerson / Concord / Mass. *Endorsed:* M M Emerson / Nov. 1840.

1. MME and RWE together read Charles Rollin, *The Ancient History of the Egyptians, Carthagenians, Assyrians, Babylonians, Medes and Persions, Macedonians, and Grecians*, trans. from the French (first American edition, 1729), when he was a boy (see *Life of RWE*, 36–37).

2. Theodore Jouffroy, *Introduction to Ethics*, trans. William H. Channing (1840), specifically addresses the question of pantheism and Spinoza's system in lectures 5 and 6; however, in the omitted portion of this letter, MME indicates she has not yet read the work.

3. Probably Elizabeth Bradford Ripley.

4. Probably "Manners" or "The Present Age," both read in the 1836–37 series, "The Philosophy of History" (see, esp., *EL* 2:139, 161).

5. Probably "Religion," no. 7 in the 1839–40 series, "The Present Age."

To Ann Sargent Gage

Thursday [1840?]

Many thanks for note & *lines* last sabbath   Yet regreted that you in concert with the mother "Queen" of poets[1] should deem a philosophy, w'h has engaged the deepest thinkers in Germany (that world of thought to w'h all you & I have read & seen are but faint resemblances of that divine power) moon shine. *What did you know of it*?? I alas, spent too much time when in the very nest of the Mass.' scholars in flouting it. I was said to be exclusively attached to one form of xianity. Mr Stone thinks the same & has not mingled a word of the transcending philosophy of Christ in his letters. But dont you believe these suspicions of either of the parties but by writing often give me your views. *Know* that I seek this philosophy only as a means of aiding one sole object of my isolated life—to bring nearer the *divine agency*! That it has done little—that I warn the two or three youths at Belfast against it's almost prophane pretentions—that I declare one of the psalms of David gives more connection—& light on our wonderfull relations than all I have studied of psychology. This I repeat to you that no need of qualifying any of your disapprobation. The only thing I want that you *know* what they would be after, in some measure, & not poetize (tho' I worship the muse as the gift of God) but assert—reason—prove one principle wrong from the exertions of your own reason, w'h I believe you can do. They are returning to Plato; they are selecting from all antient & modern philosophers—& this surely opens new vistas of thought. Vague ideas are better than none—they become clearer in time. Cousin has given me new ideas of the trinity[2] w'h may be truth—& hereafter that doctrine may be established as the mind grows—develops. But as it is not nessecary to the greater doctrines w'h Jesus preached we need not live an hour to learn it. One disinterested habit from religious faith—one living sentiment of absorption in the divine will when it crushes our dearest hopes of love—sucess in knowledge—and usefullness—is God himself in the soul! And were all other revelation extinct the soul (in the transcendental principles) would be *conscious* of the Infinite. And surely the xian with bible can say it more truly—for it has become a part of his existence without the hand maid of dialectical philosphy

I have been gratified with Phebe's *excellent* letter to Thomas.[3] You must feel very thankfull. The expression of "belonging to the people of God" sounds exclusive. Wherever there is a good person there is a church—a tempel & Jesus is its Priest & alter & inspirer whether ever they take the *external* sacraments. I should write to Frances & this would be the text—but you would not approve & I've no time. This early & often ignorant tho' well meant profession I do dread as a kind of fixture in conversion. Your children may not be injured.

Pray god every blessing attend you all
MME

Sab   I've written in haste but know that you are good at finding out. The poetry directed to my brother I intitled transendental sentiment. Bible I ought to have said—   Now[4]

MWA.

1. The "lines" are probably poetry written by ASG; the "Queen" of poets is unidentified.

2. See MME to LJE, 17 Sept. [1838].

3. Two of ASG's children, PHG and Thomas Hovey Gage (1826–1909). PHG may have written from Louisville (see MME to PHG, 2 Mar. [1840], n. 1), the reason for placing this undated letter in 1840.

4. Letter is incomplete.

1841

To Elizabeth Hoar

Vale   Ap. 8 '41

My very dear benefactress,

"Thanks to men of honorable minds is noble meed"[1] yet the interruption of a letter w'h I told you I should write no more would not exist but from a cause w'h you will or may hate to learn before I close—w'h hastens me to send before you leave that delightfull home & City—that it may be named not at Concord. Yes you are my only benefactor in letters & MMS &c—tho' Waldo writes & my brother very flattering. Yet the pictures of beauty & elegance are *very* welcome—for they inspire Hannah whose rays of genius have been more awakned than by any thing I tell her w'h is contained between pasteboard. And she has no time & I believe little taste for reading to me—but has this moment finished the "conversations"[2] and surprised me by what she understood—& of course joined me in admiring most what you said, & your letter, w'h I shall send to the Gages with explaining your flattery w'h soothes while I forget how little truth. How could you be so good as to take City time for those copies?! And the chocolate I felt as most invalids. And have imparted to the weake—more readily as a cake was sent me from the Hales who live at P. & have discovered that Bakers can be had. Remember that. The box & packet came not till this monday. May I return S.S.S.'s Coleridge with your Plato & Waldo's Faust by way of Portland to care of Miss Potters or Mr W. T?[3] The last named book w'h Waldo was so kind as to send I do not wish to retain a moment for other eyes. Have you given me the "conversations"? Am delighted with the "best hours." And *who* sent those dear works of Channing? And that precious fragmentary sermon of Frothingham? *Who* and *what* is J. Clarke?[4] And what *does* he *propose to do that* the *celestial Channing should watch him "perhaps"*? Write me, if possible, while in Boston. Dont take time for Conversations only your own opinion—but say if Clarke is going on with novelty & any like to Brownson?[5] And why are you indifferent to the spiritual Gannet?[6] w'h I infer.

And now to the letter or matter w'h filled my sick head all the tuesday night after reading one single "essay on self reliance."[7] I was lamenting it to your very image w'h was as full before me with the rich dark eyes that expressed somthing what they did when I revolted at a lecture you read. Still I determined to write—to say is this strange medly of atheism and false independence the real sane work of that man whom I idolized as a boy, so mild, candid modest obliging, before you were conscious of reason? How bitterly did I regret that he had not gone to the tomb amidst his early honors like one—who if he had lived such essays had never seen the light of a xian world—the best of w'h must disgust & revolt that faith whether it be lessened down to Priestlean or bloated with Calvinism—w'h confounds pure imperishable natural religion with the babel of real & fantastical philosophy—w'h must revolt the rational unitarian who has any modified faith in historical revelation. This the man so idolized by my imajanation and affections! And is he to go down to posterity an enymy to that faith w'h has saved millions? Oh how glad that I seperated. Yet to know that his genius & all his gifts were to be eminently blessed would add to the joys of dying. Has he no disinterested friend? Were the essays good of the kind why print now? No wife to judge? No S. A. R.? I read with pleasure Byron Hume and Gibbon. Any "method in their madness" gives us intellect. But when the highest talents wander from their God & early faith they seem insane. All common readers like me will see a partial dementing. Yesterday I kept chamber & took emetic—but were I to find a divine halo of light round the others it would not redeem that. I read Over Soul yesterday & the xian loves sometimes a sublime pantheism—but in a sentence in "spiritual" laws" about "a man who did [not] know his greatness"[8] can it mean Jesus?!!! That blessed medium to the Infinite that Alpha & Omega of human nature—that humanised God the Donor[n] & Saviour of this part of the universe! Age shrinks with sorrow. If my joys and hopes are delusive oh wake me not—but tho' not as dear as reason yet this revelation grooves with my little ray. *What do your parents say?* What the world? Write me if you have an hour. Return—would to God your own educated faith had not been shaken and you would return an Angel to one who estimates you highly. He is not happy as formerly I suspect, & the freinds who surround him you rightly described in a former letter. Burn this and may God do so and more abundantly bless you as you keep my secret & *deal* truly *with me in writing what you believe to be his real condition.* I dare not trust to my good brother & Sister at Waltham—but I may hereafter. But I must say to them that she has been one means of early infecting[n] him with infidelity. And that the happiness of w'h she boasts belongs to no one who is a world of so much sin & woe. The Athenian was always happy who was insane. The tremendous problemns w'h interest our reason & baffle it demands humility. Yours tho' I know you can't love

tho' always blessing MME

In yours of Feb. you say "were no other ladies interupting your repose." And I conjured up some Nelson[9] or his succesors[n]   His sucess is the only subject w'h draws tears. I love them partake of grief & joy. Write every thing to your lonely

but always affec[t] & gratefull
Aunt

MH: bMS Am 1280.226(1121). *Addressed:* Miss Elisabeth Hoar / Care of R. B. Storer Esq[r] / Boston / Mss. *Postmarked:* So Waterford / Apr 9.
    Donor] *possibly* Owner (*T*)
    infecting] *possibly* infesting

succesors] *possibly* accusers (*T*)

1. Attributed elsewhere to Antoninus (the emperor Marcus Aurelius), but not located in his *Meditations*.

2. MME indicates that Hannah Haskins is reading EH's transcription of some of Margaret Fuller's first series of Boston "conversations" in 1839–40, probably the MS that survives in the EPP papers (MWA). Below, MME seems to ask whether she should return the transcriptions.

3. Sarah Sherman (Hoar) Storer; Potter(s) and W. T. are unidentified.

4. Anonymous, *Reminiscences of the Best Hours of Life for the Hour of Death*, reviewed in the *Christian Examiner* 30 (Jan. 1841): 125–26. Several new editions of the *Works* of WEC were published in 1840 and 1841. Two of Nathaniel Frothingham's sermons had been published in 1840: *The Memory and Example of the Just* and *The New Idolatry: A Sermon Preached to the First Church on Sunday, 22 November 1840*. James Freeman Clarke (1810–88), Harvard Divinity School, 1833, recently returned from Louisville, established the Church of the Disciples in Boston, which caused a great stir, particularly because of the new role of the laity. He was a strongly "militant" Transcendentalist (*TR*, 43, 47). Channing welcomed Clarke's daring innovations and encouraged his parish and family to join the new society (Arthur W. Brown, *Always Young for Liberty: A Biography of William Ellery Channing* [Syracuse: Syracuse University Press, 1956], 220).

5. See George Ripley, "Brownson's Writings," *Dial* 1 (July 1840): 22–46. In his *Boston Quarterly Review*, Orestes Brownson reviewed much of the writing important to transcendentalism, including Ripley's philosophical translations, Alcott's *Conversations*, RWE's orations and essays, and the *Dial*. In 1840 he published "The Laboring Classes" (*Boston Quarterly Review* 3 [July and Oct. 1840]: 358–95, 420–512). WEC sympathized with Brownson's feelings for the "masses" (though he disliked the word), but WEC felt that Brownson exaggerated the hardships of the workingman and found his remedies for inequality of social classes "shocking or absurd" (Brown, *Always Young*, 219).

6. Ezra Stiles Gannett.

7. Printed in RWE's *Essays*, published 20 Mar. 1841.

8. "Spiritual Laws," *CW* 2:90: "The great man knew not that he was great. It took a century or two for that fact to appear"; "[not]" added in pencil by another hand.

9. Possibly an allusion to Lord Nelson's affair with Lady Emma Hamilton, which prolonged his stay in Sicily in 1798.

To RALPH WALDO EMERSON

Vale   15 May [1841]

Dear Nephew,

Your writing again and sending Essays Dials &c render thanks due & they are hearty—but the design of writing this eve. is to put a question w'h has pressed with painfull interest whenever you & Lidian ask me to visit you.[1] Is it in earnest, or to save feelings? Did I not promise—say that I w^d never spend an hour in your house, except bro't there in a liter, w'h I shall never suffer. You as *boy & youth were uncommonly true. And you never knew me else. I have tho't (at moments) of wishing to unprision mind, of taking lodgings at C. but there w^d be speculations w'h might injure the weake^n or intrude on literal truth—and when well, prefer here to any place. I remember none of the 'altercations' you name. I found for some years that I was wearisome   But was fully prepared & less mortified as this had met me in all classes. *I blame not you*, nor any living or dead, whom I had idolised—tis my fate or nature—heightens, oh how long since, the reliance on myself & One. True, of late it has lessened the delicacy of getting out of sight—when nessecity or desire of improvement have found me to be in the sight of superiors. And that I dined with you under the bewildering effect of Charle's exist^n—but ever repented. But that I justified myself in struggling with poor accomodations &c &c the evening you may refer to 'altercation' I do not blush at. Charles (my gardian) was present & it was well to make it. In greener days, when parting with your father whom I had so exclusively loved in early life, he said "I never justified myself"—but I told him I was infallible to him. I *may* have been to others?—but my lot is inevitable & it now adds to the Joy of existing for "the pleasure" of Another. I do wish at times to see you and was telling Hannah I wished you w^d make a party of wife, children, Elisbeth & some of the Ripleys & come here, I, perhaps, could find lodgings. She said it w^d be desirable to herself & parents for two of you to lodge here. I shall some time in June (with iffs) be at Portland if you fancy a journey I w^d let you know when. I put up at Thompsons Hotell. We have no idea of your coming but as a route for air & change.

And now my errands are done—shall I respect your time & say good bye? I have a multitude of things, universal & individual—but I wont intrude till my question is answered & our words can carry similar meaning.

It was pleasant to hear you had invited that amiable Allcott into your house—it bro't to mind the advantages of inequality. A condition ordain'd in wisdom and not to be rebelled at by the visions of a Brownson.[2] Where in that dawdling^n leveling of distinctions & wealth would be the exquisite virtue of the poorer—where this riot of charity in the mite? Where would God hide his richest gifts of bestowing the capasity to rejoice in the inferior gifts of the influential?

Mr A—'s "sayings" are very like "plumb pudding hot & plumb pudding cold." Were he a sound Johnsonian mind one could have faith in some of them—but I have no confidence, any more than in Palmer's, who had been deranged.[3] "Unity—synthesis"—why the secrets of existence mock them. Connected with an Infinite Unity—but seperated by chasms w'h defy imjanation to count. The facts of guilt & woe may be linked to nessecary causes w'h even the celestial executors of justice do not penetrate. I love to read Hume—it makes thought—& we kindle at the profound mathamatician who finds his god in one of the effects w'h lead us to the Cause. But I know not where to find your freinds domestic or foreign   Yet I still love the bright particular

Figure 24. Middle Street, Portland, Maine, 1844. Note Thompson's Hotel on left.

Star—"and what is that to him"? Stores of kindnesses & bright spots return to memory. And may the sweetest, brightest blessings hover over him and wife, Mother, Elisabeth & children often desires most

affectionately
MME.

Bad pen & lamp excuse scrool. I have written, I fear, proudly—it seems so for one who would not be surprised at bedridden palsy or derangment since that attack[4] but any thing rather than you s^d strain to flatter me out of my unpopularity. *Not a word.* Please send Dial. The "modern literature" interested & Walker's sermon I want   And *is* Jouffroy out?[5] I do need him. "How is my health?" Rather feeble but enjoy^n without any apprehension of a lingering disease. Am well some days & stronger

*In this "the boy is father to the man."[6] And I have not doubted your practical truth as man. The problem of invitation is unaccountable

MH: bMS Am 1280.226(903). *Addressed:* Mr R. Waldo Emerson / Concord / Mass. *Postmarked:* So Waterford / May 17th. *Endorsed:* M M Emerson / May 1841.

the weake] ⟨your influence⟩ ↑ the weake ↓

exist] *possibly* exit *intended or abbreviation for* existence

dawdling] *possibly* dandling

enjoy] ⟨in good days⟩ enjoy

1. RWE to MME, 4 May 1841, bewails their "separation" and urges her to visit and "challenge" him (*L* 2:396–98); MME's letter suggests she may have received a second letter from RWE that does not survive. She goes on to recall once again the famous disagreement that resulted in her abrupt departure from Concord in Feb. 1836.

2. RWE to WE[3], 21 Dec. 1840, says he hopes that "next April we shall make an attempt to find house room for Mr Alcott & his family under our roof" (*L* 2:371), but by 30 Mar. 1841 Mrs. Alcott had persuaded her husband not to accept the offer (*L* 2:389). For Brownson's "visions," see MME to EH, 8 Apr. 1841, n. 5.

3. Edward Palmer; the *Dial* for Oct. 1840 printed a review of Palmer's *Letter for Those Who Think*, 1840 (1:251–56).

4. Probably a reference to MME's first severe attack of erysipelas earlier in the year, most likely in Feb.

5. The *Dial* for Oct. 1840 included RWE's "Thoughts on Modern Literature" (1:137–58) and a review of James Walker's recent "Discourse before the 'Alumni of the Cambridge Theological School,'" entitled "The Connexion between Philosophy and Religion" (1:256–60). For Jouffroy, see MME to RWE, 5 Nov. 1840, n. 2.

6. Cf. Wordsworth, "Ode: Intimations of Immortality."

To Ann Sargent Gage

Wed. [May? 1841?]

Dear Ann,

The reason of my puting our Frances' name and yours (one midnight last week) in Wordworth's poems was because every night I am in habit of preparing for a sudden departure as many of my kindred have. And last week (now dont call me Bernard[1]) I had some favored omens. But whene one lives with their shadow & shroud so long as I have such things do not excite. Still I am very busy in looking or trying too over 20 MMS. How can you aid me? Your literary taste might be gratified in many quotations. Those I refer too in the trunk I dont want to leave Waldo the trouble of looking over many a womanish whim or theology he dont believe in   And such of earlier date might be there   And possibly you might like to throw some them bye[n] in your large house. If any one is alone they might in age & solitude find sympathy   But not a scrap is to see print as many deceased persons have had their papers. I wish to bring you my sectary with such as I may like him to have as he has always said he wanted them & the "woman kind" there love me & think better of me than I deserve. There is somthing pleasant in being recalled to memory by such. But if we are immortal how trilfling the love or the esteem or censure of others. If happy in God how useless—if not how idle. I regret to leave you & the children no more substantial testimony but duty forbids. I have enjoyed much thro life in expecting to quit it—for I could never act up when in tempting cercumstances to what I ought. Tho' believing myself destined to a smale condition according to my capacity here—yet it is that w'h God will appoint and it will be one of increase of virtue & the knowledge of the Infinite—   And this has hieghts & depths of goodness w'h no mortal could earn and is given in conditions explicitly named in bible.

The Doctor would think nothing farther from me than this idea of going so soon   I was warm with him—but I should be warmer for a principle at leavetaking. He will understand me better when we meet where the soul is expected to be transparent. * * *

I have to add a third letter to another freind   And when I have done all my little tolly affairs the presentiment of release may be over.

Burn this immediately & oblige   My love to D[r] & respect for what yours in love he is & showed the sabbath Stone Eve

MME

I have buried my respect & confidence for one I loved to respect D. W.[2] But those above immutable virtues can alone unite us to the divine attributes and when loved & obeyed the soul of nessecity adheres to their Source

MWA. *Addressed:* Mrs Ann Gage / Waterford / Increase Robinson will be so kind as to take this as directed. *Added in pencil:* Probably about 1840 or 41.

throw . . . bye] throw ↑ some ↓ them bye

1. Probably an allusion to Saint Bernard, a mystic; "The Life of Saint Bernard of Clairvaux, a Chapter out of the Middle Ages," *Christian Examiner* 30 (Mar. 1841), points out that he uttered prophecies, worked miracles, and experienced revelations and visions (18).

2. Probably Wilhelm M. L. De Wette (1728–95), two of whose works are cited in Samuel Osgood's essay "Christian Ethics," *Christian Examiner* 30 (May 1841): 145–

73. MME may have objected to what Osgood sums up as De Wette's emphasis on "the heart and . . . the sentimental view of duty" (171).

To LIDIAN JACKSON EMERSON

Vale   July 13 tues. Night [1841]

My dear Lidian

* * * And how are you, sister Nephew & children?

I was pleasantly reminded of him by a letter from Bowdion College this eve. A sort of novitiate in his school who tells of the extravagant praises of my freind Dr Barker of Prospect of the articles of "labour & reform."[1] And I too were I masculine could say somthing of them. Mr Pike's account of T.T. Stone refusing creeds and if insisted on asking dissmission &c interested me as I've not written him for long time. Does Waldo write him? I depend on seeing this said husband of yours in Portland and intend with his *leave* w'h will be as much as I expect to go to Waterville & hear his voice for once and the last time in publick.[2] And I need not give him any other information than to find me at Thompsons Sun Hotel or learn where I am—if sick I shall let him know & expect him here. I have today returned from Sweden Spring & feel stronge after pretty constant exercise thro a long day without reposing. But my opinion is that a sudden attack of the same kind may always be expected. In case of no other message I wish him to bring 40# from my Brother and Jouffroy to purchase at Miss Peabody's   I wrote her a week since & wished to have Plato w'h is to be purchased for a friend or any thing w'h was better. I hoped to have an answer by this mail. If you have any give away books for poor children of 6 & ten I'll be your Almoner. Where is the beggar Girl[3] for my own use? If this Jouffroy is expensive Waldo had better loan it me for it will be useless to my heirs or worse possibly. * * *

The complete famine of socity and events render one a hermit! Events of publick guilt in goverment there are enow to make one tempted to suicide— so unconnected with slavery that the very beauty of the skies becomes eclipsed and the foliage so exquisitely rich this season murmurs of oppression. I have never had Jays book on this sad subject of the Fed. gov.[4] till this week^n & wish I never had. Well may the little Sirs & Madams be hot or cold with icy indignation.

Goodnight dear Niece may the Power w'h can bring good & beauty and order from their opposites watch over you & all^n including Elisbeth ever devoutly & daily desires

MME

If you should write let me know the day & hour when Waldo is to be in Portland

I expect to go to P the last week of this month

MH: bMS Am 1280.226(784). *Addressed:* Mrs Lidian Emerson / Concord / Miss L. M. Sharpe. *Endorsed:* x M M E / 1840.

week] ⟨season⟩ ↑ week ↓

all] all ⟨always⟩

1. Probably Theodore Parker's "Thoughts on Labor" and RWE's "Man the Reformer," *Dial* 1 (Apr. 1841). Barker is unidentified. Richard Pike (1813–63) graduated from Bowdoin College in 1836 and taught for a year at the Belfast (Maine) Academy before studying divinity briefly at Harvard. From 1838 to 1841 he served as a tutor at Bowdoin while he continued his theological studies, and in 1841 he was licensed to preach by the Maine Unitarian Ministerial Association. In 1842 he became minister to the Third Church in Dorchester, Mass. MME to ASG [1837?], wrote, "Had I pen & poetry I would write of higher things to my xian friend at this silent hour of night when to use the transˡ style 'the dread ground of existence' presses on the soul—when 'consciousness' is so vivid that it seems apostacy to sleep. But how could I meet your views? Just now came a letter from Mr Pike of the new school of phi." (MWA).

2. Reference to RWE's upcoming oration at Waterville College on 11 Aug., which MME hopes to attend.

3. Possibly Martha Meredith Read's popular *Monima; or, The Beggar Girl*, first published in 1802 and reprinted in numerous pirated versions.

4. Probably William Jay (1789–1858), *Address to the Friends of Constitutional Liberty on the Violation by the United States House of Representatives of the Right to Petition* (1840), in *Miscellaneous Writings on Slavery* (New York, 1853), 397–408. Jay, a New York judge, was a son of John Jay (1745–1829), one of the authors of the *Federalist Papers*. At the 1833 meeting of the National Antislavery Convention in Philadelphia, Jay persuaded the organization to base its attack on slavery on strictly constitutional grounds (*DAB*).

To RALPH WALDO EMERSON

Windham   Au. 2   Monday [1841]

Dear Waldo,

Thanks for letters &c. Jouffroy I sent to have E.P.P. sell me and another somthing. She wrote me that his last work was not translated. It looks strange that you & brother should forget that I did not wish for Jouffroy translated by W.H.C. for I had it from Dʳ Nichols and he promised to state & clear moral questions that made me wish it tho' certain that he could do nothing of the kind in its' height or depth.[1]

That memory should turn no key on trifles is, I believe, customary for the old housekeeper yet I cannot practice the belief, & wonder that I dont have this & that w'h I desire after months applying. I was glad to hear from all & that William might possibly be seen. I am curious to know what a dozen years have done. Should be pleased to have him Judge were I not sick of any part or lot in governing or govᵗ

Portland   Tuesday   Noon   broiling. Literally "gutted & brained" after being here from 5 last eve. So weary of this City and so fond of lingering in the romantic family of Parsons[2]—take the imajanation by the scattered rays of genius. But dentist Physican salt water urged me on the route tho' I believe I should have given it up at Windham were it not for the era of meeting you & consoling myself for the lost journey. It is so mystical to be hanging about at home on the trees & rocks. Among other labours I called at the Stage office Elm House near my boarding house Geo. S. Hays *not* Thompsons Hotel a little north on the opposite side of Elm House Stage office. I went to learn how I could get on if I determined to before you & be rested for *Wed. Eve.* and hasten to say what a tedious jaunt it will give you to take the stage Tuesday 10 at 1 o'k A. M. & ride to Waterville 30 miles. Why you should exhaust kind nature by so rough usuage best known to your wisdom. I whose life so potent to society expect if able to go to Brunswick at 8 o'k saturday (w'h stage goes every day at that hour for Augusta) and pass sabbath at some publick house w'h I expect friend Richard Pike (later) to preserve for me and go to Augusta to pass monday night at the *Stage Hotel. By no means go to Sybils* for me apart from their rum & slave holding³ it is inconvenient to go across the bridge where the stage dont pass I believe. I shall send a note of information to her. It pleased them that Rebecca & her children passing from Salem alone put up at Hotel, when I reported it. They *may* be glad to see you. And perhaps they do not distill   I've never heard for two years but then it was believed to be recommencing. I should go to Waterville before you but wishing to appear on the Stage of life more respectably than usual expect to await you at Brunswick or Augusta. You shall find no difficulty in tracing me to hinder you if in my power   And I do hope better things of you than so useless a delay when all places & times can yield the interior life—except Portland. I feel weake enough to sit down only where I am known to someone as an apopletic may occur. When strong one says no matter who wraps the shroud—a crow might be parson spade & bier.

Your mind has sufered—most usefull   And so you'll excuse a letter about as empty as yours tho' your facts being very welcome about all being well— but the Plymouth folks whom I don't remember. Yours in love & much to Sister & friend Betsy.

M. M. Emerson

MH: bMS Am 1280.226(891). *Addressed:* Mr. R Waldo Emerson / Concord. *Endorsed:* 1833(?).

1. Aside from W. H. Channing's translation of Jouffroy's *Introduction to Ethics,* the only other English translation of Jouffroy available in 1841 seems to be the selections included in Ripley's *Philosophical Miscellanies: On Philosophy and Common Sense, On Skepticism, On the History of Philosophy,* and *The Faculties of the Human Soul* (1:279–383). The Reverend Ichabod Nichols (1784–1859) was minister at the First Unitarian Church, Portland, 1814–55.

2. Probably Dr. Charles Grandison Parsons and family. His brother, also a physician, was Joseph Addison Parsons.

3. Sybil Farnham Lambard of Augusta, Maine; see introduction to part 4 (p. 280).

To Ralph Waldo Emerson

Tues.   14 Sep '41

My dear Waldo,

After taking so much travel (quere in these days to call any distance so) to see you I feel as tho' I must have an answering visit by letter from you. Whatever was the effort—I shall be glad to recall the tones of your voice & the mere movements of your frame in the desk. And the wide emotions my spirit tasted. The objections it made may go up to the old Limbo for all you— Yet I would place the "extacies of nature" beside the dreams of wandering visitors to the said place[1]

When I found the meagre no.s of old Ed. Reviews with nothing else—no Dial—nothing w'h lies neglected on your & my brother's floor such as Channings pamplets—the Examiner Missellany & things unthought off when I see you—how disappointed & neglected I felt. What *were* you thinking about (I curiously ask) to come thus empty   And now I beg for a stick of black sealing wax or some black wafers. I lost the former w'h I had at Portland. It was to my taste black specked with green   And some common letter paper for I find it not easy to get this kind of w'h Elisabeth has furnished me, & I want it for day books—tho' a suspension of thought for six months has prevented a line of almanak.

I was however stirred in soul the last sabbath by finding T.T. Stone in the pulpit, of whose admittance there had been doubts by Mr Douglass who with the Society had given him out as fallen from the gospel.[2] With this conviction he came in the power of its' pristine spirit and with great lectures battered the vulgar prejudices w'h regard "tempels & priests and forms." I was unconscious of ever being sick tho' doubtfull if I could get there when going. There were many objections in his theories—those w'h respected the Christ within connected with triplicity seemed to me a pantheistic idea of Jesus & the incarnation. Tho' glad to find somthing of an explanation of his letter w'h I will inclose as a messenger to *send me the one you have kept these two* years.[3] You will not like this—but may like to see it. It has been kept secret as the first paragraph was a burst of feeling in a weak & wrong sighted moment I rather suspect. The other parts have been copied by Ann Gage & some read to allay the murmurs of his townspeople. *You will not fail to return* them by Mr Ripley who I hear is setting off tomorrow for Concord. Ill judged journey. *You will send the* Waterville lecture. A little more care in packing and directing probably than by a younger man.

You have often told me of your friends when I wished only to hear of yourself   And I have nothing to say but of T.T.S. I will return to him. I was so fortunate as to get home the day before his excellent Father was buried.[4] At the grave I met him—and he was what I wished. In praying for his Mother & children he mingled them with all the brothers & a strangers loss in a slight but touching manner—and the good Deacon received no other notice thro' the whole services. What a lesson to our most irksome minutia. In his prayers there was the transcendant spirit of a wide philosophy w'h naturally connects itself with natural but more with the late revelation. After all my excess of visitation from the spiritual world, I know that forms & conventionals can never stir an honest man from his purpose, nor erase the love of God from the spiritual. They help the common mind to employment—to them what intellect is to others. And I always shudder at every effort to remove the poor man & his offspring from Churches and schools sabbathly. They give a better external world than else where[n] to say the least.

How my heart went out after one who with as superior power as advantages, could have made the pulpit the center of attraction to the best needed classes—had his faith been only historical—but added feeling & that supernal power w'h accompanies supernal truths as naturally as attraction the magnet. But all are hastening to the future and regrets & hopes & wishes & fears wither before the fact. The millioneth obligation or chance of doing right absorbs all other ideas & renders null all splendid novelties or ghostly scarecrows

Speake of the inclosed freely & truly & oblige

your much loving Aunt
MME

The Mother wife & children have my good will   However tedious this letter it has rid me of the sense of head ache & you ca'nt expect always to be inshrined in flowers

I came here directly—not thro City, therefore could not repair the loss of stationery & had not been out of house for many days

MH: bMS Am 1280.226(906). *Addressed:* Mr R Waldo Emerson / Concord / Mss. / Rev. L. Ripley. *Endorsed:* M M Emerson / Sept. 1841.

else where] else where ⟨for them⟩

1. In his oration "The Method of Nature," which MME heard at Waterville College, 11 Aug. 1841, RWE described nature's method as "ecstacy" (*CW* 1:125, 127, 132). Writing to EH, also on 14 Sept., MME admits she left home "with reluctance, as I had been able to enjoy the beauty of spring. But if my indisposition was caused by going I cant regret it I so wished to see & hear Waldo. And the kind of life I had in hearing his voice & seeing him in publick is very memorable & dear" (MH: 1123).

2. MME suggests TTS's theology was considered too liberal or too tinged with "Germanism" for Waterford tastes.

3. TTS's letter does not survive with MME's letter.

4. MME to EH, 14 Sept. 1841, describes the death and funeral of Deacon Solomon Stone, a Waterford farmer: "A good neighbour of theirs relates that the night of the decease there was the most intire stillness with the family—and after the 'withdrawment' as his Son terms it, he prayed & the neighbour said it seemed more like a ressurection than ever he could imajine. He came forth on the sabbath in the beauty of a youthfull aspect with the eloquence of genius & the athority of a Sage—and I never remember to have been so much excited all over by Channing himself. Prayers let down the old partition walls of earth & sense— Yet they fastened the attention of all classes that

a breath seem suspended. I said to the Gages this was transcendentalism in it's reality. 'Yes!' " (MH: 1123).

To RUTH EMERSON, LIDIAN EMERSON, SARAH HOAR,
AND ELIZABETH HOAR

Madam & Mrs E. & Mrs & Miss Hoar.

Salem	No[v]. 17 [1841]

After seeing Channing yesterday I was ready to depart & tho' Mrs Cunningham invited me thro' T. W. to pass some days with her & a good accomodation but the east winds made me sick in walking home from D^r C's and it came all unexpected into my head while covered up in my back chamber at M. H. that if I were to be sick I would be at Judge White's on my way east.[1] So I came on without dinner or ability to eat & found myself most cordially received   And tho' intending to be at Portland tonight & home tomorrow night I easily gave up when I found baggage carried into a warm chamber. It is a sweet oasis in the dreary Journey of life but surrounded with so many old associations of brighter & darker days that reach thro' many a muddy & tranquil stream that it is not a bright exclusive spot in w'h we gather our favorite flowers or recall those cypress wreaths w'h we blended alone with the laurel. Age, like mine, is sometimes irked with losses of its fellows. Why Lisbeth, did you let me have nothing to say of these admirers of yours w'h would remind them you had been here in your life? Wate a silly question. You all like to know that I had a comfortable ride down to City & found E.P.P. in her store & soon came the Green & we teaed & eveed with him & Mother.[2] When I first saw him on the Couch^n at West St. I thought him an unconscious hearer of his praise as invisible spirits might. The time at Concord I lost sight of his wings—and now I believed that Waldo had done him full justice & that Miss Fuller was correct in thinking his vanity obvious. Unfortunate connection his with my friend E.P.P. Besides when one sees a youth 3 times & no moment elicits an enthusiastic impression of benvolence, we halt. I did so and became weary at 8 o'k—   One whole hour to my carriage! And roused myself by abolitionism—to w'h I found him not lukewarm but lifeless. This may account to *you* for the veil w'h I have thrown over the picture that I intended for the wilderness.—*not the case*. There are celestial spirits who may not view slavery as some do. In the long talk with Channing I was not warmed. His personal expressions of interest could not do much when one is in search of others sources of thought & faith. His pamplets paid me for the expense of riding there, however, & such a calculation may count the portion of excitment in universal ideas. If my old cloak had not sent me into a back staired chamber w'h I put up with in the pious hope that I should have a bill according (in vain) I might have had health to remain & visit Geo. R. & Emerson.[3] But this is very gratefull. Your Sister Aunt & friend in fine health & affection,

MME.

MH: bMS Am 1280.226(1124).

Couch] *possibly* Curb

1. The place of MME's meeting with WEC is uncertain ("M. H." may be an abbreviation for Marblehead). Judge Daniel A. White was living in Salem in the 1840s.

2. Because it carried foreign books and periodicals, the bookstore EPP opened on West Street in Boston in July 1840 soon became an intellectual center. There, in 1841, EPP met William Batchelder Greene (1819–78), who was looking for an English translation of Kant. She introduced him to the transcendentalist circle, and his essay "First Principles" was published in the *Dial*, Jan. 1842. RWE to Margaret Fuller, 9 Nov. 1841, says, "Mr Greene came: my Aunt stays" (*L* 2:463).

3. Probably George Ripley and GBE.

1842

To Ralph Waldo Emerson, Ruth Haskins Emerson, and Elizabeth Hoar

[1 Feb. 1842]

Blessed God how severe is thy hand   This moment sadest of many sad news my old ears have received, I read yours.[1] "Grieve"   I more than grieve—could any ills of mine have saved him—without personal attachment I did value him as an extraordinary being & wanted to hear of his soul warmed & expanded into this very old stale world—tho' I did not expect to live—yet I might. I am very much moved—forget to sympathise—vain vain all, Mother Granmother Elisbeth what a heavy sweep off of the holiest sweetest joys   I know too well those—of loving boys who looks are of^n the soul & create new prophecies   God alone who built yours can account for the calmness w'h masters your affliction—   How you could write to me at such a time & with the poetry w'h belongs only to a world free from the sad mysteries of this. You are made to live in this very one & able to breathe above its clouds & pits when your warmest affections are crushed & proudest hopes vanished

How is poor dear Lidian   God will support her and while He is preparing to take his seat in your heart & make it like the vessel laid before his alter "full of heavenly manna—within & without like pure polished gold," He will work in his own inscrutable way till he makes your genius shine over a dark world with the light of His own revealing in Christ. Farewell if you can write when poor bereaved man, you are to feel still more the loss of that bright gift do to your ever

affectionate sympathising & sadly so at this unlooked for stroke

Aunt MME

Tuesday   ½ past 3   I had the news

Feb 1

My dear Sister

How often have we suffered together. Your loss personally is grievous. I pray God to comfort you & love your Sister

MME

Dear Elisbeth

I was going to write you today (one of the few days of health I have) as Ralph goes to Boston—but I can say nor think of nothing but that beautifull face. I said little of him at Concord—but could you hear my ulogies you would be sattisfied.

Write to your aff^t Aunt. with weake nerves is almost ashamed of her agitation. But think what a pure spirit is in union with its Maker   Tell his parents of their honor. to be so connected with one who belongs to the great Restorer who still loves children. Happy boy well as he was conditioned—he has escaped that w'h we can never estimate the dangers off till there

MH: bMS Am 1280.226(910). *Addressed:* Mr R. Waldo Emerson / Concord / Mss. / Mr R T Haskins. *Postmarked:* Boston / {MAS} Feb 3. *Endorsed:* 1842.

who . . . of] who looks ⟨into⟩ ↑ are of ↓

1. RWE to MME, 28 Jan. 1842, informs her of his son Waldo's death the preceding evening (*L* 3 : 7).

To ELIZABETH HOAR

Vale   Ap 28 [1842]

* * * I never asked you to describe the particular sensation of your head ache least it should be like claiming affinity to mine—but you speake—just as I feel. I cant read but little & want that to be amusing chiefly. Wish I had some novels. I have no pain but a throbing confused sensation w'h the Faculty say is a conjestion of blood on the brain. And I am expecting one of them this Eve. to bleed me tho' some say I am too old & feeble. But extremest debility not so bad as confusion & a sort of Swift's giddiness   I would bear the giddiness with the old Dean if I could share his wit & strenght of mind. We are sad for the death of friend & Physician. Dr Gage died last sab. Alas, that late happy house. How often have I felt that the tranquil & delightfull scenery w'h surrounds it bore a natural correspondence to the gaiety of it's little inmates & the prospects of its ripening Youth. A cloud dark & heavy with sepulchral dews hangs over the scene and darkens those prospects but the wand of xian faith scatters it and the bow of promise reflected from the waters of sorrow disclose the bright & varied hues of the devine goodness.[1] I wish I had Southeys "Roderick."[2] There is a moon eclipsed by a cloud w'h scatters & ornaments. I like such kind of reading now—but I should not have applied it to these freinds, tho' they interest me much—how can it be otherwise shut up

together? That cloud so richly ornamental I have in my eye adorned a higher & gifted one. Since I began this page I have been prostrate on bed & the phlebotomist has performed his lancing—but not enough.

Love drawn deeper than the blood to Waldo L. & Sister. To know some cercumstances w'h would place me at your sides in oratory, study, dressing room & parlour of social chat, would be a cordial (not like wine for I use none) like the fragrance of Spring. Do you see the Walthamers? Will you be my messenger (sweet Iris)[3] again to your brother Waldo & say a bundle goes by the bearer of this to Thomas in w'h are W^{ms} Maucaullys M.s. My Brothers pamplets & his "Heroes."[4] Kant & Augustine there before. This frank to Boston is the first object of this letter—for I could not think of any thing to say but to know if you were able to write. Yes I feel the loss of Gage as a companion—he had force of character rather than intellect—was wide awake—high tempered yet ingeneous[n]

Called for

MH: bMS Am 1280.226(1134). *Addressed:* Miss Elisabeth Hoar / Concord, Mss / Mr J. Kennon.

ingeneous] *possibly* ingenuous (*T*)

1. A cloud . . . goodness: MME used this passage in her obituary of Leander Gage, who died 24 Apr.; the obituary was printed in the *Christian Witness* (Boston), 13 May 1842.

2. Robert Southey, *Roderick, the Last of the Goths: A Tragic Poem* (1814).

3. Greek goddess of the rainbow and a messenger of the gods.

4. Thomas Babington Macaulay's *Critical and Historical Essays* was not published until 1843; MME's reference to WE[3]'s "M.s." may refer to manuscript copies of some of Macaulay's articles in the *Edinburgh Review*; Carlyle's *On Heroes, Hero Worship, and the Heroic in History* (London, 1840; New York, 1841).

To Ann Sargent Gage

Tues   May 3. [1842]

I am glad you are so well my dear bereaved friend. I passed without speaking to you sabbath. If ever you would be alone it was on that day of mourning. & rejoicing in a Saviour—in renewing your covenant with a covenant keeping God. I hope you had some insight into the spiritual world—some realizations of the only real state. You must if willing interest my solitude with your exercises & those of the Girls. And I am hoping that the Muse tho' clad in cypress will visit your abode—her wings may be tiped with the gold & azure of faith & love—tho' dewed with tears. I had a good eve or night last & felt as tho' it might be the last—promised that I w^d write & desire you to burn *the will w'h you wittnessed* & *preserve Mr Hoars.* Better done now than to leave the responsibility on you. The below lines belonged to a letter to my B. & I want Thomas to know that I dont love professions as I urged him to study.[1] I often say if I had Sons I w^d persuade them to be farmers not that I dream I have any influence on any one *now*. The lines on the bottom of this are an addition to the obituary after sending it to you.[2] Nothing has so delighted me thro' life as to find in nature symbols of character human & divine. We do not feel the pride of a writer in metaphicks or didactics but we do feel *pleasure*—individuating us with the creations of God. It is the little sparks of poetry bestowed on all souls. I send it for I doubt if my good prose loving Brother will polish & perfect it and insert it. Had I health I should have written it anew & sent it to G. B. Emerson whose taste & judgment seem infallible. I was pleased with characterizing Sister Phebe thro' the medium of natures pictures & continue to remember it with pleasure tho' no one sympathised but H. & S.

You will pardon so rough and limited a paper but I dont love writing of late   Love to the Children from your aff.t friend

MME.

* * *

MWA.

1. B.: Brother (SR); paragraph written upside down at bottom of p. 1 omitted; MME remarks that some profession (perhaps the ministry) is the last she would "choose for a friend in these times," which she calls "gloomy & gloomier."

2. See MME to EH, 28 Apr. 1842, n. 1. The obituary survives in two undated copies, sent to ASG (MWA) and SR (MH: 1250). MME to ASG said she was sending a copy to her brother, "unless you object. I throw the responsibility on him to alter & improve as my head has rendered it a task to write."

To Ralph Waldo Emerson

Vale   Sat 28 May [1842]

And art thou become like one of us? Does nature who seemed thy favored Angel to wait thy walkings & musings and be the servator of thy Muse look askance—dreamy & like as she passes the most of her children often clad in hair cloth & at best homespun silk worm stuff? And you do not like the little grave she has dug so blindly that you cannot drop your plummet into its sad chasm. Right glad am I! Abandon her! She has been covering the earth for ages with blood & war & prisons—erected her cauldrons & swept her besoms over thrones and love & wisdom & all free beautifull things. Pass her bye— go behind her stage decorations alike with her inquisitions and prostrate thy higher capasities of enjoyment before Him who for some time of inscrutable purposes weilds her secret forces—or if you prefer, makes this proteus phenomena the palpable machine of a transient yet infinitely real discipline. Use them and all the living souls it bears or seems as shifting stones to the only real Substance. Swear by his Son, the medium of his tremendous & gracious influence, and by the record he left to live only for him, and the wide universal principles of his cross. I read by day & night (the first hours this week of receiving your lecture)[1] its transcendent ingenuity for apologizing its proud

& aristocratic retirement from laying toe on the cartlike business of publick weal. Admiration of the simple development & origin of the title to the philosphy should be made publick. I read it by night as fearing I might not be able another day. And never dreamt of writing you the syllable till this morning an hour of health from medcine & gruel gave me to life & love & faith so stronge that I scarce wished the grave. Nor can afford you unstinted sympathy for all the past nor worse in future pale years, if they be nessecery to lead you to the God of cloudy nature & brighter revelation. Yes I say to myself amidst long defeat & stupid ills

A better boon his purpose knows
A richer gift his love bestows.

And I feel "a ray kindled"[2] (tho' smale & interred) by the same Power as that which streched yours so far & wide—alas! the *contrast*[n]

I love Moore who says I feel my immortality ore "sweep all pains, ills, fears & times"[3]

Very kind & loving to Sister & Neices   If E.H. can with intire convenence perform the last mission—well—if not let me know. If I am forced to live & no better I may journey to Portland perhaps to Thomastown where I can board with acquaintance & dont wish any letter sent here. If well nothing will induce me to travel.

My daily aspirations are for you first & others with you

MME

I expect a frank sent Monday for this

MH: bMS Am 1280.226(914). *Addressed:* Mr R. Waldo Emerson / Concord / Mss. *Postmarked:* BOSTON / MS. / Jun 21. *Endorsed:* M. M. Emerson / 1843.

contrast] con{   } *in MS (torn by seal); missing letters supplied from T*

1. Rusk speculates that MME read a manuscript copy of RWE's lecture "The Transcendentalist" (first delivered 23 Dec. 1841; printed in *Dial* 3 [Jan. 1843]). MME to EH, 2 June [1842], mentions EH's "painstaking" for her "in the lecture w'h came but a few days since" and thanks her for sending some issues of the *Dial*. RWE to MME, 20 and 22 June 1842 (*L* 3:64–66) was begun before he received this letter and seems to respond to another letter from MME, written before 20 June, that does not survive. In the 22 June portion, written immediately after receipt of this letter, RWE defends himself against MME's criticism by dissociating himself as author from the "class of young persons" he describes in the lecture (*L* 3:65).

2. See MME to RWE, 7 Dec. [1843], n. 1.

3. Probably poet Thomas Moore; a new edition of his ten-volume *Poetical Works* was published in 1840–41.

To Ralph Waldo Emerson

Vale　June 27 [1842]

There was a boy who guided & gilded the steps of age for some bye gone years—and at lenght that age retired and secreted itself intending to receive no farther influence—tis crest fallen—takes the pen at every hint,[n] as tho' the mandate were royal, and like the eld of old invokes some shadow to rise. Alas, the record of fancy long since "withered weake & grey." But theres a far more potent sesame w'h tho not yet able to open the lost door to the treasure of repose—yet pierces its gloom & reads not the present fortunes of man but the future. And there tis good to see the horoscopes of all that is loved & lovely. There we expect to meet them—at last know their destiny, and willingly we leave the yet untrodden paths of their road whether prosperous or adverse it matters little when viewed from the vastness of Pisgah. Many days have gone on thier monotonous[n] course of sultry heavy weather, and I still ask why write when there is nothing to say? When this was begun T.T. Stone had roused me from sleep & I intended an abstract of his sermon but the night was far gone & the next eve. he gave a lecture here w'h I disliked for its' mysticism & adaptedness to certain calvinists so I bid him & my intended abstract good bye. He was journeying for rest to his head. Alas, I am thinking his race nearly run. He was taken in his pulpit lately with loss of mental power in prayer had to leave—says with marvelous indifference that for years he has suffered so repeatedly. As far as he can attend to his sensations his case is similar to mine—somthing probably like an apoplexy of brain. E. Hoar has sympathised with a slight attack of mine. It was the day before writing you my last letter,[1] and left no impression on my mind only to ask E.P.P. to consult some D^r (Warren I prefered) describing what could be specified by an unusual warmth in the back of head. What I mention it for is to regret that so fine a capasity as hers ca'nt remember a request not to mention it to any of my freinds. I dont wish to exhaust their sympathy on trifles—at worst 'twould scarsly demand much for a few short years. And your "wish that I s^d be well as the Angels are"[2] when fullfilled will bolt up change and shackel accidents of pain[3] of this lame bodily kind. But I never think of the future (however desirable) without the expectation of looking back with occasional shame & contempt of my littleness & sins. It is so natural to expect that when the states of wonder and joy subside that other states of mind should take place—new developments within & without　There may be some whose moral affinities are so strongly related by nature & habit to the infinite Moral Being as to escape all terror and find themselves more at home in His felt presence than when imbodied. Those who are not of this nor the Angelic order have an intuitive reason about a wonderfull Unique whose influence & love are more perceptible than that of infinity. Sybil has been here for a few days with her son and the avowal of E P P that the "unitarian Chh could not nourish her" has delighted Sib. Is it possible that any one in a xian world should complain of famine in men & Chhs I answer & this raises all my Nieces ire. So excuse my harping &

sawing. I revenged my solitude by making her read the flattery of your first page[4] & apologized for you that I was feeble & lonely & delighted with your kindness. All the rest I needed of soceity was for some D^r to tell me what this strange loss of memory meant when the old liver (weary of its task) was disordered.

Love to Sister Niece & my longing to see all of you in the Vale. I feel loathe to wander perhaps may not till Sep^r, if then. So when you can write just as well as not, do. I cant reconcile Lidians pride or indolence in not answering me. Father R. repeatedly said the books belonging once to my Father should be ours. What are they? Worth bringing? Your Aunt H. would like Moody to have some of those old folios. Oh I did not misunderstand your "biographical confessions." I alluded wholly to your letter confession of "not fathoming the chasm made under your roof."[5] Adieu. Never did I meet one so well calculated to enjoy the intellectual scenes of the other world. Do not fail of the main calculation

Yours in love

MH: bMS Am 1280.226(911). *Addressed:* Mr R. Waldo Emerson / Concord / Mass. *Postmarked:* BOSTON / MS. / JUL 16. *Endorsed:* MME / June 1842.

hint] ⟨request⟩ ↑ hint ↓
monotonous] ⟨rather⟩ monotonous
1. See MME to RWE, 28 May 1842.
2. See *L* 3:65.
3. Cf. Shakespeare, *Antony and Cleopatra,* 5.2.6.
4. RWE to MME, 20 and 22 June 1842, calls her the "lover of nature & the great heart & subtle mind—who has so woven her presence into the best threads & texture of my life" (*L* 3:64).
5. Apparently in the now lost letter written before 20 June (see MME to RWE, 28 May [1842], n. 1). MME seems to allude to their "separation" in Feb. 1836.

To ELIZABETH HOAR
Portland   lime St.   Oct. 7. [1842]
Yesterday my dear Lisbeth I ventured to put in my claim with the falling leaf now that the gorgeous summer and your gracefull troop of friends may have gone—and the leaf was as gay as the gayest—for I have had these ten days of renewed health—but while writing the news of Channing's death made away with the many thoughts I had of you thro many a month.[1] Spiritual as was his views and writings he loved old life better than I expected when I saw him[2]—besides I could not connect the reality of death with him. And hoped never to outlive him—so fondly had I ever delighted to think about him. His views of my Saviour & the plan of redemption were different from mine— & we parted not as we met. For years have I said to the youth who I wished to imbibe his spirit, what may be the disappointment—the possible regret his sainted spirit is yet to sustain in it's unbodied state! But no fear for his

cannonization. His utopian idea of human nature was the image of his own pure mind—seemed neither philosophical nor accordant to constant facts—tending to that sublime panthesm w'h spiritual natures fall into. These are set over the immense loss the world has sustained in his death. Oh how humbling to breathe & sleep when there is a world for souls like his. He spoke of nature with youthfull delight—& smiled with benevolent complacency when I said the woodsman told me they would read Channing on slavery for he was a great man. Now how wise the divine economy in loving fame & influence. Yet, yet, Lisbeth, that smile returns to me with irking. So mean—so transient all of human life that to haveⁿ a name seems little when the realities of the future open on the spirit of a Channing. But why moralize see saw to one like you. I hoped to exhaust my self last night in writing to the Waterfordians on the subject. There was some shred of genii scattered there in antient days & I love to rouse it. I think of what he has been for the slave and if there is a God & heaven he is crowned! It was there & then he forewent the love of certain fame & influence! I thought I had done. Do write as soon as you receive this, and induce Waldo to, now the Dial is done and let that come here directed to care of Rufus E. Eq^r.[3] I have been loath to leave the Vale—it was beautifull—& I dreamed easily—but knew the nessicity of salt water & air. So I shall lose the interest of seeing Hannah quit her loved home & the cheerfullness of her Sisters preparations.[4] Much as I say against matrimony—that I find no one better or happier and that probably a majority wish to be unyoked—folks will marry. And thus they lose great feelings & pursuits in individuals *sometimes*. Her elect is a sensible & honest farmer. How I could wish it were for your repose & health to come & be with me in this old Castle of house with one lone widow & domestic where nothing is seen but the opposite lights of the Exchange & half the house shut up. But I should expect & crave too much indulgence. Adieu and tell me every thing to your own Ante

MME

Mail will close I cant read what Ive written[5]

MH: bMS Am 1280.226(1138). *Addressed:* Miss Elisabeth Hoar / Care of Hon. S. Hoar / Concord / Mss. *Postmarked:* Portland / Me. / Oct 7.

have] *possibly* leave (*T*)

1. Cf. MME to ASG: "On this 6 of Oct. 42 at 4 o'k this P.M. I was astounded by hearing of the death of Channing!" She goes on to describe her thoughts and feelings about this man who always "excite[d] the mind & move[d] the heart," a "christian," "citizen," and "philantropist" (MWA). WEC died of typhoid at Bennington, Vt., on 2 Oct.—an event that MME connected with her father's death. In this same letter, 6 Oct. 1842, she writes: "I love the air of this City—but how stupid a people I have walked—& been in book stores yesterday & today—& what is more been to Mr Whitman's & got new books & not a word of Channing till a Newburyport friend called. *Is it possible that it was known* he died on sabbath at Vermont— There too & on sabbath dear Sister died our father full of piety & patriotism" (MWA).

2. See MME to RHE, LJE, Sarah Hoar, and EH, 17 Nov. [1841].

3. Rufus Emerson of Portland.
4. Niece Hannah Haskins married Augustus Parsons on 13 Oct. 1842.
5. Written on outside; badly smudged.

To ?

Tuesday Night [Oct. 1842]

Dear Sir,

You had carried me back so far that I lost sight of the present and never had a thought that I could see you tomorrow— Is it possible?[1]

I live in a great yellow house in Lime St., just opposite one side of the Exchange. The woman and domestic were absent this afternoon— When I recall the questions I had to ask, I regret not being at home.

I shall always prize Channing's[2] epistles more than ever— While ages and nations pass, the truths contained in them remains eternal. Channing! I do suspect you think that his influence was waning. But when I view him as the friend and advocate of the slave it appears to me rising to the utmost eminence. I saw him last Fall— I want to tell you how he appeared in other talks. I want to hear you speak of him and above all of Brownson's letter to him.[3] Of the philosophy so grand as far as it keeps with you in pulpit—and in affliction—if ever you should have it. Why I don't like Waldo's position is not that he left preaching— Blessed be God he has— But I want him all to himself—no Dial—no lectures—till he has returned to the centers of being and truth. And I do believe he will before death. How lovely and ingenious you knew. Surely he will return from his erratic course.

You have wakened me so completely that I should write ever so long if I had a pen and ink— But I must bid you good night for morning comes next hour— With a thousand good wishes that you may understand the whole value of Paul's mission and long bring faith sweet to the glory of God and good of men

Yours truly
MME.

Is not this late work of De Wette a desultory sententious thing? I have read now and then a page and felt as tho' it was Zimmermann—rather Goethe?[4] * * * If you can't visit, if you could write!

MH: bMS Am 1280.235(704, f. 114) [MS copy in unknown hand].

1. Although the letter is undated and the recipient unnamed, MME's comments indicate that she is writing to an acquaintance of many years, whom she has unexpectedly met while in Portland, perhaps FHH or the Newburyport friend who informed her of WEC's death in Oct. 1842 (see MME to EH, 7 Oct. [1842], n. 1). The holograph does not survive; a notation on this copy states that the letter is possibly addressed to WEC, which is clearly not the case.

2. One of several words the transcriber found difficult to decipher and bracketed and wrote in pencil. "[Charlotte's]" in MS, but "Channing's" is more likely.

3. Orestes Brownson, *The Mediatorial Life of Jesus: A Letter to Reverend William Ellery Channing, D.D.* (Boston, 1842), reviewed in the *Dial* 3 (Oct. 1842): 276–77.

4. Probably Wilhelm M. L. De Wette's *Theodore; or, The Skeptic's Conversation*, trans. J. F. Clarke, (Boston, 1841), or De Wette's *Human Life; or, Practical Ethics*, trans. Samuel Osgood (Boston, 1842); Johann Georg von Zimmermann was the author of the very popular *Solitude: Considered with Respect to Its Influence on the Mind and the Heart*, first published in English in 1797.

1843

To Elizabeth Hoar and Samuel Ripley

Vale   Jan 28   sat   '43

Dear Lisbeth,

your welcome letter is just read for the last time this winter. Your wishes gratefull for they have been realised in uncommon consciousness of the worth of existing even here, in the most unvaried solitude. Could I cast your horoscope—this year should be richer than all bye gone ones. Rather delight that it has ever been cast among the infinite ideas w'h revolve tho' sometimes in the shadows of death, yet always tending to perfection. Pleased with news— tho' I was so ignorant as to think that Lane's "announcement" [1] was almost tiresome so often repeated   That every thing is to come from within—without natural induction & the incessant education w'h fences in all, has been to me like telling children the Doctor has bro't Ma'mas baby. That "surrender to the ever active Spirit" is best known by the struggles of the moral nature, you know, when called to pass thro' those shadows w'h were to have been the bowers of^n beauty & love, and the still severer labours of every day duties & sacrifices w'h do not lift the soul to higher states as does the angel of death. However, I oppose a man of straw probably. Lane allows the scaffolding w'h gives the *within* to survey. It is the vague bold generalising irks literal me. Tho' I know it is the soul alone can feel the immortal & infinite—yet that every step on the higher rounds of the ladder of mathematics (I believe) and know that even a metaphisical hypothesis gives this feeling reason and grounds w'h imajanation & sensibility love—and would not disregard even in those religious "visitations w'h neglect prayer in its offices" [2] and would devote every tho't & every instant of it's duration to the sole idea of God w'h comprehends all others. Richter has been in the hands of the most selfish grossly worldly person I know of talents and I regret it. Impossible that she can estimate him— by artificial methods may paint him. But hear him thro' Carlyle say that he had rather give up immortality—than the existence of God—and should he not have been sacred to those who can despise wealth & jest with poverty & pain? I wish Mrs would keep to the tough old Reformers if her activity must keep in motion.[3] Dr C. called her worldly. A vague term but I had no time for definitions in that leave taking. I speake from knowledge of infant days & each succeeding ones w'h decide character. Brownson's lecture I wish I could have heard—hope he will be more of a conservative in some respects than formerly about the social order. Different ranks are among the beauties of divine economy. Who could taste the riot of charity or divine resignation in his leveling plan?[4] * * *

Thank you but know of nothing you can send me. My head wont apply to any thing steady while confined especially. It is in fine spirits riding & amusing. I teamed myself twice as far as the Gages last week in sleigh. They & these pleased with your remembrance. You are their beau ideal   The Dial you said was sent never came. I wish it *much* & the Jan. tell Waldo when he returns   I prize them altogether more than formerly

I have wanted More of sermons about Channing suppose Brother leaves to Waldo. Wrote yesterday to him for some and for Brownson's letter to Dr C. & for two or 3 last Exs w'h contain Gannets address.[5] The Standard R. T. H. takes & it comes weekly   I dont read any thing but Mrs Childs letters on other subjects. I avoid every thing of the ills & disputes. Principles are enough. If you have Miss Martineus corre. with Mrs Follen please send it.[6] Our paper goes about & gets unreadable. The 5 of Jan. you sent came the week before last. the 29 of Dec last week. Both well disposed off to the Esq[rs] & Chh. I can't but wish it were convenient for you to answer my questions earlier, as you forgot one w'h pains me. If I had not been to blame it would not. But Waldo is so kind that I wish to hear if he is offended

How is E.P.P.? I wrote by the same R. T. who carried yours in Nov. & since by mail. Ralph has been expected a month & I hoped to hear from her & a q[t] Review. What can be the *cause* of her silence perplexes me more than the silence pains. Her change of views has interested me & her attentions in going to D[r] Warren. Tonight the Standard of 12 of Jan. came. (Thanks.) w'h was at office thursday. I tried in vain to get at circulating libraries some novels to bring home   I looked for Charles G. & Porters[n] Patronage.[7] Comforts of former days.

Your aff[t] Aunt
MME

Dear Brother S. R.
        Yesterday I had no room in Uncles letter & forgot to request you to pay E.P.P. for Bellows & Clarks sermons.[8] Dont forget it

MME

I have been looking over this dislike to send it so badly written but I nightly do as tho' I were to sleep without waking & as you are kind I shall seal now & send it for I may be able to do no better for pen. I want the Dials when my Nephew returns

MH: bMS Am 1280.226(1140). *Addressed:* Miss Elisabeth Hoar / Concord / Mass. *Postmarked:* So Waterford / Jany 30. *Also on outside:* Rev. S. Ripley.
the bowers of] ⟨fraught with⟩ ↑ the bowers of ↓
Porters] *possibly* Pastors

1. Probably Charles Lane's proposal, in *Dial* 3 (Oct. 1842), "to select a spot whereon the new Eden may be planted, and man may, untempted by evil, dwell in harmony with his Creator, with himself, his fellows, and with all external relations" in New England, an early description of the Fruitlands community (246). MME's complaint—that such theories imply all is to come from "within," without discipline and education—is answered in Lane's article on Alcott in the Apr. 1843 *Dial*, which stressed the "law of industry" needed to germinate the divine "seed." She may also refer to Lane's lecture at the Concord Lyceum, 4 Jan. 1843; see *LJE L*, 114–15.

2. Probably a quotation from EH's letter, which does not survive, or from a report of Lane's lecture (see above, n. 1): see Lane's idea of "removing all hindrances to the immediate influx of Deity into the spiritual faculties" (*Dial* 3 [Oct. 1842]: 246).

3. Probably the *Life of Jean Paul Frederic Richter, Compiled from Various Sources, Together with his Autobiography,* trans. from the German (Boston, 1842), reviewed in *Dial* 3 (Jan. 1843): 404–6. Published anonymously, it was the work of Eliza Buckminster Lee; MME compares it unfavorably with Carlyle's essays on Richter in the *Edinburgh Review* and the *Foreign Review* in 1827 and 1830. See Richter's "Dream" concerning the existence of God in Carlyle's review of Richter's *Leben* (*Foreign Review* 5 [1830]): " 'I could with less pain deny Immortality than Deity' " (48). The "tough old reformers" may be in Lee's *Sketches of a New England Village* (Boston, 1838).

4. Orestes Brownson lectured on government at the Concord Lyceum, 28 Dec. 1842; MME objects to his social ideas expressed in "The Labouring Classes."

5. WEC's death in Oct. 1842 prompted numerous sermons and eulogies: the *Dial* 3 (Jan. 1843), mentioned the published discourses of Gannett, Hedge, Clarke, Parker, John Pierpont, and Henry Whitney Bellows and a recent lecture by Bancroft, while it lamented that Boston had not paid public honor to WEC (387); Orville Dewey published a *Discourse on the Character and Writings of Reverend William E. Channing, D.D.* (New York, 1843). Brownson's "letter to Dr. Channing" is *The Mediatorial Life of Jesus* (Boston, 1842).

6. *The National Antislavery Standard* (New York), edited by Lydia Maria Child, whose regular column, "Letters from New York" (separately published in 1843), was often nonpolitical. In letter 47, 19 Jan. 1843, on love and friendship, she quoted RWE. In 1844 Harriet Martineau's *Life in the Sick Room* was published with an introduction to the American edition by Eliza Follen, but their correspondence is not located.

7. Samuel Richardson's *Charles Grandison* and, probably, an unidentified novel.

8. Uncle is Lincoln Ripley. For Bellows and Clarke, see above, n. 5.

To Ann Sargent Gage

Thurs 6 [Apr.? 1843?]

Dear xian friend,

This is a day I yearn for fellowship want to join in publick confessions and deprecations of publick & private calamity.[1] Calamity how much as a Country we may fear. And when daily visited by my own conscience of falling short in temper & disposition of high & elevated purposes and of that humility so requisite so rational so demanded it seems I have only to care for one poor self. But I do think & feel for the young at these times wh foreshade revolutions   And on the whole hope more than fear that God is revolving a crisis w'h will give nations to his praise thro' the glorious plan of redemption. Oh in solitude how often is checked the blessed hour of the divine presence in some startling view of millions cruelised and of other millions who live & move in & by a Being of whom they know not. But tis the lot of xians to bow in silent adoration and humbly wait for hereafter when some of those heavy clouds will be dispersed immediately w'h conceal the throne   We know that righteousness is there   And as a Restorationist I believe in the whole race being saved or wicked annihillated[n] or I could not be happy. And the doctrine can do no harm to those who love God & virtue from the depths of their being who would not sin were there no punishment. Still I could not preach the doctrine (I think) if I were in society nor never name it unless pressed. Oh yes the redemption was for all. Dont you look forward to those bright abodes in thy long future when no created beings shall suffer?

I have been reading Wood on native depravity & I. Taylor on the bible giving no countenance to the fanaticism w'h has persecuted for ages.[2] Solemn sad reading.

If you like Taylors history on fanaticism say so. If I feel the distant murmering of the waves w'h agitate the world of religion morals & philosophy, what must you do, who have so many lives in your own to antisapate   In prayer & its effects your faith & hope will be increased my dear Ann, remember the lonely[n] passing into nest[n]

MME.

part of our barn roof fell in today   I s[d] rather have expected the house is so heavy. But every particle is held by an absolute Power and I shall not move down. A sudden remove delivers from long suffering—yet I w[d] see & feel that joyous hour if permitted.

I never remember, but once it seems I spoke of my habits of "benefit of clergy" as an apology for surprise at the extent of bills. For I should have lost the pleasure of sending for Dr G. had I to have been added to his beneficiees. I *never wished nor dreamt* it. He was kind & you have been to Rebecca and to others. I would not accept it for it would been injustice

MWA. *Addressed:* Mrs Ann S. Gage.
or . . . annihillated] or ↑ wicked ↓ annihillated (*no position marked*)
lonely] *possibly* lovely
nest] *possibly* next
    1. The first Thursday in Apr. was for many years an officially proclaimed "Day of Public Fasting, Humiliation and Prayer" in Maine and Massachusetts. The reference to doctor's bills in the last paragraph suggests that this undated latter derives from the same period as the next letter; dating in both cases is conjectural.

2. Leonard Woods, *An Essay on Natural Depravity* (Boston, 1835); Isaac Taylor, *Fanaticism* (New York and Boston, 1834); sections 9 and 10 of Taylor's work are entitled "The Religion of the Bible Not Fanatical."

To Ann Sargent Gage

Tues.   28   Night [1843?][1]

Before sleeping, almost nightly, I do as tho' it were the last. I have hunted for the bills I had seen within a fortnight in vain.[2] I believe in sweeping at dusk I saw some one or more but felt so confident of sucess that I stated no objections to taking the bill home. I had always believed that if there were later receipts than any debts it was of no consequence. Still I often asked Sarah to collect those w'h laid about falling at times from behind the glass &c. And I often took them up with sadness that I had indulged my whims in medicines w'h did not remove complaints and since that departure when the intercourse I valued the most could no longer cheer an invalid, I read, and it may be two or 3 weeks, one of these & it was 4# & add cents. I dont remember even reading the date but feel *no doubt* of it's being the receipt w'h this bill answers to. It was easy for the Doctor to make the mistake. And when I paid him in Jan. 42 for the Insurance I said in a few days I should pay his bill for the fall I had from sleigh (w'h I gave you the following sunday) he said there was a note due. I knew there was none but the one I hastily tore on sat. and gave him my idea that it was a professional way of giving. Now I think he refered to this forgetting that he had made out the bill & receipted it. When I paid him I remember being pleased that he took back some medicine—but I have no distinct memory of its being on the bill. But, my dear Ann, the probabilities (were there no receipt) is so stronge that when we go to law my learned Council will prove that I am very anxious to pay debts & have never been unable & that I was going away for an indefinite time, and that I never rested till I paid Houghton[3] whose attendance on that & the suceding day after Mr H. & I fell 1838 was merely my civility when he asked me if he should call again coming thro the messenger's zeal. 3 & lastly the latter receipts will cost you? But to be serious my dear Ann I must insist on your truthfullness to tell me if there can remain any doubt on your mind. I say tho' no one called for such a speech that I always relied on your integrity & that you had done right for I should have done the same to give me the bill. Was it not crossed on the ledger? If not it was *forgettfullness.* Your memory about *wants* is not like my tenacious one. I am always alone & when I see or hear any thing it is ingraven (if I am confident) I have never been mistaken I believe. When you were so kind as to copy my will you observed that you had forgotten Phebes remembrances. True it was a trifle but I who have time to remember the little occurences wondered at it. I dont send any papers. Let sentiment go while there is a doubt on your mind that love of money could blind my memory a moment. Could I realise my property how trifling my debts—but I should not pay twice.

MWA.

1. Note written on verso of a leaf containing one paragraph of "Almanack for '40," crossed out with several long diagonal strokes.

2. MME's note suggests that, following LG's death, ASG attempted to collect some of his unpaid bills. The note tells much about MME's disorganized financial habits, medical history, and her relationship with the Gages.

3. Lewis W. Houghton (b. 1806), a Waterford physician, held numerous town offices between 1833 and 1851.

To Ralph Waldo Emerson

Dec 7   Thursday at Me [1843]

What art thou about dear Waldo? Getting the Dial with the melody of wood notes or its richer "solitudes"   Leave these (enchanting as thou paintest) & take wing with him who visits the "cave fast by the throne"—wander to the trees of life & pluck the amaranths—for surely thou hast a "ray kindled by the same art" & tho' forbidden its native soil as yet is destined for it when the *taste* (to persume no farther) is fitted. Who made Miltons?[n1] It would have been a boon to me to have affected you with questions as a departing one (the other day) to have penetrated your inmost faith. Oh what a catecist—but the excitment of seeing you rather erased every thought.[2] Strange the admirers will say when thought was so embodied. *How is your health* and of the Sister Niece & tots? You looked thin. May I ask *why* you leave meat &c? No wine? So live I   "And how are you?" Feeble—confined as usual to solitude, but without its charms, w'h pass understanding to ones self. for I have not read even the Dial, nor but a page two or three times. The disorder lingers on my head & weakens (tho' not disfigures) one eye. Probably getting well.

But come he slow or come he fast
Death will surely come at last.[3]

And who can say I have not made my contribution to the wheels of the universe? Pain, langor & defeat—are they nothing positive? Have they not their mission—fullfill no purpose? At least, we know time & the hour go thro' the roughest day. "Do I thrive under evil"? Alas an hour of ease like this, w'h I expect to be reversed, finds me as frivolous as chipper as a child, chanting for the use of the lungs (w'h have no other play) a bit of verse or hymn, w'h I respect, tho' the latter long since had your veto as destitute of ideas. As this is the first attempt at writing I will rest the old optick. But I do want to hear a voice in the wilderness, and you are obliging.   8. Love to your mother & tell her that Sister H. has become a warm & stronge Millerite for the year past & now all her children except S.M. & Hannah are so. R.T. has been at home some weeks & goes round to missionize—to examin if the aged & young are "prepared for what he knows is coming before the end of March."[4] He omits of late the madness of knowing. But I believe him & the rest insane on *that* subject. It mortifys to lose respect for the girls reason, & they their *interest* in reading now & then an hour to me. They are kind & sweet in manner & wait on my wants. But I am a great bore to all. R.T.'s good feelings pleased me, after the fright we all had   He was absent at supper & afterwards we heard a great deal of grieflike joy up garret & it was his emotions caused by having an answer to prayer for Hannah who was here, & poor me. At first, when he came home with a lecturer, it was curious & desirable to find so stronge an instinct of immortality in those who had not one intellectual idea but I sicken at the belief now that I suspect it is attended with the doctrine of perfection & as connected with pious[n] obligations. Pardon me all the genius' of transcends,[n] if I ever, in some frivolous moment, allude to what I have heard of Allcotts &c   How we hate to see persuming hands laid on the arks of our faith & visions substituted for reason. Now I never fail to have my faith in nat. religion strenghtened by the scepticism of Hume & his admirer. Probably owing to the natural strech of mind great ones induce, at whatever eccentric point they aim. Oh your night met all my sympathies. Soon as it comes I dont feel alone or restless, tho without any one. Does the theist (for you *speculate* widely) consider the Deity as too happy to represent the idea of human joyousness—under the ideal of infinite seriousness—consciousness of possessing infinite capasities joy might be created for creatures? And even they are never sattisfied but when serious. No one is described more happy than Archimides when 'he found it,' in cold water.[5] Your real belief of what you style the Ineffable is a great desideratum with your Aunt, who has no means of streching or thinking. You spoke of the forces of nature some years since to me & I made no inquiries—the other day those *positives* seem lessened or dimed. Whether I may solicit the *truth* or not, I do hunger for it and it shall be only mine.

Thanks to Sister for the carpet w'h I had by the stage. It does very well to cover my room with the old one. Please ask Br. S.R. to send the other 10#. Rather than write for it, I have hired.[6] You may see him or chance to send very soon.

Your constantly obliged & more loving Aunt
MME.

I hate to intrude on your time. But what is the world doing? Improving? Do the reformers suceed? Persuade Lidian to answer me if you dont. Say not of R T.'s revelations &c.

Has E.H. closed her wanderings?[7] my love to her. Dont forget to send the next Dial   I expect to be reading   Are there any one of athority among the Millerites?

MH: bMS Am 1280.226(916). *Addressed:* R. Waldo Emerson Esq[r]. / Concord / Mass. *Endorsed:* M M E / Dec 1843. *Postmarked:* So. Waterford / Dec[r] 11.

Miltons] Mitons *in MS*

pious] ⟨any moral⟩ ↑ pious ↓

transcends] *probably abbreviation for* transcendentalism

1. RWE's "Woodnotes," *Dial* 1 (Oct. 1840): 242–45, and *Dial* 2 (Oct. 1841): 207–14; probably not a reference to anything in particular (below, she admits that she has not had time to read). For "amaranths," see *Paradise Lost* 3:352–53; for " 'cave . . . throne' " see *Paradise Lost* 6:4–5: "There is a Cave / Within the Mount of God, fast by his Throne"; "ray kindled" may be an allusion to *Paradise Lost* 9:634–37: "as when a wand'ring Fire . . . Kindl'd through agitation to a Flame."

2. MME to EH, 1 Aug. 1843, told how she had "started week before last for Newbury Old Town for sake of Mr Witherton's [Leonard Withington, orthodox minister at Newbury] neighbourhood—found the chamber w'h friends had engaged months before disagreably inhabited, I came here [Newburyport] & the boarding house is under the same block with my antiently formed acquaintance & freind Mrs Tracy whose daily socity is the most agreeable circumstance as yet. Feebleness has prevented renewing any other" (MH: 1142). On 30 Sept. RWE received word from Ann Tracy that the doctor feared MME's present illness could "terminate fatally"; RWE and EH left immediately by train for Newburyport, where they found MME recovering. "Whether she will forgive the Doctor for curing her, seems doubtful" (*L* 3:208), RWE reported. RWE invited MME to Concord before he left on 3 Oct.; EH remained at Newburyport for two more days. MME insisted on returning to Waterford (*L* 3:211).

3. Somewhat misquoted from Sir Walter Scott, *Marmion* 2: xxx.

4. William Miller (1782–1849), founder of an American Adventist or millenarian movement, studied the Scriptures and determined that the end of the world would come in Mar. 1843; later, he revised his prediction to Mar. 1844 and finally predicted 22 Oct. 1844 would be the end (Ahlstrom, 479–80).

5. Archimedes' "Eureka" ("I have found it"—the principle of bouyancy).

6. "I have hired": that is, borrowed at interest.

7. After seeing MME in Oct., EH visited in Boston before returning to Concord for Thanksgiving ("EH L," *SAR* 1984: 253).

1844

To Ralph Waldo Emerson

Jan. 16 Tues. '44

Yes, dear Waldo "the days are (little) gods" coming immmedeately from thier Father & ours![1] yet how many of them in touching our earth instead of strenght receive dingy feeble aspects some robed like harliquins, some habited like gaity or pomp. But this is one with the stole of thought and I bid you God speed thro' the year, and prophesy[n] its joys & ascents   *Thought* includes them all & needs no detail from your celestial demon if he is at hand. In *it* is included (scarsly when it is like a drapery w'h floats to other universes & frames other systems as did the boy at 15)[2] that "law whose characters of fire" are burned into the very essence of the spirit, & need only encouragment to develop, and find in the "spelling" w'h was once made to the world all that it needs without being driven from it's own kingdom within and finding an intire union between the antagonisms of "eating sleeping" & spiritual duties it need not a catholic instruction. Forgive this gurrelity but with my bib & hood of ignorant childhood the snatches of thought fasten me in leading strings &c so closely to much of the revelation, that I am amazed that genius, w'h seems to me the richest symbol embodied of immortality, can be bewildered in doubt (unless a Byrons) of the nature of laws w'h unite us to their Personal Source were there no rev. as naturally, and not transiently, as physical affinities adhere. Still I am worse than garrulous. I fear to write again for you are so severe on an old invalid about "burglary &c". But writing to E.P.P. who sent me a deal of information (for w'h I hunger) to tell her I could not take the three "Presents" w'h contain her "baptist", as each is 37 cents, and I do not use the eye 10 minuits a day often. And the girls dont relish such reading and have little liesure. Can you loan them to me? I may be better.

I did receive both the letters you name—the one about the woods & all fine things I made the basis of my answer on thankgiving day. The first, modesty forbad me to mention. I told the reader never was a cordial more flattering to the sick. But I read it first myself. The last I keep it might encourage less attention to the "duties" (of life) "so called" than they, who expect every day to ascend into the clouds, are willing to give.[3] I stand so worldly in their view that I liked to show them my past bright imajined spots.

Give my love & cordial wishes to yours *Cordial* for I have many happy hours w'h enable me sympathise with the favorites of Heaven & earth. Farewell God bless you my dear Waldo forever & He will. Your affectionate

and gratefull correspondent
MME

MH: bMS Am 1280.226(917). *Addressed:* R. Waldo Emerson Esq[r]. / Concord / Mass. *Postmarked:* BOSTON / MAS. / Jan 21. *Endorsed:* M. M. Emerson/ Jan. 1844.

prophesy] ⟨fain would⟩ prophesy

1. Cf. MME to LJE, 3 Mar. 1844; both letters suggest that MME is responding to an early version of RWE's poem "Days," not published until 1857.

2. Possible allusion to William Cullen Bryant's poem "Thanatopsis," published in the *North American Review* in 1817, but written when Bryant was about sixteen years old; the final two lines read, "Like one who wraps the drapery of his couch / About him, and lies down to pleasant dreams."

3. Neither letter survives; Rusk speculates that the "one about the woods" was similar to RWE to WE[3], 22 Oct. 1843 (*L* 3:218–19). MME's Thanksgiving Day letter is probably that of 7 and 8 Dec. [1843]; allusion to the Millerites.

To LIDIAN JACKSON EMERSON

March 3 Sab. '44

No one "expects the days to be good," says one who walks with some one apollo or Minerva so often

But the theist of S. Clark has the same—for this misterious time & space he calls the mode of divine existence. A glorious apriori ar.[n] And this presence

constituting time who can weary? Never were one in sound health. But now
I like to remember J. Edward's sort of axium that "God could not bring back
the hour between 11 & 12 w'h passed yesterday", when pain & langor have
finished the hour, and spontaneously bless the Auther of time & its' wings.
You, dear Neice, are somtimes feeble in body, and then do not the physical
laws w'h seem so stern, w'h are so universal hide the divine agency? Could we
but see his immediate operation, pain would never be pain. I think too much
with Horace Mann not to suffer.[1] Both err? Happily the moral laws are individual and so ingraved on us that we never doubt their immutable operation
& Agent. Are they identical? Oh no. I think if "P" on Hennell were to commit
a crime he would learn the inefficacy of naturalism.[2] Whatever bright side it
has it never appears effectual to perfect or reform. Its lustre is unquenchable
when light by the torch of rev. And how stronger are the internal wittnesses of
its inspiration when grooved into our uncorrupted convictions of conscience
& how adapted to the dark & infant ages are those points w'h meet the ob-
jector? True, there are difficulties—but how else could we expect in a rev. w'h
comes not plenary? None in its didactic. Monday. I fear my only sunday's
musings appear common cant. But when acquainted with your veiws they met
mine on the great rev. however our sensitive tempers disagreed. Oh, how often
have I repented of my faults at Plymouth. The black bile was in operation
thro' bodily humours. This real seated erriciplous brings its patience, aided
by some Graham diet, perhaps.[3] It was thought best to call a physician from
another Place & he assures me this hard numbness over part of the forehead
& eye lid will remain a year. You must not think of me as blear eyed, but pity
me the loss of it's use, accept now & then. But courage to labour at preven-
tives has never failed, tho' the task is daily tedious of swathing the forehead
& blistering the tempel neck and arm by turns, w'h I only do at expense.
The girls are as attentive to aid *as is possible,* but I must do these things. The
occasional pain is severe, and debility general of so confined a life. I stay[n]
but a few moments below, as there is nothing but Mrs H—'s tight stove & a
cooking one. But my chamber is very pleasant & my wood merchant brings
me excellent fuel. I have often thought of your stronge reliance in affliction
on a *particular* providence   I never had it so clearly, tho' the omnipresence
supplies all, and when *external* circumstances like this winter are very adverse
& confused, the provision for enjoyment is so experienced that the aspect of
the season remains pleasant. A few rich hours, whether from bodily or moral
causes, redeems the 24. And that what is universal must be particular in some
secret manner. But we hear of the miseries & oppressions of the innocent and
are sad. Carlyles "Past &c" pains me beyond any reading. The review of it
(the most I've read at a time) bore me on with interest beyond my strenght. W.
did the sick giant too good a turn for that shabby preface.[4] If I were to read
Car. through I might be wiling the world should be burnt. But I indulge the
brightest hopes that the present commotions will end in glory to God. When
this whole family (who are insane on this subject) insist on its destruction &

expect it daily,[5] I tell them of the multitudes of virtuous & happy ones, of the prosperity of their grand children. But I would care nothing about thier belief, if it were not for the number of arrogant antinomian ignorant lecturers w'h croud the house by ones & twos, & more, annexing the truths of the blessed gospel to this belief and denouncing all others and my formerly intelligent readers are lost to me, relish nothing but these doctrines   Thier singing & preaching has come thro' the doors for ten days past.

Somthing pleasant too, hearing from your "better" Self by Frances Gage is at Springfield, & sends a glowing account of his lecture & her delight. I have been very desirous to see his "life" book. He said I should. I like & love the Jan Dial & regret that but one more is coming. His review of Upham & the book I love.[6] But what I wish Waldo to know that his ingenious description in a letter of not finding what one seeks in other advantages makes an element of his wandering Aunt after health.[7] Alas, how much better & how happy I was before seeking to get rid of the disease in the back of head & the very remedy has placed it before—   I think that the love & gratitude for a home has never failed & hope never to leave it. Nothing will be said of thier millerism for they are all kindness to me. What should you think the cause of this unexpected letter dear L.? Solely to thank you for your most acceptable & handsome presents, w'h I received a month after the date of Nephews short letter, and as I was telling Sarah she must buy me a thin flannel dress if I were taken unconsciously sick.[8] I have asked you many questions w'h my total solitude induces, hoping you will add a still more delicate charity by writing me. I called you at N.P. a transparent character for you were so sincere—but you never show me a ray of it. I cannot ask the estimable daughter & Sister of your house to continue her benefactions in writing for I can never repay E. H. for this or any of her gifts in books &c. May God bless her for her love of the virtues of the dead & her charities to the living. Her last conversation excited an honest pride w'h has rendered me thus independant, or rather it's intentional kindness. My affectionate remembrance to her & parents. Her Wordsworth present lies on my table—for I try to commit lines whenever I can. Tell dear Sister I remember Mrs Grenough[9] as my early friend, possessed of a sound mind, warm heart & open hand. Tell me of your interior & exterior. Mr Haskins goes to Boston today but I hope & trust will not extend his journey to Concord   And that no packet should be given him—tho' he is not insane on Millerism but careless. Farwell. The season finds me not so well—but affc' yours

                                                             MME.
You need not give the last clause of my message to E. if it will be taken ill. I write in haste when I am well. I ride out of late

MH: bMS Am 1280.226(788). *Addressed:* Mrs R Waldo Emerson. / Concord. / Mass. *Postmarked:* So. Waterford / Mar 6. *Endorsed:* M M. E / March 1844.
    apriori ar.] apriori ↑ ar. ↓ (*the latter probably abbreviation for* argument)

stay] ⟨rarely⟩ stay

1. Horace Mann (1796–1859), secretary of the Massachusetts State Board of Education since 1837, married Mary Peabody in 1843; MME's allusion is unidentified.

2. See Theodore Parker's review, "Hennell on the Origin of Christianity," *Dial* 4 (Oct. 1843): 137–65.

3. Probably a reference to MME's first meeting with Lidian in 1835; see *LJE L*, 23–25, and Ellen Tucker Emerson, *Life of Lidian Jackson Emerson*, ed. Delores Bird Carpenter (Boston: Twayne, 1980), 50–51. Cf. reference to her "disorder" in MME to RWE, 7 Dec. [1843]; these are the earliest and most specific references to erysipelas, from which MME suffered for many years. The Reverend Sylvester Graham (1794–1851), inventor of the Graham cracker, advocated a natural health regimen.

4. In Apr. 1843 RWE arranged for the American publication of Carlyle's *Past and Present* (see *L* 3:166, 168–69); in his generally laudatory review of the book in the *Dial* for July 1843, RWE objected to the exaggerated tone of the work, saying that Carlyle "reminds us of a sick giant" (99). MME seems to say that RWE has more than repaid his debt for the preface that Carlyle wrote for the English edition of RWE's first *Essays* (London, 1841).

5. As a result of their conversion to Millerism.

6. RWE lectured at Springfield twice in the first two months of 1844, probably on topics from the New England series (Charvat); probably Thomas C. Upham, *The Principles of the Interior or Hidden Life* (Boston, 1843), reviewed by Charles Lane in *Dial* 4 (Jan. 1844); MME seems to assume that RWE wrote the review. The *Dial* ended with the Apr. 1844 issue.

7. Possibly the letter of 20 and 22 June 1842 (*L* 3:64–66).

8. MME to EH, 25 May 1844, indicates that EH fulfilled MME's request: "The robe you so kindly provided I did not need but since spring came it has been seperated & the outside given where needed & the lining I wear daily in the same form but never could use it when double & it never was finished" (MH: 1144). MME's description of how she is using the robe she received suggests that this is the origin of the "shroud" she is reputed to have worn (in several incarnations) in her later years.

9. Possibly RHE's sister Lydia Haskins Greenough (1763–1840).

To Sarah Sherman Hoar

Waterford   Ap. 23 '44

My dear Mrs Hoar,

Tho' I take the liberty to write on business & tax your wonted benevolence, I address you with many gratefull remembrances—and have preserved your notes and letter with care of long back dates. I wish to know how your Mother was affected in her late years with occasional loss of memory. Elisabeth wrote me 3 years ago (when I was unconscious of what I said or the people present for some hours) that her Granmother was thus at times, & that emetics & blisters were a remedy. Still I wish the account from your self. Did these fits prove fatal to reason memory or life?[n] Did she recover intirely? And what *was* the derangment called?[1] The physicians say here they never meet with it. I was affected, one morning some weeks since, but became after a sleep intirely myself in the afternoon, & after a day of the D^{rs} visits well as before. It seemed to have no connection with the erasippiless, which is as tenacious in its hold on part of the forehead & eyelid as ever except at intervals its lashes of pain are remitted for days almost. and the pleasure of conscious existence with a book, more fresh from the long suspension of reading.

Is Elisabeth at home? My love to her & thanks for her letter, which I hope to answer. But my writing letter days are over almost. And it is the case generally with those who have corresponded often. Whether I write or not—her letters & kindness will always be treasured up in a heart that has loved to dwell on her accomplishments & virtues and the bright and happy influence she had on one so dear to me.

My affectionate regards to Mr Hoar   How is his health? Long may it be preserved to mingle the sacred influence of conservative principles with those of reform w'h promise to raise the down trodden. I dread to look at a newspaper the gloomy prospect of Texas is so discouraging.[2] And I know so little that I prefer the hope of ignorance. And there does seem to arise the light of hope from the very disorder & darkness which prevail.

I hope your sons & daughters are well. May the rich blessings of Heaven be continued to each & all truly desires your

& their affectionate friend
M M Emerson

Love to my Sister & nephew & Niece
I have expected the Dial & more. I promised my[3]

MH: bMS Am 1280.226(1221).

reason . . . life?] reason ↑ memory ↓ or ⟨health⟩ life?

1. MME to EH, 25 May 1844, indicates that she received an answer in a "medical kind of letter from your mother" and found "the situation of your granmother distinct from my expectation" (MH: 1144).

2. A treaty agreeing to the American annexation of Texas, negotiated by Secretary of State John C. Calhoun, was signed on 12 Apr. and submitted to the Senate for approval on 22 Apr., generating fierce debates between pro- and antiannexation parties. Antislavery forces in the Senate defeated the treaty in June.

3. Remainder of letter missing.

To Ralph Waldo Emerson

Vale   August 1. [1844?]

Here I am writing to the very Orator of this auspicious day to congratulate his condition, tho' I did not on the birth of his son.[1] Why these human ties of flesh & blood how soon they corrupt under the sod. And if as many Sages believe, no *individual* soul, what a vapour w'h floats about for a few score of years? While thus swiming & shining there may be now & then an exhibition in w'h some great & little folks will hail you as the happiest of fathers. But where are the Edwards & Charles' & John Sterlings[2] & many of those whom fame & fortune cherished in her capricious nest? But what a "berrying" ground am I planting, when this morning finds me so healthy that without intention I take pen to place myself in the very ground where freedom first struck her noble blow. Yet even there I dont wish my body.[n] Yet I still love my idol muse, tho' she was early wont to stray into riegions untrod by common sense & her twin common morality bred at the celestial gate, and now Madam condescends to tread the humble ground of human emancipation with the most gracefull & fancifull drapery. Shy accomplished artist, akin to thy german defunct—thou laughest, wave like, at the enthusiasm thou kindlest, when under thy farsided wing thou livest superior to the joys & pangs of that divine gift. How else can I believe when I know not that the shrine thou inhabitest has faith in the spiritual existence of this wretched race, w'h he may call, to use his own words on another subject, the "excoria" of the nessecary creating all pervading Principle. I ask no pardon for suspicion, for I am so ignorant of any one of the sides of your interior—*that* given to this day, I've heard nothing of since you canonized Lovejoy as a "martyr"[3] Of the vague deep toned oracles of the said Muse nothing for a long time—am impatient for the *essays*—if they predict any thing of an Abdiel flight from fallen Angels to the clear throne! Oh yes, if the times, w'h some wise writers threaten, when the antagonist powers of evil shall prevail for a time over the good, you shall be found among the faithfull few, bearing a wittness worth a host of common theists, w'h God grant, and that the boy, whose birth & the safty of his truly excellent Mother was cause of immedeate joy (w'h I communicated thro' Waltham) if you be old, may bear your influence on his stronge shoulders of brave youth. His manhood will see better times or promise than ever dawned on this world of woe & guilt I ca'nt but expect—the whirl of agitation—the progress of romanism all prophesy change—& truth & love will finally cover the whole race of redeemed man & slave.

Farewell. I dont *intend* writing, for I get little but common place narration the last of all articles to a recluse so intire in ignorance, tho' blest with somthing of the Ohio senator's monnomanism, who fancies himself in another world.

However, thank G.B.[4] for his kindness in writing and there was some information about forierism tho' coulered by his feelings I thought.

I wish you would let my brother know I dont wish him to send me more cash till I ask, as I may be absent. Can you *soon* & save me writing?

Remember I appreciate his kindness. Love to my Sister, Niece E.H. & George.[5]

Yours in love and no common interest
Aunt MME.

Alas I looked for a splendid day but the winds slept & no broom was found to sweep the clouds   Well nature mourned with this poor slave part of world   May you have aided to wipe her tears. In haste if this dont go now I shall weary of it.

I was *glad* of N.A. & X Ex. long since received.[6] are they mine? And the "Presents" are they to be returned. Not much besides E P P's

MH: bMS Am 1280.226(923). *Addressed:* R Waldo Emerson Esq[r]. / Concord / Mass. *Postmarked:* So Waterford / August 2. *Endorsed:* M M Emerson / Aug 1845.
my body] my⟨self⟩ body

1. On 1 Aug. 1844 RWE delivered the address at Concord's tenth-anniversary celebration of the West Indian Emancipation Act; published on 9 Sept. in Boston and later in England (*L* 3:259), it was reprinted as "Address: Emancipation in the British West Indies" (*W* 11:99–147). Edward Waldo Emerson was born 10 July 1844.

2. Irish author John Sterling (b. 1806), a friend of Carlyle's, died 18 Sept. 1844 of tuberculosis. In 1843 he dedicated *Stratford: A Tragedy* to RWE. MME may be anticipating his death: On 5 Aug. 1844 Carlyle wrote RWE that Sterling had experienced "two successive attacks of spitting of blood" several months earlier and that recovery was not expected, information MME may have learned separately (*The Correspondence of Emerson and Carlyle*, ed. Joseph Slater [New York: Columbia University Press, 1964], 362). Or, her letter may belong to 1845, written on the first anniversary of RWE's address (see n. 1, above). Since MME is not known to have been at Vale in Aug. 1845, I have assigned the letter to 1844.

3. The Reverend Elijah Lovejoy (1802–37), publisher of an abolitionist newspaper in Alton, Ill., was killed by a mob in Nov. 1837; in his journal, RWE wrote, "The brave Lovejoy has given his breast to the bullet for his part and has died when it was better not to live" (*JMN* 5:437), an idea he used in the lecture "Heroism" (first read 24 Jan. 1838).

4. Probably SBR's brother George P. Bradford, who was living at the Emersons' in Apr. and planned to set up a school in Concord (*L* 3:259); a member of the Brook Farm community since 1841, he seems to have answered a question of MME's about Fourierism, a socialist philosophy based on the ideas of Charles Fourier (1772–1837). George Ripley's adoption of Fourierist principles early in 1844 transformed the Brook Farm experiment from a "Transcendentalist picnic into a regimented Phalanx" by Mar. 1845 (*TR*, 469).

5. Possibly EH's brother George Frisbie Hoar, then almost seventeen years old.

6. The *North American Review* and the *Christian Examiner*.

To Lidian Jackson Emerson and Ruth Haskins Emerson

Vale   Oct 30   44

The first thing I read was the address on the 1 of August[1] after my return, and the next to give it wings to some intelligent men & women, whose pleasure, if half equal to mine, was important to afford   Oh it is a capital thing in all veiws—but about England it's concessions exalt the praise & the praise impresses[n] the truths. I know you will sympathise in my enjoyment—say not

a word of this to the Auther, for all his attentions & gifts of books I never
so much as thanked him. "Why?" Why good reason, he treated me just like
a beggar, as I felt strange in being, but a little converse, a few words of light
thrown out as if there was some tie of mind—some hold on the possibility
of continuing patronage in a better state, would have graced the attentions.
But I remember now I dite this complaint by way of telling you that a score
of years for Susan to look at that likeness would not equal the good to me
of half an hours conversation. I went to Waltham unasked & unexpected but
insisted on attentions if withheld I s^d find^n & had the best time ever before.[2]
If not "they should never have had another beggar." You know the fact of this
threat. This note[3] I intended to leave with my Brother—but had only time to
tell him of it & receive a reproof the moments he & Sarah called on me the
eve. before I left Concord. Give it to my Sisters care.

And now my dear Lidian how do you get on with your "little Angels", and
your flower pots & household? Of the second objects, for w'h I gave you a
motherly reproof I will add that your "considering it a duty" is not worthy
of your high minded & sincere principles. To follow your idea of duty, you
must devote your time to study nature and in it's grandeur scenes to lose sight
of minutia (as you are not a botanist in *arranging* merely the coulers) in the
exalting veiws of the whole. By the way (as I will not quarrel with you, unless
from want of somthing to write, now that I understand you better than at our
first acquaintance) did you ever read Jean Pauls "dream of the universe"—?
not DeStale's.[4] It had an awakning effect on my narrow existence as I took it
up in the Hotel. I have wished we had time to have said more as you cannot
write more than a Slave as I see. Well never mind my lonely condition—it
passes—& hope looks over my shoulders. Have "Mama" & E. H. gone their
journey? Farwell. May the Auther of all the blessings w'h crowd arround you
continue His loving kindness prays your affectionate Aunt

MME

How is my good sisters arm?[5] * * * You feel always justly and discreetly and
conduct also better than most of us, *but* let me say you make too much of
trifles. Let us press on to the great realities w'h we so nearly approach. If I
have done or thought fastidiously or proudly towards E. or others, how soon,
if we are immortal, will all be retributed & understood—if not hereafter how
useless our character & affections, joys & ripinings

It would be as useless as difficult to try to give you my point of view in
parting with connections. * * * *Dregy* in one sense, my dear long loved fellow
traveller, is our age, but in many the best & kindest in w'h hope is no delusion
& time no ill. Yet these noisy lecturers do irritate me & their insane ravings
reach my tranquility more than flatters my self sufficiency. I thought them
done with till this night & besides I dislike their visitations on account of the
bread science.[6] Good night. My love to your Sisters, to G. P. B. & the poet &
your protoge his pretty wife.[7]

MM Emerson.

Thank your son W^m when you see or write for Macaulys essays.[8] I was hastening to Portland when I received it & knew that such things are not safe—
to lose in Hotels—so respectfully committed it to that sublime engine in the
wonderous universe, the fire. If you see E P P please say how very devoted to
me was her & hers in attentions. Was glad to have H. Mann there all the time
& went to Macreadys with us[9]

Pity my ears dear L.[10] It is not their arrogance so much in knowing the day
next sat. but^n their ignorance & nonsense. Let any man maintain the wildest
theory with talent & there is somthing to be gained; or if devotional & true
hearted one can bear with them. I wish your other self to send me another copy
of this address when the long looked for essays come. Love to Mrs Brown. I
love to hear C. Farrar's[11] idolising the same writer, he would often visit me as
would the Gages but they fear millerism from the family

                                                        Concord   Oct 15 1844
For value received I promise to pay R Waldo Emerson twenty dollars on
demand with interest

                                                        Mary M. Emerson

MH: bMS Am 1280.226(789). *Addressed:* Mrs R Waldo Emerson / Concord /
Mass. *Postmarked:* Boston / Ms / Nov 4.
   impresses] im⟨bitters⟩ ↑ presses ↓
   attentions . . . find] attentions ↑ if withheld I s^d find ↓
   arrogance . . . but] arrogance ↑ so much ↓ in knowing the day ↑ next sat. ↓ but
   1. See MME to RWE, 1 Aug. [1844], n. 1.
   2. MME visited the Ripleys in Waltham for about a week at the first of Oct.; RWE
to WE³, 4 Oct. 1844, explains he saw her in Roxbury and attempted twice to get
her to come to Concord, "but, as usual, she slipped from them both, &, in a sort of
spite, planted herself at Waltham" (*L* 3:262). SBR's description of MME, 6 Oct. 1844
(quoted in the introduction to part 5, pp. 408–9), dates from this visit.
   3. Reference to the promisory note, "Concord . . . Emerson," written upside down
at the end of the letter.
   4. Title of poem by Jean Paul Richter; de Stael reference unclear.
   5. This portion of the letter is to RHE, who "wrenched her arm & bruised her
forehead" in a fall on the stairs about 7 Oct. (*L* 3:264).
   6. Another reference to the Millerites. A "bread science" is "a science or study
pursued as a means of gaining a livelihood" (*OED*).
   7. George P. Bradford; the poet is probably William Ellery Channing (1818–1901),
nephew of the Unitarian preacher, who married Ellen Fuller in 1841, settled in Concord in 1843, and moved to a house on Lexington Road, near RWE's, in Apr. 1844
(*Days*, 171).
   8. Thomas Babington Macaulay, *Critical and Historical Essays, Contributed to
the "Edinburgh Review,"* 3 vols. (London, 1843).
   9. English actor William Charles Macready ended his 1843–44 American tour with

six performances in Boston between 2 and 14 Oct.; since SBR's letter (see above, n. 2) suggests that MME has just left Waltham after a visit of about a week, MME must have attended Macready's performance of *Hamlet* on 2 Oct. with EPP and EPP's brother-in-law, Horace Mann. Macready's description is interesting: "*Boston*, October 2.— Acted Hamlet in this barn-like stage with church-like audience, better, perhaps, altogether than I ever in my life did! The performance was too good for the place!" (*The Diaries of William Charles Macready*, ed. William Toynbee, 2 vols. [New York, 1912], 2:275–76).

10. Letter to LJE continued following the address on outside.

11. Calvin Farrar (1814–59), son of Josiah and Betsey Farrar of Waterford, graduated from Bowdoin College in 1835. His study of divinity at Harvard was cut short by illness, and he returned to Waterford, where he lived for the rest of his life. He frequently carried letters between Waterford and the Boston-Concord area.

To Christopher Gore Ripley

South Waterford   Nov 11 [1844]

Dear Gore

I send the ingraving, tho' doubtfull of it's acceptableness, as it is has become smoked &c of w'h I was not aware. Alas, too significant of the sullied fame of martial heroism, w'h will pass into oblivion as that emblem of piety, w'h accompanies it. Yet I took care to find a seal w'h I hope will omen your more lasting moral heroism. It is the likeness of La Faette. A gift from Charels C. whom I rejoice to find in your calm self collected manners a happy resemblance. And I hope the interior will be as calm & fixed amid the toils & strife of this whirling world as virtue & peace demand. You joked about the bread & cheese or cash even to me—if you are genuine Bradford & Ripley I suspect not too great a share. Oh no leave that to the vulgar & purse proud and worship at the purer shrine of immortal fame. I love to amuse the unbroken hours of invalidity & solitude by imajaning scenes of beauty and talent, wit & gaity, and lovers assiduities with thier enchantments of mystery and high plumed hopes. Oh 'tis good to forget age & the dolerous ding of newspaper parties and dolefull fears for Country & kind in these resting places. And if the visions pass into the baseless fabricks of such stuff as dreams are made off[1] and the old stage of life has a heavy curtain drawn, why there is a light w'h never fades beyond. And even here I do believe, tho' I know so little of what is promised by the history & observation of past & present, that better times are coming. Providence will progress in finally perfecting that philosophy w'h was revealed personally and is so perfectly adapted to the constitution of mans highest as his present condition. And I will add as many L Ds to your name as I feel warrented to from signs & affection. I dont forget your attentions to me as a boy at Waltham. And your father is my affectionate brother & gardian and your Mother (Heaven bless her & him) how nobly they carry on the duties of life. My visit so unintended so unexpected by me & them how glad I took it.[2] Those noble girls I had almost forgotten them. I went to see Uncle Ripley, for a strange event, and told him about each & all of w'h he was ignorant but probably forgettfull.

And now I should love to have a letter but think you too busy with more important engagements.

Good night. May God bless you with prosperity here if it hinders not your highest   Your aff^t Aunt

MM Emerson

* * *

MH: bMS Am 1280.226(1226). *Addressed:* Mrs. S. A. Ripley / Waltham / Mass. *Postmarked:* Boston / Ms / Nov / [21].

1. Cf. Shakespeare, *Tempest*, 4.1.151–58.

2. CGR graduated from Harvard College in 1841 and then studied law; for MME's visit, see MME to LJE and RHE, 30 Oct. 1844, n. 2.

To Ralph Waldo Emerson

Dec 13 '44   Vale

I have this moment laid down your Essays[1] having but few hours to run thro' them. You can better Judge of the state of mind this excited than I describe. And I somwhat bereft of power to judge and having nothing else to say, save the errand for w'h I write, will copy a line or so of the admiration of our Mountain Rustics notes w'h crowd the margin. "Experience" "What grit what bravery, what piercing eyes. How Jove like, grand & powerfull— He looks & smiles & shines surpassing Jupiter—with a stronge fresh wind sweeps away our cobweb systems & we sail, swim or fly in the immensity of all." Now a sober conservative may sigh over the youths losses, perhaps. Under the chap "Nature" "Relentless, resistless as fate he takes the "wool from the eyes" that custom system & convention has put on. We hardly thank him, tho' he seems loving, human—a man of destiny tho' dear to gods & men—yet delusions are dearly hugged & like one awoke from sleep by his best freind to see the dawn of a golden day & age & "see men as trees walking not clearly"[2]   Under "Poetry"   How grand, true, wise & beautifull—&c— exclaims the gratefull heart in it's Jubilant. But the calm of soul w'h follows is better. In your sympathy & surprise you feel that all compliment is surpurflous—who would compliment Shakespear? Who would dream of so doing to Him who is above naming as above every name? We never compliment an Angel on his divinity. So here R W E is one of the holy ones—a Seer Poet divine yet human. Those who have eyes will see & thank God for this and every "good gift". I have selected this venturing to say that if such be the effect of your writing, dearest Waldo, on many youth—there seems danger in their state of mental irreverence.

Tomorrow I give letters to C. Farrar & the ingraving of Marshall Ney to the care of E.P.P. & that if you send me the essays & any thing immediately

to her he will take them to Portland Stage as he returns not here. Did you
have a letter from me directing your packet to T.W.H.? The man returned &
said T. had left business. w'h I knew not tho' his family did. That you have not
written nor lady Lid after my polite visit[3] is not very flattering— So I owe
you nothing for your hospitable cares and shall come whenever I like without
waiting an invite. How do the Mother wife & children
Good Eve[n]

> Your affectionate Aunt
> MME.

I dont know how long C F may be in City   But well enough to send the
packet to E P P & a letter of information by mail. I regret losing the only
visitor in my young friend—whom I find much improved as a *talker*[4] * * *

MH: bMS Am 1280.226(919). *Addressed:* R. Waldo Emerson Esq[r]. / Concord /
Mass. *Endorsed:* Miss MME / Dec 1844.

Good Eve] I ⟨wish I had more of Jean Paul.⟩ Good Eve
1. *Essays, Second Series*, published in Oct.
2. Cf. Mark 8:24.
3. Perhaps after leaving Waltham (see MME to LJE and RHE, 30 Oct. 1844, n. 2).
4. Probably Calvin Farrar.

1845

To Ralph Waldo Emerson and Ruth Haskins Emerson

[16 Feb. 1845]

Amidst a crowd of spirits from antient & modern schools rose the form of
Plato whose radiant smiles gave due tolerance to many an unfortunate and
perverted shade—but on Ariel his frown was so deadly that his seat was
instantly empty. Good old Socrates never indignant, inquired of his pupil the
cause. The answer implied that as the culprit was destined to exert influence
over mortals he had dared to beseige a sometime favorite of his & somewhat
sucesfully. Besides so outrageous an assault on facts of sense and the innate
elements of reason—in every curve square or circle one part is straight—true
an infinite line can be only real in the Infinite mind who mirrors the universe
or rather is that mirrow. Liebnitz with all the dignity of a mathematician assented—however a partisan of Uriel pointed to the spectre of a monad (for
in that place even such symbols are seen) & L. blushed but still held that the
knowledge of every soul extends to infinity—tho' confused & insisted that
tho' a mirror was no argument for idealism, at w'h Burkley shrunk toward
Plato but was kindly waved. Old Kant streched out of his dark cell & averred
that a straight line was a subjective fact to the Creator & creature & no one
disputed him—and he retired. Plato was preening his wing for a singular

errand and takes the noble S. Clarke in company but first lays aside the blessed enigma of the cross for he had been to a band of mortal souls who emersed in error had not understood its character or dispised, lacking as they blindly tho't the gifts of poetry & philosophy. Now his business was to a very distant world whose inmates were possessed of intellect, in high & low measures, but without moral affections—without love for God or races. They were happy when discovering any new science and some were crying "they found it." But marvelous to tell they knew not the end of all these glittering means nor the Auther to w'h all science leads. What a field for these heireophants! What a paradise were they to open by breathing the name of the Infinite Love & wisdom in to these pure intellects who had no human passions & errors to arrest truths w'h would have demanded now & then a sacrifice. No this in- fusion of knowledge—lifes far dearer than that of Pygmations.[n] Reason had then an endless source to inlarge itself, and affections moral & immortal were developed with large harvest. This a natural reward to Plato, who found them one of the eternal ideas, and to Clarks apriori. As they returned to the Empo- rium they saw poor good natured Hume suspended in a limbo studying his maxim that one proposition was as true as another and sometimes visited by the genius of Paradox to flatter him with the return of some brighter state of heathen myths w'h might be produced by a cercle of atoms. As they passed the abode of Kant Spinoza was there & in one of his mortal returns of partial in- sanity had carried some spiders to amuse Kant by their quarrels, but it did not answer—& their recollections of pantheism were as humbling as corrosive to their immortal knowledge & appetite for happiness—still as they reasoned & lost themselves they were not deprived of that element of soul—hope—but believed that the Voltaires were—but tis possible there is provision for them, tho' they are to be ignorant of it for unknown times. Clark wore a most richly significant ensign of time & Space, w'h he had wisly prepared here, & the airy speculators scowled as he passed, even Kant drew closer into his den. And it is suspected that, however, he might believe in some essentials[n] with the mystics & old Jacob & the sublime Catholics he never sought their society. Long ages may possibly unite all the human race in sympathy.[n] But what vast distinctions in virtue & genius will ever remain. Just then came Milton & as he approached the eagle seemed all his own while Klopstock had the emblem dove   True, a few of the lower plumes of the king were with the nightangale on the eschution of Goethe   But as he still plied the artist (tho' he had sunk every pretention to universal ideas after looking at the emmet sphere he had filled) and had as many sides for XY^n and much the same as when on earth. In discussing his imp^{tn} the sainted Poet was silent—but when a celestial mes- senger arrived to solicit a missionary to the German sceptics that they might enter a state of discipline & instruction among w'h it was suspected Sch. & Richter might be in some secret correspondence Milton & Plato himself grew indignant—the latter as they had used him falsly and the former as not being of the order of those who speed he soon beheld Gabriel and went to wait near the Center. Before the conclave dispersed my humble informant thought he saw signs of favor in Plato for me & that before the lady worm had a certain rich morsel the mystery of the cross w'h included true poetry & philosophy would aid the nightingale songs of his former pupil whose affinities of genius were still related to the converted Sage.

16 Feb.   5 o'k

Dear Waldo,

At receiving your letter I threw the above for an amusement[1] & if I did not get sick of it to make up somthing—but I shant and the wish to pay attention to your mother at this short time induces me to send it.

MME

My dear Ruthy,

The wife & Mother among the most patient & indulgent and beloved, is no more—[2]   An hour since and our sister was released from sin & sorrow amidst the tears of her girls & the prayers & praises of her sons who expect soon to see her in Paridise. They insisted she was never to die & bear the disappointment with real or affected joy. Her sufferings have been severe for 5 weeks. The errasip. attacked & rested on her lungs. It was affecting to wittness the calm but efficient & excellent tendance the girls gave night & day. Would she could have died without the illusions w'h have attended the doctrines of speedy advent.[3] Would she had been able to aid in the restoration of reason & simple X^y. H—h has suffered their monomanism & Moody. God bless you dear Sister and Waldo may reflect on his kindness to this house with pleasure. You have always taken an afft interest in the deceased & will rejoice in her release. Yours in love & *haste*. I did not like you should hear of this before a direct message from your afft Sister

MME

The D^r said on friday she might continue weeks and I feared it but her ills I hope are forever past. She has enjoyed the two last years tho helpless uncommonly. Oh illusion how strange.

This Advent faith singular. Lotte & Ralph attended meeting as usual at Rebeccas while their Mother seemed to be dying in the forenoon—but I said nothing. The husband tarried at home & read his bible very calmly. appears grieved but is rational. Love to E. H. & beg her to loan me last xian Examiner   I have sent to Boston & Portland   the men too busy to get

MH: bMS Am 1280.226(920). *Addressed:* Ralph Waldo Emerson Esqr / Concord / Mass. *Postmarked:* So. Waterford / Feby 17. *Endorsed:* MME / Uriel.
Pygmations] sic; *possibly* Pygmalions *intended*
essentials] ⟨points⟩ ↑ essentials ↓
sympathy] ⟨xianity⟩ ↑ sympathy ↓
X^y] ⟨religion⟩ ↑ X^y ↓
imp^t] *probably abbreviation for* employment

1. No letter from RWE that might have inspired this response survives. (In fact, no letters to MME from RWE survive from 1844–46.)

2. Sister REH.

3. Another reference to the Haskins family's conversion to millenialism, "a doctrine of 'last things,' often based on precise and extremely individualistic interpretations of the apocalyptic books of the Bible, urging Christians to ready themselves and the world for the imminent coming of the Kingdom or Christ's second advent"; after the "Great Disappointment" (when the world did not end, as William Miller had predicted it would, by 22 Oct. 1844), many Millerites became Seventh-Day Adventists (Ahlstrom, 476, 480); but see MME to RWE, 7 Apr. 1845.

To Ralph Waldo Emerson

Vale   Ap. 7   45

I rarely write, & less so, with so little or nothing to say. But if the idea of intruding & insisting on attention rouses me, who have slept so long with indisposition, it will be usefull. I received your essays again & note immedeately, & ought to say the Express was faithfull as he spoke to my Stage friend with anxiety to know if I had not received the former. It did not come till I had written you for them. You will not grudge the trouble of sending the last if you could have seen how happy Hannah was with my giving them to her, She called at Gages ever so late that night to show her gift & I wrote Mrs Gage's name in the other after I was gone. It was a treat Hedge's review & that he said what I had felt when comparing the first & last vol.[1] I have not read all am not able to read much & prefer a brighter time. Why dear Waldo do you direct things to care of Mr Haskins? No need of any name but M.M. &c. But at this time were such a direction left to private conveyance it might never reach here. The name is a by word for fanatiscim & insanity. Not because the H—s believe in an advent, but have assumed the right to instruct families & Chhs with a severity w'h no free man would longer bear—& now they our folks^n say that there is no hope for the sinner, & to my joy, have done praying for me & the wicked world—for shut as many doors as there are & the hobgoblin noises disturb me tho' they kindly make them in kitchen when I am unwell. I dont like to indulge the sense of the ludicrous about them but yesterday they—two or 3 men strangers Sarah 'lotte & Hamlins walked up to Chamberlain's for a meeting, as they passing a good genteel house they fell on their hands & knees ("to humble themselves") and crept along, the sturdy farmer took a hoop & went to beating one of the preachers w'h presented as farcical a scene as could have been in our wilderness. I was tempted to do the same today—   Last eve came 4 stout fellows tho' some lads up stairs to search for this stranger to force him away. I coaxed them to desist, but they would carry him off & he submitted—but alas, at 10 o'k he was set free, & before light he had desecrated our lovely brook by plunging Rebecca & her daughter by way of what they call second baptism the first having taken place some months since. Sarah & lott go to Poland & were again watered.[2] Some of the first farmers (and one intelligent reader who loans me Virgil) went to Chamberlains & broke up their trough w'h had received that immaculate family before the Hamlins could be cleansed. It is wrong & idle in my neighbours to do thus, but the spontaneous disgust w'h made the whipper yesterday speaks well for human nature. I confess I am more pained at the expense of hay & food for they are here so much[n] than many would like to own. If you complain of this tedious page remember I had a whole one from you about T. when you ought to have been skirting the earth & skies to lighten my cell. I am often too anxious for the witts of these dear sensible girls to jest. On the 22 of this month is thier firm expectation of ascent. What a marvelous being is man to what mental diseases liable! Ripley is less wild, but always onesided and very pompous in condemnation—poor fellow is unwell. For every gloomy shade you are to give me a bright picture whether family or else where. How could the mistake happen in your opinion about Adams giving increased interest.[3] Why Bro. S. tells that he is done business & you have my 100. Why then did he S.R[n] pay you the 20? for w'h he is unpaid till the annuity? I'm glad the money in so good hands as yours, but my golden dream about Adams vanished. By the way, ask your good & excellent Mother to destroy the note I sent to her *care*, w'h was the 20#, and say if it be done. I dont wish to leave such memorials behind me. And the extreme forgettfullness of all makes me attentive. Have you Fuller's "Woman." I am longing to see it, & Brownson's review of it.[4] I want somthing exciting—for 'tho I get alive to thought in certain essays I have no courage to take them if I dont feel stronge   Why? Love to Lidian & E.H. I told you she must write me an account of her journey. I hoped she would have visited Mrs Cummin. I am puzzling over B—s Kant. & a deal of things lie on table   The Register does no more for your frieend than before? It noticed an english little book about "spectres & dreams" (the latter of w'h I suffer from) w'h *I do want*.[5] Miss Searle writes me of the improvement you are making in your advancement[n] & say "better & better"   I wonder if your essays would be acceptable to her. She generously gives up Richter tho' given her by a friend. E.P.P. says it may come up. Farwell dear Waldo (I hear of you with increasing interest from Polish Unitarians who swear by "Emersonean philosophy"—)

God bless you forever
MME

They know not that you are no Unitarian

MH: bMS Am 1280.226(922). *Addressed:* R. Waldo Emerson Esq[r]. / Concord / Mass. / O. Hale Esq[r]. *Postmarked:* BOSTON / MASS. / APR 14. *Endorsed:* M M Emerson / Apr. 1845.

they our folks] they ↑ our folks ↓
food . . . much] food ↑ for they are here so much ↓
he S.R] he ↑ S.R ↓

making . . . advancement] making ⟨(in theology I suppose) in your⟩ advancement; in your *probably canceled by mistake*

1. Frederic Henry Hedge, "The Writings of R. W. Emerson," *Christian Examiner* 38 (Jan. 1845): 87–106. Compared with the first *Essays*, the new book was less interesting: "It wants the point and hardiness of the other; the questionable tendencies of the author's mind are more decidedly marked in it, and the peculiar and nameless charm of his rhetoric is less apparent" (88).

2. Poland, E. Poland, W. Poland, and Poland Spring compose a cluster of small Maine towns about twenty miles southeast of Waterford. MME's nieces, Sarah (b. 1816) and Charlotte (b. 1822), the youngest children of sister Rebecca Haskins, seem to have gone to Poland Spring for another baptism. The comment at the end of this letter on RWE's reputation among "Polish Unitarians" probably refers to this community.

3. Abel Adams, a former parishioner of RWE's, who advised RWE and the family on financial matters.

4. S. Margaret Fuller, *Woman in the Nineteenth Century* (1845), was reviewed by F. D. Huntington, *Christian Examiner* 38 (May 1845): 416–17, and *Brownson's Quarterly Review* 2 (Apr. 1845): 249–57.

5. In "Things by Their Right Name," *Christian Register*, 5 Apr. 1845, a reader argues that the principle of "liberty" in a sermon by RWE's boyhood friend William Henry Furness is actually "licence"; the 29 Mar. issue prints a notice of James R. Newhall, *A Lecture on the Occult Sciences: Embracing Some Account of the New England Witchcraft, with an Attempt to Exhibit the Philosophy of Spectre-Seeing, Disease Charming, &c.* (Salem, 1845); MME's calling it "english" is unexplained.

To Ralph Waldo Emerson

Malden   August 18 Monday [1845]

Dear Waldo,

If you are at home do send me 40# as soon as you receive this. I am glad the money is in your hands as I expect to spend it shortly. Pursuit of health (how idle it seems at 70) and destitution of any aid from those Nieces who were so assiduous and received every recompence so gratefully. Both gone Charlotte thro' nessesity and Sarah by the conviction of duty. So I fumbled along for many weeks till the last few days have been at Portland & now indulging a long desired wish of visiting old haunts & reviving old friendships in the Popkin & Dexter family.[1] But my lodgings are too great a distance to walk to either and I am not suitably accomodated but expect intend to stay another week. I wish very much to see you all & if I had found house room sufficent should have immediately requested you and Elisabeth wife & children & Mother (tho' she is perhaps, scarsly rested from her more splendid journey) to visit me & the Brother & Sister at Waltham. I have the ague or irresippalas & ca'nt see to another place nor E P.P. who engaged to return with me or find me at the Vale 1^{t} of Sep. I have not written to her yet nor seen the City tho 12 cents would take me twice every day.

Those who desire to visit the paths of tho'tless innocent childhood should have gained on other roads more than I have if they expect an increase of comfort.

You have not sent me the promised book you spoke of long since. If you ca'nt come send me your Vermont address[2] & every thing to rouse a sluggish state.

Yours affectionately
M M Emerson

* * *

MH: bMS Am 1280.226(924).

1. The visit was not successful: MME to EH, 29 Aug. [1845], speaks of boarding and travel plans, and adds, "I return at 5 to *Malden & leave* as soon as possible for ever. These ugly reflections of long past failures have aided the depression of ill health & after you left the noise returned" (MH: 1146).

2. RWE's address at Middlebury College, 22 July 1845; printed as "The Scholar," W 10:259–89.

To ELIZABETH HOAR AND RALPH WALDO EMERSON

Reading   Sab. 5 Oct [1845]

My dear Eliz.,

Amidst the revival of old & almost forgotten associations of relative affections & their assiduous attentions the most interesting hour was that of locating the place of dear Charles' mortal repose.[1] I had depended on taking the Sexton & going into the Vault or tomb & discovering his well known figure, to w'h William at lenght assented, but he found the former forgettfull Intomber gone to another state—worse the Receptacle closed & sealed. But the last eve. I pressed Mr Leonard into service & we found *Carmine St Chh*. It's every stone told a tale of solemn awe—the stars had come out—the opposite lamps threw their light—and I ascended the stairs behind the Chh to view the mansions of the dead—sure that the dust so dear was there. The lessons it read of past hopes—of high aspirations—of the mede honorable w'h society gave—of the obscurity of that grave cannot be forgotten at the last moments of returning to my own so long expected—so connate with the ignorance of a long & useless life. A sadder & more painfull obscurity attended me in a feebler state of health in visiting dear Edwards. Tho I said to William how glad he was there & how delighted to rest my wearied frame beside him. And I should have rejoiced   But why I can't tell—there was a lonliness & burying to society of all that was so bright w'h left a much more gloomy impression than was natural or expected. Charles may mingle with some dust w'h was animated with great & generous principles. And so may Edwards neighbours have been. And his relatives may join him. How would the anti resurrectionists & the transcendents scorn my old habits of *feeling*—for I believe not or think not rather of literal resucitation

Why Professor Bush[2] should write so much on that subject is unexplained to me. He visited me repeatedly as a psycologist, and I was very much pleased —but regret for his sake and the worlds, that he is bent on Swendenborgianism & giving lectures. This subject took the place of my expected mesmerism (as he could not obtain the practitioner) and we were much acquainted tho' in opposite opinions. That the world (xian) needs a new rev. is absurd & dangerous?? The morning in w'h Louisa brot in W. H. Channing to see me was so interesting as to make a sort of era in my smale circle of living.

Good night—and blessed be thy sleep
MME.

I found Susan *much* as I expected & affectionatly esteem her

Dear Waldo   Thanks for your warm letter. *But* how could you expect me after the breathless messenger of your tuesday one. You have long known the least intimation of yours directs me? I ca'nt say what my little tolly "plans" are for perplexed to know whether to give up the ordination of my cousin Alfred Emersons ordination here w'h is next week *wed* 15 or M Es wedding.[3] If I am not too fatigued by that shall take car for Waltham if you & yours & E.H. can take me that very eve. to Concord?? With gratefull love for the wishes of wife & Mother to see yours truly I love

MME
Monday 6.

Dear E H   If our Poet is not at home please answer soon
in haste I am Stage going
I was right glad to see a new English review of a certain 2*d* Series & Carlyle well reproved for his[4]

MH: bMS Am 1280.226(1147). *Addressed:* Miss Eliz. Hoar / Concord / Massachusetts. *Postmarked:* South Reading / Mass / Oct.
   1. MME to EH, 29 Aug. [1845], Boston, says EPP has proposed a trip to New York (MH: 1146); RWE to WE[3], 10 Sept. 1845, warns his brother that MME is leaving for New York the next day with Christopher Cranch and EPP (*L* 3:302–3), and by 30 Sept. MME was back in New England, writing from Lancaster, Mass. (see below, n. 3). RWE to WE[3], 2 Oct. 1845, congratulates him for MME's having "passed through your house & hands so quietly," without the usual irritations caused by illness and other problems (*L* 3:305). RWE to LJE, 12 May 1836, explains that CCE's body had been temporarily buried in "a tomb of Mr Griswold a friend & connexion of Susan's" (*L* 2:19); MME's location of the burial place suggests the body was never moved to another location, and the Emerson family plot in Sleepy Hollow Cemetery at Concord contains no marker for CCE. "Edwards" below may refer to nephew EBE, buried in Puerto Rico, where he died.
   2. George Bush (1796–1859), ordained in the Presbyterian church in 1825 and professor of Hebrew at New York University from 1831 to 1847, argued against physical resurrection in *Anastasis: or, The Doctrine of the Resurrection of the Body, Rationally*

and Scripturally Considered (1844); in 1845 he published *The Soul; or, An Inquiry into Scriptural Psychology, as Developed by the Use of the Terms, Soul, Spirit, Life, Etc., Viewed in Its Bearings on the Doctrine of the Resurrection*; in Sept. 1845 the *Christian Register* printed at least two long letters from Bush defending his position.

3. Alfred Emerson (1812–97) was a great-grandson of Daniel Emerson (1716–1801), who produced a double-descended line of Emersons by marrying Hannah Emerson, daughter of the Reverend Joseph and Mary Moody Emerson of Malden, MME's grandparents. Alfred was son of the Joseph Emerson who established female seminaries at Byfield and Saugus, Mass., and Wethersfield, Ct., where MME visited him in 1830. Ordained 15 Oct. 1845, Alfred began a pastorate at South Reading, Mass. (now Wakefield); in 1847 he married Martha Eliza Vose of Lancaster. On 16 Oct., niece Mary Emerson Ripley, daughter of SBR and SR, married the Reverend George Frederick Simmons in a ceremony performed by her father at Waltham (*L* 3 : 305). By taking the train, MME managed to attend both events.

4. Possibly the review by [Charles Wicksteed] in *Prospective Review* 1 (2d quarter 1845): 252–63, which states that "Emerson has changed in attitude and tells 'less of men and more of gentlemen,' and Carlyle's prefatory note makes him seem less like a patron and more like a 'Beggar's Boy,' crying for Emerson's justly deserved sixpence" (quoted in Robert E. Burkholder and Joel Myerson, *Ralph Waldo Emerson: An Annotated Secondary Bibliography* [Pittsburgh, Pa.: University of Pittsburgh Press, 1985], 50 [item A269]).

To Ann Sargent Gage, Irene Gage, Phebe Gage, and Hannah Haskins Parsons

[4 Nov. 1845]

This night (No. 4) tho late I cannot sleep & will write you dear abolition friends of this era in my age. Have been to Fanneiul Hall and heard the bursts of eloquence in the cause of freedom & humanity.[1] No party divisions marred the sacred scene. The portraits of the venerable men who procured independence seemed to smile on the assembly. What years past in review— What depths of futurity rose from thier characters & present inheritance in the prescience of that Being whose agents they were. The object of meeting of the convention was to enter a protest against the annexsation w'h is not you know to be sealed till the next Session. Many a bright hope was raised—at least that the bay State will wash thier hands of this gigantic misery. But you will read the papers & the progress of this convention w'h sat at Cambridge repeatedly but E.H. & I was disappointed by weather & now rain & tempest was maugred. I will procure the proceedings and send them. To you dear Girls I *thought* of writing a description of a splendid crowd at a wedding, and of the interesting one of an ordination[2]—but tonight the charms of beauty & the hopes of domestic love—with the relations of pastor & people faded as all transient events & possesions—while the immutable truths of reason & humanity & religion rose in majestive perspective tho surrounded with the clouds of earthly crimes. But these will give way before that Providence whose wheels ("full of eyes")[3] move on in perfect order to bring x[t] over a woe worn world 5 Wednesday This prophetic emblem of Provision particular & universal, is often realised by the humble missionary of Christ, who unknown & unrecorded goes on his toilsome way & sows those seeds w'h bear immortal fruit like the ideal tree of life. Of all the places & folks, I have seen nothing to reveal the charms w'h attend the solitary. And tho' I shall sympathise warmly (dear Girls) in what ever situation you are placed—shall attach no value to any but such as give you to culture one sole idea—moral perfection. And you (dear I Bliss) are for the present fixed.[4] As it is a connection of virtuous affection & esteem—I congratulate you. And that you are delivered from the jargon of gossiping fashionable society congratulate you heartily. Ambition & interested motives may creep in, as the serpent did into innocent Eden— but the good Angels of faith devotion & industry will supplant him. And you will have time to attend the great questions w'h agitate the world and loosen the holds w'h selfish & family interests cling too.

Dear Phebe your butterfly pleased Mrs & M. Dewey so that she copied it. But I was more gratified at EPPs showing Eliz. H. the pages of your Mother as they met her case so dearly.[5] My copy I left at the Vale & in speaking of them to E.H. at Malden found she had read them in Boston.
* * *

Dear Hannah
We have just got a key to green trunk w'h you have packed so kindly. Hoped for a letter from you—but only a note And as you may be weary of long letters I only say that I am at P Bliss Cobb having all attentions. She went yesterday & again today after Waldo Haskins to learn how I could find his father who has moved but he said he knew nothing of Sarah & Charlotte— today he said lotte *was at Lowel.* What does this import? & Sarah was in this City. I wish verily to see them. If they have left Thomas, will one not like to go to Vale? I s[d] prefer tarrying if I had the means. But give yourself no anxiety. Waldo boarded me & the averious scamp made him pay double. Tho' Waldo never named it nor I the scolding I gave the Scamp who was not a Townsman.[6] E Hoar had read my vindication w'h you saw & never a word passed to interrupt the renewal of our affection, w'h increases. She has given me a book for you w'h is titled Margaret written by Rev Mr Judd of Augusta— & makes much stir.[7] Maine scenery beautifully described. I want all fanatics at Reading (if any) to see it—it's piety elevating—it's story romantic. What did you pay for trunk, whose key was lost probably, coming so safely? I hope soon to have a letter. I go home to R.[8] friday should have gone tomorrow but invited to pass the day at Geo. E—s & go to Lyceum eve. Have other invites but wish for *home.* Phebe B. C. sends love to you & to Phebe G. I cant send pay for this by a boy who puts it into box. Adieeu love to A & R & boy
MME

MWA. *Addressed:* Mrs Ann S. Gage / Waterford / Maine. *Postmarked:* BOSTON / MASS / NOV 7.

1. Despite a violent thunderstorm (described as "emblemmatical of the present moral and political aspects of the country!"), more than two thousand people attended the meeting at Faneuil Hall in Boston on 4 Nov. to oppose the admission of Texas as a slave state. Speakers included Charles F. Adams, John G. Palfrey, Charles Sumner, Wendell Phillips, Henry B. Stanton, George S. Hillard, and Walter Henry Channing (*The Liberator*, 7 Nov. 1845).

2. See MME to EH and RWE, 5 and 6 Oct. [1845], n. 3.

3. Ezek. 10:12: "And their whole body, and their backs, and their hands, and their wings, and the wheels were full of eyes round about."

4. Irene Bliss Gage (1824–73), third child of ASG and LG, was engaged to marry Deacon Samuel Warren of Waterford.

5. "M." is Louisa and Orville Dewey's daughter Mary; "the pages of your mother" probably refers to ASG's "The Meditations of a Widow," anonymously published in EPP's *Aesthetic Papers* (1849), 212–13.

6. RWE to WE[3], 29 Oct. 1845, says MME is boarding in Concord at Mr. Goodnow's (*L* 3:310); see also RWE to WE[3], 10 Sept. 1845, where he admits his difficulty in finding her places to board and confesses, "I make private terms with her landladies to smooth her way" (*L* 3:302). Charles Warren Goodnow (1812–56), who was born in Cambridge, Mass., graduated from Amherst College and practiced law in Concord. He was also associated with Concord Academy. In his journal for 1855, RWE told the story of MME's bowing to "Goodnow & his wife at the Lyceum, not quite knowing who they were, (G. had offended her when she boarded with them,) she afterwards went up to Goodnow, & said, 'I did not know who you were, or should never have bowed to you'" (*JMN* 13:456).

7. *Margaret: A Tale of the Real and Ideal, Blight and Bloom, including Sketches of a Place Not before Described, Called Mons Christi* (Boston, 1845), by Sylvester Judd (1813–53), Unitarian minister at Augusta, Maine, since 1840.

8. South Reading.

To Elizabeth Palmer Peabody

Vale Dec 12. 45

Last eve. C. Farrar bro't the 13 letter of E PP—the 12th he took to Rynall Hill the Gages for every one who knew the "distinguished writer" should see *that*.[1] And these alas are all I've seen since you in the very porch or vestibule[n] of the arts began reading one. But I tell them I shall read all in a book. And while they & Hannah are asking about my route with you & of you, I seem deceptive not to tell the whole truth & regret that I went to N Y, as it has lessened your esteem & confidence & caused *perhaps* an unjust resentment in the letter w'h lies by me of whose attempt to severe satire remains for some *impartial* scrutiny. I'll destroy it & beg forgiveness if I ought not to await some more independant mind. Your remark in that more witty satire is just "that smale events & acts are important." Oh *for the future*! But this silence & solitude so tomb like & sacred the far off benefactress appears to me in her wonted charm of benevolent smiles—her visits on board the boat to look after me—her hospitalities—her letters—come over me like beautifull visions that are past & clouds are hovering at moments round them—and Mr Manns supposed anathema "to take care of her purse." [2]

Yet why take time (so doubly inhanced) to name these things when my health predicts a termination to all ills owing to sin or weakness, and every object is gilded with faith in that being who has provided for perfection! Yet to ask how you feel—and whether you desire to be free from your correspondence w'h must ingross some few moments? If I live till the beauties of summer I do depend on your promised visit—it will *rest* & renew strenght & not till then am I willing to part in any respect. My body blenches to the change of climate & the erisipalas returns at intervals in spasms—but so well as to take care of self accept making fire tho' Mr Parsons & Hannah gone for a fortnight & one solitary young man is all that I am certain off. She would have removed her widow Sister [3] & daughter & little boy but I refused, & they are at a few rods distance.

I began with C. F. and his improvement in solitude—his better sense his animated spirit & high minded theories recall me to penitence for naming his outbreaks of vanity in the idle boat. Well did you say "better than him—who conceals his vanity"—   He has been able to appreciate intellectual persons— talks of those I love in Mass. & is one of the most eloquent admirers of your freind Waldo. I hope you will have time to light him   he speaks of seeing you as he is going to Boston for an uncertain time. I verily believe B.R. [4] will scarsly do better were he but in society. Will you please if meeting her, to say my regrets at not being able to call on her? Shall I send Struss & Schelling? [5] I left them with the young priest at Reading [6] at first but finding I was to go thro' Boston to get to N.P. I retook but failed to leave them at Phebe Cobbs. My hand is cold tho' in addition to an open fire I have a smale stove w'h can be moved into chamber by a long funnel. If it is possible Dr Peabody has not seen them he may like to use one in your large rooms in a morning. My affectionate regards to him & Mrs P. whose kindness I remember. Is Simmons preaching? *How?* Sucess? I was partly engaged to tea with them & Mrs Lee came for me that day but I prefered G.B.E.'s & do love him & her [7] tho' the bitter word of yours "capitalist"

Dear E P P

Night! What a blessing—its starry wand exorcises the weary dreary days of winter afternoons—dispels vapoury meannesses, & nothing less than becomes the majestic symbol & forerunner of eternity! Ah there there & then we meet. And can we meet with events more strange & grand, & transforming in that state than that of getting there? It ca'nt be even idealised—yet altogether more transforming and misterious than what we aspire too by the name of death?? This instant a letter from E. H. Bless her   she would foster the lowest shrub if Charles had left it. But alas my watch went to Reading   I shall write by this mail & (if you are willing) direct Rev. Alfred Emerson to bring it to you himself and expect a chance to send for it (I fear) before it gets to you. I hate to worry your door but my Messenger will be unwilling to go to Phebes.? Goodnight

May new blessings & honors attend you

M.M.E

MH: bMS Am 1280.226(1224). *Addressed:* Miss E. P. Peabody / West St. 13 / Boston / Mss. *Postmarked:* So Waterford / Dec 15.

porch or vestibule] ⟨tempel⟩ ↑ porch or vestibule ↓

1. Between 6 Sept. 1845 and 21 Feb. 1846, EPP published a series of twenty "Letters to a Pole on Religion in America" in the *Christian Register*. Letter 12 (29 Nov.) explores American churches in terms of a "triangle" formed by Baptists, Quakers, and Roman Catholics; letter 13 (6 Dec.), a reply to a critical reader, stresses the principle of "mutual independency" and focuses on Roger Williams.

2. Allusion to EPP to MME, 7 Oct. 1845, in which EPP discusses the problem of a letter that was left on a table by her sister Mary Peabody Mann, which MME apparently read. She contrasts what she believes would be Alcott's and Horace Mann's reactions to this event, and then she disagrees with both and substitutes her own view. While Alcott would find this evidence of a "pure & exalted mind," Mann would "tell me to take care of my purse—for a person who would do *that*—would break any commandment of the decalogue" (MWA). MME to EPP or ASG, 11 Oct. 1845, defended herself at length against the charge of "reading *private letters*" (MWA).

3. Rebecca Haskins Hamlin.

4. Possibly EH's friend Belinda Randall (1816–97), although the pronouns are confusing. MME seems to suggest Farrar as a suitor for "B. R." Tilton notes two other women courted by Farrar (*L* 8:126, n. 83); he never married.

5. David Friedrich Strauss, *The Life of Christ*, trans. from the German (New York, 1843); possibly F. W. J. von Schelling, *The Philosophy of Art: An Oration on the Relation between the Plastic Arts and Nature*, trans. A. Johnson (London, 1845), or J. Elliot Cabot's manuscript translation of Schelling's "Essay on Freedom," which RWE kept for a year between Aug. 1845 and 1846, and may have loaned to EPP.

6. Alfred Emerson; see MME to EH and RWE, 5 and 6 Oct. [1845], n. 3.

7. GBE's second wife was Mrs. Mary Rotch Fleming, whom he married in Nov. 1834.

1846

To Elizabeth Hoar

Jan Sab 11. '46

Are you well, dear Elis., that I look in vain for a letter? Are your parents & Caroline? I want to know if E.P.P. means by "*dying to our own ideal*" that of our moral perfection—our struggles after it—our *honesty* in all it's civil & conscientious relations?[1] To this we are ever alive & "complete." Does she

mean self righteousness? That in a bad sense is a truism—but inherently &
vitally demanded. How her letters increase in interest. On this paragraph of
the 16 her language whether mystical or not I dont I guess understand with
this habitual head ache   Had the divine Jesus never risen in his body I could
never believe with Paul that a sincere penitent was yet in sin. Does E P not
dwell tho' eloquently, somewhat in the letter? She offers to explain herself in
a long letter w'h she says is to be copied.

Today I could do nothing but recusitate with you. Last week excited—
(weary now) by being out late 3 nights two of wh with seeing & hearing T.T.
Stone talk one at Irene Bliss Gage's wedding[2]   He prayed once most serenely
wise, tho' not true always, like in calling marriage the holiest &c   How many
earthly passions of nessesity—some lucre (& not now) but often ambitious—
When friendships holier disinterested heaven inspired flame burns pure on
the same alter with devotion. In both the evenings beside his lectures Waldo
was the text book in some of the talk. To hear TTS about him is a serious
feast. To hear the novel history of his own first visit at Boston a pleasure." He
heard T. Parker & came away delighted & speechless for w'h he had grameys
anathema almost. He preached for Gannet and Blagden & Dr Piercie, went to
22^d at Plymouth & told an affecting story in his lecture of their apathy about
slavery—regreted that his host by a previous appointment prevented hearing
Waldo again.[3] He seems, to me, still in a transition state, speculates wide &
I fear a little less than modified conservatism as the mass are not ready.—
but bravely frank—acknowledges his belief in Ghosts visits. He preached for
Hedge & the Swedenbourgs, for the former expelled from the orthodox association, with wh he seems very easy. Some strangers & clergy at wedding
all inwraped, but when he prayed for the perpetuity of the young couples love
I saw the far off scenes of early seperation, and succesive graves & new &,
perhaps, stronger connections.

And now dear Niece, will you impart this letter to your brother Waldo. I
have met him of late on lower grounds in theory thro another & often with the
eloquent enthusiasm of my often visitor Calvin, and accept what you always
possess the warm wishes of MM Emerson

While thus desultory I meant to say how much & warmly Mrs G. Lee
lamented her engagments the morning we called. & not seeing you more when
she came to see me at Phebes & to take me home with her. I expressed pretty
clearly that she seemed not aware of the compliment I paid her in your call. I
love dearly to deal with such folks—how plainly too & they can bear it from
such bodies obscure as I. I was glad I was so pleasantly engaged at G. Emersons, with whom I went to hear H. Hudson on Othello.[4] But what a complete
humbug was the lecture. When H—h Lee asked me if I would not dispense
with the engagement to G E. I said it was preferable. Now why should the
biger folk treat the lesser me to such rudeness?

But I love to treat with them. Miss Gould I passed an hour with in N. P. &
was prevented by { } from another.[5] Mori memento of literary fame. She

deluged me with the publishers at Philadelphia pressing for her fullfillment
& those of Boston if I remember. I have at moments yearned to be interested
by some specific object—absorbed in a poem or novel—and it was good to
fathom at once the narrow limits of capasity & knowledge—may be nothing
excites more complete submission? But how can you tell? But when one comes
near to some auth*eress* the charm of employment vanishes & morbid indifference—stagnation better for even this life. The strange & healthy minded
& bodied have an object to attain—an art within to perfect at w'h all others
tho' they remain to ornament ages bear no comparison in undying zeal &
brightening hope.

Will you answer the subject of my first letter and the two pages w'h I sent
to E.P. to do the errand w'h I wished you to while beliving you in City. My
condition you will like to know improved by Hannah—tho' I tell her the
complete abstraction from this old worn world of the girls—it's poetry &
pictures are wanting to me. And the situation of the farm with Waldo's name
on it will be inhanced.[6]

Love to "Mama" Lidian & your parents. MME

Monday 12   Mr Frost wife & C. S. & the Channings & M M Brooks[7]

What is tho't or said of Bush's lectures? I cant get interested in Swen[m].[8] And
find nothing original in the synopsis. nor in extracts from doc. of resurrection.
Yet love the man & respect him. Did the man who mesmerised the Girl give
me a direction for a galvanic apparatus? If it was from Proffessor B. I think
of sending for it as my head needs somthing.

MH: bMS Am 1280.226(1155). *Addressed:* Miss Elisabeth Hoar / Concord /
C Farrar Esq[r] / to be given to Mr Emerson.

pleasure] (novelty) ↑ pleasure ↓

1. EH's sister-in-law Caroline Hoar; in the sixteenth installment of her "Letters
to a Pole on Religion in America," EPP argued that the Roman Catholic Church was
founded on a doctrine of "passive obedience" but admitted that "they understand one
part of Christianity, which . . . liberal Protestants are too apt to overlook—*the dying
to our own ideal*" (*Christian Register*, 3 Jan. 1846).

2. Irene Bliss Gage married Deacon Samuel Warren of Waterford on 8 Jan. 1846.

3. The Reverend George Washington Blagden (1802–84), pastor of the Evangelical
Church, Brighton, since 1827; possibly the Reverend John Pierce (1773–1849), minister at Brookline; probably a celebration, on 22 Dec., of the landing of the *Mayflower*
pilgrims in Dec. 1620. RWE was lecturing on representative men in Boston.

4. Shakespearean scholar Henry Norman Hudson (1814–86) graduated from
Middlebury College in 1840 and lectured widely on Shakespeare from 1844 to 1848.
He participated in Boston's winter 1845–46 Lyceum series.

5. Poet Hannah Flagg Gould published a series of prose sketches, *Gathered Leaves*,
in 1846.

6. Reference to RWE's mortgage with MME, dated 21 Jan. 1846, for the Elm Vale
farm (Oxford Cty. Registry of Deeds Book 88, p. 173). To settle a claim on the farm
and to extricate herself from Robert Haskins, MME seems to have borrowed $325

from RWE against her mortgage, which he held until the farm was sold. Letters and notes in *L* 3:371–73 and *L* 8:63–66 illuminate this situation.

7. Added at end of letter to list of people to whom she sends love: the Reverend and Mrs. Barzillai Frost, probably Caroline Sturgis, William Ellery and Ellen Fuller Channing (1820–56), who were married in 1841, and Mary Merrick Brooks.

8. Bush became a Swedenborgian in 1845 and began a career as a lecturer. He published *Statement of Reasons for Embracing the Doctrines and Disclosures of Emanuel Swedenborg* in 1846; for his ideas on resurrection, see MME to EH and RWE, 5 and 6 Oct. 1845, n. 2.

To Samuel Ripley

[24? Feb. 1846]

Dear Brother,

I have no one No. of your Edin. Review—have not for some years. You advise my selling.[1] I should like the money if I had only a little while to dispose of it—but I hope to appease Robert H. for his release by keeping it in the P—'s—if he R.ⁿ be not in insane hospital 'twill be a favor. After 5 or 600# in legacies the farm will be divided if I dont linger always between Hannah at her sole disposal & Charlotte and then the others can not be destitute   Imperious duties renders all advice useless—tho' I ca'nt but remember what you wrote last spring after Robert had been with you to take but 1100—no roof tree &c that I had no claim on the cottage land for w'h I had signed. I had before that said I would after I had advertised the place take but the sum 11 I had put in & let Robert pay his debts with the rest & have somthing to live on that is if I sold in two years. I shall be glad of more as the 400 w'h Robert added to the farm in justice belongs to my expenses in boarding here. I write this to you as your Son may read it[2] and I hope to be delivered from writing again on so irksome a business. In haste—farewell

Yours in love
MME

I should like to see the effect of all Gore's influence by reading his part of this letter.

I speake, dear brother, of duties but I have lived here so long I dont care or wish to leave & H—h may have earnt the whole of farm before I am released but Augustus speaks doubtful of remaining, tho' he thinks & calls it a splendid farm & will I beleve

MH: bMS Am 1280.235(26). *Addressed:* C. Gore Ripley Esqʳ / Boston / Mass. *Postmarked:* South Waterford / Feb 25. *Endorsed:* Mary M. Emerson / Feby 25, 1848. he R.] he ↑ R. ↓

1. This brief letter focuses many of MME's concerns about the Elm Vale farm and her relationship with Robert Haskins (see introduction to part 5, pp. 411–14).

2. Letter to SR sent with longer letter to CGR (omitted) in which she asks him to try to explain to her nephew Samuel Moody Haskins the facts concerning his father's "release" of his claim to the farm.

To Ann Sargent Gage

[Feb. 1846]

Dear Ann

Have you learnt the death or rather translation of Elis. Frye?[1] What a light from the prisons—what an alleviator of human woes & converter from guilt has departed! What a humbling lesson has her life taught to the useless & obscure—how deeply impresive now that her labours are finished in this state. Yet a thought—a faith that there is even a purer[n] lot for the most useless & isolated who love God with *one* talent—that may be for ever used & grow in adoration & study of Him—tho' they have done nothing in his cause—but with the heart—the secret care of it. Let the palms & crowns be awarded to the martyrs of virtue—it will be to the unknown to rejoice in the elections of their Father. What a divine gift of everlasting love that "the essence of virtue consists in love of Being universal," says J. Edwards.[2] E. Hoar desires remembrance to you & yours. Speaks as does EPP of C. Farrar being there. E.H. heard our beloved T.T.S. preach for J.F. Clarke. she says as I did that truly he is in the transition state. When preaching should he not be in a positive one? Mr Stringfeild dined here & thinks probably the same said every denomination claimed him. And truely is not x[y] universal in it's morals & piety? I send EPPs letter   Please return it with Ex. as soon as convenient, but more especially your ideas of what you understand from "abstract" &c   That Calvin was a "spirit of reason" revolts—for *pure* reason leads to a God far far otherwise than the modern calvinism![3] Say if my wish to impart my feelings & ask sympathy in my isolated infirm state is tedious and Ill be as silent as the grave to w'h I hasten

MME

Love to Phebe & tell her she will forget all transient ills in the view of Frye

MWA. *Addressed:* Mrs Ann Gage. *Added in pencil:* '47?.

purer] ⟨higher⟩ ↑ purer ↓

1. Elizabeth Gurney Fry, an English Quaker philanthropist and a leading advocate of reform of prisons, hospitals, and treatment of the insane in Britain and Europe, died 12 Oct. 1845. MME to SR, 6 Feb. 1846, begins with business (concerning her will and leases on the farm) and then states, "The respect & reverential love w'h Frye has inspired gives a sermon of humility to me w'h no human eloquence ever did. . . . Such as her bring to sight & sound that world where immortal spirits may expand and be ever employed in arduous & benevolent duties—what is more—far more—in losing even these in the higher & purer exercises of adoration & love to the Source of all" (MH: 225[31]).

2. Somewhat misquoted from Jonathan Edwards, *A Dissertation Concerning True Virtue*, in *Works*, 10 vols. (New York: G. and C. and H. Carville, 1830), 3:94.

3. EPP, "Letters to a Pole on Religion in America," Letter 18, *Christian Register*, 24 Jan. 1846.

To Lidian Jackson Emerson

Ap. 12, Sab P. M. [1846]

My dear Lidian

I am sad that you are not well as E P P & E.H. say—but as the cause (it seems) is other than I expected in my note to you, you will soon be better—as the beauty & warmth of the season increases. And what do you think started like a pleasant light into my thoughts the eve. of thursday last after reading those letters—nothing less than whether this mountain air w'h is novel to you might not be very restorative. And that after you had become well enough to face the north (w'h grows warm by June) you might not come & pass as short or long (longer the better) a time with us. I named it to Hannah next day & she gladly approved. Nothing but change of scene so new would give me courage to invite any one into our desert. And as you expressed a wish w'h I knew to be real, I the more speake. And at this early moment because I *want* to write you—flattering myself that if not surrounded with company &c &c it might amuse you. I have also been so torpid in health that I wish to sympathise & recover it. If sick enough to be excited why there is movement within—but I felt like Miltons description——"genial spirits droop—hopes all flat—nature in all her functions weary of herself"[1] The first thing roused me was the first pages of Wordsworth's 4 book of Excursion w'h I had not recalled for long long. Do you ever get so? No impossible if you have society—but roads bad & uninterrupted solitude gave the old prison & fetters of matter rather more predominace than the spirit was able to conquer—for the head can sustain but little reading in my case. Now & then an hour or two redeems a weary day—& the certainty that this trying season will yield to joyous flowers & green leaves gives quiet to the restless nerves. Now humour my condition by describing yours—tell of the visitations of enthuseasm when all the cares & sickness is but a trifling price for the vistas thro' w'h faith looks at great events—at sure & high modes of existence—   What is more of those times[n] when even hope is not needed—when the soul can wrap itself in the mystic charms of indifference to all present & almost all the future—somthing like the antient hindoo who expected to be so involved in the Infinite as to lose all but consciousness of that all absorbing Presence. "God only I perceive—God only I adore."[2] At such times, if shaded, there is a rich haloo about—and the miseries w'h croud our race seem so limited—so impossible that evil should be ultimate with the revelation of redemption in our hands & hearts—that no other state of mind can be desirable. Would the divine economy render it permanent—but other states—struggles—endurance & "patience more oft the victory of saints" says the Eden bard.[3] Well now say, if apart from that communion w'h is paramont to all beside, does any tho't or feeling have greater power to excite the soul than that expectation of seeing the Bards—who have attached our sympathies with their genius virtue & sufferings—with the splendid martyrs to great virtues of all times in another state? Not that it enters my head that I shall be near or converse but that

Figure 25. Lidian Jackson Emerson (1802–92) with son Edward (1844–1930).

thro' various means and some condescending satelites of theirs I may know of them—possibly see their shekinahs as they pass on some high behest thro' the lower ranks. You dear favored Child of Providence who see so much of genius (& in one is a growing mystery & fabled romance unique[n] to my dim eye) and high bred society cannot altogether sympathise with a solitude from infancy, w'h loves to wander in the reigions where spirits alone exist—and to forget in the value of bare existence it's weary ignorant modes. But rejoice that like Cowpers bobin woman[4] I am not seduced by the tempting forms of new fangled philosophy w'h float on the agitated whirlpools of time to forgo the sober truths w'h natural & revealed religion proclaim with indubitable conviction. And the lonely victims w'h for a time seem threatned with a deluge will emerge with light & love & truths fair ofspring in Gods due time—more hallowed vessels to his glory than if they had not wandered after will of wisps—perhaps!

I send no messages for your own invalid house or walk and ride in this, w'h has beguiled the tedium of afternoon returning from going twice to Chh. A rare thing for me—but the preacher whom I avoid as he never prays for abolition, was absent and I exhorted my rustic friends to attend as the very nature of worship did not depend on its stated preacher and that the time would come when every one could aid in devotion without a priest set apart. These fetters will fall when religion is understood. And I enjoyed the Deacons reading without believing half. God bless you dear Niece and may all who understand you as I do *now* love you as well hopes

MM Emerson

Be full of courage & you'll get well all the sooner & use your talents & virtues to constant high ends as ever. If E. H. knows of this letter give her the note.

MH: bMS Am 1280.226(790). *Addressed:* Mrs R. Waldo Emerson / Concord / Mass. *Postmarked:* So Waterford / April 13th. *Added in pencil:* 1850.

times] ⟨sad⟩ times

romance unique] ⟨romance⟩ ↑ unique ↓ ; *series of dots, meaning "stet," added below* romance, *possibly by MME*

1. Milton, *Samson Agonistes*, lines 549–96.

2. See MME to RWE, 26 June 1822, n. 6.

3. Possible allusion to Milton, *Paradise Lost* 9:31–33: "the better fortitude / Of patience and Heroic Martyrdom / Unsung."

4. See William Cowper, *Truth*, in *The Complete Poetical Works*, 2 vols. (1854): "Yon cottager, who weaves at her own door / Pillow and bobbins all her little store; Content though mean, and cheerful if not gay" (1:68). Cowper praises this "happy peasant," whom he contrasts with the "unhappy bard" whose reward is mere "tinsel" compared with the truth she learns from her Bible.

To Elizabeth Hoar

Elm Vale   June 12 '46

Last eve. I had your welcome letter—but I am not going to send this while so many are calling either with admiring or envious eye—with friendships spirit or its feint. But write I will—for as you are the only tie w'h acquaints me with the sympathies of life and it's varied dark and bright aspects (for many weeks as I have answered no other letters) w'h awaken interests beyond old tiresome self. It was one of my frequent wakefull nights & I wanted more particulars. * * * You noticed not *how* I should delight to see you here for *my* visitor were there any thing to intice but benevolence to me. * * * But what would the stern mountain & lake and all our wild roses w'h now crowd the windows be after New Haven with its' genius' & honorables? Write, if they permit, all about what you see & *hear* on the very spot. Waldo "an Angel" but you do any thing to"—&c   No one of body has "the species" of w'h he so often illustrates. One would think him a mahemedon from his "sense of soul" w'h they term of smells the best. Ah, dear beloved Youth—thy soul can never be sattisfied while tossed on the sea of speculation away from the center—and never may it—there alone the home of genius beauty & every form of virtue.

Thanks for the opinion of my ever respected friend and that it is what I believed the case an unjust war—tho' we suffer more for the murdered.[1] What does he think the issue? We have party papers as perhaps, all political ones are, and I could judge nothing who were aggressors. I can fear nothing for old grey self—but the expenditures of the Country and its corruptions is most painfull. You young folks will outgrow them—& I hope reap the fruits w'h may be bro't forth from the tempest and carnage by His Hand whose alchemy educes good from evil. How calm & self possessed old Goethe was in the midst of human misery. It might aid his artistic pallet w'h dwelt on the material from w'h alone he wro't (I think in ignorance) whatever was near to the spiritual beauty—for the innermost spirit as metaphysician he never comprehended. He surely may be allowed to be a fine representation of this world as an ultimate abode. No saturn presided over his birth nor did Virgils star. How came T T Stone into mind? I did not forget that you wrote of hearing his eve. lecture but he preached at Chh after noon for his acquaintance

I should like to welcome my brother to my native house of w'h you write as "graced".[2] I believe it. But the memory of a solitary recalls the idolised idea of my father whose devotion to family, freinds & Country would dignify a hovel—whose memory early gave a gloom to that beautifull spot—and latter associations give many a sadness—with long orphaned struggles. Would Waldo could have had that house w'h his grandfather built and renders sacred to my old school faith & affections. When Sarah was married nothing pleased me so much as her being the future head of that place but antagonisms of opinion & long absences have effaced her worshiped (almost) ideal. May they live to honor God and enlighten the ignorant. It makes Waldo happier their presence? I conjectured my brother grew old—in memory &c?? Let this letter aid the persian god *immediately*. The only place I could send it where you are alone as respects inquiries. Possibly they are (or he rather) chilled by my not acknowledging[n] any pleasure or gratitude for Gores professional services w'h have added to my property, perhaps, but he was Waldos agent,[n] and I felt no sattisfaction in the business as I know not the effect the relinquishment[n] w'h Mr Robert H. made of his part of my farm will have on him, till he returns. I knew nothing of it till done and I believe my right legal surely, and as surely moral established. The cause of Waldos buying[n] of an execution from us obtained Mr H—s release.[3]

Well I meant only a short letter & only see it—well you can burn without reading and I must seal this very eve. and send it to office while I am well. God bless you in every place & return you to dwell with renewed health in dear old Concord till brighter stars shine on the earth.

Your aff[t] Aunt who hopes to meet you in a higher world where her faults will never annoy any—or lessen my capasity to estimate

MM Emerson

MH: bMS Am 1280.226(1159). *Addressed:* Miss Elisabeth Hoar / Care of Hon. R. S. Baldwin / New Haven / Conn. *Postmarked:* Waterford Me / June 17.
chilled . . . acknowledging] chilled by ⟨a letter I⟩ ↑ my not ↓ acknowledging
agent,] ⟨employer⟩ ↑ agent ↓ ,
relinquishment] ⟨fancied⟩ relinquishment
buying] *possibly* levying (*T*)
1. On 12 May 1846 the U.S. Congress declared war on Mexico.
2. SR and SBR moved to the Concord Manse in Apr. 1846.
3. See MME to EH, 11 and 12 Jan. 1846, n. 6.

To Daniel Appleton White

South Waterford   June 28 [1846]

Will Judge White permit an old and gratefull friend to remind him of her continued interest in all places and instructions of w'h I hear by the Register? This paper interests me more since I learnt somthing of the Editors character from you years since.[1] And from this, and *thro' you* I venture to send the inclosed[2] that if he has a vacant page it might go in if you like it. It was written more than 15 years perhaps lost & found some days since. If it has a smack of imitating Festus, whose few pages disgusted me of dialogue, pray return or burn it.[3] I have heard of you a moment at Chh when T.T. Stone preached who hurried home, and no time to ask after Mrs White or Mary. I hope & trust they are enjoying the blessings w'h surround them. It was as unexpected as pleasant to learn that you are to have Mr S. as minister.[4] Surely his unique simplicity and beauty of genius and character will gratify you. And when I heard of it I said, to his admiring friend, that it was an important motive to wish him there as your influence must & would be nessecary to one who was born & lived in complete solitude till he went to M., & there probably. How he will appear if called to trials is uncertain. I love him & his anti slavery. I could desire your opinions of the times w'h appear to my ignorance very sad & dubious—(not dubious as they respect this *cruel* & *unjust* war on part of our odious goverment) but cannot expect you to take time from higher obligations. The sentiments you expressed at Concord—with our excellent friend Mr Hoar were what I should have expected. Elisabeth (my constant correspondent) felt sad as she related the conversation. My other friends appear by their letters to be too easy—for patriotism. I *regreted* not meeting your son,[5] who was hoped to dine with the Deweys while I was there last Autumn. I made a parting visit as well as the first to New York, as the errisiplas of w'h my last Sister died prevents much use of books or usual health— A release how desirable—tho' I find when health returns occasionally that this age is the happiest as the safest period. Did you ever hear your son speake of Henry Hudson of N.P. who graduated in '43?[6] I saw him repeatedly that year at N P & admired. Of late his Sister wrote me he was unwell & I wrote him begging him to try our mountain air & see my beautifull farm, but he is engaged to Walpole. I know nothing of him but by his family. But as E. Peabody is going to pass some time here in august it might have been pleasant. I put my signature but if improper erase it should you find any paper to tolerate the fragment.

Farewell dear friends and may God continue to bless you all forever & ever

M.M. Emerson

If it needs copying I trust Mrs Frost goodness

MH-AH. *Addressed (in another hand):* Hon. D. A. White, / Salem, / Mass. *Postmarked:* Waterford Me / June 29. *Endorsed:* Mary M. Emerson / June 28th 1846 / Ans^d. Jan 28 '47.

1. The Reverend John Hopkins Morrison (1808–96) edited the *Christian Register* from 1846 to 1851.

2. MME probably sent DAW her imaginary "Meeting of Two Friends after Long Separation by Death" ("from a fragment of 1830"), printed in the *Portland Register*, 27 June 1846, and again in the *Christian Register*, 22 Aug. 1846.

3. First published in 1839, *Festus*, by English poet Philip James Bailey, is a gigantic poem (some forty thousand lines in later editions), "semi-dramatic" in form, "a succession of fifty-two scenes in which Festus, Lucifer, and other characters engage in colloquies" (*Literary History of England*, ed. Albert C. Baugh, 2d ed. [New York: Appleton Century Crofts, 1967], 1406). MME's "Meeting" is a dialogue between two speakers designated "A." and "B."

4. Ruth Hurd Rogers became DAW's third wife in 1824. In the summer of 1846, T. T. Stone became minister of the Unitarian Church, Salem. His first pastorate was at East Machias, Maine ("M.," below). MME to DAW, 16 Sept. 1847, asks about a report she has heard that Stone was " 'tedious—that he preached 50 minutes without notes and had many repetitions' " (MH-AH).

5. William Orne White (1821–1911) received his B.A. at Harvard in 1840 and completed his studies at Harvard Divinity School in 1845; he was the son of DAW and his second wife, Eliza Orne Wetmore. In the spring of 1845 he introduced RWE to his future biographer and literary executor, James Elliot Cabot.

6. Henry James Hudson of Newburyport (1821–1901) graduated from Harvard College in 1843 and from Harvard Divinity School in 1847. Restricted in his ministry by ill health, he became active in the kindergarten and antislavery movements.

To ELIZABETH HOAR

[1846]

Do analyze EPP character w'h I never heard—nor any remarks about her   As it was known how I valued her. Is she to be *relied in statments*? Her business & crowded life I believe to have bereft her (if *ever possessed*) of clear & sensitive perceptions of truth—of understanding and honest character. She appeared wholly distinct to what I had tho't most of my acquaintance with her.[1] Seemed as I told her from her swarm of intimates &c to have lived an age. Flatters? courtier? And who wants to be one of 500? I saw her but little it is true—but that tedious   I was glad to have her so busy in writing 30 pages for publick. Chh organisations most interesting to me & letters to Kraitsir[2] & Farrar finally and to the whole family. True she offered to read to me but I could not interrupt her fun or rides & twice she read an hour or two but was indifferent to my old unitarianism &c &c   Bro't a large machine full of letters from the great & good & read them here & to Gages, whom she captivated & Hannah[n]   I was severe on her for reading such praises, & she bore it well enough. How is it that D[r] Channing & no one that I know regreted her "not being able to find food in a unitarian Chh"? She seems simple & kind—but leavened into others? Observes no sabbath—expresses no devotion yet writes with theological acuteness & athority? God bless her and we may understand each other better in another state.

Can one with mind & heart grooved into religion not feed any where & on mast that nature genius & different religions makes? I was offended at her account of certain unitarian ministers "writing to Parker with approbation &c &c & then when he came out they rejected him"   I disputed conduct w'h she represented so odious. She said she was staying at his house & saw the letters. What a deplorable account. She concealed the names   She has since broken with Parker if I remember thro' the evil influences of Brownson. & with W. Green who sent her an impudent letter. With Allcott a sad long account. He undoubtedly to blame most   But I write her that I never knew a quarrel where either was perfect—nor a separation but one & that was all my fault because I believed & do still (were it not for Charles) that I weary you. Oh this itching of errispalas crawling over my body of late. E P. appears *prodigious* to me in information in theology &c &c   What to you & others? I tho't curious to pry into family affections & views   And however always

avoided confidence in speaking except my personal opinions till last summer
felt safe in Waldos character   I took the blame of my promise.

Private for Eliz. Hoar. No other eye unless Waldo or L. should see you open
the letter & no secrets from them.

Your loving Aunt

The letter they may see if it so likes

MH: bMS Am 1280.226(1163).
captivated & Hannah] captivated ↑ & Hannah ↓
    1. In another letter, MME to EH, 14 Aug. [1846], Vale, written during EPP's first
visit to Waterford, MME says, "Miss P. busy in writing. I am glad of it as she must
rely on herself for society. In my best days can illy support it long at a time—restless
like the eel out of it's element. She was desired & very welcome— She walks & rides
and loves to be with Hannah in or out of the Lake, and the Gages are much excited &
pleased by the unremitting flow of information w'h is as novel as valuable to them, &
Hannah" (MH: 1160).
    2. Charles Kraitsir (1804–60), Hungarian philologist and political exile, in whose
school for boys EPP taught in 1845.

To Elizabeth Hoar

[1846]

    Aye, & is this indeed "calvinistic conversion"—a Specie of extravagance?
"May *I* unblamed" state opposites? Truly it is painfull to differ in case of
the only woman I rest on to lighten what some heathen called "age dark &
unlovely"—(surely to me) unlovable to society. *I should not have pretended*
"ignorance of her"[1]   How could I know one whom I only saw in company
almost wholly with Croud & those it was proper to please. I always believed
her without that earnest & delicate dignity (w'h one of her Praisers posseses)
& never trusted her with a secret or even to trade as Waldo said somthing of
her extreme carelessness   As to her "beneficence" the go betweens for sub-
scriptions are many busy old maids. Never heard a tone of commiseration for
the Lanes of guilt &c &c   As to *objective* when she took the chair here &
at others she was completely *subjective,* among the interesting artists of all
kinds her intimacy was observed[n] & even to Calvin F the story of her poor
(lunatic some what) lover[2] & another of which I had never heard   In "bestowing" "the crown of glory" is secretly increased? But if "unconscious of
exaggeration" what reliance? That she has wantonly attacked me falsly in the
letter I showed you is certain. Waldo is a nonresitant[n] to all *externals* of the
kind   had the gaurdian CC been here, I should have sent the answer, & saved
much sincerity, I *forgot* her abuse & was desirous of her visit not knowing till
she returned that the Wards[3] had invited her there. With that & after letters
to Mrs G. & C F. I deny that "she never deserved ill of any one." Why did
Green write her what she calls impudent & others w'hom she terms "devil-

ish"? That her smile & meddlesom kindness is certain & that she was born with good feelings w'h still live—but her trials & business have weakened the basis of virtue—*truth* if were inbred? I differ in regard to her talents with you & the Fuller who must be better Judges I am *sure*. Margaret said "she was good" & said no more. Her analysations of literature eccl. & phil. seem to my very limited views (& *you know* I speake honestly) bespeake an "original" genius tho' when writing^n the defects of Channing & Waldo I shrunk. Her comprehension in gaining so *much*, & the manuals of determining as she told us in childhood of knowing every thing gives me vast cause for envy if it is?? Her poetic descriptions are enviable to any one who loves the world as I *should* have done. And all these & late conversion to higher faith I was anxious to have her known to Gages & Hannah hoping that as they are destitute of society & religious means apart from Mrs Gage that she was to have given a new & holier impulse to them. But finding that it was the result of amusing poetry & conversation disliked, & prying into their relations & opinions with me, was not superior but most nervously irritable at the last. I made the most penitent confession in a letter, but she dont forgive by Farrar's letter w'h came partly written here & at Boston. In all to Hannah she exaggerates— rather creates my little capasity to a size w'h discourages if any thing could.* As to finding no food in unit^s.^n you do make an ingenious *cover* but I who never know nor talk of sects can be fed with crumbs every where. tho' I rarely enter a Chh for reasons of deseased head &c &c   If I were to see however tiresome her manners I should *forget* her injustice for my devoutest prayers attend her. Ask your Father what Lavater means by saying that he who forgives a tresspass of sentiment is as blamable as the transgressor.[4] I have not the book but this is a copy

*one so alone from infancy

MH: bMS Am 1280.226(1164).
observed] ⟨prominent⟩ ↑ observed ↓
nonresitant] sic *in MS; possibly* nonresistant *or* nonresident *intended*
writing] ⟨showing⟩ ↑ writing ↓
unit^s.] *abbreviation for* Unitarianism
　1. This undated fragment may be a response to EH's reply to MME's request, in the preceding letter, for an analysis of EPP's character.
　2. Possible reference to Dr. Charles Kraitsir (see preceding letter, n. 2). EPP to ASG, 15 Feb. 1849, describes at length the "whole truth about the Dr's [insane] wife" (MWA).
　3. Samuel Gray Ward (1817–1907) and Anna Barker (1813–1900) married in 1840.
　4. Johann Casper Lavater, *Aphorisms on Man* (1788).

1847

To Elizabeth Hoar

Vale   March 19 Eve   [1847]

"What Aunt here again? Did I not say I would write soon"? * * * And in relooking over the Mosses[1] w'h did not please much—the second part better. But in the first the old Manse (w'h by the way he makes very free with & its good old books w'h descended from my ancestors) he expresses (you may remember) a strange interest in the tradition of a boys killing, or finishing, one of those british soldiers. Nothing can be less true & if when the books return you will be so kind as to read the counter evidences w'h I inclosed & contradict H—'s whim I will be glad. His imajanation is very fertile & entertaining. What interests me is the "Apple man" so much that I want to know who he is as probably it is your nieghbouring object.[n] Your father or my brother may know him & his family. I suspect H. may have not reached the bottom of the sigh & folded arms. Why not some deep grief? Or why not "the divine idea" of the world w'h Fitche describes as rendering all transient interests useless? True, the slight anxiety with he so carefully eyes the apples & replaces a sale looks against my notion. And H. closes so piously the character that we lose sight of sadness, but not my curiosity. How much superior was the silence of the lorn man than cricket[n] alertness—   And one (whom I need not name) reminds me of the large class of those whom even you speake off as being happy. He came in one day after being arrested in the street by Dr Pierce with some local historical inquiry, and said "he could not think of any subject that good D[r] could lay hold on in the spirit world." How often that saying with it's *manner* occurs. And may there not be large classes in that pure world who may live on external influence without the power of inner?? And how many Hastings[2] crowd the bright banquets that are *called* happy, to whose eye nations & individuals affect but as flickering images   Since writing the above I read with zest "the celestial rail road" except the caricature of transcendentism.[n] At seeing the title when they first came supposed it some jest, and Farrar took them. Do tell me about Hawthorne. If F. cant take all my packet I'll keep these as finding some tedious threw by the things. Next summer when *I do* expect to see you W. & L. you can take them. How you keep telling of portraits & minitures my dear E. No wonder Sarah's was imperfect   She can never look, *so look,* as in the first. Grey hairs no ornament on canvass.[3] Tell me that yours is taken and I will congratulate your present & future connections. It is passing strange that they do not insist on your consent. Forty years hence & beauty of woman has not it's appropriate expression. True, the aged hero of high order is an improvement on youth, and every furrow bears the stamp of being worn in others service. If nothing more have a miniture & then it can visit me. I know you will feel that the best charm is wanting[—]that of the eyes of one who *loved.*

Figure 26. Sarah Bradford Ripley (1793–1867), in a crayon portrait by
Seth Wells Cheney, about 1846. Courtesy Concord Free Public Library.

About your head—it grieves me—the more as I believe it may be cured by care in youth.

There are great & real cures for heads like yours in hydropathy. The former partner of Mr Parsons[4] left farming thro' eyrisipalas—humour in head w'h a german Dr said was *not* ey. but has almost cured him by the sweating process & after dry blankets a cold bathing   He was here lately & continued the remydy. Farewell dear E. I wrote last eve. & today in haste but you can spell it out. I have to write by the same mail to my friend Ann T.

Yours aff[t] as Aunt friend &cc
MME

20 Sat.   Pardon the trouble (w'h you need not take) of spelling out more than the errand. My head very troublesome & could do nothing but write to forget the idleness of living

MH: bMS Am 1280.226(1169). *Addressed:* Miss Elisabeth Hoar / if absent Mrs Waldo Emerson / Concord / Mass. *Postmarked:* So. Waterford Me / March 22.

object *possibly* despot; depot *in T*

cricket] ⟨the critic⟩ ↑ cricket ↓

road" . . . transcendentism] road" ↑ except . . . transcendentism ↓

1. Nathaniel Hawthorne's *Mosses from an Old Manse*, published in 1846.

2. Warren Hastings (1732–1818), first governor general of British India (1774–84); on his return to England he was charged by Edmund Burke with high crimes and impeached (1787), but he was acquitted in 1795.

3. The crayon portrait by Seth Wells Cheney (1810–56), made about 1846, now in the Old Manse (figure 26).

4. Hannah's husband, Augustus Parsons.

To Ralph Waldo Emerson

On the 21 of March '47 at ½ past 11 'k night I on a lowly seat before the racking up fire ask Waldo dear to pardon my persumption in penciling the "Destination" now & then a sentence of Fitche's.[1] I knew it could be rubed out by my Sister in her liesure hour. It is well you know of it as you may loan it. Many thanks for the two smale books of his   Much excitment at some great tho'ts tho' mystically expressed the meaning applies to the simpel. And his faith (from idealism?) is good. if I comprehend it with my incapasity of head to apply. Happy soul to have escaped & gone where he will find somthing to rely on & derive from beside poor "one sided human nature." If my friend Lidian should still remember to ask after poor Aunt & wonder at my letters often being dated near midnight say I am better then. half the day taken up often in getting alive this curdling season

God bless you says
MME

There is no prospect (as there was) of a water establishment to increase the value of the land as yet. Expect to send your books tomorrow to Boston West St.[2]

MH: bMS Am 1280.226(931). *Addressed:* Mr R W Emerson / C Farrar Esqr. *Endorsed:* M M Emerson / March 1847.

1. Johann Gottlieb Fichte, *The Destination of Man*, trans. Mrs. Percy Sinnett (London, 1846). Fichte's *On the Nature of the Scholar and Its Manifestations*, trans. William Smith (London, 1845), is in RWE's library (Walter Harding, *Emerson's Library* [Charlottesville: University Press of Va., 1967]).

2. Location of EPP's bookstore. For the watercure, see MME to RWE, 17 July [1847], n. 3.

To Ralph Waldo Emerson

Vale   July 17 Sat. [1847]

Dear Waldo,

I was pleased with your letter—apoligies for silence however unaceptable to the higher folks—to me was even flattering—that attention w'h is constrained is welcome to the solitary. It may be that all notice is to one who is positively content with an unloved & unloveable destiny. But the fact that you expect to go to England was good & is good. Strange as it is that my opinion did not send you there before. Health not the least motive, will be all the firmer. And you have lectured enough for your best friends in the Yankee world, who are not so well prepared for novelties. Could you go commissioned with thundering terrors to that goverment about these slavery plans to supply the west indies! I never suspected them of the crime till the 12 of June's Register.[1] And another thought as I have read more of your works lately   I wish that you could get into Miltons old room & blind yourself to all but real poetry w'h would lead you to the Center of all truth just, almost, as in the revelations, not as the Poet viewed them—only to think of his materilasm! Now how it is possible for a mind represented as his (besides poetry) could exist—even in his age & not go before it in phylosophy? You will pity my perplexity at what may appear no problem to you. *Well*   You may pity my ignorance & be offended too for I said to Mrs Gage & Miss Pea. that if you were blind & fixed in good faith you could write "Paridise Lost" and avoid the wearisome parts. Blind I mean shut up in yourself & alone with that Muse who like Plato smiled high promise on your dawn. The "poems" have led me to think of their defects and the injustice you have done to the unique lady above named.[2] And to compare what I knew of the sainted benefactor to *poetry*. Now for the cause of this letter—wh was br'ot forth day before yesterday at Mrs G—s with Miss Pea. whom I beleive knows somthing of every thing ("without that under laid character the largest part of whose power is talent") and whose malformation of w'h Dr Bush says "thier is nessisity of lying." So I asked her if the water bath would not be good for our Lidian adding all that value for her high principles & *truth*fullness w'h I always bore Miss Pea. in some form or other. She said it would kill or cure then I revolted at the experiment. However, commissioned her to consult with Dr K[3] & if favorable urge it on you. I afterwards dined with a friend from Dorchester

Figure 27. The stagecoach arrives at the Lake House, South Waterford, location of the watercure. Courtesy L. Elizabeth Lord, Bethel, Maine.

and was certain that L. could not board there. And the Lady complained of bread often. And L. must be with the Doctor. In common cases he visits. And could she be with me it would *delight*. But our market famished and help none. Now here comes the cause of my injunctions—"old maidish timid smale"— Well! It is well with me. But should you see or communicate with Pea. say not a word of the diet or any thing w'h she can model into an accusation to K or C. F. who provides the table for it would be inconsistent with my pleasant reception of their attentions. And it certain she has injured me with Gage's & Hannah by prying into our relations owing I hope not to malice at first, but a desire to know every thing. Besides when I met Dr K. in going to dine I named Lidians coming with her character. "And he said too high he had common folks" And he was crowded sometimes & knew nothing when he was to change one set for another. I have taken leave of Pea.[4] I hope & should not name bread nor any thing to Gages[n] tho' Hannah has unfortunately done it that very eve. "Now how idle & persuming that Aunt should beleive we dont know every thing about the water cure & have the best advise and there is North Hampton & Brattleborogh" Well I am ashamed of the whole commission but I wanted if L. went any where it be here. And would not have Pea. know of my alteration or its *cause*. If you can read without any scorn let me know how Pea. manages she goes[n] Monday. MME. *Write soon*

MH: bMS Am 1280.226(933). *Addressed:* R. Waldo Emerson Esq[r]. / If absent Mrs R. W. Emerson / Concord / Mass. *Postmarked:* So Waterford / July 19th. *Endorsed:* M M Emerson / July 1847.

Gages] *illegible; possibly* her (T)

goes] goes ⟨I hope⟩

1. "Reinstitution of the African Slave Trade by the British Government," *Christian Register*, 12 June 1847.

2. Reference to RWE's *Poems* (published late in 1846); the "lady" is probably the muse, but possibly an allusion to RWE's failure to appreciate the poetry of ASG.

3. Calvin Farrar was so pleased with the "water cure" he experienced at Brattleboro, Vt., that in 1847 he established his own "hydropathic institution" at Waterford and persuaded Dr. Edward A. Kittredge of Lynn, Mass., to join him.

4. Several letters written by MME and by EPP in 1846 and 1847 suggest reasons for this rupture in their friendship, probably during EPP's second trip to Waterford in 1847. EPP, in particular, describes MME's irrational requests and sudden changes of mind as well as her irritation and jealousies, demanding nature, and failure to understand EPP's religious views. At the end of one undated letter (Apr.? 1847?) to Frances Gage, she writes, "Miss E told me tonight we should part now *forever*. There were to be no more illusions in her mind *about me*" (MWA). MME to EH, 16 June [1849], responds to EPP's magazine, *Aesthetic Papers* (published in May) and goes on to say of Peabody, "What stores of history? I wish I had explored her resources if able when here instead of quarreling so unmercifully with her meddling" (MH: 1190).

To Ralph Waldo Emerson and Elizabeth Hoar

Vale   Aug. 15 '47

No day but accords with the sacredness of bidding my most——   —most to me *for the future* unwavering faith—most interesting fellow being *farewell*.[1] I shall not be the subject of low fears of insanity in any of it's happy or ill forms—of bodily apathies—or what is altogether worse—what renders this world apparently "accursed of it's Auther"—deformity of thought or word! No if there is any thing in omens w'h have spoken on other occasions I shall see one no more whose early years gave a new interest to my wearied age. And think what you use to—I even I shall know of the intellectual orders some time or other—yea if for ages their destiny seperates them as now it *appears* from the supernatural Medium thro' whom a human degraded race communes with infinite Holiness & joy—at some *ordained* & most glorious period (perhaps of all eternal rewards most misterious) the humblest literal believer of certain immutable truths w'h have recieved no polish or mutalation, will be permitted to mingle with those whose genius she respected without understanding—to recall the beams of thier young dawning virtues & bow to thier larger^n vision. That sympathy w'h has so long been the richest gift of ignorance & imprisonment will increase for ever!

Go and if Neptune or Nature give favorable winds & waves—well. Go and the God & Father of the divine Head & Redeemer of man protect you and prolong a life to the coming promotion of that religion w'h Angels admire.

Aunt M M E.

The *govt* of England respecting a "modified slavery" is odious & damning. God grant you to lecture on it. Lidian is saintly to consent to your going & she so feeble

Dear Elis.   What of the evil sprites w'h envy me my visitor spoke of "crowded"—Hannah has rarely been without two—mostly 3 spare beds. Bring Edward.[2] This water practice is sucesfull with many—   Oh I wish your Mother would come—nervous complaints flee before it   I shall try it perhaps if my head gets no cooler—but I expected you & would not be in a "wet sheet." I ought to have written before & let you know where I was—waited a week & more to hear from Waldo and thus of you—but you know always where I am? Days shorten and tho' the dear long nights are hastening I want you before the leaves "seer." You say you'll write if prevented write at the *moment* but not I trust to disappoint your Aunt

MME

We are two miles off from the Common & only the sprightly ones call mornings & evenings   Had yours last thurs. How is it that it took 6 days for mine to go? *The object* of *this was to hope* that one week was not all after expecting a number. Rest for you & reviving for me   Haste   Sabbath

Aug. 15

MH: bMS Am 1280.226(934). *Addressed:* R. Waldo Emerson Esqr. / Or Mrs R.W. Emerson / Concord / Mass. *Postmarked:* Waterford Me / Aug 16. *Endorsed:* M M Emerson / Aug. 1847.

larger] ⟨higher⟩ larger

1. RWE sailed from Boston for Liverpool on 5 Oct. 1847; he was gone for almost a year.

2. Probably Edward Hoar. EH and LJE's visit to Waterford began on 23 Aug.; LJE left on about 29 Aug.

To Elizabeth Hoar

Vale   Tues. 7 Sep. [1847]

This is good of you dear dear Child to get me a letter this very night and of so much lenght to give each of the family a pleasure   I never read letters but all heard this but Charlie who is to have his kiss from 'father'[1]   I shall prize the Vale more for your approbation. Mr Sumner & Mrs Porter[2] called the day after you went and Mr Harris who spoke of the seeing just as he should. The others & those at the Common surprised at your short stay as I had expected weeks and the days were very short.[3] I assured them I was resigned as you went before being weary of our monotonous life. Now were you at home with *it* why you could give it life by duty & inward pleasure. Short as it was it gave me a pleasant persuasion that if solitude were to be part of your sojourn it would not be irksome—tho' no one's element as it is mine & those bro't up in it. It's rainbow hours do not depend on clouds—for these are vapoury—but the dun rich days w'h shade the skies become inmates of welcome converse. Surely I will get me to sleep for my 11 o'k hastens. Yet so tenuous is the little fiber by w'h the brain retains reason that I would not sleep without leaving my sense of this and the many kindnesses bestowed thro many a long & often infirm year. May the gifts of heaven rest on you forever prays your Aunt

MME

Wed.   I've just put down the starry sights at C. in the Register.[4] Would you were here to explain! Endymion why—what is *that*. I thought I might be acquainted with the pretty myth—and now what is it? Night before last there rose over the mountain a fine large star—   Now how I wanted you. Is it the same I watched last winter as it rose higher & higher? This was before midnight paralell to the pliedies some y^{ds} south. "Why on earth struggle to know the names & times of the stars when so near to that article of certainty by w'h the poorest spirit will see them without lenses?" Why need of more active & higher pursuits w'h eye forbids. And besides if the spirit should for a time wander without senses will not the remembrance these wonders excite devotion? Ah vapoury—   The naked spirit may be suffered to contemplate the first great Spirit—source of all in matter & mind (whether the matter w'h *may?* have been eternal and have taken these glorious forms & forces by the *designs* of the delegated Creator how indifferent) and then how useless all science if not promotive of love. What truisms—and how obscurely have I run on with thoughts crowded on each other—thats the priveledge of writing to thee, who if you can't spell out writing or meanings never trouble yourself or me with complaints   And I trust to the lamp lighting. Where was it that Milton inserted that lady & chair of a constellation?[5] I've been read-ing a few pages of Vestiges—[6]   Why these laws w'h have bro't matter & animals without reason may have operated unknown ages and the true theist exulting says what are natures greatest or smalest *laws* but names for Gods agency and he spurns the atheism. And when if the Auther dares to say that man is thus generated he knows nothing of phisical or meta. philosophy and is beneath criticism. And even the instincts of brutes are beyond him. He is bold & ignorant(?) to speake lightly of Whewell.[7] He never read the whole of that history. Above all he never was blest with the internal gift and of course can do no harm to thinkers who are honest   That his heart remains in a *"fish"* state is evident. Oh how many have never shed their scales. Well good night dear Child of immortality—   Thurs. Eve. Here is a voluntire visitors D[r] K wife & friend   I can only say I left the letter to say how S. Beck does.[8] Alas she has been very low—fever—pain weakness—her husband came sab Eve   Mother on tuesday the day her hus. moved her to Mrs Gages. Today she seemed better—but in bed—yet hopefull. Tis' well I've no time to say how sorry & then glad to have her moved & Mother there. All inquier—   Never forget the Gages. Write soon of yourself & stars & houses & how Caroline is

MH: bMS Am 1280.226(1173). *Addressed:* Miss Elisabeth Hoar / Care Hon S. Hoar / Concord / Mass. *Postmarked:* Waterford Me / Sept 11.

1. Charlie appears in several Waterford letters for this period; he may be the same child mentioned by ASG in June 1850, the son of a boarder, Mrs. W— (MWA).

2. See MME to EH, 27 Jan. 1849, n. 4.

3. EH left Waterford about 1 Sept.; see MME to RWE and EH, 15 Aug. 1847, n. 2.

4. "The Great Telescope at Cambridge," *Christian Register*, 4 Sept. 1847.

5. The constellation Cassiopeia's Chair; possible allusion to Milton, *Paradise Lost* 2:929–31: "Thence many a League / As in a cloudy Chair ascending rides / Audacious."

6. Robert Chambers anonymously published *Vestiges of the Natural History of Creation*, in 1845, and *Explanations: A Sequel to "Vestiges . . . ,"* in 1846.

7. William Whewell, *The Philosophy of the Inductive Sciences* (1840, 1847); in a note on pp. 73–74 of *Explanations*, Chambers rebuts Whewell's criticism of some of his ideas in the 1845 *Vestiges*. MME's reproof may derive from a review of J. S. Mill's *Logic*, "Fundamental Laws of Reasoning," *Christian Examiner* 40 (1846): 363–84, which states that Whewell's philosophy "may well be termed 'transcendental.' By this we mean he asserts the power of the mind to originate ideas independently of sen-sation" (365) and that this sort of logic may be seen as a means to the "intellectual regeneration of the world" (383).

8. Dr. Kittredge; Mrs. Beck was probably a watercure patient whom EH had met during her visit.

To Elizabeth Hoar

South Paris   No[v]. 6, '47

Dear Elisabeth H.

Thanks for the kind labour you've thus performed. I knew you must be busy but what could have become of my letter w'h was sent Oct. 21 and I waited a fortnight before yours came dated "*30 of Nov.*" w'h you called friday & had mine only the monday before. Now how trifling to go over your mistakes when the time was stolen from sickness   *But* had you seen me opening a letter (tho' I had *not* expected sucess) w'h I received yesterday (at some miles distant from home on my way the eveg before) w'h the stagman would not permit me to read if I came on with him—but I caught the terms &c & concluded to search further rain as it might in an open waggon, and in the vast events of my journey this most dolerous ride figured strongly. True it was equal to some events of a M. Theressa or that of the bride of Napoleon when he steped into her carriage as she also was finding a new home or like Vitoria's visits to foreign continents[1] but it answered all the same to me and here I am at the Cape an obscure Villiage 3 miles from the Shire of Paris Hill. In such a Nook would I linger away & hide my deformities of character & tongue & of body. Pride & humility often hug. The minister has long been here a close solemn calvinist.[2] Well that implies a somthing—when one has lived alone & the old head refuses to read we want—need *somthing*. The house large & well furnished—but nothing but cook stoves & sitting room afflictions, but they will let me have their large spare chamber with open fire place instead of a lower room w'h I expected. Yet shame to say I can't decide—when a decision of such a being seems in wiser moments so trifling. But I can board at your calling place with more home feelings—tis society I need for this wearisome head. And Mrs Aber Ball "can make me comfortable."[3] Oh to board with some others where there need be no making *me* comfortable. I have made myself more so alone *night* & day the fortnight after H—h left.[4] I still hope some human form will appear to take some of the house and leave me to take care of *self* w'h forbids laziness & book. *Your* farmers ask as much as Mrs Ball it seems & I prefer near the Chh & lectures & my brother if he wont feel too much the care as Miss Lowel said Mr Gardiner did (*save the obscurity*). They ask here 15 ⅝ & find wood oil &c—

But I think to do better if with more expense if conscience dont revolt. I estimate your *kindness* & need not have said it. Who was Mrs Ball before marriage. I have dreamt of *boarding* with Lidian??[n] Would it come in competion with a hasty promise "never to spend an hour in visiting Waldo?? unless carried on a litter"   Have Mama's chamber & even airtight tho' any other back or before? This a sudden thought. Sat eve 13. I fear I've done wrong to keep Mrs B in suspence but you said a week or more. Dont let her lose a boarder but I hope to keep in this nighbourhood   You are still in the sick close room I fear—so I send this kind of hobglobin letter thro' my Brother to whom I must at last come tho' I do hate to present my tolly self & cares after so long years he got me a proper good table. Tow objects I have either cheapness or good society in house with good bread & half the time fresh meat for w'h I can afford to pay for I inclose in this very letter 40# for Mr Ripley to take care off as seems him fit. Neighbour Hale offered more for the land than A P gave for all & paid me. But I am so giddy headed I cant take care of it & the besides it may be unpleasant to deny loan to any who had better be without it

Your afft Aunt
MME

* * *

MH: bMS Am 1280.226(1175). *Addressed:* For Elisabeth Hoar / After S. A. Ripley / please read it including / 20# for Mr R—s care.

Lidian??] Lidian?? ⟨or Mrs Brown⟩

1. Marie Therese (1638–83), Queen of France, or Empress Maria Theresa (1717–80); probably the Empress Josephine (1763–1814); probably Queen Victoria (1819–1901).

2. Paris, Maine, is the "shire" town, or county seat, of Oxford County; from 1821 to 1851, the Congregational minister at Paris was the Reverend Joseph Walker.

3. Abner Ball and Sarah Farrar, both of Concord, married in 1823; in the 1840s Mrs. Ball's rooming house was on the Lexington Road near the Concord town center.

4. MME to EH, 19 Oct. 1847, describes Hannah and Augustus Parsons's preparations to leave the Vale and explains that Charlotte Haskins had already left for New York, where she was going to teach school (MH: 1174).

1848

To Lidian Jackson Emerson

Jan 28 '48   Friday

Thanks dear Lidian for your letter. Sympathy with you for the editorial of your loved Waldo[1]   Indeed my old heart burnt with pleasure to find him beyond the mists & rainbow visions of transcendental philosophy (however it has truths of nature) and once more mingle with the woes & cares of *practical* life. True I had wearied of the bustle of reformers w'h seemed to bring forth no reform, and ceased to pine for his name in healthy missions, but now hope that the pent up fires will breake thro' the ashes (what to old xianity & first principles appears like those of some ruinous volcano) and assume the phenix of indisputable truth & salvation. How bold & noble his disclousers of the great mountain men! God bless him for fearlessness on true sacred ground. Ask our dear Elis. H. if the "review" is Mr Geo Bradfords or mine? Ask her take charge of the 100# wh Gore will deliver her for the bank. Ask her for her patronage is unwaried to look over your husbands periodcals & see if there is any one review of the Vestiges & of Whewell's review. If she is absent you or

Mrs Brown will take the task. And I want the last Xian Ex. any who criticize Bellows wonderous good sermon lately at Brookline.[2] * * * You may ask why I seek these— Why the short review of Assazis.[3] Happy that an antagonist to the Auther of Vestiges appears in so famed a naturalist. Yet the Ves. can do no harm as poor Chever feared.[4] And even were the whole earth & the race a seedling w'h untold eyes were maturing and were its spiritual part (tho' no true philosopher you know would admit that to be possible) is any thing to be developed too hard for the *Infinite*! Have not our spirits a sort of platonic pre-existence in *that*? How does it delight to have lived in the purposes of God— and verily to have been objects of the redemptive plan before any foundations of the material were formed into growth. I know your sympathies with me will make no excuses for giving myself society in this very close Cell. I am looking for the said packet as you are so good as to inclose "husband letters." Miss Searle is offering every thing & A. Tracy—but they dont meet my *scientific* pursuits. Pray dont E.H. read this *word*. I read but little of any thing & ignorant of phisical science altogether all know   But in reviews (foreign) of Whewell I found his transcendental spiritual use of them and understood to^n *name* the delight with w'h I had inducted a moral fact from a phisical.[5]

I regret for your sake that Charlotte is called to S. M. H—'s imperiously by the death of his valuable wife,[6] and for C. who prefered being with you, & I did as fully. but it seems was expected after her labours at Roberts. in spring

A letter from Louisa Dewey tells she has written to our widowed Sarah.[7] Dear L. in her sweet tranquility does not feel with you & I of the task to speake & write to one who has lived in other beliefs & indefinable abstractions to *me*. Long since I sat at her shrine & am ignorant of "the word w'h Waldo alone could speake." Farewell dear & estimable Niece

from yours truly   MME.

The errands to E.H & Gore please remember.

To an affectionate Aunt L D—'s letters are sensible & enlightened by literature & husband—piety rich.

MH: bMS Am 1280.226(793). *Addressed:* Mrs R. Waldo Emerson / Concord / Mass. *Postmarked:* Waterford Me / Jan 31.

to] ⟨why⟩ ↑ to ↓

1. LJE's letter does not survive; probably a reference to the editor's address in the first number of the *Massachusetts Quarterly Review* (Dec. 1847), which RWE wrote before sailing for Europe in Oct.; MME's "sympathy" parallels RWE's dismay at discovering he was listed as one of the editors (along with Theodore Parker and J. Elliot Cabot).

2. Henry Whitney Bellows, *The Relation of Christianity to Human Nature*, sermon preached at the ordination of F. N. Knapp, Brookline, 6 Oct. 1847 (Boston, 1847); briefly mentioned in *Christian Examiner* 44 (Jan. 1848): 150.

3. Probably [J. Elliot Cabot], "The Life and Writings of Agassiz," *Massachusetts Quarterly Review* 1 (Dec. 1847): 96–119.

4. George Barrell Cheever (1807–90) wrote the introduction to the second American edition of Chambers's *Vestiges of the Natural History of Creation* (1846).

5. See MME to EH, 7 Sept. [1847], n. 7, although the review cited there is not "foreign."

6. Nephew Samuel Moody Haskins of Williamsburgh had married Adaline Peck in 1842.

7. MME's half brother SR died suddenly on 24 Nov. 1847.

To Elizabeth Hoar

So Paris   March 13 '48

* * * If any mode of rest to one wearied by strange & unwelcome sounds & new or famished means of "keeping soul & body together," it is to a solitary like me a new novel. And whatever *the* reviewer says I love James' & without that rest all winter I found one here.[1] To go at once into scenes of heroism & beauty &c what an escape. True were the trials such as to bear on the good spirits of patience & fortitude—but they would scorn to aid such sickly wants. Did you ever read Cecelia? I loved the Mother of Delville & C. & the gay witty young Countess. But have been oftener led to think of Briggs having a resemblance to him in a Mrs Briggs.[2] But I've escaped—& from an iron stove to one of her connections across the street & am comfortably fed—regreted to lose a thinker (tho icy) in the rev. companion. The snows are high but will go in time while they are nurturing your flowers & walks & preparing the beauty of the Elm Vale. Memory of the past year is sweet & excites gratitude. Never went into the east & north chambers, after they were winter naked, without the pleasure of their visitants short stay returning to me with gratitude.[3] Poor dear L. I grieve tell her for sufferings tho' they are past—and light always succeeds darkness. Happy that Mrs B.[4] was with her. Hannahs last letter gave no account when she could return to N. Yarmouth their intended home for she has the sole care of Sam[ls] babes & family who has lost his excellent wife and Charlotte cant leave her brother's sick wife—[5]   And who would willingly die without her Madonna aspects & unceasing care. Hannah's situation assorts with her virtue & kind impulses— and I doubt not she pleases the society who call much. Glad am I to have you name the deserted manse—of w'h I often think and send many a loving wish to Sarah whose socety you justly prize. And Mrs J. Barret has gone.[6] Her peculiar looks & manner (even the kind of bold romance by w'h she gained her husband) use to interest me. She was so innocent in face & the family so affectionate that if Marm Bonds gossip was correct it never disgusted. But how these gossips rise over the very grave—not to darken it's repose for surely there were embaressments enow to retribute. I have been writing to Gore and fear (*shame*) he will mistrust me too far tell him I've been reading Edwards on will & somthing of that sort with more clearness than 30 years ago. I have suspected it might be owing to spare diet, however.

Love to your parents. How could the Hon. say *lady*—he whom for 40 or more years I've respected and loved as a *freind*

Your aunt in love

MME.

If my Nephew dont come on sat. please inclose the answer about Monroe soon

MH: bMS Am 1280.226(1180).

1. George Paine Rainsford James (1801?–60), English writer who published over one hundred romantic historical novels between 1825 and 1850. One reviewer found James's rapid production "appalling" and charged him with "diffuseness," "an incontinent discharge of verbosity," "flatness, and tediousness," *Christian Examiner* 42 (Jan. 1847): 108.

2. Fanny Burney, *Cecilia; or, Memoirs of an Heiress* (1782); Delvile is Cecilia's secret lover; Briggs is a miserly character. MME's hostess was probably Mrs. Joseph Walker.

3. Reference to EH and LJE's short visit to Waterford in late Aug. 1847.

4. Probably LJE's sister, Mrs. Lucy Jackson Brown.

5. MME indicates that Hannah Parsons is helping out with the children at Williamsburgh while Charlotte Haskins is now serving as nurse in the family of possibly another Haskins brother.

6. Sophia Fay Barrett, wife of Joseph Barrett, died 18 Feb. 1848. She was a descendant of the Reverend Peter Bulkeley.

To Elizabeth Hoar

Ap 14   Friday '48

You have been good to copy—a task—unless there was more of "the *possible*" (w'h you do most justly say in a former letter) this brother so deals in.[1] And while sending thine eye (so able to dissect) over my poor "self possession," you limit it most truly to keeping soul & body together in difficulties rather than temper, as I interpret the wise limitation. I ca'nt get the letter unpacked for I am sadly clutered at Rail Road House hoping to have got home on tuesday but the stage full & I poorly sadly with a cold for the past & present week. You are my resort when weary of myself & every body I've seen since the absence from home. Oh how quietly (as puss own self) did I use in early years to pass from Mother to Aunt from Sister to Sister for all was without mentality & to keep souls & bodies together. I had to sit all day after leaving Paris in the sitting room as no chamber was vacant and I read a whole book of stories "The Consuls Daughter" was the outside title   And never was a finer love tale. Since "the Simple Story" and all "John Adams' letters."[2] Many of w'h *I* thought might have been omitted—was weary of the same high patriotism with so much self sacrifices named. All well for his wife be sure. Disgusted with his inaugural assurance that a *decent* respect for XY &c. Better no word than decency? The wine & punch sound very different from they did then. I wish I had some for there has been none in the Vale since one pint winter before last. And I dont like to ask if they have any here

Sat 16

Glad you pursue the scientific in the material   Likely I told you when I first found in such a fact spiritual truth how delighted—'twas so novel tho' I had always seen the stars & earth   But design in the minute brings the finite so near to catch a glimps of—of! I now recall a winter letter of yours w'h closed with sublime aspiration. One ray from the interior is like going into the sanctom of existence in human sympathy. But shall I intrude? Shall I tell of experience infinitly dearer? The last winter of solitary confinement renewed old tho'ts and sins &c &c   But the wraping up my poor little unoccupied (? "I know not I judge not myself") talent—my utter "poverty of nature" to attack or benefit, my wandering thoughts when constitution forbids them to fix—the huddle of associations—the epicurean charm of quietude too much indulged(?) I say I find all this host surrounding me   I am wholly willing to be the nothing alotted—aye & to do nothing forever but remain a contemplator of God & his works or omit the latter. Unknown unloved & solitary forever the enjoyment would be perfect naturally if in harmony with Him the spirit seeks! You *cannot* surrounded—born & bred in love & friendship & influence & success—impossible. I knew nothing of either—but I love existence & the medium of salvation! I have seen more of the disgusting in avarice pride & selfishness in forms of piety & even good sense than ever in the time. Alas, they in gross & uneducated shapes are but the true expression of the world in all ages. & the publick voice of accusing parties. Well then may the hermit love his shell—bind himself to obscurity forever than partake even of an Angel's ambition? Ah beloved Ed. & C C. Happy your escape   And thus it always seemed. Delightfull is the hope that France however fickle, may be a means of shaking every throne.[3] Yet what insues? Nothing but miracle can improve human nature! Yet may you long live to aid it eminently is oft the prayer of

yours ever
MME

* * *

MH: bMS Am 1280.226(1181). *Addressed:* Miss Elisabeth Hoar / Concord / Mass.

1. MME to EH, 13 Mar. 1848, reminds her that she is still hoping to "hear from oversea & have Lidians promised budget" (MH: 1180). LJE to RWE (still in Europe on his lecture tour), [17 May 1848], but apparently continued later, says EH has recently "copied what she knew would most interest Aunt Mary & sent it. She said it was best not to send the originals, lest her name not being mentioned in any, might hurt her feelings" (*LJE L*, 152), and encloses a recent "affectionate note" from MME, possibly MME to LJE, 18 [May] 1848 (MH: 794). In this context, MME's comment indicates she would have liked more than these few passages from RWE.

2. Elizabeth Simpson Inchbald, *A Simple Story* (1793); John Adams, *Letters . . . Addressed to His Wife*, 2 vols. (Boston, 1841).

3. Reference to the February Revolution (1848) in France, which overthrew King Louis Philippe and established the Second Republic.

To Lidian Jackson Emerson

Elm Vale　July 22　Sat. 48

My dear benefactress & Neice,

Husband or none I'll wait no longer to console your suspense or welcome his arival—¹ Surely not—to thank you for the packet of letters and your own welcome invelop.² Truly amid your preparations 'twas good good! And sweet to read in my dear home. Oh glad I did not go further. A number of places disturbed any decision & the best was *home,* where I can have every quarter of the atmosphere—tho' tedious to open & close the windows as often as light & air prevails. *Has he come?* Will the agitations be like or good as the sole possesion of the interior? "What a question none but a solitary celebrate wraped perhaps in self possesion could make such an icy one— ignorant of the richest gifts of human life." Pardon me　I have been reading a number of certain essays even at midnight last eve. and all all of genius &c &c seem to terminate in zero at times—again the ignis fatuus of genius bewildered & lost a smale brain. I have of late repeatedly read them when I found nothing w'h induced *thought* in the salons & coteries of weary aristocratic London. Oh forgive my ingratitude, thou high minded *xian,* but Lords & ladies are but shadows to one who is passing into realities. So dont you & dear E.H. regret my absence—for if ever I come and see & hear him it will be when his ideal world is more positive than men & women. I hope you have not written to P.³ I came a week since * * * Waldos letter, you so graciously sent, was very welcome. Enough for a general view of London or English good & bad. Pen & ink bad & I'll wait for this post to hear. See that your other self makes no pecuniary bargains if I sᵈ *need* come—for that *Scamp* of Goodnow made as tho' for my friendship the board low & I lived as his boys did & then he lied so. I ca'nt bear him for a teacher. One of his first talks at table was deceptive　What a wicked price. I *can* pay & will reasonably　At the best table in Portland (tho' true an upper chamber) the hostess asked but 2# I shall (if forced thro' health) take the Hotell for a little time w'h E H has provided　Sab Morn. 23. No letter. "*Well*" nothing could add I think to the charms of this morn. What a presentiment of the higher rest where there will be alternations of perfect rest in consciousness of the Infinite? It seems impossible but a disinterred soul should gain constant accessions of all the virtues known here & there discovered from the natural effects of the divine *presence?* Besides, to the obtuse of humans the fact of intercourse with that wonder of the universe!—the humanised divine Head of our poor race will be a certain means of communicating with his God and Father and ours (primarily) and we shall resemble him more & more! One of these mortal days you will have time to read Cudworth & Plotinus. "The reasons of philosophy that prove the soul's immortality (tho' firm and demonstrative in themselves) yet are so thin & subtle to vulgar apprehensions that they glide away." Cud.[4] I have purchased a little memoir of Madame Adorna edited by Nieghbour Upham of Brunswick.[5] But her apparent ignorance of the nature of mind gives no spring to one of this century. Nothing approaching to the experience of Plotinus who "four times was conscious of individuation with the Infinite." Blessed inspirations of the All Good who never left any without some "wittness" of His presence & athority! And what a wittness to the mass (tho' *the best need*[n] *the plan*) was the condescention of the xian revelation! It's institutions it's *sabbaths* as humane for this life as nessecary for means of another. What patriot would take the ewe lamb from the poor. Garrison & Phillips have greived thier admirers.[6] Again I crave mercy   But as I have not had publick worship except two or three half days the year past I often spend some in writing to Ann Tracy & F. Searle who are sabbatharians. Social & publick sympathies are not lost in the Cell where no life but of birds & breezes are heard. I am not favored with abstractions, w'h you seem to have even in your own house & among visitors of high note. I felt a secret envy mingle with dislike. Well here is a disordered paper & so I'll cover it. Farewell

May the accession of new blessings lead you to higher & holier ones. Yours truly

MME

Love & gratulations to Sister. And beg E.H. to write to her ever gratefull Aunt. Dear Nephews positive annihilations abstract me oft times. He cant write.

MH: bMS Am 1280.226(795). *Endorsed:* M M Emerson.

need] *possibly rec'd (abbreviation for* received)

1. On 27 July RWE returned to Boston after traveling on a lecture circuit for almost ten months in England and France.

2. LJE's packet probably included RWE's letter of 22 June, which Rusk says is the only one that RWE wrote MME during his trip (*L* 4:90).

3. Probably Portland.

4. Ralph Cudworth, *The True Intellectual System of the Universe.*

5. Thomas C. Upham, *The Life of Madame Catharine Adorna: Including Some Leading Facts and Traits in Her Religious Experience* (Boston, 1845).

6. The *Liberator* of 31 Mar. 1848 tells of a recent two-hour speech by Wendell Phillips (1811–84) before the Judiciary Committee of the Massachusetts legislature. Phillips, who favored disunion, failed to persuade his audience that "the sacrifice of our glorious Union" would benefit anyone. By the time that William Lloyd Garrison (1805–79) came to speak, most of the audience had left.

1849

To Elizabeth Hoar

Vale   Jan. 27   sat. '49

Dear Elisabeth

Tho' no one asked, yet I believe the three houses will like to hear that the body they were so kind too (for we love whatever we have favored) is not petrified among the glaciers of Me, or unable to say where or what it might be. I should have written soon but a tedious spell of errasipalas has confined me & affected eyes externally that they resemble red forested[n] peepers. Tho' extremly cold weather, I suspect it was not that, but the disease has been in same shape for the time at C.[1] for I had a scarcity of brain in thought, w'h was employed ? in clearing it by disease for indeed it has been more active— or mentally it was owing to my expecting all excitment without, and when geting a glimsp wanted more. I did not go to "whip a top" w'h never rolled, but the hope w'h has hung long that the little shallop w'h had always paddled in stagnant pools might recieve a new oar. Idle for age! And if your cares had been less in all houses I should return to rely "on the hidden light"   But the last & lasting lesson was the wretched Inn at W. and the long painfull walk in quest of the Hill whose house I believed nigh. But the spirit of Scotus had gone thro' those pages for I found it not. Still the Ex. (worm) might illicit talk and the beautifull history of Bartol's cloud—and his reply was "it was not accurately scientific!" Ah good Bartoll may never have seen the *mountains* of Maine where belike clouds are formed without any aid from oceans w'h cover human miseries blood & slavery—such as Angels might have been clothed with from the hills of Judea when they missioned for the first Chh. Do you re- member B—s article on "Providence"?[2] He explained nothing, and who can what is purposely wild? Wat noble things Epic. & A. M. say about the senses (w'h dear Ellery talks of better than nothing)[3] and in thier best men was re- fered to! But all that Plato & his say, tho' sublime, pass away like rainbows when real affliction from the heart disease assails thro' the rod of connection in perplexities. I was so badly off with what the tenant had done & what engagment neglected so insolently that I read, when able, nothing but stories where all vice is so natural "as the rose." Well I would be quiet—but better & higher athority was needed to forgive & treat with kindness. True, in cases of the vulgar, one's pride or affection is never disturbed. I was better too for the woman who used kindness to that boy your father related. How many ques- tions I intended to ask of still higher sort of him but after exhausting myself in encountering "Mothers" wit. But *if I had been well.* The beautifull prospect from the west chamber remains with the memories of that south part of the Manse w'h remains as when built by one whose soul was composed of love & joy & dreamt of those of his idolisied family, who were so soon consigned to long & painfull sorrows. "Well!" It was when Sarah was engaged I rejoiced that the fate of the house would be changed at some time   That a composition of genius talent & good temper would nurse all that was harmonious with other queer possessions. Alas that genius has brooded over the chaos of mystery (?) till that very intellect (w'h leads so directly to the bible God) seems to my limits, like an ignus fatuus, and gives delight in penetrating laws of matter w'h do not seem to relate her to thier divinity. But she cannot with her mind but recognize this Being & when with the simple faith w'h reason demands she takes the revelation what a spirit! I want to hear all about her journey & Mary. * * * And now for my often benefactor. Oh could Martha's opening the door return to my unaided solitude of confinement, the pleasure I then felt would be smale indeed compared.[4] Many a time has your image & those of the others returned to me but I came believing it right have regreted nothing for to *me* is that *right* as important as was the sacrifice of La-fayette when in dungeons & the greatest of sacrifices, he presented a principle of liberty to the world. Besides tell Martha this day of healthy life gives me all I need—that the promised letter to her was to have been written on a sat. Eve w'h I past there. And if will answer me I'll write still—this a family surtificate that I live. This *continuance* reminds me of all I've seen of Gages. And that was Thomas who came on wed. in the full bloom of manly beauty & additional grace of being touched by the death of a friend who boarded with them. Mrs Porter you may have seen.[5] But the errand he came on was a sort of home welcome w'h reminded me of Sarah's. His mother wished to know if I were willing that this stranger should be buried near her husband as I had engaged the place immediately at his head Stone. I was willing for every thing & place I told him. But she was not to take mine &c. There is no room for me near your Aunts & I liked this spot w'h was large & might possibly lead some inquirer to my grave w'h was always to be stoneless. Oh no flower nor tree I ask. Natures wildest pebbles & sleet & waring winds are welcome. It was not the thing however for Mrs P. to ask for the left *side* as the family are large. Farewell dear dear E—   Eye complains

Yours & Charles Aunt I hope forever.
MM Emerson

MH: bMS Am 1280.226(1187).

forested] *apparently* forneted *in MS; T reads* bonneted

1. C.: Concord, where MME boarded in Nov. and Dec. 1848.

2. Probably Cyrus Bartol, but no article on Providence published before 1853 located.

3. Stoic philosophers Epictetus and Marcus Aurelius; Ellery Channing.

4. Probably Martha Bartlett, SBR's sister; MME suggests that she is considering boarding with her in Concord.

5. Aurora F. Porter (b. 1815), wife of Oliver Porter of Lynn, Mass., died at Waterford on 21 Jan. 1849. In 1853 ASG sold her property to Porter.

To Sarah Bradford Ripley

[July? 1849]

Dearest of Sisters

(If I may be allowed the word w'h you never use to lonely Me.) How do you this hot day? And all the rest of you? Has E. B. returned from Marys & how did she leave them? I called at Uncle's[1] yesterday (who has moved half a mile or more beyond his old lodgings w'h the owner needed to his expensive ones with one room & a bit of garrett but a very dear freind of his & Marthas,[2] who has rivaled me, for as soon as heard of the plan I urged them to take the rooms I use in Vale & would never sell in his life time) and they engaged me to tell you how very acceptable your kindness was—so that Mr R. often repeats his gratitude that you should think of him. I intended to write to Martha B.[3] soon & promised to send thanks—for we read that it is noble mede to honorable minds,[4] but have not time to write a long letter to her. I think oftener of you since seeing you than ever. Was glad that the faith of unlearned gave you a moments pleasure. Much as I like Morell want no "scientific" grounds of the certitude of my knowledge—better like his views of the "intuitions." You never refused a request of poor Me. *Will you read those 4 short lectures?*[5] One two hours will put you in rapid possesion. And then what is more give me your opinion. Tho' nothing profound but that those described in Positivism I thought were rather vacilating like all speculators. Pardon me but the farther you reach thro the spectacles of science it *seems* to my limitations, the less positive hold you have of solution of the only questions of infinite importance & many are merely in a transition state w'h I can never know where to find. The superficial ones I meet lose the Being you believe in. Yet how overwhelming to me that your relation to Him is—is— The greatest problem I ever met.

Yours for the earliest of your career for ever & ever

MME

—& of your destiny for me in any true science but that w'h leads from reason to God & his rev. of immortality for man * * *

MH: bMS Am 1280.226(1291). *Addressed:* Mrs S. A. Ripley.
1. LR.
2. Probably Martha Robinson.
3. Martha Bartlett.
4. Quotation attributed elsewhere to Marcus Aurelius.
5. John Daniel Morell, *On the Philosophical Tendencies of the Age: Four Lectures Delivered at Edinburgh and Glasgow, January 1848* (London, 1848). MME to WE[3], 5 July 1849, urges him to read these same lectures (MH: 220[75]), the source for the date assigned to this undated letter.

To Martha Bartlett

Vale   Nov. 22   Thurs. [1849]

Dear Martha,

Can you spare time from your delightfull walks to the Manse Elisabeth's &c this fine weather to tell me where your & mine Elis. is? I expected to have heard from her before this and how her Mother is and if she has returned home? And of you I always like to hear by your pen. Are all well at your & your Aunts?[1] Do you ever meet with M. Thoreau?[2] My love to her & thanks for the cap w'h I begin to use & you'll excuse the renewal of the message. Do not fail to tell me of Miss Bremer[3]   Where she is in Boston and who sees her and what is said of her? I hope she will approve the better taste of the English & Americans she dont have their good characters drink & swear like some of hers & mix great drops of tears with their meat & about cleaning noses. Her latest works I ca'nt get. She is said by reports to be at the good tranquil age of 50 rather gross & not handsome. Surely her taste for beauty & love was not taken from her mirror. What does my Sarah read? And what does *she say of* Esthetic Papers?[4] And what does the reviews say? And what does *S.A.R. say of* S.M.F. marriage?[5] I never was more curious to hear of a stranger & see him than the ex Marquis. Surely W.E.C.[6] must appear and is a delightfull contrast to me.

If you will tell me what the past & coming seasons do for your mind & heart I shall know how to fill a sheet. Do you read "Night tho'ts"?[7] I hoped to have forgotten them by years, and had in some sort the 9th w'h roused the old jaded imajanation & I laid bye the modern pages of philosophy &c to dwell in the glories of the nocturnal Muse & wished every young aspirant to know them. Now the immediate reason of taking your bright moments is to request my benefactress, if absent, Mr W. E. to invest 20# in bank as soon as Gore[8] gives it, & let the rest remain till I send. I believe Elisabeth's benevolence too large to be exhausted yet by my cares & hope she is well.

With love to the four houses w'h I often visit in mind and Mr Channing I continue tho ever so much in haste your afft friend

MME.

MH: bMS Am 1280.226(624). *Addressed:* Miss Martha Bartlett / Care of J. Bartlett M D / Concord / Mass. *Postmarked:* So Waterford Me / Nov 23.

1. Martha Bartlett (1824–90) was the daughter of Concord physician Dr. Josiah Bartlett and Martha Bradford Bartlett, sister of SBR, MME's sister-in-law.

2. HDT's aunt, Maria Thoreau.

3. Swedish author Frederika Bremer arrived in the United States in Oct. 1849; she visited Concord on 3 Dec. 1849 (*Homes of the New World* 1:116–17) and returned for another visit in January.

4. The single issue of EPP's *Aesthetic Papers* was published in May 1849.

5. RWE to WE[3], 17 Oct. 1849, reports that Sarah Margaret Fuller "has been near two years married" to the Marchese Giovanni Angelo Ossoli (*L* 4:168); their son was

born in Sept. 1848. Whether Margaret and Ossoli actually were married is uncertain; in his letter RWE mentions their plans to travel to the United States.

6. William Ellery Channing, the younger, was married to Ellen Fuller, sister of Margaret.

7. Edward Young's *Night Thoughts*, a perennial favorite of MME's.

8. CGR.

To Lidian Jackson Emerson

Sab Eve   23 Dec. '49

And then, dear Lidian, you have not forsaken your aged Aunt. Many thanks for so long and welcome a letter[1]   And will you send me Miss B—'s book? If you will stop & send it when your other self can send Morell's "phi. of religion" and somthing new, w'h will come surely. Miss Searle sent by Express the 'modern Painters' with letter inclosed, but I have not but looked at it as kind of thing I dont need at this time of evening.[2] Glad to hear of the genius &c but more of the xian virtues of that lady. Yet can't but smile at your hearty unaffected enthusiasm & intimacy with a days acquaintance. It is good, oh how good, I should think, to find congenial sentiments—the opinions of mere theology not so great. Her sattisfaction on the office of our divine Saviour (w'h I saw a page of in Ex.) appeared to *me* slightly gained on a subject w'h presents to the old school of arianism so many difficulties—   Yet none that I suffer from now as I am no teacher. But in my faith there are rich grounds of certitude. And when formerly you conversed with me a sacred sympathy. Why "dont I care to hear" of F. B.? I respect & now love her virtues. I dislike her taste in many respects, and that novel where Bruno is. Unnatural in our climate such violent passions & deaths for love. I used to like Burney & Porters—felt at home. And James I never weary of tho his Reviewe's do.[3] Wish I had somthing of his new & Bremer's, when weary with labours of body, mind & the uninterrupted (of *society*) solitude   Yet how dear past defining have been the days & hours of past weeks of ability to read little & enjoy, you know, what is better. The 1^t vol of Waldos essays have interested me & some with greater vision

I hoped to have heard your opinions of poor Dr P—s sad manner of exit.[4] Distressing as the event is to his connections (with whom I was early acquainted) and to his wife, good will come of it (as all evils finally) already   What a terror it gives to those who believed the suspected Prof. so always good.* And to the votaries of material science what a lesson! How useless to insure principle & habits of piety. Whatever doubts it give to the Naturalist or rationalist it gives not one to the simple bibleist.

To return to your new friend the death bed of Elda is a description w'h can never fail to elevate the reader or gain respect for it's auther. But of all opinions about Waldo that of hers that he is American is beside all my expectations.[5] If ever a writer was universal as unique, it is that very man—scarsly of this poor disastrous earth unless there was an Eden. If you can see him wholly unoccupied before Jan. please to say I must give an obligation for a deed before he moves all from Gorham. and whether it be then nessecary to have Gore come down?

Your affectionate letter my dear L. gave pleasant feelings to the violent storm of last night. No "Ghost complaining rode" on its strides but rather seemed as tho' the winds might be echos of "trumpets sounded by Angels." Aye, and why not? May not these very laws we vaguely call *nature* be connected with the agency of Spirits who alone understand the secrets of matter— and what is the most delightfull harmonious musick in higher riegions become the baser notes to earth? rather the bass of their tunes? Pardon me if I indulge fancies on paper for I carry the barreness of my self with many a one & find myself making little rhymns. I begged dear Elis. to say nothing of any "annoyance" about farm &c. And they touch not my heart nor rob me of ought within. Good night   Love to Sister husband & children and Mrs Brown

Your with esteem & love and gratefull memories

MME

*E. H—s letter

MH: bMS Am 1280.226(799). *Addressed:* For / Mrs R. Waldo Emerson / Concord / Mass. *Postmarked:* So Waterford Me / Dec 24. *Endorsed:* M M Emerson / 1849.

1. See LJE to MME, 16 Dec. 1849 (*LJE L*, 168–69); letter is incomplete.

2. MME refers to a novel by Frederika Bremer; John Daniel Morell, *The Philosophy of Religion* (London and New York, 1849); and John Ruskin's *Modern Painters* (1848).

3. LJE's letter tells of Bremer's visit on the Monday following Thanksgiving; Bremer's theology is discussed in a review of her *Morning Watches: A Few Words on 'Strauss and the Gospels': The Confession of Faith of Frederika Bremer* (Boston, 1843), in the *Christian Examiner* 36 (Jan. 1844): 98–103. Bruno is a violent character in Bremer's *Neighbors* (London and New York, 1842; Boston, 1843); novelists Fanny Burney, probably Anna Maria Porter, and G. P. R. James.

4. One of the most sensational Boston-area crimes of this period was the murder, on 23 Nov. 1849, of Dr. George Parkman, a Boston philanthropist who had recently endowed the new building of the Harvard Medical College and the Parkman professorship. On 8 Dec. the *Christian Register* reported that Dr. John W. Webster, professor of chemistry and metallurgy at Harvard, had been charged with the crime after parts of Parkman's body were found in a vault below his office. Webster was found guilty and sentenced to death following a two-week trial (19 Mar.–1 Apr. 1850).

5. "Elda" is MME's misspelling of Edla, the heroine of Bremer's *President's Daughters* and *Nina*; in a letter dated 20 Oct. 1849, Bremer calls Emerson the "American Thorild" (*America in the Fifties: The Letters of Fredericka Bremer* [New York and London, 1924], 13).

1850

To Frances Gage

Thurs.   13 June '50

Dear France

I return with thanks your kindness in loaning this little work.[1] The story at the beginning I run thro' in weariness & mindlessness   But certain I should approve it no better. The very milky childish bride is not, I believe a specimen of the general character of the age, who cannot but know that happiness is not allied to any condition   Mental & moral strenght give individual reliance and leave each of the pair room for happiness without quarelling for constant or even occasional devotion & explanation. Hapless the husband who is yoked to a mere flower whether pious or not   Trials are the divine economy—what if matrimonial or solitary say the wise. I really wish Bremer had been married tho', for her sorrowfull disappointment has left a strange predilection for mating. In her works you now & then find such exaggerated description of its happiness—in one (Mardont Hall was it?) it seems over charged if there is another life scarcely—but what is a set off (rather quere) the wife is afflicted with constant remorse for she has a former husband & daughter. I regret the many difficulties I meet in Bremers works for her own xian sweetness modesty unpretendedness is sublime. But the orthodox sudden conversion of some of her subjects & the misery of an Alina without giving the true cause (*want* of a *religious character*) undivorced from the rapturous love of the senses & human aid. I wish you were not so busy or I should like to give you the last half page of De Isreal's "Conisby" worth much of female painting, unless the character w'h Elda (?) attained finally.[2] An auther that could so ably describe a death should basis all her descriptions on real xiananity

But you are young—and this is my farewell for weddings are not the place or time to talk—but to think & sympathize—but little gratulation or sympathy from me do any get as I have never met with any realities in *my* (besure, very limited acquaintance) observation w'h increased but lessened happiness. Now dont rave at me as some have done. But to say adieu to one who has always given me kind attentions is the often sad errand of life. May your happy temperment & good principles secure you, as of course, their effects. And when the cares and novelties of change have subsided, may you possess (if not now) the richest of all Gods gifts,—communion with Himself—*love* of Him for Himself is the only idea of *disinterested* love. And then how indifferent the toils or pleasures of this passing scene—how superior—how happy to yourself—and your amiable husband able to lessen all his cares—to your children an Angel to guide them to Heaven. If thrown in view of the great & good & wealthy how pure your gratitude to the Giver of their gifts & what is holier your sympathy with them. The faith in the special appointments of Providence is the secret of a happiness w'h nothing else can bestow. Love & gratulations to the husband w'h I always bestow, as I did to S. Warren.[3] I remember well the sattisfaction I enjoyed in your parents union & in their children—since they have grown I am very little acquainted them. Adieu Gods blessing prays your aged well Wisher

MM Emerson

If Mrs Gage has leisure to find out this hurried writing Please read it to Frances Gage to whom it belongs if not too sad.

MWA.

1. Possibly Bremer's *Neighbors*, which MME was reading in Dec.; at the beginning of the novel, the narrator, Mrs. Werner, is a simple, young bride.

2. Alina and Mardont Hall are unidentified; for "Elda," see MME to LJE, 23 Dec. 1849, n. 5; Benjamin Disraeli's *Coningsby; or, The New Generation* (London and New York, 1844).

3. Frances Gage married Humphrey Cousens on 26 June 1850 ("husband" refers to the "husband to be"). Frances's sister Irene married Samuel Warren on 8 Jan. 1846.

To LIDIAN JACKSON EMERSON

Vale   June 26 '50

My dear Niece,

I hear with sad regret by E.H. that you are not well. *What is the case?* That a journey—absence from all care, or the water cure will not take your notice. When you last wrote you were certain of the best way to promote your health ect. Is it maternal increase? Or what can retard health? The late Journal of Water cure N. York, if true, has repeated instances of pregnant difficulties being wholly removed & health taking place of weak & distressing nerves.[1] I thought much of you today when dining at C. F's, whose house is in fine repair & *some* what interesting patients but mediocer—much mirth in bowling &c with good musick I witnessed. I expressed my belief that the water & absence from care w'h cares prevent your own water uses probably   Now your other self has returned & I hope after his inlarged portion of life & pleasure at Niag. will dole me out one of his hasty letters. But it's description of what he saw & *more* what was *felt* will give a tone to non entity almost. And so little of existence for some months that I can not account for but the season. The blessed Autumn approaches and the sun is hastening with comfort & long nights. The close confinement without any horse in the Town almost to be had. I have always feared that the cooking could not answer for one of your life long customs in this place or the best chambers might be taken up and the shell[n] w'h surrounds you has prevented my saying ought of my belief in this place. The prospect of being with you constantly (as my boarding place w'h I sometimes take for a week or days, is so near) has been desirable to my heart, w'h the ice gathers round at times. Today has been quite genial. Went to France Gage's wedding & saw a deal of happy faces. And she tho' given to lachrymary went off with much controul for Boston at 11 o'k P. M. tonight. If ever a happy girl is to be pitied it is the first year of leaving a good home & mother. After that the yoke becomes easier and bye & bye after a few years dragged out in mutual efforts for the pockets prosperity they became nessececeary to each other. F. is in love for some years (strange) with this gentlemanly man, who has sufficient property.[2] I was so glad of getting an airing & tried to talk of the great question. Our Gerry has done well in his speech. & Wilmots! have you read it?[3] These publick dangers ought to make us forget & do at times stupid body

Love to "Mama" & husband, whom I venture to solicit alms for *thinking,* & the other houses. How is Mrs Hoar? I do wish to see Elis. but dare not urge her to visit me so destitute of a Hannah. If she comes of her own accord *well!* and if she comes with you far better. The same chamber you had is now the Owner of the house says at E—'s service & she will board you & E.H. with all meals.[4] She has so good bread that I shall rarely send to Norway. She expects to get fresh meat half the time. Will a mere journey be usefull to you. Love to Elis. & hope for good news in her letter.

Farewell—whether sick or well—your faith w'h never fails will every moment keep you in that communion w'h is the sole of all virtue & happiness   Your

aff^t Aunt in haste
MME

A journey here I suspect gives you a greater change of air than to Plymouth if you dont need that native atmosphere   What if Waldo comes!? Water Cure can take him without being ducked

Sarah dear will not come to W. I fear never

Dear Elis.,

Please speake of Miss Binley, whom S J G is lamenting, & says you & your brother Waldo esteemed. Miss Goddard seemed hurt last summer that I had never heard you name her.[5]

MH: bMS Am 1280.226(801). *Addressed:* Mrs R. Waldo Emerson / If absent Miss E. Hoar / Concord Mass. *Postmarked:* So Waterford Me / June 28. *Endorsed:* M M E / 1850.

shell] *possibly* skill (*T*)

1. EH to MME, 23 Nov. 1849, discusses LJE's poor health ("EH L," *SAR* 1986, 165–66); no more recent letter on this subject survives. The *Water-Cure Journal* (*WCJ*) (New York, 1845–62) frequently touted the virtues of the hydropathic approach to prenatal and obstetrical care; see, for example, Joel Shew, "The Water-Cure in Pregnancy and Childbirth," *WCJ* 7 (1849); R. T. Trall, "Allopathic Midwifery," *WCJ* 9 (1850); and M. L. S., "Childbirth: Three Cases from My Note Book," *WCJ* 9 (1850). LJE to MME, 11 Aug. 1850, answers MME's question about possible pregnancy by

stating that seven-year-old Eddy was her "baby . . . and will never be superseded by one younger" (*LJE L*, 174).

2. In 1845, Frances's husband, "Colonel" Humphrey Cousens, a Portland native, bought a large share of the very profitable Waterford-Portland stagecoach line; in the *History of Waterford*, Cousens is described as "the beau ideal of a stage-driver; tall, courteous, capable, and generous to a fault" (*Waterford*, 173–74).

3. Probably part of the U.S. House of Representatives' debate over slavery and the annexation of Texas, which culminated in the Compromise of 1850: Waterford native Elbridge Gerry (1813–86) served one term in the U.S. House of Representatives, 1849–51; however, the *Congressional Globe* includes no record of his making a significant speech in Congress. Pennsylvania representative David Wilmot (1814–68) sponsored the Wilmot Proviso (1846), which sought to prohibit slavery in territory added following the Mexican War; on 3 May 1850 he spoke on the admission of California.

4. In Apr. 1850 MME sold the Elm Vale farm and house to John and Mary Howe of nearby Norway.

5. Probably Sally Jackson Gardner of Boston and Lucy Goddard, an "antislavery friend of Lidian" (*LJE L*, 121 n. 1).

To LIDIAN JACKSON EMERSON

Vale [July] 26 Sat. [1850]

My dear Lidian,

You ca'nt be able to write tho' Elis—'s last letter said "well as usual", or you would have answered mine, or induced your other self to revive my heart (almost petrified of late by &c feeble health w'h is today yeilding to better)   Has he returned? What of the finest scene in nature does he say?! Is the loss of the table rock lamentable? Surely. I regret he was not at the 19 celebration.[1] What did *you* feel? One name of an ancestor (to me so idolized from childhood so mourned at every lenghtening heavy footed year of the loss of those advantages w'h would have cultured *affection* & intellect) I would fain have seen among the famed speakers. But W. could not, perhaps, with all his artistic eloquence have breathed life into the memory of one so long forgotten. That anniversary roused every publick & private feeling of w'h my narrow limits are capable. And tearing eyes w'h moisten not for years. Why Lidian, if you could know my fathers character as I do from his childhood (living with a doating Sister) you would have your natural enthusiasm roused—his high principles—his enthusiastic desire to sacrifice for the publick & xian[t]—for family he could make none, for he so doated on them— with the most frank and ingenuous character. The times, the theology of his stronge puritanic parents & Ancestors forbad development of his talents of w'h I know nothing. Tho' I was well pleased to hear a publick character, in a stage who as a stranger passed by the old Chh & said to his companions "there I first heard eloquence." C. Farnham[2] & I heard it said of our parent. Yes, it was his burning zeal that sowed many of the seeds w'h were ulogized of the good Middlesex. Why dear Niece if you had seen his beauty & known him

Figure 28. Concord in Mary Emerson's first year: *A View of the Town of Concord* (Apr. 1775), by Ralph Earle, engraved by Amos Doolittle. Courtesy Concord Free Public Library.

you would have rejoiced that your children are his descendants. You would have seen that I had the pamplet soon.[3] Could I have passed that day in the attic of the house he built, and to which he *looked,* as the road was about to hide it, as few men look—for he was taking a leave & he turned his horses head—a ploughman saw it & told me. In secret would I have passed the day & interfered with none, the sight of publick parades has always pleased & the musick would have made an impression to accompany many a midnight pleasure. But *I know* it was *not* best or I should apprised of the event— Still I hate to stirr every day more & more & should not unless I had read apriori the history of the anniversary.[4]

Well Lidian I have said more as a long mourner to you than to any one. With faith like ours, perhaps you may say it is too much. Well write it—and we will resolve to pass all earthly cares, w'h cark & *disturb* devotion. And when I read periodicals where unitarian clergy are named, who had no pretention to talents—who had sculked behind orthodox phrases, when my brother was as open (in his unpopular humanitarianism) as the light of day—but his name is not with the Thayers & Thachers.[5] True, he took no controversial part, and was never (when I saw him) in the health & ardor of days & years gone bye. When young he came on the stage with like beauty & popularity of his father, but the chill w'h orphan years gave him who was the very idol of parental doatage, returned, I thought, in the City life[n]

* * *

Love to Sister, if at home, Nephew & his younglings—want to hear from each. In reading the above I think your very vivid ima[nn] will take range over sea & land & ask what name so lifted & criticized as E.? And I myself have been flattered at Water Cure as enough to give me immortality thro' this synosure. And I look in papers &c I love his name remembering his platonic element　But he is related to no family or Father or teacher—an exotic. And you are tho' esteemed by your freinds a Nonpareil—are somwhat past common comprehension. Well matched. Oh that raving letter about F— G—s wedding[6]—& looking at dark side of matrimony, I forgot—never seem to think you married. Did you think it generally true? Adieu

Your aff[t] Aunt　MME

MH: bMS Am 1280.226(802). *Addressed:* Mrs Waldo Emerson / If absent, Miss E. Hoar / Concord / Mass. *Postmarked:* So. Waterford Me / July 29. *Endorsed:* Miss M. M. Emerson / July 1850.

City life] ⟨later⟩ ↑ City ↓ life

ima[n]] *abbreviation for* imagination

1. RWE left Concord in mid-May for an extensive lecture tour that took him, for the first time, as far west as Niagara Falls ("the finest scene") and the Mississippi River (*Life of RWE*, 380), but he had returned by 30 June 1850 (*L* 4:214). The last section of Table Rock, a flat projection on the Canadian side of Horseshoe Falls, fell into the Niagara River Gorge in June 1850. Since RWE did attend the annual celebration of the Concord fight on 19 Apr. 1850, MME may be expressing her disappointment that he

was not among the speakers, who included Robert Rantoul, Jr., Ebenezer Rockwood Hoar, Rufus Choate, and Edward Everett (*JMN* 11:250 n. 207) and her wish that her father's heroic death in the revolution be noted at this celebration.

2. Charlotte Farnham.

3. *An Oration Delivered at Concord, on the Celebration of the Seventy-fifth Anniversary of the Events of April 19, 1775*, by Robert Rantoul, Jr., and *A Brief Account of the Celebration of the Nineteenth of April*, at Concord (Boston, 1850).

4. LJE to MME, 11 Aug. 1850, explains that her own disgust with hypocritical patriotic displays (in the face of "our National Shame"—slavery) had blinded her to the possibility that MME could be interested in attending the celebration; she responds also to other matters that MME brings up here and in her 26 June 1850 letter (*LJE L*, 172–74).

5. Nathaniel Thayer (1769–1840), minister at Lancaster, preached the installation sermon for WE[2] at Boston in 1799. The Thachers were a notable clerical dynasty, beginning with the first Peter Thacher, minister at Boston's Brattle Street Church, 1785–1802, and including Thomas Thacher (1756–1812) of the Dedham Third Church and Samuel Cooper Thacher of New South, Boston, 1811–18.

6. See MME to LJE, 26 June 1850.

To Ralph Waldo Emerson

Vale   Au. 16 '50   Friday

Dear Waldo,

Ca'nt delay to say somthing—least I should be awake another night as to think of yours received last night. And yet how idle will fall my opinion (tho' too kind to dispise my feelings)   As to the men who are seranading presses, they ask what that they dont value I guess—is it so? The sacred treasure of my first & deepest affections & hopes I should keep from their hands if I could. Were there extra events or changes in mind of the departed—let the eager empty publick be indulged—or what is infinitely more—had sacrifices to it or principles be made or needed—then let gold & saphire stampt them. But an unhappy time for education—narrowed modes of living in a smale compass—yes—always for in Boston at that time & society what to awaken thought and admiration? Could you have seen the Subject[1] in College—in soceity admired for beauty frankness and youthfull enthusiasm ingenuity & truth—one of the first scholars & "who ought to have the first part," your prophecy would have kindled. But the romance of life was first chilled by disappointed affection in one of the most captivating of women, at that day. And my richest remisience is on that occasion. I believe there was a nominal or virtual engag^t I heard. And the old Lee Castle, now Barretts, was much assailed by admirers of the Sisters.

The one I aim at was attended by a bright Lawyer the paternal Uncle of Judge Fay. The noble lover promised that if he ever again saw that man's horse at her door, he would never renew his addresses—he saw it & kept *his truth*, tho' he might surely have taken possession of what he had won. No other did for long years. Again & he nobly sought a poor orphan for her worth beauty & genius, and again intended union with a fine woman Miss Doubleday.[2] Phebe & I went to dine with her at Stow & met him from Harvard. A most pleasant day. Health & joy attended. How often I recall few such social days. The next week we attended her funeral! It was designed that the lovely tempered and dignified Ruth should be the wife. As to his advantages—too poorly prepared—and settled too soon in an undeserving society. His patience rather affected his manners &c. An old man now good in this place, was a parisher & tells me how he was forborne with by his minister, who once carried him a good book but he refused it & the visit. Still poor as society was there how often since his decayed years of health, & the compitions of new & brilliant men like Holley & the young B.[3] devoted to please. Alas, dear poor B. how didst thou fail in vanity I believe after returning from Europe the first time, from a secure & witty sarcasm I heard given thee by old Mr Eliot.[4] Mild & lowly—yet never able to touch (from what I've read) the deep recesses of the heart or make one *think*. And are his sermons better more affecting than my subject's? Those of the unitarians I heard at thursday lectures were except Channing & Holleys. Have you read those printed? But why? *You* cannot be interested. Besides, I am not as I should have been, nor the xian world had he not been a Priestlean altogether. That most most stulifying faith (if faith it be) was fatal to his young enthusiasm & pulpit. His prayers tho' were the best of any almost. And all I believe higher & sermons[n] than the sermons of his celebrated Predessor, Clarke.[5] But I write on without having reminisnces. For I knew him but little after settling at H. or before only by glimpses, at w'h *I wished his glory* tho' I might never see it or him. His theology seperated all sympathy, thro my imprudence, perhaps, & my obstinate aversion to fashion. You alone are the best judge of committing to common hands his memory. And I grow indifferent to every thing. But would say with Antoninus, "it is pleasant to die if there be gods—and sad to live if there be none"[6]—so of memoirs, if immortal they are useless— — except[n] those w'h throw new light & strenght. And in going after such as I have found in some of the Germans I could but respect Priestleys quiet grave compared to the will of wisps w'h they conjured up & dreamed them into the spiritual world.

I hope you will suceed in do justice to your lamented friend[7] & give energy to it's readers. I think if she had survived only her husband—and been impressed with that kind of grief w'h gives a zest of immortality to certain minds we read about, her expression &c &c I may as well confess—that in taking an interest in her fate I do not love to remember her want of beauty. She looked very sensible but as if contending with ill health & duties. Had I been favored with one sparkel of her fine wit—one argument for her dissent, from her fine mind what a treasure to memory. She laid all the day & eve. on soffa & catechised me who told my literal "traditions" like any any old bobin woman.[8] Well you'll never read half this as you are so full of business so adieu dear W.

MME.

Send me somthing to make *think*. And I have been going for long to ask your Mother to send me a vol. of your fathers sermons   Long years & I loaned them to one who has lost them.

Good night & good days *forever*   In reading over this hasty written letter with bad spirits I find I did not say what I meant & often believe that in solitude books & healthy piety the Recluse of Harvard would have been a happier wiser man—somewhat resembling his ancestors who knew not the name of ambition—and his native elements expanded with patriotism & benevolence equal to his early aspirations   Preistly left for S. Clarke. Pious Locke for the good sensible scotch school. Pardon my garullity

Sab Eve   I fear you will scorn my sending the scrap but you ca'nt feel as I all alone & nothing to do. Can it or not influence you I know not but believe *not*. Who *is* the Editor?

MH: bMS Am 1280.226(935). *Addressed: Only* for Mr Emerson to open. *Endorsed:* M. M. E. / Aug. 1850.

higher & sermons] higher ↑ & sermons ↓

useless— — except] useless—(if not idle)— except

1. Rusk describes this letter as "mainly a history of [MME's] love life" (*L* 4:226), but the story MME begins here concerns her brother's youth; RWE may have asked about him in his letter. Her story is not clear, but it involves a number of known Concord events. Dr. Joseph Lee (1716–97) built a "venerable mansion" on his "grand farm" in the Nawshawtuct Hill area of Concord, on the triangle between the Sudbury and Assabet rivers; however, none of his female descendants seems a likely choice for the admired sister of MME's tale. By 1821 the farm was owned by members of the Fay and Barrett families (who were connected by marriage). Jonathan Fay (ca. 1754–1811), a Harvard College classmate of EzR's, was a postrevolutionary lawyer in Concord; one of his daughters married Joseph Barrett, who took over the property in 1825. In 1852 their son Richard Barrett (who became owner in 1844) sold the property to Samuel G. Wheeler, who renovated it (Grindall Reynolds, "Story of a Concord Farm and Its Owners," in *A Collection of Historical and Other Papers*, ed. Alice Reynolds Keyes [Concord, 1895], 147–73; John S. Keyes, *The Story of an Old House* [Concord Antiquarian Society, n.d.]; MS records in the Concord Free Public Library).

2. "Doudleday" in MS; MME may confuse Miss Doubleday with Lucy Grosvenor, whose funeral she attended on 11 Feb. 1795 with sister Phebe and EzR (MH; see MME to WE[3], 29 July 1793).

3. Joseph Stevens Buckminster.

4. Probably John Eliot (1754–1813), minister of New North Church, Boston, 1779–1813.

5. John Clarke (1755–98), minister of First Church, Boston, 1778–98.

6. Paraphrased from *The Meditations of the Emperor Marcus Aurelius Antoninus; A New Translation from the Greek Original . . .* by R. Graves (London, 1811), 28–29. RWE used MME's version in "Worship," *W* 6:240.

7. RWE was working on the *Memoir* of Margaret Fuller Ossoli, who died 19 July in a shipwreck off Fire Island, N.Y.

8. Cowper's "bobbin woman."

To LIDIAN JACKSON EMERSON

Vale   Oct 15 '50

My dear Lidian,

Why have you not written to me anathamatising the odious *Bill* for returning the poor slave—you so well denounced the omission of thier cause
on the *19*?[1] Are you all silent & acquiesent in Concord?! It was ill timed to
visit Sybill[2] after years (long) absenting on antislavery reasons   She invited
me so kindly and I desirous to be rid[n] of the *slavery* w'h domestic cares forced
(not by stern respected nessesity) but from an unapeasable apprehension of
some thing being amiss in house or dress gentility that I escaped knowing for
certainty that I should never in body nor willingly in spirit visit that place
w'h always obstructed thought & damped feeling when boarding there long
months. Mr Frothingham *aged* rather from never having a *soul* to any appearance, passes all his reading hours in Dicken's works or French novels &
newspapers. Ellen a handsome & devoted lover of poetry seems apathised as
her parents to all but the tangible wants of the present life. An old maid Sister
of my once loved Lydia more avercious for amusement & property than is
usual—[3] But I forget myself and you & will describe no longer. At Sybils I
became aware of the bill & the sattisfaction of the family. With the kindest
attentions & a peace w'h I intended to maintain I remained about ten days, &
hastened to Winthrop Hotel, where for two days I was waiting to see an old
& revered friend in the person of the Pastor devoted to abolition, in vain. In
both places I had as much solitude with books as I could use—w'h solitude
agreed with visitor & hosts. *Business* & its sweet results occupied Mr L. &
his sons one of whom a very likely man soon to be married to a rich Judge's
daughter—the grown daughter's heart far away in California where her be-
trothed has been 5 years—these with Jenny Lind, whom the father & son had
just come from hearing were an innocent amusement to me, with fine houses
& costly presents for the Belfast bride.[4] These descendants of my father are
naturally fine children—but immersed in the whirl of the present times Alas!
Thier interesting images followed my lone & tedious journey in the Carrs,
whose occasional howls reminded me of the Cerebus who watches misery,
& the volumns of steam w'h vanish into "thin air" of those who pursue *only*
this poor world, whether in it's refined arts its human affections or grosser
wealths. An hour with Paulfrey (rev.) Judd[5] & especially my friend D[r] Bacon
dentist at Portland left me something of existence. Tis dusk. In haste for dear
Elisabeth to send me 10#   And as soon as convenent. I have such dear things
to say to her that I shall write soon if she is at home & speaks to me.

Love to him who thinks not of your
aff[t] Aunt MME

* * *

MH: bMS Am 1280.226(804). *Addressed:* Mrs R. Waldo Emerson / or Miss E.
Hoar / Concord / Mass. *Postmarked:* So. Waterford Me / Oct 16. *Endorsed:* M M E /
Oct 1850.

desirous . . . rid] ⟨anxious⟩ desirous to ⟨avoid⟩ be rid

    1. The Fugitive Slave Act went into effect on 18 Sept. 1850; for LJE's denunciation, see LJE to MME, 11 Aug. 1850, *LJE L*, 172–74.

    2. Possibly MME's first attempt to visit niece Sybil Farnham Lambard since her aborted visit in Aug. 1833; when temperance reform made distilling unprofitable, Allen Lambard turned his business into an iron foundry.

    3. William and Lydia Frothingham of Belfast and daughter Ellen (1835–1902); probably Lydia's sister Rebecca Prentiss (1794–1873).

    4. MME's great-nephew Charles A. Lambard and Frances E. Johnson of Belfast married on 29 Oct. 1850.

    5. Cazneau Palfrey (1805–88) succeeded Frothingham as pastor at Belfast, Maine, in 1848; Sylvester Judd.

To Ralph Waldo Emerson

This letter *only* for Waldo of no consequence, perhaps, even to him—but no one else to read[1]

                                        Vale   Nov. 27   Wed   [1850]

    You will recur to the past w'h I always "bury."[2] As to resemblance between parents & offspring there is none naturally between souls. My Father left no trace of his ardent unselfism on one of us. A irritable hot temper come thro' organisation of the flesh. Bliss & Emerson were united neither of w'h were calm in temper—but in all the memories w'h my Uncles & Aunts could collect—nothing but the candid & kind & *giving* never spoke of saving was in their idolised brother. And yet I've often said that never were more unamiable tempers than my two respected pious usefull departed S.s^n A long scene of severer discipline was the nessceary gift of Heaven—& mine alas, how much longer & forlorn may it be. My remembrances of one who seemed destined for love & respect are, when he characterised with pleasure the genius of Kirkland saying that he possessed more than Thayer & himself—praises of Buck. Thacher & Holley.[3] He had some life left after a dolorous dull life in domestic econimees & solitude at Harvard & with "Priestley's Corruptions."[4] But he went to City believing he should disappoint society—was out of health & alas for his clerical & domestic education, respected society too much & his whole being too little. Had he one friend, superior, to whom he could closly communicated himself what a continuance of his youthfull fame. One remembrance I cherish (more than limited views gave me then) in his last days he said to me of that "robe so needed"—not any thing like the fanatics or antinomian's corruption. And where is the mystery—whence came the beauty & worth of the excited mind? And in higher wants why not richer gifts? Yes I love to think of his future. And of yours—of the vast variety spirits pass. The doctrine of transmigrations of high order is founded in nature— w'h is in many of its' instincts in unison with XY. And some *antipodal beyond* interpretation. What changes? After forming some close intimacies with a platonic Angel—his mission is for ages remote from yours—w'h call you to some distant world, where intellects alone without affections is the order of existence (and why such ca'nt be happy like Archimedes I dont see)   For how many sorrows cluster round love here. But you who have tasted celestial— wont be sattisfied—and will surely avoid the "dull heaven" & silly loves of the sainted Swede.[5] You will never go where the last pages of that lecture will not be approved, I dont believe! It was very nectar to my soul. His mesmeritic state was not tinged with one hue of the love of the Infinite, abstracted as it's nature is able to be from all others! Oh how puerile to that spirit who has entered the more immediate Presence are the praises & censures of this almost crazy world! And how contemptously you will recall the subject of correspondences—little tongues & all those whims w'h crazed him by too much useless stuff. When new worlds of new & undreamt of sciences open on regenerated minds—touch with new raptures every law of existence where will be any material vestige? Surely we have more than enough here. Not but great respect is due to phi. sciences w'h lead the young to theism & show that there are no forces in nature without a Mover. But they get no "robe" for "*inherent* evil" w'h the Examiner believes, without showing any remedy.[6] Pray forbear to flout my "sniffling" w'h I could not resist without laughing. *I do pray to know* what *ails* your eyes. Disease? theres science. Decay? then glasses at night as others & S.A.R. use. I was surprised & anxious the night of last tues. when your letter came   And wrote a number of prescriptions by midnight. Recollected myself & waited for Elis—'s letter, who is a kind & intelligent narrator, & was silent & destroyed the old saws. Still permit me to say that I've doctored mine well. Avoid all violent changes from dark to light & night walks. A paper of rum (or brandy w'h I never have) put on soon as the light is out restores strenght. And why did I snuffle about your eyes   Surely we need an epic. I know no one who can do so well blind—your images will return constantly and new ones & more distant—more at home where all germs are breathed. I can't see any resemblance to C. C. in Ellen rather in the mild & obedient Eddy. I could not become acquainted with Ellen   I know her talents uncommon and her flatterers of fashion & influence. Dear Edith how does she come on?[7] I am curious to know if my directions have restored my Sister's eyes. She used no nights. No love to Lidian till she forgets her labours & writes

Farewell dear Waldo with unfailing respect for your genius & ever love for your sucess

M M E

Please be kind to C.F.[8] if you meet. He was gentlemanly in his account to me for board w'h I would not accept gratis. He was so pleased with your gift of Platto he would not loan it me & it was not what I needed   Thanks for Wordsworth w'h I loaned & I've never read. When I saw how much light you used I tho't of the birds who become blind you know on snow mountains.

MH: bMS Am 1280.226(938). *Addressed:* R. Waldo Emerson Esq[r]. / If absent to remain unopened / Concord / Mass. *Postmarked:* So. Waterford Me / Nov 29. *Endorsed:* M M Emerson / Nov. 1850.

S.s] *probably abbreviation for* Sisters

1. Written on outside.

2. MME responds to a letter from RWE, written about 24 Nov., which does not survive (*L* 4:235); RWE seems to have asked about his grandfather, WE[1], or his father, WE[2] (the "one" she begins to remember below); cf. MME to RWE, 16 Aug. 1850.

3. All ministers in Boston and contemporaries of WE[2]: John Kirkland (1770–1840), at New South Church, and president of Harvard College from 1810 to 1828; Joseph Stevens Buckminster (1784–1812), at Brattle Street Church; Samuel Cooper Thacher (1785–1818), Kirkland's successor at New South beginning in 1811; Horace Holley (1781–1827), at South End Church (Hollis Street) beginning in 1809.

4. Joseph Priestley, *A History of the Corruptions of Christianity*, 2 vols., first published in 1782.

5. RWE's lecture on Swedenborg in 1845 became the basis for his essay on the Swedish mystic in *Representative Men*, published in Jan. 1850.

6. Probably a reference to C. A. Bartol, "Modern Scepticism," *Christian Examiner* 49 (Nov. 1850): 317–40.

7. RWE and LJE's three children, Ellen (1839–1909), Edith (1841–1929), and Edward (1844–1930).

8. Calvin Farrar.

1851

To Ralph Waldo Emerson
Only for R W E to read[1]

Vale   Feb '51

Dear Nephew,

The first object is to say, please convince Gore that A. Parsons gave 100 to the cause of his father H. in Cottage debt—that you paid 300 for w'h you had the deed w'h you transfered to me. Reasons of request to so dull a case.[2] viz. Last spring after hearing of sale of farm A.P. wrote for 100 (to pay the pressure of the Creditor at Providence) for barn. I instantly wrote to Gore & his answer was implicating sadly A.P. that I owed him nothing of the 100 he had produced that Mr R.H. owned that I had relinquished 60 or 80 acres long since   Now *those* were merely crowded into my deed for a cover. Besides R.H. had a claim w'h his brothers contrived to sattisfy him of 400 on my farm. So that must be paid & A.P. an honest man must have his 100 out of the 4 tis possible R.H. has given.* I have never answered my Councillor's letter, as A.P. wrote that if I had received nothing that he would quiet Matherson till this spring   Why I've had no rent before, nor why Gore took a mortage of farm from Howe, I never inquired nor knew till lately. Was rather pleased & obeyed you my long accounted Sir in asking no question & Gore desired me not to come into the parlour at W. Cure till he called me to sign a deed I believe. As his children maintain R.H. it matters not who has the 100. Some acres of poor land beginning under the barn the girls say their father lays claim too not legally rather morally they think— I have told them no moral one can exist after my mode of spending my anuity on myself, but as a millioneth chance of honesty, as the land was not the neighbours say on the Pollard place, I intend to sattisfy the claim in my will & if possible before. Alas I wrote the poor fragment while sick & inclose it to see if the Executor approves its form. That indisposition w'h had been hanging for winter somewhat came on lungs so hopefully that I was confident it was consumption. And avoided your knowledge as determined that none of you should know till after burial (such is the state of snow & cold here). If this hacking hopefull cough continues & is an answer to natural hourly petitions in May you L.[,] S.A & E.H. must come & see me—*that is when I personally* request it. Who is to arrange my last offices? Why Mr O. Hale. He has paid the taxes & no Monroe near. He has a heart at the bottom of a seared conscience. Who was it wrote that a "whole villian was preferable to a half"? *Pray* explain & tell me the Author, as it suits my feelings so well. If Howe had been at home I should have chosen a long known neighbour. Howe while I was writing the conditions of the bargain I sent you at the moment of about to write 1500 took advantage (I think) of my nervous anxiety for his wife's safty with a young horse, to ask a reduction of 50 w'h I instantly yielded saying the care & assistance of theirs rendered price indifferent. A single month convinced me that mamon was their idol & their childrens early imbued with one sole pursuit. He & his oldest son & girl are carrying on a large establishment in keeping workmen to build a large Hotell so only Mother & youngers at home. No horse to use & his early & insolent assumption of an entry &c sickens me. Yet when well as I have been accostomed to imprisonment & contest with ignorance & privation[n] most of all my years makes no change in the inward content. But as poor forgotten Scott says—

"its very nakedness had power
    to aid the feelings of the hour."

But not like the Kantian school whose only point is "the inward active consciousness bro't out by a vigorous will." Alas my will is a poor thing till roused for executorship. In wealth & ease & friendship how unable to controul— how much poorer & vainer & prouder would you have found the future character of your poor Aunte. *Wealth* my dear Waldo how could *you*—you gifted to rouse the interior to make even xians think & feel at certain high sentiments—how—under what illusion could you lecture to Concord of it's advantages?![3] *You* sap the foundations of all that is great & independant. Oh send the young to Brothels & intemperance, 'tis possible the *spirit* may retain generosity under *bodily* guilt—but never does the miser. You born to suggest *ideas*—to new dress old eternal ones. You who have steadily stood for the *rights* of the slave are riveting his chains & pursuing the fugitive with increasing the rage the mania for wealth. Were you poor (and the papers speak of your high taxes) what a beautifull vision might you have drawn of it's baseless fabrick while you awakned charity in it's depths & glory. Forgive me if I offend, & send me the lecture. Thanks for your last letter note and its book & bottle of a kind of high spirits[n] better than lavender for my bathings. Tell "Mama" her muff came in time to loan a poor nice widow whose I hope it to be. I dont go out but 2 or 3 times the winter by Hale's means & then Lidian's answered. No one tell dear E.H & the rest need be anxious if I am sick "S. or Charlotte can come at an hours warning" I shall write to E. as soon as I am well. w'h I fear—but however deep the disappointment I still hope it not lasting. What is the usual expense from N.Y.? I believe E. has ten # w'h I wish you to inclose to your aff^t Aunt

MME

H. S. & C. sent word that any provision for Uncle R. was very hearty And long years of aid & home for children deserves more than I have given—only Justice—for myself I could find no sympathy nor but little hospitality there. And I could not think it but right. And Sister Phebe when I went to thank her said "only forgive." Martha has never made effort to pass a sick day with since her Aunts death. I have had no D^r but by acident once & twice It is inconsistant to be desirous of going. I might be moved to one Monroes but get on with many comforts

I dont regret selling as I felt it was best. The spiders web is no less geometrical & designed than the first of men. Who paid Gore for his coming— Howe? And for what he did about Matherson? I thought of giving him a 100 in will, as he said his executorship s^d cost nothing to the heirs. I insisted he should make charges. This years since. And I can *never* get near that nephew. Love to M.B. & glad she tho't "no Emerson could lecture on wealth."

*A. P. a deed of strawberry hill farm but A feels no security & cant sell

MH: bMS Am 1280.226(940). *Addressed:* R. Waldo Emerson Esqr. / Concord / Mss. *Postmarked:* Waterford Me / Mar 3. *Endorsed:* M M E / March 1851.
     privation] pri— *in ms*
     high spirits] ⟨alcohol⟩ ↑ high spirits ↓

     1. Written on outside.

     2. This is one of many letters in which MME attempts to explain her side of the questions surrounding her sale of the Elm Vale farm. Persons named or mentioned include CGR, who acted as MME's lawyer in the transaction; Augustus Parsons ("A.P."), who married niece Hannah Haskins ("H."); her brother-in-law Robert Haskins ("H." and "R.H."); Allen C. Mathewson ("Matherson"), to whom MME had sold or given twenty-five acres in 1845, which RWE bought back for MME later that year for $325; Oliver Hale (Sr. or Jr.), one of MME's closest neighbors; probably William Monroe, who sometimes handled business for MME and whose wife, Betsey Atherton Monroe, boarded MME for a while in Waterford; John Howe, who bought the farm in 1850; nieces Sarah Ripley Haskins ("S.") and Charlotte Haskins ("C.").

     3. According to Concord Lyceum minutes, RWE read "Property" on 6 Dec. 1850; no title is given for the lecture read on 19 Feb. 1851 (*Lyceum* and Charvat). Either could have been an early version of "Wealth," which became the third lecture in the series on the conduct of life.

To Ann Sargent Gage

Concord   July 2 Wed. 51

My dear Ann,

Nessesity & you'll excuse my unasked letter. * * * "Did you suceed at Shakers?"[1] I never felt beyond Glocestor there finding no boarders taken. Had a sickly sad night of wakfullness thro fatigue ect. and it came most graciously to mind to go to N. Port instead of passing the sab. at Portland Hotel & there I rested till tuesday noon from w'h I reached here at 4 o'k. These alternations of ease & pain w'h are wisely designed to school us I rarely experienced so much as in that short Journey finding myself in company with one of the most interesting men the eve. of getting there. It was Ex. Proffesor Crosley of Yale College—who has devoted himself to the consolation of his sickly & afflicted Mother in law since the death of his only Child (his wife) dead some years since & the two last years lost her affectionate husband. This *Son* indeed dont leave her, but his study is opposite her parlour & if he goes out for some hours calls Louisa Tracy to sit with her. His rubing her arms every morning was a singular & affecting affair.

This bereaved Mother has long been a friend to me and I put up at their boarding house. Afraid of exciting the lately weakned nerves of Ann Tracy I let her know of my being there & who came sab Morn. but S.J. Gardiner with her! And most of the time we were together. Mrs Tracy better than when last I heard. We spoke of my condition w'h is impossible to avoid with Ann and of course how lonely I had lived. We spoke of you in another way for the very first walk on saturday was to see Miss Gould with my poem & verses. I had only known her as an autheress. I wanted to learn her taste & sympathies—so showed her the Basin lines first expected her to kindle at the cave & description—[2]   No   She was filled with saturday sewing "had no time to read any thing was continally called upon for supplying out of Town publications"   I therefore read those pages (w'h I never weary off)   "she could not enter into the situation of their auther." I felt indignant for her neglect of me but *more* for want of taste. I told her if she never read how could she progress or Judge what it was &c. Moreover that I thought her poetry—(not to me surely) had fallen off. She saw how it was & *owned* (I *think*) that "she was envious." Well my pronouns came on stronge when relating to the Tracy house all the above. Oh Mrs. T. was shocked at my telling her the last sentence. I did not leave till I had seen & heard Mr Crosley read all & hear all that past. Was it not a duty I insisted (the resentment impelled)? to let every writer know every friends opinion? He said it was good for the writer. I was sattisfied with the pleasure & interest he discovered at reading—he is a disciplined man in every way. And I dont expect to find any one who feels those pages with me.

Miss G. says her living depends on writing. Unhappy.

There is somthing so sacred in new thoughts of religion that to sell them— alas! And to use the muse for bread, Alas, But what would the world be were it not so ordained that bread is often thus had—& surely more respectable than to write for fame—that very toy w'h time so often obliterates as the east winds of autumn blights & burns the flowers of summer. I found Sister E. confined with a disjointed hip—but so comfortable "so rich in nurses & Charlotte the prominent one to her" that tears of affection fell while she drawed me to her embrace—today E. H. & I rode down again and she was comfortable.[3] The eve was with some of the three families today   I ca'nt feel like going to dine among any of them for it is so good to sit still & find such good lodgings

Mrs Hoar I saw a few moments & her spirits yet good. Elis. had engaged the lodgings & to furnish the room so here lies a carpet & bed stead & she will soon be here to sit. It is near her. & S.A.R. I expect. This is a new kind of pronouns for rarely so great a contrast. The best eve. I remember of a social kind in Maine was the last spent with you. I beg you to write in pity to my wishes to hear from Max—& money   I send this by Express to Boston but not whether it can be paid here last night Waldo & E.H. said it would go sooner

Fare well   I hope you will write long for they will expect to hear it.

Your aff[t] friend

MM Emerson

I hope never to end an acquaintance thro' your writings as I have with the lady who I dont think is wholly dependant on her pen. Lives in a fine house tho' no domestic.

Please say to Mr Max.[4] I wrote paid & meant to have carried his letter myself but the man took it when I was absent

MWA. *Addressed:* Mrs Ann S. Gage / Waterford / Maine. *Postmarked:* Concord, 2 July.

1. EH and MME visited Rebecca Haskins Hamlin, who was living in the Shaker colony at Harvard, Mass., about 28 July 1851 ("EH L," *SAR* 1984:257).

2. MME frequently used ASG's poem, "The Basins" (a reference to the Albany Basins, a romantic waterfall about eight miles from Waterford) to test the taste of those she met, as she did here with the Newburyport poet, Hannah Gould.

> In God's true temples the whole heart cries out
> For transformation, harmony with truth,
> With all true forms, the vast and the minute.
> The holy service needs not human speech.
> The tall old Hierarchs from out their cores
> Dispense the healing word, the Gilead balm,
> The Balsam for torn hearts by discord rent.
> The orchestra pours forth from inmost throat
> A rich mellifluence of sacred song;
> And the large blessing waits for ready hearts,
> True Word of Life, distilling as the dew.
> Sweet soothing Power, so softly breathing love,
> Distil on us, attune our jarring strings,
> And join our song in unison with thine.

[TS, MWA; dated 10 Aug. 1849; "Visited 'the Basins' in Albany Aug. 9th."]

3. RHE broke her hip on 26 July 1851; niece Charlotte Haskins served as RHE's nurse from 15 June 1851 to 30 Jan. 1852.

4. Probably Eliakim Maxfield, an owner and manager of the Waterford Stagecoach line.

To Samuel Moody Haskins and Hannah Haskins Parsons

Harvard   Aug. 14 '51

Rev. S. M. Haskins

I have been loathe to state many of the facts w'h I believed all your family knew and had told you. Still more disgusted at relating facts wh would infer any justification of my known character[n] with their bad defects— But Mr Waldo Emerson whose practice & character as well as his kindnesses to me among a numerous beneficances renders his opinion oracler wished me to state the facts of my posessing the farm. And I believe he wished Mr Gore Ripley to *see* them sent to you. They render yours fabulous. In 1805 your father took a deed of the farm & in 1809 Mr Ralph Haskins found it nessecary to relieve his brother took a deed of him, & in two or 3 years hired a thousand # of me & gave me a mortage, w'h (after many intreaties to be saved the consequence of having my little property in a place w'h I did not desire to be *obliged* to live in) he turned into a deed. I feel smale at remembering how painfull was the sacrifice & the displesure your father felt that a mortage from him had not been the case. And when I named giving the whole 1500 "he would never work on a farm without ownership"—so his brothers provided that I gave him a bond for the 7 or 10 years w'h my lease to him extended & he thus "owned," and the world of waterford never discovered, I believe, till after '45 the all important (it seems by your letter) fact. Your father often blest with gentlemanly impulses said I "was good" in secrecy & as it required no deception was no trouble. This *bond* renders me I tho't legally due to the Haskins and I have written this once & again to my benefactor & agent that the mortage I gave his cousin Waldo for money to save the Cottage was I believed due on that hand morally if not legally. But such has[n] been my haste or incapasity when addressing Gore (& feeling a stronge reluctance to have him amidst the toils of constant engagments with my little toly affairs) that he never perceived or saw the affair as I did. Nor have I been less, but more unintelligible in speaking of asking "no rent" but the interest of 1100#. Every one knew I lived on the interest when there & when desired to board elsewhere the interest was paid chiefly, till ceasing, I was obliged to return. Your uncle Ralph charged 80 for yearly rent, I know for one year while boarding with your Mother at her request (before your birth & after)   I allowed Mr Ralph a year 70, w'h interest he owed me. Nor did Mr C.G. Ripley find me advanced in giving an exact statment (or what I beleved one) of the relinquishment of land to your father, w'h he discovered by his friend Emery[1] giving him copies of all my concerns, without my knowledge—such & so generous has been his care of me that I feel a debt of gratitude w'h nothing pecuniary in my power can repay—he fullfills an assurance his ever noble father gave that "while Gore lived, I should never miss one to take a friend's care." It is true there might have been a deed to w'h the Lawyer refers, (besides those relinquishments wh were lands put this deed) to cover what belonged to your father & wh I had no right but to sign away when desired[n] wh I gave to Mr Haskins in Sep. 1828[2] under the immediate impulse of showing my confidence and good will. As I was walking near him one very fine morning in Sep. he kindly asked me to give him a little piece of land

Pointing to it I *told him to take what he pleased*—soon after he asked me to call as I was passing & sign the deed. I did call & about to sign, Whitman[3] *advised* me to *read*. I could not have understood perhaps, & haste to mount my horse desired him to alter what would indanger my right to the house lands &c. He did I believe, tho' in my haste to sign before commencing a long absence to east Andover, never knew it's contents, and Mr H. engaged that no record should take place, *naturally* for his organized memory he forgot & recorded it. He was as apt to forget his own as other interests, and *I have not blamed him for omissions or commissions* to any one. *It* is the worst mishap that attends *un*organized memories, or what is called bad (better called none) ones, that the imajanation takes part with the passions for wealth or power or influential consequence, that the images by constant habitual indulgence *assume the nature of facts,* even in persons of good sense, if also excited temperments & imajanations. That the hallucinations of believing the farm his own honestly, and saying to my deceased Agent,[4] "that *I had no rights" is* one living instance of many an illusive belief. It is innocent till it injures justice to character. And such must my Nephew C.G.R. find, if he should ever be acquainted with my habits & disposition from the "self denials & labours of your Sisters as represented thro' your ignorance, of sacrifices w'h nothing but looking to Heaven" can repay. And ingratitude the worst of crimes must be infered for me. It has been my humble lot to make none worth naming. My constant regret was till the H—h & Sarah grew up that I did no more work, or could afford no more aid in money than supplying my own monied wants. Could I have done as the gifted with means, I should have learnt by bitter self knowledge that I had no human claims to look to Heaven for justification.

Adieu dear Rector, little personal acquaintance have we ever, & less likely from our distance to have any more. I have sympathised in your afflictions & present prosperity, esteemed you as an affectionate son & brother. Wishing you & your amiable wife those blessings w'h last forever[5] I bid you kindly

farewell.

MM Emerson

Dear Hannah,

I should have written before, but waited to fullfill my promise of sending 70# to make a 100 for the barn with receipts for more than 90 w'h I sent copies off by R.T.H. last March. Your husband (whose understanding and judgment are good) fails about memory—this attribute of mind is said (or rather was said) & adopted by my Father Ripley, that a sound judgment & sound memory not usual to meet. I whose organ for *events* merely is strong, often verify his belief. Mr P. forgets the deed he wrote for me to Mr R W E for supplying 29# to pay a back tax of your fathers w'h deed returned as not acknowledged and a note on interest accepted by Gore in its stead for his cousin whose confidence in Gore is of the first rate. Your fruitfull imajanation has raised such tragic images about rights w'h no divine or human eye ever saw in my chamber with you or any watcher after dissmissing the kind watchers, that I wrote a long & minute history of each winter & one spring seperated by years—but do not send it. No my *much* loved child, in your growing life, and my consolation in some of my later eye confinements I retain it—but have ever refered to that state where memory will restore every instance & circumstance to connect us in a lasting union. Mr P. kindness in keeping a rightous account of all I had of eatables & wood w'h left me 30 or more # excites my gratitude as information that I had been of less expense to your father than I sometimes feared. I do believe I shall be able to give some other proof of both your kindnesses

some time before or after death.
Your loving MME.

MH: bMS Am 1280.226(1082).

character] ⟨habits⟩ ↑ character ↓

has] as *in MS*

to cover . . . desired] *written vertically in the margin; position for insertion not marked*

1. George F. Emery, Waterville lawyer.

2. In an 1846 account (MH: 225[27]), MME recalls the year as 1827, but she tells essentially the same story; in 1855, she again recalls giving to "R H. in Sep. about or less than 30 years since a deed of some of my land. He requested it as a favor and I impulsive & silly told him to take what he wanted   Some days after he asked me to stop & sign the deed   The lawyer asked if I knew its contents   he said it included the land on w'h the house stood. So he altered it but I never saw it" (MH: 950). MME's memory for specific dates and facts is quite reliable: it was Sept. 1827 when she felt so "irk'd" by her relations with Robert Haskins that she was ready to "clear out," and soon she left Waterford for Andover.

3. Charles Whitman.

4. Levi Brown (father of American humorist "Artemas Ward" [Charles Farrar Browne]) was serving as MME's "agent" in her negotiations concerning the farm when he died suddenly in Dec. 1847 (MH: 1178 and 225[28]).

5. See MME to LJE, 28 Jan. 1848, n. 6. In 1851 Haskins married Sarah B. Knickerbacker. MME's very cool statements here contrast markedly with the warmth of her note to Haskins's sister Hannah.

To Martha Bartlett and Elizabeth Hoar

Lancaster   Sep. 30 [1851] Tuesday

Dear Martha,

If I think of you oftener than usual 'tis from a new house & then the wonted discontent of change makes every freind & each of thier calls & kindnesses reappear to stir some pain & past pleasure. And now for the immediate cause for you to let the other houses know where I am. * * * At Harvard Stow & Bolton I became content but in the first the kind Angels of death hastened me the next was only transient as the first place the stage stoped— so the last—the Towns were indifferent only a home. And *this* promises— but a week with present ease is enough for age to calculate. It is well called a beautifull place—but not equal to dear old flat sandy Concord. Flatt also— no mountains like the late famed Waterford, where the stars tell of other ascending worlds at midnight & in the mornings when the crescent is paling before *the* star—then & there are tales. But tis any where & any star to w'h habit attaches—so kindly is human nature fashioned that the alternations of pleasure & pain darkness & light accostom the mind to find it's own place & prefer its associations to brighter scenes where no image of the past appears— nor it's very ghost—but to be silent long before cock crowing. I hope to like Bartol whose brother I love in his vol. of sermons.[1] Get them do—better while you read them than Martineaues "Endeavors." And this last may be too fond of his beloved Harriet.[2] To love is an earnest of Heaven—yet how dangerous if the object causes a single deviation from that *straight path* w'h leads there.[n]
* * *

Love to your parents & Aunt

Your afft friend M. M. Emerson

Has Mr Foster gone? Alas that he goes at all. Mr Packard I shall find friendly but not like Foster a brave man[3]

Oct 1   Wed   I cant let this go dear Elis. without asking what claim J.F C. has to be put before or at side of Bushnell?[4] If at home pray write soon. I came here night before last & resemble as usual a hen with her head taken out of wing—   No excitment or like wine it would *sedate*—but dudds lying in *my* way. I just found yours & this the consequence. I have been much taken with Uphams "Union."[5] One of the most original (to me) of all ideas & the whole chap. 12 is as opposed to all nat. & revealed religion as I ever saw thought or felt. Now & then one lights on a chap as the book opens w'h rouse & delight   You'll have the whole—   And Morells Philosophy of religion! better what I read than his 1t.

Antie MME

Martha will excuse me   I cant find a bit of paper for my impulse of &c

Tell Elis. H. I do expect another letter when she is settled. But not the least calculation of society—   It is called an aristocratic place—but not of the kind to allure me & all best for me in naming the clergy & some other D^rs family I added these lines.

MH: bMS Am 1280.226(621). *Addressed:* Miss Martha Bartlett / Care of J. Bartlett, M. D. / Concord / Mass. *Postmarked:* Lancaster / Ms. / Oct 1.

there] ⟨above⟩ there

1. The minister at Lancaster was George M. Bartol, brother of Cyrus A. Bartol, minister at Boston's West Church since 1837. C. A. Bartol's sermons were published in 1850 as *Discourses on the Christian Spirit and Life.*

2. James M. Martineau (Harriet's brother), *Endeavors after the Christian Life,* (1843).

3. Daniel Foster (1816–64), acting minister of the Second Congregational (Trinitarian) Church, Concord, in 1850 and 1851. MME suggests he is to be succeeded by Packard (unidentified).

4. James Freeman Clarke; Horace Bushnell; allusion not located.

5. Thomas Cogswell Upham, *A Treatise on Divine Union, Designed to Point Out Some of the Intimate Relations between God and Man in the Higher Forms of Religious Experience* (Boston, 1851).

To Lidian Jackson Emerson

* * *

[2 Dec. 1851]

Dear L.   The other page obsolete now I've seen your welcome   But it goes & were it not 12 o'k would sympathise with you about the lecture.[1] *What* was the mystery. No *record of her faith in imm^t!*^n Had she been xian! What a spirit! And thro' the future what a bright & burning one who could be so generous   *And her truth*   Oh what an eternity awaits. And we forget all if with her powers & influence as like the waves wh so soon ceased the feeble agitations w'h interred her remains

Good night

MH: bMS Am 1280.220(74). *Addressed:* Mrs R. W. Emerson / or Mr Emerson. *Endorsed:* M M Emerson / 1851.

imm^t!] *probably abbreviation for* immortality

1. In the first part of this letter, MME apologizes for her "oft disagreeable impulses," apparently correcting or preaching to LJE on Saturday evening. RWE lectured on Margaret Fuller Ossoli at the Concord Lyceum on 2 Dec. 1851.

To Ralph Waldo Emerson

Tues. [16 Dec. 1851] 4 ok PM.   I've just laid down your Commonwealth venturing to detain it. And after the vociferations of the City trust you will not take the task of reading it. But I hunger for your opinion on Kossuth's errand.[1] It affects my patriotism illy. A war! How great it sounds for universal peace principles & disinterested benvolence. But as yet I ca'nt approve it thro' the telescope of the most refined morality abroad. Where the cry from the Genius of peace? Does eloquence from a foreigner dim that of equal heros of our own? Is it xian or true philan. for him (already so filled with the generosity of this Country) to *broach* it? Are our great folks easily led away? You know them. I like a conscience war as did our kindred. And the antient ones were no worse(?) than any other penal deserts w'h dear grand natures ingulphed & burnt. However important my opinion to you I can instruct no longer

Mamas love   MME

The stars bring thought—& asks for the lectures w'h S A R says you have   A course on the "*conduct* of life".[2] Now these are what I long to see. If the *conduct* is to follow the "advantages of wealth" woe to the world! What *conduct* can but be farcical whose nessecary connections are not to be platform? This stirrs my curiosty   How better the generations who sleep forever or transformed into pretty beasts or weeds. And what all the arts & Baconish improvements of this life to them & their children who are like Henry's "scuttle of dirt"?[3] I know you believe in some infinite series w'h they tell me is immortality. Much highers you than your sympathiers. But to the point of this paper's existence. I mean to remain (God permitting w'h is glorious as a decree free will in all duress) in this place for one of the stirring motives w'h bro't me, till I *read some lectures*!

Mary M. Emerson

Wittness the 16 of Dec 1851

MH: bMS Am 1280.226(945). *Endorsed:* Dec 1851.
  1. The *Boston Daily Commonwealth* was filled with stories about Louis Kossuth, the "Hotspur Hungarian" (19 Dec. 1851), from the time of his arrival in New York on 5 Dec. On 16 Dec., the front-page story, titled "Kossuth's Mission," explored the question of intervention by other nations in the Hungarian struggle for freedom; the *Commonwealth* viewed the noninterventionist argument as "absurd" and "obsolete," even if U.S. aid to the freedom fighters should lead to war.
  2. RWE's Boston series of lectures on the conduct of life began 22 Dec. 1851.
  3. See Thoreau's journal for 27 Oct. 1851 (PJ 4:155).

To RALPH WALDO EMERSON

[1851?]

If RWE Will send me his Fate works[1] it will *oblige*. Alas your covetousness in this way increased my zeal for the places I sought in other Towns. Had there been else but inanity I should have more regreted my vain enterprise. I intend to try at Amherst if I fail here.[2] But I *never fail* if I have a week at ease enough. But there should be no ease in a house of liqor perhaps & never shall be with a man pleased with the slave bill.

I have written a sort of draft of my notions or dream of *fate*, But will not show it before yours— And you or the very nearness to you locally always stops pen like the beaver whose architecture[n] always subsides before men.

Bless you in search of truth & glory prays
MME

I was told Mr Angier[3] did not come here on account of[n] I said I did not *know* nor you it was not a temperance

I wish there was nothing worse in the world but drunkness w'h is only a *bodily sin*

MH: bMS Am 1280.226(939).
architecture] ⟨artist⟩ architecture
of] *possibly* of —

1. RWE read "Fate," the first lecture in the conduct of life series, at Boston on 22 Dec. 1851. MME's note may be a response to RWE to MME (*L* 8:573–74), which Tilton dates [23? Aug.? 1858?]. If so, RWE's note would belong to 1851 or 1852.

2. After spending some time in Concord in July, MME traveled to at least six towns before returning to Concord in Dec. (see Calendar of Residences), making her present location difficult to determine; her reference to liquor and support of slavery suggests another attempt to visit Sybil Farnham Lambard.

3. Luther H. Angier (1810–98), minister at the Second Congregational (Trinitarian) Church in Concord from 1851 to 1858.

Part 6

1852–1862

1852   Concord, Lancaster (Jan.); Concord [Wheeler's] (Feb.–June?); Alfred, Maine (July–Aug.?); Kennebunkport, Bolton?, Maine (Sept.–Dec.?).

1853   Concord, Kennebunkport?, Newburyport? (Jan.–Feb.?); Ashfield, Mass. [house no. 1] with possible trip to Providence, Waterford, and Conway; WE[3] visits in Sept. (Mar.–Dec.).

1854   Ashfield [house no. 2] (Jan.–June?); trip to Staten Island, N.Y., with EH (June); Charlemont, Mass. (summer); Harvard, Mass. (Aug.); ? (Sept.); Shelburne Falls and Amherst, Mass. (Oct.); ? (Nov.–Dec.).

1855   ? (Jan.); Ashfield [house no. 3] (Feb.–June); Deerfield, Mass. (July?); Montague, Mass. (Aug.–Sept.) [Lucia G. Merrill's?]; Concord (Oct.–Dec.).

1856   Concord [Deacon Reuben Brown's] (Jan.–July); Goshen, Mass. (July–Aug.); ? (Sept.–Dec.).

1857   Cummington, Mass. (?–Mar.?); ? (Mar.–Oct.); Savoy [Hotel] (Nov.); Ashfield (Dec.).

1858   ? (Jan.–June), Concord [Mrs. Wright's], with visits in Boston (July–Oct.); Boston [P. B. Cobb's] (Oct.–Nov.); Concord (Dec.); Williamsburgh, N.Y. (Dec.).

1859   Williamsburgh [Hannah Parsons's] (all year).

1860   Williamsburgh (all year).

1861   Williamsburgh [ETE visits in Jan.].

1862   Williamsburgh.

1863   Williamsburgh; 26 Apr. Hannah Parsons sends word to Concord that the end is near; MME dies 1 May.

It is astonishing to realize that these letters from the 1850s were written by a woman who became eighty years old in 1854. Mary Emerson's moves from town to town and house to house are prodigious, as she continues her spiritual journey and search for a "home." In these years her quest is marked by a new kind of faith, a grand acquiescence to her situation. Gone are the anxieties about the future that troubled her in the 1840s. She realizes that she has never been at a loss for a place to stay; and even the occasional weeks spent searching for the house, family, quiet, and library she requires, all at "low board for a lady," occupy high points in her memory. She refuses to let Waldo know where she is when she is not settled, lest he jump in and urge her once again to Concord.

The many question marks in the Calendar of Residences for this part indicate how difficult it is to follow her movements in the first half of the decade. From 1852 to 1863, about eighty-seven letters survive (dating in this period becomes increasingly difficult, and letters are more often fragmentary); thirty-eight are printed here. Her correspondence widens to include several great-nieces and -nephews at the same time that old correspondences diminish (only seven letters to Elizabeth Hoar can definitely be assigned to this period, despite frequent references to Elizabeth as her "human Angel" and "executrix"). She continues to correspond somewhat regularly with Waldo and Lidian Emerson, but without the letters to Ann Gage, to whom a full third are addressed, we would have only a limited picture of these years.

For the first six years of this period, Mary continued her pilgrim life, boarding and visiting in New England, usually alternating between northwestern Massachusetts and the Concord-Boston area. About 1857–58, the quality of her writing begins to deteriorate significantly. In 1859 she moved to Williamsburgh (now Brooklyn), New York, to live out the rest of her days with niece Hannah Parsons. From 1859 through the first third of 1861, we can follow her adjustment to a new life in New York, both through her letters and through others' descriptions of her. The last surviving letter is undated and could come from 1862; nothing else survives from after May 1861. She was well cared for by Hannah.

In this period Mary Emerson became separated from the personal belongings she left behind in Waterford with her friends Betsey Monroe, Mary E. Millett, and Mrs. Joe Hale, perhaps because she never really believed she would not go back: her bed, blankets, carpet, a trunk full of manuscripts, her engravings, portraits, and medallion of Charles Emerson, many books and her bookcase all become leitmotifs in these letters. Some she sold or tried to give to favorite relatives and friends; many she tried to retrieve; but few returned to her. Although she often mentions her desire to board in Waterford, there is no firm evidence to indicate she ever returned after she left for Concord about May or June of 1851. She tried Concord twice again in the next two years, as well as about nine other places, mostly in Maine, before settling at Ashfield (northwest of Northampton) in March 1853.

Ashfield was a wonderful place to board. The main attraction was one of her favorite nieces, Charlotte Haskins Cleveland, who in November 1852 married the Episcopal minister of this small western Massachusetts town. Charlotte was the youngest of more than two dozen nieces and nephews who survived infancy. Born at Elm Vale in 1822, she was a full generation younger than her eldest Emerson cousin, John Hay Farnham, born in 1791. Long after most of her older siblings had left home, Charlotte continued to help out her family by teaching school and caring for their father and motherless or fatherless nieces and nephews, and she spent much of 1851–52 in Concord, caring for Ruth Emerson after she broke her hip in 1851 (although she left more than a year before Ruth's death on 16 November 1853). With Hannah Haskins Parsons in New York, Charlotte's new life was a godsend for Mary.

The letters from Ashfield in 1853 indicate that this was the earthly home she sought, a "pleasant roomly house & the hostess & daughter tiring me with kindnesses," on a "pleasant farm" about a mile from the "very pleasant Villiage" of Ashfield, where Charlotte and her "hospitable & gentlemanly" husband (the "C.C.'s") live. She found a friend in the orthodox minister and discovered other intellectual attractions. All she needed was her Waterford blankets. But, by January 1854, Mary was reminded again of the vanity of human wishes, when her wonderful landlady (or "hostess," as she always called the women with whom she boarded) became ill, requiring Mary to find new lodgings. By fall this kind and animated woman, mother of a "small family," was dead, following a miscarriage at the age of forty-five.

In June 1854, Miss Emerson traveled to Staten Island with Elizabeth Hoar to visit the William Emersons for about a month, and after their return to New England she explored at least three other boarding places (in Charlemont, near Ashfield, and Harvard and Amherst, Massachusetts) before returning to Ashfield early in 1855. Once again, she seemed happily situated with a good family, in a separate cottage; but by June 1855, the marriage of one of the daughters in this family required her to relinquish the cottage. This led her to board in at least seven more places over the next two and a half years. She accepts all of these events gracefully, gratefully, always ready to discover what new adventure awaits in the unfinished plot of her life.

The portraits of Mary Moody Emerson drawn by others, mostly people in Concord in these years, are the stuff of which legends are made. It was during her first stay at Concord in 1851–52 that Henry Thoreau described her as witty, vivacious, the woman "most profitable to meet—the least frivolous, who will most surely provoke to good conversation and the expression of what is in you," a "genius" capable of a "masculine appreciation of poetry & philosophy" (PJ 4:181–82). Frank Sanborn recalled that he first met Miss Emerson when she was eighty-one, which would have been during her 1856 Concord visit. He described her as four feet three inches tall and marked by "some of the deformities of old age" (*Recollections* 2:382, 363).

Sanborn's best story re-creates a Bronson Alcott "conversation" in Mrs. Emerson's parlor in December 1858, attended by Henry and Sophia Thoreau, Sam Ward, the poet Channing, Henry James, Sr., and several others, where "Mary Emerson distinguished herself." Sanborn wonderfully describes how James, "not understanding the law of an Alcottian conversation," began displaying his own wit, a "flow of . . . semi-Hibernian rhetoric" that stopped the conversation cold. No one quite knew how to turn James off: Sanborn prints Thoreau's statement that James uttered " '*quasi* philanthropic doctrines in a metaphysic dress, but [was] very crude,—charging society with all the crime committed, and praising the criminal for committing it.' " Mary Emerson listened "with rising wrath," and she lost her patience when James spoke scornfully of the moral law: "Rising from her chair at the west side of the room, and turning her oddly-garnished head toward the south side, where the offender smilingly sat, she clasped her little wrinkled hands and raised them toward the black band over her left temple (a habit she had when deeply moved), and began her answer to these doctrines of Satan, as she thought them" (2:384). He goes on to describe her defense of the moral law, her appeal to her favorite authorities, the Bible and Samuel Clarke, and her sound denunciation of her worthy opponent, all delivered across the room. When she had finished, she sat down quietly, and, Sanborn adds, she "was complimented by the smiling James, who then perhaps for the first time had felt the force of her untaught rhetoric" (2:385). Several years later, James himself recalled "that confabulation at Mr Emerson's" when he was " 'shamefully treated' by the old Lady from Maine." He, too, admired what he saw that day: really, he claimed, he felt "soothed and delighted. The old lady had the flavour to me of primitive woods wherein the wolf howls, and the owl has never been dislodged; and I enjoyed the novelty of her apparition in those days too much to mind the few scratches I got in making her better acquaintance."[1] The similarity between James's metaphors and those used by Elizabeth Peabody more than a decade earlier is striking.

The Concord antiquarian George Tolman, who, in 1901–2, in a beautifully clear hand, painstakingly transcribed the majority of the letters and "Almanack" for Edward Emerson, got to know Miss Emerson in the 1850s. He claims only a "slight and superficial knowledge of her . . . most marked and most publicly exhibited eccentricities of manner" in the 1850s; that is, he never knew her in her prime. Edward detected a negative "tone" in Tolman's portrayal, suggesting that some memory of his subject as a querulous old woman from his college days had colored his picture. Indeed, Tolman's monograph contains much loaded language, such as "clamorous," "annoying," and "proud old soul" (all from p. 29). However, he suggests that his portrait, derived as it is more from his close acquaintance with her writings than from any personal relationship, may "represent her as she was" (1) better than Waldo Emerson's well-known essay, "Mary Moody Emerson."

One other description comes from Susan Loring, a friend of Edith Emerson's, who was about twelve when she visited Concord in 1851–52. She, too, remembered Miss Emerson as tiny, standing near the pulpit in the old church, "hardly taller than a girl of twelve—and . . . dressed in a white woolen 'shroud.'" Susan's description helps to explain Sanborn's mention of Mary Emerson's "oddly-garnished head": Miss Emerson wore a small, close-fitting, black "cottage bonnet" with a black veil that "instead of hanging was drawn up at the side and fastened in a great bunch or knob on the top." Susan also told the anecdote about Mary's having tea with a woman friend. When asked if she would have "tea, coffee or chocolate," Miss Emerson replied, "All," and, when asked whether she wished separate cups or all together, the answer was "*All together*." So she "poured a little of each into a cup and she drank it" (15).

Stories like these preserve both this woman's eccentricities and her sharp mind, undiminished in conversation (although in writing she increasingly omits important letters or syllables from words, writing "specien" for "specimen," "orthody" for "orthodoxy," "physian" for "physician," and so on). Her interest in ideas continues unabated, and, in contrast to the debilitation experienced in the 1840s, which greatly limited her, she seems now to have more energy for reading omnivorously and commenting profusely. Waldo's claim that she chose her lodgings on the basis of reading potential is borne out by frequent mentions of the libraries of her "hosts."

Mary Emerson remained open to everything new in the world of ideas: she looked into mesmerism and galvinism as cures for her continuing erysipelas; continued to read J. D. Morell's lectures on philosophy and *Philosophy of Religion*; devoured sermons and discourses by Frederic Dan Huntington (the Unitarian preacher at Harvard who would soon become an Episcopal bishop), Hitchcock's *Religion of Geology*, Thomas Cogswell Upham's several books, Isaac Taylor and George Bush on the possibility of physical survival after death, Neander's life of Christ, and many other current writers. She was disappointed in a lecture by Louis Agassiz, whose reply to the fatalistic ideas of Robert Chambers she had admired in the late 1840s; and she confessed a strong interest in science, as interpreted by William Whewell. As the decade progressed, and she read Stowe's *Uncle Tom's Cabin*, Beecher's *Conflict of Ages* and James's response, *The Nature of Evil*, antislavery tracts and newspapers, Dewey, Stone, the Beechers, Palfrey, and Channing on slavery, she anticipated the coming conflict in the millenarian terms used by Taylor, whose "prophecy" about the "crisis" that would "revolutionize the world" and bring "good out of evil" she frequently quoted.

In November 1858, Mary Emerson spent her last Thanksgiving at Concord, and a few weeks later she had arrived at Williamsburgh. Niece Hannah was the "angel" provided for her last years. By all reports, Hannah was an extremely warm, capable, and attractive woman, immediately likable. Now forty-four years old, she was a skilled nurse: she had cared first for her mother until her death in 1839 in Waterford, then had kept house for her aging father after her own marriage in 1842. She had gone to Williamsburgh, in about 1848, to help raise brother Samuel's children after their mother died. After Samuel remarried in 1851, she began to care for aunts Betsey and Fanny Haskins (who died there in 1854), her father (who died there in 1855), and, finally, Mary. Later, William Emerson described how devoted Hannah Parsons was to her aunt, day and night. "Providence has mercifully ordained that she should be childless, so that she might be a martyr to Aunt Mary's infirmities, & those of several other excellent old and young people, whose path through this world has been smoothed by her tender care" (MT/MH). Hannah attended to her many needs, and Mary quickly adjusted to her new life.

It was near the end of Mary's first two years in New York, when she was still getting out to walk and visit occasionally and was somewhat regularly writing letters, that twenty-two-year-old Ellen Emerson visited and made her famous coup of the Mary Moody Emerson treasures. Ellen also gives us one of our last glimpses of a remarkable woman whose life was drawing to a close. In January 1861 Ellen went to New York with her father, who then "disappeared" to deliver lectures in various places while she stayed with her uncle William and aunt Susan. She made several trips to Williamsburgh to visit her great aunt, playing the role that Mary had imagined for years, described in dreams in which "a wife" or "daughter" of her nephews would come to treasure her manuscripts.

In two letters to her sister Edith, dated 10 and 15 January, Ellen, in her chatty way, tells us much about her aunt's condition. For Ellen's first visit, probably 8 January, Mary had insisted on being dressed entirely in black. Going upstairs to the bedroom from which Aunt was crying, "Here—here," Ellen endured a half hour of anxieties about her comfort and the setting, the weather, and other trifles before "business begins"—funny stories about Mary's luck with "Ministers and Doctors in Williamsburgh" (*ETE L* 1:222–23). On her second visit, the following Thursday, "after the preliminaries," Ellen worked the conversation around from family history to her aunt's papers, and she ventured to ask whether she had any. To her surprise ("mirabile dictu"), Mary "trotted up" to a chest full of letters and journals and offered Ellen whatever she wanted. Ellen left, filled with feelings of triumph. The next day, Friday, she returned, and this time Mary brought out old letters and told stories of grandmothers and great-grandmothers and aunts and cousins (Ellen's "What

I Can Remember of Stories of Our Ancestors Told Me by Aunt Mary Moody Emerson," MH). Ellen's list of what she found in Brooklyn (see *ETE L* 1:224) reveals how important her coup was for Emerson family archives.

At Mary's urging, Ellen slept that night in a bedroom adjoining her great-aunt's; the next morning she looked over the letters before going for dinner at cousin Charlotte Cleveland's three miles away. After dinner, Charlotte brought out more family papers for Ellen to take to Concord, including more journals. When she returned to Williamsburgh on Monday, 14 January, Ellen found Mary not well and perhaps not entirely lucid. They met downstairs this time, and Mary sent Hannah to fetch her "pall," a black shawl, from her room; she spoke of a "coffin across the street which she could see, 'the emblem of Peace.'" She was irritable, and her mind seemed to wander again during Ellen's last visit the next day, when she gave Ellen more letters and "talked again of the Symbol of Tranquillity" (*ETE L* 1:226).

After Ellen and her father returned to Concord with her treasure trove of manuscripts, Mary wrote at least four more letters, the last of which (to Sarah Bradford Ripley) may come from 1862. The only other evidence for these last two years comes from William's letters to his brother. In November 1861 he described her "painful" situation and Hannah's difficulties in coping with her. "Her mind is much shattered," he said, and he was dissuading old acquaintances from trying to visit her (MT/EW). When he visited her six months later, he found her "very quiet & even gentle, & extremely forgetful. To use her own expression, 'My capacity is gone.'" They were trying again to get a photograph of her; the first one was so poor that William urged Hannah to destroy it at once (MT/EW). His only other surviving communication is dated less than a week before Mary's death, when she had slipped into unconsciousness. "She has not taken any food for more than a week; only wine & water; & the doctor has administered a little morphine, to quiet her restless nerves; so she is much wasted, & her eyes are very dim. No trace of that quick wit, that bright fancy, that stinging satire that have made her so remarkable" (MT/MH). William also described the funeral service, probably Episcopal, she had requested in New York, to be read by a friend of Samuel Haskins, a Rev. Mr. Clapp. Following the funeral, she wished that her body be sent to Concord for burial, "with no service of any kind."

After the burial in Concord, when Mary Emerson's body found its final home in the family plot in the Sleepy Hollow burial ground, above the town her ancestors had founded and defended, the family gathered and reminisced. Ellen remembered particularly Hannah's stories about what a hard time she had had with Aunt in those last three years. Waldo, however, remembered the one about the bed "made in the form of a coffin; and [that she] delighted in the figure of a coffin made daily on her wall by the shadow of a church" (*JMN* 15:343). This was the coffin Mary had tried to show to Ellen.[2] The two coffins coalesce, creating an image of Mary Moody Emerson in her bed in Brooklyn, with moonlight or streetlight streaming through the windows, casting shadows of the church across the street into her bedroom, the strange angles created by the church's outline distorted even more as they strike the walls, ceiling, and floor of her room and bounce off furniture and mirrors. They could have reminded her of the obtuse angles that characterize the shapes of coffins.

Perhaps it is not necessary to read more into the "bed in the form of a coffin." Here is a fit icon for the end of Mary Emerson's life: the infinite, in the ageless and feminine symbolic shape of the moon, throws its light on and defines the finite, Mary's aging body on that bed in a strange land, far from everything she had ever dreamed of for her end. In the home of her beloved niece Hannah, who in her young life had helped so many to die in peace, Mary found her final home.

Three days after Mary's death in New York on 1 May, a hearse brought her body back to Concord, where she had been born eighty-nine years before. The Emersons—Lidian, Waldo, Edith, and Ellen—and Hannah Parsons went to the depot when the train arrived, where they met Elizabeth Hoar and two of the Ripley girls, and the lone nephew and the seven women followed the hearse up to the Emerson family plot near the top of a hill in Sleepy Hollow. Ellen describes the little funeral procession, arriving at the newly dug grave, "made in line with Grandma's [Ruth Emerson's]. They opened the coffin for us and every one looked at her and then they lowered it and as we came away Aunt Lizzy said it was just the day Aunt Mary would have chosen for her funeral, soft and pleasant, but with no sun" (*ETE L* 1:310).

NOTES

1. Henry James to Mrs. Carter, 27 Jan. 1862 [Knox College]; I am grateful to Eleanor Tilton for bringing this letter to my attention.

2. RWE changed the wording of Hannah's story in the essay "MME": she "delighted herself with the discovery of the figure of a coffin made every evening on their sidewalk, by the shadow of a church tower which adjoined the house" (*W* 10:428).

1852

To DANIEL APPLETON WHITE

Concord   Jan 6   Wed Eve. 52

With this new year accept, dear Sir, for yourself, wife & daughters my fervent wishes that each of its' revolutions may be as influential for you & happiness for all as our infinite Father sees good and a continuance of the peculiar gifts of the past. I wrote timidly before but Waldo bro't all your kind inquiries—& your letter woke up my heart, around w'h the ice will now & then gather. I take the liberty to ask you to put the inclosed into the Register if think proper. I have been so sad with a new "reformer" who preaches up no sacred or commanded sabbath—no inspiration of the Decalogue or special inspiration in the rev that I have written a piece in the Concord Freeman on the sabbath which met with Mr Frost & Mr Hoars approbation so fully that when I attended Mrs E Oakes' Smith's lecture last week I wrote the inclosed.[1] I was amused & my young Townswoman[n] said I was for "the rights," of which I desired to be rid of the suspicion. But the Editor is timid or "too full of matters more appropriate to his smale paper." And tonight he returns it. As he had refused one more weeks since theological[n] I told him that I would submit it to you, who had once sent an article of mine to Mr Morrison.[2] I respect & love the Register and if it is not troublesome to you or if it needs correction. My copiest has made trifling mistakes of which I know not the consequence. I will not intrude longer on your time but gladly remain your long friend with respect

M M Emerson

You may be absent and Mrs White will send it & she must forget the lover of her early youth.

As to violent Reformer Rev. Daniel Foster he was noble on Boston warf when poor Simms was carried off. But since he writes in a printed sermon of the pious Rogers & Orville Dewey that "they are traitors to Christ."[3] I believe verily that Mr Dewey believes in the xian religion. As to F—s preaching, that the bible is not specially inspired is it not dangerous? Plenary inspiration no thinker for long years has recognised it as such I think. A restorationist I have *felt* always but no one who loves virtue & his God will ever be injured? He would not sin knowingly if no omniscient eye were on him. But this man is a radical. I dislike the sentence I wrote in haste about the woman of feverish affection intitling to Martyrdom. I can't get the letter in tonight so trouble you more.

Pardon an aged friend

MH-AH. *Addressed:* Hon. D. A. White. / If absent, Mrs. White / Salem / Mass. *Endorsed:* Mary M. Emerson / Jan. 6, '52 / Ans[d]. " 12 ".

Townswoman] ⟨friend⟩ ↑ Townswoman ↓

weeks . . . theological] ↑ weeks since ↓ theological

1. MME's "The Sabbath" was printed in the *Middlesex Freeman* (Concord), 14 Nov. 1851. Elizabeth Oakes Smith lectured on "Womanhood" at the Concord Lyceum, 31 Dec. 1851. A draft of the "substance" of DAW's response to MME's ideas on "the rights" (of women) indicates he returned the piece (which does not survive) to her in befuddlement as to her meaning and in despair about making it sufficiently grammatical for publication (MH-AH). However, Phyllis Cole has located a brief piece entitled " 'The Woman': A Reminiscence," *Christian Register*, 24 Jan. 1852, by "An Octogenarian," which may be a heavily edited version of what MME wrote.

2. John Hopkins Morrison.

3. Thomas Sims, a seventeen-year-old escaped slave, was arrested in Boston on 3 Apr. 1851; despite the efforts of area abolitionists to rescue Sims, he was "escorted by federal marshals and city militia to a ship waiting in the harbor and shipped back to

Georgia" (*Days*, 314–15). Tilton notes that Foster "distinguished himself on April 12, 1851, by his prayer on the Boston wharf as the ship carrying . . . Sims was about to depart" (*L* 8 : 552 n. 23). In his Fast Day Sermon, *Our Nation's Sins and the Christian's Duty* (Boston, 1851), Foster denounced the "well-known Mr. Rogers of the Winter Street Church" for preaching obedience to laws supporting slavery (7) and included Dewey among "*men of treason against Christ*" because he "affirmed his readiness to surrender child or mother if necessary to preserve this Union" (14).

To Henry David Thoreau

[1852?]

If Mr Thoreau took the least dislike at the close of his last visit to me—why it is not the home of genius to notice trifles. Why not have visited my deeper solitude? Why not bring me the Plymouth lecture?[1] And a budget of literary news? Are you under no obligation to benefit or gratify your neighbours? Age loves the old fashion of catechising the young. Love to your parents & Aunts & forget not

MME.

ViU. *Addressed:* Mr H. D. Thoreau / Proffessor of lectures.

1. On 22 Feb. 1852 HDT lectured at Plymouth on his experiment at Walden. In his journal he reports visiting with MME on 13 Nov. 1851 and 8 Jan. 1852 (PJ 4 :183–84, 242).

To Martha Bartlett

Wed. Night   25 [Feb.? 1852]

Dear Martha,

I have thought often of your indisposition but as an Optimist knew every thing eventually for good. Glad to hear that you are so cheerfull out of your favorite element of air & earthly activity. I have hastened to finish the painfull task of following so monsterous a temperment as Margarets that you might have it.[1] You will find classical information to reward the reading undoubtedly. And when the hopefull sport of her *best* & *real* existence occurs it invites a hope. But the highest exstacies of imajanation reach not the xian demands, & they did not save her from her natural feverishness. Her opinion of our divine Saviour prevented any advance to the Infinite but thro instinct, paganism & being unhappily steeped in Goetheism. RWE has done justly by her & the publick I believe. And every good disposition & xian taught person will rejoice in their comparitive ignorance & hermit obscurity. The last line of the 23d[n] page beginns a sentence which redeems many a sad sympathy with the noble minded deceased & honors the biographer.[2] So somewhere in this 1[t] vol. the Editor & perhaps the extraordinary subject, allows that there "may lie fallow some of the best thoughts." It were pitiable to our future hopes if every thing were to be expended on this passing whirling stage, where theatricals abound & are suceeded continually. When reading her ulogists I could but regret the loss of so unique a mind. But I think her old age would have been very dark, if reason had continued Our own dear Elis. shall not hear of my late opinion. I hope to go over the life when in better health. There seems an evident tendency to halluciations & "queenly" demands. Your kindness to your aged friend will inquire how I am situated. Very easily & with a kindest hostess. I did get attached to my Cave as one generally does. And if for the last month I could have reposed under healthy circumstances which failed me in Feb. a month trying to billious subjects I should have enjoyed the memorial. Oh I sympathised with Margaret in her "regret at remorials." Love to my long loved S. A. R. & your parents. Waldo sent for me to Lyceum tonight but I disliked the lecture he read to me yesterday[3] & I felt rather feeble. Good night dear Martha

M.M.E.

You can well know how almost every cold or infirm day was brightened by Elis. It was a constant expectation & I ought to learn my old habits of expecting no *outward* event. *One* sole idea makes all events & hopes. better than all created ones. May the blessing of that Presence always attend thy steps & motives

MH: bMS Am 1280.220(70). *Addressed:* Martha Bartlett / Concord.

23d] *possibly* 232

1. *Memoirs of Margaret Fuller Ossoli*, ed. William Henry Channing, Ralph Waldo Emerson, and James Freeman Clarke, 2 vols., published in Boston in early Feb. 1852.

2. Possibly this passage: "So gratuitous, indeed, appeared her hypercriticism, that I could not refrain from remonstrance, and to one of my appeals she thus replied: 'If a horror for the mania of little great men . . . if this be to offend, then I have offended'" (*Memoirs* 2:23–24).

3. On 25 Feb. 1852 RWE read "Economy" at the Concord Lyceum.

To Haven and Charles Emerson

Concord   May 15 '52

Dear Nephews, Haven & Charles

How do you and your parents & brother do? All well I trust. I have sent you thanks for your handsome box intending to write, as you favored me with a welcome note, but for want of a safe place to keep my box your Aunt Elis. H. kept it till a week or two; it is established on a table & serves me so well that I shall keep it with me & carry it when I move to Kennebunk. I promised to show it to some little friends whenever I could open its valuables. How could you contrive so many dear boys? They benefit me—but the *lasting* pleasure they afford is the memory of your dispositions to add to the gratifications of your aged Aunt, whom you, Charles, dont remember, and Haven if he had not come to bid me farewell, one bright morning last August. I like to take its pure & brilliant contents for omens of your future good characters, and of *influence* to the solitary and whoever *needs* the essential comforts of life and *liberty* like my coulered brethren & Sisters.

I thought of you & your brother & the descendants of my Father very much the 11 (last tuesday) when Kossuth spoke of the honor derived to your uncle Waldo in bearing the name of E—n[1]   As you will see the papers I need not explain. As to the highly talented Guest, I shared none of the extreme excitement w'h seemed or really did possess my friends & the ladies who have had in Cities a mania of admiration. If it had been a LaFaette a Clarkson[2] or some of our own patriots like W—n or the Adams' 'twere natural & like gratitude. But while deeply interested in Hungary and all the oppressed by despotism I am more affected by the unhappy state of our beloved Country on whom a corrupt gov^t encourages the blackest crime of slavery. And as to K—s urging a war in defence of Hungary, I dont see its disinterested love of peace & prosperity for the *whole*. It *seems* to me that were his warm & noble spirit actuated[n] by the love of the *universal principle* of freedom he would have been kind & affectionate to those oppressed coulered people who attended him with a speech. But as your father is on the spot he can instruct you & me as to the circumstances which I read in passing a newspaper, weeks since. But this I know in all my ignorance of political affairs, that a gentlemanly notice of the oppressed could interfere with no state or national goverm^t. If England & Poland should join America there might be a prospect of success, and such events as would render America's interference by the sword expected & constitutional. But I am writing of my own private opinions, w'h the above mention of England & Poland give an expression to, and w'h I read yesterday in the "Commonwealth"   I hope your Father or brother will answer these queries. Your uncle Waldo, I perceive by his eloquent speech, if I understand him, leans to the errand of the Stranger   But I dont see Mr. E. long enough since he has been so busy to state my opinions[n] of the publick, at w'h he & my elder Nephew may smile. And I would not wait any longer an hour to assure you both, dear descendants of your sainted & patriotic Grandfather, of my remembrance & hopes that his name will receive new recollections from you as men & xians.

Your aff^t Aunt
M M Emerson

MH: bMS Am 1280.220(73).
actuated] *possibly* activated
opinions] ⟨affairs⟩ ↑ opinions ↓

1. Louis Kossuth, exiled Hungarian patriot, visited Concord on 11 May 1852. A cavalcade escorted him from Lexington to the Concord town hall, where RWE read a brief welcome (W 11:397–401). Lavishly thanking RWE, Kossuth claimed there was "meaning in the very fact that it is you" by whom he was welcomed. "Your honored name is Emerson," he said, recalling WE[1]'s action in the revolution as an "augury" of the progress of religion and philosophy in America (quoted in W 11:624).

2. Thomas Clarkson (1760–1846), English antislavery crusader and author of *His-*

tory of the Rise, Progress, and Accomplishment of the Abolition of the African Slave Trade, 2 vols., 1808.

To Ruth Haskins Emerson

Alfred   July 7 [1852]   Wed. after 11 A M

My dear Sister

I expected to see you before leaving but did not much desire it   There is somthing undesirable in biding adieue for the last time to one with whom our earliest remembrance is individuated, and with one whose cares sorrows & joys have been so long connected   That we may both linger (you surrounded with every comfort to render life a blessing) and with those (w'h no disturbance except dispepsia w'h prevents appetite &c) w'h are very mercifull to me. And when we meet in other states how short will be our seperation in recalling a score of years if such are appointed. Whatever ills of pain or privations they will all add to our rest in peace I trust. But I feel sure that my duty to others, and myself of course, will prevent my ever trying to board in dear loved Concord again. Wheelers house,[1] tho' I had many days of health & enjoyment, will warn me against being "obliged" as they called it again. Your dear child E.H. will visit me in all situations. I beged her to write by M. Bartlett but the errand not done I think. Well you have lost Charlotte, and she writes long & happily, for w'h I do rejoice   Did William or Susan know of Mr Cleveland?[2] The post goes out at 12 and I must look up the boy who seems absent—therefore you will excuse the haste of this as I think Mr Ripley will get the inclosed sooner if sent immediately than if I interrupt him again with a letter on business. My best love of the benevolent kind & best wishes to your Son & daughter, Ellen & the other children & Mrs Brown

Your affectionate Sister & friend

MM Emerson

Writing has been a task this season. I am pleasantly situated at present   I dont venture to ask to hear from Waldo as he nor L. asked to hear from the pilgrim

MH: bMS Am 1280.226(1043). *Addressed:* Mrs Ruth Emerson / Care of R.W. Emerson Esqr. / Concord / Massachusetts. *Postmarked:* ALFRED / MAINE / July 7. *Endorsed:* Miss M M E / 1852.

1. Where MME had boarded in Concord, probably with one of the Wheeler families on the Sudbury Road.

2. Charlotte Haskins had left Concord (see MME to ASG, 2 July 1851, n. 3) in Jan. to attend her sister (probably Hannah Haskins Parsons), who was ill in Williamsburgh; there she met an Episcopal minister, Charles Cleveland, whom she married in Nov. 1852.

1853

To Ann Sargent Gage

Ashfield   March 15 '53

I should have written long since you asked me about a lodging for I had before resolved to come here where Charlotte had got good ones, and I waited to speake of this place as having somthing out of the old track, tho' desirous to hear whether any new bargain had been started & where Dr Gage *was*.[1] Probably waiting to know where you will be. For 4 weeks I was prepared to leave K. Port as the boarders were coming for thier rooms but weather & loathness to move from Concord kept me till Waldo was coming to Springfield last sat. I came here. At N. P. a day or two at N with A. Tracy with whom we talked of you and I regreted that among many valuables I had lost those pages w'h I needed to try Mr Cleveland's taste.[2] You will be good enough to send me another copy I trust. And here I am but the C.Cs have gone to see his mother in Vermont and Sarah R.[3] came & passed the day with me yesterday w'h made it very wakefull to my wearied soul & body. Alas this homesickness for old lodgings the very inconveninces of w'h we get habited to—better than the novelty of new ones. This a pleasant roomly house & the hostess & daughter tiring me with kindnesses. Well did Pope say he "hated to part with an old post—he would swear to its beauty." But time never stops his winged speed^n and we pass to all that makes existence. How strange were it not that our misterious destiny calls for discipline that we seem like nonexistences at times of feeble health. When you do move where can go the portraits & Dante & Madalion? I expect to go or send in the warm weather for my books & blankets & etcs. Oh for one blanket. The houses crouded with every thing but blankets of the right sort. Here is snow & extreme cold the last 24 hours. It is like coldest winter. My last place of boarding was wanting & needed another lodger at Concord but I was stupid not to move there from Waldos where he induced me to go as we came from N Port. And after visiting the Bliss house dear E. H. & M.M Brooks I *left Concord*! Sarah R. is obliged to go to Providence as Frances is unwell. We are sorry   Will you be my voice in more welcome accents than I can offer to our pious Connection & Martha[4] and do do do write me while I am helpless. Love to Phebe & George. How do Lois & Mary in health? And all the others. What do you say to the new President. Alas for his inagural speech.[5] S.A.R. has given me at the Manse & in calls some dear hours. She was pleased with T.H.G. Inquires about Uncle & hopes to be able to do somthing, I add if nessecary. She is earning somthing by a scholar generally.

Farewell dear Ann, and do not forget how I prize your letters and the poem.

Your aff^t friend
MM Emerson

MWA. *Addressed:* Mrs A. S. Gage. / Waterford, Maine. *Postmarked:* ASHFIELD / MASS / Mch 17.

speed] sic *in MS; possibly* steed *intended (cf.* stops] spots *in MS)*

1. Thomas Hovey Gage (1826–1909) completed his medical studies at Harvard in 1852.

2. Charlotte Haskins married the Reverend Charles Cleveland on 4 Nov. 1852. Cleveland served as rector of Saint John's Episcopal Church, Ashfield, from 1853 to 1857; MME often refers to them as the "C.Cs." MME went to Ashfield to be near them. See MME to ASG, 2 July 1851, n. 2, on MME's use of ASG's poetry to "try" one's "taste"; "pages" may also refer to the poems of ASG printed as "Meditations of a Widow" in the *Aesthetic.*

3. Possibly Sarah Stone Ripley (b. 1793), daughter of EzR's brother Noah, or niece Sarah Ripley Haskins.

4. Lincoln Ripley and Martha Robinson.

5. Franklin Pierce became president on 4 Mar. 1853; in his inaugural address, which he had memorized, he promised to support the compromise of 1850.

To Ellen Emerson

Ashfield   Aug. 22 [1853] Monday

Dear Ellen,

I am so pleased with your attention in making time (out of your need-full & nessecary pursuits) to write me so many fine discriptions, that I hasten while the letter is fresh to thank you. If I did not do it under the first impression, I should be apt to neglect it as I do some others. It is a frequent subject of sattisfaction that you are with Mrs S.   And you name another long loved sound, the niece of *Mrs* Childs.[1] These early friendships (if they decay as every event & object of affection is fluctuating) are highly important to develop your more *disinterested* affections, and may yours continue a permanent advantage   I wished for more of the *internal* impression on your *heart* from every new view of your Heavenly Fathers bountifull beauties—   But perhaps you chose to kept them sacred as secret. Madam De Stale, a dear & early favorite *writer,* speaks of the lasting couler w'h the soul receives from the new scenes of nature—that they remain to characterise it. What companions do the trees become, w'h surround this uncommon pleasant farm—so high & thick round the house that the sun & moon give a most delightfull light thro' their rich foliage. But there is a higher sentiment of domestic poetry w'h our much prized and beloved Elisabeth H., gave me of your gracefull & quiet success in attention to the lamps one eve. She gave a minute detail, tho' she had just come from Niagra's wonders! Of all the descriptions of that place I dont remember to have read any w'h have met me so deeply as a letter in the Mirror of the young minister of Kennebunk Port.[2] It was his *pulpit* library &c w'h induced my tarry in that place. But no accounts of any place stir any desire to move at my extreme age. How will our own dear beautifull world & its related system vanish before the majority of higher regions and larger planets—worlds we trust that are free from the ills w'h thousands in this suffer hourly thro' long years of poverty and the blackest of all many thro' vice. There & then alone my dear Niece, will you realise *true* happiness in the increase of every virtue, whose *foundation* is laid in this chequered & disciplinary state—there & then will such freindship and *love* itself alone be perfected.

But time & poor pens hasten me to relieve your patience. Do write when you can to dear Charlotte whose sight always gave me pleasure & Mr C. whose gentleman attentions are welcome tho' their new & increasing society prevent much intercourse.

Love to your Mother whose loss of you must be a trial.

Your Aunt MME.

I had William Emersons company an hour or two as he passed thro' this place some days since. I urged him to remain a day or two with his Chum, as this large house likes company. We talked of you & many others. I like him. Do you? I preserve the Tribune in wh his performances was related.

MH: bMS Am 1280.226(760). *Addressed:* Miss Ellen T. Emerson / At Mrs Sedg-wick's / Lenox / Mass. *Postmarked:* Ashfield Mass. / Aug 23. *Endorsed:* Aunt / Aug 22nd.

1. In June Ellen Emerson went away to Lenox, Mass., as a boarding student at the school conducted by Elizabeth Dwight Sedgwick. One of Ellen's school friends was Hatty Francis, probably the daughter of Child's brother Convers Francis (*ETE L*).

2. The *Portland Christian Mirror* of 5 Oct. 1852 printed an unsigned letter dated 13 Sept. 1852 from Niagara Falls.

To ANN SARGENT GAGE

Ashfield   Nov. 2   Wed.   '53

My dear Friend,

And you are gone from that scene of beauty—of long loved associa-tions—and where the memory of one so richly endeared by his private & publick influence was so ingraved with every object of beauty & interest.[1] But you part with none of these memories—they may serve more to bring you nearer to those higher & holier scenes where love shall be perfected in individuals and in what a higher & holier nature towards the Infinite Source of all that is great & desirable in existence. And you are not going to any City where I always tho't you were   And that Society in other forms & other sympathies would be calling your talents into new exercise. This situation is wholly unexpected to me. But surely better & safer & happier than any with-out full independence of means. And for the *future*—of all that prepares & gives "the taste of the powers" of that future how desirable how blessed your retirement with none but to love & bless. And when leaving the society of the litteratie, how smale the advantage (& "peace w'h passeth understanding" not found) to those of the closet meditation & the indefinable communion w'h results. Do do write— You can more—no care of providing for body. Pray write and as usual be particular of our good Uncle. You were very kind in the note to E. Hoar. I have mislaid it without understanding whether the furniture were at Hale's. I shall reward her trouble. And where the portraits & Madallion? Oh my blankets & carpet tho' the last is unnessecary. But the comforters—the quilts if I did not have Charlotts in cold weather. I wish that I had more resolution & means of expense to journey. I could not trust R.T.H. tho' there was no certainty of his route. Here is a full rich house & so at Hotels but not blankets sufficient. And for draws my papers are confused. Yours I can find and the Deweys and E H—s and Hannahs—but notes & accounts. I often wish to send you the New Y— Inquirer—but if the Puritan is in repute perhaps these will not go well. The unitarian's are much engaged, and some with increasing spirituality and some with the mania of novel views w'h are rejected. Have you read Uphams "Interior life"? I have been reading looking at the famed & sainted Neander's "life of Christ," and his review of John's Epistles.[2] Oh do tell me of *T.T. Stone*! He the child of our love— our mutual interest. I see his name no where. That last time how he rode in my wagon, and how you came out at my return. Have you seen him since? And Harris my favorite. Do let me recall interests so dear. I thought of these absent ones last wed. when anxious to hear Prof. Aggisiz at the convention for the Institute, and how disappointed. Since reading some pages of his w'h fully defeated the "Vestiges" Man it appeared such a prize and Conway is but an hour's ride.[3] He lectured on geology—but it's elements chiefly and it sattisfied me never to seek foreign means when so many are closeted. There to I borrowed Neander for the few days I staid and intend to own the smale work of the seraphic deciple. Will you add to your cares, dear Ann, that of sending some private conveyance Maucaully's two Vols to Dr Charles Parsons—with the cherished remembrance of the times past in his house and his kindnesses. Please take any vol. you or Phebe like in lieu of the book given to Caroline Stone. I hope Phebe's Muse will rekindle amid the wide prospect of hills and Vales.[4] Do represent me better I can to your father & my Uncle to Martha with a never slackned interest. And if any inquire after me thanks & to Mr & Mrs Warren love.[5]

Farewell long cherished friend with each of your children. I feel decay— weakness &c Take my love & write soon It is so duskey cant continue to say all I want of Charlotte & the Rector & the W^mburghers

M M Emerson

MWA. *Addressed:* Mrs Ann S. Gage / Waterford, Me. *Postmarked:* Ashfield / Mass / Nov 4.

reading looking at] reading ↑ looking at ↓

1. Although this letter is addressed to Waterford, ASG had sold the Gage farm to Oliver Porter on 13 Sept. 1853; ASG to THG, 25 Sept. 1853, is largely about packing up to leave (MWA).

2. Thomas C. Upham, *Principles of the Interior or Hidden Life*; August Neander, *The Life of Jesus Christ . . .*, trans. John M'Clintock and Charles E. Blumenthal (New York, 1848); *The First Epistle of John, Practically Explained by Dr. Augustus Neander*, trans. Mrs. H. C. Conant (New York, 1852).

3. MME to EH, 19 Oct. 1847, reports she recently spent several days "at Harrison & chiefly at Bridgton hoping to board a little in the latter Villiage & hear Mr. Harris" (MH: 1174). She may refer to Dr. Samuel Harris (1814–99), who had served as pastor of Congregational churches in Conway and Pittsfield, Mass., before becoming professor of systematic theology at the Bangor Theological Seminary in 1855, where he remained until 1867. MME suggests she heard the Swiss naturalist Louis Agassiz speak on an unidentified occasion in Conway, Mass. A review of *Vestiges of the Natural History of Creation* in the *Christian Examiner* 40 (May 1846): 333–49, concludes that Chambers's system leads to "*fatalism*" (344). MME may have read Cabot, "Life and Writings of Agassiz": in contrast to Chambers's naturalistic theories, Agassiz emphasized the "relation of the Creator to the universe" and the existence of a "Superior Intelligence" responsible for the order of the universe (107).

4. PHG published at least one poem (undated newspaper clipping, MWA).

5. Probably Irene Gage and her husband, Samuel Warren, with whom ASG and her daughter Phebe seem to be staying in Waterford.

To William Emerson[3]

Ashfield   Dec. 1   53

My Dear Nephew,

How is your shoulder? Have you returned to Office? I love your solitude, in the sanctuary of soul you may return to that "enthusiasm" of w'h you speake as "past." Not I hope—why age itself kindles with new delights as its scene is closing. Your character so well established in the voice of private friends, like *the dear Deweys,* and by publick will bear a good deal of enthusiasm on the only subject w'h is worth it—religion! In this reason shines with new vigor as the emotions are strenghtened by faith. And "faith is the daughter of reason" says the sainted Young.[1] Enthusiasm, that holy wine, can be illy spent on our inslaved Country. What a sadening doefull portrait does its history of succumbing to the Slave tyrants present by Palfrey the brave & patriotic![2] Since reading it (w'h was lost before I knew it had come among newspapers) I have almost forgotten the friend & Sister I was grieving for, & rejoice at every good one's release.[3] But not to congratulate you on the happy influence you so early shed on her widowhood and had so long the priviledge of giving light & joy by your & Susan's visits & sending attentions. She loved you both sincerely without gifts. What an infinite treasure had God bestowed on her very nature—*truth*—that prime virtue in Heaven & earth, from all created universe! Yet what an infected atmosphere we breathe. It is not the gay Dandys and frivolus Bells that exaggeration is labeled with poetic florishes, but sober well meant Adults, when they are overcome with ill or good fluctuations that sincerity is defiled   I've just read the notice of your excellent mother's exist.[n4] And marveled who put it in? It seems strange that

Figure 29. "Judge" William Emerson (1801–68), nephew of
Mary Emerson.

her husband's relation was not first named. But singular as it has constantly
been that neglect of finding his mention among other unitarians to this day,
and even when Evertt preached Abbots funeral sermon the predossors were
stopt at his.[5] How angry I felt as injustice to him & his sons—for of many
of the contenders at that time, how many of unitarians practised somthing
of that basest jesuitism, from w'h he was pure. He was as radical, it is true,
as Dr Freeman.[6] but he took no part in proslyting or deceiving. But what I
was going to say about the secondary notice is that he smiles as I do now on
earthly neglect. And if he has after seeing it's cloudy futility, regret his early
love of fame, w'h promised in his youth to weave many a laurel—that regret
or sadness may establish solid happiness finally, and his early enthusiasm return adorned^n by the only amaranthine flower and him^n to influence other
inmates of higher discipline   It is unaccountable to think that men, superior,
can be so led & hoodwinked by the mere breath of human approbation who
soon die & sooner forgotten. How we love to dwell on the hermits whether
of philosophy or xianian^{ty} who dwelt in caves & mountains to be rid of their
vanity.

Many thanks, dear William, for letter papers & Palfrey. At the sadness his
views cast, one ca'nt but wish he had recurred to that eternal Cause whose
providence is working under the tempest current, but will bring truth out re-
splendent. But his object was foreign. Love to Wm Haven & Charlie & many
blessings on parents & ofspring

from Aunt Emerson

I hope Susan will have the pleasure of a visit from your Cousin Sophy Ripley.[7]
She is with a daughter of Patrick Jackson but I dont remember her husband
name. You will not tire about the *house* so *left*, that our estimable Elisabeth
feels it so "desolate." And so will Lidian whose provident care has never re-
lapsed and Waldos has been genuine. My Charlotte knew to prize her dear
Aunt—but was so thankfull she had not lived beyond reason & affection.

MH: bMS Am 1280.220(75). *Addressed:* Hon. William Emerson / New York. / No
10 Wall St.

exist.] sic *in MS; possibly* exit. *intended*

return adorned] return ⟨sanctified⟩ ↑ adorned ↓

him] ⟨lend⟩ him

1. Probably Edward Young; quotation not located.

2. Possibly John Gorham Palfrey, *Remarks on the Proposed State Constitution:
By a Free Soiler from the Start* (Boston, 1853).

3. RHE died 16 Nov. 1853.

4. An obituary notice, "Madam Ruth Emerson," was printed in the *Christian
Examiner* 56 (Jan. 1854): 163–64.

5. Edward Everett, *An Address, Pronounced October Twenty-first, at the Funeral
of John Lovejoy Abbot, Pastor of the First Church of Christ in Boston* (Boston, 1814).
In the printed version of the address, WE[2] was included: quoting from Abbot's 1811
funeral sermon for WE[2], Everett says, " 'I find in looking over the list of predecessors,

the names of Colman, Foxcroft, Cooper, Chauncy, Clarke, Thacher, and now, alas, Emerson'" (5).

6. Probably James Freeman (1759–1835) the "Anglican-turned Unitarian minister of King's Chapel" (Howe, 310).

7. Sophia Bradford Ripley (1833–1914), youngest child of SR and SBR.

1854

To Ann Sargent Gage

Ashfield   Jan   Sab. 15 '54

I received yours, my dear Friend, last friday eve. Should that eve. have spoken my heart to it, but delayed to look up a review by G.G. Elisses w'h is the first thing that has interested me about the "Conflict" w'h I found tedious as I read a little reviewed in N York & Boston.[1] Or rather the idea of his "preexistence." To age, surely any new mode of belief is a nullity. The "reminiscences & persistence of Plato & the Hindoo" is palatable. And so any new light thrown on any of the obscure passages of scripture. But for me, who never think of literary society, & my wants make me *hunger* & *thirst* only to feel *old truths* like the divine sermon of our Saviour. Any means by w'h a *consciousness* of the divine Presence can be indulged & inlarged and felt. Then all ills & infirmities of flesh, & such as Paul gloried in, are light— & happy if they bring xian graces! Yesterday I devoted to Ellis, as a man of talents & one of the Xian Ex—'s editors, and found it so good that I was for sending it to you * * * Mrs Tracy (whom I wish you w^d name, expressed much sympathy at your leaving the beautifull house) sent me a smale book entitled "Tho'ts that help & cheer"[2] at Nicols store in Boston. I wondered at it at first, but found it would do more than tomes of polemic theology. And I am going to borrow the "Andover Sacra. biblical Review" & "Stewarts Apocalypse" of the orthodox minister, when my head grows stronger.[3] You will think well of Beecher after reading Ellis. His family excites much gossip w'h is groundless? I cant find the work on Infidelity you speak off named & can't look over heaps of Newspapers w'h Wm Emerson sends of the Xian Inquirer & E.H. of the Register. * * * Does my friends the Douglass' take an interest in the increasing agitations of Chhs' & Countrys? The "Conflict" may awaken Calvinists to see the evils of some of thier preaching w'h has hardened the sinners & sent them to the altars^n of universalism. Are you a Restorationist in heart if not in theory? I have always been one in feeling, and it is a constant Joy, when the clouds of Providence hang over national goverments & chhs in worldly tempers & private societies & individuals. Inexplicables—then we know that rightiousness & judgment are the Habitation of all! Oh my long loved Ann how I do wish you to read Bartolls two last vol's, one of the spirit & the other on the "Forms & body" of xian^n They are life & spirit.[4] Never felt the significance of baptism so before. Tho't how Uncle R. would like 'em. A Restorationist without doubt & one line I erased before lending a vol. to youth. How often I tho't (as before) of P.H.[5] saying some years since "she could not see the significance of the supper." And is it possible she could leave *you*? And be happy and you resigned? * * * The Pilgrims, whose light still lingers in history, passed but a month at a place. They had duties to strenghten them but I none. * * *

I seldom go to Chh as the heat is not good for head. Tho' I do love to go in mornings for the liturgy and Mr C.[6] is an earnest preacher of his order. I left my dear large chamber & open fire place owing to sickness in family & am hardly got over homesickness these days. Do you use stoves? Oh dear   No such thing beside my other large large house. It is growing dark   And I must say fare well. S.A.R. well & her daughter writes me. Good night   I cant but hope you will come here & see those who will be delighted & more than all

MME

MWA.

altars] *possibly* ultras

xian^y] ⟨religion⟩ xian^y

1. George Edward Ellis was an editor of the *Christian Examiner* from 1849 to 1857; see review of Edward Beecher, *The Conflict of Ages; or, The Great Debate on the Moral Relations of God and Man* (Boston, 1853), *Christian Examiner* 55 (Nov. 1853): 394–425.

2. Anonymous, *Thoughts to Help and to Cheer* (Boston, 1854).

3. The *Bibliotheca Sacra and Theological Review*, published at Andover; Stuart, *A Commentary on the Apocalypse*, 2 vols. (Andover, 1845).

4. C. A. Bartol, *Discourses on the Christian Spirit and Life* (Boston, 1850); *Discourses on the Christian Body and Form* (Boston, 1853).

5. Phebe Hovey Gage.

6. Cleveland.

To Ann Sargent Gage

Friday Night 31 Marche [1854]

My dear dear friend,

This moment laid down yours with a sympathy not often moved, in my life bereft of most I loved & relied on. Oh, what does that "*cloud*" contain or omen! To *know* would be better than suspense. Yet why express a sympathy w'h cannot "line" that cloud, w'h as yet conceals a bright inside, and in the best & fittest moment and season will reveal the light & wisdom of your covenant God & Father. I will imitate your silence and respect it. As to our friend T.T.S. are you "startled" least he is grown cold to that Being whose agency is the joy & absolute support of every being from the highest arch Angel to the humblest intelligence who hangs on Him in faith & love. I shall inclose his letter or part of it as I know your interest in him. Tho' how he came & went without seeing you (at times?) or me, who was less interesting to him as to every one. He is very remote from the usual modes of feeling & acting—perhaps owing to his early education? He does not sympathise in publick calamity tho' a noble defender of the slave, or he would have spoken of the political agitations in our unhappy goverment tho' this infamous bill to intail slavery on an extended plan & to injure the always injured Indians might not have taken form when he wrote.[1] He should write again & express his patriotism—yet every member of our indangered Country must *feel* the agitations w'h billow up with sad omens. The crisis w'h some of the wise & pious, Isaac Taylor 12 years since, prophesied would revolutionize the world, probably by some great suffering to the Chh w'h might bring good out of evil &c.[2] Age can not fear nor hope *personally* but you & your children full of promise & hope, must be much occupied in these days. But your faith & resignation failed you not in the greatest of losses where your mutual affection was very happy & your virtues appreciated by a man of no common worth. Every lesser trial will only have a tendency to draw you nearer to that *consciousness* of the ever present God w'h constitutes that peace w'h *passeth understanding.* And does indeed shed light when cercumstances & bereavments have been darkest, if so poor and inactive a being as your unprogressive friend may so speake. I w^d tell you of a late loss in the death of a hostess, the kindest & most attached to me I have had on some accounts—tho many I have had very much prized—but in this I felt at home for the future with age & infirmity. Her husband equally kind & her death by miscarriage sudden. I will send you some time her obituary. I hasten to write now tho' bad pen to tell you what will cure your eyes. & how I regret to hear you will write "less & less." A loss to me w'h I shall think you ought not to allow if not nessecary. I go not out as not inclined & love to hear your opinions of books & our times, and of your *interior self.* I am with my good Charlotte till the weather warms & her husband urged my immediate removal. She sends her aff^t respects & begs you to call her Charlotte. I need a chamber fire. and not to take a front room. She copies poetry for me sometimes, & my senior *Ann* T. has sent me a *new* book of daily comforts, w'h includes fine lines of poetry.

And now farewell dear Ann, let me soon hear if you love   M.ME.

My late good Sister[3] at her extreme age was troubled with watery eyes and the use of alum water cured them, w'h she added cologn & then rose water. If yours have irritation or inflamation a little cotton wool diped in tincture of flies put behind the ears or *ear* (I use whenever the errisippal gets any way down to it cures it in a few hours or night & day). Air & good diet keep mine in capasity to read all evenings. Adieu—write to one who has always felt a pilgrim from childhood & that circumstances have become easy however undesired.

I have found it difficult to procure stamps till this week for many weeks. Perhaps you may. Do take the liberty to inclose part of mine. I felt anxious at

your long silence. Thanks to our good father[4] in piety for his letter   But as
he has "correspondents" I shall not write soon as my time presses. Hannah
writes me of a room but I dont feel disposed to go. W^m E & his wife would
render their vicinity pleasant & so would Sarah R.

Sab Eve   Ap 2.

But since EPP was a seperation between us the intercourse cannot be as once
so beloved. Nor can I ever think of my ill tempered resentment to EPP before Frances without shame & penitence. There will be an hereafter when my
provocation may be known perhaps

Love to Frances tho' she neglects my leter. Glad you have been visiting

MWA.

1. Beginning in Jan. 1854, the Kansas-Nebraska Act, which in effect repealed the
Missouri Compromise of 1820, was hotly debated in Congress and bitterly opposed
by antislavery northerners; the bill was passed by the Senate on 26 May 1854.

2. Cf. Isaac Taylor in *Natural History of Enthusiasm*: "Great and happy revolutions usually stand ready and latent for a time, until accident brings them forward. Such
a change and renovation we believe to be at the door of the Christian Church" (96).

3. Probably RHE, who died in 1853; possibly REH, who died in 1845.

4. LR.

To Ann Sargent Gage

Amherst   Oct. 3   Tues.   54

This eve. I read for the third time and can stay no longer without telling
how long I looked for it and how glad to have it. Oh right glad that you are at
home, and it is a beautifull place. Is there *minister & society?*[n] You are glad
to get from W.? If it were possible to get a place there for the last remove how
w^d I go and again be near you   What a world of memories I s^d feel *at home* it
seems. I have *felt* your changes before, but since I wrote more than ever. I lost
a *most kind* host & hostess, the latter by an unexpected death. A fine farm &
large house smale family and the best table in Ashfield   She was *animated—*
in the midst of life 45. The pall of the destroyer rarely appeared heavier—
And dear Charlotte to lose but I tried in vain for open fire places or open stove
or even any place. I came to Charlemont (20 miles from pleasant Ashfield)
where I had a connection, & after puting up at the hotel a week he found me
one good place but an new accession to their family defeated me & the next
remove was without inquiry & most unpleasant. But if I^d not been unwell s^d
have enjoyed life as there are always hours dear to memory every where. All
at once this same second Cousin[1] unexpected to me recommended this place
very strongly & as my room was only engag^d till cold weather, here I came to
a beautifull house & grounds and as it was retired from Villiage I tho't I was
at home. But as dear T.T.S. says "he has had such dreams." Where & how he
is I hear nothing since the letter I spoke about. Dont T.H.G. know of him? I

have been unwell all the time about writing & all externals or s^d have written to T.T.S. and to Dr G. but he did not ask it and I know he's engage^d—dont wish it.

I grew very prostrate in "the nervous system" (while with C.C.)[2] after the bereavment of my hostess the Doctor said he could do nothing but a little cordials. I believed myself going & the disapp^t was depressing & I hope humbling. Elisabeth was hovering over her infirm charge, came to Charlemont for me to go to Staten I. where I had promised William who came to me in my prosperity (the life of my hostess) and I promised him to go if I s^d be unwell. I went and we staid a month in all the elegance & luxuries of a large new house but that did not do much to restore. I spent 2 or three days with Hannah whose animated attentions and affection awaknd old & good feelings. I w^d have lived with her as she had proposed it before and had a spare room, w'h had now but the noise of W^g was insupportable as my nerves are rather naked But I had been very glad to return to Charlemont to a new place and a *very* good girl to tend me. She was gone, and the three months I staid were those of a confessional I called them as to diet & social existance, however better on the whole (the *latter*) than the present, tho' the landlady among the most fashionable & smattered with books. Indeed this partial dash of literature is infringing the simplicity & modesty of former old times. However that w^d not disgust me *but*—let them rest   I hope to have a new door opened as usual. There have been from 23 years old an intire sattisfaction (to say the least) when a week was before me (at times & thro' many years)   So kindly & mercifully are the "winds tempered."[3] And how many boarding *homes* that were good! Deacon Warrens[4] as a specimem. It is natural that a single boarder must bear the natural results & disadvantages. These people urge my stay^n & were going to buy an open stove but I assured them I should move by leave of Providence in a week or two. I have found a most affectionate friend in a daughter of "Aunt Sheppard,"[5] so richly situated that I dont think of asking board, but she thinks she can find some place in this or near Town. I wrote her that what she w^d call too humble I s^d approve   I give & have for months 3 # hope to do better in summer. And after these tedious details w'h I avoid to every other one whom w^d send me invitations at Concord &c. Indeed I never write to them when out of a place

Good night dear Ann & return me as full account after *burning this*

Wed. Morn 5 Oct.   "What I read"? You surely have more means of what is new in the world of politick (poor bad state!) and theology than I shut up in Charlemont. All my reading after some part of summer was confined to Channings memoirs w'h were given by good Susan.[6] And there I found full cause for my confessial when I compared his deep humility & fervent charity. I knew it not of him till his diary. I have been wholly taken with a smale portion of "*his works*" since I found them here almost a fortnight since. I read slowly always & when *here* takes a day almost to get one charge at ordination (some years since) there was so much of gospel light and exalted virtue in it, & there were charges to two ministers ordained "at large" to visit the City poor. Never was a more apostalic view of Christ. But *Bushnell* has interested for the first of his publishing   And here is his "God in Christ."[7] Have you seen it? *Do* and tell me what think & feel. I'm on the meta^{ln} chap. It rather disturbs my old *intuition* of the *Absolute nessecary Being* whose idea is an element of the soul? Dearer than all meta$^{s.n}$ It is natural theology, the ground & preparation for the glorious rich charter of revelation by Jesus Christ, the *arian* high scheme   Dr B. *seems* yet in the *transition* state. But I shall understand him better in health. He is *meeting* it *seems* the unitarians who are also meeting bible orthodoxy. But at my age, I dont enjoy any thing like the bible, & Ware's pages, beginning at page 100. *Do* read his wife's biography.[8] It but 1 vol. but I ca'nt indulge in the details. I have received among other presents Mrs Stowes "army Memoirs."[9] The young & lover of fine arts will be delighted & benefited by it. It is all the light reading Ive had and my health needed it. But I've gone over not half. I long for my old book case & the ones you have. But glad they are safe with you   I s^d never read them all get thro' the fewest of any school girl. Where is the trunk of papers & my blankets &c &c   I ca'nt find blankets enough & my chairs & table that belonged to Susan Stone after my death? No matter if she has them. Have you given Maucallys *essays to Dr C. Parsons? He deserves them.* * * *

One favor I wish to insist on   A copy of those 3 pages for the year &c   I made close liking to a Baptist minster & wife at Shelburn Falls and he is a stronge abolitionist. I have some pamplets in sermons of his   I past 3 or 4 days in coming here and as they had a girl or some else had Felicia Hemans I told them of a poet bro't up in the pure mountain air who exceeded all I had ever seen of Mrs H. and I engaged to send them a copy.[10] I told them the occasion. I hate to pester you with my poor steel pen & think you ca'nt read. * * * But what an aid w^d you be in my reading now that I'm old & infirm. But ever your first of friends and hereafter where freinds meet to part no more. If you write soon it find me

in Amherst Mass.
MME.

There is nothing sure of a place but you had better write soon

MWA.
society] *underlined twice*
stay] stage *in MS*
meta^l] *abbreviation for* metaphysical
meta^s] *abbreviation for* metaphysics
1. Probably Sabra Cobb Clark Snell (1807–83), a granddaughter of John Emerson of Conway, who in 1828 married Ebenezer S. Snell, professor of mathematics at Amherst, 1834–76. Rusk identifies the writer of an unsigned letter to MME, dated

6 Oct. 1853, Amherst (MH: 226), as Sabra Cobb (Emerson) Snell and the only descendant of John of Conway living at Amherst in 1853. Mrs. Snell's parents were Rebecca Emerson (1777–1822) and Scotto Clark (1767–1851).

2. Charles or Charlotte Cleveland.

3. Opening quotation mark missing in MS; possible allusion to proverb quoted by Maria in Laurence Sterne's *Sentimental Journey*: "God tempers the winds."

4. Possibly Deacon William Warren (b. 1794), a farmer and cabinetmaker in North Waterford, or Irene Gage's husband, Samuel Warren.

5. Possibly RHE's sister Deborah (1765–1841), who married the Reverend Mase Shepard of Little Compton, R.I.

6. *Memoir of William Ellery Channing, with Extracts from His Correspondence and Manuscripts*, ed. W. H. Channing, 3 vols. (Boston, 1848).

7. Horace Bushnell, *God in Christ: Three Lectures Delivered at New Haven, Cambridge, and Andover, with a Preliminary Dissertation on Language* (Hartford, 1849).

8. Possibly John Ware, *Memoir of the Life of Henry Ware, Jr.* (Boston, 1846, 1854). Edward Brooks Hall, *Memoir of Mary L. Ware, Wife of Henry Ware, Jr.* (Boston, 1852).

9. Not identified. Sir George Stephen, *Antislavery Recollections: In a Series of Letters, Addressed to Mrs. Beecher Stowe, Written at Her Request*, was published in 1854, but it does not seem to fit MME's label "light reading," which follows.

10. Felicia Hemans (1793–1835), very popular British romantic poet; ASG's "Meditations of a Widow"; a MS copy by ASG survives with MME's endorsement: "Ann S Gage to the / friend of her earliest life" (MH).

1855

To Ralph Waldo Emerson

Ashfield   Feb. 16 / '55

My dear & valued Lecturer of the 26 of Jan![1] Shall I offer my "applause" after the most eminent—for worthy must have been the lovers of it's stand points of morals adorned by the illustrations of *justice* & *liberty*—and gilt with the *bravest* exposure of titled governor and judges, wealth & station. Yes, you must value the delight it gave to a solitary who loves her country and kind. At the first reading I was so much overcome with pleasure, that the hopeless wish to find any one to be inlightend in this Town by it, that I put it bye with regret & admiration. After a week came the schoolmaster for two or three eve[s]— An obscure & unpopular man here, but an *intelligent* reader & *think*er, and read it with animation. Judge of my surprise & gratification. And *now* I've gone over every line that was legible, and beg for a number. Can't it come in pamplet form that it may spread? I know one farmer who deserves it and I have no other intercourse but to give it him. I dont know how my kind Rector will enjoy it, he has been I hear a sufferer, it seems, by disappoin[t] in trying to aid abolitionists. But I know nothing of his life or history. The distance of long tow miles, weather & health, has prevented my going to see dear

Charlotte for weeks till last week, & I then named *the* lecture, he said he had been at Boston since & heard Edward Haskins offer to get it for him, "that many were displeased with the mention of Jesus." I said it was regreted—but if the trinitarian did, it might be answered, that was the *humanity,* that else where, our divine & human Master and xianity was recalled to mind with respect that I persumed Ed. H. & all objectors did not understand the drift of the lecture. No the Seer & aged look with *faith* on the auther[n] of that lecture, and behold in vision the time when it is appointed for him to find the home of genius in the only ark of patriotism, *true* freedom & endless morals[n] & *disinterested* humanity in christianity! That if he *seems* to place too much on freedom, he will one day feel how much may be given up of political liberty and all transcient good for citizenship in all the rights to w'h this wonderfull Jesus will influence the race, thro' connecting it with the first Cause!

Love, here & after forever for Lidian. She would write if she knew amidst Dewey & dear Elisabeths letters I look for hers. In haste I must seal this or I may have no chance till sunday to get it to the office. God bless you the daily wish of Aunt

M.M.E.

MH: bMS Am 1280.226(951). *Endorsed:* Miss M. M. Emerson / 1855.

auther] ⟨performer⟩ ↑ auther ↓

freedom & endless morals] freedom ↑ & endless morals ↓ ; & *possibly canceled or an asterisk*

1. On 25 Jan. 1855, RWE read his "American Slavery Address" before the Boston Antislavery Society at Tremont Temple. The address was never published; MME's comments suggest she read the "very complete account" Gougeon states was published in the *Boston Evening Traveller* on 26 Jan. and hopes for more copies ("a number," below) (*Virtue's Hero,* 207; for a summary of the lecture, see Gougeon, 207–12).

To Ann Sargent Gage

Ashfield   June 1 '55

My Dear Friend,

Are *you well*? are all dear well? I have wondered that you did not write, perhaps my last did not reach? Did I offend by recalling any of my grieving? Then forgive, nothing was less expected—nor more useless and when viewed in the light of the future and happy hours more smale & needless. I have tho't often of you in intire solitude & decay of health. And the expectation of meeting hereafter was very pleasant. There every tho't and desposition will be remembered & freindship such as mine for your early years will appear welcome. Did I tell you how age had its increasing infirmities—debility & rhumatism but little pain, and every letter I write 'tis with the hope of a farewell. I want to know how you have felt & expected from the tumults of foreign war & the corruptions of our own gov[t] and the good signs w'h prevail in missionary projects and increased publick charities and the hardness of times with the laboring classes. If I knew what newspapers and books you read I could better know when I read what you thought. Have you read all Mr Stones Sermons? Then you w^d particularise. No one has I can't spare them Have you read Clarks smale book on prayer?[1] I want to know your opinion. He is a remarkable for piety charity &c   I s^d send the Register now & then when full of interest but I dont but you have it. The Independant of N.Y. is full of interest but I read but little on account of irresipal.

You have enjoyed Mrs Stowes travels?[2] Well I *once* met a young reader, and told him somthing of the eastern scenery, that it was poetic, that much as I loved the author of "Uncle Tom" she could not have written certain pages wh were &c from one who never had any of the early advantages of Mrs Stowe and the lines at Albany[3]   You have neglected my request. No matter. If I am found in Christ I shall not care about even the poetry of Angels. The contemplation of the Infinite will fill eternal ages with employment sufficient even without society or the sciences of Heaven. If we are blest with moments here w'h bring a foretaste of feeling some glimpes of His presence tho' it banishes every idea of ourselves and our nothingness is realised, we have an idea of "true *Being!*" as a late Author describes it. Tis *Morell*. have you seen his "Philosophy of Religion." The 3 & 4th chapters I have read "the essence of religion." His views of *inspiration* & *tradition* are not approved by the orthodox. I have owned it at times for 2 years but so little able to read. You dont believe in plenary inspiration I suppose. I have in secret and when reading the holy rev. for years, never could believe it. If a smale part of its morals were inspired as we know there were from Jesus, there is truth enough to save a world. And to humble me & wean from the wish of worldly prosperity. You can bear it. But so excitable & impulsive a weak thing as your poor freind cannot. And tis the goodness of Providence to have left me ignorant. The last year & more, since I lost my home by the death of my kind hostess I have been tried with unfortunate places till the last 6 or 7 months. And this retired spot has been I trust has left some memories for the future thro' close confinement on account of bad roads & extreme cold. You will ask after Charlotte. She is all attention, & gets here since the roads mend but I dont encourage her coming often for she has no help and no horse but Mr C. ever kind brings her when a hired one can be found. And I have been there once in 3 or 4 weeks as there is means of riding on this farm where they are very indulgent and fond of a boarder. But as the daughter is about marrying I believe they will need the whole of this Cottage. And I mean to journey for health about this reigion. So I want you to write as soon as you can. I want to go to Montague & board near Lucillia Griswold (that was)[4] but the family she engaged last fall have moved   But I'm well housed, & there will be another door open. In the Villiage w'h I like & near to C.C. there is no room. There is a room Hannah writes to C C in her house for me as there was long since but more expence than I choose and less of quiet & solitude. So at Concord—the facinations of Waldo's society is not what I can venture nor is it   I should go to Waterford & look up my book case & blankets & carpet w'h I needed in winter but expense & unable to go alone. I know Elisabeth whose unfailing attentions to my comforts & wants would go with me if I asked it. But I dont know how we could be accomodated

And now my dear Ann, I have gratified your curiosty if you have any time for me and if I have not exhausted your patience, you will let me know by being as particular in your telling me what you read and how each child is & where they are & with what prospects. If it is a releif to my Cell to read & sympathise with publick ills & hopes (and without spontaneous sympathy what were human kind) what must be that of friendship! I think Irene cannot value that old fashioned ring,[5] would she not be willing to exchange it for books. And have you any of mine to repay her? I wish for the ring to bestow on Phebe Bliss Ripley who said she would like it not knowing it was given. That family have ever be affectionate & Gore is my benefactor

Farewell my xian friend ever estimable to her affectionate

MM Emerson

How does good Father & Uncle. I hope Mr Cummings[6] will remember him now in his wealth   What & who is your pastor? I've not been to Chh but once these many months

MWA. *Addressed:* Mrs Gage only to read. If she is unwell let it lie bye.

1. TTS, *Sermons* (Boston, 1854); James Freeman Clarke, *The Christian Doctrine of Prayer* (Boston, 1854). MME to ASG, 28 Mar. 1855, states that she has borrowed "a little book on the *nature* & methods of *prayer* [by] James F Clark w'h is of actual & immediate importance to every xian whether weary or stronge" and which she would like to send to her; it is "a little thing but great truths in simple style" (MWA).

2. Harriet Beecher Stowe, *Sunny Memories of Foreign Lands* (Boston, 1854).

3. See MME to ASG, 2 July 1851, n. 2.

4. Lucia Griswold of Fryeburg married James Hervey Merrill in 1839.

5. See MME to PHG, 2 Mar. 1840.

6. "Father & Uncle" is LR, now ninety-four years old; his support was a continuing matter of concern for MME. Cummings is probably a son of Dr. Stephen Cummings, who moved from Waterford to Portland and "became a physician of great distinction." He died at Cape Elizabeth in 1854 (*Waterford*, 238). MME to ASG, 17 Aug. 1855, says, "How is our patron saint? I saw in paper that Dr Cummings was possessed of wealth. Does he know Mr R—s need? Shall I acquaint him? I think Mrs Tracy has done [so]" (MWA).

To Ralph Waldo Emerson

Montague Au 10 55

Dear Waldo,

You got home safely & found your treasures well I trust. Dont have a thought that I need wine for it is uncertain in its use. And I determined not to have any brot *for me* last summer were the worst to happen. It allways seemed improper to use it when we preached against spirit for the laborious. Am glad the express wont take it. This book seemed at first promising, as the Beecher had so failed and the Missisipi man had pretended to write a theodaci with no title to success. And Squire more persumptous. But on finding this man a trinitarian w'h seems to violate the first laws of mind I rested. That strange & awfull secret of the origin lies deep in the abysses of eternity. God exists by nesscity of nature Clarke says but what mystery in that *nature*.[1] Evil may exist by a nessicity w'h God cannot annihilate but thro' ages of the sufferings of it's victims. The redemption (misterious and grand) may be the final means of its end. Surely of our ephemeral race! And there are others, beside the bobin woman,[2] who confide with unshaken confidence that if the soul had but one hour to exist, and *that filled with a consciousness of God* it would ask for nothing but his will. It may be a strong instinct of immortality that would forbid realisation of ending.

But what am I doing? No dream of any thing but the possibility of your attempt to send somthing. I felt that your visit was to end as usual every moment and forgot to ask if you ever T. T. Stone, and notice him? If you do tell him I wish for his sermons w'h he has offered in a letter and have them sent to Concord to Elisabeth   I lost those she gave at a Hotel

Love to Lidian again & tell Ellen not to expend her fine spirits and lovely temper on musick or too much gaiety but study the character & doings of Florence N. to read the 2^d I do know w'h Register of her character & achivements. Oh that I could look into the mind of Simmons[3] says & thinks your afft Aunt

MME

But its bars are closed tighter than ever I think
Let me know your tho'ts of Mr Merrill   I have not seen any one

MH: bMS Am 1280.226(952).
    1. Beecher's *Conflict of Ages*; Albert Taylor Bledsoe (of Mississippi), *A Theodicy; or, Vindication of the Divine Glory as Manifested in the Constitution and Government of the Moral World* (New York, 1853); Miles P. Squier, *The Problem Solved; or, Sin Not of God* (New York, 1855), was one of many responses to Beecher's controversial book. Probably Samuel Clarke.
    2. Cowper's "bobbin woman."
    3. Florence Nightingale (1820–1910) first achieved prominence for her work in hospitals during the Crimean War, 1854–56; George F. Simmons.

To Elizabeth Hoar

[Aug.? 1855]

Dear Tutelar,
    Constant proofs of your devotion to duty in kindness. The purse what can I do with so splendid an article. *Why were your hands so long employed* And the book, is it mine? I can part with it as of no use to loan, to me very desirable to read once   But your letters don't fail me there. When do you go

in a few days I believe. You will not stay at this time while Simmons lives I dare to hope.[1] I feel lost at C— if you dont often write. I've heard nothing since your letter, of the effect w'h the knowledge of his case? Waldo had not seen him since—but he feels the sadness of the expected loss to poor dear Mary & the children. Give my love to the returned travellers, but to what houses of affliction[2]   And do they speake of the sad state of England. Do they sympathise with publik? Did they hear of the heroine F Nightingale. her sensibility and disinterestedness and what she did to create order and comfort? They seem happy to get home, contentment from transient sucess will never induce that quiet Angel to reside with the restless. And ones own gratification is a very narrow sphere. I was much disgusted with some connections who visited my lodgings in Deerfield. Such a fullness of mirth & emptiness and glut of earth. I can always tell you when I escape bores than when met. *I* failed to bore them with Pope's story of the Idiot who when her Master's son died, ran round the house exclaiming "So an't I."[3] Picture of poor human nature. Not a speck of it rises with the fragrance of colong. nor the sparkel of gilt. But I have most of a bottle of the first. Write as soon as this gets to you. And if you go away can't Martha inform me often of the afflicted. I dont ask Lidian for I know at times how she suffers in her head. Thanks for the papers. Sad view of English losses. Yours in head ache so I could not finish last eve. & it must go. I direct to Waldo (by the bye I was so excited with seeing him I lost all calmness the whole eve) as I am childish to think the post O. folks will think I take too much of your time or that I am idle. Mori memento, now that I am very ambitious. I seem to have forgotten that sick chamber in my trifling. But I shall not write often. Your Aunt

MH: bMS Am 1280.226(1202). *Endorsed:* Miss M M Emerson / 1855.

1. Undated letter was written shortly before the death of George Simmons (see MME to WE[3], 24 Sept. 1855). MME to ASG, 17 Aug. 1855, explains, "Mr Simmons who married Mary E. Ripley is about to die. After a life devoted to study & religion after 3 changes caused by his antislavery and when happily for less than a year at Albany New Y. he was taken with a lung fever w'h has left him in a consumption. He was removed to Concord with great care (so very feeble) and is at his Mothers near to the manse where are the three children the infant with Mary and him. Here is a prospect of dependence & struggle for Mother & Children. They will live with S.A.R. Mary is all industry & said she feared not poverty but it was before desolation appeared. But I grieve at the publick loss of such a preacher. I never heard him but once and I believed his manner for simplicity & sanctity before even Channings" (MWA).

2. RWE to Abel Adams, 6 Aug. 1855, reports that he has recently taken a "pair of holidays" (*L* 4:524) and that on 8 Aug. he read a commencement address at Amherst. He extended his trip to visit MME (see reference to seeing him, below); MME to ASG, "Montague Aug. 17 '55," states that "Waldo has been to see me when at Greenfield," a town about ten miles northwest of Montague and twenty miles northwest of Amherst (MWA). Other "travellers" not identified.

3. Story not from Pope but Laurence Sterne, *Tristram Shandy*, vol. 5, chap. 7.

To William Emerson[3]

Montague   Sep. 24   55

Thanks for your letter. Like the visits w'h are "far & few between"   And those visits may often come with ills in a world misteriously (and when we know all) fitted for sufferings of every kind to the good & bad, but preparatory to virtue and high degrees of felicity if used bravely—certainly if religiously I forbear preaching on "morals" as W^m Jr. would say. I had not Charlotts of grief, till afterwards. It is singular the success of Samuel in life in excellent wives & in his pastoral efforts.[1] This I hope will help him to depend more on the truest means of happiness, *within* his heart & its relations to the Source. I am glad that all has been so prosperous with dear Susan and the sons. If any body can be *full* in happy circumstances without injury or even a look of as-sumption, *tis Susan*. How much easier 'tis to sympathise with the happy than the afflicted. We know that all is for the best even now, for sorrow "cometh not out of the dust,"[2] nor by that mongrel non existence chance.

You speake truly of Geo. Simmons. He suffered from Neuralogy the winter they passed in the Manse and Mary was devoted night & day to him & Anne Loring. C. Simmons who went to Albany to assist her, calls her a "miracle" (in describing) of endurance and cheerfullness.[3] She knew not his danger then. She has a devoted Mother & many friends   She said in that dark winter "no fear of poverty while she could work"   How slim do literary accomplishment appear before such as hers. She had none of them. I never expected to see him but I cherish the memory of his attentions & believe I have lost a friend. Nobody I ever saw could get near him. I have lost one more,[n] of many a long year in solitude, Mrs Ann Sargent Gage.[4] I had hoped felt sure w^d out live me, & perhaps when her children were settled I could pass my last days in her soceity, in her poetry I loved, believed her Mountain Muse superior to F. Hemans. But these recent losses not the cause of low spirits but the health w'h gave way to age the year & more and wh promises no crisis, but will finally and at the fittest time. I thank you, dear William, for your offer of books. Tenneson[5] I dont appreciate. My own Tutelar[6] has sent me of him. But I should like somthing new. Have you Hitchcocks "Religion of geology."[7] A book highly to be prized in these days for the youth, for age as long as life

If you find any review w'h puts *down* H. James new book[8] do let me have it. The Independant of N. Y is very desirable   Any thing you can send by Charlotte who stays with S. I dont how long or short. I hope for a letter & what you can bestow soon, next week I *may* move to Orange[9]   This house cannot comfort me no fire nor stove w'h I hope to avoid but stoves are potent. I have an acquisition in Rev. Lawrence Bradford. He delighted me by remem-bering your doing a disinterested kindness to him a stranger—'twas advice. I dont what the occasion. He wished me to ask you if he was remembered   He married Maria Bradford double consin to S A R and I shall prefer Montague but can't get the humblest accommodation I suspect, for my other clerical

friend for whose socety I came here has tried. Hannah is going to take S. &
family to board.[10] That is good. Your true well wisher

& aff^t Aunt MME

MH: bMS Am 1280.220(75). *Endorsed:* Aunt Mary.

more,] more ⟨near⟩,

1. Probably a reference to death of Samuel Moody Haskins's second wife, Sarah
Knickerbacker, whom he married in 1851; he married for a third time in 1859.

2. Cf. Job 5:6–7.

3. George Simmons died 5 Sept. 1855, age forty; MME's niece Ann Dunkin Ripley
Loring (1829–52) was his sister-in-law. Niece Mary Ripley Simmons nursed both
George and Ann the year the Simmonses lived at the Manse, 1852; Charles Francis
Simmons was his brother.

4. ASG lived until 1876, but either she was very sick or some rumor led MME to
believe she had died. MME to ASG, 26 Nov. [1855], begins, "You are alive & I am
thankfull for the gift of your restoration," and goes on to explain how she felt "when
doubtfull": "Not as you & C C expected. For you seem dead to me since moving from
W. And no word of hope ever occurs that we are to meet in Me or Mass" (MWA).

5. Possibly Tennyson's *"Maud" and Other Poems*, published in 1855.

6. EH (see preceding letter).

7. Edward Hitchcock, *The Religion of Geology and Its Connected Sciences* (Boston, 1851). Hitchcock was president of Amherst College.

8. Henry James, Sr., *The Nature of Evil, Considered in a Letter to the Reverend
Edward Beecher, D.D., the Author of "The Conflict of Ages"* (New York, 1855).

9. A town about fifteen miles northeast of Montague (which is north of Amherst).

10. Probably Samuel Haskins; see above, n. 1.

To Ralph Waldo Emerson

[1855?]

Dear Waldo

If I go before seeing you Please send for the Clevelands by telegraph. I
have expressed my desires for years to be buried by Chh. service & wrote to
them that I desired Mr C. to attend my funeral— Yet in your haste forgot
to mention *Sarah* & Elisabeth knows it. Send for Phebe Bliss Cobb. I cant go
to sleep this desire is so & so. If I should not meet you till long times have
passed over us. How then & where? For me the discipline may be of ignorance for not doing better but more & more surely I expect for not *feeling* &
doing better. But thro' ages of *what* is impossible to know—but finally that
work of redemption now in sort veiled, but glory & *infinite love* shines & will
be perfected we shall meet if my happiness is to be complete & genius will
sympathize with its admirers!

Night friday late but tho' in haste I could not sleep without naming the
C. C.s & they knowledge that you were acquainted therewith

I surely meant to write only that

MH: bMS Am 1280.226(953). *Addressed:* Mr R Waldo Emerson / To be given him / immediately.

1856

To ANN SARGENT GAGE

Concord   March 2, Sab '56

My dear Ann

How long it is since I've heard from you except Martha said they seldom did, and were it not for hoping to, I could not write as I am not well enough to read but little & have much that urges me to read of new and high works respecting the times of religion and of politicks so as not to be ignorant of the welfare & woes of my Country & kind— How disgracefull to shut one's up in ease (even in the hopes of the great salvation) in ignorance of the great wheels of Providence whether gloomy or bright. Some glimpses I get & try to forget the bodily & mental wants & ails. And one expectation has engaged me habitually when I came & been impressed since by some omen w'h Waldo says are not superstitions   But the hope fades and that state of soul which nears death dont comfort and were it approaching what it be it would not insure nothing when sin is remembered but faith in the glorious grave w'h Jesus bro't to light and a perfect confidence that whatever portion is allotted is the best wisest & welcome. Who would elect their retribution and appoint their station thro' eternity?? or wait for better improvemet after no native duties remain. Should I not always fail? I asked how you felt when you came to reason about going   But apart from your beloved ties you have a desire to live & learn & enjoy? S.A.R. has just an hour. And what deep & cloudy views with new light in a scientific, rather meta^{ln} A rousing of old tenacious ever stronge intutions. Her patience and benevolence in bearing such a bore as my limited self & oft told tale! She knows I love her & when she was on old ground with me was my oracle in *knowledge* as she ever remains   With Waldo (tho see but little of him so busy & absent) so attentive with Elisabeth H. and Lidian tho much of the time enduring debility. As to E.H. I received the gift from God   Her years of attention—

Twelve o'k   I was obliged to go to bed at 12 generally as I cant have fire early & love to sit late when all is still. With all these 3 families you'll say how happy. Yes tis a blessing to see them   But tell my young freinds if they have not experienced enough of life and the faith in the great Guide of all events that happiness depends not on place or circumstancs. That a famine of soceity which has so much of my life has been my lot and in seclusion in the best places my choice as I always enjoy more in the best soceity than the hope of giving pleasure, and the excitment &&c makes solitude more dear than most else. Now then the maxim I started with went in all cases. But it is a general truth with all thinkers that prosperity is not promotive of the best happiness & that effort patience & fortitude increase under meagre means in a manner that cant be accounted for but the wise ordinance of Providence in this misterious state where redemption was begun & perfected in the Saviour by his sufferings. You have had a great loss in a beloved husband and the consequences, still you have not lived long enough nor been obliged to meet so much variety of the same dull round. That round how weary—yet what joy has attended it when health favored solitude. Now you must write soon & answer. You say "you dont speake of yourself." Then you have no friends out your family that you love? I well know how often when returning in fine spirits that I have recalled what I taxed Hannah Sawyer Lee with that it was egotism of a refined & proud kind occupied her silence on this score of self. Now do you *forgive me what I've written*? Do probably the last offence. And remember that the great & pious Lavater dont approve of so reserve. I would fill up both pages with an account of *my* feeling it nessecary (for Hon. S Hoar says it) to make a new will before death.[1] * * * I think to go to W. this spring if extra expenses for the last year permits. Your letter was usefull as well as interesting, to learn that Mrs Ann Tracy had not forgotten My Uncle & your Father. I thanked her. S A R. sent by me 5 & I added 3 Mr Hoar some I see by a note from Martha so that her uncle[2] will be comfortable a good while. Waldo is going to—the non payment of rail roads has pestered him. I acted from your saying "the means not equal to the pence" but no complaint   And I wrote to Moody[3]   I reminded him of the affections and touched on the attentions of his Uncle & Aunt. He returned such an excellent letter of gratitude to him & resolution he would sacrifice any thing than he s^d suffer any comfort that he had sent so. He had understood that a Mr Ripley of NY. had the care of him   How came this report? M. says he a young man & poor. Moody is in debt some 1000 I know but this of *gratitude* is *sacred*. Did you ever send *Maucaulys essays to Dr Parsons*?? I am in debt to him for low board & many liberties. Pray write soon I have said any thing so much as I feel in my heart but 'tis 4 days since I began and have not got good means of writing. But if I dont write again how clear and most desirable to communicate in this world of spirits if I am permitted to enjoy pious friends

Your aff^t friend
MME

I cant read this over   I want to seal tonight. Pray for your aged   I expect to go back soon as roads good

MWA.
meta^l] *abbreviation for* metaphysical
   1. In the omitted portion of this letter, MME discusses particulars of her will.
   2. LR.
   3. Nephew Samuel Moody Haskins.

To Calvin Farrar

Concord   June 17 '56

Dear Friend

This day had your kind & interesting letter. Some weeks when first due it (pardonne) it would have bro't me, but for so short a time it would not answer as I want now a winter home & always (w'h God in mercy grant short) oh who desires to live in this state of things as we are sure of other; whether Heaven is granted to us till other and severer disciplines is needed—but it will rid us of the sight of such accumulations of human crimes & oppressed millions!? I wish to know the terms if I come after August but I shall not take too much room for Mrs F—s company.[1] And after summer I fear you ll be gone? I spent some weeks at Goshen the attraction is there to be near to dear Charlotte in Ashfield. And I had nearly concluded to go in a fortnight. But the dear air the rich lakes & the noble mountains and my book case & its contents you & your library turn my eyes and associations to the Vale & the common. Where is Mrs Joe Hale   I like to board there from the week there? Time prevents the many notices of your letter & a wish for an *immediate* answer. I board at the house of Deacon R Brown & ca'nt see my human angel E Hoar & Mr & Mrs Emerson to send their remembrances. Your aged & true freind

M M Emerson

terms of board at Goshen 2½. Here in winter 3½. I prefer Goshen for duty.

You know the holy scriptures and theology therefore I spoke rapidly of the greatness of our change from earth to Heaven but not irreverently. Isaac Taylor the great writer in "Sat. Eveg" says we know not what sufferings may intervene or somthing of that sort.[2] But *do you* have Morrel's Philosophy and Religion. The Chap's on the essence of religion & essence of x^{t}ianity wonderfull. My interest in you *points* only to the future!! Woe or weal here is nothing but as they prepare

MH: bMS Am 1280.948. *Addressed:* Calvin Farrar Esqr. / Waterford / Maine. *Postmarked:* concord / Mass. 18 Jun. *Endorsed:* Calvin Farrar / 1856 / Containing a letter from M. M. Emerson written to Mr. Farrer.

1. Calvin Farrar sent MME's letter on to RWE and added a note (dated 19 June 1856) concerning the question of finding MME a suitable boarding place for life in Waterford. Farrar does not want to proceed without advice from RWE and EH.

2. Isaac Taylor, *Saturday Evening* (Boston and New York, 1832).

To Henry David Thoreau

Sab Noon [12 July 1856][1]

Will my young friend visit me tomorrow early as he can—   This eve. my Sister Ripley sends word she will come & go to see Mrs William Emerson who is in Town. I wish for your writings—hoping they will give me a clearer clue to your faith—its nature its destination & *Object*! While excited by your original visit & thoughts, I lose sight, perhaps, of the motive & end & infinite responsibility of talent in any of its endless consequences. To enter the interior of a peculiar organization of mind is desirable to all who think & read in intermited solitude. They believe when the novelty of genius opens on their unpractised eye that the *spirit* itself must own and feel its natural relations to their God of revelation where alone every talent can be perfected and bring its' *additions* to the Owner—that faith in the discipline towards moral excellence can alone insure an immortal fame or even sucess & happiness here.

God bless you & thus make you usefull to your Country & kind prays
MME.

ViU. *Addressed:* H. D. Thoreau Esq.

1. Dating from F. B. Sanborn in the *Critic*; however, 12 July did not fall on Sunday in 1856.

To the THOREAUS

17 July [1856]

It is a pleasure I've depended on for weeks to visit you and was sure last eve. When I returned from the Manse that I should spent part of this day at your house. But the weather is extremely trying when visiting and I conclude I must forgo the gratification of seeing your sons library and daughters drawings. And having my good wishes with Mr Thoreau and family personally But they will exist without vow that you may all be prepared to meet your friends and the good of all nations & denominations in a world delivered from the alternations of woes caused by the passions of undisciplined men & rulers. Affectionately adieu

MM Emerson

Thurs. eve   July 17.

Dear Henry,

I expect to set out tomorrow Morn. for *Goshen*. A place where "wit & gaity never comes that comes to all" But hopes lives & travels on with the speed of suns & stars. And when there are none but clouds in the sky its very nakedness has power to aid the hour says old Sir Walter. But however the "old Bobin woman was steady to her bible"[1] where each page unfolded worlds of comfort & asurance, yet the memory of intelligence extensive mentality will never fail to give a vivid pleasure to reflections if shaded by the faith of future uncertainties—tis well to admit the devices of unerring rectitude. If you write to M E it will brighten the solitude so desired. Had I not been detained by nothing but weather—but I must pack up by day light

ViU. *Addressed:* Mr & Mrs Thoreau & family.

1. Cowper's "bobbin woman."

To Ann Sargent Gage

Goshen   Au sabbath   11 Agu [1856]

My dear Ann

I just came from hearing a sermon from the minister whose sermon I heard 2 years since induced me to come to this place after I lost by death & marriage two good ones in Ashfield. It reminded me of what I once heard your adopted mother say on the temptations of Satan that she never had any she did not trace to herself * * * Last friday I had a letter from *the friend* of *Ann* Tracy with the heavy news of her being given over by Dr Gale & all. Alass, the bereavment of my last & earliest womanly cotemporary. It is a selfish sorrow in most respects for none except her husband loses the last. I knew her when 15 & I two more   And she I *think* prefered life, as she was usefull & devoted to charity—I'm not acquainted with him. I am ignorant whether she lives as I was in case of my other Ann.[1] She has been unable to write very feeble but falling down has deprived her of the use of her body except above the place of her shoulders. Tow friends and a good nurse yet was alone & lost her ballence. Ann was of that sort of early & late devotion to freindship & society that she would have sorrowed for me more than I do. If I had been at Concord I should perhaps seen her. The letter was sent there after I came here and it takes some days to get from Ashfield where I was at the time it went to Concord tho' but 6 miles. It was pleasant to go there as Saml Hannah & Mr Chap^n and the children were there for some weeks. They bro't me here & since H—h came with Henry Haskins who has horses. A son of Wm's to say good bye again.

You wanted me tell you of the H—s. They are very affectionate towards thier only aged Aunt. H—h dont like this out^n the place and thinks she can get one in the Country at her reach. * * * The memory of past days & months of high health I had for years can't be recalled, for age is run down so fast within 2 & 3 years. Are you & family as healthy? I could have remained at my board in Concord but it was more expensive and no retirement & stillness as here, nor the needs of a proud heart so well supplied with means of penitence where friendship was for cheering every day. Ah "the hours of human dull & common" ones pass & return no more but endurance & patience, however humble & obscure, bear an import of immense incalculable beyond.

I have procured the Esthetic papers & given the poem to Waldo & Ellery Channing and the verdict is the best line is where the departed no "longer can die to beauty." What a picture of most reveries. Not that W. did not appreciate all   And I beleive they w^d have better liked the verses at Albany— less of death &c &c[2]   I had not time to get my human angel (E.H) to copy them before coming & know not her admiration. She came with me to A. & left me asleep next morning. Now I hope you will write me as fully your self & children pursuits & reading & ministers company &c. I expected when I began to fill the sheet on religious subjects but am weary. You dont care about Kansas nor Sumner[3] but man. This is large & philosophical—   But individuals goverments are specimens of immediate *sympathy* and call for the xians point or centre of observation? Perhaps I did not take your exact meaning. The whole history of man as given by sacred & profane opens volumns of wonder and often eclipes faith in the unpious reader & wonder in all & *mystery*. Token of individuals and exalts and delights. The martyrs in all ages and this Florence N. & D. Dix[4] with other women do the same. It is for minds like my own & only Ann (I fear) to discrimate judge & bring to light the stars that appoint!

Your affectionate & lasting freind I hope thus forever
M M Emerson

To tell gentlemen that I had the best Poet from the mountains rather than Cities where Hemans was not a prepassing plan   I am better for lying down but writing an effort but I need a letter from *you*

Will you write soon & tell me of Mr Ripley   Has he heard from W.E. of late? R^n has?

MWA.

Chap] *possibly* Clough

out] *illegible; possibly* sort *or* rent

R] *illegible; possibly* he *or* K

1. See MME to WE[3], 24 Sept. 1855.

2. ASG's poem, "The Meditations of a Widow"; the admired passage reads, "*Thou, thou* hast passed all change of human life, / And not again to *thee* shall Beauty die." For the "verses at Albany," see MME to ASG, 2 July 1851, n. 2.

3. Charles Sumner (1811–74), U.S. Senator from Massachusetts, was attacked on the Senate floor following his antislavery speech, "Crime Against Kansas."

4. Florence Nightingale and Dorothea Dix.

To RALPH WALDO EMERSON

[1856]

Spare me once most Oracler Man, a few more days, if I spoke to injure the beautifull Sirs feelings   But somthing spoke undesignely by me ("behind" to use a idea of yours)[1] & I spoke of the religous use of *showing* out, that not a new ribbon or flower would pass untho't of & talked about thro' the day. But I wish you to treat as matter of *taste* & the opinion of *true aristocracy* not to show out in tempels dedicated to worship. The poor suffer in their means of living & all social duties. Your father said once as returning from Boston with your blessed Mother with a new bonnet that the "blue band would come off before it was seen at Harvard, for the wheels would be put away"

Your feeble weak & obliged Aunt
MME

God bless you & wife & children

MH: bMS Am 1280.226(955). *Addressed:* Mr Emerson / Solus. *Endorsed:* M M Emerson / 1856.

1. See "The Method of Nature," CW 1:129.

1857

To Ralph Waldo Emerson

* * *

[6 Jan. 1857]

Dear Waldo

I know only by Sybil like prophecy of your inward life   But a letter from my Angel Medium, speaks real things (deepened by human nature arts or juglers) that you have lectured on the times gained 500 & given it to Kansas.[1] A bright & worthy laurel feather in your cap! But some confidential friends among the platonic spirits talked of it, who are acquainted with the secrets of our Revelators genius & unique econymy agreed that the best gem in your collection was the private little donation to an object the most obscure from birth to extremest age, whose humble and untarnished virtues might lay claim to justice from that Power whom we dare to think of as if all His Attributes might be resolved in the pure and infinitely perfect idea of justice? But the mystery w'h attends the guilt & terrible history of our race and all clothes this sublime holy attribute with clouds & terror. But there is a remedy w'h scatters every cloud & in due time restore the part of creation w'h suffers under the origin of evil and with the glory of that not surely more misterious than the insolvable *origin* of sin, enoble poor frail man to understand the harmony & love w'h presides in the Infinite! As I took Edwards as a table to write on by fire two lines on "justification by faith"   What a mercifull provision for beings who never are perfect to say of the best. If I intrude this scrool it will to thank you for both your letters & for the beautifull traits rather realities of our deceased & revered friend. You cant wish nor I should not have written but the violence of the storm prevented reading & my usual time of sleep w'h is generally nearer one than 12. All good be in store for you & yours
Jan. 6 midnight   Could get no paper tho' there is plenty[2]

MH: bMS Am 1280.226(949). *Addressed:* to Waldo Solus / if absent burn it.

1. RWE spoke twice at Kansas-aid meetings in 1856, at Concord in June ($962 was raised immediately and another $640 by mid-Sept.; Gougeon, 223), and at Cambridge on 10 Sept., where he read "Speech on Affairs in Kansas," his "most militant antislavery speech to this date," at the request of the Middlesex County Committee for Aid to Kansas (Gougeon, 225–26). Her "Angel Medium" is EH.

2. Letter written on leaf with "Almanack" dated "July 15 [1853] Ashfield" (omitted).

To Ralph Waldo Emerson

Commington   March 7   57

Dear Waldo,

Love to Lidian to send into my Cell that which "blind love" betrays her good taste in dress & furniture?[1] I want somthing (if anything) that awakens intellect in its chamber or rather very limited closet, to multiply this infortunate likenes! It Is a problemn among the misteries, not of *nature*, w'h always inspires the theist to it's magnificent Cause and invites the great chambers of study & indefinable wonder & delight! I can't "cut it out" for if I did it must be burnt. What genius averse to the arts, or to *you* as its rival in the better ones of scholarship & its higher sources presides over the wrong headed painter is strange, but the marvel is certain, & that all but mine (w'h I wished returned) should be of this caricature description with a face w'h the cultured socity approve & can admire. If it were with that adverrted & unhealthy cast of eye it might do for a description of the doefull[n] and warped condition of our unhappy Country. No, your pardon, the views of *nature* do not tyrannise over all (true) speculations in any age altogether? Are there not thousands w'h have not bowed to the idols of the sordid, & worshipers of fortune & fame? How humane & elevated the politics of the Jewish nation, tho they were a rude & semi barbarous race? And the tyrannical Romans, how elevated their *codes*? I think of your wishes for a disunion of our quarrelsom, once so so prosperous and I felt glad, but now I tremble at my cherished hopes. But ignorance knows not what to desire or expect   Some deep & enlightened politican it seems would set the mind at rest or inkindle it. Churches are in their last sleep and I have not been to any some time thro' infirmity or thinking so, and from a reluctance to hear a man who dont pray for the slave and whose heart seems to have no accession from its very smalest embryo.[n] Well I'll tease you no longer for this long page was wholly undesigned till just as it grew doing   It was bro't thus far by an interesting lady (the sole fine one in the Town) coming in and was desirous of taking the present of Lidian to her husband, but I would not let her till I had pasted another paper over the skeleton, for I knew his curiosty to see you, & as he is a stranger, except an hour or so, could not trust him. He has a great desire to read. Your books have opened an intelligent mind— A devoted Abolionist, sends me the Liberator if I wish it. A mechanic & my only acquaintance. An invalid or I s[d] often have him come. I hear from our own most precious Elisabeth often, with some xian E.s & her welcome letters and in one she is so earnest in admiring Arora w'h you sent her that I forgot all Mrs B's wearisoms.[2] Among other articles, Mrs Lowels "seed"[3] w'h I soon sent to my friends, for I am always a slow reader and these months scarsly any. Forget how to spell and shorten it. No, I dreamt not of you but intending when March was over (if alive on this whirling earth) to answer the kind Deweys who have bro't me into debt, and Sophy & Maria C.[4] but believe I shall never to that admirable woman, for a Reviewer calls her this, a "snake in the grass" as to my faith. Farewell with many a desire that

Figure 30. Ralph Waldo Emerson, in a crayon drawing by
Samuel W. Rowse in 1857.

your gifts may be sacred to the best interests of your Country as they may yet
bear *directly* on the most sacred connetion with the blessed truths directly
from Heaven   They skirt the heavy clouds of earth with light brighter than
the wings of seraphs. They give to many an aged believer to rejoice tho' they
expect this a crisis w'h may terminate in a great and severe judgment to a
world & Chh, and feel willing to share thier short part of it if it may improve
a wicked world. Your letter would have ended the first page but I wanted to
send love to the beloved children and tell Ellen May will restore her strenght
Love to Mrs Brown   Your affectionate

MME

Bad pens & lamps. You need not read it if you could

I ca'nt write as I meant to this post to my Tutelar.
Ask her to send Xian. Ex. for I have read its articles, tho' I dont think it
burning with celestial fire in these portentous days   If you dont forgive my
first complaints we will meet at some spirit clad Philipi[5] & so good night

MME.

Pray let Elizabeth if sees this in the office hear of the pressing cause. of my
letter   I wish you w^d go to Europe and have a real portrait where only I *think*
Dr Channing had a good one. My sympathy & love to Mr W E Chaning[6]   I
was surprised at Dr Deweys first letter to his impudent assailant.[7] What do
you all think of it   Ask E.H. to tell me for you'll never write least I should
answer

MH: bMS Am 1280.226(956). *Endorsed:* M M Emerson / 1857.

for . . . doefull] ⟨it might do⟩ for ↑ a ↓ description of ⟨our⟩ ↑ the ↓ doefull (it
might do *probably inadvertently canceled*)

embryo] embro'y *in MS*

1. MME seems to respond to a portrait or photograph that LJE has sent; some of
her comments suggest the Samuel W. Rowse crayon drawing of RWE made in 1857.
According to Edward Waldo Emerson, Rowse was dissatisfied with the first crayon,
which he destroyed, but not before the family had a photograph made of it; the second drawing survives (*W* 6, "List of Illustrations"). Other comments suggest instead a
group photograph that includes MME (the "skeleton" she pastes over before showing
the picture).

2. Elizabeth Barrett Browning's *Aurora Leigh* (London, 1857).

3. Anna Cabot Jackson Lowell (1819–74), compiler of *Seed Grain for Thought
and Discussion* (Boston, 1856).

4. Probably Sophia Bradford Ripley and Lydia Maria Child; one letter from Child
to MME, dated 6 Jan. 1857, survives in the Houghton Library. Below, MME probably
refers to a review of Child's *Progress of Religious Ideas through Successive Ages*, 2 vols.
(New York, 1855), in the *Christian Examiner* 60 (Jan. 1856), 148–151, or possibly J. F.
Clarke's "Comparative Theology of Heathen Religions," *Christian Examiner* 62 (Mar.
1857), which calls her study "unreliable" (190).

5. See MME to EBE, 7 Oct. [1823], n. 2.

6. Ellen Fuller Channing died 22 Sept. 1856.

7. Possibly a reference to Moses Stuart's "unmanly & disingenuous attack on Dr. Dewey and Mrs. Dana, in his late volume of *Miscellanies*" (*Christian Examiner* 41 [Nov. 1846]: 452). This review of Dewey's *Discourses and Reviews upon Questions in Controversial Theology and Practical Religion* (New York, 1846) finds one of the notes an admirable "reply" to Stuart's "attack." Probably Mary Dana (later Shindler), who in 1845 published *Letters Addressed to Relatives and Friends, Chiefly in Reply to Arguments in Support of the Doctrine of the Trinity.*

To Ann Sargent Gage

Ashfeild   Dec 29 '57

Dear to me by the memory of those kind of pleasures w'h are immortal, those w'h your youthfull, scarsly escaped from childhood, opened on the wilderness where I had lived some time. But you have forgotten my old age, why not answer my last inquiries about Phebe & each of yours   How Ann L. comes on—where Dr T. and George, & how Irene is and Mrs Cousins & Lois.[1] Sybil writes that M.R. says Uncle fails very fast.[2] Happy saint to enjoy so much of Heaven that he is not impatient to escape a world w'h runs over with so much publick guilt in our gov^t and increase of human coldness in saints & sufferings in lower of coulered & white people. But RWE. writes that "the panic has made people thoughtfull & believe there is a Providence"[3] Do let me know your veiws & observances on times & Chhs & people   I live from all socity amid mountains w'h conceal the sabbath bells a place & smale family I was pleased with in the pleasant season but too far from the C.C.s and milder winds have an invite to move to the widow & Mother of a fine physian & if cercumstances are permissive shall move into villiage till summer tho' I do not expect to see it in this world not that my health fails, nothing retards activity but irresipalas & rhumatism in knees. You spoke as tho' Uncle could no feel a dependance on Nephews   M. has nothing but to mention his wants to Waldo & Samuel.[4] I have with a contribution from Charlotte sent him a smale token of love—   But Sybil is now in New E. & I intend to ask Waldo & S.M. about my applying to Dr Dewey for an application to the Society to relieve destitute clergymen who ever deserved it more. And his adherence to the orthodox faith will make no odds with the unitarian society. Mr D. is going to pass the last of his days in the pastoral office at Chh Green in City. His health forbids preaching more than ½ day he hopes his plan. Louisa loves her retirement but enjoys the society where she most friends   And no situation found her assuming nor ought but the humble & retiring xian. Yet I did write to her as I have to others who are successfull in these sad times when we seem like slaves under our corrupt gov^t that one cant but think of dear old Popes relating the fact of going to see a nobleman in loss of an only Son that the *idiot* met all the visitors with her merry asurance that "*so ant* I."[5] Charles Dewey is a farmer but the eldest daughter & young one are at home. Now tell me what Goverment has done to aid the unhappy sufferers of Kansas, and what you think of the times? Is some great crisis at hand that will bring God's goverment more prevalent? I Taylor expected it 12 years since. Does antislavery prevail with your companions? Do the great questions of theology prevail? I hoped you would tell me about Huntingtons sermons & his views.[6] They are like rich beams of love & devotion   And Bartol keeps close to the cross and mans fears & hopes   But it is Dr Bushnell w'h I wish you to see so much. It is here borrowed from South Adams where I went from the need of a short journey and to see the daughters of my late Cousin.[7] They are under an unhappy delusion of having the spirits of the departed visit & one is a medium. My earnest exhortations answered no purpose. And I left them after ten days of kindnesses from them in their wealth (the husband of one) with no great desire to hear more. But paid richly by the vol. of sermons wh put bye those of H. & B & our dear T.T.S. The one on the "attonement" not finished but intend rereading. A subject always sublime when treated by the Arian Dr S. Clarke of England in the last Century   If you choose not to part with the feeble & aged let me know what you think of the questions so agitated (and improved as to speculation since) the contention has softened within some years and more union—   This was preached at H. university

And now dear Ann I must say that if ought against the connection has arisen with you, duly let us part as former friends. It best than keep up forms. No wonder you might have been disgusted with my improper treatment of Miss E P   A rediculous pet. When knowing her propensity to meddle & divide freinds it well to part. A letter from Dr Channing in his second vol. of memoirs contain kind reproof of Poets at which surprise is the least emotion.[8] Errors in religion leading to infidelity & arrogance. Do you know of her and correspond? Burn this information for she may yet be a sincere redeemed saint. Love to each and if death hastens as I often feel sure, how delightfull the hope of meeting in a better higher state. How is Uncle?

Affectionately your freind
MME

If Charlotte knew of this oppy she would send much love

Tell me of Phebe & *the place*   If I live I may gladly go there.[9] I write in haste for a chance to send to office

MWA. *Addressed:* Mrs Gage / If absent the letter may not be opened.

1. MME asks about seven of ASG's eight children.

2. Sybil Farnham Lambard, Martha Robinson, Uncle LR (who died the following July).

3. See RWE to MME, 10 Dec. 1857, on the panic of 1857 (*L* 5:91–92).

4. Samuel Moody Haskins.

5. The "foolish Scullion" in Sterne's *Tristram Shandy*.

6. MME to ASG, 21 Apr. 1857, exclaims, "Oh how I wish you had Dr Huntington's vol. of sermons. They are intitled 'for the people.' What a remarkable event that he should be the preacher for the university at C. It is a kind Providence. His sermons are full of orthodoxy of the bible kind, and they were well known in a magazine he

edited. A no. are on the trials & duties of women. I have skiped these as yet, his trinitarian faith is stronge" (MWA). Frederic Dan Huntington (1819–1904) became preacher to the university and Plummer Professor of Christian Morals at Harvard in Sept. 1855; *Sermons for the People* (Boston, 1856); in her Apr. letter MME quotes from sermon 12, "The Christian Woman." From 1856 to 1858 he edited the *Monthly Religious Magazine and Independent Journal*.

7. Possibly Horace Bushnell's *Sermons for the New Life* (New York, 1857); probably Sabra Emerson Field, who died in 1837.

8. *Memoir of William Ellery Channing*, possibly 2:448.

9. ASG to Lucius Manlius Sargent, 8 Jan. 1852, describes her eldest daughter Phebe's condition and states that she is almost deaf (MWA). MME to ASG, 21 Apr. 1857, asks about Phebe and continues, " 'She is content.' Well I never felt about insanity as most" (MWA); LR to ASG, 1856, mentions that Phebe is now in the asylum at Augusta (MWA).

1858

To Ralph Waldo Emerson

Monday 25 Au. [1858] Birth day of 84. Cant give to its usual joy because the image of a beautifull being just budding into existence. A stranger to me dont know whether her existence is noted by any communion with reality—or only a kind of painting an influx of images of delight to eye & ear, fancy & the deep root of ambition (alas how abased[n] in our sensual world from its noble destiny) to shine in the cellars of our world w'h demands the *light* (so called) of natural science. What do we learn of its uses except to its adepths to earn bread & fame? How many have found shelter in stoicism or insane hospitals of its greatest scholars? Oh save this precious being one more year to learn the value of life from its purest sources! Poetry even of heathen will verrify[n] like Virgil in riegions of death the native powers of immortality, studied in the sacred home far from the croud of constant changedness & all its distracting agitations. Who could better (once!) give original ideas of *natural religion* than him who is responsible for her? The sublime idea of *nessesity* w'h gives our existance to be connected by *it's nature* to the only Source of life and joy & virtue! Enough to know that every mode of being is caused by Him whose very being causes *time* & *space*! Who but the usefull drudges of natural science would peep into bugs & turtles to find a Cause for every reptile? That the odious reptiles devour man & beast is among other misteries w'h viel the eternal throne, but the torch of revelation assures its belevers that rightious is the "habitation" of that throne.* And that virtue in its mere moralities cannot florish and grow without toils & sacrifes of early study & experience. Oh let her learn that solitude affords the purest joys, w'h cannot be explained by the host of learned men. Milton tho' blind knew them in obscurity. Archemides knew them for a transient run. But do we ever hear of his triumph over disease

& the grim mesenger of death? But what kind of excitment has led me into this persumption? Is it Margarets restless demon?[1] No a more tranquil healthy day has never come in this season   So forgive & burn if you cant read.

Yours with respect for Gods gifts

*And *true* philosophy whether by nature &c or revelation teach that Infinite Being must be infinitely good![2]

"From today dates, not nor yet from yesterday; but
From eternity, the moment known to none"!
Sophloces

You see dates are nought. The day of my illustrious birth was 25 of August. Napolens the 24 of August

A scroll for Mr Emerson who asked long since for the old Almanaks and will never see else

MH: bMs Am 1280.226(957). *Endorsed:* M M E. / on her 84th / birthday / 1858.
abased] *possibly* abused
verrify] *possibly* vivify (*T*)
   1. Cf. MME's response to reading the *Memoirs of Margaret Fuller Ossoli* (MME to Martha Bartlett, 25 [Feb.? 1852]).
   2. Remainder of letter written upside down on opposite half of leaf.

To Ellen Emerson

Aug. 27, '58

Dear Ellen,

Thanks for attending my request of a letter. I take this rainy day & *lame* confinement to inform you that the valuable Register I send contains an important article, I believe, about Dr Jackson.[1] Been standing at the door to find a look of the amiable Alice,[2] in vain. Your Mother and Mrs B. will like it if it is as new to them as to me. An interesting notice from Dr Gannet about the telegraph.[3] But I want to ask him if it will tend to the benefit of 3 millions *of our fellow men*? England has a right to rejoicie in every thing for they have done bravely at great expense to the freedom of slaves! It would be well if that respectable preacher were questioned on the divine Telegraph who descended 18 centuries since to preach *truth Justice* and *charity,* yet the world in its *mania* for *fashion amusements, literature* & *fame* remain in full pursuit of the very world his doctrines opposed, and for which he suffered to reclaim from. There is much told of a new version of bible. Age dreads such versions whatever need there may be, it seems the man is not born in the 19 cent. not in Mass. if such opinions as Mr Parkers are tolerated with the falshoods like this in Register.[4] To those who are not learning to be troubled with the plenary theory or belief there seems no startling difficulties to arrest the highest attainments in morals and what infintely more important in christianity the way *to* morals and their strongest or supposed[n] basis. The xian Mirrow must go to the Manse, S. A. R. wishes her children to see it, & send the biography of thier Uncle to E.R.[5] It is beleaved that if this means of conveying intelligence had existed there would have been no war with our Mother land at the last war. If peace of nations contributes to invidual virtue may the world well rejoice. But what a vast desire there is in persons and gov[ts] for war, till the Prince of peace comes and reforms by power the passions. And tis hoped & believed by such as Taylor, he is coming! May you and your parents live long and happier days. I speake not to a child—if I write it must be on the few subjects that run in my diseased brain before going to the regular[n] composure of hospitals

Your Father can rectify you. He is said to be the most industrious student known. If haste is a token he is. It is most desirable to see the fruits. He said I might have the last Atlantik; *do send* it[6] I was desirous you should get me to S A Rs because Phebe Bliss insisted on sending for me I intended to have gone on my own score else. If convenient to carry me to a part of town where · I have business, the begining of next week—if not Tod has horses & carriges

Love to parents & Aunt and E W E. & Edie.

from your fond & aged Aunt
MME.

Opend the letter to beg you *return* the Register[7]

MH: bMS Am 1280.226(761). *Addressed:* Miss Ellen T. Emerson / Present.
strongest or supposed] ⟨eternal⟩ ↑ strongest or supposed ↓
regular] ⟨happy⟩ ↑ regular ↓

1. The *Christian Register*, 21 Aug. 1858, printed an article, "Invention of the Telegraph," which claimed that LJE's brother, Dr. Charles Jackson, and not Samuel F. B. Morse, was the inventor of the magnetic telegraph.

2. Probably Alice Forbes, sister of William H. Forbes, who would marry Edith Emerson in 1865. The Emersons visted the Forbeses at Naushon in late Aug. 1858, and ETE to EE, Naushon, 1 Sept. 1858, mentions Alice (*ETE L*, 150–51).

3. The *Christian Register*, 28 Aug. 1858, printed a notice of Ezra Stiles Gannett's recent sermon on the Atlantic telegraph (Boston, 1858); for several weeks the *Register* had carried news of the cable's completion, which it compared to the voyage of Columbus (14 Aug.) and called the "great event of the age" (21 Aug.).

4. The *New Translation of the Bible*, by the Reverend Leicester Ambrose Sawyer (Boston, 1858), was advertised in the *Christian Register*; in a brief notice, the reviewer asked, "Is a greatly improved translation of the Bible practicable?" (28 Aug. 1858); allusion to [Theodore?] Parker unclear. References to this number of the *Christian Register* indicate MME's letter is probably misdated.

5. LR died 14 July 1858 at the age of ninety-six years, ten months. The obituary was on the front page of the *Christian Mirror* (Portland) for 24 Aug. 1858.

6. RWE's essay "Eloquence" was published in the *Atlantic Monthly* 2 (Sept. 1858): 385–97.

7. Written on outside.

To Ann Sargent Gage and Martha Robinson

Night
Concord   Sep   Sab 24 '58

Dear Freind

Yours so full of interest I could not answer (of some months since) then, but now if I could find it where frends have put up in their order, I should rejoice to bring you to habits of discussion for our mutual interest. The old maxim that thoughts increase and improve by communiation. I can't read but little the past summer thro' debility. But that little shows me my own ignorance & short commings and how much there is to know. And the great blessed enjoyment of being *to think*. But to be a *thinker* is great—yet what have thinkers become thro' false views if not insane worse of scepcists. The natural sciences reported so important to great truths sometimes lead on to pride & loss of spiritual causes. Not so with Hugh Miller but to xianity. Have you seen much of his works. "The wittness of the Rocks" is the only work I've got for a time but expect to read all of it.[1] Rev. Thomas Hill of Waltham a great Mathematican, in his address at Cambridge closes with saying that the one science of math., "to study a 1000 years would not exhaust it," or somthing of the sort, but I can't find the address.[2] It is so desirable to find these uses of learning   But the peace w'h passeth understanding like the "Bobin womans." "Blessed is the man *whose sins are forgiven*", says the psalm,[3] and the xian says he needs no other, to shorten the lingering hours. What an eternity of increasing knowledge may he not expect of that greatest of sciences theology! That science w'h comes cloudy at times thro' deficient men & books whose few simple precepts lead to *greatness*, and whose promises, founded on the rock who is the redeeming Agent of a fallen race, inrich the poorest

And now Dear Ann   Tell me of your self & loved ones. * * * You know by Martha that I'm about to be deprived by a year of my providential Angel E.H. I rejoice in her going   She has much care since the loss of the best of Fathers & men and needs change for health.[4] * * *

Good night the best of it when its morning twilight becomes a symbol of the advent of the once appearance of a star in the east. May you be eminently devoted to God and the cause of Jesus w'h is one & undivided.

Your afft friend
MM Emerson

* * *5

If you wish for the blankets take them with my love. Do you know any thing about Mr Hows folks   Or my treasures there? in the book case. Of my loved Medallion & the portraits? If Mrs Gage would send Coleridges Conffesions[6] or any book w'h she thinks I need it would oblige me when you come here. I can't ask E.H. for the list Ann sent me for Elisabeth is crouded with items

MWA. *Addressed:* Mrs Gage & Miss M. R.
   1. Hugh Miller, *The Testimony of the Rocks; or, Geology in Its Bearings on the Two Theologies, Natural and Revealed* (Boston, 1857).

2. The Reverend Thomas Hill (1818–91) was ordained pastor of the Independent Congregational Church, Waltham, in 1845; his Phi Beta Kappa address at Harvard in July 1858 was titled "Liberal Education." In 1862 he became the twentieth president of Harvard University.

3. Cowper's "bobbin woman"; Ps. 32:1.

4. Samuel Hoar died 2 Nov. 1856; on 6 Oct. 1858 EH sailed from Boston for Liverpool with her brother Edward and Elizabeth Pritchard.

5. The following is from a note to Martha Robinson, dated "Monday," mostly omitted.

6. Samuel Taylor Coleridge, *Confessions of an Inquiring Spirit*, ed. H. N. Coleridge (Boston, 1841).

To Ralph Waldo Emerson

[Sept.? 1858]

Good morning to thy pursuits of the beauty honor & golden uses of earth. Rapidly run its races   And some morning no fairer needs, will wrap up these clayey rags, and give a revolution in w'h no foolish will blunder about but be mingled with the wise in a new essence "involving all & in a perfect whole uniting." Rather may the smalest individual possess it's mite of identity—if so belong to the Original!

Well the messengers gone. I wanted to know if you would give me the "paper" containing the poetry, fed from the magic of lakes & wizard mountains, where no voice of science, oratory or civil law intrudes its proses, or human mists obscure the open vision[1]

Please send the paper & if I must not carry it away It shall be copied

Your obliged MME

MH: bMS Am 1280.226(958). *Addressed:* Mr R W Emerson / H. Hoar. *Written on verso in pencil by ETE:* Aunt M. M. E. to Father in Sept. 1858 or 9 asking for Adirondac verses / Brought by Hatty Hoar daughter of Mrs Clark with whom Aunt was boarding.

1. RWE's poem "Waldeinsamkeit," probably written in the summer of 1857; the "paper" may be the *Atlantic Monthly*: RWE to Sarah Swain Forbes, 18 Sept. 1858, complains about the publication in the Oct. *Atlantic* (vol. 2, 551; published 18 Sept.) of an unauthorized version of his poem (*L* 5:118–19).

To Ralph Waldo Emerson

[1858?]

Dear W.

If you are not engaged long in the use of your valuable opticks, & if it dont rain, & &c cant you give me an hour? & oblige a pilgrim   At what hour & moment? MME

1 o'k   The sun has gone so has the Winter. His muse sleeps today and the adjutant took place. O Vanity or that element of self love w'h make part of

all Intelligent creatures is innocent & may become holy. But here on earth it becomes at least a little toe in the cloven foot, and ripens into a vampire that leaves but the skeleton of *man,* not wholly woman whose constitution is prepared for a weaker vesel.

Mr Emerson
Please return answer

MH: bMS Am 1280.148. MS attached to p. 73 of RWE's MME Notebook 3. Before his transcription of MME's note, RWE wrote, "Here is one of the last notes received from her when in Concord, on a scrap of paper."

1859

To Ellen Emerson

W^m' June 1 1859.

My dear Ellen,
    Yesterday your Uncle wrote me of Bulkleys death.[1] Poor dear child his sufferings are ended. His little hopes & fears quited. It is sad to me—that I saw him scarsly at Thankgiving That I never urged him to stay with me more—but he made me sad and I had nothing to entertain in that house & no Elisabeths to walk to. He was not well & affected me more than usual. This the usual complaint of people when they lose a friend. Somthing omitted past recall. I congratulate you all as you parents & children were all his comfort. It pleased me to hear you call Uncle Bulkley. When a child of 3 & 5 I was at Boston but rarely he pleased the family of Bradfords so much that they often called to take him to walk. Full of spirit and shrewdness but the wit of his remarks and his gaity attracted notice then and at Waterford after the death of his father he past a year with his aunt Ripley who took him on a visit to lessen the cares of his Mother. And this *ancestral* relative of yours spent much of her time in the care of children, not her own, as the Haskins took in a sick neighbour. Mrs S. A. Ripley was very indignant to hear that the inscription on her gravestone was "that she did what she could." She had never read Huntingtons sermon from that text, that of the highest as the test of true devotedness.[2] When do you go to Maine? Hannah & I talk of going—but come to no resolve while the expense is uncertain but the articles are needed.[3]
    How is your Mother's health? My love to her I think of her kindness. Is it not better to think more & say less? When have you heard where my human Angel is? Does your father speake of their journey being made under disadvantage owing to the warlike state of Europe? Alas how dark & gloomy the state of war and the distress it will involve. Were they nations of a semi barbarous kind they might promote civilisation at least. What does your young heart feel in this (to you) new sights & sounds? May no personal & family

prosperity render you indifferent to the publick evil which is fertile to diffusion. Did you ever hear the story of Popes Idoet?[4] In other sources she exults in saying "So a'nt I"   Good bye dear Ellen   I did not know how blessed at seeing you pass Mrss W—s house & thinking of Ellen & Ediths & Edwards

Aunt M Emerson

MH: bMS Am 1280.220(72).

1. RBE died 27 May 1859.

2. "She hath done what she could" (Mark 14:8), the epitaph on the grave of Phebe Emerson Ripley in Elm Vale Cemetery, Waterford, Maine, served as the text for F. D. Huntington's sermon "Acceptance of the Heart," *Sermons for the People*, 134–48.

3. Probably another reference to the belongings left at Waterford: her bed, blankets, books, bookcase, pictures, and medallion of CCE.

4. Actually, Sterne's "foolish scullion."

1860

To Lidian Jackson Emerson

Wmsburgh   Feb 16, /60

My dear Niece,

Last Sat. Night I received your very handsome presents with much pleasure, as tokens of friendship more than of their special uses, tho' those were affectionately accepted. And my Niece expressed much pleasure. Today Charlotte came from a party at Rev. Mr's New Y. where she & her husband, met Samuel & wife,[1] who told her of the handsome dress. "*The times*" are still interested in appearances. I am glad to congratulate you on improved health. And how much better is your other Self? Wm who often sends me kind notes and to my inquiries of Waldo favorable. Last was from Mr Ralph H. who met him & heard him lecture somewhere at the West much to Ralphs delight.[2] I ought to have answerd before (but writing becomes a task to infirm age) and said my gifts from Edith tho daily worn will hold good as I seldom walk further than the garden w'h ample for City. I had the excellent sermon you sent. I sent it to two clergymen whom I like to hear preach & they were glad. One of them advanced rather came to see since I have been confined by reason of weather and I asked him to pray as usual, and *for the slaves* nothing personal as to disease. Alas, that among so many thousands it is not apparent there is one anti slavery to care." Wm E. sends me the "National anti" every week. I fear he is too disinterested and dont read them himself. It requires better strenght than mine. Mr & Mrs P. read some to me tho' they have others How painfull & lasting a loss to the University & the publick is Mr H—s resignation. His last vol. w'h my book benefactress E.H. sent me, have you seen it?[3] Have you seen D[r] Bushneels on "Nature & supernatural"?[4] I am impatient to understand more of him—much interested in his views of the supernatural in dreams "premotions" &c &c w'h I flatter myself our own oracular W. will not sneer at; tho' many other objections made will be made to some of his opinions about instances of conversion, in a work w'h seems to aim at metaphisiks.

But I am so desirous of health to read more of this and H's last vol. that I have applied to a phycian who reads this (or has it) and is an educated gentleman. I give him no hope of curing old age, nor do I wish it. Comes twice in a week and probably that *one* week will do   But one Doctor about omens & "premonitions" I will keep to till the realities of the unseen state is opened, in *mercy* & *forgiveness*, on so unworthy a subject. Have you seen the verses of our favored M. Childs on the Martyr Brown kissing a coulered infant when going to death.[5] Do thank her for me in giving to print that most delightfull characteristic of the man.

Mrs Stows novel has come here by Charles who has been reading it in his office. I dislike the tone of its first pages & the title, and with her leaving the Country at such a time, to get *copy right*[6]   How irksome to give up a favorite. But if the Beecher family as the Anti S. intimates that that family is lowering, why how natural that changes must occur and how best. May they rise with power & virtue increased *I hope*

Is Mrs & Miss Hoar *well*? How Miss Hoar sounds to one who has been to me like a providential Angel so many solitary years. I felt when I saw her go away that I was Concord sick, But H—h has carried me thro so cheerfully that I had nothing to regret, but much to be thankfull for. And I give her the flanel dress as a token *special* tho' I left her the disposal of all things personal. Ask Ellen to write & be a comunication between me & the beloved family at Manse. Is Edward recovered intirely? The Phycians advise with D[r] Jackson of Boston, wine & tonics. I tried them when the climate first over set me but to my joy did no real benefit, and I tell W. E that his *good* wine did me no good. But the good beer is usefull w'h the family use. Life is not desirable to one so useless with the habit of tonics. Did you send the stockings & gloves *thank* you. Elisabeth has given me enough for each my surviving Nieces. I have not even worn two best dresses. I had no particular call but should if I had feared the Citizens would have feared I was a pauper. If I could give any pleasure to Edith & Edward by writing I should with any certainty they answer me. Ellen I depend on   I remember that you expressed a desire that I would take my last sleep in your lot[7]   And it would be gratify if the season is favorable. I desire W[m] E to take the direction if convenint & directed the episcopal services here in a private way. May the blessing of God continue to watch over each of the three houses

Is Mrs Brown at home? I have inquired & sent love no answer. The house where E.H. SAR & you are the three named. but the writing so poor the whole may be a task. And another where Mary S. lives will be dear.[8]

MH: bMS Am 1280.226(809). *Endorsed:* M. M. Emerson, 1860.

care] *illegible; T reads* one

1. The Charles Clevelands and the Samuel Moody Haskinses.

2. Probably Ralph T. Haskins; in mid-Jan. RWE set out on an extensive lecture tour that took him to twenty-three cities before the date of this letter, including Buffalo, Rochester, Toronto, Toledo, Cincinnati, Chicago, Madison, and Milwaukee; he stopped at another eleven cities before arriving home at the end of Feb.

3. F. D. Huntington left his position at Harvard in 1860; his latest book was *Christian Believing and Learning: Sermons* (Boston, 1859).

4. Horace Bushnell, *Natural and Supernatural* (New York, 1858).

5. Lydia Maria Child edited the *National Antislavery Standard*, a New York weekly that advocated "the peaceful, immediate, unconditional abolition of slavery"; the 11 Feb. 1860 number told of a recent *National Antislavery Standard* subscription anniversary celebration, at which a choir sang a sort of hymn by Child, "The Hero's Heart," which depicted John Brown's stopping, on his way from the "jail to the gallows," to "kiss a colored child that stood near" (p. 3). Brown was executed 2 Dec. 1859.

6. Probably Stowe's *Minister's Wooing* (New York, 1859); Stowe sailed to Europe with most of her family in Aug. 1859; her European letters were printed in the *New York Independent* almost weekly between 1 Dec. 1859 and 23 Aug. 1860.

7. In Sleepy Hollow Cemetery, Concord; RWE gave the dedicatory address in 1855.

8. Paragraph written upside down at top of p. 1.

1861

To WILLIAM EMERSON[3] AND SUSAN HAVEN EMERSON

8 [Feb. 1861]

Dear Nephew,

It is long since I saw you or yours   And I cant wish to have you come & walk while the weather is unpleasant. *How does William* do? I hope he avoids this ungentle weather. Is he & Charles absent? How do you view the sad aspect of the times? With philosophy I persume—with somthing higher and stronger also. It is the sure refuge of women to rely on that Infinite Being whose agency is forever operating and bringing good out evil thro' all the misterious clouds which darken the history of the Church, and the universe, eventually. But the discipline is long and severe, tho' never too much if it improve morals in a nation by faith in the faith which xianity offers. And how individuals are often able to take the higher steps of virtue & piety thro' tribulation   Excuse me dear William for troubling you with so trifling an errand after asking your opinion on subjects so interesting. I wish you to send me a paper I intrusted to you, an account of some my possessions on a smale paper.

Your Sister Exextric[1] I wish her to have and explain. My health or rather lameness increases so fast that I wish to see it before closing my will

Wishing you blessings which rest not on certainties I bid you farewell

MME.

My dear Susan, How is your health? Ellen tells a fine story of her visit, and then you were well.[2] Yesterday[n] Mrs G Ripley was buried from the Catholic Chh.[3] Did you know her? She was a fine woman and pious xian. My close confinement for some time prevented the desire to visit her. Her husband wrote me an afft letter, and I depend on his calling. It is a great while since I had the comfort of seeing you but think of you with good wishes and good prospects of your ripening for happier scenes than mortal life can ever give

Love to Haven Your afft Aunt

MME.

Friday 8 Jan.[4]

MH: bMS Am 1280.220(75). *Addressed:* William Emerson Esq[r] / New York. *Endorsed:* M. M. Emerson / Feb. 8 / 61 / Answered—.

Yesterday] ⟨Today⟩ ↑ Yesterday ↓

1. EH.

2. For Ellen Emerson's account of her visit to New York and of seeing MME, see *ETE L* 1:221–27 and introduction to part 6, pp. 547–48.

3. Sophia Dana Ripley, wife of George Ripley, converted to Roman Catholicism soon after the collapse of Brook Farm in 1847; she died 4 Feb. 1861.

4. Sic *in MS;* 8 Feb. fell on Friday in 1861 (and see endorsement).

To LIDIAN JACKSON EMERSON

Williamsburgh March 18th. [1861]

Dear Lidian

I wished to write to you through Ellen and thank you for your invitation but I had not the strength and she gave it to me in Such haste that it did not make much impression. But there is another invitation that you implied that I want to attend to. When I was journeying once you asked me if I should like to be brought to Concord after death—? I replied that it was a matter of indifference to me where I was buried. Then you said "Are you *willing* to come"? Now I feel very desirous to do so. I long to see Concord and to lie by my old friends there. I have given Hannah directions to have my executor take all the care of sending me & if the weather be warm to have the body embalmed. I think it probable that my executerix (E. H.) will be here. Give my love to Waldo and ask him if he adds to the invitation if not, I will go to the old hill burying ground.[1] I believe there is no dust of a friend to slavery on that Hill.

A merciful Providence *seems* to improve our public prospects for which I am glad for you, your husband & children, & all my freinds sake　　your afft.

　　　　　　　　　　　　　　　　　　　　　　　Aunt　M.M.E.

MH: bMS Am 1280.226(810). *Added at top of p. 1:* Letter from M. M. E. dictated to Charlotte Haskins—.

1. This is probably the letter LJE sent to Ellen Emerson "for [her] delectation" (Mar.? 1861), "which though on so mournful a subject made [me] laugh till I cried while Papa and Aunt Elizabeth [Hoar] kept me company in the laughing I mean" (*LJE L,* 207–8). RWE to MME, 29 June 1861, assured her of a place in Sleepy Hollow (*L* 5:249).

To Sarah Bradford Ripley

　　　　　　　　　　　　　　　　　　　　　Wmsburch　March 25　61

My long loved Friend & Sister,

　　　tho' I never used the last dear word　Avoided it for I had no such claims tho' my brother was estimable to me. I was old and you young　I was unlearned & you learned, known, & prized by friends and strangers. How vanished all these distinctions when your life was endangered! And so all the highest & the lowest do when the strongest elements of our nature over take the shadowy ones which hide in the dust with body! This Divine gift asserts its right from the everlasting Creator. But His love & bounty is giving you to mortals. What a gift did I, even departing by disease, rejoice to have you left to fullfill the compass of duties, and recieve the fullness of that great glorious faith which pours light and strenght on every doubt of the mere understanding, and already makes eternity to be *inheritance* of its lovers. Even then and there I may be permitted to share some of your society. There even the unscientific may be able to understand the higher light which is enjoyed by those of the more enlightened. That great & boundless truth of the *nessissity* of the Infinite Existence will be unfolded forever, in all its relations to all beings & histories? You once alluded to it. And I wont weary you any longer but your letter which I love to read often forbad me to restrain the joy of your recovery. Elisabeth H. knows to appreciate your soceity & you and she will sometimes mention one who loves you both. And Waldo & Lidian & their children I congratulate in heart for your restoration. But it is your dear children I want to write to. Tell them I joy for them

　　　　　　　　　　　　And now beloved Sarah farewell from
　　　　　　　　　　　　　　　　　　　　　MM Emerson
I wish to write to E. R. but I dont use the pen often it wearies me.

MH: bMS Am 1280.226(1292). *Endorsed:* Miss M. M. Emerson / 1861.

To LIDIAN JACKSON EMERSON

W^msburgh   May 1/ 60 [1]

Dear Niece

How do you all? I tho't you might not be well not noticing my letter. Never mind. You have been kind. Lotte is not near me so I must write. I dont like to go to bed as the D^rs tell me the welcome news that I have sure signs of death by a conjestion of blood on the brain. And when I feel able to write I do it before sleeping. I am thinking of your presents to me long since but when Ellen (dear Girl) was here I said "we can buy our clothes"   I refered to Hannahs & my bundle   It has haunted me since tho' spoken thotlessly and last week H. went out & wore your handsome present w'h I had never seen. I had given this one to me & never worn in the house but to ride. And here is that nice flannel & a black silk which I leave to Lotte

What do [you] and Mrs Brown think of the war? If it is to free the slaves & effects that shall we all be thankfull to Providence!? H—h has just come and says I made this apology in Lottes letter. My memory fails—but I dont mind it. If I must be fetters of this life & recover health memory will recover her loved { }ks that very ill furnished articles. And I sh{all recover to} have power to perceive the Angel look of inte{lligence}^n I tost^n on reading a page of Waldos con{sci}ous." [2] It seemed there was no other world but this   I wish I could see what W. writes & thinks about this great sad cruel^n war. I well remember what his earliest was on slavery that "thiers was the right." I have not well so as to finish. And as you gave no welcome to my intention of lying in your cementary, I shall see where dear S.R is going to lie or E.H. How selfish I feel in preparing a *place* when multitudes are going to die for the publick. Our house has lost its youthfull light & beauty in Charles *zeal* to join the army. I am in feeble health or would say more & more

You & yours with love & good wishes
MME.

May 24. Friday

MH: bMS Am 1280.226(811). *Endorsed:* M. M. E. to L. E. / May 24, 1861.
sh{all . . . inte{lligence}] *several words lost due to large blot; bracketed letters from T*
tost] sic *in MS; possibly* lost *intended*
cruel] *possibly* civil (*T*)
    1. References to the war and Ellen Emerson's visit indicate letter written in 1861.
    2. con{sci}ous] badly blotted at line break; left blank in T; MME possibly means RWE's *Conduct of Life*, published in 1860.

1862

To [SARAH BRADFORD RIPLEY]

Sat Night   9 'ok   [1862?]

Dear—admired for long years for talents which I could not with your education well understand but {believe} I *never* envied.ⁿ Oh no! Your last letter was every way delightfull except somthing I could understand as simple truth What raised my spirits but could not comprehend that I could be of spiritual comfort as implied. The comfort and desire for the world where my feet thro the aid of the divine Son. But it occurs always in that intellectual, where spirits will *naturally* associate I can be no intimate. *Well I shall admire* and rejoice in you on the same principles as when here I *do believe*. I have never felt like writing since I have been here. And as to immortality if you did not feel & believe there was nothing tisⁿ   May the God of love & wisdom draw you so near to communion with Him that you may long remain to bless your gifts of children. Commend me to Gore whose obligations to me will go with. To each dear object among the rest may the blessings of the devine gospel be an ornament of their lives and a sacred obligation to others. I had the desire of my heart to see dear E. H. but was too unwell to enjoy it as usual. Farewell dear & beloved Sister & friend

MH: bMS Am 1280.226(959). *Written on back by Ellen Emerson:* Aunt Mary's last.

never] *underlined three times;* envied: *possibly* injured (*T*). Letter is marred by a large ink spill and is written in a badly deteriorated hand

tis] *possibly* to s (*T*) (*possibly* to say *intended*)

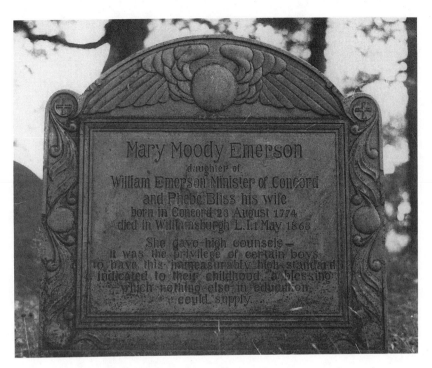

Figure 31. Mary Emerson's grave, Sleepy Hollow Cemetery, Concord.
Photograph by Nancy Craig Simmons.

Index

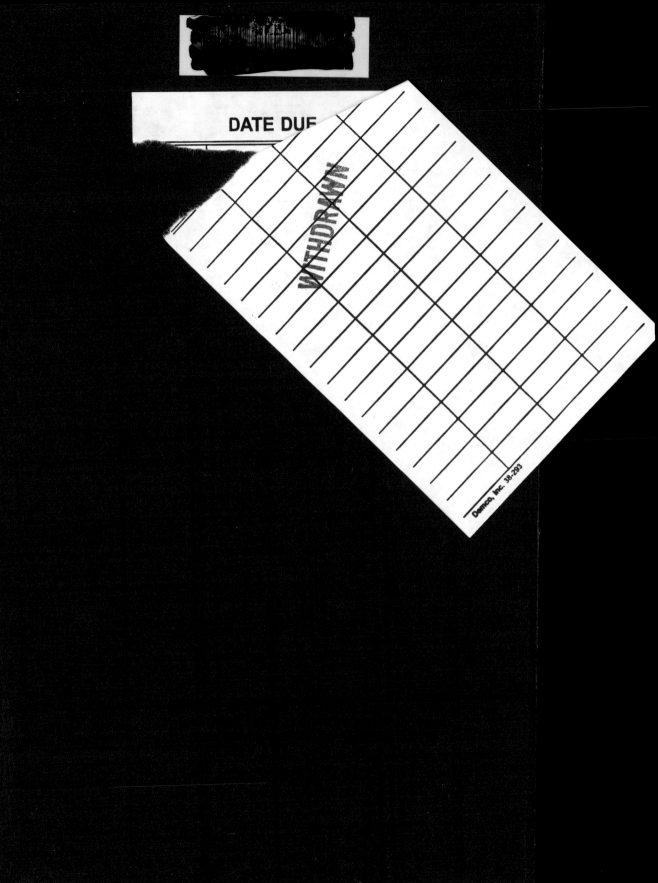